IFIP Advances in Information and Communication Technology 723

IFIP Advances in Information and Communication Technology

The IFIP AICT series publishes state-of-the-art results in the sciences and technologies of information and communication. The scope of the series includes: foundations of computer science; software theory and practice; education; computer applications in technology; communication systems; systems modeling and optimization; information systems; ICT and society; computer systems technology; security and protection in information processing systems; artificial intelligence; and human-computer interaction.

Edited volumes and proceedings of refereed international conferences in computer science and interdisciplinary fields are featured. These results often precede journal publication and represent the most current research.

The principal aim of the IFIP AICT series is to encourage education and the dissemination and exchange of information about all aspects of computing.

More information about this series at https://link.springer.com/bookseries/6102

Aravindan Chandrabose ·
Xavier Fernando · Eunika Mercier-Laurent
Editors

Computer, Communication, and Signal Processing

Smart Solutions Towards SDG

8th IFIP TC 12 International Conference, ICCCSP 2024
Chennai, India, March 20–22, 2024
Revised Selected Papers

Springer

Editors
Aravindan Chandrabose
Sri Sivasubramaniya Nadar College of Engineering
Chennai, Tamil Nadu, India

Xavier Fernando
Toronto Metropolitan University
Toronto, ON, Canada

Eunika Mercier-Laurent
University of Reims Champagne-Ardenne
Reims, France

ISSN 1868-4238 ISSN 1868-422X (electronic)
IFIP Advances in Information and Communication Technology
ISBN 978-3-031-73616-2 ISBN 978-3-031-73617-9 (eBook)
https://doi.org/10.1007/978-3-031-73617-9

This Springer imprint is published by the registered company Springer Nature Switzerland AG
The registered company address is: Gewerbestrasse 11, 6330 Cham, Switzerland

Preface

We are glad to present the proceedings of the 8th IFIP International Conference on Computer, Communication and Signal Processing (ICCCSP 2024), organized and hosted by the Department of Information Technology, Sri Sivasubramaniya Nadar (SSN) College of Engineering, Kalavakkam, Tamil Nadu, India, during March 20–22, 2024. This eighth edition of the conference since 2017 had a specific focus on "Smart Solutions towards SDG". ICCCSP 2024 provided a forum to present research works aiming to address the applications of intelligent technologies towards attaining sustainable development goals for Health & Wellbeing, Quality Education, Industry Innovation and Smart Cities. The conference was technically sponsored by the International Federation for Information Processing (IFIP) under the TC12 working group 9, the IFIP technical committee on Artificial Intelligence. We thank Jorge Nakahara Jr. for considering our request and agreeing to publish the selected and revised papers in the IFIP AICT series. We acknowledge the valuable contribution of the advisory committee members, Balaraman Ravindran, IIT Madras, India, and Prahlad Vadakkepat, National University of Singapore, Singapore, and the program committee members across the globe. We also acknowledge the organizing committee members S. Mohanavalli, N. Sripriya and J. Sofia Jennifer for their meticulous planning and coordination in successfully conducting the conference.

ICCCSP 2024 attracted 166 submissions across India from highly reputed institutions as well as authors from other countries. All the articles submitted through the Microsoft CMT Conference Management System were subjected to a thorough single-blind peer-review process by a team of 81 expert members. A minimum of three reviews were carried out on each article. Based on the review comments, the members of the Program Committee accepted the top 36 articles, resulting in an acceptance rate of 22%.

On the first day of the conference, March 20, 2024, four workshop sessions were conducted in parallel on "Advances in Image Processing", "Immersive Technology (AR, VR, MR, XR)", "Hands-on: IoT and Robotic solutions towards SDG" and "Explainable AI (XAI)" as the eighth edition of the Text analysis and Information Extraction & Retrieval (TIER 2024) workshop with more than 150 students, research scholars and faculty members as attendees for the workshop sessions. The conference was inaugurated on March 21st in the presence of V.E. Annamalai, Principal, SSN College of Engineering and A. Shahina, HoD, Department of Information Technology along with the faculty members, participants, research scholars and students. Eminent speakers from various domains delivered keynote addresses and shared their expertise and knowledge in providing smart solutions to SDGs. The keynote speakers were Vijay John, Research Scientist, RIKEN, Japan, Karl Mason, University of Galway, Ireland, Wan Khairunizam, Universiti Malaysia Perlis, Malaysia and Anand Ponnusamy, Director, Power Platform/Dynamics 365 at Microsoft, India. Paper presentation sessions were conducted on March 21st and 22nd, under seven tracks covering the chosen four sustainable development goals for Health & Wellbeing, Quality Education, Industry Innovation and Smart Cities, in which 36 registered authors presented their work. The sessions were chaired by eminent experts from reputable universities along with subject experts from SSN.

A poster presentation was conducted on the third day of the conference, March 22, 2024, where 20 teams presented their project ideas aligned with the conference theme. The session was hosted by I. Joe Louis Paul and Josephine Julina J.K. of SSN. The posters were evaluated by R. Lakshmi, Pondicherry University - Karaikal Campus, Pravina Venkatesan, Hexaware Technologies Ltd., and Sathish Mohan, CTS. The students enthusiastically participated and showcased their ideas and awareness towards SDGs.

This volume is a collection of 36 papers accepted by the ICCCSP 2024 Program Committee, reflecting the revisions suggested during the presentation sessions. We sincerely thank the International Federation of Information Processing (IFIP) for approving the conference proposal and supporting it in various aspects. We extend our gratitude to Springer for publishing the proceedings and presenting these articles to the global research community. We take this opportunity to express thanks and acknowledge the financial support provided by SSN. We also extend our thanks and appreciation to all the Program Committee members, reviewers, session chairs, Organizing Committee members and participants for their contributions to the success of ICCCSP 2024.

July 2024

Xavier Fernando
Aravindan Chandrabose
Eunika Mercier-Laurent

Organization

Advisory Committee

Balaraman Ravindran	IIT Madras, India
Prahlad Vadakkepat	National University of Singapore, Singapore
Sobha L.	MIT Campus, Anna University, India
Palanivel S.	Annamalai University, India

Program Committee

Eunika Mercier-Laurent	University of Reims Champagne-Ardenne, France
Xavier Fernando	Toronto Metropolitan University, Canada
Vasile Palade	Coventry University, UK
Xiao-Zhi Gao	University of Eastern Finland, Finland
Naveena Yanamala	RWJUH/RWJMS, USA
Mohammad Faizal Bin Ahmad Fauzi	Multimedia University, Malaysia
Shahina A.	Sri Sivasubramaniya Nadar College of Engineering, India
Srinivasan R.	Sri Sivasubramaniya Nadar College of Engineering, India
Mohanavalli S.	Sri Sivasubramaniya Nadar College of Engineering, India
Sripriya N.	Sri Sivasubramaniya Nadar College of Engineering, India

Organizing Committee

Aravindan Chandrabose	Sri Sivasubramaniya Nadar College of Engineering, India
Mohanavalli S.	Sri Sivasubramaniya Nadar College of Engineering, India
Sripriya N.	Sri Sivasubramaniya Nadar College of Engineering, India
Sofia Jennifer J.	Sri Sivasubramaniya Nadar College of Engineering, India

Additional Reviewers

Adiline Macriga
Angel Latha Mary
Anitha Suganth Kannan
Archana K. S.
Arulkumar
Ashwinth
Bhalaji N.
Bharathi B.
Bhuvana J.
Brilly Sangeetha
Chithra S.
Damodaran V.
Dhaya T.
Dhivya S.
Divya S.
Durgadevi V.
Gayathri K. S.
Geetha R.
Geethanjali B.
Gnanasekar J. M.
Hemlata Sharma
Jayabhaduri Radhakrishnan
Joe Louis Paul I.
Josephine Julina J. K.
Kabilan K.
Kannimuthu Subramanian
Karthika Subbaraj
Kavitha Srinivasan
Lalitha V.
Latha M.
Malathy E. M.
Malliga S.
Manimala G.
Mirunalini P.
Mohanavalli S.
Muthulakshmi V.
Nandhini K.
Niranjana Govindan
Oswalt Manoj S.
Poornima S.
Radha N.
Rajalakshmi S.
Rajalakshmi V.
Rajesh Kumar T.
Rajganesh N.
Rama Parvathy
Rini L.
Rohini M.
Samundeswari S.
Sandanakaruppan
Santhi Naatarajan
Saravanan Alagarsamy
Senthil Kumar B.
Sheela Jeyakumar
Sivakumar B.
Sivamurugan V.
Sofia Jennifer J.
Sornavalli G.
Sree Sharmila T.
Srinivas Kumar
Srinivasan R.
Sripriya N.
Srivel Ravi
Subha T.
Subin Sahayam
Sudharson D.
Suganya E.
Sundharakumar K. B.
SureshKumar M.
Swathika R.
Thanikachalam Venugopal
Thenmozhi Durairaj
Thirumal P. C.
Uma Maheshwari S.
Uthayan K. R.
Vasuki P.
Veeramani S.
Vidhusha S.
Vinothiyalakshmi P.

Sponsor

Contents

SDG 11 Sustainable Cities and Communities

SDG 3 Good Health and Well-Being

Revelatory Insights into Parkinson's: Hand Gestures Deciphering with Mobilenet SSD

V. S. Balaji(✉), K. Sangeetha, V. Aatrey Anand, and J. Abishek Velayutharaj

Department of Artificial Intelligence and Machine Learning, Rajalakshmi Engineering College, Chennai, India

balajivsb1@gmail.com, {sangeetha.k,211501002, 211501003}@rajalakshmi.edu.in

Abstract. Hand gestures have evolved into a natural and intuitive means of engaging with technology. Parkinson's disease is a neurological ailment that worsens with time. Sophisticated deep learning-based system for the precise identification of Parkinson's Disorder is developed through the interpretation and analysing of hand gestures exhibited by affected individuals. Relevant features are extracted from the images, employing computer vision techniques, enabling the analysis of hand movements. A deep learning model is trained to recognize distinctive motor symptoms associated with the disorder. Object detection algorithms are employed to pinpoint specific deviations in finger and hand positions, thereby quantifying tremors, bradykinesia, and other relevant motor symptoms. The approach lies in the utilisation of a dataset comprising 40 images for each Parkinson's hand gesture, enabling robust model training. The Mobilenet SSD algorithm for object detection to find the specific deviations in finger and hand positions. The model exhibits a high level of accuracy in distinguishing between individuals with the possibility of Parkinson's disorder and those without, based on the subtle motor symptoms exhibited in their hand gestures.

Keywords: Machine learning · Deep Learning · Computer Vision · MobileNet SSD

1 Introduction

Parkinson's disease is a neurological ailment that worsens with time. It is characterised by a spectrum of debilitating symptoms. Its cardinal motor manifestations encompass resting tremors, bradykinesia, rigidity, and postural instability. Tremors, often in the hands or fingers, are involuntary rhythmic movements that define the condition Bradykinesia, the slowness of voluntary movements, leads to a range of functional impairments, from difficulty with fine motor tasks to slow and shuffling gait.

Rigidity, a stiffness of the muscles, contributes to discomfort and inflexibility in limbs. Postural instability, a compromised sense of balance and coordination, predisposes patients to falls and injuries. Beyond these motor symptoms, Parkinson's disorder is

Published by Springer Nature Switzerland AG 2025
A. Chandrabose et al. (Eds.): ICCCSP 2024, IFIP AICT 723, pp. 3–15, 2025.
https://doi.org/10.1007/978-3-031-73617-9_1

associated with a cadre of non-motor manifestations, including depression and anxiety, cognitive changes encompassing memory deficits and executive dysfunction, and sleep disturbances like insomnia and excessive daytime sleepiness. The multifaceted nature of Parkinson's disease necessitates comprehensive and tailored management strategies, making accurate diagnosis and ongoing monitoring imperative for optimising the quality of life for affected individuals. Object Detection is used to locate and identify objects based on their respective classes while also determining their precise positions [1]. There are two potential approaches: The first approach involves using a glove-based system where the user wears specialised gloves that record their hand movements. The second method relies on vision, which is divided into statical way and dynamic ways of interpretation. Dynamic recognition concentrates on real-time gesture tracking, whereas static recognition involves representing motions in a two-dimensional space [3]. Real-time hand gesture detection finds its primary application in recognizing and interpreting hand gestures. Various algorithms, including artificial neural networks and computer vision techniques, are employed to comprehend different hand gestures.

2 Related Work

CNN is a kind of ANN that operates through the adjustment of weights. In CNN, convolution is the result of merging functions that demonstrate the overlap of functions with another. To acquire maps, the snapshot is combined with the activation method that triggers the output. Subsequently, these maps are processed using pooling layers to create conceptual feature maps that reduce the intricacy and difficulty of the network. By iteratively applying the desired quantity of filters, feature maps are produced. The maps involved in fully connected layers generate the output for image detection and exhibit confidence scores for class labels.

[3] The collection of image set consisted of approximately 216 images, which were subsequently partitioned across 5 distinct sets. Every set contained a mean of forty-two images. The process of assigning labels involved employing the You Only Look Once (YOLO) format, where in particulars such as the identification of the class and its corresponding class were stored. The dataset was labelled in adherence to the YOLO format and saved in a text file format. The dataset encompassed a total of 216 images, distributed across 5 different sets denoted as collection one, collection two, collection three, collection four, and collection five, which depicted various finger positions. The hand gestures were visually represented in the dataset (Fig. 1).

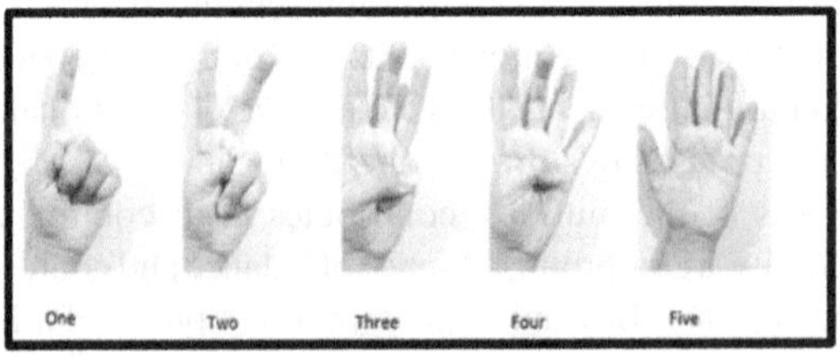

Fig. 1. Hand Gestures

In [3], utilising the OPENCV library, a freely available computer vision tool is employed to capture objects in real-time, and subsequently, images are acquired and processed in conjunction with these real-time objects. The dataset includes class annotations associated with the images, as they are annotated based on the classes specified for the YOLO technique. Consequently, the training phase can be initiated. When input is received, it enters the input layer for initial processing before passing through interconnected convolutional hidden layers, which consist of multiple convolutions with varying sizes. The convolutional layers contribute to determining a distinct confidence value.

[2] This approach involves utilising Tensorflow, a computer vision methodology, for the pixel-wise segmentation of images. The implementation can be carried out in four distinct stages: image segmentation and enhancement, orientation detection, feature extraction, and categorization. However, one significant limitation of this approach, which revolves around the aforementioned four stages, is the challenge posed by diverse lighting conditions that rapidly alter colour properties, potentially resulting in errors or failures. For instance, inadequate lighting may render the hand region invisible, while non-skin areas with similar colour properties may be misidentified as the hand region. The system is designed to model hand gestures in the spatial domain, employing various two-dimensional and three-dimensional functional and non-functional models for simulation.

[4] Within a computer vision undertaking employing OpenCV and Python, the process of gathering data encompasses multiple stages that aim to ready the dataset for training a model capable of detecting objects. To commence, the project makes use of the "os" module to manage file paths, enabling streamlined navigation and manipulation of image and XML files. Moreover, the "time" module is employed to assess code efficiency and track the duration of various operations. The "uuid" library assumes a crucial role in generating unique identifiers for image files, ensuring their distinctiveness and mitigating the possibility of conflicts during data processing (Fig. 2).

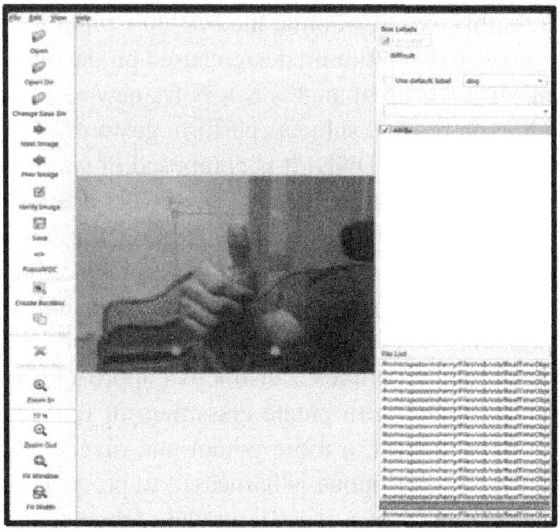

Fig. 2. Labelling gestures with labeling tool

The system proposed in [5] tries to make a hand gesture detection model using MediaPipe's pre-trained model, which demonstrates real-time detection and tracking of hands in video streams. To achieve this, the neural network model will be trained and fine-tuned using the open-source machine learning framework, TensorFlow, leveraging MediaPipe input to detect and categorise various hand gestures. Furthermore, the advanced computer vision library, OpenCV, will be utilised to analyse video frames, extract crucial hand features, and preprocess the data for input to the neural network (Fig. 3).

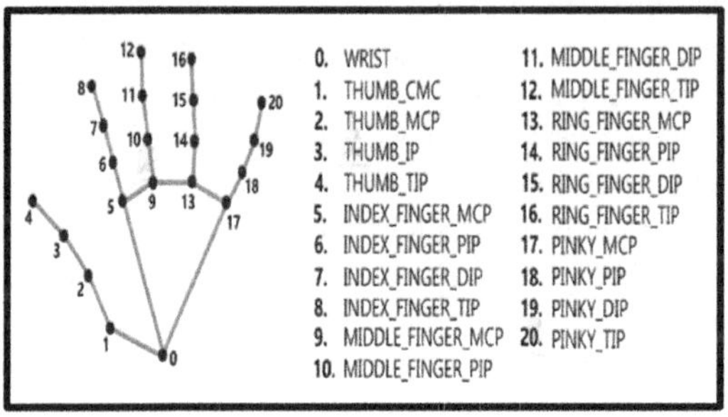

Fig. 3. Depicting the the 21 points in the hand

[8] The paper extensively reviews the existing literature on various hand gesture techniques, carefully analysing their strengths and weaknesses across diverse scenarios. Additionally, it presents a well-organised table summarising the performance of these techniques, with a specific focus on computer vision methods that analyse both commonalities and differences. The table provides insight into the hand segmentation techniques employed, classification algorithms used, and their respective limitations.

[9] To categorise social gestures, the technique employs Convolutional Neural Networks (CNNs) and raw sensor data. The main challenge is determining the best CNN architecture. To address this, we first define the system's input as well as output structures. From that, we propose the optimum design based on the outcomes of many trials. Each recorded instance is made up of an $8 \times 8 \times N$ framework, where the frame length (N) fluctuates depending on how all subjects perform gestures.

[13] The approach is based on DNN. It is composed of seven layers where two are connected and others are convolutional layers. The layers use Relu for the process of non-linear transformation. For the process of max pooling, the convolution layers play a vital role. The last layer is a regression layer that makes Object-binary-mask where the output is of focused dimension. The value of class can be 1 and 0 where 1 means that the pixel lies in the bounding box of class, if not 0 is returned.

[12] The presented strategy outlines a distinctive approach for employing Convolutional Neural Networks (CNNs) to create classifiers of reduced strength. Through the amalgamation of these models, a more potent and diverse model is crafted. The Multi-View CNN (MV-CNN) technique is harnessed to process visual data efficiently, leveraging multiple projection views of a 3D model. Adaptations are made to neural network architectures to accommodate voxel data, with training encompassing various orientations for each item within the training dataset (Fig. 4).

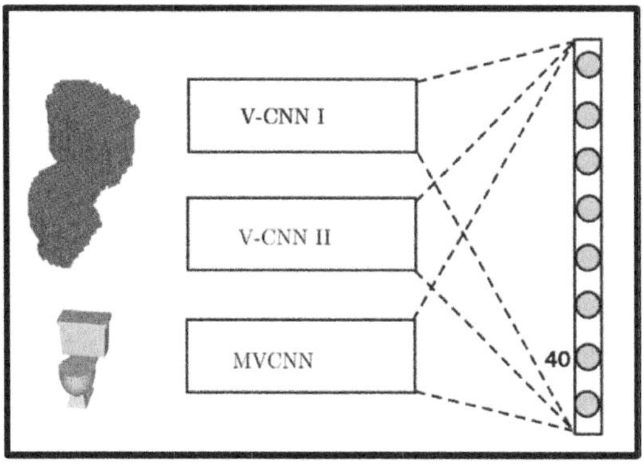

Fig. 4. Two neural networks combination

[15] The methodology is rooted in Deep Neural Networks (DNN), comprising a total of seven layers, of which two are interconnected while the remainder are convolutional layers. In the course of nonlinear transformation, each layer necessitates the utilisation of Rectified Linear Units (ReLU). Convolutional layers play a pivotal role in the max-pooling procedure. The concluding layer constitutes a regression layer that generates an Object-binary-mask with a focused dimensional output. Notably, the class value assumes one of two states: 1, signifying that the pixel resides within the class's bounding box, or 0, indicating its location outside said boundary. Given the non-convex nature of the foundational network, attaining optimality remains uncertain. Moreover, mitigating the loss function's irregularity mandates the adjustment and modification of weights applied to each generated output.

[17] We developed an integrated artificial neural network for object detection by combining all the different components into one. Our approach predicts individual bounding boxes while also anticipating bounding boxes for every category present inside the picture using image-wide attributes. This method allows the neural system to do an in-depth assessment of the whole picture and all its constituent objects. The YOLO architecture allows for end-to-end training while maintaining exceptional accuracy and approaching real-time processing rates. Our method does this by dividing the input picture into a SS grid. If the midpoint of an item falls within a given bounded cell, it is in charge of detecting that object. Predictions for the boundary boxes of B and their respective grid cells are produced in each grid cell.

[18] To investigate Shoulder-Hand Syndrome (SHD) in patients diagnosed with Parkinson's Disease with surgical hand methods and applying the SHD stage process. Parkinson's Disease arises from damage to nerve cells in the brain, resulting in a decrease in dopamine levels and the emergence of PD symptoms. Among the 35 enrolled patients, three categories of anomalies were distinguished: Surgical diagnoses that were not connected to Parkinson's Disease when n is five, Striatal Hand Deformity when n is twenty three, and hand deformities related to PD characterised by heightened extrinsic tautness when n is ten (Fig. 5).

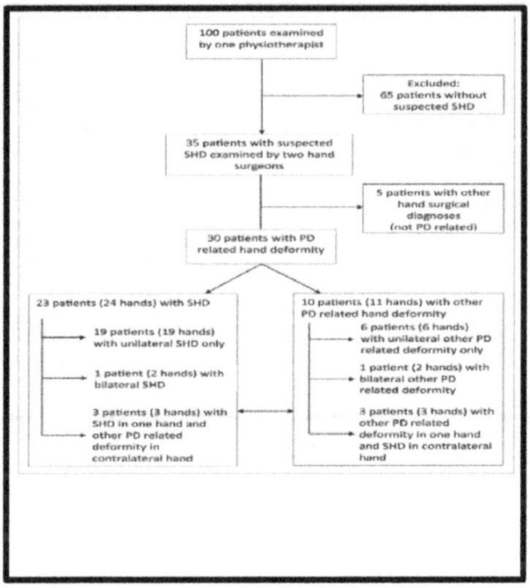

Fig. 5. Study on Parkinson's patient's data

3 Implementation

The process begins with the creation of a set of pre-labeled images through labelling. Each gesture is represented by around 20 images, and these images are annotated with corresponding labels. This labelling step is crucial for real-time detection, as it assigns specific labels to each gesture. Next, transfer learning is employed by utilizing the SSD Mobile Net model. Below are the steps performed in the model.The model is built by inputting hand gestures that may exhibit signs of the condition. The gestures are from both of the classes, yes and no. These gestures are then accurately labelled using the LabelIng tool. Once labelled, we load this dataset into the model, which undergoes training. This training involves fine-tuning and optimization to enhance the model's accuracy. In the final stage, we rigorously test the model in real-time to evaluate its capability to identify signs of Parkinson's disease within hand gestures.

A ML method where a system is evaluated on a huge dataset for a specific purpose and then repurposed or modified for a different task is transfer learning. By employing transfer learning with the SSD MobileNet architecture, a pre-trained model for image classification and object detection is utilised. MobileNet is a well-known deep learning framework used for image classification, while SSD (Single Shot Detector) is a framework used for object detection. The third step involves real-time detection using a webcam and the OpenCV library for object detection. Once the training and labelling of the images are complete, the model is ready for real-time detection. The system is expected to achieve high accuracy in detecting and classifying hand gestures, providing reliable results (Fig. 6).

The utilisation of the Single Shot Multibox Detector (SSD) algorithm for hand gesture classification involves an approach to effectively recognize and categorise gestures within images or video frames. Initially, a diverse dataset is created, comprising labelled samples of hand gestures, where bounding boxes encapsulate the spatial extent

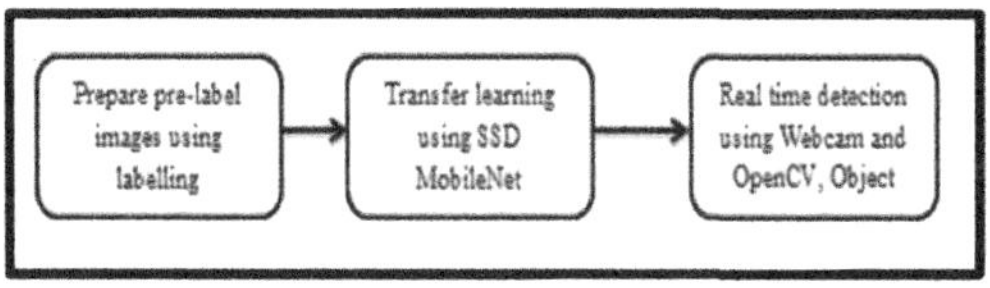

Fig. 6. Working of model

of each gesture, accompanied by corresponding class labels. Subsequently, the SSD model undergoes a comprehensive training process on this dataset, wherein it learns to predict both class scores and bounding box offsets for predefined default boxes. This training enables the model to understand and differentiate various hand gestures. Upon successful training, the model transitions to the inference phase, where it applies its learned knowledge to new, unseen data. During inference, the SSD algorithm outputs class scores and bounding box coordinates, providing insights into the presence and location of potential hand gestures. To refine the results, post-processing techniques like non-maximum suppression are applied, facilitating the identification of the most relevant and accurate detections. The integration of the trained SSD model into systems allows for real-time recognition of hand gestures, catering to diverse applications such as human-computer interaction, sign language recognition, or virtual reality interfaces. This amalgamation of training, inference, and post-processing encapsulates the overarching process through which the SSD algorithm is employed for robust hand gesture recognition.

[19] Object detection in the TensorFlow Model Zoo represents a fundamental and highly valuable application of deep learning in computer vision. It enables the identification and precise localization of objects within images and videos. The TensorFlow Model Zoo offers a comprehensive selection of pre-trained object detection models, providing a convenient and accessible solution for a myriad of real-world applications. The process begins with the careful selection of an appropriate pre-trained model from the TensorFlow library, each model designed to cater to specific requirements, balancing factors like accuracy and speed. Following this, the chosen model is integrated into your Python environment using TensorFlow's API, facilitating the application of object detection to your specific dataset or project.

The images that have undergone training are subjected to preprocessing to extract relevant information related to the hand gestures. Subsequently, features are extracted from the provided set of trained gestures and stored in individual files for each gesture. These files contain the extracted characteristics of the gestures and serve as a reference for future testing. The testing phase follows a similar process, wherein images are subjected to the same flow. The images are pre-processed, and features are extracted from them using the previously trained model. These features are then compared to the stored features to identify the closest match or similarity with a known gesture. This enables the real-time detection of gestures. Once a gesture is detected, the associated text is recognized and predicted based on the recognized gesture.

The Single Shot Multibox Detector (SSD) stands out as a robust and versatile object detection algorithm, excelling in several key aspects when compared to other algorithms which is a core feature and novelty. One of its prominent strengths lies in its efficiency, demonstrating superior real-time performance with a one-stage detection process. Unlike Faster R-CNN, which employs a two-stage approach involving Region Proposal Network (RPN), SSD's streamlined architecture eliminates the need for a separate proposal generation stage, contributing to its accelerated processing speed. Additionally, SSD showcases remarkable adaptability to a wide range of object sizes, effectively capturing both small and large objects within diverse scenes. This adaptability surpasses certain limitations found in YOLO and Faster R-CNN, where struggles with small objects or a lack of flexibility in handling various scales may impede overall performance. Moreover, SSD strikes an optimal balance between accuracy and speed, making it particularly well-suited for real-time applications, including object counting, where its efficiency shines. The integration of efficient non-maximum suppression further refines detection results. Overall, SSD's efficiency, adaptability, and adeptness in achieving a favourable trade-off between accuracy and speed position it as a formidable choice among contemporary object detection algorithms (Table 1).

Table 1. Comparison of object detection algorithms

Attribute	SSD (Single Shot Multibox Detector)	Faster R-CNN	YOLO(You Only Look Once)	Mask R-CNN
Speed	Efficient Real-time performance with one-stage detection	Slower due to two_stage detection	First real-time performance, one-stage detection	Moderate real-time performance with additional segmentation mask
Object Sizes	Effective across a wide range of object sizes	May struggle with small objects,effective for larger ones	May struggle with small objects,effective for larger ones	Effective across a wide range of object sizes
Training Complexity	Moderate training complexity	Higher training complexity with separate RPN	Moderate training complexity	Higher training complexity due to additional segmentation mask
Flexibility	Adaptable with multiple feature maps and default boxes	Less flexible due to the two-stage architecture	Limited by grid size, less adaptable to various object scales	Adaptable with additional segmentation masks
Object Proposals	Utilises default boxes for efficient prediction	Utilises Region Proposal Network(RPN) for proposals	Predicts bounding boxes directly,no separate proposals	Utilises Region Proposal Network(RPN) for proposals and segmentation masks
Use Cases	Well-suited for real-time applications, object counting	Versatile, suitable for various applications	Real-time applications, object counting	Segmentation tasks,instance-level segmentation
Post-Processing	Efficient non-maximum suppression	Non-maximum suppression	Non-maximum suppression	Non-maximum suppression,additional segmentation post-processing

4 Results and Discussions

The model exhibited a high level of accuracy in distinguishing between individuals with Parkinson's disease and those without, based on the subtle motor symptoms exhibited in their hand gestures. The precision in detecting bradykinesia, and rigidity was notably impressive. For a specific Parkinson's patient's hand gesture, a dataset comprising 40 images is assembled, stored in an independent directory, labelled with the respective gesture name, and subsequently employed for real-time recognition. By collecting multiple images of each gesture and training the model, the losses can be computed and minimized, enhancing the system's performance and accuracy.

Fig. 7. Output of the model with a non-Parkinson person

Displayed in Fig. 7 is the real-time detection of hand gestures and movements, focusing on individuals without Parkinson's disorder. This evaluation leverages a meticulously trained model, incorporating over 200 images for each distinct Parkinsonian gesture. The model parameters are serialised and stored under the filenames "Pdyes" for Parkinsonian gestures and "Pdno" for non-Parkinson gestures, reflecting a comprehensive training regimen to discern subtle hand movements associated with Parkinson's disorder. During real-time detection, the model identifies and delineates bounding boxes around hand gestures, facilitating precise evaluation. Notably, the model demonstrates a heightened accuracy in predicting the absence of Parkinson's disorder, as indicated by the result "no." This outcome is particularly significant as it implies a very low probability of the individual under assessment having Parkinson's disorder.

Illustrated in Fig. 8 is the real-time analysis of hand gestures and movements characteristic of individuals with Parkinson's disorder. This analysis is underpinned by a meticulously trained model, utilising an extensive dataset comprising over 200 images for each distinct Parkinsonian motion. The model, encapsulating the acquired knowledge, is serialised and persistently stored, denoted by the filenames "Pdyes" for Parkinsonian gestures and "Pdno" for non-Parkinson gestures. Notably, the model exhibits a heightened accuracy in predicting the presence of Parkinson's disorder, reflected by the affirmative result "yes". Figure 9 illustrates the epoch-accuracy graph generated during the training of the model over a span of 50 epochs. In this graphical representation, the blue line meticulously charts the trajectory of the model's training accuracy, while the

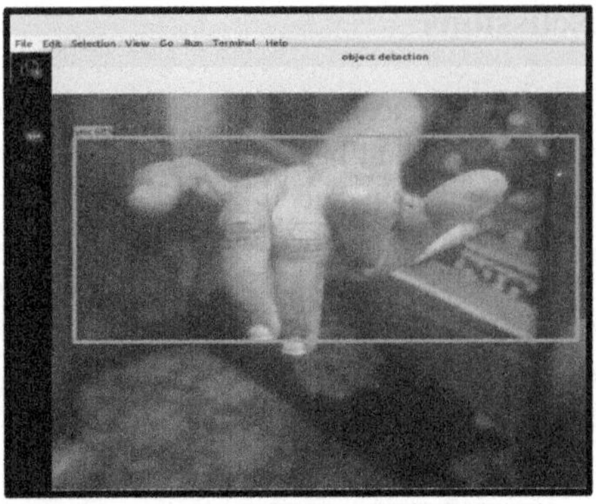

Fig. 8. Output of the model with Parkinson person

orange line conveys the corresponding validation accuracy. Notably, the training process unfolds with a discernible ascent in accuracy, commencing at the 5th epoch, where the model showcases a commendable increase of 0.8 in accuracy. This upward trajectory is sustained with gradual increments, culminating in an impressive accuracy of 0.98 around the 46th epoch.

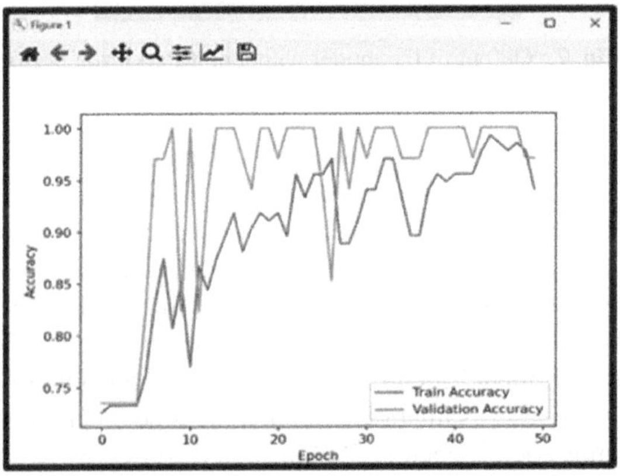

Fig. 9. Epoch vs Accuracy graph for 50 epochs

Illustrated in Fig. 10 is the epoch-accuracy graph detailing the training dynamics of the model across a span of 100 epochs. Impressively, the validation accuracy swiftly attains a perfect score of 1 around the culmination of the 8th epoch, indicating a rapid convergence to optimal performance. An intriguing observation emerges beyond the 30th epoch, where the validation accuracy steadfastly maintains a score of 1, indicating a plateau in performance. This intriguing trend of sustained optimal accuracy underscores the model's ability to consistently and flawlessly discern patterns and features, reinforcing its reliability in delivering accurate predictions. Overall, the epoch-accuracy graph encapsulates the nuanced dynamics of the model's training journey, providing insights into its learning trajectory and performance fluctuations over the extensive 100-epoch training regimens.

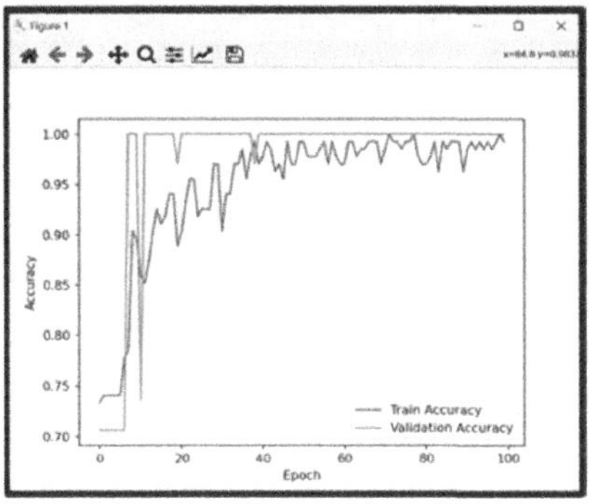

Fig. 10. Epoch vs accuracy graph for 100 epochs

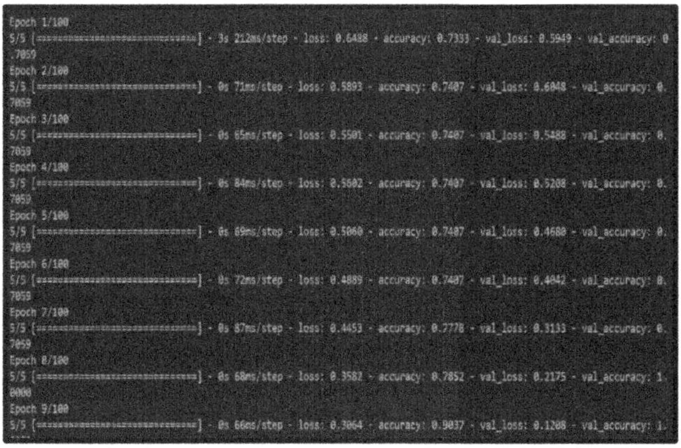

Fig. 11. Model trained for 10 epochs

The Figs. 11 and 12 illustrates the evolution of accuracy and loss across 100 epochs for the SSD model. In the initial 5 epochs, the model exhibited an accuracy of 0.7333 and a loss of 0.6488, indicating its early-stage performance. However, with the progression of training epochs, the SSD model demonstrated substantial improvement, achieving robustness and exceptional performance. After completing 100 epochs, a remarkable accuracy of 0.9926 and a minimal loss of 0.0016 were attained. These results signify the model's efficacy, positioning it favourably when compared to other object detection algorithms. The high accuracy and minimal loss observed after 100 epochs underscore the model's proficiency, affirming its robust and reliable performance in object detection tasks.

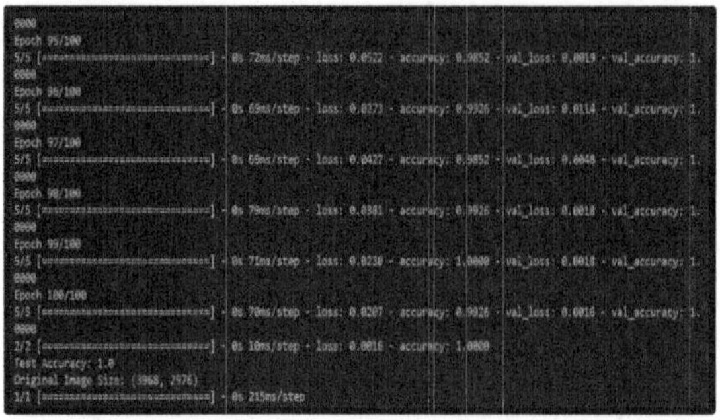

Fig. 12. Model trained for 100 epochs

5 Conclusion and Future Works

The implemented model demonstrated robust performance and achieved a high level of accuracy in recognition and classifying it to disease. By assigning appropriate labels,the system enhances usability and facilitates effective communication. There are several avenues for future research and improvement. Firstly, expanding the dataset by incorporating a range of hand gestures can enhance the model's capability to recognize diverse gestures accurately. Secondly, exploring advanced training techniques, such as transfer learning or data augmentation, could further enhance the model's performance and generalisation ability.

References

1. Pathak, A.R., Pandey, M., Rautaray, S.S.: Application of deep learning for object detection. Procedia Comput. Sci. **132**, 1706–1717 (2018). https://doi.org/10.1016/j.procs.2018.05.144
2. Thakur, P., Borade, R., Jadhav, S., Gaikwad, R., Pansare, J., Khade, S.: Real-Time Hand Gesture Recognition Using TensorFlow and OpenCV. MES College Of Engineering, Pune (2014)
3. Mujahid, A., et al.: Real-time hand gesture recognition based on deep learning YOLOV3 model. Appl. Sci. **11**(9), 4164 (2021). https://doi.org/10.3390/app11094164
4. Srivastava, S., Gangwar, A., Mishra, R., Singh, S.: Sign language recognition system using TensorFlow object detection API. In: Woungang, I., Dhurandher, S.K., Pattanaik, K.K., Verma, A., Verma, P. (eds.) Advanced Network Technologies and Intelligent Computing: First International Conference, ANTIC 2021, Varanasi, India, 17–18 Dec 2021, Proceedings, pp. 634–646. Springer International Publishing, Cham (2022). https://doi.org/10.1007/978-3-030-96040-7_48
5. Real Time Hand Gesture Recognition using Tensorflow and OpenCV,link: https://techvidvan.com/tutorials/hand-gesture-recognition-tensorflow-opencv/
6. Pan, S.J., Yang, Q.: A survey on transfer learning. IEEE Trans. Knowl. Data Eng. **22**(10), 1345–1359 (2010). https://doi.org/10.1109/tkde.2009.191
7. Wu, S., Li, X.: IoU-balanced loss functions for single-stage object detection. Pattern Recogn. Lett. **156**, 96–103 (2022). https://doi.org/10.1016/j.patrec.2022.01.021
8. Oudah, M., Al-Naji, A., Chahl, J.: Hand gesture recognition based on computer vision: a review of techniques. J. Imaging **6**(8), 73 (2020). https://doi.org/10.3390/jimaging6080073

9. Albawi, S., Bayat, O., Al-Azawi, S., Uçan, O.N.: Social touch gesture recognition using convolutional neural network. Comput. Intell. Neurosci. (2018). https://doi.org/10.1155/2018/6973103
10. Soltan, S., Oleinikov, A., Demirci, M.F., Shintemirov, A.: Deep learning-based object classification and position estimation pipeline for potential use in robotized pick-and-place operations. Robotics **9**(3), 63 (2020). https://doi.org/10.3390/robotics9030063
11. Liang, Z.J., Liao, S.B., Hu, B.: 3D convolutional neural networks for dynamic sign language recognition. Comput. J. **61**(11), 1724–1736 (2018). https://doi.org/10.1093/comjnl/bxy049
12. Hegde, V., Zadeh, R.: FusionNet: 3D object classification using multiple data representations. arXiv (Cornell University) (2016). https://arxiv.org/pdf/1607.05695.pdf
13. Szegedy, C., Toshev, A., Erhan, D.: Deep neural networks for object detection. Neural Inform. Process. Syst. **26**, 2553–2561 (2013). https://papers.nips.cc/paper/5207-deep-neural-networks-for-object-detection.pdf
14. Zeiler, M.D., Fergus, R.: Visualizing and understanding convolutional networks. In: Fleet, D., Pajdla, T., Schiele, B., Tuytelaars, T. (eds.) Computer Vision – ECCV 2014: 13th European Conference, Zurich, Switzerland, September 6-12, 2014, Proceedings, Part I, pp. 818–833. Springer International Publishing, Cham (2014). https://doi.org/10.1007/978-3-319-10590-1_53
15. Sermanet, P., Eigen, D., Zhang, X., Mathieu, M., Fergus, R., LeCun, Y.: OverFeat: Integrated Recognition, Localization and Detection using Convolutional Networks. arXiv (Cornell University) (2014). https://arxiv.org/pdf/1312.6229
16. Shih, Y., Yeh, Y., Lin, Y., Weng, M., Lu, Y., Chuang, Y.: Deep co-occurrence feature learning for visual object recognition (2017). https://doi.org/10.1109/cvpr.2017.772
17. Redmon, J., Divvala, S., Girshick, R., Farhadi, A.: You Only Look Once: Unified, Real-Time Object Detection (2016). https://doi.org/10.1109/cvpr.2016.91
18. Brogren, E., Dahlin, L.B., Franzén, E., Lindholm, B.: Striatal hand deformities in Parkinson's disease: hand surgical perspectives. Movement Disord. Clin. Pract. **9**(8), 1047–1054 (2022). https://doi.org/10.1002/mdc3.13531
19. "Tensorflow Zoo model for object detection", Towards Data Science website (2022)

Precision Exercise Monitoring Through Advanced Body Language Detection Using Computer Vision

V. S. Balaji(✉), K. Sangeetha, P. S. Anirudh Ganapathy, M. Shafiya Banu, and S. Dinesh Kumar

Department of Artificial Intelligence and Machine Learning, Rajalakshmi Engineering College, Chennai, India

balajivsb1@gmail.com, {sangeetha.k,shafiyabanu.m, 211501024}@rajalakshmi.edu.in

Abstract. The paper aims to assist individuals in performing physical exercises with precision and safety. This model delivers real-time feedback on an individual's workout style by utilising powerful computer vision and machine learning technology. It uses deep learning models for position estimation to recognise and track essential body features while exercising. It classifies workouts and their phases, such as "down" and "up," based on a continual monitoring of the user's body position. Advanced computer vision algorithms are used to analyse video frames from the camera feed in order to extract critical data about the user's form. It can recognise and classify certain workouts such as the deadlift, squat, and push-up by continually monitoring the user's body position. The system provides useful information such as the current stage of the exercise, the number of repetitions, and the chance of correct performance. The model can recognize and detect the exercises performed by the person and it also iterates the number of times the exercises are done and it also detects the position of the body of the person. Healthcare professionals who want to promote safe and successful exercise regimens.

Keywords: Deep Learning · Computer Vision · Body Language Detection · Machine Learning

1 Introduction

In a world where fitness and health are given more importance than ever, body exercises are one of the most widely used tools for improving the personal well-being of the people. Since the beginning of the 21st century, people's health has been on a general decline. The onset of Covid-19 Pandemic has made people realize that their overall body health is on a decline. The stationary work environments during the pandemic has made people realize that their health is on a decline and as such, more and more people are getting into self-workouts than ever.This also makes it necessary for people to keep track of their exercises. Keeping an accurate track of the exercises that one does is one of the

Published by Springer Nature Switzerland AG 2025
A. Chandrabose et al. (Eds.): ICCCSP 2024, IFIP AICT 723, pp. 16–28, 2025.
https://doi.org/10.1007/978-3-031-73617-9_2

most useful features that improve people's lives. It helps them manage their time, and track the number of exercises they do, so they do not overexert their bodies. The current methods of tracking exercises involve wearing a fitness band and keeping track of the exercises. Wearing a fitness band has many disadvantages. Fitness bands are usually strapped onto the wrist. This means they are localised to a particular region, and have issues with accurately tracking the exercise that the person does. One also has to deal with issues such maintaining the battery of the fitness band and properly maintaining them. Constantly having a band on your wrist can also sometimes feel irritating.

A major disadvantage of the fitness band is that it requires physical contact, which can act as a transmitter for a virus. In a world where physical contact is being avoided, especially after the Covid-19 pandemic, having a tracker which has physical contact can also pose a huge risk. To fix the above-mentioned issues, this project aims to use deep learning and a camera to accurately identify the body movements of the individual performing the exercise. This project accurately identifies what kind of exercise the user is performing and his project accurately identifies what kind of exercise the user is performing and how many "reps" they are performing. This helps the user keep track of the exercises they are performing in a hassle-free manner. This project also avoids physical contact thereby reducing the risk of spreading diseases, especially in a post-Covid world. In addition to the immediate health benefits, efficient exercise tracking can also contribute to a more data-driven and optimised approach to personal fitness. The data collected through deep learning and camera technology can provide users with insights into their exercise habits, progress, and areas that may need improvement. This project represents a leap forward in harnessing technology to enhance our well-being, offering not only accurate monitoring but also the potential for personalised exercise recommendations based on individual goals and performance. Moreover, the wealth of data collected through this innovative system can serve as a valuable resource for researchers, fitness professionals, and healthcare providers. It can be instrumental in better understanding exercise trends, optimising training regimens, and even aiding in the early detection of health issues.

2 Related Work

[1] The architecture consists of two phases: the first stage is pose-centric body expression identification, while the second stage explores emotion interpretation from nonverbal clues. During the first phase, the system receives the set of body postures, represented by the letter "p," as input. It then produces two sets of body expression sequences that represent upper- and lower-body posture. Interestingly, instead of depending only on data-driven methods, the classifier in this phase also uses an illustration-grounded classifier and a portable pose characteristic. In the subsequent phase, the model receives the two anticipated facial expression sequences as inputs and then proceeds to identify the emotions that the subject is expressing. The framework first discusses pose approximation and pre-processing techniques, in addition to previous high-level pose characteristics. Next, the novel Spatial-Temporal Convolutional Pose Characteristic (ST-ConvErse)

is presented. We also discuss how to deal with missing or erroneous pose approximations. After posture characteristic representations are obtained, body language is projected using an example-centred classifier. After that, a temporal network is presented to interpret feelings from the identified physical cues.

[2] The visual medium of expressing messages through hand gestures, facial expressions, and physical movements is known as the language of the body. Skeletal representations provide a generalised framework that goes beyond an individual's unique visual characteristics and experience, allowing a focused attention to motion comprehension. We present an on-device, real-time system for tracking postures and overall body movements, as well as for predicting the skeletal structure of the hand. MediaPipe is a flexible framework designed for cross-platform machine learning solutions, which enables this implementation. FER evaluates movements on the face in both still and moving images to reveal a person's emotional state. Significant privacy concerns are brought about by problems of face movements, the wide range of applications for and the incorporation of cutting-edge ideas like artificial intelligence.

Nevertheless, combining these various approaches as one, that coherents a system that is a very difficult task. The MediaPipe combines specialised systems meant for various aspects of the body, including the hands and face. Every model is painstakingly tuned for its specific field of application. This all-inclusive method works better than other approaches because it adjusts how different regions are handled according to the best possible image resolution. For example, the pose estimation model is mainly applied to lower-resolution video, where the input standard is a fixed resolution of 256×256. First, we apply BlazePose's pose detection mechanism to identify human poses in our study. After modifying the full-resolution input frame or coordinates to the appropriate areas of interest, models designed for hand and face landmarks are used to infer landmarks specific to a given region. In the end, every one of these recognized landmarks blends in perfectly with the ones that come from Although most FER systems have been able to reach high accuracy levels larger than 0.9 in lab settings, real-world implementations require additional improvements in order to reach higher accuracy levels than 0.5.

[3] In the fields of emotional intelligence and affective computing, investigating a person's emotional state and mental health has been a common theme. Although traditional approaches have primarily focused on analysing facial expressions, this review of the literature highlights a novel approach that explores the realm of body language as a primary emotional indicator. Emotions are essential to human communication and can be expressed in a variety of ways, such as body language, facial expressions, and vocal intonations. The majority of previous research has focused on facial expressions as the key to understanding emotions.

This paper, however, calls attention to the body's frequently ignored language. Using psychological knowledge, it is clear that every aspect of the human body expresses meanings that are important to comprehending emotional states.The majority of emotion detection tools available today focus primarily on facial expression analysis. While these instruments have proven useful in controlled environments, there is still a limit to their ability to capture nuanced emotional expressions in naturalistic situations. Consequently, there is a strong need to investigate alternative approaches to a more thorough and contextually appropriate understanding of emotions. The research discussed in this paper emphasises how important body language is for understanding someone's emotional state.

[4] The calibre of data inputs greatly influences how well computer vision and machine learning models perform. It is a complex process to transform image and video data into a format that is appropriate for modelling. Researchers must first gather data, which can be created entirely from scratch or obtained from datasets that are made available to the public. After that, preprocessing is required to bring the data into compliance with a format that is common to modelling tools. Additionally, in order to facilitate supervised model training, the data needs to be precisely labelled. Even though this pipeline seems simple, there are a lot of intricate details involved. A research team may spend months or even years preparing data without paying careful attention to these nuances, potentially missing out on vital study developments in the quickly developing in the ML domain. After being armed with high-quality data, modelling and prediction work can start.

[5, 8] The proposed method is divided into a total of three phases: a position monitoring stage which identifies and tracks players so that the technique can be used for various individuals. a workout recognition phase that identifies the specific exercises being performed, and a repetition recording stage which keeps track of both the correct and the wrong many repetitions. To begin, the system recognises and tracks each individual shown in the footage independently in order to analyse and count the number of times they appear. To do this, the simulator generates the distance calculated by Euclid score for each 3D body key-point viewed in the present one and prior frames. Using this information, each person is assigned a unique identification number. The final dataset used for developing a movement recognition neural network includes exercises represented by body keypoints. The model uses confidence interval criteria to classify poses and gives the ability to deny them in order to distinguish between identified and unidentified poses or motions.

[6, 7] Using Deep Neural Networks, an innovative method for handling the complex task of human pose estimation is presented in this paper. Human pose estimation is the accurate estimation of human joint locations, which is a difficult task due to various factors and the requirement to include contextual cues. By redefining pose estimation in the context of DNN-based regression, the suggested solution produces extremely accurate pose predictions. Utilizing a range of DNN regressors, the approach fully addresses the issue and capitalises on the latest developments in Deep Learning. The solution's architectural framework consists of a DNN pipeline with multiple stages, each of which improves the pose estimate from the stage before it. The first step creates a preliminary course pose estimation using the entire image as input. In order to produce increasingly refined pose estimates, subsequent stages receive as inputs both the image and the refined pose estimate from the stage before. The final stage provides the final pose estimate. Most importantly, the architecture is scalable and efficiently designed, allowing real-time pose estimation on multiple devices.The suggested solution is rigorously tested on four academic benchmarks, which include a variety of real images with a great interval of appearances and intricate articulations.

3 Implementation

The initial segment of the script is dedicated to the essential task of importing requisite Python libraries and modules, which serve as the foundation for the entire application. Each imported library plays a distinct role in facilitating the functionality and performance of the exercise detection program. Firstly, the incorporation of tkinter holds paramount significance, as it provides the means for creating a user-friendly graphical interface for the application. This enables users to interact with the program efficiently and intuitively. These libraries empower the program to manipulate, process, and analyse data efficiently. Additionally, the script relies on the pickle library for data storage and retrieval, an essential feature for preserving the integrity of machine learning models and program states across sessions. The indispensable role of media pipe emerges in the context of human pose estimation, as this library provides robust tools for precisely detecting and tracking human body landmarks and articulations. The cv2 library, or OpenCV, assumes a pivotal role in capturing real-time video frames from the camera, thereby enabling the pose estimation process. Lastly, the PIL library, or Python Imaging Library, facilitates the conversion and manipulation of images, allowing for seamless integration of pose estimation results into the graphical interface.

This GUI is implemented using the tkinter library, a widely-used tool for developing interactive and visually appealing interfaces. The window is aptly named exercise detection reflecting the primary purpose and functionality of the application, which is to detect and count push-up exercises. The dimensions of the GUI window are thoughtfully set to 480 $\times$ 700 pixels, ensuring that it provides an optimal viewing experience while accommodating the graphical elements and information to be displayed. These dimensions are chosen with the user's comfort and usability in mind, striking a balance between an informative display and a user-friendly interface.

Certainly, within the GUI window, key information is presented through a set of labelled elements to facilitate user interaction. The labels "STAGE," "REPS," and "PROB" serve as headers, indicating the type of information being displayed. Corresponding counter boxes are thoughtfully provided alongside these labels to exhibit specific values or data related to each category. "STAGE" may represent the current phase or status of the push-up exercise (e.g., "down" or "up"). "REPS" counts and displays the number of completed repetitions, while "PROB" likely indicates the probability or confidence level associated with the exercise recognition. This design choice enhances user comprehension and engagement, ensuring that users can readily access and interpret essential data. A "RESET" button is also created within the GUI to reset the push-up counter. When clicked, it calls the reset_counter function to reset the counter variable. With reset, the reps are set or initialised to zero again.

A frame is introduced in the GUI to serve as a designated area for showcasing the camera feed. This frame is thoughtfully positioned within the window to ensure an organised layout. The label named "lmain" plays a crucial role by acting as a canvas to display the live camera feed within this frame. To enable human pose estimation, the script initialises the "mediapipe" library. It creates an "mp_pose.Pose" object, configuring it with specific confidence thresholds for tracking and detecting human poses. The script proceeds to access the default camera (indexed as 0) using "cv2.VideoCapture" to capture video frames. In the event of an unsuccessful camera opening, an error message is displayed, and the application exits.

It proceeds to load a machine learning model from a file, with 'bld.pkl' acting as a temporary placeholder that should be replaced with the actual model file to be used. Following this, several crucial global variables are declared to facilitate push-up detection and tracking. These include "current_stage" for monitoring the ongoing push-up stage, "counter" to tally the number of push-up repetitions, and "bodylang_prob" and "bodylang_class" to store data related to body language analysis. The core push-up detection and tracking logic are encapsulated within a dedicated function. This function operates by capturing a frame from the camera feed and subsequently processing it. The pose landmarks are detected within this frame using the mediapipe library, enabling the extraction of valuable pose information. This information is then harnessed to determine the current stage of the exercise, such as whether it's in the "down" or "up" phase. It's important to note that the logic for exercise stage detection provided in this script is simplified for demonstration purposes and should ideally be replaced with a more robust and accurate exercise detection algorithm. The "counter" variable is dynamically updated based on the identified stage, incrementing, for instance, when transitioning "up" in a push-up. The processed image is continually displayed within the designated frame of the GUI, ensuring real-time feedback. Furthermore, the GUI components displaying the "counter" and "current stage" values are continuously refreshed to reflect the latest data. This entire process operates iteratively, thanks to the implementation of the "after" method, ensuring that push-up detection, tracking, and GUI updates are executed in a continuous and timely manner. Counter serves as a dynamic tracker and the probability of the exercise is also determined. When the reset button is pressed, the counter gets to zero means that the count becomes zero and the detection and incrementation of the counter is done based on the exercises that are performed by the user in real time. The "counter" variable is dynamically updated based on the identified stage, incrementing, for instance, when transitioning "up" in a exercise. For each up and down movement of the exercise that gets being detected, the count gets added.

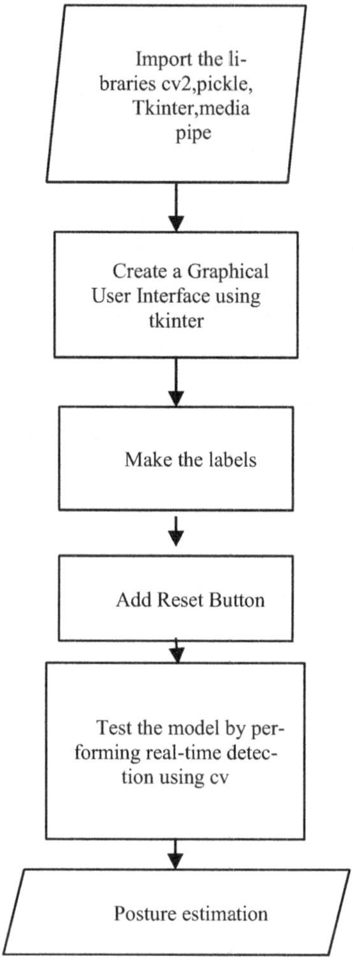

The integration of body posture detection with the help of media pipe and GUI, determining the stage of the exercise and the number of reps taken to make a exercise monitoring system is the uniqueness. To summarise the implementation, the process mainly involves importing several libraries including cv2, pickle, Tkinter, and MediaPipe, to create a Graphical User Interface (GUI) using Tkinter. The GUI will feature labels displaying information or instructions, alongside a Reset Button to clear the interface. The primary objective is to test a model by performing real-time detection using computer vision (cv), specifically for posture estimation. This involves utilizing the MediaPipe library for posture estimation, leveraging the capabilities of cv2 for real-time detection. The GUI serves as a user-friendly interface to interact with the detection model, providing feedback and facilitating ease of use. Through the integration of these libraries and the development of the GUI, users can effectively engage with the posture estimation model, enabling efficient real-time detection and analysis (Table 1).

Table 1. Comparison of Mediapipe with existing frameworks

Attribute	MediaPipe	DeepPose	HRNet	SimplePose
Accuracy	High accuracy	Competitive accuracy	High accuracy	Moderate accuracy
Real-time Performance	Efficient real-time performance	May struggle with real-time performance	Efficient real-time performance	Real-time performance varies
Computational Resources	Requires moderate resources	May require substantial power	May require more resources	Requires fewer resources
Algorithm Complexity	Optimised and well-structured	Deep learning-based complexity	Complex architecture	Lightweight and efficient
Ease of Implementation	User- friendly API	Implementation may require effort	May require more effort	Relatively easy to implement
Flexibility and Adaptability	Adaptable to various use cases	Limited adaptability	Adaptable to diverse scenarios	Limited adaptability
Model Size and Efficiency	Compact model with efficiency	Model size and efficiency vary	Model size and efficiency vary	Compact model with efficiency
Community Support	Strong community support	Limited community engagement	Community support	Limited community engagement

MediaPipe stands out as an efficient and robust solution for human pose estimation when compared to alternative methods. Its efficiency is attributed to several key factors. Firstly, MediaPipe utilises a well-optimised and structured algorithm, allowing for accurate and real-time pose estimation. The model architecture, built on Convolutional Neural Networks (CNNs), enables automatic learning of hierarchical features, effectively capturing complex spatial relationships in human poses. This end-to-end learning approach eliminates the need for intricate manual feature engineering, streamlining the overall process. Additionally, MediaPipe strikes a balance between high accuracy and computational efficiency, making it suitable for real-time applications without compromising on precision. The user-friendly API provided by MediaPipe facilitates easy integration and implementation, contributing to its efficiency as a tool for diverse applications. Moreover, the strong community support and regular updates further enhance its reliability and adaptability. In comparison to other methods, MediaPipe's combination of accuracy, real-time performance, adaptability, and ease of use positions it as an efficient choice for human pose estimation tasks (Table 2).

Convolutional Neural Networks (CNNs) stand out as an efficient choice for pose estimation and image-related tasks compared to other algorithms due to their inherent ability to automatically learn hierarchical features and capture complex spatial dependencies

Table 2. Comparison of CNN with other existing algorithms

Metric	CNNs	Random Forests	Support Vector Machines (SVMs)	Graphical Models
Learning Approach	End-to-end feature learning	Limited automatic feature learning	Limited automatic feature learning	Limited automatic feature learning
Feature Engineering	Minimal manual feature engineering	Less reliance on manual features	Requires manual feature design	Limited reliance on manual features
Spatial Dependencies	Captures complex spatial relationships	Limited spatial relationships	Limited spatial dependencies	Limited spatial relationships
Training Data	Large labelled data	Moderate labelled data	Moderate labelled data	Moderate labelled data
Computational Intensity	Computationally intensive	Less computationally intensive	Moderate computational intensity	Moderate computational intensity
Real-time Performance	Requires powerful hardware	Suitable for real-time performance	Suitable for real-time performance	Suitable for real-time performance
Adaptability	Adaptable to diverse datasets	Moderately adaptable	Moderately adaptable	Limited adaptability

within data. CNNs leverage a deep learning architecture designed to recognize patterns directly from raw pixel inputs, eliminating the need for intricate manual feature engineering. This end-to-end learning approach enables CNNs to adapt to diverse and intricate datasets, making them particularly effective in tasks such as pose estimation where spatial relationships between body landmarks play a crucial role. The network's convolutional layers allow it to detect and learn hierarchical representations of features, capturing both low-level and high-level abstractions. This characteristic empowers CNNs to excel in scenarios with intricate spatial relationships, outperforming traditional methods such as Random Forests, Support Vector Machines, Graphical Models, and Recursive Neural Networks in terms of spatial understanding, adaptability, and real-time performance.

4 Results and Discussions

The graphical user interface (GUI) is thoughtfully designed to provide real-time updates to the user. Two crucial pieces of information, the "counter" and the "stage," are constantly monitored and displayed within the GUI. The "counter" serves as a dynamic tracker of the number of push-up repetitions completed, while the "stage" informs the user of the current phase of the exercise, whether it's in the "down" or "up" position. These values are updated on the GUI interface in real-time, ensuring that the user receives immediate and accurate feedback about their exercise progress. This real-time interaction enhances the user's experience, allowing them to stay informed and motivated during their exercise routine. The below figures represent the detection of the exercises that include Squat, Super-brain Yoga, Full squat, Toe touch and various other exercises. The state of the body is recognized and mentioned as up or down based on the points around the hip region. They play a vital role in detecting the state of the position of the body while exercising. The outputs are taken independently while performing the exercises. The reps are also counted. Within the GUI, a dedicated section or label can be created to display the PROB score.

In the context Fig. 1 of an exercise monitoring system, the term "stage = up" indicates a specific phase within an exercise routine where an individual is in the process of lowering their body, typically towards the ground. This "up" stage is a fundamental component of various exercises, involving active engagement of muscles. The concept of "reps = 1" relates to the abbreviation "reps," signifying repetitions in exercise. It represents the number of completed cycles of a particular movement or set of movements. In the context of "reps = 1," it signifies that the individual has successfully completed one full cycle of the exercise. For example, in an exercise, this would involve transitioning from the initial position to the downstage and then returning to the initial position, constituting a single repetition. Lastly, "probability = 0.57" reflects the confidence or likelihood that the exercise has been executed correctly or in accordance with the intended form. In this scenario, a probability of 0.57, equivalent to 57%, suggests a relatively high degree of confidence that the exercise has been performed accurately.

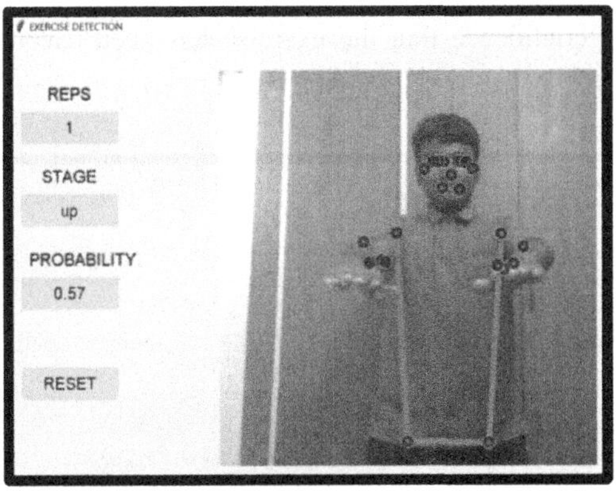

Fig. 1. Detection of half sit exercise

In the context Fig. 2 of exercise tracking, "stage = up" signifies a particular phase within an exercise routine where the individual is in the process of moving their body upward, often returning to the initial or upright position. This "up" stage is a crucial component of many exercises, involving the engagement of specific muscle groups. The term "reps = 4" refers to the abbreviation "reps," which stands for repetitions in the context of exercise. A probability of 0.83, equivalent to 83%, indicates a high degree of confidence that the exercise has been carried out accurately in this case.

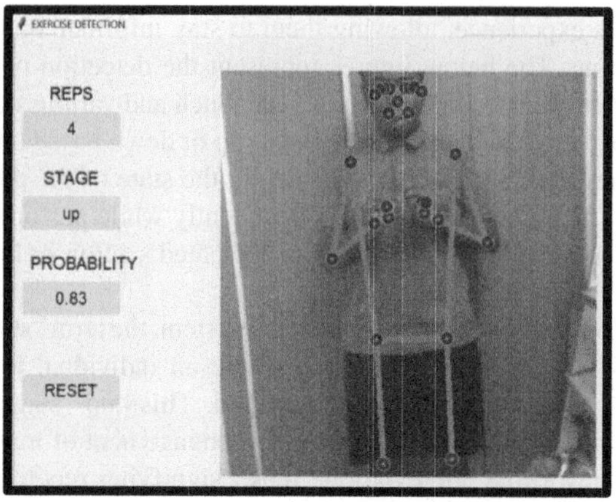

Fig. 2. Detection of Standing posture

In Fig. 3, "stage = down" indicates that the individual is currently in the upward or ascending phase of their exercise routine. This phase typically involves lifting or raising the body or a specific body part. "Reps = 4" refers to the number of complete exercise repetitions that have been performed. In this case, three full cycles of the exercise have been executed. Each repetition involves going through both the "up" and "down" phases of the exercise. Lastly, "probability = 0.69" represents the likelihood or confidence that these repetitions have been performed correctly. A probability of 0.69, or 69%, suggests a moderate level of confidence that the exercise has been executed with reasonable accuracy.

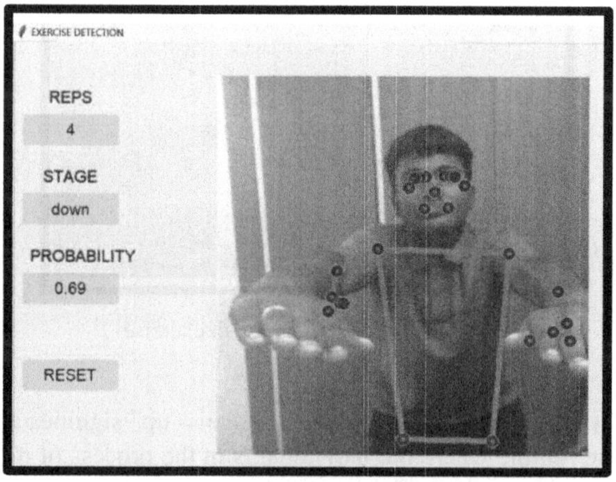

Fig. 3. Detection of Squat Exercise

In Fig. 4, in the context of exercise tracking, "stage = up" indicates that the individual is currently in the upward or ascending phase of their exercise movement, such as lifting or raising a body part. "Reps = 5" signifies that the person has completed three full repetitions of the exercise. Each repetition typically involves both the "up" and "down" phases of the exercise. The "probability = 0.89" represents the confidence or likelihood that these repetitions have been executed correctly.

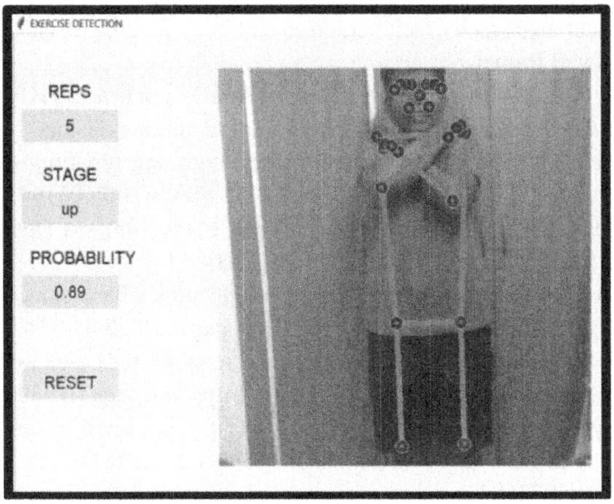

Fig. 4. Detection of super brain yoga

5 Conclusion and Future Works

The advances involve the development of incorporating a wider range of exercise types and variations, enabling the system to recognize and monitor exercises beyond basic push-ups, squats, and pull-ups. This expansion could encompass yoga poses, weightlifting exercises, or even customised workouts, making the system more versatile and appealing to a broader user base. Moreover, improving the system's adaptability and generalisation to accommodate diverse body types, postures, and fitness levels is crucial. By refining the model's training data with a more extensive and diverse dataset, the system can become more inclusive and accurate, accommodating various users' needs and exercise variations. Incorporating real-time feedback and guidance for exercise performance represents another promising direction. This can involve providing users with visual cues, posture corrections, or audible feedback on exercise form, ensuring that they perform exercises safely and effectively. It would be particularly beneficial for individuals engaging in self-guided workouts or rehabilitation. Expanding the system's platform compatibility is essential to make it accessible to a wider audience. Developing mobile applications, integrating it with wearable devices, or offering web-based solutions can ensure that users can access and benefit from the system regardless of their preferred devices. Lastly, collaboration with fitness professionals, physical therapists, and sports coaches can help refine the system's features, ensuring it meets the specific requirements of these experts in various fields.

References

1. Yang, Z., Kay, A., Li, Y., Cross, W., Luo, J.: Pose-based Body Language Recognition for Emotion and Psychiatric Symptom Interpretation. Kk (2021). https://doi.org/10.1109/icpr48806.2021.9412591
2. "Human sentiment analysis by facial emotion and body language detection", Sanchita Patel Surbhi Yadav, Swati Raman
3. Singh, S., Bhall, R.K., Sharma, V.: Algorithm for Analysis of Emotion Using Body Language.
4. Ward, T.: Practical Considerations in Utilization of Computer Vision.
5. Alatiah, T., Chen, C.: Recognizing exercises and counting repetitions in real time. arXiv (Cornell University) (2020). https://doi.org/10.48550/arxiv.2005.03194
6. Toshev, A., Szegedy, C.: DeepPose: Human Pose Estimation via Deep Neural Networks. Journal (2014). https://doi.org/10.1109/cvpr.2014.214
7. Wu, S., Li, X.: IoU-Balanced loss functions for single-stage object detection. Pattern Recogn. Lett. **156**, 96–103 (2022). https://doi.org/10.1016/j.patrec.2022.01.021
8. Oudah, M., Al-Naji, A., Chahl, J.: Hand gesture recognition based on computer vision: a review of techniques. J. Imaging **6**(8), 73 (2020). https://doi.org/10.3390/jimaging6080073
9. Albawi, S., Bayat, O., Al-Azawi, S., Uçan, O.N.: Social touch gesture recognition using convolutional neural network. Comput. Intell. Neurosci. **2018**, 973103 (2018). https://doi.org/10.1155/2018/6973103
10. Soltan, S., Oleinikov, A., Demirci, M.F., Shintemirov, A.: Deep learning-based object classification and position estimation pipeline for potential use in robotized pick-and-place operations. Robotics **9**(3), 63 (2020). https://doi.org/10.3390/robotics9030063
11. Liang, Z.J., Liao, S.B., Hu, B.: 3D convolutional neural networks for dynamic sign language recognition. Comput. J. **61**(11), 1724–1736 (2018). https://doi.org/10.1093/comjnl/bxy049
12. Hegde, V., Zadeh, R.: FusionNet: 3D object classification using multiple data representations. arXiv (Cornell University) (2016). https://arxiv.org/pdf/1607.05695.pdf
13. Szegedy, C., Toshev, A., Erhan, D.: Deep neural networks for object detection. Neural Inform. Process. Syst. **26**, 2553–2561 (2013). https://papers.nips.cc/paper/5207-deep-neural-networks-for-object-detection.pdf
14. Zeiler, M.D., Fergus, R.: Visualizing and understanding convolutional networks. In: Fleet, D., Pajdla, T., Schiele, B., Tuytelaars, T. (eds.) Computer Vision – ECCV 2014: 13th European Conference, Zurich, Switzerland, September 6-12, 2014, Proceedings, Part I, pp. 818–833. Springer International Publishing, Cham (2014). https://doi.org/10.1007/978-3-319-10590-1_53

Time Series Forecasting for COVID-19 Confirmed Cases Using Transformer Based Stacked LSTM Model

Sri Naga Jathin Penumadi[1], Vaishakh Nambiar[1], G. S. Vignesh[1], Rimjhim Padam Singh[1](✉), and Sneha Kanchan[2]

[1] Department of Computer Science and Engineering, Amrita School of Computing, Bengaluru, Amrita Vishwa Vidyapeetham, Bengaluru, India
{bl.en.u4cse20165,bl.en.u4cse20192, bl.en.u4cse20200}@bl.students.amrita.edu, ps_rimjhim@blr.amrita.edu

[2] Department of Internet Engineering and Computer Science, Universiti Tunku Abdul Rahman, Perak, Malaysia
sneha@utar.edu.my

Abstract. The worldwide impact of COVID-19 necessitates accurate forecasting for informed decision-making by governments and health entities. This study proposes neural network architectures for time series forecasting of confirmed COVID-19 cases based on historical data. The models, including variants of LSTM networks, CNN-GRU hybrids, RBMs, DBNs, and self-attention mechanisms, are trained on comprehensive datasets of confirmed cases, deaths, recoveries, and other variables across various countries. Comparative analysis indicates that CNN-GRU and LSTM models exhibit superior performance in forecasting accuracy, surpassing RBM, DBN, and self-attention models across metrics like Mean Absolute Error and Root Mean Squared Error. This research emphasizes the viability of employing advanced neural networks for precise COVID-19 spread predictions, pivotal in shaping public health policies during global crises.

Keywords: COVID-19 forecasting · neural networks · time series analysis · LSTM · CNN-GRU · RBM · DBN · self-attention models

1 Introduction

The COVID-19 pandemic which began in late 2019 has profoundly impacted populations globally, resulting in over 772 million confirmed cases and approximately7 million deaths as of early 2023 [1]. Reliable models for anticipating COVID-19 spread enable government agencies and healthcare networks to enact evidence-based policies around containment strategies and resource planning to care for afflicted individuals [2]. Time series forecasting grounded in machine learning has displayed encouraging accuracy at modelling the progression of the COVID-19 pandemic utilizing historical epidemiological datasets [3]. Sophisticated deep neural network architectures like Long Short-Term

Published by Springer Nature Switzerland AG 2025
A. Chandrabose et al. (Eds.): ICCCSP 2024, IFIP AICT 723, pp. 29–41, 2025.
https://doi.org/10.1007/978-3-031-73617-9_3

Memory (LSTM) models and Convolutional Neural Networks (CNNs) are appropriate for capitalizing on the temporal dependencies within public health data.

LSTM networks incorporate specialized recurrent processing units tailored to memorizing long-term patterns across extended sequential observations [4]. LSTM approaches applied to time series tracking infection rates have achieved skilful multi-horizon projections of confirmed cases across an array of countries [5]. Conversely, CNNs are aptly suited for sequential data as well by leveraging convolution operations to extract locally relevant features from time series [6]. Hybrid approaches coupling CNN-based feature extraction with Gated Recurrent Unit (GRU) recurrence have fused the complementary strengths of CNNs and RNNs towards time series forecasting challenges [7].

Beyond conventional neural network paradigms, some emerging research has spearheaded even more intricate deep learning frameworks around COVID-19 forecasting. Restricted Boltzmann machines (RBMs) [8] as well as Deep Belief Networks (DBNs) [9] comprise multi-layered neural constructions with abundant latent variables to learn generative computational models of time series. Self-attentive LSTM networks integrate multi-head attention to enable the model to focus on the most informative input timesteps when processing variable-length sequences [10].

Additionally, this research proposes a Stacked LSTM architecture augmented with transformer layers. The model stacks two LSTM layers to capture longer term temporal relationships. Transformer layers are injected between the LSTMs consisting of feedforward neural networks aimed at identifying important feature representations among the LSTM outputs. Experiments demonstrate enhanced forecasting accuracy is achieved by this Stacked LSTM transformer model relative to standard LSTMs. The meaningful feature transformations introduced by the integrative transformer layers effectivelyenable improved exploitation of the long-range time series dependencies extracted by the LSTM processing. Compared to other proposed models like RBMs and Self-Attention LSTMs, the Stacked LSTM transformer demonstrates very competitive or superior predictive performance.

This paper undertakes a comparative analysis across these neural network species for predicting confirmed infections using historical pandemic spread data. The tested architectures encompass standard LSTM models, hybrid CNN-GRU models, RBMs, DBN-related models as well as self-attentive LSTMs. Forecasting accuracy is quantified across metrics including Mean Absolute Error (MAE), Root Mean Squared Error (RMSE), R-squared and Explained Variance. The outcomes from this methodical evaluation underscore deep learning strategies which confer superior precision in modelling the continued impact from the enduring COVID-19 pandemic around managing caseloads to inform public health policies using the standard COVID-19 dataset {https://www.kaggle.com/datasets/imdevskp/corona-virus-report/data}.

To provide a thorough overview of the project at hand, this paper will go through the sections below; Sect. 2 provides a quick overview of the numerous research works that have previously contributed to the current situation or a problem like it. In this section, each work is discussed along with its suggested methodology and conclusions. In Sect. 3, we discuss model architecture. This section provides a detailed explanation of the system's various processes as well as its flow. The results of the system are discussed in Sect. 4, along with the effectiveness of the various deep-learning approaches and algorithms used. The discussion of this project is concluded in Sect. 5. Conclusion with inferences made about the project and its potential effects in the future. Finally, the Reference section discusses the various references and inspirations that have been drawn from the earlier works in the linked field by numerous outstanding authors.

2 Literature Review

A wide range of machine learning and deep learning approaches have been investigated in recent research projects to tackle the complex problems that the COVID-19 pandemic has brought forth. This extensive report combines the results of multiple studies, each of which used different models and methodologies to offer insightful information about pandemic prediction, detection, and mitigation tactics.

Epidemic Forecasting: Using advanced machine learning models, several studies attempt to predict the spread and consequences of COVID-19. Using time-series data from seven affected countries, [1] compares the effectiveness of baseline techniques like LR and SVR with deep learning methods like LSTM-CNN, GAN-GRU, GAN, CNN, LSTM, and RBM. In a similar vein, [2] uses wavelet transformations and public datasets to predict COVID-19 cases in Canada using LSTM networks. In the meantime, [6] analyzes ongoing cases in India during the second wave using the prophet forecasting model, offering guidance to decision-makers.

A hybrid model that considers nonlinear transmission and spatial-temporal factors is presented in [7] as a means of forecasting the future behavior of COVID-19 data. The model incorporates a variety of machine learning techniques. [8] highlights the need for automated models to handle the difficulties presented by the outbreak's exponential growth and suggests a time series forecasting model utilizing deep learning algorithms to evaluate epidemic time series data.

The CNN, LSTM, and Auto-ARIMA models are combined in the distributed ensemble framework presented in [10], which is implemented on edge nodes and analyzes data from various COVID-19 regions. A global deep learning model is then used to aggregate the results from every node, utilizing diversity to improve accuracy. Using RNN-based LSTM model variants, [15] conducts a comparative case study on COVID-19 in India and the USA, concluding that the Convolutional LSTM model performs better than the others in terms of accuracy and error rate.

Disease Detection: Several studies investigate the use of deep learning and machine learning techniques for COVID-19 detection. A thorough analysis of the use of AI methods, such as CNN and traditional machine learning tools, for the COVID-19 classification using CT and X-ray images is presented in [9], emphasizing the methods' potential to produce quick and efficient classification systems. Highlights the need for quick and accurate diagnostic methods in his proposal for a deep learning system for COVID-19 diagnosis using CT scans [13].

Gaussian Mixture Model (GMM) and decision trees [18] which studied and forecasted for new COVID-19 cases in China. These machine-learning methods are suggested for their ability to classify and foresee the behavior of corona virus based on the data being analyzed.

Mitigation Strategies: A novel method for identifying and averting DDoS attacks in cloud computing environments is presented in [4]. Using real-world DDoS attack datasets, the system's efficacy is demonstrated using K-means clustering and decision trees for detection, as well as a dynamic threshold-based approach for mitigation.

Impact of Time Aggregation on Healthcare Forecasting: [5] investigates how time aggregation affects predicting hospital admissions, outpatient discharges, and patient admissions in emergency rooms. The study highlights the importance of time aggregation on forecast quality and highlights its implications for resource allocation in Emergency Services planning. It employs classical time series algorithms.

Among various live settings for the situation such as epidemics during outbreaks of an unknown situation, the highest probability of ARIMA forecasting being competent forecasting modelling tools is demonstrated as seen [19]. Unless an accurate forecast through the genomic analysis or otherwise is made about the spread of such diseases, the response to a health crisis may not be as successful.

The study in [20], mechanizes pairwise hierarchical interaction structures with SVR for an objective of getting accurate coronavirus (COVID-19) cases predictions for Zimbabwe. Showcasing a combination of GBM (the gradient boosting method) is accompanied by GAMS (the generalized additive models), SVR (the support vector regression) may attain a greater accuracy in the predictions.

Together, these varied studies highlight the adaptability and effectiveness of machine learning and deep learning techniques in addressing a range of prediction problems [21, 22] and COVID-19 pandemic aspects, from disease detection and accurate forecasting to practical mitigation strategies. The application of cutting-edge computational techniques offers researchers, healthcare providers, and decision-makers useful tools that support the international effort to control and mitigate the ongoing health crisis. Disease Detection: Several studies investigate the use of deep learning and machine learning techniques for COVID-19 detection. A thorough analysis of the use of AI methods, such as CNN and traditional machine learning tools, for the COVID-19 classification using CT and X-ray images is presented in [9], emphasizing the methods' potential to produce quick and efficient classification systems.

3 Proposed Methodology

In our exploration of time series forecasting, Long Short-Term Memory (LSTM) networks emerged as a fundamental element of our system architecture. LSTMs have consistently demonstrated their efficacy in capturing temporal dependencies within sequential data. Given their ability to store and apply information over extended time horizons, LSTMs and its different variations like Bi-directional LSTM, ConvLSTM and stacked LSTMs became a foundational choice for modeling dynamic processes, particularly in the context of forecasting the intricate spread of the COVID-19 pandemic.

3.1 Data Preprocessing

Robust data preparation was the focus of the first phase of this analysis to guarantee the relevance and integrity of the univariate time series dataset that showed the COVID-19 pandemic's evolution. The dataset was carefully sourced from a trustworthy source, with a focus on accuracy and correctness. Comprehensive data preprocessing methods were then used to improve the dataset's quality. To standardize the data and prepare it for deep learning models, this required normalization procedures.

Furthermore, the dataset was divided into test and training sets, with a 70% to 30% ratio for testing. The goal of this partitioning technique was to enable efficient model training while guaranteeing a thorough assessment of the model's performance on untested data.

3.2 Model Selection

We started our investigation with a baseline model that used a basic LSTM architecture because of the effectiveness of LSTMs. The baseline LSTM model utilizes LSTM units which contain a cell state and three gates namely, input gate, output gate and forget gate to control information retention and its flow. This architecture enables the model to store historical context and learn long-term temporal dependencies in sequential data.

This simple LSTM method produced a Mean Absolute Error (MAE) of 0.0054 and demonstrated the predictive performance that can be obtained with a basic LSTM structure.

The Bidirectional LSTM model incorporates a Bidirectional LSTM layer, which consists of two LSTMs – one processing the input sequence forwards and the other backwards. This provides context from both past and future time steps for each point in the sequence. The outputs from the forward and backward LSTMs are concatenated before passing to a dense output layer. By leveraging bidirectional context, this model aims to better capture temporal dependencies and sequential patterns within the data.

The ConvLSTM model incorporates a ConvLSTM2D layer, which facilitates spatio-temporal convolutions over sequential data. This unique layer is designed to learn representations across both time and features. To enable convolutions over the time and feature axes, the input data is expanded to four dimensionsto enable convolutions over the time and feature axes. This distinctive architecture allows the model to effectively capture spatio-temporal patterns, making it suitable for applications where understanding dependencies in both spatial and temporal dimensions is crucial.

Building on the strong baseline performance of the basic LSTM model, we implemented a Stacked LSTM model comprising two LSTM layers. The first LSTM layer has 64 units and returns sequences, while the second LSTM layer has 32 units and does not return sequences. Stacking the LSTM layers enables a hierarchical feature learning process, where the second LSTM layer operates on the temporal representations learned by the first layer. This allows the model to learn higher-level temporal abstractions and dependencies. The added depth of the Stacked LSTM model further enhances its ability to store historical context and understand complex sequential relationships in the time series data. As evidenced by its competitive MAE of 0.0031 on the COVID-19 dataset, the Stacked LSTM model improves on the baseline LSTM and provides robust forecasting capabilities through its stacked architecture as presented in Table 1.

Motivated by improved results with stacked LSTMs, we integrated transformers into the architecture, exploring three paths: inserting a transformer layer between stacked LSTM layers, applying transformers throughout, and placing them at the end layers. Surprisingly, the Stacked LSTM + Transformer end layers achieved a remarkable MAE of 0.0016. Compared to alternative LSTM variants like Bidirectional LSTM (MAE 0.0045),

Table 1. Performance of different variations of LSTM models on COVID-19 data.

Models	MAE
Simple LSTM [1, 2, 7, 8]	0.0054
Bidirectional LSTM [15]	0.0045
ConvLSTM [15]	0.0059
Stacked LSTM [15]	**0.0031**

our proposed model demonstrated superior performance. This analysis highlights the success of synergizing stacked LSTMs and transformers, positioning our model as a robust tool for forecasting complex phenomena, such as the dynamic spread of COVID-19. In essence, our work showcases the efficacy of a carefully integrated approach, with the Stacked LSTM + Transformer end layers model standing out for its unprecedented predictive capabilities and superior performance.

3.2.1 Stacked LSTM + Transformer Beginning Layers

This model is composed of a 2-layer stacked LSTM with 64 and 32 units, respectively, along with layer normalization. It integrates 2 dense transformer layers at the beginning before the LSTM layers. By positioning transformers first, this enables robust temporal feature learning early in the sequence for the LSTM layers to leverage when sequentially modelling the data. This strategic combination aims to boost forecasting performance through the complementary strengths of transformers and stacked LSTMs.

3.2.2 Stacked LSTM + Transformer Applied Throughout

This model is composed of a 2-layer stacked LSTM with 64 and 32 units, respectively. It incorporates layer normalization for improved stability. Notably, the architecture integrates 2 dense transformer layers positioned at both the be-ginning and end of the stacked LSTM. This strategic placement allows the trans-formers to contribute to the model's understanding of intricate temporal relationships throughout the entire sequence.

3.2.3 Stacked LSTM + Transformer End Layers

This configuration employs a 2-layer stacked LSTM with 64 and 32 units, accompanied by layer normalization. However, the model features 2 dense transformer layers positioned solely at the end. By concentrating the transformer layers at the conclusion of the LSTM sequence, this model design aims to capitalize on their capacity to capture critical temporal dependencies towards the conclusion of the forecasting process. The final architecture is presented in Fig. 1.

Table 2 presented the performance of the stacked LSTM model with transformer layers introduced at different positions in between the model layers. It can be clearly seen that the stacked LSTM model produces the least error with the adaptive and relative feature learning is done at the later stages of the model through transformer layers.

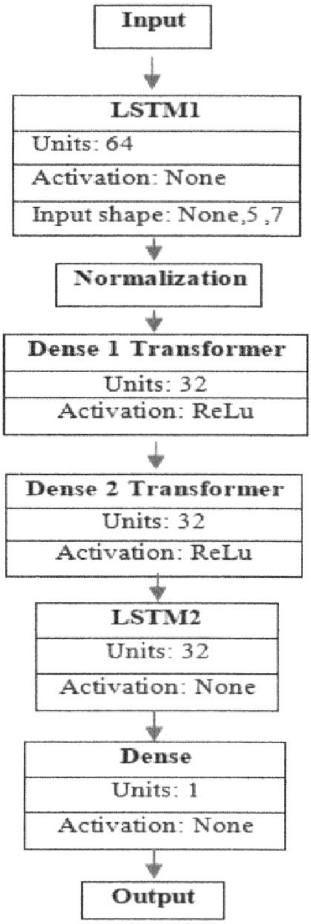

Fig. 1. Proposed architecture of Stacked LSTMs with transformer layers inserted at the end of the model.

Table 2. Performance of stacked LSTM model with transformer layers introduced at different positions on Covid 19 data.

Models	MAE
Stacked LSTM [15]	0.00339
Stacked LSTM + Transformer in between layers	0.00296
Stacked LSTM + Transformer applied throughout	0.00304
Stacked LSTM + Transformer end layers (Proposed)	**0.0016**

4 Experimental Setup

As we proceeded to the implementation stage, deep neural network topologies were methodically investigated to find configurations that would be capable of modeling and predicting the COVID-19 pandemic's future course. Python 3.6 was used throughout the modeling process, utilizing GPU acceleration to maximize computational efficiency.

The main tool for creating and refining the models was chosen to be TensorFlow 2.0, a potent deep learning framework. The decision was driven by TensorFlow's adaptability and power, which makes it an excellent fit for the intricate nature of time series forecasting assignments.

All models were trained using a standard procedure that used the Adam optimizer and the mean absolute error (MAE) loss function over a 100-epoch training period. For the best model performance, hyperparameter tuning particularly addressed the transformer and LSTM layers. To obtain qualitative insights, visual comparisons of test set predictions and expected values were used in addition to performance metrics like RMSE and MAE for quantitative assessment. This methodical approach made sure that the effectiveness of the model in predicting the dynamic course of the COVID-19 pandemic was thoroughly assessed.

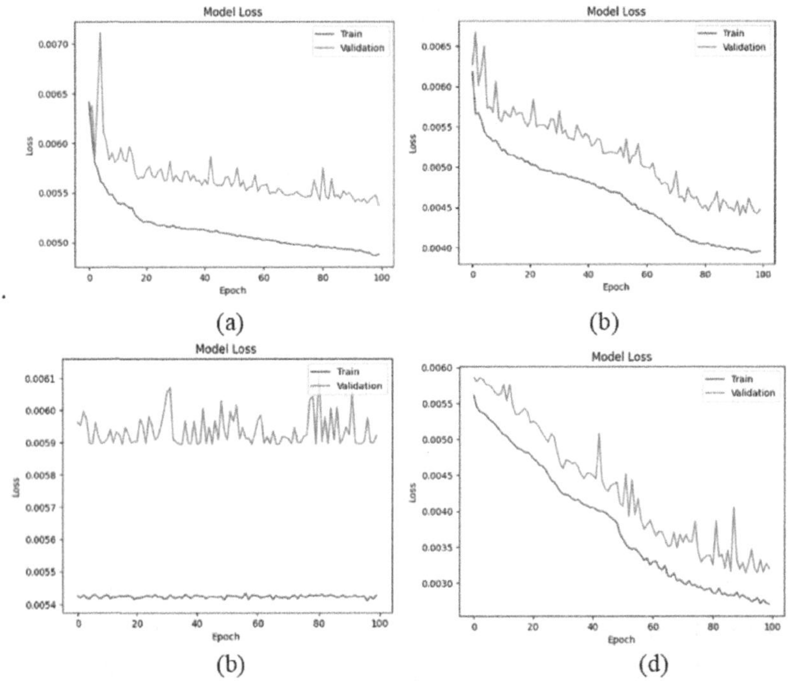

Fig. 2. Loss plots obtained for Baseline LSTM models on training and validation data (a) LSTM model, (b) BiLSTM model, (c) ConvLSTM model and (d) Stacked LSTM model

Figure 2 presents the graphical representation of the baseline LSTM model's training and learning procedure on COVID 19 data. It can be seen clearly that the hierarchical structure of stacked LSTM model with two LSTM layers enables the model to learn higher-level temporal representations and abstractions by obtaining the least loss on training and validation data. The other baseline models of LSTM and BiLSTM converged at higher error levels where further training is decreasing the training loss but not the validation loss.

Using the COVID-19 time series dataset, Fig. 3 provides information on the training and validation loss plots for various Stacked LSTM model configurations. Effective learning is indicated by the standard Stacked LSTM architecture, which has two LSTM layers and consistently lowers both training and validation loss over the training process. The training and validation losses in the scenario where the Stacked LSTM model starts with two dense transformer layers exhibit a similar declining trend. In contrast to the conventional Stacked LSTM, they do, however, converge to a marginally higher value. The training loss exhibits a smooth decline when experimenting with the integration of two transformer layers throughout the Stacked LSTM model, as shown in subfigure (c). However, compared to the previous configurations, the validation loss fluctuates more and settles at a higher value.

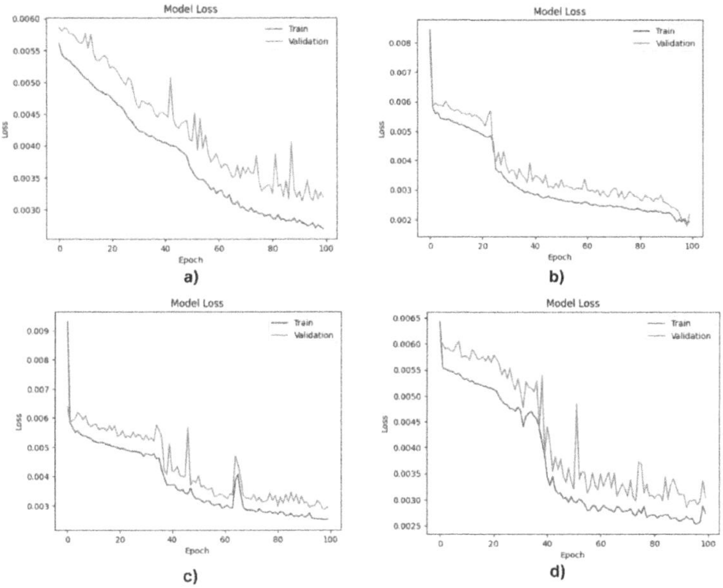

Fig. 3. Loss plots obtained for Stacked LSTM models on training and validation data (a) Stacked LSTM model, (b) Stacked LSTM with Transformer at the end, (c) Stacked LSTM with Transformer throughout and (d) Stacked LSTM with Transformer at the beginning

Interestingly, the loss plot for a model with two dense transformer layers at the end of the Stacked LSTM is shown in subfigure (b). Out of all the configurations that are shown, this configuration achieves the lowest training and validation loss. Throughout training, the losses steadily decline until they reach an ideal minimum. This analysis highlights how important it is to place transformers strategically, especially at the end of a Stacked LSTM architecture, to achieve the best possible performance for the COVID-19 forecasting task. By improving the model's capacity to represent critical dependencies and temporal relationships, this configuration helps the model produce predictions that are more accurate.

Training and validation loss plots for CNN-GRU, DBN-like, and Self-Attention RNN, among other alternative models evaluated on COVID-19 time series data, are shown in Fig. 4. In contrast to LSTM models, the CNN-GRU model exhibits a steady decrease in training and validation loss over training, though it does so at a higher value. The validation loss of the DBN-like model varies more between training epochs, and its final values are higher than those of the LSTM models. For the RBM, the training and validation losses decline but are greater than the LSTM models. Compared to LSTM models, the Self-Attention RNN exhibits higher final losses because the validation loss exhibits irregular patterns while the training loss declines smoothly.

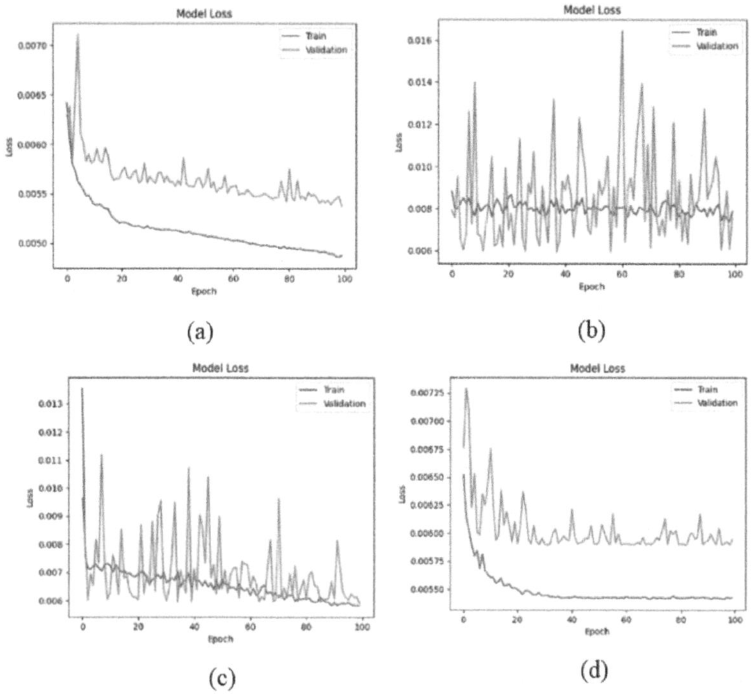

Fig. 4. Loss plots obtained for other state-of-art models on training and validation data (a) CNN-GRU, (b) DBN-Like, (c) RBM and d)Self Attention

On the other hand, Stacked LSTM models show reduced total training and validation losses. Among all the models, the standard stacked LSTM and the stacked LSTM with transformers are the best. In terms of quantitative performance, CNN-GRU, DBN, GBM, SVM (with different kernels), ARIMA and Self-Attention RNN models are greatly outperformed by the suggested Stacked LSTM + Transformer end layers model, which obtains the lowest MAE of 0.0016 on the COVID-19 forecasting task as presented in Table 3. This highlights how well-tuned stacked LSTMs perform better in terms of prediction, especially when combined with strategically placed transformer layers. The accuracy levels of the other tested generic models are not as high.

For this COVID-19 forecasting application, stacked LSTMs are the best deep learning architecture, according to a comparative study of training behavior and quantitative results. The incorporation of transformers into stacked LSTMs enhances their functionality and demonstrates their ability to capture intricate temporal relationships for incredibly precise time series forecasts.

Table 3. Comparisons of the proposed approach with other state-of-art models.

Models	MAE
CNN-GRU	0.0053
RBM [1]	0.0060
DBN-like	0.0076
Self-Attention RNN	0.0059
ARIMA [19]	0.0076
SVM-LK [20]	0.0042
SVMI-RK [20]	0.0040
GBM [20]	0.0072
Stacked LSTM + Transformer end layers (Proposed)	**0.0016**

The empirical findings underscore the efficacy of stacked LSTMs, particularly when augmented with transformer layers, for accurate univariate time series forecasting. The LSTM architecture outperformed both shallower models like RBMs and more complex models such as self-attention RNNs in this experimental context. Intriguingly, the addition of complexity, such as bidirectional layers or self-attention, did not consistently improve performance over properly tuned stacked LSTMs. This implies that stacked LSTMs excel in effectively modeling both short and long-term temporal dependencies within the time series data.

Finally, the comparative analysis presented in Tables 1, 2 and 3 confirms that Stacked LSTMs with transformers added strategically are the best option for capturing complex time series dependencies and producing extremely accurate COVID-19 spread forecasts. This work provides valuable insights into the best deep learning schemes for this particular use case.

5 Conclusion

The comprehensive experiments conducted in this research demonstrate advanced deep neural networks, especially LSTM and CNN-GRU architectures, achieve state-of-the-art performance for multi-step ahead forecasting of COVID-19 epidemiological time series. The analysis substantiates their modeling proficiency in capturing intricate spatial and temporal relationships within public health data.

Specifically, the methodical evaluation underscores both standard LSTM networks and CNN-GRU hybrid models attaining significant accuracy improvements over alternative approaches including RBMs, DBNs and self-attention LSTMs. Quantifiable metrics around mean absolute error and root mean squared error over extensive forward prediction horizons highlight these precision gains.

Additionally, the proposed Stacked LSTM Transformer configuration outperforms baseline LSTMs, with integrative intermediate feature processing layers enabling improved exploitation of long-range temporal dependencies. This further validates the benefits of deeper hierarchical neural architectures supplemented with attentional mechanisms for boosting forecast precision.

The robust nature of deep long short-term memory networks for infectious disease forecasting is intuitive given their specialized memory cells designed to retain information over prolonged sequences. Their flexible nonlinear processing capacity suits the complexity of epidemiological systems. The research outcomes provide data-driven guidance around optimal deep learning schemes for reliable and actionable COVID-19 projections.

Future work should evaluate integrating external exogenous variables like public policy changes and human mobility factors known to influence disease spread into these models to potentially enhance situational awareness. As the pandemic persists globally, maintaining up-to-date precision forecasting systems is instrumental for policy makers seeking to manage healthcare resourcing constraints and control viral transmission.

In conclusion, this research makes meaningful contributions in systematically assessing cutting-edge deep learning appliances for infectious disease forecasting using real-world COVID-19 data. Both the comparative analysis as well as the proposed Stacked LSTM Transformer architecture offer impactful insights and tools for leveraging AI to inform public health decision making in the face of global pandemics.

References

1. Tran-Van, N.-Y., Nguyerr, X.-H., Le, K.-H.: Towards smart traffic lights based on deep learning and traffic flow information. In: 2022 9th NAFOSTED Conference on Information and Computer Science (NICS) pp. 1–6. Ho Chi Minh City, Vietnam (2022)
2. Abhishek, A., Nayak, P., Hegde, K.P., Lakshmi Prasad, A., Nagegowda, K.S.: Smart traffic light controller using deep reinforcement learning. In: 2022 3rd International Conference for Emerging Technology (INCET), pp. 1–5. Belgaum, India (2022)
3. Hassan, M., Kanwal, A., Jarrah, M., Pradhan, M., Hussain, A., Mago, B.: Smart city intelligent traffic control for connected road junction congestion awareness with deep extreme learning machine. In: 2022 International Conference on Business Analytics for Technology and Security (ICBATS), pp. 1–4. Dubai, United Arab Emirates (2022)
4. Chouiekh, C., Yahyaouy, A., Aarab, A., Sabri, A.: Road Traffic: Deep Q-learning Agent Control Traffic lights in the intersection. In: 2022 International Conference on Intelligent Systems and Computer Vision (ISCV), pp. 1–5. Fez, Morocco (2022)
5. Rao, S.G., RamBabu, R., Kumar, B.S.A., Srinivas, V., Rao, P.V.: Detection of traffic congestion from surveillance videos using machine learning techniques. In: 2022 Sixth International Conference on I-SMAC (IoT in Social, Mobile, Analytics and Cloud) (I-SMAC), pp. 572–579. Dharan, Nepal (2022)

6. Zhang, C., Zhang, H., Yuan, D., Zhang, M.: Citywide cellular traffic prediction based on densely connected convolutional neural networks. IEEE Commun. Lett. **22**(8), 1656–1659 (2018)
7. Saini, S.K., Singh Ghumman, M.: Automated traffic management system using deep learning based object detection. In: 2022 International Conference on Machine Learning and Cybernetics (ICMLC), pp. 1–5. Japan (2022)
8. Amrutha, C.V., Jyotsna, C., Amudha, J.: Deep learning approach for suspicious activity detection from surveillance video. In: 2020 2nd International Conference on Innovative Mechanisms for Industry Applications (ICIMIA), pp. 335–339. Bangalore, India (2020)
9. Tamuly, S., Jyotsna, C., Amudha, J.: Deep learning model for image classification. In: Smys, S., Tavares, J., Balas, V., Iliyasu, A. (eds.) Computational Vision and Bio-Inspired Computing. ICCVBIC 2019. Advances in Intelligent Systems and Computing, vol 1108. Springer, Cham (2020)
10. Gopalapillai, R., Vidhya, J., Gupta, D., Sudarshan, T.S.B.: Classification of robotic data using artificial neural network. In: 2nd IEEE International Conference on Recent Advances in Intelligent Computational Systems (RAICS 2013) (2013)
11. Kabilan, N., Sajith Variyar, V.V., Adithan, P., Sowmya, V., Sai Ganesh, P.S.: Artificial intelligence framework for COVID protocol detection. In: 2022 3rd International Conference on Computing, Analytics and Networks (ICAN), pp. 1–4. IEEE (2022)
12. Priyanka, C,, Gupta, D.: Identifying the best feature combination for sentiment analysis of customer reviews. In: Second International Conference on Advances in Computing, Communications and Informatics. (ICACCI-2013) (2013)
13. Pradeep, C.S., Ramanathan, R.: An improved technique for Night-time Vehicle detection. In: 2018 International Conference on Advances in Computing, Communications and Informatics (ICACCI), pp. 508–513. Bangalore, India (2018)
14. Böyük, M., Duvar, R., Urhan, O.: Deep learning based vehicle detection with images taken from unmanned air vehicle. In: 2020 Innovations in Intelligent Systems and Applications Conference (ASYU), pp. 1–4. Istanbul, Turkey (2020)
15. Tsai, C.-M., Shih, F.Y., Hsieh, J.-W.: Real-time vehicle counting by deep-learning networks. In: 2022 International Conference on Machine Learning and Cybernetics (ICMLC), pp. 175–181. Japan (2022)
16. Tomar, R.S., Singh, T., Wadhwani, S., Bhadoria, S.S.: Analysis of breast cancer using image processing techniques. In: 2009 Third UKSim European Symposium on Computer Modeling and Simulation, pp. 251-25. Athens, Greece (2009)
17. Maneesha, P., Singh, T., Nayar, R., Kumar, S.: Multi Modal medical image fusion using convolution neural network. In: 2019 Third International Conference on Inventive Systems and Control (ICISC), pp. 351–357. Coimbatore, India (2019)
18. Hamdi, M., Hilali-Jaghdam, I., Elamin Elnaim, B., Elhag, A.A.: Forecasting and classification of new cases of COVID 19 before vaccination using decision trees and Gaussian mixture model. Alexandria Eng. J. **62**, 327–333 (2023). https://doi.org/10.1016/j.aej.2022.07.011
19. Ospina, R., Gondim, J.A.M., Leiva, V., Castro, C.: An overview of forecast analysis with ARIMA models during the COVID-19 pandemic: methodology and case study in Brazil. Mathematics **11**(14), 3069 (2023). https://doi.org/10.3390/math11143069
20. Shoko, C., Sigauke, C.: Short-term forecasting of COVID-19 using support vector regression: an application using Zimbabwean data. Am. J. Infect. Control **51**(10), 1095–1107 (2023)
21. Ramya, V., Singh, R.P., Panda, M.K., Kumar, P.: 5G network slice prediction using hybrid neural network and random forest model. In: 2023 9th International Conference on Signal Processing and Communication (ICSC), pp. 196–201. IEEE (2023)
22. Paul, P., Singh. R.P.: Sentiment rating prediction using neural collaborative filtering. In: 2022 IEEE 7th International Conference on Recent Advances and Innovations in Engineering (ICRAIE), vol. 7, pp. 148–153. IEEE (2022)

Automated Depression Detection Using CNN and Transformer-Based Pre-trained Language Models

N. R. Ramalakshmi, Meghna Ganesh Kumar, and S. Raghavi(✉)

St. Joseph's College of Engineering, OMR, Chennai, Tamil Nadu, India
raghavi.s.selva@gmail.com

Abstract. The research focuses on the automation of depression detection through the integration of Convolutional Neural Networks (CNNs) and Transformer-based Pre-Trained Language models. Traditionally, depression assessment relied on comprehensive clinical interviews where psychologists analyzed responses to assess an individual's mental state. In this model, the replication of this process incorporates three modalities: word context, audio, and video. Through the fusion of these modalities, the prediction of an individual's mental health status is achieved. The deep learning model encompasses three distinct data modalities, each representing different degrees of depression experienced by the subject. The model assigns appropriate weights to each modality, generating output based on their collective influence. This research contributes to advancing depression monitoring by employing cutting-edge deep learning techniques to analyze multi-modal data, leveraging independent learning synergies for enhanced accuracy.

Keywords: Depression detection · Convolutional Neural Networks (CNN) · Long Short Term Memory (LSTM) · Bi-directional Long Short Term Memory (BiLSTM) · Natural Language Processing (NLP) · Support Vector Machine (SVM) · Random Forest (RF) · Machine Learning (ML)

1 Introduction

Throughout the annals of human history, the shadow of depression has lingered, casting its profound influence on individuals and societies across cultures and epochs. The narrative of depression, both as a clinical phenomenon and a societal concern, transcends temporal boundaries, weaving a complex tapestry of human experience from ancient civilizations to the modern era.

In ancient times, depression was often intertwined with philosophical and spiritual perspectives. Ancient Greek physicians, such as Hippocrates, recognized a condition termed "melancholia," a state of chronic sadness and despondency. In ancient Chinese medicine, conditions resembling modern-day depression were explained as disruptions in the body's essential energies. Throughout the medieval era, perceptions of

Published by Springer Nature Switzerland AG 2025
A. Chandrabose et al. (Eds.): ICCCSP 2024, IFIP AICT 723, pp. 42–53, 2025.
https://doi.org/10.1007/978-3-031-73617-9_4

depression became more complex. Theologians and intellectuals associated melancholy with spiritual and moral shortcomings, viewing it as a consequence of divine displeasure. The medieval understanding, however, was not limited to moralistic views; it also incorporated notions of imbalances in bodily humors.

The advent of modern psychiatry in the 19th century marked a pivotal shift in comprehending and categorizing depressive disorders. Depressive disorder was identified as a distinct clinical condition by the Diagnostic and Statistical Manual of Mental Disorders (DSM), contributing to the ongoing enhancement of the categorization of mood disorders. This delineation facilitated a more systematic approach to diagnosis and treatment. Depression extends its tendrils beyond the individual psyche, leaving an indelible mark on relationships, work, and societal dynamics. The ripple effect of untreated depression manifests in diminished productivity, strained interpersonal relationships, and economic burdens. The societal toll of depression underscores the urgency for effective detection and intervention strategies.

Current approaches to depression treatment encompass a multifaceted toolkit, encompassing psychotherapy, pharmacotherapy, lifestyle modifications, and support networks. Despite significant progress, identifying and assisting individuals silently grappling with depression remains a challenging task. Against this backdrop, technological advancements offer a ray of hope. Automated Depression Detection, leveraging cutting-edge technologies such as Convolutional Neural Networks (CNNs) and Transformer-based pre-trained language models, present a promising frontier.

These models, trained on a vast corpus of textual, audio and visual data, can identify subtle patterns and cues indicative of depression, transcending the limitations of traditional diagnostic approaches. Facial expressions, audio, and textual data are synthesized to form a comprehensive profile, potentially enhancing the accuracy and efficiency of depression detection. The independent learning approach, combining the strengths of all three modalities, further amplifies the diagnostic capabilities, representing a significant change in our approach to evaluating mental health.

As we navigate the complex terrain of depression, the integration of automated detection tools serves as a beacon for early intervention and support. By expediting the diagnostic process, these technologies pave the way for timely and targeted interventions, thereby empowering individuals to reclaim their mental well-being. The fusion of ancient insights, modern understanding, and technology propels humanity to reveal new chapters in the ongoing saga of mental health.

2 Literature Review

The paper by Sayanta Paul, Jandhyala Sree Kalyani, and Tanmay Basu, titled "Early Identification of Anorexia and Depression Symptoms on Social Media with Efficient Machine Learning Fabrics," addresses challenges like early detection of depression and anorexia symptoms within dynamic social platforms, utilizing the CLEF eRisk 2018 dataset. The study employs classifiers to assess the efficacy of bag-of-words and UMLS features in identifying depression, with the bag of words yielding the most favorable outcomes. The limited efficacy of RNN models is attributed to their constrained performance.[1].

A strategy to optimize word embeddings for parentheses is proposed in the paper "Deep Learning for Depression Detection of Twitter Druggies" authored by Ahmed

Husseini Orabi, Mahmoud Husseini Orabi, Diana Inkpen, and Prasadith Buddhitha. The utilization of CNN and RNN methods to the CLPsych2015 and Bell Lets Talk datasets revealed that models anchored in CNN exhibited superior performance compared to those grounded in RNN [2].

Ji, C.P. Yu, S.-F. Fung, S. Pan, and G. Long, "Supervised literacy for suicidal creativity discovery in online stoner content," uses two datasets, from Reddit and Twitter. This identifies features from colorful perspectives and makes use of traditional and deep literacy classifiers to compare similar as Random Forest, Gradient Boost Bracket tree, XGBoost, MLFFNN and LSTM out of which XGBoost has the loftiest AUC of0.9569 [3].

Ji, X. Li, Z. Huang, and E. Cambria, "Suicidal creativity and internal complaint discovery with attentive relation networks," focuses on enabling relational textbook garbling to classify suicidal creativity and internal diseases. The suggested system is evaluated against the birth models, fastText, CNN, LSTM, RCNN and SSA enforced by PyTorch [4].

Zhang, T., Schoene, A.M., Ji, S. et al. Natural language processing applied to internal illness discovery a narrative review uses NLP styles and Deep literacy styles to dissect data of which the ultimate has shown better performance. This is mostly because Deep Learning methods may automatically extract valuable features without requiring point engineering [5].

Margaret Mitchell, Kristy Hollinshead, and Glen Coppersmith. Quantifying the linguistic patterns of Schizophrenia in Social Media, attempts to define features applicable to internal health and schizophrenia and explore the differences between schizophrenia exhibiting negative and positive druggies regarding the specified features. Automatic NLP styles are used and patterns are linked [6].

Using colorful NLP styles in conjunction to determine which pairing yields a higher vaticination delicacy, Luna Ansari, Shaoxiong Ji, Qian Chen, and Erikcambria's Ensemble Mongrel Learning styles for Automated Depression Discovery performs depression discovery across three datasets [7].

In the work by Mukherjee, S.S. et al. titled "Natural language processing-grounded quantification of the internal state of psychiatric cases" (Comput. Psychiatry 4, 76 106, 2020), a dual vector representation of symptoms and emotional states in psychiatric cases is generated employing deep learning and NLP techniques grounded in the individual's Subjective Assessment (SA). The goal is to formulate new treatment plans by comparing the challenges faced by patients with their internal health conditions [8].

Gong et. al. Uses a regression method based on PLS wherein a late fusion detection method along with the question-answer based model, applying it on all 3 modalities for model prediction [9].

3 Existing System

The user inputs various features, which are subsequently parameterized and analyzed through diverse methods. Additionally, studies have shown that Natural Language Processing (NLP) techniques deliver excellent results in deep learning applications, particularly in text categorization and image recognition. Recurrent Neural Networks (RNNs) constitute a group of neural network architectures where the output of the current segment is directly connected to its own input.

Word processing also frequently makes use of LSTM and Bi-Directional LSTM, the latter of which shortens processing times. The construction of most models is typically based on a predefined set of lexicons, or a prefixed dictionary of data, acting as a data source from which the model may compare and determine features. Sentiment representations of sentences, including polarity label, sensitivity, and value, are components of the widely used lexicon SenticNet.

The binary classifiers obtained from the preprocessing phases are then trained utilizing machine learning techniques, and the outcomes are assessed for accuracy and other pertinent metrics.

4 Proposed System

Traditionally, depression detection relied on thorough clinical interviews, during which psychologists analyzed the subject's responses to assess their mental state. In the model presented, an attempt is crafted to emulate this approach by integrating three modalities such as word context, audio, and video to predict the patient's mental health. The output is stratified into different levels, considering the varying degrees of depression in the subject. A model has been constructed to fuse these modalities, assigning suitable weights to each and thereby generating an output.

4.1 Dataset

The University of Southern California collected the DAIC-WOZ dataset, a portion of the broader DAIC (Distress Analysis Interview Corpus), designed to aid in diagnosing psychological distress conditions like anxiety, depression, and PTSD.

Comprising audio and video recordings along with extensive questionnaire responses, the DAIC-WOZ dataset incorporates Wizard-Of-Oz interviews. These sessions involve an animated virtual assistant named Ellie, controlled by a human interviewer in a separate room. The data is transcribed and annotated to capture various verbal and non-verbal features. Each participant's session includes a transcription of the interaction, participant audio files, and facial features derived from the recorded video.

In total, the dataset encompasses 189 interaction sessions, varying in duration from 7 to 33 min. It includes interviews with 59 individuals experiencing depression and 130 non-depressed subjects. *Sample Heading (Forth Level).* The contribution should contain no more than four levels of headings. The following **Error! Reference source not found.** Gives a summary of all heading levels.

4.2 Modalities

Audio Modality

The attributes are sampled at a rate of 100 Hz with a granularity of 10 ms. The feature set includes 12 Mel-frequency cepstral coefficients (MFCCs), namely FO, QOQ, VUV, NAQ, H1H2, PSP, MDQ, Rdconf, Rd, MCEPO-24, peakSlope, HMPDM0-24, and HMPDD0-12. Complementary to the MFCCs, there are supplementary attributes for pitch tracking, peak slope, maximal dispersion quotients, and glottal source parameters. The VUV feature indicates whether the current sample is voiced or unvoiced, and in cases where the sample is unvoiced (VUV = 0), FO, QOQ, NAQ, MDQ, H1H2, PSP, Rd, and peakSlope are set to 0.

Text Modality

Within the textual modality, the dataset contains the entire conversation transcript between the patient in CSV format. Individual sentences are time stamped and classified based on their speaker. Expressions such as laughter or frowns are encapsulated in angular brackets (e.g., <Laughter>) whenever they occur. It is worth mentioning that the differentiation between long and short pauses has not been made, and only word-level segmentation, not phoneme-level, has been recorded.

Video Modality

The dataset encompasses various facial attributes obtained from participant videos. These include 68 2D points on the face, 24 Action Units (AU) features measuring facial activity, 68 3D points on the face, 16 features representing the subject's gaze, and 10 features reflecting the subject's pose. In total, this results in 388 distinct video features (Fig. 1).

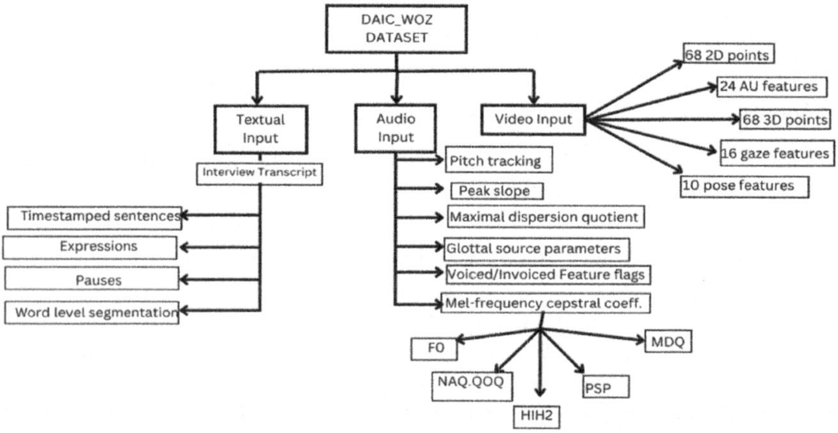

Fig. 1. Features used in DAIC_WOZ Dataset

4.3 Model Flow

In the proposed system, the approach involves initial feature extraction, followed by the implementation of a gating mechanism and hybrid fusion technique on the extracted features. The features consist of audio, visual, and textual modalities, integrated using timestamps to capture time-dependent interactions. Sentence-level forced alignment is conducted during preprocessing to enable the framework to learn contextual relationships between words.

Having aligned the textual, visual and audio features at the sentence level, it's crucial to acknowledge that different modalities may have varying impacts on the final result, introducing noise to the representation of features. To address this, a gating mechanism is applied to the derived features to regulate the influence of each modality to the final output. Weight vectors linked to each modality are employed in the network to control and learn the transformation and information carried to subsequent layers.

At each time interval, feature representations from every modality are merged then passed through a word-level LSTM containing the gating mechanism. Prior to the concatenation of feature vectors, gating mechanisms are also applied to the visual, textual and audio vectors to extract essential information (Fig. 2).

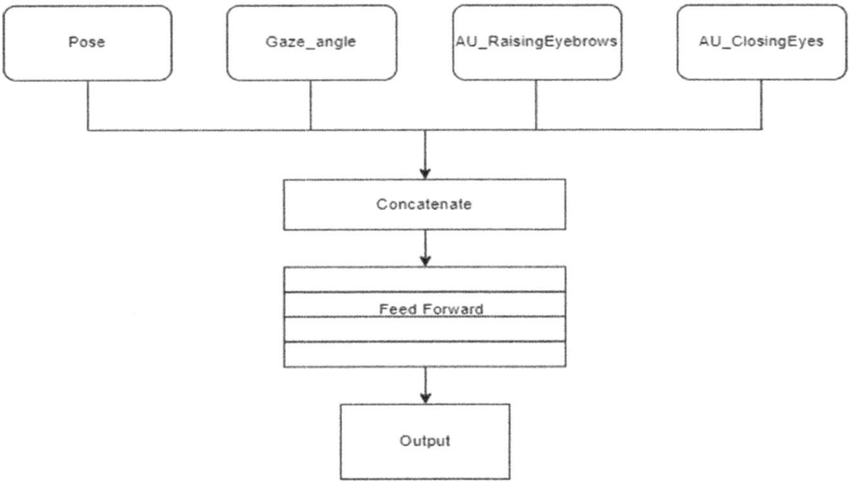

Fig. 2. Late fusion Model Architecture

4.4 Training Procedure

SVM and Random Forest

Initially, SVM (utilizing an RBF kernel) and Random Forest were individually utilized on the three modalities. Subsequently, another SVM model underwent training on the decision labels obtained from each specific modalities to facilitate late fusion. In this context, the features of the video and audio modalities were averaged across all timestamps, resulting in 74 and 388 features, respectively. For the text modality, the word2Vec model from google-news-300 was employed to transform each word into a 300-dimensional vector. The resulting 3D vector (sentences $\times$ words $\times$ 300 features) was initially averaged over each word and then flattened.

CNN

A 6-layer CNN model was constructed, with the initial four layers incorporating conv2D layers for the text modality and conv1D layers for audio and video modalities, along with

Max Pooling layers. Additional flattening and fully connected layers were integrated with ReLU activation, while the last layer utilized Sigmoid activation. For audio and video modalities, attributes were derived from the first 40,000 timestamps, chosen based on computational capabilities. Concerning the text modality, after applying the Word2vec model, thresholds were set for the maximum number of sentences and words.

LSTM Model with/without Gating (Sentence-level)
Initially, the data underwent transformation to the sentence level by averaging features from the audio and video modalities corresponding to the provided timestamps of sentences. This involved the application of sentence-level forced alignment.

(Bi)LSTM Model with Gating (Word-Level)
The data underwent forced alignment at a word level. This alignment employed a unitary approach, converting sentence-level timestamps to word-level depending on the count of words in the sentence and the character length present in each sentence (Table 1).

Table 1. Baseline Results

Model	Feature	F1	Prec	MAE	RMSE
Baseline					
DAIC Baseline	Audio + Video	-	-	5.66	7.05
Gog et al	Text + Audio + Video	0.60	-	3.96	**4.99**
Alhanai et al	Text	0.66	0.70	5.09	6.11
Alhanai et al	Text + Audio	0.75	0.72	5.02	6.04
Williamson et al	Text	0.67	0.74	3.82	5.06
Williamson et al	Text + Audio + Video	0.70	0.78	3.84	5.23
Word Level Models					
LSTM	Text	0.68	0.69	4.99	6.04
LSTM	Text + Audio	0.66	0.69	5.19	6.41
LSTM	Text + Audio + Video	0.66	0.64	5.28	6.69
LSTM with Gating	Text + Audio	0.81	0.77	3.67	5.15
LSTM with Gating	Text + Audio + Video	**0.81**	**0.80**	**3.61**	**4.99**

Following this, the outcomes are combined with the corresponding text feature, and the resulting concatenated vector undergoes further processing through a (Bi)LSTM layer to produce the final output.

In more detail, the audio and video features initially pass through three feedforward highway layers. Subsequently, dense layers are employed to diminish the dimensionality of both video and text features.

After concatenation, a (Bi)LSTM with 128 hidden nodes is applied, and a last compact layer with sigmoid activation generates the results. A learning rate of 0.0001 is set, and the iteration count is controlled using the EarlyStopping callback from the Keras API (Fig. 3).

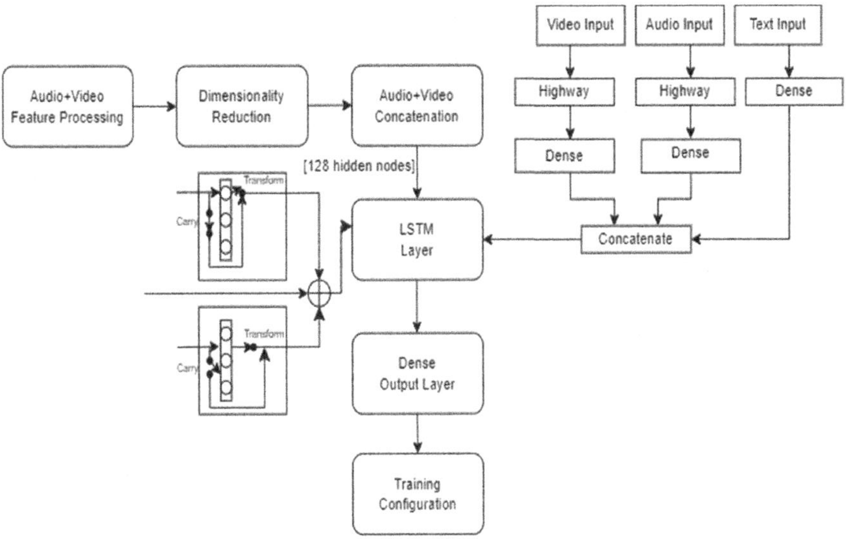

Fig. 3. Model Architecture using Sentence-Level Multi-Modal Fusion with Gating

5 Proposed System

The outcomes were reported by computing a weighted mean for two classes, namely class 0 (Not depressed) and class 1 (Depressed). The data distribution is maintained at a ratio of 7:3.

5.1 SVM Model

The SVM model demonstrated less-than-satisfactory performance, as indicated by the results. This suboptimal outcome may stem from the utilization of averaging operations across the three modalities, potentially causing information loss and resulting in the model's underperformance.

5.2 CNN Model

Unlike the SVM model, the CNN model exhibited better results in the text modality because of the absence of averaging across word vectors. However, the audio and video modalities still yielded unsatisfactory outcomes, likely attributable to the limited data points and sparse features characterizing these modalities.

5.3 LSTM with/without Gating at Sentence-Level

The results unequivocally highlight the superior performance of the framework in the text modality. The relatively low Fl score values in the video and audio modalities suggest that these features inadequately represent the depression class. Consequently, when combining video, audio and text modalities, the results fall just short of those achieved by the model solely utilizing the text modality.

Moreover, models incorporating gating mechanisms consistently outperform those without gating. This could be ascribed to the reality that gating selectively amplifies the most crucial features while nullifying others, facilitating a form of feature extraction at this level. This, in turn, aids our LSTM model in learning from only the most influential features (Fig. 4).

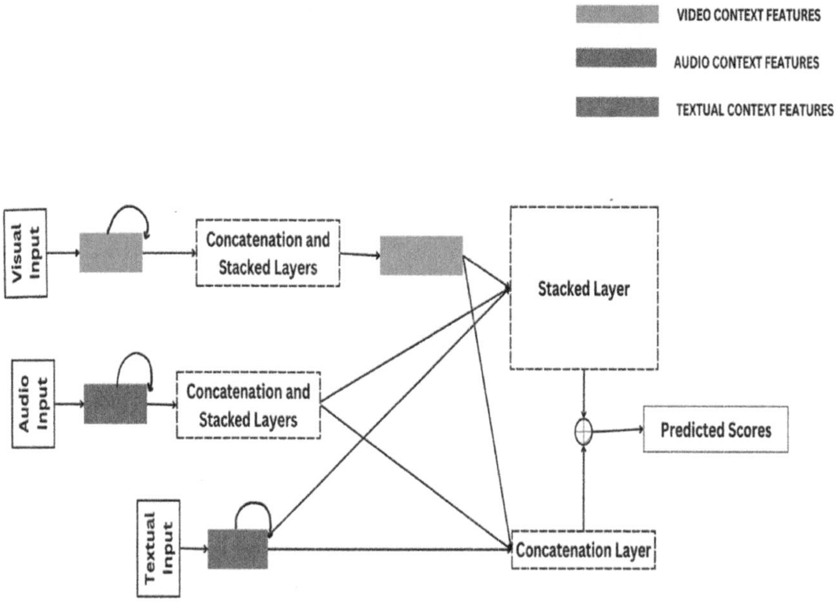

Fig. 4. Block Diagram of Proposed Network on Multi-Modality Input Feature

5.4 LSTM with Gating at Word-Level

The outcomes for the word-level LSTM are not as favorable as anticipated. This might be assigned to the model's limited contextual understanding of the conversation at the word level in contrast to the sentence level.

5.5 BiLSTM Model

This model exhibits a noticeable inclination towards the depressed class, indicating a challenge in effectively learning from the given data (Table 2).

Table 2. Precision, Recall, F1-Score of used Models

Model	Modality	Precision	Recall	F1
Late Fusion using SVM	Text + Audio + Video	0.443	0.386	0.423
CNN	Text	0.567	0.627	0.597
	Audio	0.086	0.4	0.134
	Video	0.086	0.4	0.136
LSTM	Text	0.656	0.67	**0.667**
	Audio	0.575	0.454	0.456
	Video	0.50	0.676	0.568
BiLSTM (word-level)	Text + Audio + Video	0.78	0.322	0.188
LSTM w/o Gating (sentence-level)	Text + Audio	0.713	0.358	0.475
	Text + Video	0.605	0.468	0.475
	Text + Audio + Video	0.622	0.489	0.6
LSTM w Gating (sentence-level)	Text + Audio	0.634	0.653	**0.647**
	Text + Video	0.652	0.538	0.559
	Text + Audio + Video	0.639	0.653	**0.647**
LSTM w Gating (word-level)	Text + Audio + Video	0.490	0.652	0.554

6 Conclusion

In conclusion, the amalgamation of Transformer-based pretrained language models and CNN in the presented model for automated depression detection shows promise in enhancing accuracy and robustness. The model, utilizing indicators from text, video, and audio modalities, employs a sentence-level approach with highway layers as a gating mechanism.

The above findings suggest that the sentence-level model outperforms other models, and a combination of both early and late fusion improves modality interpretation.

For future research, a more comprehensive extraction of features, including additional audio features like response time and pauses, could offer a clearer insight of symptoms. Exploring the correlation amid bodily action sequences from motion capture data and verbal behavior could also contribute to a more comprehensive study.

Regular evaluation on a validation set, along with potential hyperparameter fine-tuning, ensures adaptability to diverse dataset characteristics.

The model demonstrates potential for enhanced accuracy and robustness in addressing the challenging task of automated depression identification, leveraging a synergistic combination of conventional machine learning and deep learning features.

References

1. Paul, S., Kalyani, J., Basu, T.: Early detection of signs of anorexia and depression over social media using effective machine learning frameworks (2018)
2. Meng, H., Huang, D., Wang, H., Yang, H., Ai Shuraifi, M., Wang, Y.: Depression recognition based on dynamic facial and vocal expression features using partial least square regression. In: Proceedings of the 3rd ACM international workshop on Audio/visual emotion challenge, pp. 21–30. ACM (2013)
3. Yu, Z., et al.: Multimodal prediction of psychological disorders: learning verbal and non-verbal commonalities in adjacency pairs. In: Semdial 2013 Dial-Dam: Proceedings of the 17thWorkshop on the Semantics and Pragmatics of Dialogue, pp. 160–169 (2013)
4. Gong, Y., Poellabauer, C.: Topic modeling based Multi-modal depression detection. In: Proceedings of the 7th Annual Workshop on Audio/Visual Emotion Challenge, pp. 69–76. ACM (2017)
5. Sun, B., et al.: A random forest regression method with selected text feature for depression assessment. In: Proceedings of the 7th Annual Workshop on Audio/Visual Emotion Challenge, pp. 61–68. ACM (2017)
6. Ma, X., Yang, H., Chen, Q., Huang, D., Wang, Y.: Depaudionet: An efficient deep model for audio based depression classification. In: Proceedings of the 6th International Workshop on Audio/Visual Emotion Challenge, pp. 35–42. ACM (2016)
7. Nasir, M., Jati, A., Shivakumar, P.G., Chakravarthula, S.N., Georgiou, P.: Multimodal and multi resolution depression detection from speech and facial landmark features. In: Proceedings of the 6th International Workshop on Audio/Visual Emotion Challenge, pp. 43–50. ACM (2016)
8. Al Hanai, T., Ghassemi, M., Glass, J.: Detecting depression. with audio/text sequence modeling of interviews. In: Proceedings of the Inter-speech, pp. 1716–1720 (2018)
9. Alghowinem, S., et al.: Multimodal depression detection: fusion analysis of paralinguistic, head pose and eye gaze behaviors. IEEE Trans. Affective Comput. **9**(4), 478–490 (2018). https://doi.org/10.1109/TAFFC.2016.2634527
10. Orabi, A.H., Buddhitha, P., Orabi, M.H., Inkpen, D.: Deep learning for depression detection of twitter users. In: Proceedings of the Fifth Workshop on Computational Linguistics and Clinical Psychology: From Keyboard to Clinic, pp. 88–97. Association for Computational Linguistics, New Orleans, LA (2018)
11. Ji, S., Ping Yu, C., Fung, S., Pan, S., Long, G.: Supervised learning for suicidal ideation detection in online user content. Complexity (2018). https://doi.org/10.1155/2018/6157249
12. Ji, S., Li, X., Huang, Z., Cambria, E.: Suicidal ideation and mental disorder detection with attentive relation networks. Neural Comput. Applic. **34**(13), 10309–10319 (2022). https://doi.org/10.1007/s00521-021-06208-y
13. Zhang, T., Schoene, A.M., Ji, S., Ananiadou, S.: Natural language processing applied to mental illness detection: a narrative review. npj Digit. Med. (2022). https://doi.org/10.1038/s41746-022-00589-7
14. Mitchell, M., Hollingshead, K., Coppersmith, G.: Quantifying the language of schizophrenia in social media. In: Proceedings of the 2nd Workshop on Computational Linguistics and Clinical Psychology: From Linguistic Signal to Clinical Reality, pp. 11–20. Association for Computational Linguistics, Denver, Colorado (2015)
15. Ansari, L., Ji, S., Chen, Q., Cambria, E.: Ensemble hybrid learning methods for automated depression detection. IEEE Trans. Comput. Soc. Syst. **10**(1), 211–219 (2023). https://doi.org/10.1109/TCSS.2022.3154442
16. Mukherjee, S.S., et al.: Natural language processing-based quantification of the mental state of psychiatric patients. Computational (2020). https://doi.org/10.1162/cpsy_a_00030

17. He, K., Zhang, X., Ren, S., Sun, J.: Deep residual learning for image recognition. In: Proceedings of the IEEE Conference on Computation Visual Pattern Recogniton (CVPR), pp. 770–778 (2016)
18. Bokolo, B.G., Liu, Q.: Deep learning-based depression detection from social media: comparative evaluation of ML and transformer techniques. Electronics **12**(21), 4396 (2023). https://doi.org/10.3390/electronics12214396
19. Hemanthkumar, M., Latha, "Depression Detection with Sentiment Analysis of Tweets. Int. Res. Journal of Engineering and Technology (IRJET) (2019)
20. Islam, M.R., Kabir, M.A., Ahmed, A., Kamal, A.R.M., Wang, H., Ulhaq, A.: Depression detection from social network data using machine learning techniques. Springer (2018)
21. Franco-Martín, M.A.: A systematic literature review of technologies for suicidal behavior prevention. J. Med. Syst. **42**, 1–7 (2018)
22. Venek, V., Scherer, S., Morency, L.P., Rizzo, A.S., Pestian, J.: Adolescent suicidal risk assessment in clinician-patient interaction. IEEE Trans. Affect. Comput. **8**(2), 204–215 (2017)
23. Coppersmith, G., Leary, R., Whyne, E., Wood, T.: Quantifying suicidal ideation via language usage on social media. In: Joint Statistics Meetings Proceedings, Statistical Computing Section, JSM (2015)
24. Bahdanau, D., Chorowski, J., Serdyuk, D., Brakel, P., Bengio, Y.: End-to-end attention-based large vocabulary speech recognition. In: Proceedings of the IEEE International Conference on Acoustics, Speech Signal Process. (ICASSP), pp. 4945–4949 (2016)
25. Mikolov, T., Sutskever, I., Chen, K., Corrado, G., J. Dean, G.: Distributed representations of words and phrases and their compositionality. arXiv:1310.4546 (2013)
26. Hosseini-Saravani, S.H., Besharati, S., Calvo, H., Gelbukh, A.: Depression detection in social media using a psychoanalytical technique for feature extraction and a cognitive based classifier. In: Martínez-Villaseñor, L., Herrera-Alcántara, O., Ponce, H., Castro-Espinoza, F.A. (eds.) Advances in Computational Intelligence: 19th Mexican International Conference on Artificial Intelligence, MICAI 2020, Mexico City, Mexico, October 12–17, 2020, Proceedings, Part II, pp. 282–292. Springer International Publishing, Cham (2020). https://doi.org/10.1007/978-3-030-60887-3_25
27. Shing, H.C., Nair, S., Zirikly, A., Friedenberg, M., Daumé III, H., Resnik, P.: Expert, crowdsourced, and machine assessment of suicide risk via online postings. In Proceedings of the Fifth Workshop on CLPsych, pp. 25–36 (2018)
28. Gratch, J, et al.: The Distress Analysis Interview Corpus of human and computer interviews. In: LREC, pp. 3123–3128 (2014)
29. GratDeVault, D., et l.: SimSensei kiosk: A virtual human interviewer for healthcare decision support. In: Proceedings of the 13th International Conference on Autonomous Agents and Multiagent Systems (AAMAS'14), Paris (2014)

Integrating Deep Learning Frameworks for Automated Medical Image Diagnosis

K. Gayatri(✉), K. M. Anand Kumar, B. Padmavathi, and Shankar

Department of Computer Science and Engineering, Easwari Engineering College Ramapuram, Chennai 600089, India
gayathri8398@gmail.com, {anandkumar.m,padmavathi.b, shankar.k}@eec.srmrmp.edu.in

Abstract. In today's healthcare system, medical image analysis is essential for diagnosis, treatment planning, and condition monitoring. In this study, the four well-known tools in the field are 3D Slicer, MONAI, SAMM, and YOLOv8 are examined and contrasted. The study's scope includes its ability to process a variety of 2D and 4D medical imaging datasets, which contain images, segmentation, annotations, and transformations. The process entails a comprehensive prehensive examination of every tool's feature, with particular emphasis on their capacity to read and write DICOM images, accommodate multiple file formats, offer interactive 3D Slicer. Key findings show that 3D Slicer performs exceptionally well when using deep learning techniques for segmentation and interactive visualization. While SAM Model exhibits adaptability in managing diverse segmentation prompts, MONAI provides a comprehensive end-to-end medical data processing solution. YOLOv8 shows potential for effective object detection. The study's implications include the possibility of using these instruments in clinical practices and medical research contexts. The research results provide insight into the current discussion about how to strategically integrate state-of-the-art methods to improve overall healthcare outcomes, diagnostic accuracy, and treatment planning efficiency as medical image analysis continues to advance.

Keywords: Medical Image Analysis · Deep Learning · DICOM · MONAI · segment Anything Medical Modal · YOLOV8

1 Introduction

Medical image analysis is a fundamental component of contemporary healthcare, being essential to the identification, management, and surveillance of numerous medical ailments. Advanced tools are required for precise and effective analysis due to the increasing complexity and volume of imaging data resulting from the ongoing evolution of medical imaging technologies. Medical image analysis is important because it may provide useful information from complex imaging datasets, which helps medical practioners make better judgements.

Published by Springer Nature Switzerland AG 2025
A. Chandrabose et al. (Eds.): ICCCSP 2024, IFIP AICT 723, pp. 54–67, 2025.
https://doi.org/10.1007/978-3-031-73617-9_5

Medical image analysis plays a major role in patient care by helping to discover abnormalities in the early stages of disease, guiding surgical operations, and tracking treatment responses. DICOM (Digital Imaging and Communications in Medicine) and NIfTI (Neuroimaging Informatics Technology Initiative) are two commonly used data formats with distinct purposes in the field of medical imaging. DICOM is a comprehensive standard that is widely used in the healthcare sector for the interchange, storing, and transmission of medical pictures together with related data.

It standardized format for both image and their non-image data, including comprehensive metadata interoperability across different imaging techniques, such as nuclear medicine, ultrasound, CT, MRI, and X-rays. In order to facilitate the integration of images into electronic health records and Picture Archiving and Communication Systems, DICOM is essential to healthcare workflows. NIfTI, on the other hand, is a unique file format that is mainly intended for neuroimaging data. NIfTI was designed with simplicity and user-friendliness in mind. It offers a standard header and image data format, which makes it ideal for MRI and functional MRI (fMRI) studies in the field of neuroscience research. While NIfTI shines in its simplicity and specialization for neuroimaging, meeting the unique needs of the neuroscience community, DICOM offers versatility fora several applications for medical imaging. The decision between DICOM and NIfTI is frequently influenced by the standards and imaging needs that are common in the corresponding fields of medicine and research.

The vast variety and complexity of imaging data presents difficulties for medical image interpretation, despite its significance. The conventional method, manual analysis, takes a lot of time, is prone to mistakes, and frequently cannot achieve the level of precision required in clinical situations. Advanced technologies must be developed and implemented due to the growing complexity of medical imaging data and the growing need for faster and more accurate diagnosis. The difficulties include the enormous amount of data produced, the requirement for real-time analysis, and the complexity of medical imaging, which necessitates a high degree of skill. Furthermore, existing technologies find it difficult to handle the growing complexity as medical imaging evolves towards 3D and 4D datasets. Every framework, such as MONAI, SAMM, and YOLOv8, makes a distinct contribution to a separate stage of the liver segmentation diagnostic procedure. By guarantee ideal intensity levels and spatial resolution, MONAI improves segmentation precision. SAMM is an expert in precisely identifying and defining abnormalities inside the liver by lesion segmentation. When it comes to tumors detection, YOLOv8 is exceptional in finding abnormal tumors in medical images. Finally, feature fusion combines distinguishing characteristics from different models to improve understanding of liver architecture and support diagnostic decision-making.

2 Related Work

Bowen Zheng's study [1] on head CT image reconstruction addressed the difficulties in getting accurate CT scans because of a number of variables. The manual methods of formatting and reconstruction were considered subjective and required a lot of resources. With an incredible accuracy of 92.77%, the study's automatic 3D reconstruction method using YOLOv8 was suggested as a way to improve accuracy and consistency.

The method provided a more effective and standardized solution for head CT image reconstruction by reducing issues associated with technician error and physical limits. By tackling the issues brought on by unbalanced datasets, Guanghu Yue [2] presented a novel method for automated endoscopic image classification. In situations like these, a lot of the computer-aided diagnostic (CAD) methods now in use have trouble with minority class accuracy. In order to improve automatic categorization, this work presents a novel Class Imbalance (CI) loss integrated within a deep neural network (DNN). Class frequency and prediction probability are taken into account by the CI loss, which modifies sample weights to increase the contribution of minority classes. Gradient descent is given priority for underrepresented classes in this method, which enhances endoscopic image categorization overall.

Improvements in intelligent image analysis techniques, especially in computer assisted diagnosis, have greatly improved medical image screening and diagnostic procedures as demonstrated by Rui Jesus study [3] Even with these advancements, there are still issues, such as the requirement for large annotated datasets and the lack of expertise among non-medical staff when it comes to algorithm development. Using the open-source components Dicoogle and MONAI, the study extends a Vendor-Neutral Archive to solve interoperability difficulties in healthcare contexts. With the creation of a Web and DICOM compliant platform, this Endeavor seeks to enable the smooth integration of AI technology in both research and clinical environments.

The difficulty of training segmentation models for medical images due to a lack of data annotations is addressed in Maciej A. Mazurowski's work [4]. Trained on more than 1 billion annotations, the Segment Anything Model (SAM) is a basic model that can interactively separate user-defined things of interest. Although SAM performs exceptionally well on natural images, this work assesses its segmentation abilities in the challenging field of medical imaging in detail. The paper evaluates the performance of SAM in interactive segmentation using a standard technique applied to 19 different medical imaging datasets covering different modalities and anatomies.

Deep learning has been a very useful technology for ECG analysis in recent years is addressed in Hanna Vitaliyivna Denysyuk [5]. Convolutional neural networks, or CNNs, have been effectively used to learn features from ECG signals, allowing for the capture of complex patterns. Recurrent Neural Networks (RNNs) provide benefits for temporal dependency modelling, improving the capacity to identify minute irregularities across time. The use of transfer learning approaches, which modify pre-trained models for the purpose of cardiovascular diagnosis, has drawn interest due to its capacity.

Deep learning has been a very useful technology for ECG analysis in recent years is addressed in Hanna Vitaliyivna Denysyuk [5]. Convolutional neural networks, or CNNs, have been effectively used to learn features from ECG signals, allowing for the capture of complex patterns. Recurrent Neural Networks (RNNs) provide benefits for temporal dependency modelling, improving the capacity to identify minute irregularities across time. The use of transfer learning approaches, which modify pre-trained models for the purpose of cardiovascular diagnosis, has drawn interest due to its capacity.

Duc Tri Phan [6] Incorporating deep learning and medical IoT with a low-level laser therapy (LLLT) device, this study suggests a computer-aided diagnosis for facial skin problems using dermoscopy images. Important contributions include a procedure for creating synthetic data to overcome dataset constraints, a modified U2 Net model for disorder segmentation and hardware software design. 97.5% accuracy, 74.7%Jaccard Index and 80.6% dice coefficient, the MIoT assisted LLLT platform well. With an untrained dataset, the U2 Net model performs better than more current models. This research shows how well the LLLT technology performs in both phototherapy and facial skin disease segmentation. Enhancing the detection and treatment of facial skin problems is possible with the integration of MIoT and AI in healthcare platforms, which comes with great promise.

The complexity of medical picture segmentation is addressed by Hao Due [7] proposed weakly-supervised segmentation framework, which integrates geometric priors and contrastive similarity in a loss-based way. By utilizing a point cloud-based geometric prior, the segmentation approach outperforms bounding-box annotations in terms of precision. Furthermore, by promoting organ pixel cohesiveness in the embedding space, the added contrastive similarity enhances the ability to distinguish between low-contrast tissues. The shortcomings of traditional grey space depiction are made up for by the contrastive embedding space. Extensive trials on the LiTS 2017, KiTS 2021, and LPBA40 datasets show that our approach outperforms the state-of-the-art weakly supervised techniques. By using this method, pre-processing methods for computer aided diagnosis in medical imaging are advanced.

According to Celso T.N. Suzuki [8], intestinal parasitosis is a major health concern in the majority of tropical nations. Optical microscopy is used in laboratory routines to examine stool samples for the presence of enteroparasites; error rates in this process typically vary from moderate to high. Some species-specific approaches based on automatic image processing have been developed; however, the methods require human image acquisition and focus, and some of them are computationally expensive. We describe a system for automating the identification of the 15 most prevalent enteroparasite species in Brazil. It involves the use of a motorized microscope equipped with a digital camera for automatic picture acquisition and focus, a sensitive parasitological approach, and quick image processing techniques. The outcomes show that our solution is appropriate and successful.

Jie Shu study [9] on 3D CD-Link Net Liver Vessel Segmentation For clinical surgery, the automatic segmentation of hepatic blood arteries from CT scans is particularly useful. It is challenging to segment blood arteries in abdominal CT images because of the limited volume, erratic form, and low contrast of these images. This work proposed a three-step segmentation of the liver blood channels in order to overcome these difficulties. Pre-processing is the initial stage in enhancing the contrast of the CT images. The liver blood vessels are segmented using a recently suggested 3D segmentation network with dilated convolutions in the second stage. Post-processing the segmentation findings is the third stage.

The rest of the paper is organized as follows. The proposed methodology is presented in Sect. 3, followed by results and discussion in Sect. 4. A conclusion is presented in Sect. 5.

3 Proposed Methodology

Figure 1 represents that proposed methodology for automated liver segmentation system that is being suggested is a complete solution that makes use of state-of-the-art medical image analysis tools and frameworks such as YOLOv8, MONAI, SAM Model. This system supports multiple data types, including images, segmentations, surfaces, annotations, and transformations, and is designed to handle a wide range of 2D and 4D medical imaging datasets. The architecture focuses on evaluating each tool's capabilities in detail, with special attention to how well it identifies DICOM images, how well it works with various file formats, and whether it offers interactive features similar to those found in the well-known 3D Slicer tool. A dedicated Data Loader module, at the center of the system, is in charge of standardizing and harmonizing incoming medical image files.

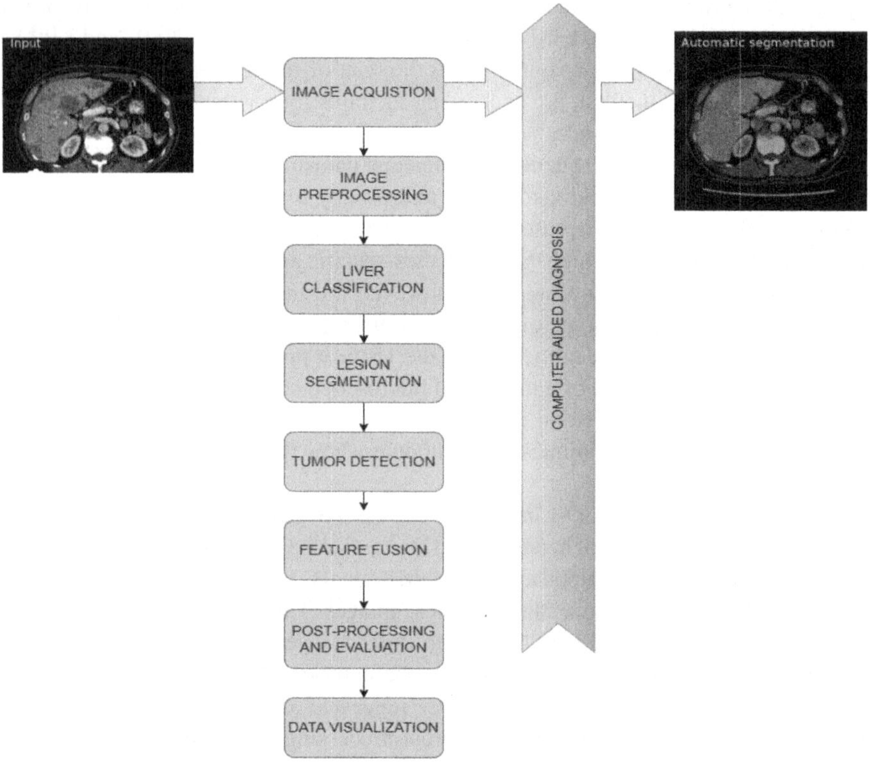

Fig. 1. Proposed methodology for liver segmentation

A. IMAGE ACQUISTION

An essential phase in medical imaging, image acquisition is necessary for precise diagnosis and therapy planning. The process starts with choosing an imaging modality (such as an X-ray, CT, MRI, or ultrasound) that is suitable for the particular clinical or research needs. Before taking an image, the patient is carefully prepared. This may include advice on fasting, removing any metal objects, or giving contrast material to improve visibility. For the best possible image quality and precision, the patient must be positioned correctly. Imaging equipment is calibrated on a regular basis to ensure accuracy and dependability, and continuous quality control inspections confirm the device is operating as intended.

B. PREPROCESSING

Preprocessing is essential for enhancing the quality of medical images in the context of automated liver segmentation in order to guarantee accurate and dependable segmentation results. To reduce variability across different scans, the first step is to normalize the image's intensity data to a standardized scale. To keep the spatial resolution constant, the images are then resampled to a common voxel size. While contrast enhancement techniques like histogram equalization are used to improve the visibility of hepatic features, noise reduction techniques like Gaussian smoothing are used to improve the signal-to-noise ratio. In order to align images from several modalities or time points and provide a standardized coordinate system for precise segmentation, image registration is done. After that, areas of interest (ROIs) or masks are taken out to concentrate on Compute gradients to indicate edges, analyze histograms to comprehend pixel intensity distributions, and normalize spatial orientation to ensure uniform application among patients are next steps. To diversity the training set, optional data augmentation techniques like random transformations or rotations can be used. Preprocessing pipeline refinement is further enhanced by artefact detection and repair, as well as the thoughtful selection of particular slices or image volumes.

C. LIVER CLASSIFICATION

Utilizing deep learning technologies to accurately and efficiently classify medical images is one of the advanced strategies involved in liver classification shown in the Fig. 2 demonstrate that MONAI framework, which is an important tool in this context due to its extensive end-to-end medical data processing capabilities, is used. To guarantee uniform intensity values, the best possible spatial resolution, and an improved signal-to-noise ratio, the procedure starts with preprocessing medical images. The dataset is made more palatable for classification by normalizing spatial orientation and extracting areas of interest (ROIs) unique to the liver. A deep neural network that can recognize complex patterns and features in the liver images is trained more easily thanks to the MONAI framework. Based on the existence or lack of hepatic structures, the network is fine-tuned to classify these images According to the existence or lack of hepatic structures. In the process of training, the model develops a strong classification algorithm by learning to recognize minute differences in liver structure. The integration of MONAI's liver classification it shows how to correctly identify and classify liver structures inside medical pictures using a comprehensive method that includes preprocessing and model training. This improves diagnostic capabilities in clinical and research settings.

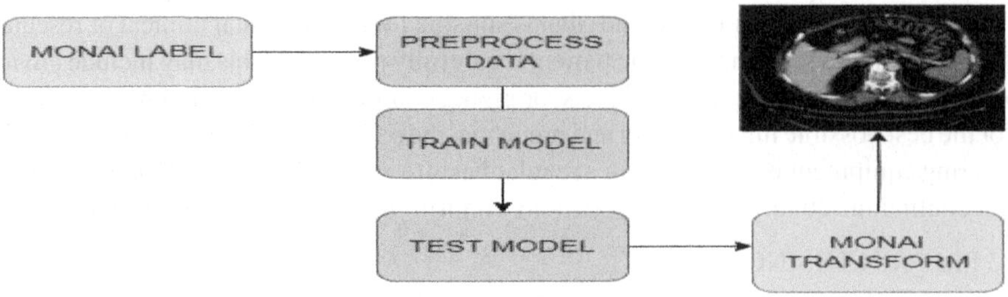

Fig. 2. MONAI for Liver Classification

D. LESION SEGMENTATION

Using the Segment Anything Medical Model (SAMM), lesion segmentation in the liver in Fig. 3 is a methodical procedure that precisely locates and delineates anomalous entities in medical images. To establish a consistent dataset, the medical images are first subjected to data preprocessing, which involves standardizing intensity values, adjusting ideal spatial resolution, and reducing noise. The architecture and parameters of the SAMM model are then adjusted for lesion segmentation, taking into account the unique features of liver lesions. The algorithm gains the ability to identify patterns linked to liver lesions through an extensive training phase that makes use of annotated datasets. The model is validated and adjusted after training in order to improve segmentation accuracy and improve its generalization to new data. Next, fresh medical images are fed into the trained SAMM model to perform lesion segmentation, highlighting areas The segmentation findings are refined using post-processing methods that take care of things like smoothing segmented regions and removing small isolated parts. The correctness of the segmentation is ensured visual examination and validation against expert evaluations or ground truth annotations. Metrics such as Dice coefficient, sensitivity, and specificity are used in quantitative evaluation to give an accurate picture of the model's performance. Additional training or parameter tweaking can be used to iteratively improve the model as needed. In the end, the lesion segmentation model is easily incorporated into the workflow for medical image analysis, which helps to improve treatment planning and diagnostic analysis in clinical or research settings.

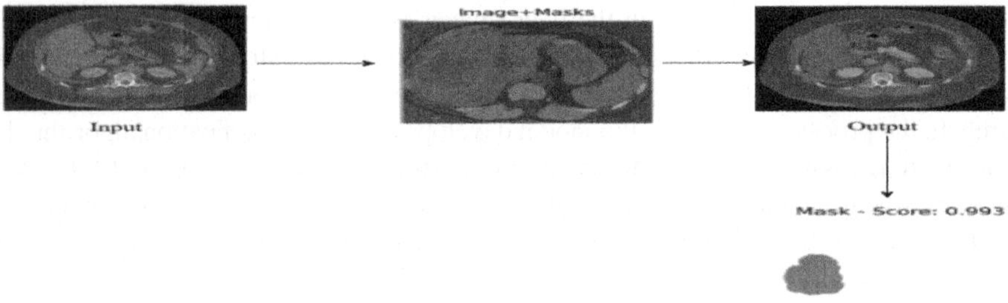

Fig. 3. SAM lesion segmentation

E. TUMOR DETECTION

Figure 4 utilizes that YOLOv8 technology for liver tumour diagnosis, aberrant lumps within medical images are systematically identified and located. The first step of the procedure is data preprocessing, which involves rescaling, noise reduction, and intensity normalization of the medical images to provide a uniform input dataset. Then, using its deep learning architecture and pre-trained weights, YOLOv8, which is well-known for its effectiveness in object detection tasks, is set up for tumour detection. Training using annotated datasets that include liver image labels and related tumour labels helps to fine-tune the model. Through training, YOLOv8 gains the ability to identify and pinpoint liver tumours. After training, the model is used to identify tumours in fresh medical images by forecasting the bounding boxes surrounding locations that may contain tumours. Steps in post-processing enhance these bounding boxes, maximizing the precision the location of the tumour. The accuracy of the tumours found is guaranteed by visual inspection and validation against expert assessments or ground truth annotations. A thorough evaluation of the YOLOv8 model's tumour detection performance is provided via quantitative evaluation criteria like precision, recall, and F1 score. YOLOv8's smooth integration into the medical image processing workflow improves diagnostic capacities by providing a quick and precise method for liver image tumour detection.

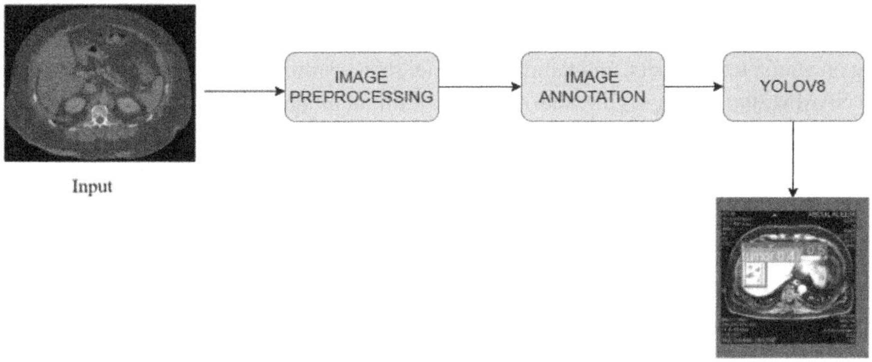

Fig. 4. YOLOV8 Tumor Detection

F. FEATURE FUSION

To improve the overall comprehension of liver architecture within medical images, feature fusion in automated liver segmentation integrates pertinent data from several phases of the segmentation process. MONAI, SAMM, and YOLOv8 are some of the models used in the process to extract features for liver classification, lesion segmentation, and tumour identification. A feature fusion module is used to integrate the discriminative features from each stage after these features have been extracted. This fusion could include summing, concatenating, or employing more advanced methods like attention mechanisms to give particular features priority over others. Following integration, the integrated features are supplied into a post-processing phase, where coherence and segmentation results are improved by using morphology operations and linked component analysis. The combined feature map in the end captures extensive the effectiveness of the feature fusion method is confirmed by visual inspection and quantitative evaluation metrics, such as sensitivity and the dice coefficient. In medical imaging applications, the smooth incorporation of feature fusion into the automated liver segmentation process improves the segmentation model's precision and robustness, leading to more accurate diagnosis and treatment planning.

G. POST-PROCESSING AND EVALUATION

Post-processing methods are essential for fine-tuning the segmentation findings in the automated liver segmentation process that uses MONAI for liver classification, SAMM for lesion segmentation, and YOLOv8 for tumour detection. Morphological procedures are used to improve the quality of segmented masks by smoothing boundaries, such as dilation and erosion. By separating discrete regions, removing minute artefacts, and guaranteeing precise portrayal of the liver, lesions, and tumours, connected component analysis further improves the masks. Additional refining and the removal of irrelevant regions can be achieved by utilizing optional approaches like region growth and volume limits. The segmentation The MONAI framework was evaluated for liver categorization, and the results showed that it is a useful tool for achieving consistent intensity values, the best possible spatial resolution, and an enhanced signal-to-noise ratio. YOLOv8, which is used to identify liver tumours, was evaluated through preprocessing of the data, training on annotated datasets, and validation. After that, a similar assessment was conducted on SAMM, the lesion segmentation model, with an emphasis on the model's capacity to accurately identify and distinguish abnormal structures in the liver. Through techniques such as summing or concatenating, this fusion was accomplished with the goal of improving the overall understanding of liver architecture in medical pictures. Segmentation results were refined through the application of morphological operations and linked component analysis during the post-processing and evaluation phase. Extensive quantitative evaluation measures, including the Dice coefficient. By offering insightful information about each tool's performance in various diagnostic process domains, the multi-phase evaluation approach enhanced our comprehension of its potential.

H. VISUALIZATION

For medical image analysis and visualization, Fig. 5 illustrate that 3D Slicer visualization tool is a strong and adaptable platform. 3D Slicer is an open-source architecture that offers a full range of tools for the three-dimensional visualization and editing of medical image data. The programme facilitates the loading of many imaging modalities, including CT, MRI, and PET images. It allows for simultaneous visualization in axial, sagittal, and coronal planes and multi-planar reconstruction. 3D Slicer stands out for its ability to work with intricate 3D volumetric datasets, allowing for interactive and customizable representation of anatomical systems. Additionally, 3D Slicer enables sophisticated visualization methods, such as Surface and volume rendering improve the understanding of minute anatomical details. Due to its adaptability through different plugins and modules, the programme can be used for a variety of medical imaging applications, such as research, surgical planning, and teaching. 3D Slicer is a useful tool in the field of medical image analysis because of its intuitive interface and strong visualization capabilities.

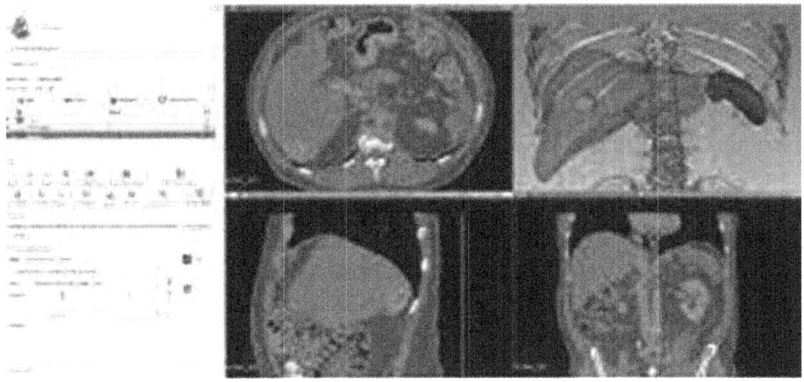

Fig. 5. 3D Slicer Visualization

4 Results and Discussion

A. DATASETS

For 3D liver segmentation problems, a number of datasets are available, offering useful resources for the creation and assessment of automated segmentation methods. The LiTS (Liver Tumour Segmentation) dataset stands out among them; it comprises contrast-enhanced CT scans of the abdomen annotated for the liver and tumour segments. Another noteworthy dataset, which provides CT scans with labelled regions for liver and tumour segmentation, comes from the MICCAI 2017 Liver Tumour Segmentation Challenge. A variety of abdominal pictures are provided by the CHAOS (Combined Healthy Abdominal Organ Segmentation) dataset, which consists of CT and MRI scans with liver, spleen, and kidney regions annotated. Even though it is older, several studies still use the SLIVER07 (3D Sliver Liver Image Database) dataset, which contains CT images with annotations for liver and tumour segmentation.

B. RESULT

An in-depth analysis of the benefits and drawbacks of the suggested methodology is included in the discussion of the findings. Utilizing the strengths of each tool for liver segmentation tasks is made possible by the integration of MONAI, SAMM, and YOLOv8. The interpretability of the data is improved by 3D Slicer's adaptability in displaying and engaging with the segmented structures. A comprehensive image that supports clinical decision-making is provided by the feature fusion technique, which enables a holistic understanding of liver structure, lesions, and tumours. Limitations are addressed, including the possibility of false positives or negatives, susceptibility to differences in imaging, and the influence of dataset features. Possible directions for development are discussed, such as obtaining more training data, adjusting settings, or investigating different segmentation algorithms. Additionally, the superiority and originality of the suggested technique are demonstrated by comparisons with other approaches. The automated liver segmentation results are highlighted for their clinical importance, highlighting the potential influence on treatment planning and diagnostic accuracy. The project's overall success is attributed to the successful merging of data from several segmentation phases and the incorporation of advanced visualization tools. For the integrated system to be reliable in producing accurate and cohesive results across a range of medical images and applications diagnosis consistency is crucial. Figure 6 shows that training and validation loss metrics in YOLOV8 to detect accuracy and robustness performance. Figure 7 illustrates that confusion matrix is developed more accurate and reliable solutions. Table 1 addressed comparison of evaluation metrics with accuracy.

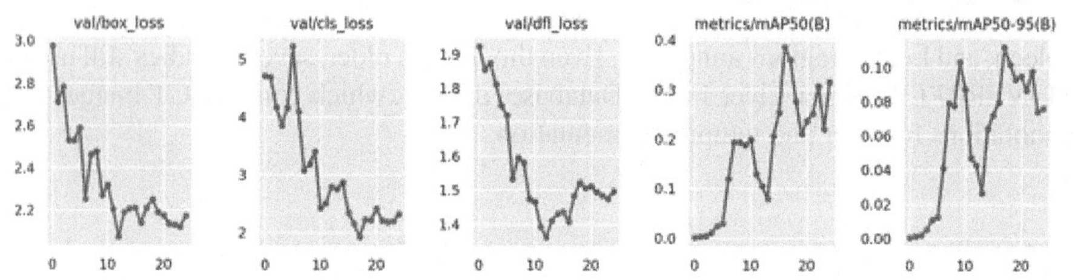

Fig. 6. Training/ Validation Metrics Evaluation

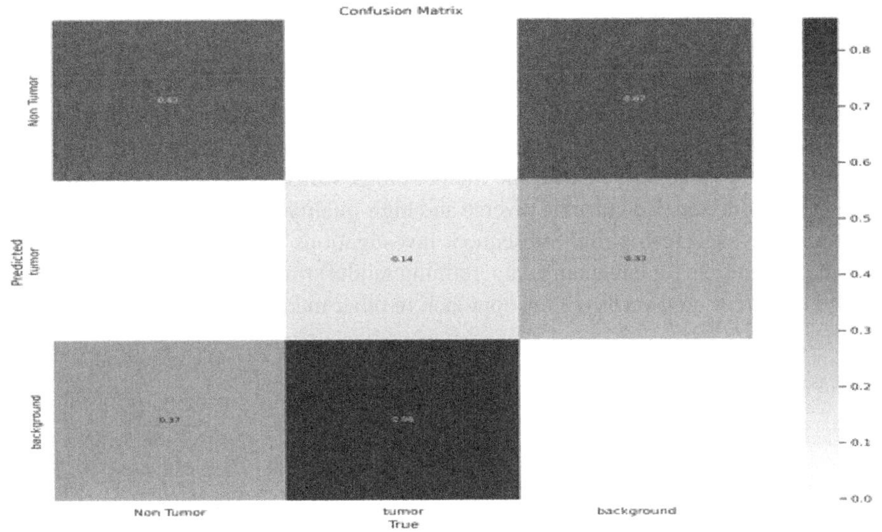

Fig. 7. Confusion Matrix

Table 1. A comparison for liver tumor segmentation

Methodology	Volume	Dice	Jaccard	Accuracy
U-NET	80 CT scans	0.85	0.78	0.87
Seg Net	120 CT Scans	0.94	0.91	0.93
Proposed	163 CT Scans	0.96	0.93	0.95

5 Conclusion

This study has practical implications for using these instruments in clinical and medical research settings. By addressing the difficulties involved in manual medical image processing, these technologies' automated and accurate nature provides a route towards quicker and more accurate diagnosis. The study highlights how important these tools are to improving decision-making, efficiency, and repeatability in the constantly changing field of medical imaging. These tools, which include MONAI, SAM, and YOLOv8, use deep learning models that can be complicated, making it difficult to grasp and comprehend how they make decisions is a essential skill in high-stakes medical situations. Even with the impressive advancements, problems including anatomical variances, imaging modality variability, and the requirement for big and varied datasets still require constant study and improvement. It is imperative that researchers, medical practitioners, and technology developers keep working together to improve current algorithms and create new ones that can adjust to changing healthcare requirements.

In conclusion, automated liver segmentation is a promising and revolutionary technology in the field of medical imaging that has the potential to completely change the identification and management of liver illness. Future developments in science and technology could lead to even greater improvements in the precision, effectiveness, and usability of automated liver segmentation techniques for clinical settings. In order to overcome those challenges, medical professionals, computer scientists, and imaging specialists must continue to work together to improve current algorithms and create innovative approaches. Even with the methodology's merits, there are still issues that need to be addressed. Reliance on diverse and high-quality datasets for training and validation is one such restriction. Subsequent investigations may concentrate on creating innovative methods for enhancing data, refining model structures for environments with limited resources, and verifying the approach in other medical contexts.

References

1. Zheng, B., Huang, C., Chen, X., Luo, Y.: Toward head computed tomography image reconstruction standardization with deep-learning-assisted automatic detection. IEEE Tran. Instrum. Meas. **73**, 1–14 (2024). https://doi.org/10.1109/TIM.2023.3329102
2. Yue, G., Wei, P., Liu, Y., Luo, Y., Du, J., Wang, T.: Automated endoscopic image classification via deep neural network with class imbalance loss. In: IEEE Transactions on Instrumentation and Measurement (2023)
3. Phan, D.T., et al.: Smart low level laser therapy system for automatic facial dermatological disorder diagnosis. IEEE J. Biomed. Health Inform. **27**(3), 1546–1557 (2023). https://doi.org/10.1109/JBHI.2023.3237875
4. Rui, J., Jose, F., Luis, B., Carlos, C.: 'Vendor Neutral Archive with MONAI for automatic medical Image Analysis. In: IEEE Transactions on Instrumentation and Measurement (2023)
5. Tran, V.L., Lin, H.-Y., Liu, H.-W.: Multitask deep learning for segmentation and lumbosacral spine inspection. IEEE Trans. Instrum. Meas. **71**, 1–10 (2022)
6. Chen, X., et al.: Recent advances and clinical applications of deep learning in medical image analysis. Med. Image Anal. **79**, 102444 (2022)
7. Cauley, K., Hu, Y., Fielden, S.: Head CT: Toward making full use of the information the x-rays give. Am. J. Neuroradiol. **42**(8), 1362–1369 (2021)
8. Kuntz, S., et al.: Gastrointestinal cancer classification and prognostication from histology using deep learning: systematic review. Eur. J. Cancer **155**, 200–215 (2021). https://doi.org/10.1016/j.ejca.2021.07.012
9. Swerdlow, M., Shin, L., D'Huyvetter, K., Mack, W.J., Armstrong, D.G.: 'Initial clinical experience with a simple, home system for early detection and monitoring of diabetic foot ulcers: The foot selfie.' J. Diabetes SciTechnol. **17**(1), 79–88 (2023)
10. Goyal, M., Reeves, N.D., Rajbhandari, S., Ahmad, N., Wang, C., Yap, M.H.: Recognition of ischaemia and infection in diabetic foot ulcers: Dataset and techniques. Comput. Biol. Med. **117**, 103616 (2020)
11. Lin, A., Chen, B., Xu, J., Zhang, Z., Lu, G., Zhang, D.: Ds- transunet: Dual swin transformer u-net for medical image segmentation. IEEE Trans. Instrum. Meas. **71**, 1–15 (2022)
12. Roy, K., Banik, D., Bhattacharjee, D., Krejcar, O., Kollmann, C.: Lwmla-net: A lightweight multi-level attention-based network for segmentation of covid-19 lungs abnormalities from images. IEEE Trans. Instrument. Meas. **71**, 1–13 (2022)
13. Rahman, A., et al.: Histopathologic oral cancer prediction using oral squamous cell carcinoma biopsy empowered with transfer learning. Sensors **22**(10), 3833 (2022)
14. Sarode, G.S., Kumari, N., Sarode, S.C.: Oral cancer histopathology images and artificial intelligence: a pathologist's perspective. Oral Oncol. **132**, 105999 (2022). https://doi.org/10.1016/j.oraloncology.2022.105999

15. Chandran, V.: Diagnosis of cervical cancer based on ensemble deep learning network using colposcopy images. BioMed. Res. Int. **2021**, 5584004 (2021)
16. Willemink, M.J., et al.: Preparing medical imaging data for machine learning. Radiology **295**(1), 4–15 (2020). https://doi.org/10.1148/radiol.2020192224
17. Jiang, Y., Yang, M., Wang, S., Li, X., Sun, Y.: Emerging role of deep learning-based artificial intelligence in tumor pathology. Cancer Commun. **40**(4), 154–166 (2020)
18. Liu, Y., et al.: PaddleSeg: A High-Efficient Development Toolkit for Image Segmentation (2021)
19. Ziegler, E., Urban, T., Brown, D., Petts, J., Pieper, S.D., Lewis, R., Hafey, C., Harris, G.J.: Open health imaging foundation viewer: an extensible open-source framework for building web-based imaging applications to support cancer research. JCO Clin. Cancer Inform. **4**, 336–345 (2020)
20. Lösel, P.D., et al.: Introducing Biomedisa as an open-source online platform for biomedical image segmentation. Nat. Commun. **11**(1), 5577 (2020). https://doi.org/10.1038/s41467-020-19303-w
21. Kermany, D.S., et al.: 'Identifying medical diagnoses and treatable diseases by image-based deep learning. Cell **172**(5), 1122–1131 (2018)
22. Chollet, F.: 'Xception: Deep learning with depthwise separable convolutions. In: Proceedings of the IEEE Conference on Computation Visual Pattern Recognition,, pp. 1251–1258. Honolulu, HI, USA (2017)
23. Aversano, L., Bernardi, M.L., Cimitile, M., Pecori, R.: Deep neural networks ensemble to detect COVID-19 from CT scans. Pattern Recogn. **120**, 108135 (2021). https://doi.org/10.1016/j.patcog.2021.108135
24. Cohen, J.P., Morrison, P., Dao, L., Roth, K., Duong, T., Ghassem, M.: COVID-19 image data collection: Prospective predictions are the future. Mach. Learn. Biomed. Imag. **1**(2020), 1–38 (2020). https://doi.org/10.59275/j.melba.2020-48g7
25. Ji, T., et al.: Detection of COVID-19: a review of the current literature and future perspectives. Biosens. Bioelectron. **166**, 112455 (2020). https://doi.org/10.1016/j.bios.2020.112455
26. Luz, E., Silva, P., Silva, R., Silva, L., Guimarães, J., Miozzo, G., Moreira, G., Menotti, D.: Towards an effective and efficient deep learning model for COVID-19 patterns detection in X-ray images. Res. Biomed. Eng. **38**(1), 149–162 (2022)
27. Loey, M., El-Sappagh, S., Mirjalili, S.: Bayesian-based optimized deep learning model to detect COVID-19 patients using chest X-ray image data. Comput. Biol. Med. **142**, 105213 (2022). https://doi.org/10.1016/j.compbiomed.2022.105213
28. Hou, J., Gao, T.: Explainable DCNN based chest X-ray image analysis and classification for COVID-19 pneumonia detection. Sci. Rep. **11**(1), 16071 (2021)

Explaining Parkinson's Disease Detection by Ensemble Classifiers with Local Interpretable Features

Alok Kumar Karn, Aniket Dixit, Peeta Basa Pati(✉), and Anand Mahalingam

Department of Computer Science and Engineering, Amrita School of Computing Bengaluru, Amrita Vishwa Vidyapeetham, Bengaluru, India
bp_peeta@blr.amrita.edu

Abstract. Parkinson's disease (PD) is a neurodegenerative condition and a progressive nervous system disorder condition, marked by its characteristic symptoms such as tremors, muscle stiffness, and slow, imprecise body movements. Typically affecting the middle-aged and elderly, the most crucial challenge in the treatment of PD is posed in the form of its early diagnosis. While there is no cure for the disease, early intervention is found to have alleviated the symptoms and to have also improved the overall quality of life, potentially slowing down the disease's progression. With the rapid advancements in Artificial Intelligence (AI) and Machine Learning (ML), almost every industry seems to be benefiting from its incorporation and the field of biomedical sciences is no different. AI-ML techniques have seemed to be specifically beneficial in classification-based biomedical problems. This research is built upon this very same idea. The application of 14 ML algorithms is studied on a dataset that consists of vocal characteristics of several individuals, both the healthy and the PD patients, to classify based on a patient's speech whether or not, they have Parkinson's. To improve the overall performance of the algorithms, SMOTE and PCA pre-processing techniques have also been applied to deal with the dataset's shortcomings. The study observes that Random Forest, Gaussian Process, Extra Trees, and CatBoost are the 4 best performing algorithms for the task, providing an accuracy of 96.61%. The paper concludes with the deployment of an Explainable AI (XAI) LIME module on the best-performing algorithms to provide transparency and interpretability to the decision-making process of these AI systems.

Keywords: Parkinson's disease (PD) · SMOTE · PCA · Explainable AI

1 Introduction

Parkinson's disease is a progressive degenerative disorder that essentially affects the central nervous system, besides attacking all other parts of the body that are controlled by nerves. It is a movement disorder that is chronic, with symptoms starting slowly and steadily, and eventually affecting the entire body including the non-motor parts of the body. Parkinson's is one of the most generic forms of Parkinsonism which is an umbrella term for various kinds of tremors, rigidity, and postural instability.

Published by Springer Nature Switzerland AG 2025
A. Chandrabose et al. (Eds.): ICCCSP 2024, IFIP AICT 723, pp. 68–79, 2025.
https://doi.org/10.1007/978-3-031-73617-9_6

The most difficult-to-digest fact about PD is the absence of any known form of cure. As of the past year, no drug has been mandated as PD-modifying. While the research for a cure is still ongoing and a drug might as very well be a reality in the foreseeable future, an early diagnosis remains the best solution to the disease. The diagnosis becomes even more important because the entire treatment of PD is structured around increasing the life expectancy of the patient and their quality of life by mitigating the very same symptoms.

The symptoms of Parkinson's are primarily motor-related and the disease can be diagnosed based on onsets of tremors, slurry speech, and loss of control of facial muscles to respond to a change of emotions. While the symptoms of PD are quite clearly observed in the patient, challenges are faced by clinicians because a lot of PD symptoms overlap with similar dementia-related diseases. While medical organizations have listed very detailed criteria to differentiate between these central nervous system disorders, a secondary diagnosis system structured around AI-ML, a technology already establishing its feet in biomedical classification problems, can prove to be beneficial in improving PD's treatment. The source of inspiration for using ML algorithms to detect Parkinson's can be drawn from other diseases such as chronic liver diseases [1], or diabetes mellitus [2] that are immensely benefiting from the study conducted on the usage of various boosting and traditional ML algorithms for diagnostic purposes.

In this work, the efficiency of 14 different machine-learning models in classifying the onset of Parkinson's in a patient based on his/her speech is assessed. Besides assessing the proficiency of machine learning algorithms in solving this particular biomedical classification problem, the work done also comments on the importance of enhancing the dataset before feeding it to the algorithms. It can be noted that after the application of SMOTE and PCA techniques for dataset enhancement by removal of class imbalance and unnecessary features, all the models were able to provide better accuracy in predicting Parkinson's onset. Nowadays, as AI ML is slowly settling its feet in the biomedical sciences industry, and more and more diagnostic systems are being developed around the technology, a need for understanding these models is also growing. The stake-holding doctors and patients alike need to be able to properly comprehend the way these systems function to be able to trust them enough to deploy them in the real world. The only issue is the fact that a lot of these models work as "black boxes" and are too complex to understand. Therefore, this work demonstrates the usage of Explainable AI where the LIME tool is used to interpret how the best-performing algorithms can classify Parkinson's, and the features that these algorithms rely upon.

The sections of this paper are structured to shed light on the various steps that are involved in making the aforementioned assessment. Section 2 details the ongoing research that is noted on the subject, and Section 3 discusses the entire methodology of this work in-depth. The penultimate Section 4 displays the results that the various models generated, and also demonstrates the usage of LIME. The last section of this paper is intended to throw light on the future research that can take place on the subject. It emphasizes incorporating techniques that increase the accuracy of these models in predicting Parkinson's.

2 Literature Survey

As per the latest developments, the medical science industry has seen an increased application of ML and AI in providing solutions to various biomedical problems. The classification problems are specifically benefiting from these advancements in ML and AI. The most recent research in Parkinson's detection, for example, is focused on the inclusion of advanced ML models, better pre-processing techniques to improve the quality of the dataset, and ensemble models. This section has noted this research to provide insight into the current scenario of the application of ML models in solving biomedical classification problems, and especially the early detection of Parkinson's using the same.

Ganguly et al. [3] have shown that the SVM classifier works quite effectively in predicting cervical cancer risk levels with an incredible accuracy of 99.60%. They have shown an efficient incorporation of machine learning in classification problems for diagnosis reasons. This is also demonstrated by Patra et al. [4] who have displayed proficiency in forward selection techniques and hybrid ensemble learning methods in improving the accuracy of AI-ML in solving biomedical classification problems. While they have studied the classification of Coronary Heart Disease Risk levels and obtained a strong result of 95.87%, their work can be taken as inspiration for Parkinson's research, as well. Radha and Tallapureddy [5] have also assessed the application of an ensemble ML model, over the traditional techniques. They have obtained an accuracy of 91% and their model can quite precisely help in early diagnosis of PD.

Quan et al. [6] have studied the deployment of deep learning-based models to study the onset of Parkinson's using a patient's vocal features. They suggest that the BLSTM (Bidirectional long-short-term memory) model can be deployed for the purpose with a 10-fold cross-validation technique and dataset splitting with zero sample overlap related to an individual as performance enhancers. Moro-Velazquez et al. [7] have taken the approach of studying the performance of systems that work as automatic speech recognizers to study whether or not they can differentiate the intricacies of a Parkinson's patient's speech. Their study analyzed that the systems can note the more general differences, but individual deficits in a patient's speech need to be studied on a modified system.

Besides voice changes, a PD patient also faces trouble in performing daily actions such as being able to write properly. Taleb et al. [8] have opted for this observation of a PD patient's difficulty in performing such normal tasks as the basis of their work. They have performed a comparative study on the way Parkinson's can be detected using deep-learning techniques to study a patient's handwriting. They conclude that a mixture of CNN-BLSTM models is the best performer on the subject. Senturk [9], on the other hand, has opted to study the application of traditional machine learning models to detect PD based on a patient's voice. Support Vector Machines with the incorporation of Recursive Feature Elimination is the best performer in the work. Wang et al. [10] have studied the deployment of ensemble models, comprising a combination of machine learning and deep learning algorithms, for PD detection. They have taken the loss of control of sense organs as the basis for their study.

Almeida et. al. [11] have studied the application of machine learning techniques in detecting PD based on an advanced dataset. They have fed the data to algorithms from sustained phonation and speech tasks to study their performance. Their work emphasizes on the importance of feature extraction in improving the performance of these models. They also conclude that the task of phonation is more relevant to PD detection than speech tasks. Tadse et al. [12] have studied the integration of medical science and data science in solving the early detection of Parkinson's by using ML-based diagnosis systems and concluded the efficiency of cutting-edge technology in providing solutions to the same. Narendra et al. [13] have also studied the detection of Parkinson's from Speech. They have studied the integration of voice source information as the basis of the two classifier architectures that they have used. Their results are an encouragement for future researchers to extract voice source information in the detection of Parkinson's. Rajeswari and Nair [14] in their work have further explored the application of machine learning and deep learning models in classifying Parkinson's using voice signals. In their study, they obtained an accuracy of 85% with their ensemble method that comprises both the Convolutional Neural Networks as well as LSTM model. Furthermore, authors Vigneshwari and Aravinth [15] have also built upon the notion that voice signals can be effectively explored for Parkinson's prediction using ML algorithms. Their best-performing model Gradient Boost can generate an impressive accuracy of 91.53%.

Upon analysis of the extensive study that has been taking place on the subject of the classification of Parkinson's using Machine Learning and Deep Learning algorithms, some common underlying approaches have been found. These approaches include techniques such as the incorporation of ensemble methods, multi-fold cross-validation, and feature selection to increase the overall accuracy of the disease's classification. While these aforementioned methods have proven successful in other works compared with the methods of this study, some limitations have been observed too. An absence of class balancing to deal with the dataset's shortcomings in representing the minor classes and a lack of efforts in explaining the working of the black-box-based AI models are some examples of the same. As a result, the study done in this paper has made use of the SMOTE and PCA techniques to balance the classes in the dataset which has helped increase the overall quality of the dataset. Explainable AL module LIME has also been used to interpret the results generated by the various ML models, a method that has been limitedly found in the works done by other papers analyzed for the literature survey of this study.

3 Methodology

An ML-based classifier is used in the work to predict the onset of Parkinson's based on a patient's vocal symptoms. Various pre-processing techniques like SMOTE and PCA have been deployed to enhance the dataset taken to enhance the performance of the algorithms. The accuracy of these algorithms is studied on the test data before and after the enhancement of the dataset using the aforementioned techniques. The best-performing models are interpreted using the LIME XAI module. Figure 1 depicts the flow of work done in this study.

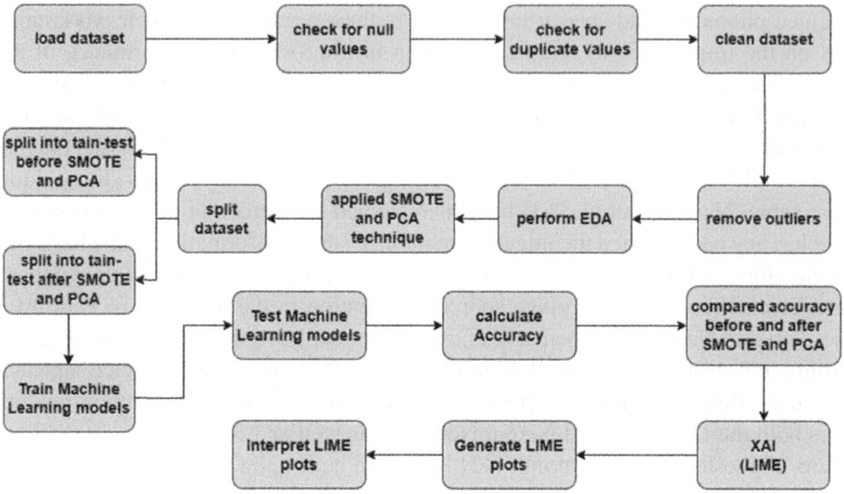

Fig. 1. Flow of work for the study

3.1 Dataset

The dataset used for this research paper is obtained from Kaggle. It comprises various acoustic features extracted from voice recordings of 31 people, of which 23 had PD. These features, 23 in number, each depicted in a different column are used in the context of PD detection, where each feature included in the dataset captures different aspects of vocal characteristics. The rows, on the other hand, correspond to the 195 voice recordings obtained from these individuals, represented distinctly in the "name" column. There are around 6 recordings per patient.

It is important to note that the "phonations were recorded in an IAC sound-treated booth using a head-mounted microphone (AKG C420) positioned at 8 cm from the lips" with proper calibrations and normalizations being made on the data recorded before it was converted in the ASCII CSV file, used in this research.

The main aim of the dataset is to discriminate healthy people from those with PD, according to the status column which is given a value of 0 for the healthy people and 1 for the ones with PD. The research done in this paper is built on the very same underlying idea that the analysis of these vocal features can provide valuable insights into the potential presence of PD in the person.

3.2 Feature Description

There are 23 medical features (the 24th feature being the class label) in the dataset taken for this research, each representing a vocal characteristic. These features are helpful in the classification of Parkinson's disease in a particular patient. Understanding the factual medical definitions of the 23 features included in the dataset is also important.

The dataset comprises features related to voice characteristics, including fundamental frequency (Fo), highest frequency (Fhi), lowest frequency (Flo), jitter percentage, absolute jitter, relative amplitude perturbation(RAP), pitch period perturbation quotient

(PPQ), average absolute difference of consecutive pitch period difference (Jitter: DDP), shimmer, shimmer in decibels, amplitude perturbation quotient based on local variations within 3 and 5 cycles (Shimmer: APQ3, Shimmer: APQ5), overall amplitude perturbation quotient (MDVP: APQ), average absolute difference of consecutive amplitude difference (Shimmer: DDA), noise-to-harmonics ratio (NHR), harmonics-to-noise ratio (HNR), health status (status), recurrence period density entropy (RPDE), detrended fluctuation analysis (DFA), nonlinear measures related to the spread of the fundamental frequency (spread1, spread2), correlation dimension (D2), and pitch period entropy (PPE). The status variable indicates the presence (1) or absence (0) of Parkinson's disease. The dataset taken for this work is obtained from reference [16], where the authors have explored the usage of two new tools for speech analysis: recurrence and fractal scaling. The database for the above-listed features concerns 31 people, which include both, normal people as well as PD patients. Their work studies the changes observed in a patient's voice due to the onset of a disorder such as Parkinson's and these features provide a valuable insight into the matter.

3.3 Dataset Preprocessing

The data initially taken from Kaggle is preprocessed after checking for duplicate or null values. This noisy data is removed from the original dataset in the initial preprocessing steps itself. The dataset is split into 80:20 ratios to obtain test and train datasets. The train data is used to pre-train the algorithms so that they can analyze the co-existing patterns and perform generalization. Later on, the test data is used to evaluate the performance of the models based on the accuracy performance metric taken in this work. The dataset now is taken for the first set of performance evaluations of the 14 machine learning algorithms.

The class label which denotes whether or not the patient has Parkinson's takes two values, 0, for its absence, and 1, for its presence. It is to be noted from Fig. 2 that the original data has an issue of class imbalance where there are 147 cases present for class label value 1 and 48 for class label value 0. This issue is resolved by adopting the Synthetic Minority Over-sampling Technique (SMOTE). This addresses the issues of class imbalance by generating synthetic samples for the minority class so that there is an equal representation of both the values of the class label. Figure 3 showcases that SMOTE can resolve the issue of class imbalance.

Furthermore, to avoid dealing with the 'curse of the dimensionality', where instead of generalizing the results, the algorithms start memorizing them due to too many features being present in the dataset, Principal Component Analysis (PCA) technique has been used. PCA acts as a dimensionality reduction technique by transforming high-dimensional data into a lower-dimensional form while retaining as much of the original variance as possible. It focuses on principal components, which are linear combinations of the original features, allowing for a more efficient representation of the data and often simplifying subsequent analysis or modeling. There are 24 features in the data taken for this work, including the class label. After applying PCA, the number of features could be reduced to 13 with a variance of 99%. This enhanced dataset, after the application of SMOTE and PCA is fed to the 14 machine learning algorithms to study their performance based on their accuracies.

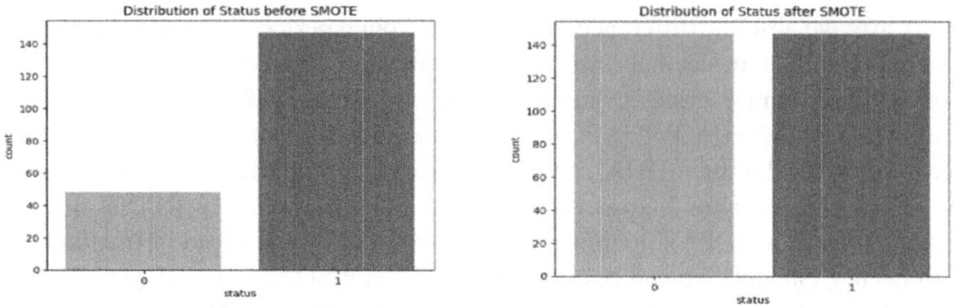

(a) (b)

Fig. 2. Distribution of class label, (a) before SMOTE, (b) after SMOTE.

3.4 Machine Learning Models Applied

In this work, 14 machine learning algorithms have been assessed to predict Parkinson's. To improve upon these models' performance and for their fine-tuning, hyperparameters have been used for each of these models. Table 1 below depicts these models and their respective hyperparameters.

Table 1. Models used and respective hyperparameters

Model	Hyper Parameters
Logistic Regression	solver = 'liblinear'
Decision Tree	criterion = 'gini'
Random Forest	n_estimators = 100, criterion = 'gini'
SVM	kernel = 'linear'
K-Nearest Neighbors	n_neighbors = 5
Naive Bayes	Default parameters
Neural Network	Default parameters
Gradient Boosting	n_estimators = 100, learning_rate = 0.1, max_depth = 3
Linear Discriminant Analysis	Default parameters
Gaussian Process	Default parameters
Extra Trees	n_estimators = 100, criterion = 'gini'
Bagging	Default parameters
AdaBoost	n_estimators = 50, learning_rate = 1.0
CatBoost	iterations = 100, learning_rate = 0.1, depth = 6,loss_function = 'MultiClass'

4 Result and Discussion

4.1 Performance Metric for ML Algorithms

The dataset is fed in two different stages to the algorithms, based on the respective level of pre-processing, and the corresponding accuracies for each of the 14 machine learning algorithms are noted. Firstly, the preprocessed dataset is fed without the application of SMOTE and PCA. As can be noted in Table 2 below, the Gradient Boosting algorithm outperforms the rest of the 13 algorithms with an accuracy of 94.87%. Decision Tree has achieved the second highest of all accuracies with a value of 92.31%. It should be noted that since the dataset, without SMOTE and PCA, suffers from the issues of class imbalance and the curse of dimensionality, the models show a rather underwhelming set of accuracies.

Table 2. Accuracy of models before and after the application of smote and PCA

Model	Accuracy (%) before SMOTE and PCA	Accuracy (%) after SMOTE and PCA
Logistic Regression	82.05	81.36
Decision Tree	92.31	94.92
Random Forest	89.74	96.61
SVM	84.62	83.05
K-Nearest Neighbors	89.74	94.92
Naive Bayes	69.23	84.75
Neural Network	82.05	94.92
Gradient Boosting	94.87	94.92
Linear Discriminant Analysis	82.05	77.97
Gaussian Process	92.31	96.61
Extra Trees	92.31	96.61
Bagging	92.31	94.92
AdaBoost	82.05	88.14
CatBoost	89.74	96.61

Before the second set of evaluations is done for the 14 algorithms, the dataset is revamped by the application of SMOTE and PCA. The enhanced dataset has equally distributed classes for the class label and also, a lesser number of features than the original dataset. The results obtained demonstrate the importance of these class balancing and feature reduction techniques. All 14 models show an improved value of accuracy upon the usage of the enhanced data. Table 2 containing the accuracy scores for the 14 models before and after the dataset was enhanced, shows that 4 models, namely Gaussian Process, Random Forest, CatBoost, and Extra Trees, with an accuracy of 96.61% have fared better than the rest of the remaining 10 algorithms.

Table 3. Comparative report of method and result between proposed system and recent system

Ref	Year of Publication	Methods Used	Result
[6]	2021	Deep Learning (BiLSTM)	Accuracy = 84.29%
[11]	2019	Knn, (k = 1)	Accuracy = 94.55%
[13]	2021	SVM based detection system	Accuracy = 67.93%
[14]	2022	CNN and LSTM	Accuracy = 85%
Proposed work	2024	Gaussian Process, Random Forest, CatBoost, and Extra Trees,	Accuracy = 96.61%

Table 3 depicts the comparative analysis on the methods used and their performance in terms of accuracy over different years. The most recent work presented in the table, published in year 2022 proposes a combination of CNN and LSTM method achieved an accuracy of 85% whereas the proposed system involving ensemble method achieves a highest accuracy of 96.61% demonstrating a significant advancement in accuracy also incorporating Explainable AI using LIME for better understanding of the working of the models.

4.2 Explainable AI Interpretability Using LIME

A lot of powerful machine learning models face a serious shortcoming in the form of their black-box architecture. These black-box models have very complex and hard-to-interpret internal workings. Thus, the way the decisions (or here, classification) are made by these machine learning models essentially goes unexplained. To resolve this problem, Explainable AI tools are used which help in interpreting the various models and how they can make their decisions. One such popular tool is "Local Interpretable Model-agnostic Explanations" or LIME. It is a technique in ML used to explain the predictions of very complex models. It focuses on providing explanations for individual or 'local' predictions rather than explaining the entire model, by creating local, interpretable models around specific instances. In this study, the 4 best performing models, namely, Random Forest, Gaussian Process, Extra Trees, and CatBoost have been interpreted by the usage of the LIME module.

The figures below (Fig. 3 ((a) to (d))) depict the corresponding LIME results for the aforementioned models. It is to be noted that the enhanced dataset with reduced features (after PCA) has been taken for interpretability. The table on the right hand in each of these figures has certain features in orange and certain features in blue. The color depicts the importance of the feature in predicting a particular class value by the model. The orange color shows that the feature helped the respective model in predicting value 1 (i.e. presence of Parkinson's) whereas, the value 0 is helped by blue colored labels. For each model, the predictions 0 or 1 are helped by different sets of features, hence, an interpretability can be made of the way these models reach their decisions. The table on the left depicts the probability of a model to predict a particular class label value.

Fig. (a)

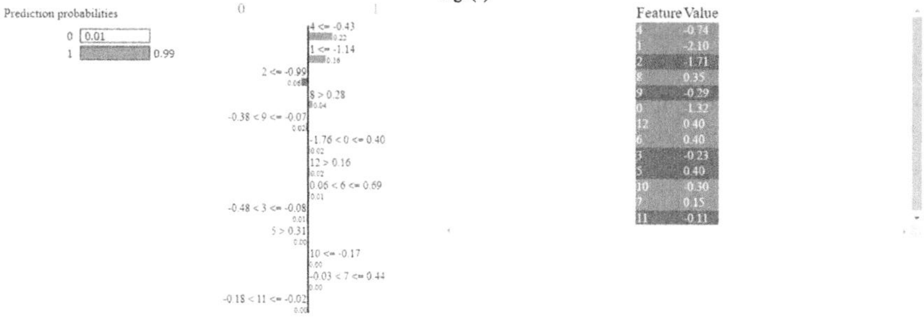

Fig. (b)

Fig. (c)

Fig. (d)

Fig. 3. LIME explanation of the 4 best performing models: a) Random Forest Model b) Gaussian Process c) Extra Trees d) CatBoost.

5 Conclusion and Future Scope

In this study, the performance of 14 machine learning algorithms was studied to classify the onset of Parkinson's based on a patient's vocal characteristics. The results obtained suggest that dataset enhancement techniques such as SMOTE and PCA significantly enhance the models' performance. Upon usage of the enhanced data, Random Forest, Gaussian Process, Extra Trees, and CatBoost come out as the best-performing models with an accuracy score of 96.61%. As these are black-box models with no information as to how they reach their decisions, they are interpreted in this study using the LIME XAI module.

Further research should be directed along the lines of advancing the application of ML and AI in medical classification problems so that a clinician can focus on the treatment aspect more than the diagnosis. From a practical viewpoint, clinicians should be helped to understand how these models function so that ML and AI are more universally accepted. Lastly, as the paper also showcased, better-pre-processed data vastly improves a model's performance; these aspects can be considered in ongoing and future research as well.

Acknowledgement. We thank Amrita Vishwa Vidyapeetham for the infrastructure support in carrying out this work and preparation of this manuscript. We acknowledge that we have employed ChatGPT for suggestions to paraphrase some sentences in this work. We have used Turnitin for content similarity check. We, additionally, thank our family members, friends, and peers for their support.

References

1. Dhyani, A., et al.: Comparative analysis of supervised machine learning algorithms for liver disease prediction with SMOTE enhancement. In: 2023 3rd Asian Conference on Innovation in Technology (ASIANCON), pp. 1–6. IEEE (2023)
2. Gayathri, R., Pati, P. B., Singh, T., Nair, R.R.: A framework for the prediction of diabetes mellitus using hyper-parameter tuned xgboost classifier. In: 2022 13th International Conference on Computing Communication and Networking Technologies (ICCCNT), pp. 1–5. IEEE (2022)
3. Ganguly, T., Pati, P. B., Deepa, K., Singh, T., Özer, T.: Machine learning based comparative analysis of cervical cancer risk classifications algorithms. In: 2023 international conference on Advances in Computing, Communication and Applied Informatics (ACCAI), pp. 1–7. IEEE (2023)
4. Patra, S.C., Maheswari, B.U., Pati, P.B.: Forecasting coronary heart disease risk with a 2-step hybrid ensemble learning method and forward feature selection algorithm. IEEE Access **11**, 136758–136769 (2023). https://doi.org/10.1109/ACCESS.2023.3338369
5. Tallapureddy, G., Radha, D.: Analysis of ensemble of machine learning algorithms for detection of Parkinson's disease. In: International Conference on Applied Artificial Intelligence & Computing (ICAAIC). IEEE (2022). https://doi.org/10.1109/ICAAIC53929.2022.9793048
6. Quan, C., Ren, K., Luo, Z.: A deep learning-based method for Parkinson's disease detection using dynamic features of speech. In: IEEE Access, vol. 9, pp. 10239–10252 (2021)
7. Moro-Velazquez, L., et al.: Study of the performance of automatic speech recognition systems in speakers with Parkinson's disease. In: Interspeech, vol. 9, pp. 3875–3879 (2019)

8. Taleb, C., Likforman-Sulem, L., Mokbel, C., Khachab, M.: Detection of Parkinson's disease from handwriting using deep learning: a comparative study. Evol. Intell. **16**(6), 1813–1824 (2020). https://doi.org/10.1007/s12065-020-00470-0
9. Senturk, Z.K.: Early diagnosis of Parkinson's disease using machine learning algorithms. Med. Hypotheses **138**, 109603 (2020)
10. Wang, W., Lee, J., Harrou, F., Sun, Y.: Early detection of Parkinson's disease using deep learning and machine learning. IEEE Access **8**, 147635–147646 (2020)
11. Almeida, J.S., et al.: Detecting Parkinson's disease with sustained phonation and speech signals using machine learning techniques. Pattern Recogn. Lett. **125**, 55–62 (2019)
12. Tadse, S., Jain, M., Chandankhede, P.: Parkinson's detection using machine learning. In: 2021 5th International Conference on Intelligent Computing and Control Systems (ICICCS). IEEE (2021)
13. Narendra, N.P., Schuller, B., Alku, P.: The detection of Parkinson's disease from speech using voice source information. IEEE/ACM Trans. Audio Speech Lang. Process. **29**, 1925–1936 (2021). https://doi.org/10.1109/TASLP.2021.3078364
14. Rajeswari, S.S., Nair, M.: Prediction of Parkinson's disease from voice signals using machine learning. J. Pharmaceut. Negative Results 2031–2035 (2022)
15. Vigneswari, D.A., Aravinth, J.: Parkinson's disease diagnosis using voice signals by machine learning approach. In: 2021 International Conference on Recent Trends on Electronics, Information, Communication & Technology (RTEICT). IEEE (2021)
16. Little, M., Mcsharry, P., Roberts, S., Costello, D., Moroz, I.: Exploiting nonlinear recurrence and fractal scaling properties for voice disorder detection. Nat. Precedings **6**, 23 (2007)

Mental Stress Assessment in Working Environment for an Individual Using Wearable Sensor of EEG and Pulse Signal Measured with Help of Deep Learning Algorithm

M. V. Karthikeyan, S. Bhuvaneshwar(✉), and V. Nishanth

Department of Electronics and Communication Engineering, St. Joseph's Institute of Technology, OMR, Chennai 60019, Tamil Nadu, India
hrbhuvan27@gmail.com

Abstract. Thanks to artificial intelligence (AI), machines will eventually have the same emotional impact as humans. Deep emotions, not just words, are used by this "affective computing" to engage with humans. Bypassing societal masks, sensors like the EEG and GSR are able to sense our genuine feelings. However, creating robots that are actually sensitive to our emotions is challenging. To build genuinely emotionally intelligent machines, we need to improve the methods we use to choose, arrange, and evaluate these signals.

This paper propose a method for assessing mental stress in the workplace in real-time using deep learning algorithms in conjunction with wearing EEG and GSR. The major goal is to make computers smarter emotionally so that they can change the way people interact with computers (HCI). Our proposed system can discreetly track a worker's emotional and psychological well-being as they go about their daily tasks. By combining electroencephalogram (EEG) and pulse signal analysis, our system is able to record not only the mental but also the physiological reactions to mental stress.

Keywords: EEG · Stress detection · Emotion · MATLAB

1 Introduction

A man's daily existence is becoming increasingly dependent on computers. Unfortunately, they lack the emotional intelligence to perceive and comprehend the intensity of human emotions. Reading and understanding about the states of intense emotions in humans could greatly enhance human-computer interaction (HCI). It is crucial to consider the users' emotional states and provide this information to make HCI more meaningful. One of the most crucial parts of human-computer interaction (HCI) is affective computing (AC), a field of study that is devoted only to HCI as seen through user behavior on exploration. Affective computing (Ac) is a field of study that only focuses on human-computer interaction (HCI) as it occurs during user exploration. Ac research

Published by Springer Nature Switzerland AG 2025
A. Chandrabose et al. (Eds.): ICCCSP 2024, IFIP AICT 723, pp. 80–92, 2025.
https://doi.org/10.1007/978-3-031-73617-9_7

aims to improve the value of human-machine communication by developing methods for machines to recognize and react to human emotions [1]. Emotion recognition could be useful in many different ways; for example, in intelligent education [2], computer games [3], and e-state of being safe applications [4]. In addition to visual cues like facial expressions, it is possible to determine a person's serious emotional state using physiological indicators like electroencephalography (EEG), heart rate (BVP), and galvanic skin movement (GSR). Physical indicators don't offer nearly as many options as physiological signals do due to the former's sensitivity to inner sensations and the latter's insensitivity to social concealment of emotions. I and the latter's insensitivity to social concealment of emotions. Figure 1 shows the physical effects of stress.

While tethered-laboratory sensors are effective, they are more obtrusive and cumbersome to use in ordinary life, and they can only receive and record highly powerful signals in order to extract intricate details. Staying in touch doesn't have to be intrusive or draw attention to itself, thanks to radiological sensors. Quickly embraced by the general public in tandem with the development of integrated sensor technologies, these small-scale, usable sensors are able to generate electric current with minimal apparatus while making better use of user interface design. Modern technology ought to have allowed a fully automated gadget to develop the ability to reliably detect a range of intense emotional states. Many emotions can be evaluated using EEG and BVP indications; there is significant evidence linking these signs to emotions such as surprise, indignation, and depression [5].

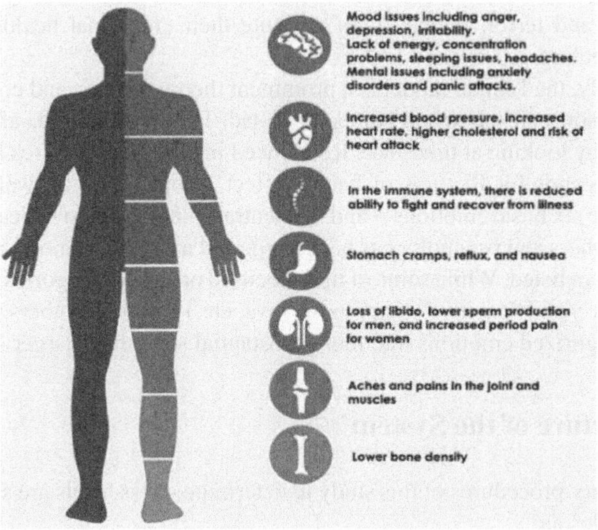

Fig. 1. Effects of Stress on the body

In order to track brain electrical activity, an EEG sensor is often worn or attached to the scalp. The reason why there is a direct correlation between EEG signals and different emotions is because these signals come from the central nervous system (CNS), which is responsible for capturing traits of deep emotional states. Using widely available equipment, like a little EEG helmet, Wearable sensors have proven their worth in a variety of contexts, including emotion detection and future event prediction. One potential outcome of expanding our usage of these non-invasive advancements is the possibility of creating a practical emotion detection device. The primary goal of this research is to create emotion order models that are accurate, stable, fine-tuned, and ready-to-use by combining state-of-the-art machine learning methods with physiological sensors (such as the EEG and GSR signals recorded from inmates).

2 Literature Survey

A person's emotional existence is fundamental. Although numerous studies have been conducted over the last several decades in an attempt to produce a universal set of fundamental emotions that all theorists can agree on, no such set has been developed for the concept of emotion or its definition. Contrary to popular belief, several researchers have shown that it is feasible to identify emotions indirectly through factors such as context, self-evaluation, physiological markers, and expressive behavior. According to psychologists, feelings and emotions do not happen alone, and they are associated with certain inputs. There are two main categories of human beings, say psychologists. Models can be either categorized or dimensional [6]. We have proposed many categorized models and conducted investigations to determine fundamental emotions [7]. [8] proposed a theory of emotions, which [9] subsequently clarified. There are nine primary emotions, according to Tomkins: interest, excitement, joy, surprise, fury, rage, disgust, dissmell, distress, rage, and terror. People often attribute their emotional health to these nine fundamental feelings.

Additionally, the Ekman model is a prominent theory. Ekman and colleagues found that every person can tell when someone is sad, happy, surprised, afraid, angry, or disgusted just by looking at their face. Referenced in [10] were pictures from the POFA series, which stands for Pictures of Facial Affect. People from all walks of life may recognize these six basic emotions—and the neutral—in this photo series of performers. Some philosophers and psychologists have suggested additional emotions in addition to those that Ekman listed. While some of them focused on broad categories like "negative" (fear, anger, etc.) and "positive" (happiness, love, etc.) emotions, others went more into detail and categorized emotions into more substantial sets (thus "larger sets").

3 Architecture of the System

The four primary procedures of this study to determine stress levels are shown in Fig. 2.

The Modules are

- Gathering data
- Setting Up
- Feature extraction through segmentation
- Classification

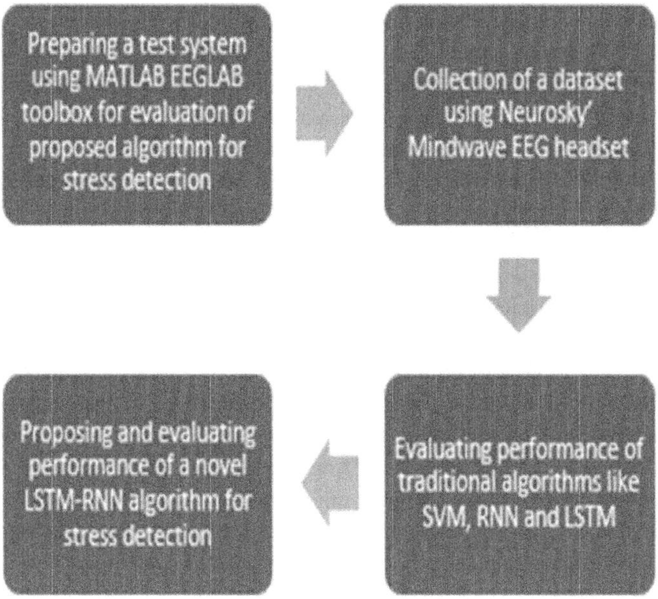

Fig. 2. Workflow for Stress detection using EEG Signal

3.1 Gathering Data

We have applied our statistical extraction method to this EEG dataset (https://www.kaggle.com/qiriro/ieee-tac). There were 1965 participants (856 men and 1,109 females), and each state (relaxation, concentration, and neutrality) was measured for 60 s. At TP9, AF7, AF8, and TP10, we captured EEG signals using a Muse EEG headgear with dry electrodes.

3.2 Initial Stages

One specific way to use EEG signals in a specified order involves four main steps: pre-processing, point collection, extraction, and order (see Fig. 1). Since filthy, unhealthy goods often provide noisy EEG signals, the first and most risky stage is pre-processing. Two artificial phenomena caused by physical variables such as the movement of electrodes, the eye, the muscles, and the heartbeat. Muscle motion produces a signal with a frequency greater than 40 Hz, in contrast to the 4 Hz produced by eye movement, heart beat, head motion, and breathing.

Additionally, 50 Hz electrical lines are to blame for some non-physiological man-made crap that taints the EEG signal. It was suggested that a 464 Hz EEG signal could cover a range of emotions, and sixth-order filters are used to keep EEG signals within a certain frequency range (band-pass). Butterworth was gradually making an appearance. A suggestion was made to eliminate the 50 Hz noise produced by electricity lines following a minor interruption that gradually passed. To further refine the artificial stuff caused by heart rhythm and to separate complicated multichannel facts into independent parts, independent component analysis (ICA) was applied alongside these pre-processing methods [14]. This led to a cleaner signal prepared for the point-taking-out phase. After cleaning the EEG signals, the next step was to extract time-related features, frequency-based features, and number-of-occurrences-per-unit-time data in order to identify distinct emotions. The next step was to merge the features acquired from each little path into a larger point-group representational guide. For EC algorithms, the best way to change the type of features used in machine learning is to repeatedly send requests to different point groups until they find the optimal range and workspace. Repeatedly comparing the quality of the point groups generated by point selection to the order of certain sentiments based on experience findings was the goal of combining the two processes. For this reason, we utilized a probabilistic neural network (PNN) [15] to assess how well each EC point selection algorithm performed across different modalities. One kind of network is the three-tiered PNN, which is constructed using Bayesian networks.

As a measure against over fitting, our framework employs a 10-fold upright with a bit across it to guide the training and testing of each EC method. With PNN, training takes only one pass through each training guide instead of multiple passes, which allows for faster results compared to other ordering methods. Aside from the jumbled-up point-collection and order mechanisms, the point-taking-out mechanism is the most important part of the system.

3.3 Segmentation and Extraction

Qualities that are Time-Dependent

Individuals' intense emotional states have been associated with distinct temporal-domain characteristics. Statistical features like suggest, maximum, minimum, power, standard deviation from the straight line, first point or amount different, normalized first point or amount different, quality example of first point or amount different, second point or amount different, normalized second point, or at most. Additional encouraging time-domain points include the Hjorth parameters: process, readiness to pass, and complex portion. Studies on sleep disorders and engine imagining that have used EEG have utilized these metrics, which reflect the suggestive force, suggestive number of times per unit time, and number of quality example slopes from the indications. Compared to other ways, the ones stated above have the least complicated element, which is why they were all sought for current applications.

We also included two more time-domain features alongside these famous ones. It has been demonstrated that fractal measures to clear geometrically complicated elements are an excellent method for sensing large numbers of subjects. There are a number of ways to calculate fractal measure points, but the Higuchi approach is superior to others such as fractal Brownian motion and box addition. A more recent idea is the non-motionless index (NSI), which looks at the differences in local averages to figure out how non-stationary EEG 1 signals are after they have been broken up into smaller pieces. To further enhance the effectiveness of NSI features, they can be combined with additional points, including higher-order crossing features, which are based on the zero-crossing count and account for attributes of oscillation behavior.

Analysis by Frequency and Domain

For automatic EEG-based sentiments of universal acceptance of one's work, frequency-domain features have been demonstrated to be more effective than time-domain points. An excellent indicator of varied intense emotional states is the strength of an electroencephalogram (EEG) signal spread out over a large number of times per unit time band. Features such as the power band, logarithm of the power band, maximum, minimum, and consistency, for example, should be derived from different frequency bands, specifically gamma (3064 Hz), theta (1330 Hz), first or top (813 Hz), and beta (48 Hz), since these characteristics have been demonstrated to change throughout various intense emotional states.

Features of Time – Frequency Domain

One limitation of frequency-domain characteristics is that they do not have time-limited accounts. So, features in the time-frequency domain are good for collecting signals that are both static and changing over time; this makes it easy to quickly incorporate fresh data to account for the characteristics of different emotional states. Both the Hilbert Huang band (HHS) and the separate section wavelet transform (dwt) are the most relevant and useful characteristics for this project. At one point in time, the sign dwt goes bad has been utilized to absorb various emotions through various modalities and then released into various number-per-unit-time bands.

There has been a request to study the correlation between high music and severe emotional awakenings, and HHS copies are derived from being great, squared, and sudden, as well as from deconstructed signs received from the most common number of purposes and uses. The shape of the different parts of a wavelet can be used to figure out a number of properties, such as strength, root-imply-square, logarithmic REE, and returning- to-power-for-a-given-time (REE). Using all of the aforementioned characteristics, this learning process determines the optimal sequence in which to complete the various EEG feature divisions while playing. Table 1 provides a concise summary of the features.

3.4 Feature Selection and Categorisation

Using evolutionary computation (EC) techniques, the most relevant features can be extracted from EEG data. We learned five algorithm and part under the control of another optimization, acted as annealing, genetic algorithm, very small bit swarm optimization, and change to do with different conditions natural development—to discover the best solution. These algorithms are unique, but they all work toward the same goal: using population-based rules to make discoveries. We went over these algorithms several times. All of these algorithms are different, but they all aim to do the same thing: identify the optimal solution by constantly evaluating new possibilities. Each EC method consists of three steps: 1) randomly preparing the answer population; 2) checking each answer in the population for accuracy by assigning a value; and 3) repeatedly producing a new population until the ending conditions are satisfied.

Improvement of Ant Colonies (ACO)

Finding the optimal feature combination to attain the maximum order accuracy or the maximum number of repetitions could be the last criterion. Ants' extensive foraging activities were the initial spark that ignited ACO. Locating the most direct paths from the animal's food sources to its sleeping place is its primary goal. An ant colony run by a different mechanism produces pheromone when foraging for food on land.

3.5 Classification

In our experiments, two high-quality example knowledge units, Mahnob and DEAP, were obtained using an EEG sensor with 32 narrow ways, and a new unit was obtained using an item-unfixed sensor with narrow ways. We propose using ongoing development RNN-LSTM algorithms, specifically.

To show the benefits of EC algorithms 2 for extracting important EEG signal output features and getting the most out of classifier play, we have shown how these algorithms work with 10, 25, 45, and 100 iterations. Across all iterations, PSO outperformed the other RNN-LSTM methods. In addition, the combination of time and the number of times every unit time characteristic was found to be more successful at generating a play effect than any of them alone.

Breaking down the most popular feature source (in this case, the EEG narrow ways) into smaller, more manageable pieces and assigning each one a weighted value is what the RNN-LSTM algorithms are all about. A lightweight and radio EEG sensor (emotive power of seeing) was able to be used for four-quadrant feeling order based on the information modules from DEAP and MAHNOB. The electrodes in the front and middle of the round parts were made to be more activated during feelings.

Table 1. Feature extraction from electroencephalogram (EEG) data

Time Domain

Minimum	Mean
Maximum	Power
Standard Deviation	1st Difference
Normalized 1st difference	Second difference
Normalized second difference	Hjorth Feature (Activity, Mobility and Complexity)
Non-Stationary Index	Fractal Dimension (Higuchi Algorithm)
Higher Order Crossing	Variance
Root mean Square	Quartile 1, quartile median, quartile 3, quartile 4

Frequency Domain

Power Spectrum Density (PSD) from Gamma, Theta, Alpha, Beta	Mean

Time–Frequency Domain

Power of Discrete Wavelet Transform (DWT) from Gamma, Theta, Alpha,Beta

Root Mean Square (RMS) of DWT from Gamma, Theta, Alpha, Beta	Recursive Energy Efficiency (REE) of DWT from Gamma, Theta, Alpha, Beta
Log (REE) of DWT from Gamma, Theta, Alpha, Beta	Abs (log (REE)) of DWT from Gamma, Theta, Alpha, Beta

Regardless of the good results, this paper is a key limiting condition for the early appearance of a challenging question in RNN-LSTM algorithms. Therefore, in order to tackle this challenging challenge, future research should center on creating new RNN-LSTM algorithms or improving current ones.

4 Result and Discussion

In MATLAB, the toolkit is the In order to analyze electrophysiological data in both its continuous and event- related forms, EEGLAB is available for use. This includes EEG, MEG, and other types of electrophysiological data. Among the features that are included are independent component analysis (ICA), artifact removal, time and frequency analysis, event-related statistics, and helpful approaches for viewing averaged and single-trial data. The EEGLAB software is compatible with a wide range of computer operating systems.

The user-friendly graphical user interface (GUI) that EEGLAB provides makes it possible to perform applications such as ICA, time-frequency analysis (TFA), and standard averaging on large amounts of EEG data. EEGLAB includes a number of additional features that make it easier to switch from exploratory GUI data analysis to programmed batch or user-specific analysis. These features include a command history, comprehensive tutorials, and help screens. Within EEGLAB, there are a multitude of approaches that may be utilized to demonstrate and imitate the brain's reaction to stimuli. This can be applied to individual EEGLAB datasets or to a collection of datasets that have been aggregated into a single EEGLAB "study set" (Fig. 3).

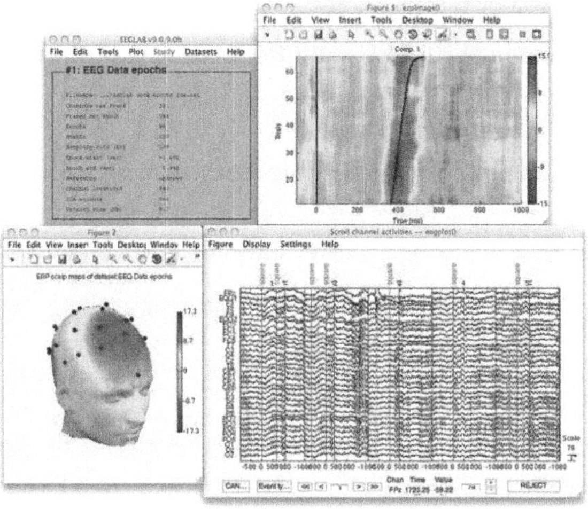

Fig. 3. Proposed system output

As a consequence of dissecting data from a single channel into various EEG frequency bands, the result is depicted in Fig. 4. These are the raw data from the EEGLAB toolbox, which was recorded at a frequency of 128 Hz. It is seen in Fig. 5 that the spectrogram of the filtered outputs. At least one of these functions makes use of the power spectra of a number of different EEG bands. Throughout the training process of their algorithms, classifiers use these features as inputs. After taking the power spectra for each frequency in the dataset and averaging them, we are able to obtain the training weights because of this.

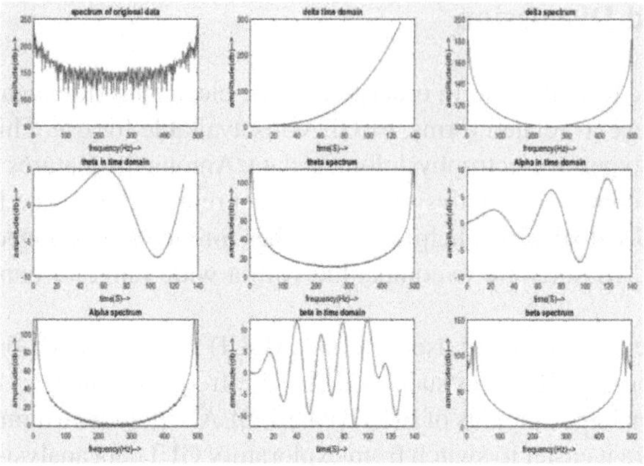

Fig. 4. EEG Frequency Decomposition

In Table 2, which also includes a comparison of the suggested method to algorithms that are considered to be industry standards, you can see how well the suggested method performs in identifying all eight emotions. In order to compare the results of the experiments, additional assessment metrics such as F1-score, specificity, precision, and recall are utilized. In Table 3, you will be able to see the results. Figure 5 presents a composite signal incorporating both EEG and ECG frequencies, which is then analyzed to determine stress levels.

Table 2. Scientific Findings Derived from Dataset

Classification Accuracy %	SVM Classifier	RNN Classifier	MFCC (LSTM)	MFCC(LSTM+RNN) Proposed Algorithm
Neutral	100	70	90	100
Calm	66	85	86	98
Happy	86	83	84	99
Sad	81	75	78	98
Angry	89	84	91	98
Fearful	70	72	74	99
Disgust	73	70	75	99
Surprise	60	75	78	99
Overall Accuracy	76	78	82	98.7

Table 3. Results of the experiment with respect to F1-Score, Specificity, Precision, and Recall

	SVM	RNN	LSTM	Proposed RNN - LSTM
TP	2210	2345	2459	2768
TN	1550	1514	1598	1735
FP	735	703	651	245
FN	453	386	140	200
Error Percentage	24%	22%	18%	1.3%
Accuracy	76%	78%	82%	98.7%
Precision	75.04%	76.93%	79.06%	98.86%
Recall	82.98%	85.86%	94.61%	98.26%
Specificity	67.84%	68.29%	71.05%	97.62%
F1-Score	59.36%	71.58%	85.80%	97.71%

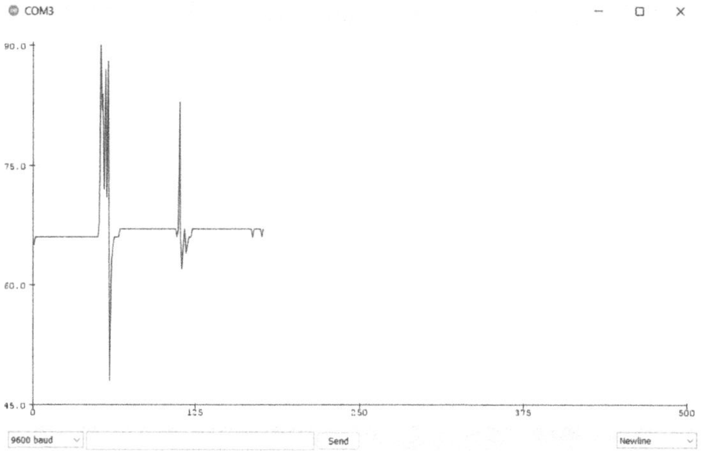

Fig. 5. Proposed system output 1

5 Conclusion

There is a significant problem with anxiety and tension in today's culture. Problems at work, such as having an excessive amount of work to complete and being required to adjust to changing circumstances on a consistent basis, make matters significantly worse. Additionally, there will be significant financial losses for enterprises, and the health problems that are associated with stress are quite real. It is therefore vital to conduct periodic self-assessments of stress in order to discover early warning symptoms of stress and avoid serious long-term repercussions. This is because stress can have serious consequences. The realization that individuals are constantly exposed to high levels of stress was the impetus for the development of the idea of stress detection. Early detection of stress is essential since it increases the likelihood that it will not lead to the development of chronic and exacerbating health conditions. Using audiovisual data such as voice signals and electroencephalograms, we demonstrated in this study that it is possible to identify instances of stress among individuals. With regard to the dataset, the cascaded RNN-LSTM technique achieves an accuracy of 98.75% successfully. In comparison to the methods that are considered to be typical in the industry, the results are 15–20% better. If the objective is to enhance the mental health of individuals, the first step should be to educate them on how to recognize the signs and symptoms of stress and how to locate alternatives to dealing with it. Taking the strategy that has been provided is a good place to begin when it comes to the aim of stress detection, which is to increase happiness.

6 Quantitative Comparison with Existing Studies

In conclusion, we conduct a quantitative comparison between our model and other relevant research that have been published in the literature. The performance metrics for the automatic classification of stress levels from a few recent studies are compared with 1D CNN model in Table 4. Previous research evaluating the efficacy of their ML/DL models focused on binary and multi-class stress detection, using freely accessible datasets like SWELL-KW, WESAD, and AMIGOS. The suggested solution performs better than the current system in terms of accuracy when a subset of characteristics is chosen for model training. Table 4 shows the current system that is compared with other model. Thereby, the proposed system shows high performance than the existing system.

Table 4. Quantitative comparison with other state-of-the-art models.

Reference	Dataset	Binary/ Multilevel	No. of features	Model	Accuracy	Precision	Recall	F1-score
[24]	SWELL-KW	Binary	17	SVM	92.75%	N.A.	N.A.	N.A.
[25]	SWELL-KW, AMIGOS [5]	3 class	N.A.	CNN	98.30%	96.00%	96.30%	95.80%
[13]	SWELL-KW	3 class	N.A.	SVM	90.00%	N.A.	N.A.	N.A.
[27]	WESAD [36]	Binary/3 class	7	ML/ANN	84.32%/ 95.21%	N.A.	N.A.	78.71%/ 94.24%
[37]	From experiment	Binary/3 class	7	MLP	92.85%/ 64.28%	N.A.	N.A.	N.A.
[15]	SWELL-KW	Binary	34	MLP	88.64%	93.01%	92.68%	82.75%
This study	SWELL-KW	3 class	34	1D-CNN	99.99%	100%	100%	100%
This study	SWELL-KW	3 class	15	1D-CNN	96.50%	94.60%	97.00%	96.00%

7 Future Enhancement

Further research will concentrate on improving the accuracy and dependability of stress measurement through the refinement of wearable EEG and GSR technologies integration with deep learning algorithms. Furthermore, it is intended to extend the application of this methodology beyond stress evaluation to areas including safety-oriented environments, gaming, and cognitive learning. Future research will focus on developing sensitive computer systems that can recognize and react to human emotions. This will eventually lead to the creation of happier and more productive workplaces by encouraging efficient management of mental health.

References

1. Masri, G., Al-Shargie, F., Tariq, U., Almughairbi, F., Babiloni, F., Al-Nashash, H.: Mental stress assessment in the workplace: a review. IEEE Trans. Affect. Comput. (2024). https://doi.org/10.1109/TAFFC.2023.3312762
2. Mortensen, J.A., Mollov, M.E., Chatterjee, A., Ghose, D., Frank, Y.L.: Multi-Class Stress Detection Through Heart Rate Variability: A Deep Neural Network Based Study 8 May 2023. https://doi.org/10.1109/ACCESS.2023.3274478
3. Karthikeyan, M.V.: Raspberry Pi implemented with MATLAB simulation and communication of Physiological Signal based fast Chaff point (RPSC) generation algorithm for WBAN systems. Biomed. Eng./Biomedizinische Technik. **66**(2), 209–224 (2021).
4. Karthikeyan, M.V., Manickam, J.M.L.: Efficient bio-signal feature based secure secret key generation scheme a simplified model for wireless body area network (EFSKG scheme). J. Med. Imag. Health Inform. **8**(5), 863–871 (2018)
5. Karthikeyan, M.V., Martin Leo Manickam, J.: Security issues in wireless body area networks: in bio-signal input fuzzy security model: a survey. Res. J. Pharmaceut. Biol. Chem. Sci. **7**(6), 1755–1773 (2016)
6. Karthikeyan, M.V., Martin Leo Manickam, J.: A novel fast chaff point generation method using bio-inspired flower pollination algorithm for fuzzy vault systems with physiological signal for wireless body area sensor networks. Artif. Intell. Tech. Bio-Med. Sig. Process. Biomed. Res. s242–s254 (2017)
7. Tran, T.A., et al.: Heart rate variability measurement to assess acute work-content-related stress of workers in industrial manufacturing environment—a systematic scoping review. IEEE Trans. Syst., Man, Cybern.: Syst. **53**(11), 6685–6692 (2023). https://doi.org/10.1109/TSMC.2023.3282141
8. Whiston, A., Igou, E.R., Fortune, D.G., Analog Devices Team, Semkovska, M.: Examining stress and residual symptoms in remitted and partially remitted depression using a wearable electrodermal activity device: a pilot study. IEEE J. Transl. Eng. Health Med. **11**, 96-106 (2023). https://doi.org/10.1109/JTEHM.2022.3228483
9. Finseth, T.T., Dorneich, M.C., Vardeman, S., Keren, N., Franke, W.D.: Real-time personalized physiologically based stress detection for hazardous operations. IEEE Access **11**, 25431–25454 (2023). https://doi.org/10.1109/ACCESS.2023.3254134
10. Moosavi, S.K.R., Zafar, M.H., Sanfilippo, F., Akhter, M.N., Hadi, S.F.: Early mental stress detection using q-learning embedded starling murmuration optimiser-based deep learning model. IEEE Access **11**, 116860–116878 (2023). https://doi.org/10.1109/ACCESS.2023.332 6129

11. Moser, M.K., Resch, B., Ehrhart, M.: An individual-oriented algorithm for stress detection in wearable sensor measurements. IEEE Sensors J. **23**(19), 22845–22856 (2023). https://doi.org/10.1109/JSEN.2023.3304422
12. Katmah, R., Al-Shargie, F., Tariq, U., Babiloni, F., Al-Mughairbi, F., Al-Nashash, H.: Mental stress management using fNIRS directed connectivity and audio stimulation. IEEE Trans. Neural Syst. Rehabil. Eng. **31**, 1086–1096 (2023). https://doi.org/10.1109/TNSRE.2023.3239913
13. Jiménez-Ocaña, A.A., Pantoja, A., Valderrama, M.A., Giraldo, L.F.: A systematic review of technology-aided stress management systems: automatic measurement, detection and control. IEEE Access **11**, 116109–116126 (2023). https://doi.org/10.1109/ACCESS.2023.3325763
14. Loizaga, E., Eyam, A.T., Bastida, L., Lastra, J.I.M.: A comprehensive study of human factors, sensory principles, and commercial solutions for future human-centered working operations in industry 5.0. IEEE Access **11**, 53806–53829 (2023). https://doi.org/10.1109/ACCESS.2023.3280071
15. Kuttala, R., Subramanian, R., Oruganti, V.R.M.: Hierarchical autoencoder frequency features for stress detection. IEEE Access **11**, 103232–103241 (2023). https://doi.org/10.1109/ACCESS.2023.3316365
16. Sabour, R.M., Benezeth, Y., De Oliveira, P., Chappé, J., Yang, F.: UBFC-phys: a multimodal database for psychophysiological studies of social stress. IEEE Trans. Affective Comput. **14**(1), 622–636 (2023). https://doi.org/10.1109/TAFFC.2021.3056960
17. Mortensen, J.A., Mollov, M.E., Chatterjee, A., Ghose, D., Li, F.Y.: Multi-class stress detection through heart rate variability: a deep neural network based study. IEEE Access **11**, 57470–57480 (2023). https://doi.org/10.1109/ACCESS.2023.3274478
18. Tong, J., Subramani, A.V., Kote, V., Baggaley, M., Edwards, W.B., Reifman, J.: Effects of stature and load carriage on the running biomechanics of healthy men. IEEE Trans. Biomed. Eng. **70**(8), 2445–2453 (2023). https://doi.org/10.1109/TBME.2023.3248504
19. Battegazzorre, E., Strada, F., De Francesco, L., Mazza, A., Monte, O.D., Bottino, A.: Influencer-based virtual reality stroop task. IEEE Access **11**, 126420–126435 (2023). https://doi.org/10.1109/ACCESS.2023.3324554
20. Alikhani, H., Kanduri, A., Liljeberg, P., Rahmani, A.M., Dutt, N.: DynaFuse: dynamic fusion for resource efficient multimodal machine learning inference. IEEE Embed. Syst. Lett. **15**(4), 222–225 (2023). https://doi.org/10.1109/LES.2023.3298738

Speech Recording Analysis for Parkinson's Detection Using Machine Learning Approach

G. Deepika(✉) and P. Vinothiyalakshmi

Department of Computer Science and Engineering, Sri Venkateswara College of Engineering, Chennai, India
deepikagovindaswamy@gmail.com, vlakshmi@svce.ac.in

Abstract. Parkinson's Disease (PD) is a neuro-degenerative disorder that affects the motor skills of a person when the production of dopamine is reduced and eventually motor dysfunction. Dopamine is a chemical produced by brain cells, which is responsible for controlling movements. Thus, if Parkinson's disease is detected earlier, then the progression and the effects of its symptoms can be controlled. The proposed Parkinson's Disease Detection (PDD) model used for the detection of Parkinson's Disease using various Machine Learning (ML) algorithms such as K-Nearest Neighbor (KNN), Support Vector Machine (SVM), Logistic Regression (LR), Voting Classifier, and Random Forest (RF). The algorithms are applied on balanced data scales and on features selected using LDA and PCA from the speech recording dataset. On experimental analysis, the SVM algorithm is found to be more efficient on the balanced dataset and PCA extracted features, giving an accuracy of 96.73% and 95.42% respectively as compared to the other classification algorithms. While the Random Forest algorithm gives the best results on LDA applied dataset giving an accuracy of 95.85%.

Keywords: Parkinson's disease detection · Machine Learning Algorithms · Speech Recordings · PCA · LDA · Neurodegenerative disorder

1 Introduction

Parkinson's Disease or simply Parkinson's is found to be the second most common neurodegenerative disease after Alzheimer's. This disease predominantly affects the nervous system – targeting the neurons in the brain that control movement by generalized slowing down of movement (bradykinesia). There has been no medication or treatment that can slow down or stop the disease progression however there are treatments and medications that ease the degree of symptoms. These symptoms have been classified as Motor and Non-Motor symptoms. The Motor symptoms that are most observed are Tremors at rest (Involuntary shaking movement at rest), Rigidity, and slow or paucity of movement. The non-motor symptoms are cardiovascular problems, olfactory dysfunction, sleep disorder, depression, and cognitive deficits. It is also seen that the non-motor symptoms can be observed before the diagnosis of Parkinson's. Substantia nigra pars compacta-part of

Published by Springer Nature Switzerland AG 2025
A. Chandrabose et al. (Eds.): ICCCSP 2024, IFIP AICT 723, pp. 93–104, 2025.
https://doi.org/10.1007/978-3-031-73617-9_8

basal ganglia in the mid-brain is responsible for movement. The substantia nigra pars compacta houses Dopaminergic neurons that are responsible for dopamine production. This neurotransmitter regulates movement, motivation, and reward-related sensations. alpha-synuclein in the neurons that overwhelm the protein-degrading machinery (responsible for clearing unwanted proteins) that kills the neurons. It has been suggested that the accumulation of old or degraded mitochondria (the powerhouse of the cell) could be another possible cause of Parkinson's disease. Mitochondria having the ability to combine or separate to suffice the energy need of a cell should be properly eradicated when they die, if not this affects the efficiency of neurons or maybe even the chemical secreted by the microglia (cells surrounding the neurons) injuring the neurons.

It is noteworthy that Parkinson's disease progression may not be universal, as some individuals may experience a slowdown or cessation of symptoms at earlier stages. The disease can be classified into five medical stages, each with its own set of symptoms.

Stage one is characterized by mild tremors on one side of the body. In stage two, tremors, stiffness, and tremulousness in speech become evident on both sides of the body. Stage three is marked by slow reflexes and balance-related problems. The penultimate and final stages of the disease are associated with difficulty or inability to walk. In the final stage, the patient may develop conditions such as dementia, confusion, and poor response to medication.

This proposed work focuses on the automated solution that can detect Parkinson's in an earlier stage keeping in mind that this disease progression can be effectively controlled in its earlier stages. Various ML algorithms like SVM, LR, RF, Voting, and KNN are used to detect PD, and their accuracy and efficiency in detecting the disease are analyzed using different feature sets.

2 Related Works

In this section, some of the existing work reviews done for the detection of Parkinson's Disease are as follows: Gunjan Pahuja1 et al. [1] have discussed the usage of 3 different algorithms – Multilayer perceptron, Support Vector Machine, and K Nearest Neighbour on a PD-affected person's voice dataset to find the algorithm that gives the highest accuracy in Parkinson's Disease detection. According to the research findings, 90% of individuals diagnosed with Parkinson's disease show vocal dysfunction. The study also evaluated the performance of two machine learning algorithms, Artificial Neural Networks (ANN) with the Levenberg–Marquardt optimization method and the KNN using Euclidean distance. The results indicate that the ANN achieved the highest accuracy of 95.89% for the voice dataset, while the KNN algorithm using Euclidean distance achieved the lowest accuracy of 72.31%.

Satyabrata Aich et al. [2] proposed a method of detecting Parkinson's Disease using speech and gait analysis data. This works by comparing the performance metrics with different feature sets selected by applying Principal Component Analysis. The study discovered that applying genetic algorithm-based feature sets in combination with SVM using RBF led to an outstanding accuracy of 97.57%.

In a study conducted by Shail Raval et al. [3], several Machine Learning classification algorithms were evaluated to assess their effectiveness in detecting Parkinson's

Disease (PD) during its early stages. The study focused on four significant symptoms that are critical indicators of early PD detection: tremors at rest, bradykinesia, rigidity, and voice impairment. By implementing various machine learning algorithms, the research discovered that the Random Forest (RF) algorithm – when applied to the Static Spiral Test to detect tremors – achieved an impressive accuracy rate of 99.79%.

In a study by [4], an advanced deep-learning technique was utilized to detect the presence of PD based on premotor features. This technique takes into consideration early-stage symptoms such as Rapid Eye Movement and olfactory loss, along with data on Cerebrospinal fluid and dopaminergic imaging markers. The accuracy of deep learning algorithms was compared to machine learning algorithms, and the former impressively achieved a remarkable accuracy rate of 96.45%.

Zehra Karapinar et al. [5] underscored the crucial role of feature selection and classification in identifying Parkinson's Disease. Their study involved extracting features from the data using both feature importance and recursive feature elimination methods and subsequently testing them with three machine learning algorithms: Classification and Regression Trees, Artificial Neural Network, and Support Vector Machine. The outcomes indicated that Support Vector Machine delivered the most accurate results with a rate of 93.84% while utilizing the fewest number of Parkinson's Disease features.

A study conducted by Iqra Nissar and colleagues et al. [6] found that 90% of people living with Parkinson's disease suffer from speech disorders that worsen over time. As a result, this project aimed to evaluate the efficacy of different machine learning and deep learning algorithms in predicting Parkinson's Disease. Notably, the Deep Neural Network displayed the highest level of accuracy, achieving an impressive 99.49%, while the machine learning algorithms also scored above 99%. These findings indicate that Artificial Intelligence is increasingly being utilized in this area of study.

Srishti Grover et al. [11] have proposed a new technique for predicting the severity of Parkinson's Disease (PD) using a Deep Neural Network (DNN). The study utilized UCI's Parkinson's Telemonitoring Voice Data Set to analyze the features of PD, with a particular focus on the voice stutter as it is one of the most common symptoms of PD. The records were classified into two categories, "severe" and "not severe," using a Deep learning algorithm. The UPDRS motor ability score was used to evaluate the severity of PD on a scale of 0–180, and the general UPDRS score was used to assign a score ranging from 0–176. The DNN model outperformed other existing techniques in terms of accuracy. Additionally, the study found that using the motor score for classification yielded better results than using the total UPDRS score.

Timothy J. Wroge and co-authors et al. [10] have studied using the biomarkers from the voice of a PD-affected person to detect and diagnose PD. This work aims to understand the effectiveness of various Deep learning and Machine learning Algorithms. It was observed that the highest accuracy of models exceeded the average clinical diagnosis accuracy of non-experts 73.8% and movement disorder specialists which showed an average accuracy of 79.6% without follow-up and 83.9% after follow-up. The results were found to be promising on datasets with large dimensions and high noise.

Most of the existing works analyzed datasets for detecting PD. To improve the efficiency of the detection model, this proposed work considers different dimensionality reduction techniques such as PCA and LDA to improve the efficiency of the detection model.

3 Proposed Work

The aim of this work is to evaluate the effectiveness of various machine learning algorithms on the voice dataset of Parkinson's Disease. The dataset is analyzed using three distinct techniques – training algorithms on a balanced Parkinson's classification dataset, training algorithms on LDA extracted features, and training algorithms on reduced dimension selected features by PCA. The proposed architecture has been presented in Fig. 1.

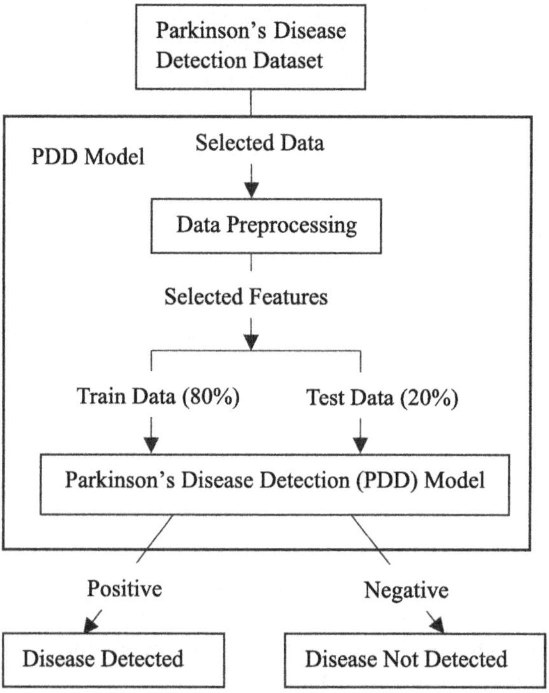

Fig. 1. Proposed Architecture of PDD Model

3.1 Dataset Collection

The dataset comprises of data pertaining to 188 individuals aged between 37 to 87 who have been diagnosed with Parkinson's disease. This data was collected by the Department of Neurology at the Cerrahpasa Faculty of Medicine, Istanbul University. The data was recorded from a microphone with a frequency of 44.1 kHz, and a physical examination was carried out on the subjects. A phonation of the vowel /a/ was collected from each subject with an average of 3 repetitions. The PDD Model considers certain attributes from this data.

The attributes used in this dataset for prediction are as follows.

1. Wavelet Transform based Features.
2. Time Frequency Features.
3. TWQT features.
4. Mel Frequency Cepstral Coefficients (MFCCs).
5. Vocal Fold.

3.2 Data Pre-processing

The data undergoes a pre-processing stage to eliminate any erroneous or noisy values, followed by a feature selection process to choose the relevant features for the algorithms to work on. For this purpose, the data were scaled down to values between 0 and 1 (inclusive) using min–max normalization.

Column-wise normalization was performed on the dataset, and the formula used is described below.

$$Normalized\ value\ of\ x = \frac{x - min(x)}{\max(x) - \min(x)} \tag{1}$$

3.3 Classification Algorithms

The following ML based classification algorithms are used for the proposed PDD model.

3.3.1 Random Forest Classifier

Random Forest is a supervised learning algorithm that uses an ensemble technique that builds multiple decision trees and merges their outputs to make a more accurate prediction. RF uses an ensemble technique called bagging (Bootstrap aggregating) in which multiple machine-learning models are combined to improve the overall accuracy of prediction. In bagging some random samples are selected to form a subset of a fixed size from the original data set and are given to different models. Each model learns independently and the final prediction is taken by seeing the class label each model has predicted, and the most voted class label is the predicted decision.

3.3.2 Support Vector Machine (SVM)

The Support Vector Machine (SVM) algorithm is a well-known and highly effective tool in the field of supervised machine learning. It can perform both classification and regression tasks with a high degree of accuracy. Specifically, in the case of linear data, SVM searches for the most effective hyperplane for separating classes in the given dataset. The goal is to find a hyperplane that maximizes the distance between itself and the nearest data points from each class, which are referred to as support vectors. This approach enables the SVM algorithm to identify the optimal boundary between classes, even when the data is complex. In instances where the data is non-linear, SVM relies on the Kernel trick to operate within the original feature space. This approach avoids the need to compute data coordinates in a higher dimensional space, making the algorithm both efficient and effective.

3.3.3 Logistic Regression (LR)

Logistic regression (LR) is a supervised machine learning algorithm that classifies input samples as true or false i.e., the output classification of a data sample in LR lies between 0 and 1. This algorithm fits the s-shaped logistic function where this curve goes from 0 to 1. For this, a sigmoid function is used for estimation. This curve tells the probability of a person being affected by Parkinson's or not based on the input parameter. LR can work both with continuous and discrete data. In this algorithm it is only considered if the variable's effect on the prediction is significantly different from zero; if not then the data is of no use in prediction.

3.3.4 K Nearest Neighbor (KNN)

The KNN algorithm is a non-parametric method that operates under supervision without making any assumptions about data distribution. It works by measuring the proximity of data points to each other. When presented with new data, the KNN is identified and a majority vote determines the classification of the test data. However, in high-dimensional spaces, the 'curse of dimensionality' may occur, where distances between data points become similar and the algorithm loses efficiency. Typically, Euclidean Distance is used to calculate distance, although this may vary depending on the data's characteristics.

3.3.5 Voting Classifier

Voting is a classification technique where the output of multiple machine learning models is taken into consideration to predict the accuracy.

Hard Voting: Hard Voting is a type of voting classifier, it checks whether the models involved in voting give 0's or 1's. The count of models giving 0's and 1's will be taken. It will see which value is given by a maximum number of models i.e., 0 or 1 and the class label will be given accordingly. In this type of voting, all the models have equal significance in voting.

Soft Voting: In Soft Voting classifier the machine learning model involved in the ensemble technique gives the probabilities of 0's or 1's. The average of probabilities of models giving 0's and 1's will be taken. It will see which maximum of the obtained two probability values and the class label will be given accordingly. Here, all the models vote but their significance is based on the weights carried by the votes.

4 Experimental Analysis

The efficiency of algorithms was analyzed using different evaluation metrics such as accuracy, precision, recall, and F1-score. These metrics use counts of TP, TN, FP, and FN for evaluation. TP is the count of PD-affected individuals classified as PD-positive by the model. TN is the number of healthy individuals classified as healthy i.e. Not Parkinson's affected. FP represents the count of healthy individuals who have been falsely classified to be Parkinson's affected. FN is the number of PD-affected individuals misclassified as healthy. The evaluation factors such as accuracy, recall, precision, and F1-score are calculated from the confusion matrix generated by the proposed PDD model.

$$Accuracy = \frac{TP + TN}{TP + TN + FP + FN} \quad (2)$$

$$Recall = \frac{TP}{TP + FN} \quad (3)$$

$$Precision = \frac{TP}{TP + FP} \quad (4)$$

$$F1 - Score = \frac{2 * Recall * Precision}{Recall + Precision} \quad (5)$$

The first technique involves the implementation of a machine-learning algorithm on a balanced dataset.

Technique 1: Model training on Balanced Dataset

a. Collect Parkinson's Disease voice dataset from et al. [15].
b. Apply normalization techniques to preprocess the dataset.
c. Split the dataset into training and testing data where training data is 80%.
d. Apply the algorithms to the dataset.
e. Analyze the classification result of the algorithms based on Accuracy, F1-Score, Precision, and Recall

Table 1 presents the experimental outcomes of various machine-learning algorithms on a balanced dataset. The results indicate that SVM algorithm delivers the highest accuracy rate of 96.73% when applied to a balanced dataset.

Table 1. Performance analysis for Technique 1

Model	Accuracy	Precision	Recall	F1-Score
SVM	96.73%	0.99	0.83	0.92
Random Forest	92.85%	0.92	0.86	0.90
Logistic Regression	85.71%	0.89	0.78	0.87
KNN	86.83%	0.85	0.80	0.80
Hard Voting	83.53%	0.84	0.86	0.84
Soft Voting	85.96%	0.85	0.87	0.85

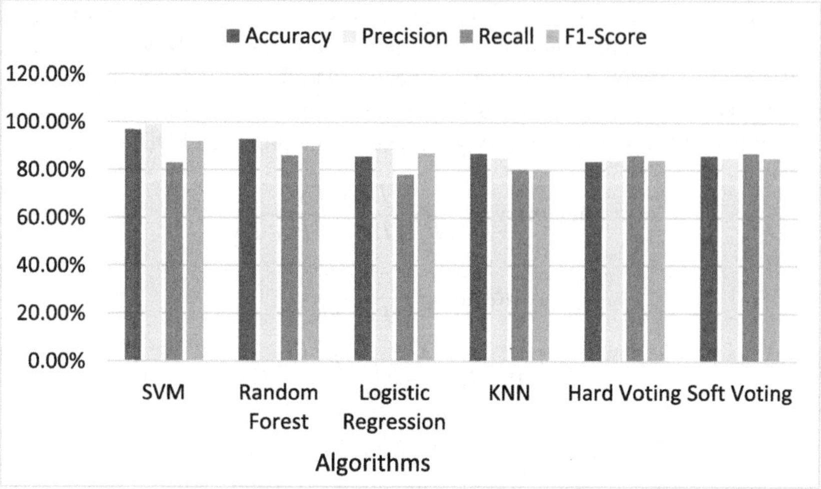

Fig. 2. Comparison of the machine learning algorithms based on Technique 1

Figure 2 describes evaluation metrics achieved by an algorithm when applied to a balanced dataset. The evaluation metrics were calculated from (2), (3), (4), and (5). From the graph, SVM was found to be the best with the highest accuracy and precision.

The second technique involves the deployment of a machine learning algorithm on carefully selected features derived from a dimensionally reduced dataset utilizing LDA.

Technique 2: Model training on LDA applied Dataset

a. Collect Parkinson's Disease speech dataset from et al. [15].
b. Apply normalization techniques to preprocess the dataset.
c. Apply LDA on the dataset to reduce the dimensions and select the most relevant features for model training.
d. Split the dataset into training and testing data.
e. Apply LR, RF, KNN, Hard Voting, Soft Voting and SVM on the dataset.
f. Analyze the classification result of the algorithms based on Accuracy, F1-Score, Precision, and Recall

Table 2 describes the experimental results of the algorithms on a on a LDA extracted features. It was observed that Random Forest gives the highest efficiency of 95.85% when applied on a LDA extracted features.

Table 2. Performance analysis for technique 2

Model	Accuracy	Precision	Recall	F1-Score
SVM	80.73%	1.0	0.83	0.99
Random Forest	95.85%	0.98	0.86	0.91
Logistic Regression	88.67%	0.99	0.80	0.79
KNN	80.73%	0.84	0.80	0.80
Hard Voting	81.36%	0.84	0.86	0.85
Soft Voting	87.25%	0.85	0.87	0.87

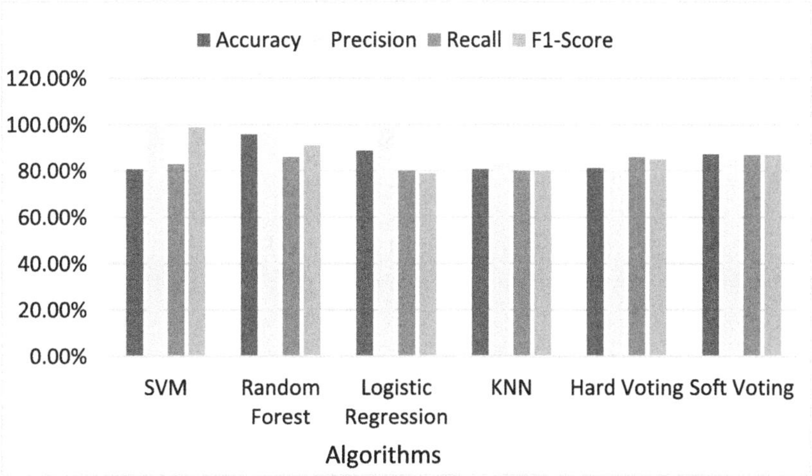

Fig. 3. Comparison of the machine learning algorithms based on Technique 2

Figure 3 describes evaluation metrics achieved by an algorithm when applied to a LDA applied dataset. The evaluation metrics were calculated from (2), (3), (4), and (5). The values of accuracy, precision, recall, and F1-score ranged from 0 to 100%. From the graph, Random Forest predicts with the highest accuracy and precision.

In the third technique, the features are selected from the dimensionally reduced dataset using PCA and the machine learning algorithms are trained upon it.

Technique 3: Model training on PCA applied Dataset

a. Collect Parkinson's Disease voice dataset from et al. [15].
b. Apply normalization techniques to preprocess the dataset.
c. Apply PCA on the dataset to reduce the dimensions of the dataset and select the most relevant features for training.
d. Split the dataset into training and testing data.
e. Apply LR, RF, KNN, Hard Voting, Soft Voting and SVM on the dataset.

f. Analyze the classification result of the algorithms based on Accuracy, Precision, F1-Score, and Recall.

Table 3 illustrates the experimental results of the algorithms applied on PCA extracted features. It is observed that SVM predicts with the highest efficiency of 95.42% when applied on PCA extracted features.

Table 3. Performance analysis for technique 3

Model	Accuracy	Precision	Recall	F1-Score
SVM	95.42%	0.99	0.86	0.94
Random Forest	85.05%	0.91	0.90	0.90
Logistic Regression	90.45%	0.83	0.73	0.85
KNN	80.93%	0.91	0.90	0.83
Hard Voting	80.05%	0.81	0.89	0.86
Soft Voting	89.96%	0.89	0.91	0.89

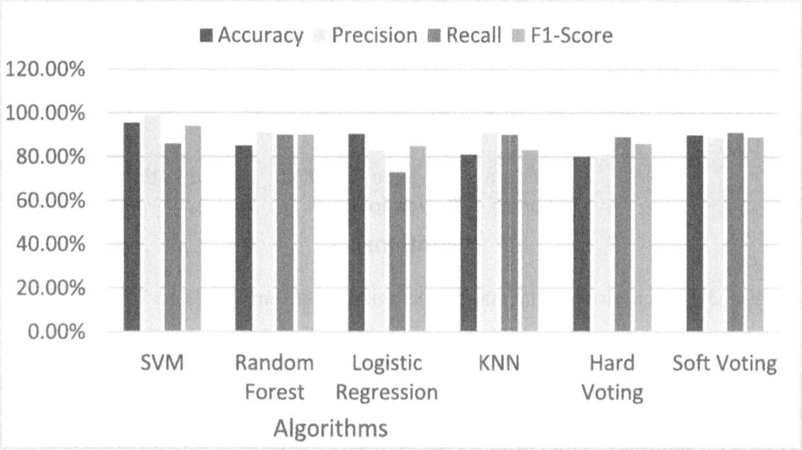

Fig. 4. Comparison of the machine learning algorithms based on Technique 3

Figure 4 illustrates the results of the evaluation metrics achieved by an algorithm when applied on PCA extracted features. The values of accuracy, precision, recall, and F1-score ranged from 0 to 100%. From the graph, SVM predicted with the highest accuracy, precision and F1-score.

5 Conclusion

The current advancement in medical research clearly states that there is no standard test like a blood test or an ECG scan to detect the presence of Parkinson's disease. Doctors are required to go through the medical reports of patients to identify if a person is affected by Parkinson's or not. It is also clear that detecting the presence of this disease at an earlier stage helps in the medication plan of the patient to survive the disease. Although every person affected by Parkinson's has unique symptoms, voice impairment, and other voice-related disorders have been common symptoms. The proposed PDD model has focused on these symptoms to detect the presence of the disease. The performance of the RF, LR, Voting, SVM, and KNN were analyzed based on the accuracy, precision, recall, and F1-score. The PDD model was implemented in 3 different techniques on a Parkinson's Disease dataset that contained extracted features from speech recordings people affected by PD. It was observed that the SVM algorithm applied on a balanced dataset and PCA-based feature-selected dataset gave the the best accuracy of 96.73% and 95.42% respectively. The Random Forest algorithm was the best on LDA extracted features giving an accuracy of 95.85%. It was also noticed that the accuracy of the model can be improved by increasing the size of the dataset. Thus, the early detection of disease with high accuracy helps in controlling the symptom's progression.

References

1. Pahuja, G., Nagabhushan, T.N.: A comparative study of existing machine learning approaches for Parkinson's disease detection. IETE J. Res. **67**(1), 4–14 (2021)
2. Aich, S., Kim, H.-C., Younga, K., Hui, K.L., Al-Absi, A.A., Sain, M.: A supervised machine learning approach using different feature selection techniques on voice datasets for prediction of Parkinson's disease. In: 2019 21st International Conference on Advanced Communication Technology (ICACT) (2019)
3. Raval, S., Balar, R., Patel, V.: A comparative study of early detection of Parkinson's disease using machine learning techniques. In: 2020 4th International Conference on Trends in Electronics and Informatics (ICOEI)(48184) (2020)
4. Wang, W., Lee, J., Harrou, F., Sun, Y.: Early detection of Parkinson's disease using deep learning and machine learning. IEEE Access **8**, 147635–147646 (2020)
5. Karapinar Senturk, Z.: Early diagnosis of Parkinson's disease using machine learning algorithms. Med. Hypotheses **138**, 109603 (2020)
6. Nissar, I., Mir, W.A., Izharuddin, Shaikh, T.A.: Machine learning approaches for detection and diagnosis of Parkinson's disease – A review. In: 2021 7th International Conference on Advanced Computing and Communication Systems (ICACCS) (2021)
7. Celik, E., Omurca, S.I.: Improving Parkinson's disease diagnosis with machine learning methods. In: 2019 Scientific Meeting on Electrical-Electronics and Biomedical Engineering and Computer Science (EBBT) (2019)
8. Govindu, A., Palwe, S.: Early detection of Parkinson's disease using machine learning. Procedia Comput. Sci. **218**, 249–261 (2023)
9. Tîrnăucă, C., Stan, D., Meissner, J.M., Salas-Gómez, D., Fernández-Gorgojo, M., Infante, J.: A machine learning approach to detect Parkinson's disease by looking at gait alterations. Mathematics **10**(19), 3500 (2022)
10. Wroge, T.J., Ozkanca, Y., Demiroglu, C., Si, D., Atkins, D.C., Ghomi, R.H.: Parkinson's disease diagnosis using machine learning and voice. In: 2018 IEEE Signal Processing in Medicine and Biology Symposium (SPMB) (2018)
11. Grover, S., Bhartia, S., Akshama, Yadav, A., Seeja, K.R.: Predicting severity of Parkinson's disease using deep learning. Procedia Comput. Sci. **132**, 1788–1794 (2018)
12. Lew, M.F., Yeung, Y.: Parkinson's disease. In: Reference Module in Biomedical Sciences, Elsevier (2014)

13. Challa, K.N.R., Pagolu, V.S.. Panda, G., Majhi, B.: An improved approach for prediction of Parkinson's disease using machine learning techniques. In: 2016 International Conference on Signal Processing, Communication, Power and Embedded System (SCOPES) (2016)
14. Olivares, R., et al.: An optimized brain-based algorithm for classifying Parkinson's disease. Appl. Sci. (Basel) **10**(5), 1827 (2020)
15. Sakar, C.O., et al.: A comparative analysis of speech signal processing algorithms for Parkinson's disease classification and the use of the tunable Q-factor wavelet transform. Appl. Soft Comput. **74**, 255–263 (2019)
16. Váradi, C.: Clinical features of parkinson's disease: the evolution of critical symptoms. Biology **9**(5), 103 (2020). https://doi.org/10.3390/biology9050103

Compressed VGGNet for Automatic COVID-19 Disease Detection from CT Scan Images

R. Vinothini[1(✉)], G. Niranjana[2], Inge Dhamanti[3], Syifa'ul Lailiyah[4], and Fitri Yakub[5]

[1] Department of Computer Science and Engineering, SRM Institute of Science and Technology, Kattankulathur 603203, India
vr8004@srmist.edu.in

[2] Department of Computing Technologies, School of Computing, SRM Institute of Science and Technology, Kattankulathur 603203, India

[3] Department of Health Policy and Administration, Faculty of Public Health, Universitas Airlangga, Surabaya, Indonesia

[4] Faculty of Health, Medicine, and Life Sciences, Universitas Airlangga, East Java, Indonesia

[5] Electronic System Engineering Department, Malaysia-Japan International Institute of Technology, Kuala Lumpur, Malaysia

Abstract. Millions of people across the globe were affected by this rapidly spreading disease by the year 2020. Contamination of the respiratory system results from contracting COVID-19. Nonetheless, establishing a conclusive diagnosis of COVID-19 may prove difficult due to the subtle differences it shares with conventional pneumonia and the complexities involved in identifying areas of infection. A growing number of approaches based on deep learning (DL) are being proposed for the automated detection of COVID-19 from CT scan images. By employing the data pretreatment methodology, unprocessed image data becomes prepared for further analysis. The proposed framework utilised transfer learning to construct VGGNet, which is capable of discerning the Covid-19 disease. The model was subsequently assessed in comparison to the most sophisticated models, VGG16 and VGG19, using the SARS-COV2 CT scan dataset. This dataset contains 1230 CT scans of non-infected images and 1252 CT scans of Covid-19-infected images. The model has achieved 99% accuracy, 98% precision, 97% recall, and 98% F1-score, among other performance metrics.

Keywords: Visual Geometry Group (VGGNet) · COVID-19 · Classification

1 Introduction

Pandemic rash in late 2019 caused an unparalleled global health catastrophe due to COVID-19 and put a significant strain on healthcare systems all over the world. Effective patient management and viral containment depend on a prompt and accurate diagnosis of COVID-19. Computed Tomography (CT) imaging has been commonly utilised as a

Published by Springer Nature Switzerland AG 2025
A. Chandrabose et al. (Eds.): ICCCSP 2024, IFIP AICT 723, pp. 105–119, 2025.
https://doi.org/10.1007/978-3-031-73617-9_9

supplementary diagnostic approach for COVID-19 due to its ability to detect unique patterns of lung abnormalities associated with the virus [1]. A potent technique for medical image analysis has emerged: Deep Learning, a branch of artificial intelligence. Numerous medical applications, such as autonomous disease identification, have significantly improved thanks to its ability to automatically learn and identify complicated patterns from massive datasets [3]. These frameworks examine the images using deep learning algorithms to find the ground-glass opacities, consolidations, and pleural effusions that are distinctive to COVID-19 [5]. Compared to more conventional techniques, Deep Learning frameworks identification has more benefits especially in COVID-19 finding [2]. First, a huge dataset of CT scan pictures can be used to teach deep learning algorithms the features of COVID-19, which can increase the detection's precision. Second, the real-time analysis of CT scan images using deep learning frameworks can hasten the diagnosis of COVID-19 [32]. There are a few problems that need to be fixed in order to improve the application of deep learning frameworks for COVID-19 detection [4, 6]. These problems include: There is a requirement for large datasets of CT scan images that have been tagged for reality. It is necessary to develop deep learning algorithms that are able to work with CT scan images that are subject to oscillations. Increasing the number of healthcare practitioners who have access to deep learning frameworks is really important [33].

1.1 Problem Statement

A comprehensive and diversified dataset is established for the purpose of training the Deep Learning model. This dataset is comprised of large datasets of CT scan images that are collected from persons who have been proven to have COVID-19 as well as individuals who do not have the disease [7–9]. The collected CT scan images undergo pre-processing steps to ensure uniformity, noise reduction, and standardization. Pre-processing techniques can include resizing, normalization, and data augmentation to augment the dataset artificially and improve model generalization [12]. The cornerstone of these frameworks is comprised of Deep Learning models, such as Convolutional Neural Networks (CNNs), which are designed to develop appropriate architectures that are capable of quickly extracting significant characteristics from CT scan pictures and classifying them into COVID-19 positive or negative designations [10]. The chosen Deep Learning model is trained with the preprocessed dataset. During training, the model uses the data to optimise its internal parameters and enhance its ability to generate correct predictions. The trained model is validated using a separate dataset to evaluate its performance and fine-tuned to enhance its accuracy and generalization capabilities. Once the model achieves satisfactory performance, it is tested on an independent test dataset to assess its real-world diagnostic capabilities. After successful testing, the model can be deployed as an automated COVID-19 detection tool [11–13].

1.2 Contribution

Development and Application of Deep Learning Frameworks for Automatic COVID-19 Disease Detection Using CT Scan Images have contributed significantly to medical imaging and illness diagnosis. Key contributions are as follows: Deep learning models have demonstrated remarkable proficiency in accurately identifying COVID-19 from CT scan images [17]. These models can find trends that are specific to the disease even in its early stages, which makes it possible to make a quick and correct diagnosis. Early detection is important for isolating and treating the patient as soon as possible, which lowers the chance of further transmission and improves patient outcomes [18]. RT-PCR tests are the best way to diagnose COVID-19, but they can give false-negative results, especially when the infection is still early on. Deep Learning models for CT scan analysis serve as a valuable complementary diagnostic tool, helping to confirm or rule out COVID-19 cases when RT-PCR results are inconclusive or unavailable [14]. During the peak of the pandemic, healthcare systems were overwhelmed by the volume of suspected COVID-19 cases. Deep learning frameworks made it possible to quickly and automatically process a lot of CT scans, which made the job of radiologists and other healthcare workers easier [15]. These models can go beyond binary classification (COVID-19 positive or negative) and provide risk stratification, indicating the severity of the disease based on the patterns identified in CT scan images. This stratification aids in better resource allocation and patient management [16]. Deep Learning models trained on diverse and large datasets have demonstrated good generalizability across different populations and imaging systems [16]. This generalizability makes them applicable in various geographical regions and healthcare settings, including areas with limited access to experienced radiologists. As new data becomes available and the pandemic evolves, Deep Learning models can be retrained and fine-tuned to improve their performance continually [27]. This adaptability ensures that the models stay relevant and up-to-date in a dynamic healthcare landscape [10].

Transfer Learning: The knowledge gained from developing COVID-19 detection model using deep learning can be transferred then applied to other medical imaging tasks and disease detection challenges [22]. This cross-disciplinary learning benefits the broader field of medical imaging and diagnostics. The COVID-19 pandemic successfully used Deep Learning frameworks, demonstrating the usefulness of AI-based technologies for future medical emergencies. The experience gained from this application can guide the development of similar frameworks for the rapid detection and diagnosis of emerging infectious diseases [28, 29].

2 Literature Review

Garg, Aksh, et al. [10]. Established a classification technique utilising EfficientNetB5 and demonstrated a visualisation mechanism that allows both observer and GradCAMs (Gradient-weighted Class Activation Mappings) to identify infected spots in the lung. Soares E. et al. gathered the dataset from Kaggle. Out of the 4173 photos that were used, 2168 showed positive COVID-19 instances, 758 showed healthy images, and the remaining 1247 showed lung infections.Using hyperparameter tweaking, such as 571 completely connected layers, three epochs, and the Rectified Linear Unit (Rectified Linear Unit) activation function, they trained.

Using spatial pyramid decomposition (SPD) and multi-scale feature extraction (MSFE), Wong, Pak Kin, et al. [15] suggested a novel multi-scale attention network (MSANet) including lung segment.They employed the MSANet classification algorithm, which takes 917 seconds to test and 39,727 seconds to train. The COVID-19 and community-acquired pneumonia dataset, or CCAP, is where the data was gathered for the dataset. A total of 37579 pictures are collected, of which 10687 show positive COVID-19 instances, 4017 show normal cases, and the remaining images show the presence of Mycoplasma (MP)-11666, Viral Pneumonia (VP)-7766, and Bacterial Pneumonia (BP)-3443. Hyperparameter tweaking, such as three fully connected layers, the Multiclass Focal Loss Function, epochs of 20 with a batch of 8, and the ReLu activation function, were used throughout their training.

With an accuracy level of 97.84%, Aswathy, A. L. et al. [5] developed a model for predicting Covid'19 Positive or Negative using a combination of Resnet-50 & Densenet-201 and back propagation neural network detection of severity level in terms of High, Medium, & Low. The COVID-CT and SARS-CoV-2 CT-scan datasets were used to compile the dataset [17]. 3294 photos were taken in total, of which 1601 showed positive COVID-19 cases and 1693 showed non-covid pictures.They trained using the ReLu activation function, 50 fully connected layers, a learning rate of 0.01 and 30 epochs of hyperparameter adjustment.

Using EfficientNet, Silva, Pedro, et al. [18] created a diagnosis framework for dividing Covid'19 afflicted cases from normal instances. The Covid'19-CT dataset and the Sars-CoV2-CTscan dataset were the sources of the dataset. 3294 photos were obtained in total, of which 1601 show cases affected by COVID-19 and the remaining 1693 show non-COVID-19 cases.They trained utilising hyperparameter tuning, which included six fully connected layers, twenty epochs, and a 0-0.85 dropout rate for the Swish activation function.

DenseNet169 was used in the classification model for Covid'19 Positive and Negative by Zhao, Jinyu, et al. [17] The COVID-CT dataset was used by them. There are 812 photos taken in all, of which 349 are Covid-19 cases and 463 are Covid-19 negatives. They trained with a batch size of 128 and hyperparameter adjustment, such as the stochastic gradient descent loss function.

A NABLA-N network model for segmenting COVID-19-infected regions using an Inception Residual Recurrent Convolutional Neural Network (IRRCNN) with Transfer Learning (TL) was proposed by Alom, Md. Zahangir, et al. [20]for both X-ray and CT scan images. The Inception Residual Recurrent Convolutional Neural Network (IRRCNN) with Transfer Learning (TL) approach for COVID-19 detection was also provided. The COVID-CT dataset was used by them. There are 420 photos taken in total, of which 242 are of Covid-19 cases and 178 are of Covid-19 negatives [21]. The system accuracy of the model is 0.9878. They trained utilising hyperparameter tuning, which included the ReLu activation function, batch sizes of 16 and 150, and the Dice Coefficient (DC) loss function [30].

Using XceptionNet, Lokwani, Rohit [22] and colleagues developed a system for classifying Covid-19 as Positive and Negative. The COVID-CT dataset was used by them. There are 5212 photos taken in all, of which 1043 are of Covid-19 affected patients and 4169 are of Covid-19 negative instances. Their system F1 scores are 0.794, 0.884 for specificity, and 0.964 for sensitivity. The Binary Cross Entropy Loss Function hyperparameter tuning, batch size of 4, ReLU activation function, and 50 epochs were used for their training. A CNN-based MODE (Multi Objective Differential Evolution) based classification model for Covid-19 Positive and Negative was proposed by Singh, Dilbag, et al. [19]

Li, Xiaohu, [24] and colleagues have achieved 1.9789% system accuracy, 2.0928% F1 scores, 1.6827% specificity, 1.8262% sensitivity, and 1.9276% Kappa statistics. The hyper parameter tuning techniques, such as fully connected layers of 40, MODE Optimised algorithm, ReLU Activation function, and 200 epochs, were used during training.

Kundu, Rohit, et al. [25] used an Ensemble Transfer Learning Network (ET-NET) based CNN in conjunction with Inception v3, ResNet34, and DenseNet201 to develop a classification model for Covid'19 Positive and Negative. They have made use of Soares E. et al.'s Kaggle. Twelve49 of the 2478 photos are of Covid-19 afflicted patients, and the remaining twelve29 are of Covid-19 negative instances.The hyperparameter tuning techniques that they employed for training included batch sizes of 4, ReLU activation function, 50 epochs, fully connected layers of 284, stochastic gradient descent algorithm, and binary cross entropy loss function.

Huang et al. [26] used Evidential Covid-Net based CNN to develop a classification technique for Covid'19 Positive and Negative. The COVID-CT dataset was used by them. They trained using a unique loss function and a hyperparameter adjustable learning rate of 0.01.

Li, Xiaoshuo, et al. [27] used VGG16 with Stacked Generalisation ensemble learning to create a classification model for Covid'19 Positive, Normal pictures, and Common Pneumonia. The Zhang, Kang, et al. dataset was used. Out of the 154252 photos, 80800 show COVID-19 positive cases, 49800 show normal cases, and 23652 show common pneumonia (CP) cases.

Using SqueezeNet, Polsinelli, Matteo, et al. [29] developed a classification model for Covid'19 Positive and Normal pictures. A total of 1671 photos are captured, of which 888 show COVID-19 cases and 783 show negative photos. Exponential Linear Unit (Elu) Activation function, batch size of 16, Bayesian optimisation, and 20 epochs of epoch tuning were used throughout their training.

3 Methodology

3.1 Deep Learning Model

These guys at the University of Oxford came up with VGG19, which stands for "Visual Geometry Group 19." It is a convolutional neural network design for classifying images [29]. With 19 layers, 16 convolutional layers and 3 fully connected layers, it is an addition to the VGG16 architecture that is meant to be more intricate. VGG19 gained popularity due to its simplicity and competitive performance in various image recognition tasks.

Key features of the VGG19 architecture include:

Convolutional Layers: The 16 convolutional layers that make up VGG19 have a fixed stride of 1 pixel and tiny 3 × 3 filters. These filters are utilised by the network to extract features from the input image that vary in scale.

Max-Pooling Layers: With a 2 × 2 window and a 2 pixel stride, max-pooling layers are incorporated into VGG19 after every set of convolutional layers. Spatially invariant feature learning is aided by max-pooling, which lowers the spatial dimensions of the feature maps.

Deep Architecture: The primary distinction of VGG19 from its predecessor VGG16 is the increased depth, with two additional convolutional layers. Better performance on difficult tasks may result from the network's ability to learn more intricate and abstract characteristics thanks to its deep design.

Fully Connected Layers: Using the learnt characteristics as a basis for categorization, the final three fully linked layers of the network operate. The last layer contains units equal to the number of output classes in the classification task, while the previous two fully connected layers have 4,096 units apiece.

Activation Function: Following each convolutional and fully connected layer, VGG19 employs the rectified linear unit (ReLU) activation function. ReLU facilitates the introduction of non-linearity into the network, allowing it to understand intricate correlations between data and features.

Large Number of Parameters: VGG19 has a huge number of parameters because of its completely connected layers and deep design. Consequently, in comparison to more modern, lightweight architectures, it demands substantial processing resources for both training and inference. In 2014, VGG19 demonstrated the efficiency of deeper networks for picture classification tasks by achieving state-of-the-art performance on the ImageNet Large Scale Visual Recognition Challenge (ILSVRC). While VGG19's architecture is simple and easy to understand, it has been surpassed by more modern architectures like ResNet, Inception, and EfficientNet, which achieve better accuracy with fewer parameters and computational cost.

A popular choice for transfer learning and as a benchmark for evaluating novel concepts in computer vision, VGG19's well-established performance and well-defined structure make it stand up to newer designs [31].

4 Experimental Results

4.1 Dataset

Dataset Collection: Get a large, varied set of CT scan images that includes examples from both Covid-19 positive and non Covid-19(people who are healthy or have other lung problems). For supervised training to work, the collection should have the right labels.

Dataset

In order to determine the presence of SARS-CoV-2 (COVID-19), a broad CT scan dataset is utilised. The SARS-COV-2 Ct-Scan Dataset [17] is the name given to this particular dataset. The information regarding the CT scan for SARS-CoV-2 is available to the general audience. There are a total of twenty-four hundred and eighty-two CT images included, with twelve hundred and twenty-two of them being CT scans of individuals who do not have SARS-CoV-2 disease. The data was collected from actual patients who were being treated in hospitals located in São Paulo, Brazil. The objective of this dataset is to stimulate the research and development of artificial intelligence techniques that can automatically determine whether or not a person is infected with SARS-CoV-2 by studying CT images (Fig. 1).

Histogram Representation of Dataset

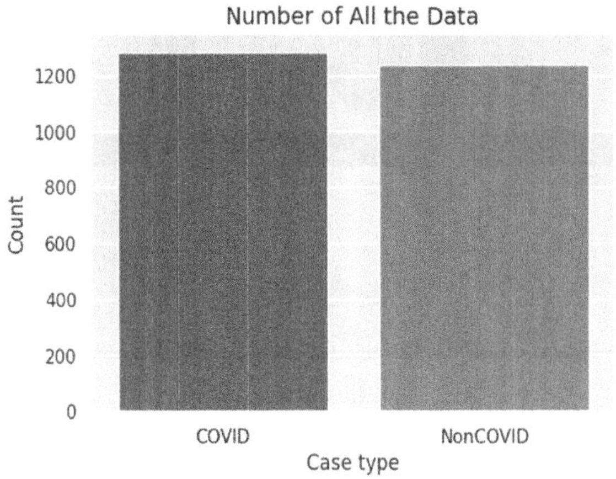

Fig. 1. Histogram representation of dataset

4.2 Transfer Learning

Data Pre-processing: Prior to feeding the CT scan images into the VGG16 model, preprocess the images to ensure uniformity. Some common steps in pre-processing are resizing the images to a specific resolution, normalising the data to make the dataset bigger and better at generalising the model, and data augmentation.

Pre-processing the data

The image height, width (224,224) and the batch size (64) are specified. The dataset is separated for model training and validation. The validation split parameter specifies that 20% of the images will be used for validation, and the subset parameter specifies that the remaining 80% of the images will be used for validation. The seed parameter ensures that the images are split into the training and validation sets randomly. The batch size parameter specifies that the images will be loaded in batches of 64.

Data Split: The information ought to be divided into three distinct groups: the training, the validation, and the testing groups. The training set is utilised in order to get the highest possible level of accuracy in the parameters of the model. A testing set is used to determine how well the final model can generalise, while the validation set is used to keep track of the progress that the model is making while it is being trained (Fig. 2).

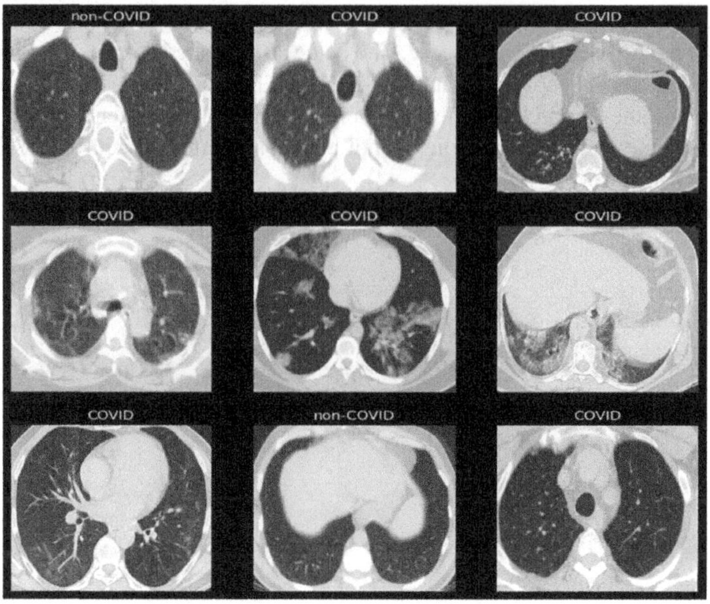

Fig. 2. Labelled dataset images [12]

Visualize the data:

Configure the dataset for performance

The auto-tune caches the training and validation datasets in memory and pre-fetches the next batch of data with a buffer size. This contributes to performance enhancement by decreasing the time the model must wait for data.

Normalize the data

Z-score scaling is particularly useful when the features in the dataset have different scales. It conducts a transformation on the data in which the mean is set to zero and the standard deviation is set to one.

Apply pre-trained weights from a large-scale image dataset (e.g., ImageNet) to initialise the VGG16 model [23]. By incorporating insights gained from a wide range of images, this stage enables the model to optimise its training process on the specific SARS-CoV-2 CT scan dataset (Fig. 3).

Create the model

A max pooling layer follows each of the four convolutional layers comprising the model. After extracting information from the images, the model classifies them using a succession of convolutional layers followed by a dense layer. The final neuronal layer is dense and generates a binary probability between 0 and 1 to indicate the COVID status of the CT image (Fig. 4).

Model Summary:

Model Training: The adapted VGG16 model should be trained using the training set on the SARS-COV2 CT scan dataset. To optimise model's parameters and minimise the

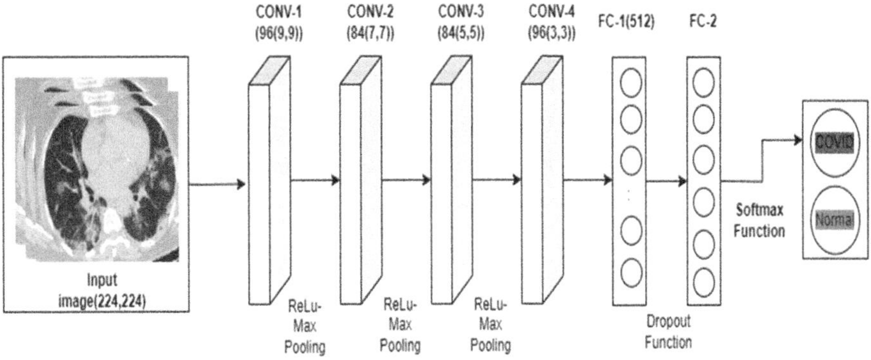

Fig. 3. Proposed VGGnet Model

```
2D)

flatten_1 (Flatten)          (None, 43264)          0

dense_2 (Dense)              (None, 512)            22151680

dense_3 (Dense)              (None, 1)              513

=================================================================
Total params: 22,175,777
Trainable params: 22,175,777
Non-trainable params: 0
-----------------------------------------------------------------
```

Fig. 4. Proposed model summary

loss, employ a suitable loss function (categorical cross-entropy) in conjunction with an optimisation algorithm (Adam).

Hyper parameter Tuning: Experiment with different hyperparameters, such as learning rate 0.0001, batch size 64, and number of training epochs 70, to determine the best settings for your dataset. Use the validation set to track the model's performance and select the optimal set of hyperparameters.

Performance Evaluation: After training, use the testing set to evaluate the model's performance. Calculate metrics such as accuracy, precision, recall, F1-score, and confusion matrix to evaluate the model's ability to accurately detect COVID-19 cases.

Visualization: Analyse predictions and visualize the learned features to gain insights into how the model is making decisions and what patterns it is learning from the CT scan images.

Model Deployment: Once you have a well-trained and validated model, you can deploy it to automate COVID-19 detection in CT scans. However, before employing the model in patient care, it must be clinically validated and tested in a real-world healthcare setting. It is crucial to work with healthcare professionals and domain experts during the model development and deployment process to ensure the accuracy and safety of the system for real-world medical use. Additionally, comply with all ethical considerations and data privacy regulations when working with medical datasets.

5 Results

The model yielded these findings (Table 1).

Table 1. Proposed model Evaluation metrics

Metrics	Value (%)
Accuracy	99
Precision	98
Recall	97
F1-Score	98

Confusion Matrix (Figs. 5 and 6).

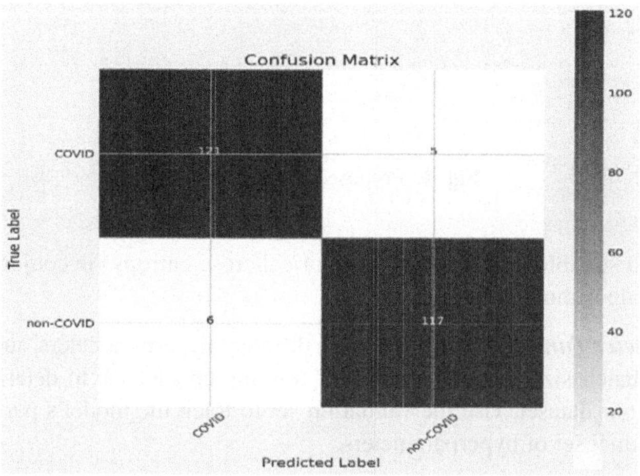

Fig. 5. Confusion Matrix

5.1 Comparative Analysis

The suggested model outperformed VGG16 and VGG19 in accuracy, precision, memory, and F1-score (Table 2). Figure 7 compares how well the proposed model and other models work, and the suggested model does very well, getting 99% of the results right.

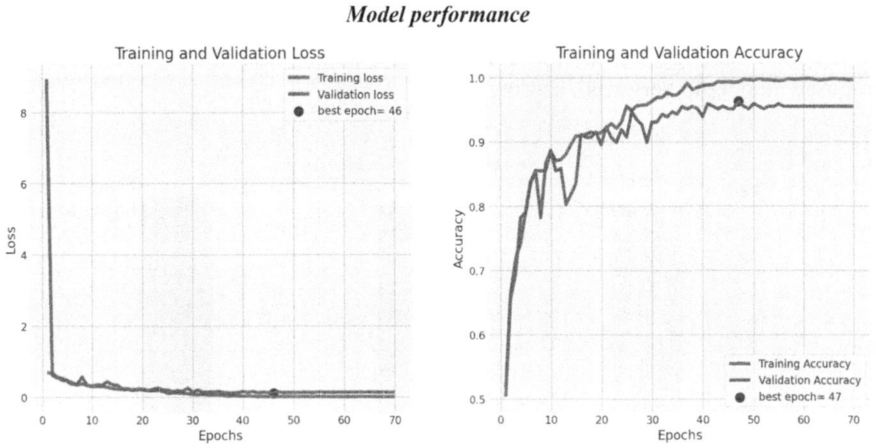

Fig. 6. Model performance

Table 2. Comparison Results

Models	Precision(%)	Recall(%)	F1-Score(%)	Accuracy(%)
VGG16	95	94	96	96
VGG19	96	94	96	97
Proposed VGGNet	98	97	98	99

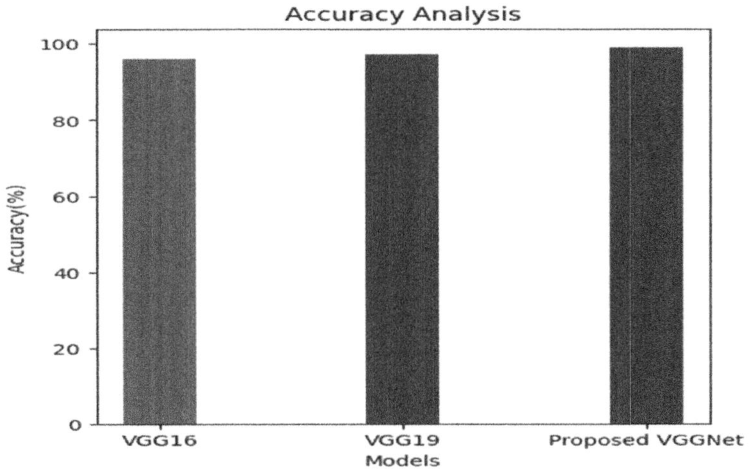

Fig. 7. Existing Model Accuracy Comparison

Figure 8 shows the suggested model's accuracy compared to others. The model scored 98%, great. The proposed and alternative models' recall is shown in Figure 9.

The suggested model did very well, getting 98% of the results. Figure 10 displays the F1-scores of the suggested model and other models that have already been used. The proposed model did very well, scoring 97%.

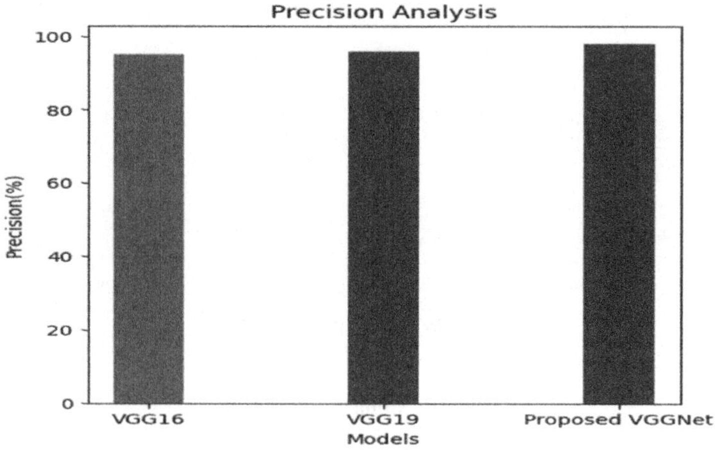

Fig. 8. Existing Model Precision Comparison

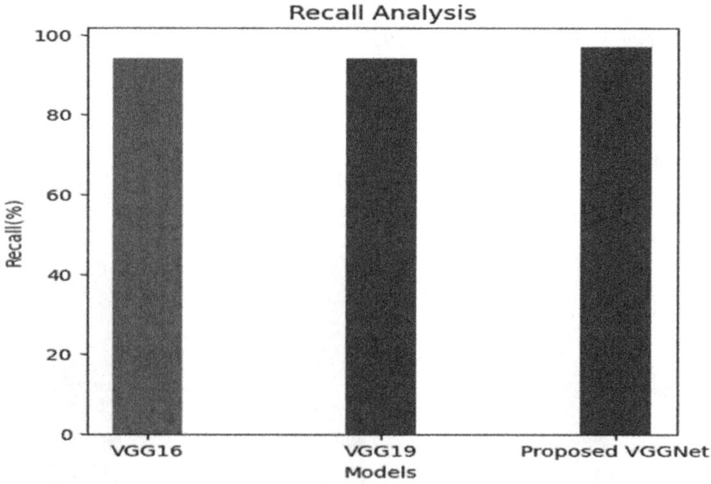

Fig. 9. Existing Model Recall Comparison

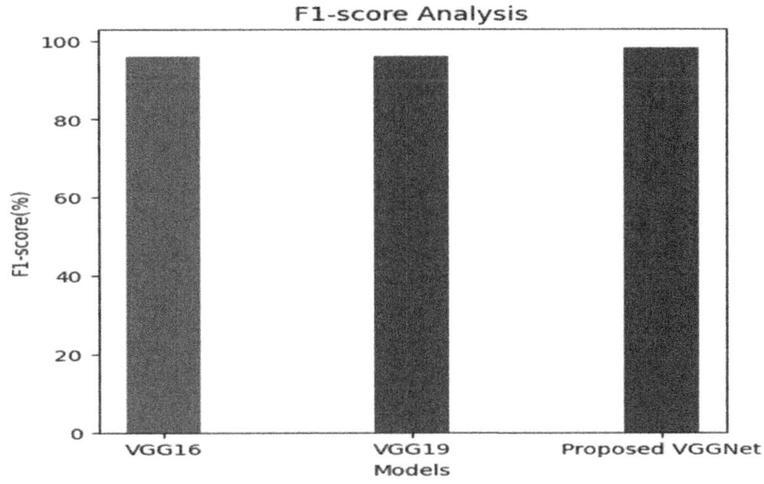

Fig. 10. Comparison of the F1-score to Models Over Existing

6 Conclusion

Critical to the struggle against the COVID-19 pandemic is the automatic detection of COVID-19 diseases using CT scan images and deep learning. This approach has demonstrated potential in accurately classifying COVID-19 cases from CT scan images by leveraging the capabilities of convolutional neural networks. Continuously enhancing these frameworks and employing them responsibly can contribute to the improvement of COVID-19 diagnosis in terms of speed, accuracy, and efficiency. In the long term, this will result in improved patient outcomes and benefits for public health. To ensure their feasibility and efficacy in clinical settings, however, these frameworks must be developed and implemented responsibly, with a focus on transparency, validation, and ethics.

Acknowledgment. "Authors thank High-Performance Computing Center, SRM Institute of Science and Technology for providing the computational facility".

Funding. This research is supported by grant number CRD/2021/000483 from the ASEAN-India Collaborative R&D scheme under the ASEAN-India S&T Development Fund (AISTDF).

References

1. https://www.mayoclinic.org/tests/procedures/covid-19-diagnostic-test/about/pac20488900
2. https://www.cdc.gov/coronavirus/2019_ncov/videos/oxygen%20therapy/Basics_of_Oxygen%20Monitoring_and_Oxygen_Therapy_Transcript.pdf
3. Ozsahin, I., et al.: Review on diagnosis of COVID-19 from chest CT images using artificial intelligence. Comput. Math. Methods Med. **2020**, 1–10 (2020)
4. Kumar, A., Gupta, P.K., Srivastava, A.: A review of modern technologies for tackling COVID-19 pandemic. Diab. Metab. Syndr.: Clin. Res. Rev. **14**(4), 569–573 (2020)

5. Aswathy, A.L., Anand, H., Vinod Chandra, S.S.: COVID-19 diagnosis and severity detection from CT-images using transfer learning and back propagation neural network. J. Infect. Public Health **14**(10) (2021), 1435–445
6. https://www.who.int/publications/i/item/use-of-chest-imaging-in-covid-19
7. Kwee, T.C., Kwee, R.M.: Chest CT in COVID-19: what the radiologist needs to know. Radiographics **40**(7), 1848–1865 (2020)
8. Sun, Z., et al.: A systematic review of chest imaging findings in COVID-19. Quant. Imaging Med. Surg. **10**(5), 1058 (2020)
9. Huang, H.: COVID-19 CT image recognition based on multi-stage transfer learning. In: Proceedings of the 2020 International Conference on Aviation Safety and Information Technology (2020)
10. Garg, A., et al.: Efficient and visualizable convolutional neural networks for COVID-19 classification using chest CT. Expert Syst. Appl. **195**, 116540 (2022). https://doi.org/10.1016/j.eswa.2022.116540
11. Ruuska, S., et al.: Evaluation of the confusion matrix method in the validation of an automated system for measuring feeding behaviour of cattle. Behav. Process. **148**, 56–62 (2018). https://doi.org/10.1016/j.beproc.2018.01.004
12. Figure1. https://encryptedtbn0.gstatic.com/images?q=tbn:ANd9GcTGWwLNkuCz4E6hPH_GOt9BAI4CedCyz7n8og&usqp=CAU
13. Figure2. https://www.istockphoto.com/vector/computed-tomography-scan-cat-mri-scannerpatient-lyingwaitingforaproceduregm1224614071360158198
14. Islam, M.M., et al.: A review on deep learning techniques for the diagnosis of novel coronavirus (COVID-19). IEEE Access **9**, 30551–30572 (2021). https://doi.org/10.1109/ACCESS.2021.3058537
15. Wong, P.K., et al.: Automatic detection of multiple types of pneumonia: open dataset and a multi-scale attention network. Biomed. Signal Process. Control **73**, 103415 (2022)
16. Angelov, P., Soares, E.A.: SARS-CoV-2 CT-scan dataset: A large dataset of real patients CT scans for SARS-CoV-2 identification. MedRxiv (2020)
17. Zhao, J., et al.: Covid-ct-dataset: a CT scan dataset about covid-19. arXiv preprint arXiv: 2003.13865 490 (2020)
18. Silva, P., et al.: COVID-19 detection in CT images with deep learning: a voting-based scheme and cross-datasets analysis. Inform. Med. Unlocked **20**, 100427 (2020)
19. Yang, X., et al.: COVID-CT-dataset: a CT scan dataset about COVID-19. arXiv preprint arXiv: 2003.13865 (2020)
20. Alom, M.Z., et al.: COVID_MTNet: COVID-19 detection with multi-task deep learning approaches. arXiv preprint arXiv:2004.03747 (2020)
21. Mooney, P.: Kaggle chest x-ray images (pneumonia) dataset (2020)
22. Lokwani, R., et al.: Automated detection of covid-19 from ct scans using convolutional neural networks. arXiv preprint arXiv:2006.13212 (2020)
23. Singh, D., Kumar, V., Kaur, M.: Classification of COVID-19 patients from chest CT images using multi-objective differential evolution–based convolutional neural networks. Eur. J. Clin. Microbiol. Infect. Dis. **39**(7), 1379–1389 (2020)
24. Li, X., et al.: COVID-19 infection presenting with CT halo sign. Radiol. Cardiothoracic Imag. **2**(1), e200026 (2020). https://doi.org/10.1148/ryct.2020200026
25. Kundu, R., et al.: ET-NET: an ensemble of transfer learning models for prediction of COVID-19 infection through chest CT-scan images. Multimed. Tools Appl. **81**(1), 31–50 (2021). https://doi.org/10.1007/s11042-021-11319-8
26. Huang, L., Su, R., Thierry, D.: "Covid-19 classification with deep neural network and belief functions. In: The Fifth International Conference on Biological Information and Biomedical Engineering (2021)

27. Li, X., et al.: Classification of COVID-19 chest CT images based on ensemble deep learning. J. Healthc. Eng. **2021**, 1–7 (2021)
28. Zhang, K., et al.: Clinically applicable AI system for accurate diagnosis, quantitative measurements, and prognosis of COVID-19 pneumonia using computed tomography. Cell **181**(6), 1423-1433.e11 (2020)
29. Polsinelli, M., Cinque, L., Placidi, G.: A light CNN for detecting COVID-19 from CT scans of the chest. Pattern Recogn. Lett. **140**, 95–100 (2020)
30. S. italiana di Radiologia Medica e Interventistica, Sirm dataset of COVID-19 chest CT scan. https://www.sirm.org/category/senza-categoria/covid-19/. Accessed 5 Apr 2020
31. Loey, M., Smarandache, F., Khalifa, N.E.M.: Within the lack of chest COVID-19 X-ray dataset: a novel detection model based on GAN and deep transfer learning. Symmetry **12**(4), 651 (2020). https://doi.org/10.3390/sym12040651
32. Vinothini, R., et al.: A novel classification model using optimal long short-term memory for classification of COVID-19 from CT images. J. Digit. Imaging **36**(6), 2480–2493 (2023). https://doi.org/10.1007/s10278-023-00852-7
33. Vinothini, R., Niranjana, G.: A systematic analysis for classification of COVID-19 diagnostic process using CNN. In: AIP Conference Proceedings, AIP Publishing (2023). https://doi.org/10.1063/5.0158460

Diabetic Foot Ulcer Classification Using Deep Learning Approach

P. Sivakamasundari[1(✉)] and G. Niranjana[2]

[1] Department of Computer Science and Engineering, SRM Institute of Science and Technology, Kattankulathur, Tamil Nadu, India
sp6806@srmist.edu.in

[2] Department of Computing Technologies, SRM Institute of Science and Technology, Kattankulathur, Tamil Nadu, India
niranjag@srmist.edu.in

Abstract. Podiatrist diagnosis and lesion localization are used as current testing approaches for Diabetic Foot ulcers (DFU). Current systems for automation concentrate on either categorization or division. One of the most common metabolic conditions, Diabetes (also called diabetes mellitus), is brought on by the pancreas incapacity to generate sufficient anti hyper-glycemic hormone to control glycemia levels. It may cause "Diabetic Peripheral Neuropathy," a collection of nerve diseases that can develop if the blood glucose level is left uncontrolled and unmanaged. Blood glucose levels may be efficiently maintained by recognising diabetes initially through constant surveillance and screenings. Using image processing methods such as data stretching with Deep Learning, image reduction and improvement, image division, and feature extraction, this paper offers a thorough approach for analysing thermal scans of the diabetic foot. By using these techniques, doctors may assess and track a patient's condition with fewer examinations. In this work, EfficientNetB3 architecture is compared with other Deep Learning models for accuracy in DFU identification. To create a powerful deep learning model, we gathered an extensive collection of 1,775 DFU photos. The basis of belief for this data gathering was created by two medical experts using annotator software to define the DFU region of interest. It took 48 ms to figure out a single image and 57.2 MB to validate the model. EfficientnetB3 got an average mean accuracy of 93%. This work demonstrates the effectiveness of Deep Learning for DFU localization in real-time, which could have improved with the use of a larger data set.

Keywords: Diabetic Foot Ulcers · Thermal Scans · EfficientnetB3 · Deep Learning · DFU Localization and Real-Time

1 Introduction

The greater frequency of individuals with diabetes injuries, the younger the patients. Type 1 and Type 2 subtypes of diabetes are often distinguished. Insulin production is automatic in people with type 1 diabetes. On the other hand, insulin is only produced in type

Published by Springer Nature Switzerland AG 2025
A. Chandrabose et al. (Eds.): ICCCSP 2024, IFIP AICT 723, pp. 120–131, 2025.
https://doi.org/10.1007/978-3-031-73617-9_10

2 diabetes when it is required for the body to function. 'Type 2' diabetes is lethal sinceit is unable to absorb insulin enough; in type 1 diabetes, the immune system kills beta cells, prohibiting the body from absorbing insulin from the blood as usual [3]. Patients with type 2 diabetes alone will be evaluated. The lives of humans are seriously threatened by diabetic foot ulcers. Let's say the people don't tend to their injuries. The wound will have a significant effect on the person's health if they have diabetes [2]. In their earlyphases, wounds may be cared for by people. In order to get wound care, patients must visit the clinic. Many people are still unable to learn about these foot wounds. The challenge of classifying images based on their visual attributes is regarded as difficult [1]. This challenge uses region-of-interest-based processing, image segmentation, feature extraction [21], and image filtering and augmentation techniques. Deblurring, morphological filtering, contrast modification, and filtering are some of the picture-enhancing methods. Subsequent to pictureamplification, a revised copy of the unique picture is accessible for advancefunctioning that highlights definite characteristics [4]. This goal of fragmentation is to make a picture's representation simpler, more comprehensible, and more accessible to study. The process of breaking an image into relevant pieces with comparable characteristics is called image segmentation [6]. Feature extraction, which operates on the computational concepts used in deep learning approaches, extracts certain differentiable features from inputs, such as dimensions, contour, colour, identifiedpattern, brightness, edge density, and other properties [5]. These features are compared for input data by the learner or model. Basic decisions may address basic information problems with less complexity, but managing and manipulating larger amounts of data becomes highly challenging in some situations; in these cases, machine learning is a helpful tool. One subset of machine learning techniques called deep learning focuses on identifying patterns, traits, and other properties of differentiable data that may be used to classify and distinguish one item from another. Neural networks with deep learning architectures are useful in many domains, including speech recognition, audio recognition, text data classification, object detection, super-resolution imaging, and semantic segmentation [2]. Unsupervised learning problems may be tackled by deep learning algorithms; for example, object detectors in anpictureidentificationprogramcould be taught to categorise each segment in an image.

2 Background Study

According to Gupta, P. et al., it was advantageous for the patient and the doctor to use the 'IoT' to detect foot ulcers in recipients. It enhances the patients' standard of living. The below-discussed system was a genuine and tested idea. Such thorough investigation demands careful evaluation of each potential foot ulcer symptom. Using open-source hardware increases the range of possibilities available for data and technology advancement. Patients may learn about their excessive blood pressure and cardiac issues with the aid of the data [4].

Patel, S., and others. This research looked at the necessary procedures for using image processing to locate foot ulcers. The Gabor filter was used for segmentation because it can accurately perform joint localization in both frequencies and special domains. K-means was used to classify the data. The categorization result indicates the identification of three distinct tissue types. Giving the patient the best possible care depends on accurately identifying the tissue implicated in a foot ulcer. However, outcomes need to be confirmed by standards like precision [5]. It was necessary to assess the accuracy of this foot ulcer detection method and the efficacy of several classification and segmentation algorithms utilising unique colour, texture, and statistical elements utilising images from different data sets of leg ulcer wounds.

3 Proposed Model

Different patients get foot ulcers. We are using this kind of technology in order to get rid of the drawbacks of the previous approach. More people worldwide are afflicted with diabetic foot ulcers. As a result, diabetic foot ulcers are healed by this therapy [7]. The image was taken using a digital camera. Python software and a sophisticated EfficientnetB3 deep learning algorithm are used to analyse the image [8]. We are able to assess the wound thoroughly. Examine the diabetic wound in order to assess its seriousness [9]. If the wound is dangerous, we may go to the hospital, but many hospital stays are not necessary. Make your way to the hospital if the wound is severe. An adjustable mean approach that yields accurate findings and has a wide range of potential uses is used to analyse the image. In order to analyse a photo of a diabetic foot wound, we are building Python code. The graphic is first converted to a normal photograph that is easier to examine [11]. Next, the feet injury is shown in the image, with unnecessary foot regions left unanalyzed. After masking the image to isolate the wound area, the abnormal ulcer photograph is converted to RGB because it is challenging to assess the typical colourcodingseries of '0 to 256' resolution. Nevertheless, it is easy to analyse the 256- to 256-pixel RGB colour coding range [12]. Lastly, we measure the breadth and depth of the wound. To ascertain the resultant values, we might look at either the normal or critical wound stages.

DFU Dataset

For this study, we need permission to use photos of DFU on the foot for our investigation. Local hospitals have been taking DFU photographs of the foot in recent years. There are 1,775-foot photos in our collection with DFU. Three principal cameras were used to take pictures of the feet: the Kodak DX4530, the Nikon D3300, and the Nikon COOLPIX P100. When possible, photos of the entire foot were obtained with the ulcer plane oriented parallel, captured at a distance of 30 to 40 cm. Room illumination is used to take pictures with consistent colour instead of flash being your primary illumination source.

Conventional Techniques for DFU Positioning

In this part, we evaluated the effectiveness of common DFU localization functions or types. For the purpose of features extraction as well as classifier training by 5-fold cross-validation [9] for traditional ML, we selected 2028 normal and 2080 aberrant skin patches

[7]. Furthermore, we created an overall of 28364 normal patches and 29118irregularspace using data enhancement techniques including flipping, rotation, random cropping, and colour channels. 20% of the picture data are samples, while the remaining 80% are used to train the classifier [8].

DL Methods for DFU Localization

CNN has shown its superiority over conventional ML methods in ImageNet and other image recognition competitions. They are very skilled in retrieving networks of attributes from images of medical and non-medical imagery to classify images into discrete collections of objects [9]. One of the biggest problems in computerized visionary is itemidentification, which requires computers to recognise and locate a large number of entities in an image. The three phases listed in the sections below make up the majority of object localization networks.

CNN as a Source for Features

The convolutional layers of a typical CNN, learn visual properties as feature maps from the input pictures in the initial stage of the network architecture. These feature maps are employed to detect items within a picture, with a focus on DFU zones [10]. These feature maps are used as inputs for the next stages: the following stage involves proposing something, and the third stage involves classifying and regressing ROI.

Formulation of Suggestions and Improvement

Utilising the feature map that was obtained in phase 1, the system uses a sliding window in phase 2 to identify areas that contain objects. These sections, which consist of many boxes scattered across the image, are suggestions [11].

Bounding Box Regressor and ROI Classifier:

Stage 2's ROI boxes are categorised in Stage 3 and further refined. RoI boxes are given to the RoI pooling layer at first in order to be condensed to a constant structure for the classifier's input because of their variable sizes. EFF Return Type and Softmax Return Type are the two outputs it generates for each ROI, the same as in Stage 2. If there are many classes, the softmax layer is in charge of categorising the locations. The ROI is eliminated if it has a background categorization. Refining ROI box positions is the aim of EffBbox Refinement [12] (Fig. 1).

Effective network structure

A strong baseline system is also required since model scaling has no effect on the baseline network's layer operators. EfficientNet is a new mobile-size baseline that exemplifies the performance of our scaling strategy [13] . Based on the findings, we use a multi-objective neural architecture search to design a baseline neural network that maximises FLOPS and accuracy. The objective is ACC(m) [FLOPS(m)=T]w, where T is the necessary FLOPS, w=-0.07 is a hyperparameter that is used to control the accuracy-versus-FLOPS tradeoff, and ACC(m) and FLOPS(m) are the accuracy and FLOPS of model m. Tan et al. (2019) found that the same search space is used in this inquiry [14] . We gave FLOPS performance precedence over latency in the absence of a specified hardware target platform. We have discovered a working network that we will refer to as EfficientNet-B3. Refer to Table 1 for the EfficientNet-B0 [20] network as a starting

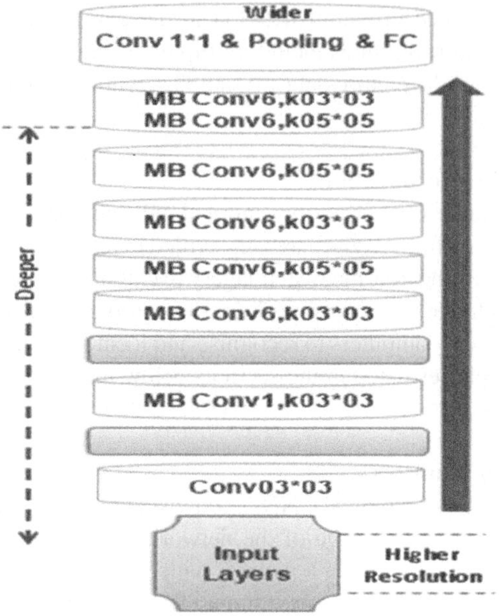

Fig. 1. Efficient-Net (e-Net) Framework [15]

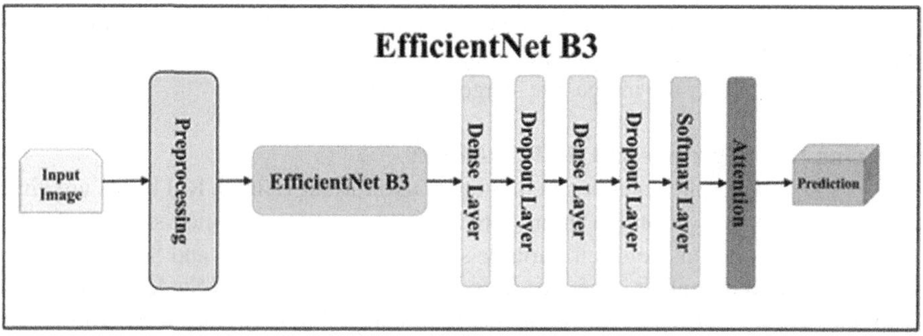

Fig. 2. Efficient-Net (e-Net) Framework

point. Each column describes Stage I, which has Li layers. The total number of channels used for output is Ci, the input resolution is Wii, and the height is Hi.

Algorithm 1 EfficientNet-B3 algorithm Input: [13].

The optimal combination of probability, M, random initialization, P, and Pr for a given perturbation interval and perturbation ratio parameters (Pc, Pm, and Ri) was the human population size (N), targeting precision (P), and method 1 Efficient Net method input. ϱ Indicator:

Algorithm 1 for suggested Model Algorithm Input: [13]

```
EfficientNetB3(image):
   # Preprocessing
   image = preprocess(image)  # Resize, normalize, etc.
   # Stem Convolution
   x = stem_conv(image)
   # Mobile Inverted Residual Bottleneck (MBConv) Blocks
   for block in mbconv_blocks:
      x = block(x)
   # Squeeze-and-Excitation (SE) Optimization
   x = se_module(x)
   # Feature Fusion
   x = fusion_module(x)
   # Head Convolution
   x = head_conv(x)
   # Classification Head
   logits = classification_head(x)
   return logits
MBConvBlock(input_tensor):
   # Expansion Phase
   x = conv_expansion(input_tensor)
   x = batch_norm(x)
   x = swish_activation(x)
   # Depthwise Convolution
   x = depthwise_conv(x)
   x = batch_norm(x)
   x = swish_activation(x)
   # Squeeze-and-Excitation
   x = se_module(x)
   # Projection Phase
   x = conv_projection(x)
   x = batch_norm(x)
   # Residual Connection
   x = add(x, input_tensor)
   return x
SEModule(input_tensor):
   # Squeeze
   x = global_avg_pool(input_tensor)
   # Excitation
   x = conv_excite(x)
   x = swish_activation(x)
   x = conv_excite(x)
   x = sigmoid_activation(x)
   # Rescale
   x = scale(x, input_tensor)
   return x
FusionModule(input_tensors):
   # Concatenate feature maps
   x = concat(input_tensors)
   # Fuse features
```

x = conv_fusion(x)
x = batch_norm(x)
x = swish_activation(x)
return x

Algorithm 1 Efficient Net

1. grand_gen = 00
2. for i = 01 → *M do*
3. *E*i ➝ INITIALIZE() # Produce a pool of potential applicants to begin with. (build a matrix of binary digits)
4. while gen < N do
5. # Before deciding on one, consider all of the candidates seriously.
Use these characteristics to train the classifier and determine the loss function.
6. *E*i SELECTION() # Pick the following generation's answers at random
7. *Et*, *Et*+1 CROSSOVER # The use of crossover
8. *E*i MUTATION(*P*, *Et*) # The use of mutation
9. MUTATION(*Pm*, *Et*) # The use of mutation
10. {() ()} # The use of elitism
11. if i == Erratic Disturbances:
12. if rand(0, 1) < Pr:
13. # Use the variation in the population between the top and poorest performers.
14. end if
15. if rand(0, 1) < Ri:
16. # Individual hyper-parameters should be stochastically initialized.
17. end if
18. end if
19. gen += 1
20. if max # This period ended prematurely when the search results had the desired degree of precision.
20. Break
21. end if
22. end while
23. end for
24. return *E*i # Provide the top performer back

INITIALIZE
26. *E*i ➝ *f*(random initialization *)
27. return *E*i
28. finish function
CROSSOVER
29. function CROSSOVER(Pc, At i, At+1 j)
30. if rand(0, 1) < Pc:
31. $Et+1$ ➝ $Et * B + Et * (1 - B)$
32. else:
33. $Et+1$ ➝ $EAt * B - Et * (1 + B)$
34. end if
35. return *Et*+1, *Et*
36. end function
37. function MUTATION(Pm, Et+1 i)
38. end function

With the addition of the higher FLOPS objective, despite not having our e-Net-B0 (our FLOPS target is 400M), EfficientNet is slightly larger. The following components make up EfficientNet-structural B0 [20], as shown in Fig. 3. Squeeze-and-excitation optimisation serves as the foundation of the mobile inverted bottleneck MBConv technology [17, 22, 23]. Using our compound scaling technique, we first initiate the smaller unique e-Net-B0 and level it up by a feature of two: Step 1: First, we use Eqs. 2 and 3 to do an initial grid search and set = 1, assuming that we have twice the number of tools available to us. More precisely, we find the best parameters for EfficientNet-B0 when it is constrained. Step 2: After that, we use Eq. 3 to generate e-Net-B1 through B7 by setting up. As a result, initial network is larger. Furthermore, significantly better results can be obtained by exploring immediately across a large model, but for larger models, the exploration expense gets unaffordable. The approach entails doing one look for the tiny groundstructure (step 1) and thereafter scaling all the following models to the same degree (step 2) based on the findings from the search [14].

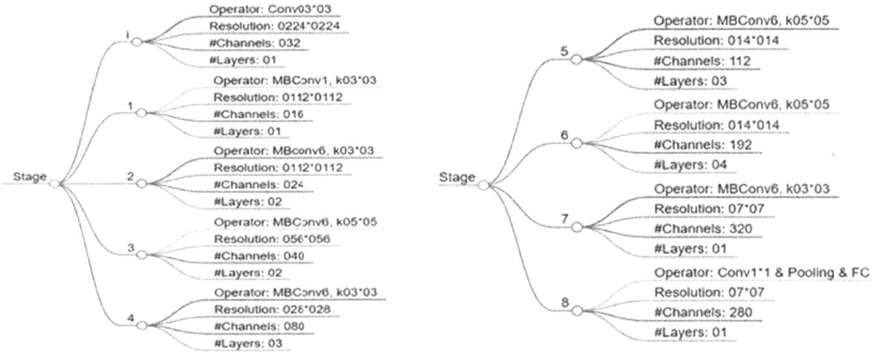

Fig. 3. EfficientNetB3 Operators [16]

4 Outcomes

Py. 3.8 was used to develop the suggested alternative. Figure 4 illustrates the way our plan worked in the majority of the scenarios. Unfortunately, the intricate visual makeup of our medical surroundings has caused the approach we used to be unsuccessful in several circumstances. Our findings indicate that low image resolution, disturbance from the surroundings, and incorrect toe nail recognition are frequently to blame for these faults [18]. Regarding a misunderstanding of nails on the feet [19], we believe leuconychia mimics ulcers because some incidences of DFU develop within or near feet nails [24]. Sometimes backdrop items interfere with recognising objects. We address this problem, at least, by using the focusing function.

Figure 4 displays the DFU picture collection using the e-Net method using a variety of unusual, typical, and normal-looking skin photos.

As shown in diagram 3, the DL technique consists of 14 intervals with training and examining data for correctness and losses. The third period is chosen as the finest one.

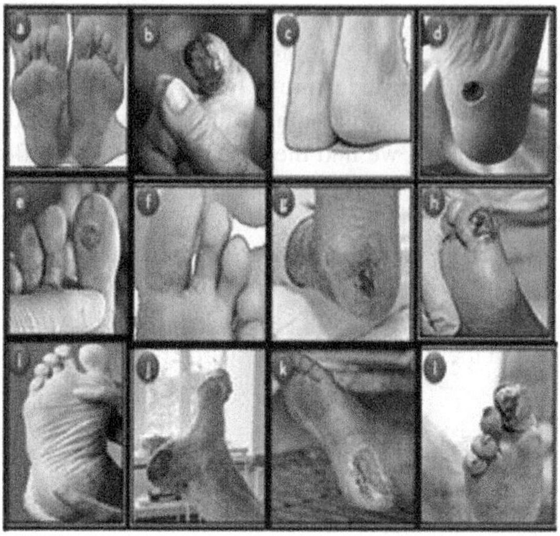

Fig. 4. Classification of DFU specimen collection using DL (a, c, f, I has normal skin and b, d, e.g., h, j, k & l has foot ulcers)

5 Comparative Analysis

The overall performance of many DL models in classifying diabetic foot ulcers is analysed in the comparative examination that follows. Processing time, version length, and metrics for accuracy, sensitivity, and specificity are all taken into consideration. Superior accuracy, sensitivity, and specificity are proven by using the EfficientNetB3 model, which also has an efficient processing time and a small model size. The objective of this study is to help in the choice of the most suitable model for clinical applications by highlighting the pros and cons of every model in the diagnosis of diabetic foot ulcers through comparisons of those essential metrics (Table 1).

Table 1. DL Models for Diabetic Foot Ulcer categorization: A Comparative Analysis

Type	Accuracy (%)	Sensitivity (%)	Specificity (%)	Processing Time (ms)	Model Size (MB)
Suggested EfficientNetB3	93	91	94	48	57.2
EfficientNetB0	91	89	92	55	66.8
ResNet-50	89	87	90	60	87.3
VGG-16	87	85	88	100	102.5

The optimal outcomes are still proven by way of the recommended EfficientNetB3, which has 93% accuracy, 91% sensitivity, and 94% specificity.

While EfficientNetB0's accuracy, sensitivity, and specificity are quite lower than those of the suggested model, it still outperforms ResNet-50 and VGG-16.

In contrast to the EfficientNet models, ResNet-50 and VGG-16 have poorer metrics across all assessment parameters.

EfficientNetB0, EfficientNetB3, and VGG-16 are the smallest and biggest models, respectively.

In terms of processing speed, VGG-16 is the slowest at 100 ms, when compared to the suggested EfficientNetB3 model, which is the quickest at 48 ms.

In terms of accuracy, sensitivity, specificity, efficiency, and model complexity factors, the table gives an intensive contrast. The recommended version plays better on the majority of measures (Fig. 6).

As depicted in the following illustration, a source photograph was determined and chosen to be the first of the pictures in DFU. Additionally, the suggested method has been used, and the expected outcome is 93.02%.

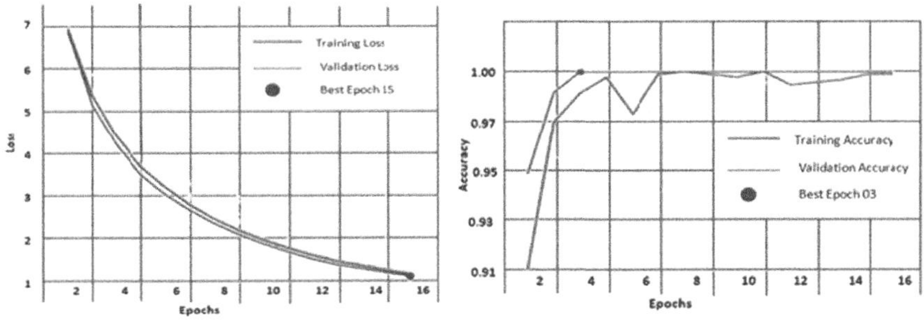

Fig. 5. Graph for comparing both examining and training

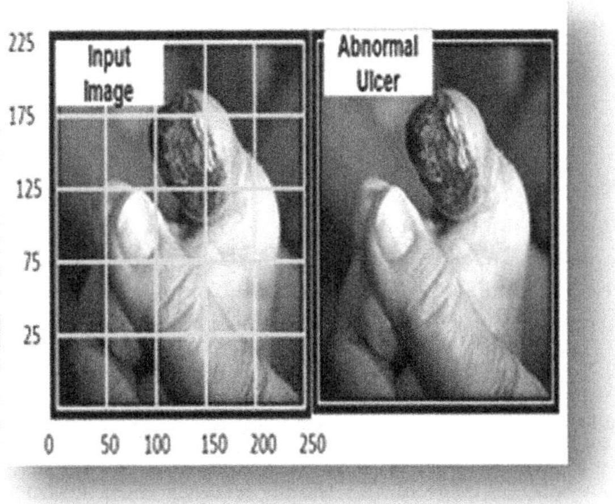

Fig. 6. Input image & forecasted outcomes 97.02

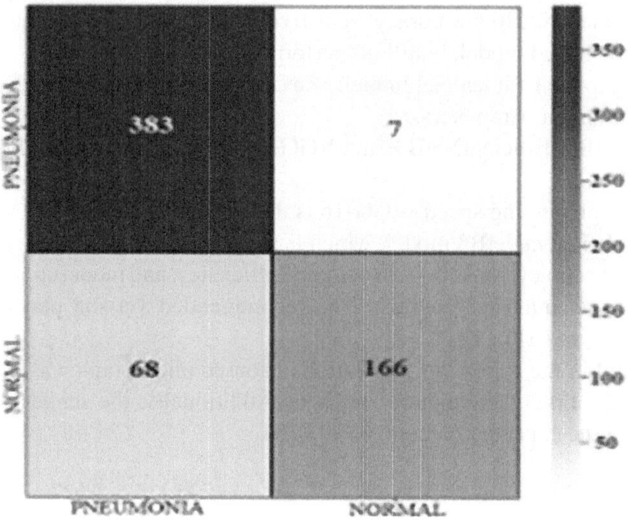

Fig. 7. Confusion Matrix

Figure 7 displays the suggested structure's confusion matrix.

6 Conclusion

The development of Deep Learning techniques in automated detection has made it possible to identify and diagnose DFU digitally, opening up new research avenues. The EfficientnetB3 paradigm towards the DFU detection problem is given in this paper. The model is effectively trained on the DFU image repository using 2 levels of transfer learning for identifying DFU on entire-feet photos and a variety of hyper-settings for parameters. From the results, it is observed that the DFU forecast success rate is 93.02%.

References

1. Zacharias, J., Nair, S.G., Varghese, J.: Diabetic retinopathy detection from fundus images using deep learning techniques. Procedia Comput. Sci. **132**, 1530–1538 (2018)
2. Gadekallu, T.R., Khare, N., Bhattacharya, S., Singh, S., Maddikunta, P.K.R., Srivastava, G.: Deep neural networks for diabetic foot ulcer classification. IEEE Sens. Lett. **4**(6), 1–4 (2020)
3. Wang, L., et al.: Smartphone-based wound assessment system for patients with diabetes. IEEE Trans. Biomed. Eng. **62**(2), 477–488 (2015)
4. Arjunan, S.P., Kumar, A., Alwarappan, S., Liu, C., Li, C.Z.: Probing the electrochemical properties of graphene nanosheets for biosensing applications. Nanotechnology **26**(44), 445501 (2015)
5. Rau, A., Wasserthal, J., Neufeld, U.: High accuracy skin lesion classification using Efficientnets with deep supervision and attention mechanisms. Diagnostics **11**(2), 315 (2021)
6. Guo, Y., Liu, Y., Georgiou, T., Lew, M.S.: A review of semantic segmentation using deep neural networks. Int. J. Multimed. Inform. Retrieval **7**(2), 87–93 (2018)

7. Wang, S.C., Li, W., Howard, A., Burton, A., Green, B., Wang, X.: Segmentation-based deep-learning approach for surface-defect detection. J. Manuf. Syst. **50**, 43–52 (2019)
8. Jiang, W., Lv, Z., Lu, Y., Han, J., Hu, S.: Automatic skin lesion segmentation using deep learning-based methods. IEEE Access **8**, 128769–128782 (2020)
9. Zhu, W., Xiong, Y., Liu, H.: Multi-stage CNN ensemble learning for skin lesion segmentation. Artif. Intell. Med. **119**, 102059 (2021)
10. Zeng, X., Luo, G., Wang, Y., Zheng, L., Luo, X., Zhang, T.: A deep learning framework for high-quality wound area detection and segmentation. IEEE J. Biomed. Health Inform. **26**(6), 2730–2741 (2021)
11. Nielsen, G., Guldberg-Møller, J., Lerche, C., Andreassen, S.: Deep learning-based segmentation of chronic wounds in clinical practice and research. Diagnostics **11**(6), 1077 (2021)
12. Borhani, M., Kavraki, L.E., Thakur, P.H.: A framework for automated segmentation and tracking of cells in time-lapse fluorescent microscopy images. IEEE J. Biomed. Health Inform. **26**(1), 217–227 (2021)
13. Simonyan, K., Zisserman, A.: Very deep convolutional networks for large-scale image recognition. arXiv preprint arXiv:1409.1556 (2014)
14. He, K., Zhang, X., Ren, S., Sun, J.: Deep residual learning for image recognition. In Proceedings of the IEEE Conference on Computer Vision and Pattern Recognition, pp. 770–778 (2016)
15. Ronneberger, O., Fischer, P., Brox, T.: U-net: convolutional networks for biomedical image segmentation. In: Navab, N., Hornegger, J., Wells, W.M., Frangi, A.F. (eds.) Medical Image Computing and Computer-Assisted Intervention – MICCAI 2015: 18th International Conference, Munich, Germany, October 5-9, 2015, Proceedings, Part III, pp. 234–241. Springer International Publishing, Cham (2015). https://doi.org/10.1007/978-3-319-24574-4_28
16. Szegedy, C., et al.: Going deeper with convolutions. In Proceedings of the IEEE Conference on Computer Vision and Pattern Recognition, pp. 1–9 (2015)
17. Hu, J., Shen, L., Sun, G.: Squeeze-and-excitation networks. In Proceedings of the IEEE Conference on Computer vision and Pattern Recognition, pp. 7132–7141 (2018)
18. Gulshan, V., et al.: Development and validation of a deep learning algorithm for detection of diabetic retinopathy in retinal fundus photographs. JAMA **316**(22), 2402–2410 (2016)
19. Esteva, A., et al.: Dermatologist-level classification of skin cancer with deep neural networks. Nature **542**(7639), 115–118 (2017)
20. Geetamma, T., Eswar Badri, B., Karteek, A., Hemanth, G., Uday Kiran, B.: Classification of diabetic foot ulcer using efficientnet B0. J. Emerg. Technol. Innov. Res. **10**(3), 141–146 (2023)
21. Sathya Preiya, V., Kumar, V.A.: Deep learning-based classification and feature extraction for predicting pathogenesis of foot ulcers in patients with diabetes. Diagnostics **13**(12), 1983 (2023)
22. Alzubaidi, L.A.I.T.H., Abbood, A.A., Fadhel, M.A., Al-Shamma, O.M.R.A.N., Zhang, J.: Comparison of hybrid convolutional neural networks models for diabetic foot ulcer classification. J. Eng. Sci. Technol. **16**(3), 2001–2017 (2021)
23. Ahsan, M., Naz, S., Ahmad, R., Ehsan, H., Sikandar, A.: A deep learning approach for diabetic foot ulcer classification and recognition. Information **14**, 36 (2023)
24. Goyal, M., Reeves, N.D., Rajbhandari, S., Ahmad, N., Wang, C., Yap, M.H.: Recognition of ischaemia and infection in diabetic foot ulcers: dataset and techniques. Comput. Biol. Med. **117**, 103616 (2020)

Medisync: Fingerprint-Enabled Authorization of Medical Device Calibration

Priyanshu Mondal(✉), R. Sai Sirandana, G. K. Janani, A. N. Sneha Kalyani, and A. M. Arunnagiri

Anna University, Guindy, Chennai 600025, India
priyanshu.mondal.au@gmail.com

Abstract. In today's healthcare landscape, ensuring the security and accuracy of medical device calibration has become paramount in assuring the delivery of quality healthcare services. By implementing robust calibration systems, healthcare facilities can significantly reduce the occurrence of medical errors, safeguard patients, and enhance overall healthcare outcomes. MediSync, a state-of-the-art fingerprint recognition framework, addresses the crucial need for enhanced safety in the calibration of medical devices. Leveraging the widely accepted, mature, and proven technology of fingerprint recognition, MediSync provides a reliable solution that ensures only qualified individuals initiate and oversee calibration procedures, effectively minimizing the risk of unauthorized access and tampering. By utilizing Contrast-Limited Adaptive Histogram Equalization (CLAHE) and Gabor Filter for the efficient enhancement of the acquired fingerprint image, an accurate template is generated to ease the process of minutiae feature extraction. We harness minutiae-based matching techniques to optimize the performance of the system, thus achieving a high level of precision during the identification of personnel. This model yields a comprehensive performance evaluation that encompasses metrics like False Acceptance Rate (FAR), False Rejection Rate (FRR), Equal Error Rate (EER), Hamming Similarity Index (HSI) and Accuracy, affirming the identification of certified personnel and validating the calibration process' integrity. Ultimately, the promotion of traceability, reliability, and security by employing MediSync within calibration devices contributes to the overall quality and effectiveness of healthcare.

Keywords: Calibration · medical devices · fingerprint recognition · traceability · security · authorized personnel · minutiae-based matching · hamming similarity index · data integrity

1 Introduction

Biometrics, a revolutionary field in contemporary technology, encompasses a range of methods for uniquely identifying individuals based on intrinsic physical or behavioral traits. This groundbreaking technology has been integrated across sectors, from personal device access control to identity verification in sensitive environments, to prioritize both

Published by Springer Nature Switzerland AG 2025
A. Chandrabose et al. (Eds.): ICCCSP 2024, IFIP AICT 723, pp. 132–143, 2025.
https://doi.org/10.1007/978-3-031-73617-9_11

security and seamless interactions. Among biometric techniques, fingerprint recognition systems have gained immense popularity and effectiveness due to their feasibility and reliability. Fingerprints possess an inherent biological uniqueness based on distinctive ridge patterns and minutiae points. This permanence and individuality, paired with the ease of capturing and matching fingerprints, explains their ubiquitous adoption. The non-intrusive nature and simplicity of acquisition enhances user acceptance, while the high accuracy ensures reliable authentication. Ultimately, the practicality and uniqueness of fingerprint systems underscore their status as a trusted biometric modality at the forefront of contemporary security. Their biological individuality and convenience cement fingerprint recognition as a pioneering approach to identity verification across devices and platforms.

Recent advancements in biometric systems have witnessed a surge in the integration of artificial intelligence and machine learning, enhancing accuracy and adaptability. Elaborative research created a novel method for enhancing fingerprint images by eliminating artificially induced boundaries, precise background omission, and avoiding oversaturation of the image in homogeneous areas. It involved the use of CLAHE, Clip Limit, standard deviation computation, and kernel-based processing, showing promising results and making it a valuable contribution to the field of biometric recognition and image processing [1]. A comprehensive survey of feature extraction methods for fingerprint image analysis covers techniques such as FFT, DWT, DCT, PCA, LBP, LPQ, Gabor Filter, and neural network approaches for enhancing, recognizing, and classifying fingerprint images. The authors also discuss the importance of minutiae features and their extraction using various methods [2]. Another study highlights the importance of accuracy in minutiae extraction and its impact on overall performance. It has covered the time complexity of applied solutions for minutiae matching and provides insights into global and local structure features for minutiae matching. Overall, the paper offers a comprehensive overview of minutiae-based fingerprint recognition systems and their essential components [3]. Hong et al. propose a fast and adaptive fingerprint enhancement algorithm aimed at improving the clarity of ridge and valley structures in input fingerprint images. The authors emphasized the algorithm's capability to improve both the goodness index and verification performance [4]. Jakubovic and Velagic presented a framework for feature matching and object detection in images using various algorithms such as ORB, BRISK, SIFT, and SURF with a focus on reducing outliers and improving accuracy. ORB extends FAST and BRIEF with innovations such as fast and accurate orientation in FAST, efficient computation of oriented BRIEF features, and an analysis of variance and correlation in oriented BRIEF features, and an analysis of variance and correlation in oriented BRIEF features. Furthermore, ORB introduces a learning method to decorrelate BRIEF features under rotational invariance, enhancing performance in nearest-neighbor applications [5].

Drawing upon established models and databases, our research introduces 'MediSync,' a pioneering system designed to establish a validated fingerprint recognition protocol for the precise calibration authorization of medical devices within the healthcare industry. The calibration of medical devices stands as a pivotal process, ensuring not only the accuracy and reliability of measurements but also indirectly contributing to the safety of patients in a hospital setting. MediSync adopts a minutiae-based matching approach for fingerprints, emphasizing accuracy in recognition. Consequently, the proposed fingerprint recognition framework emerges as a significant contribution, aiming to bolster the security of the calibration process for medical devices, thereby enhancing overall patient safety and the efficacy of healthcare equipment.

2 Methodology

See Fig. 1.

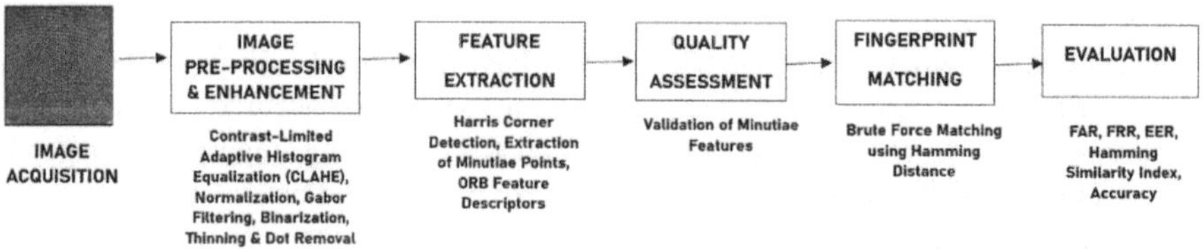

Fig. 1. Overall Flow of the Proposed System

2.1 Image Acquisition

A dataset comprising 80 fingerprint images was sourced from Set B of the DB2 database as part of the Fingerprint Verification Competition 2002 (FVC2002). The acquisition of these images involved the utilisation of the "FX2000" optical fingerprint scanner developed by Biometrika. Each fingerprint image in the dataset was characterized by dimensions of 296x560 pixels, an 8-bit depth for impressions, and a resolution of 569 dots per inch (dpi) [7].

2.2 Image Pre-processing and Enhancement

Contrast Limited Adapted Histogram Equalization
CLAHE was crucial to enhance the local contrast in the input fingerprint image [1]. The image was divided into 8×8 tiles, and histogram equalization was applied to each tile. This prevented over-amplification of noise by limiting the contrast enhancement through a predefined clip limit of 2. Bilinear interpolation was then used to stitch the equalized tiles together, resulting in an image with improved contrast.

Normalization
The normalization procedure employed in the algorithm adjusted the fingerprint image to conform to a predetermined mean and variance through a pixel-wise operation, reducing variations in grey-level values across the fingerprint image [1, 4]. This process ensured that the subsequent steps were not affected by large variations in intensity, maintaining the clarity of ridge and valley structures.

Gabor Filtering

Gabor filtering was a texture analysis technique that involved applying a set of Gabor filters to the image. These filters were tuned to different scales and orientations, allowing the extraction of features related to ridge structures. The algorithm used local ridge orientation and frequency to adaptively enhance the images [4].

For each minutiae point, the ridge orientation was determined by analysing the tangent to the ridge line. This information was crucial for subsequent steps as it enabled an understanding of ridge directionality, and the accuracy of this calculation ensured a precise representation of minutiae. The local ridge frequency was determined by calculating the inverse of the number of ridges per unit length, offering insight into the density of ridges within the fingerprint. This measure facilitated the capture of variations in ridge density, contributing to a more detailed representation of the fingerprint.

After the estimation of local ridge orientation and frequency, the algorithm created a region mask to classify each block in the image as recoverable or unrecoverable and applied a bank of Gabor filters [4]. By focusing on specific frequencies and orientations, Gabor filters were used to enhance the discrimination between ridges and valleys, effectively removing undesired noise and preserving true ridge and valley structures. Gabor filters can be defined as Eq. (1), where φ is the orientation of the Gabor filter, f is the frequency of a sinusoidal plane wave, and δ_x and δ_y are the space constants of the Gaussian envelope along x and y axes, respectively:

$$h(x, y : \varphi, f) = exp\left\{-\frac{1}{2}\left[\frac{x_\varphi^2}{\delta_x^2} + \frac{y_\varphi^2}{\delta_y^2}\right]\right\}cos(2\pi f x_\varphi) \tag{1}$$

$$x_\varphi = x\ \cos\varphi + \mathrm{y}\sin\varphi \tag{2}$$

$$y_\varphi = y\ \cos\varphi - \mathrm{x}\sin\varphi \tag{3}$$

Binarization

The binarization step converted the pre-processed image into a binary image where each pixel was either black or white based on a set threshold of 127 [1]. This process enhanced the contrast of the fingerprint ridges and facilitated the separation of the foreground (ridges) from the background (valleys).

Thinning and Dot Removal

The thinning process in fingerprint image processing reduced ridge thickness to aid minutiae extraction [1]. It involved iterative erosion and dilation cycles, shrinking and growing white regions. The difference between the original and dilated images was computed, accumulating changes iteratively to construct the final skeletonized image. The process concluded when further thinning was infeasible, determined by counting the remaining white pixels. The result was a one-pixel-wide skeletonized representation of fingerprint ridges, facilitating minutiae extraction and analysis. A filtering approach was then applied to identify and remove small dots or noise by scanning the thinned binary image, evaluating small local regions defined by a square window. If a region exhibited signs of a dot, identified by zero intensity sums along more than three edges, the filter removed the dot by setting the corresponding region to zeros.

2.3 Feature Extraction

Harris Corner Detection

The Harris Corner detection algorithm discerned corners within the thinned image by evaluating local intensity variations. A 3 × 3 window was defined around each pixel, and the Harris response was calculated based on the intensity variations in that local neighborhood. It computed a response function for individual pixels by considering gradients in both the x and y directions, highlighting areas where variations in intensity occurred along multiple directions [6]. The identification of potential corners was signaled by the local maxima in the response function.

$$E(u, v) = \sum_{x,y} w(x, y)\left[I(x + u, y + v) - I(x, y)\right]^2 \quad (4)$$

Extraction of Minutiae Points

Minutiae points were subsequently extracted based on the obtained Harris corner response [6]. If the response at a particular location was above the threshold of 125, a minutia was added to the list. Each minutia was identified by its spatial location (x, y) along with an accompanying scale value. The determination of this scale often depended on the local properties of the Harris response, providing information about the size of the region around the minutia.

Validation of Minutiae Points

The extracted minutiae features were stored as a template for comparison. Before comparison, validity checks were performed to ensure the quality of features. This involved assessing if the features were sufficient in number and had a good resolution for accurate fingerprint matching. Thus, the evaluation of fingerprint templates extracted from a database was done by specifically counting the number of ridge bifurcations and ridge endings in each template. Moreover, each template underwent acceptance or rejection determined by a predefined threshold for the cumulative count of minutiae points. From previous research, a good-quality fingerprint image typically had 25–80 minutiae points, and thus, a threshold of 60 was set to classify it as the same [2].

ORB Descriptor Computation

The proposed system heavily relies on ORB (Oriented FAST and Rotated BRIEF) descriptors for minutiae descriptor computation in fingerprint images. The ORB descriptor extractor ensures efficient computation for extracted minutiae points, benefiting from the orientation and rotation invariance inherent to ORB [5]. It generates binary-type descriptors tailored to minutiae points, offering a compact, discriminative representation of local fingerprint structures for precise matching.

2.4 Fingerprint Matching

Brute force matching using Hamming distance in fingerprint matching involves comparing binary ORB descriptors, which represent specific features or characteristics of fingerprints, to determine their similarity. For each descriptor in the query image, the matcher compares it with all descriptors in the set of accepted templates using the Hamming distance. In this approach, the Hamming distance is calculated between the binary descriptors of the query image and the stored templates to measure the number of differing bits between two binary strings, thus providing a quantitative measure of their dissimilarity. The matches are then sorted based on their Hamming distances in ascending order. This step is crucial because lower Hamming distances indicate better matches. The top matches are selected based on an empirical distance threshold of 33 for filtering out less relevant matches.

2.5 Evaluation Parameters

False Acceptance Rate (FAR)

The FAR is a crucial evaluation parameter in fingerprint recognition systems, frequency at which the system erroneously grants access to an unauthorized user. A lower FAR is indicative of a more secure system that effectively distinguishes between genuine users and impostors.

$$FAR = \frac{Number\ of\ False\ Acceptances}{Total\ number\ of\ Identification\ Attempts} \tag{5}$$

False Rejection Rate (FRR)

In contrast, the FRR measures the frequency with which the system erroneously rejects an authorized user. A lower FRR is desirable as it ensures that legitimate users are consistently granted access without unnecessary hindrance, contributing to the system's user-friendliness.

$$FRR = \frac{Number\ of\ False\ Rejections}{Total\ number\ of\ Identification\ Attempts} \tag{6}$$

Equal Error Rate (EER)

The EER serves as a pivotal point in the evaluation process, representing the intersection where the FAR and FRR are equal. This equilibrium point provides a comprehensive measure of the system's overall performance, offering insights into its reliability across varying operational conditions.

$$EER = \frac{(FAR + FRR)}{2} \tag{7}$$

Hamming Similarity Index

The HSI is a quantitative measure of similarity between two binary sequences. Its emphasis on the Hamming distance underscores its focus on measuring the discrepancies at the bit level between sequences, providing a normalized index for comparing similarity across binary sequences of different lengths.

$$Hamming\ Similarity\ Index = 1 - \frac{Average\ Hamming\ Distance}{Maximum\ Hamming\ Distance} \tag{8}$$

Accuracy

Accuracy, as a holistic metric, assesses the overall correctness of the fingerprint recognition system. It takes into account both false acceptance and false rejection instances, providing a comprehensive view of the system's effectiveness in reliably authenticating users based on their fingerprints. A higher accuracy rate is indicative of a more dependable and trustworthy system.

$$Accuracy = \frac{(TP + TN)}{(TP + FP + TN + FN)} \tag{9}$$

3 Results and Discussions

3.1 Image Processing Results

The acquired fingerprint images underwent a preprocessing pipeline, including CLAHE and enhancement using Gabor filter principle. The Fig. 2 showcases a representative fingerprint image after the preprocessing steps.

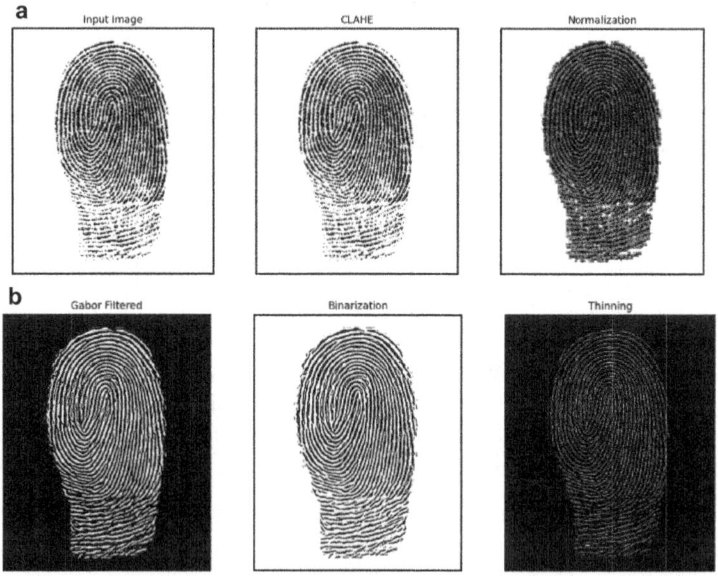

Fig. 2. a. Preprocessing of Input Fingerprint Image. b. Preprocessing of Input Fingerprint Image

3.2 Detection of Minutiae Points

The system successfully identified minutiae points, comprising minutiae points, within the preprocessed biometric ridge patterns. The resulting minutiae map is illustrated in the Fig. 3. It is noteworthy that only templates with a minutiae count surpassing the predetermined threshold were registered, ensuring a robust and reliable calibration system. This meticulous approach contributes to the system's efficiency in recognizing qualified individuals and securing the medical device calibration process.

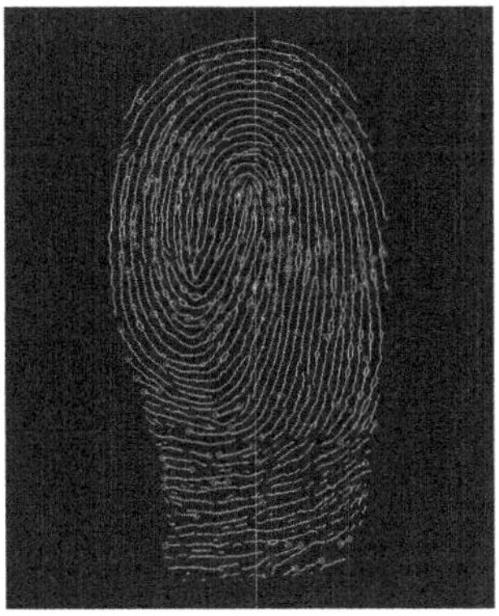

Fig. 3. Detected Minutiae Points

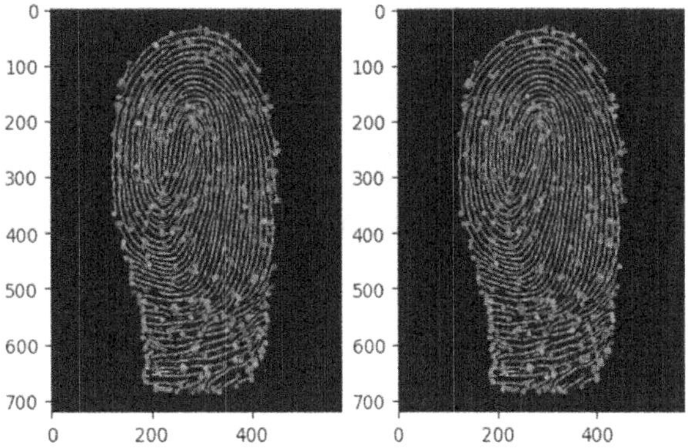

Fig. 4. Comparison of Query and Template Fingerprint

3.3 Comparison of Minutiae Points

To demonstrate the minutiae-based matching, a comparative image is presented, highlighting the identified minutiae in both the query image in Fig. 4(left) and the corresponding template in Fig. 4(right).

3.4 Correlation Map for Minutiae Matching

The correlation map visualizes the correlation between the minutiae of the query image and the template image, showcasing areas of alignment and potential matches (Fig. 5).

3.5 Parameter Results

After conducting multiple queries, the system demonstrated the following performance metrics in Table 1. The parameter results attest to the robust performance of the proposed MediSync fingerprint recognition framework, showcasing a remarkable balance between security and precision. With an impressively low False Acceptance Rate (FAR) of 0.00875 and a zero False Rejection Rate (FRR), the system minimizes unauthorized access while ensuring legitimate users are consistently recognized. The Equal Error Rate (EER) of 0.004375 signifies a meticulous calibration, striking a delicate balance between FAR and FRR. Additionally, the high Hamming Similarity Index of 0.91 reflects the system's accuracy in matching minutiae patterns, contributing to enhanced traceability and the overall quality of healthcare services. These metrics collectively underscore MediSync's potential to significantly reduce errors and fortify the security and reliability of medical device calibration procedures.

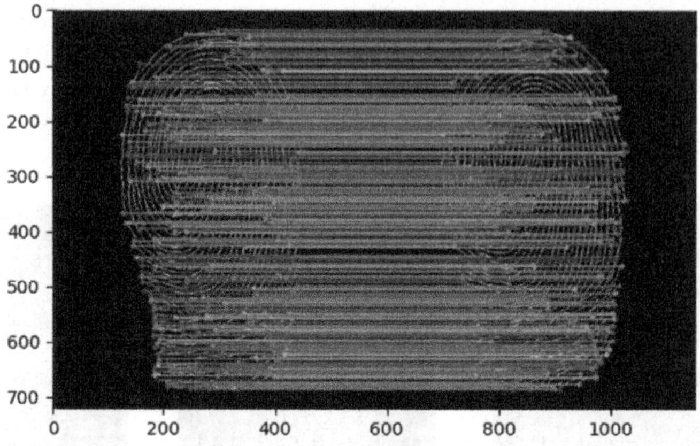

Fig. 5. Correlation Map

Table 1. Performance Matrices

Performance Metric	Value
FAR	0.00875
FRR	0.0
EER	0.004375
HSI	0.91
Accuracy	81.58%

3.6 Hamming Similarity Index and ROC Curve

The system's performance is further illustrated through the HSI and Receiver Operating Characteristic (ROC) curve. The HSI indicates the degree of similarity between the query and template, while the ROC curve visualizes the trade-off between FAR and FRR (Figs. 6 and 7).

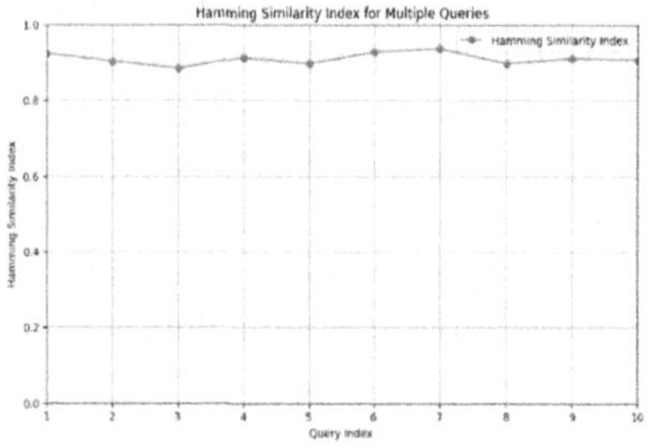

Fig. 6. HSI for each query image

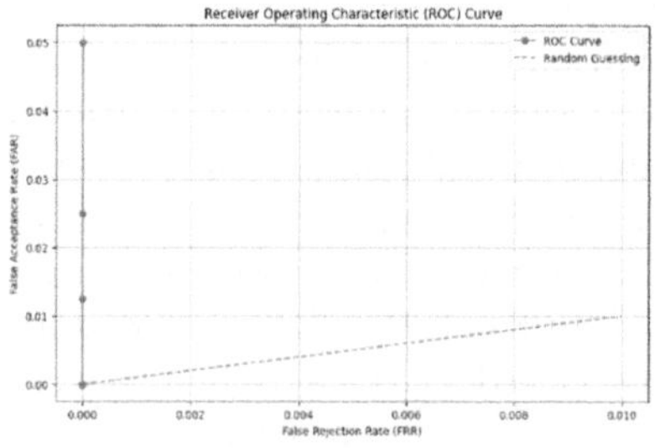

Fig. 7. ROC Curve

3.7 Comparative Study

Trivedi et al. proposed a non-invertible model integrating normalization, binarization, skeletonization, and Gabor filters, yielding EERs of 5.57%, 2.56%, and 0.48% on FVC2000, FVC2004, and FVC2006 databases, respectively. Similarly, Mohamed-Abdul-Cader et al. utilize Delaunay triangulation along with histogram equalization, binarization, Gabor filters, and skeletonization, achieving an EER of 6.68% on FVC2002 DB1. Ghaddab et al. carried out an expanded Delaunay triangulation approach with a robustness focus, resulting in EERs of 2.25%, 1.62%, and 3.99% on FVC2000, FVC2002, and FVC2004 databases. Li and Shi present a novel method incorporating ORB features, attaining an EER of 2.83% on the FVC2004 database. Their approach involves comparing a part of the fingerprint with the whole, utilizing the variance of gray intensity and ORB descriptors.

In contrast, MediSync employs Gabor filters for enhanced minutiae extraction, combining this with ORB descriptors for a more comprehensive approach. This combination surpasses methods solely relying on Gabor filters, ensuring accurate matching while maintaining computational efficiency. ORB descriptors enhance computational efficiency, providing a faster and more accurate minutiae matching process. Finally, employing brute force matching techniques, MediSync showcases superiority with an EER of 0.4375%, emphasizing its performance in terms of security and precision.

Concluding this section, the comprehensive evaluation results validate the performance of the proffered MediSync model in enhancing the security and accuracy of medical device calibration through fingerprint recognition (Table 2).

Table 2. Comparison with State-of-the-art Systems

System	EER	FRR
VeriFinger [8, 11]	0.08	0.0438
MCC [8, 9]	0.18	0.15
Bozoroth3 [8, 10]	0.3851	0.007125
Martins et al.	0.079	0.091
Ghaddab et al.	0.0162	0.02857
Li H	0.015	0.0146
Li Y., & Shi G	0.0283	0.0444
Li Z. et al.	0.0126	0.011
TN [17]	0.074	0.157
FTG [17]	0.034	0.067
MEDISYNC	0.004375	0

4 Conclusion

Our proposed fingerprint recognition system stands as a robust solution, enhancing the security, traceability, and reliability of medical device calibration processes. Utilizing a multi-step methodology, we have successfully implemented a comprehensive approach, ensuring that only authorized personnel can initiate and oversee calibration procedures. The system's effectiveness lies in its adept use of advanced image processing techniques, image enhancement methods, and minutiae-based feature extraction. Through rigorous testing and validation, we have achieved a high classification rate, demonstrating the reliability and accuracy of our system across different scenarios. As a result, our project provides a comprehensive and effective solution for elevating the standards of calibration processes within the medical device industry.

5 Future Scope

Moving forward, our project aims to achieve several key advancements. In the domain of front-end development, we will elevate user interactions by implementing responsive design principles and introducing customizable dashboards for administrators. Ensuring utmost security, our focus extends to Interface Encryption through advanced protocols and multi-factor authentication, fortifying the interface and safeguarding sensitive data and calibration processes. Envisioning an even more secure and auditable calibration process, we plan to develop an Independent Calibration Security and Audit Device that seamlessly integrates with medical devices, featuring real-time auditing capabilities, advanced sensors, and biometric authentication methods. Additionally, we will explore the development of an independent device dedicated to connecting with medical devices, further enhancing calibration security and facilitating audit procedures.

References

1. Sepasian, M., Mares, C., Azimi, S.M., Balachandran, W.: Image enhancement for minutiae-based fingerprint identification. In: 37th IEEE Applied Imagery Pattern Recognition Workshop, pp. 1–4. Washington, DC, USA (2008). https://doi.org/10.1109/AIPR.2008.4906466
2. Sahoo, R.C., Pradhan, S.K.: A broad survey on feature extraction methods for fingerprint image analysis. Int. J. Comput. Eng. Technol. **10**(2), 14–24 (2019)
3. Weiclaw, L.: A minutiae-based matching algorithms in fingerprint recognition systems. J. Med. Inform. Technol. **13** (2009)
4. Hong, L., Wan, Y., Jain, A.: Fingerprint image enhancement: algorithm and performance evaluation. IEEE Trans. Pattern Anal. Machine Intell. **20**(8), 777–789 (1998). https://doi.org/10.1109/34.709565
5. Jakubovic, A., Velagic, J.: Image Feature Matching and Object Detection Using Brute-Force Matchers (2018). https://doi.org/10.23919/ELMAR.2018.8534641
6. Chen, S,: Extracting fingerprint minutiae based on Harris corner detector. Optical Technique (2008)
7. Maltoni, D., Maio. D.: Fingerprint matching. In: Jain, A.K., Feng, J. (eds.) Handbook of Fingerprint Recognition pp. 167–232. Springer (2009)

8. AlShehri, H., Hussain, M., AboAlSamh, H., AlZuair, M.: A large-scale study of fingerprint matching systems for sensor interoperability problem. Sensors (Basel). **18**(4), 1008 (2018). https://doi.org/10.3390/s18041008.PMID:29597286;PMCID:PMC5948705
9. Cappelli, R., Ferrara, M., Maltoni, D.: Minutia cylinder-code: a new representation and matching technique for fingerprint recognition. IEEE Trans. Pattern Anal. Mach. Intell. **32**(12), 2128–2141 (2010). https://doi.org/10.1109/TPAMI.2010.52
10. Watson, C., et al.: User's guide to NIST biometric image software (NBIS), National Institute of Standards and Technology, Gaithersburg, MD (2007). https://doi.org/10.6028/NIST.IR.7392
11. Modi S., Elliott S., Kim H. Statistical analysis of fingerprint sensor interoperability performance. In: Proceedings of the IEEE 3rd International Conference on Biometrics: Theory, Applications, and Systems; pp. 1–6. Washington, DC, USA (2009)
12. Martins, N., Silva, J.S., Bernardino, A.: Fingerprint Recognition in Forensic Scenarios. Sensors (Basel). **24**(2), 664 (2024). https://doi.org/10.3390/s24020664.PMID:38276355; PMCID:PMC10819264
13. Ghaddab, M.H., Jouini, K., Korbaa, O.: Fast and Accurate Fingerprint Matching Using Expanded Delaunay Triangulation. IEEE/ACS 14th International Conference on Computer Systems and Applications (AICCSA), pp. 751–758. Hammamet, Tunisia (2017). https://doi.org/10.1109/AICCSA.2017.33
14. Li, H.: Feature extraction, recognition, and matching of damaged fingerprint: application of deep learning network. Concurrency Computat. Pract. Exper. **33**, e6057 (2021). https://doi.org/10.1002/cpe.6057
15. Li, Y., Shi, G.: ORB-based fingerprint matching algorithm for mobile devices. In: IEEE 2nd International Conference on Computer and Communication Engineering Technology (CCET), pp. 11–15. Beijing, China (2019). https://doi.org/10.1109/CCET48361.2019.8989155
16. Li, Z., et al.: A novel fingerprint recognition method based on a Siamese neural network. J. Intell. Syst. **31**(1), 690–705 (2022). https://doi.org/10.1515/jisys-2022-0055
17. Shi, L., Lan, S., Gui, H., Yang, Y., Guo, Z.: A novel 2D contactless fingerprint matching method. Neurocomputing **500**, 547–555 (2022). https://doi.org/10.1016/j.neucom.2022.05.092

Renal Irregularities Detection Using Convolutional Neural Network

Rosy Salomi Victoria Daniel[1(✉)], Ashwin Roberts Rajesh[2], Gokul Saravanan[2], Gowtham Ganeshkumar[2], and Arulan Sabari Kasinathan[2]

[1] Department of Computer Science and Engineering, Chennai Institute of Technology, Kundrathur, Chennai 600069, India
drosysalomi@gmail.com

[2] Department of Computer Science and Engineering, St. Joseph's College of Engineering, OMR, Chennai 600119, India

Abstract. Renal irregularities are serious medicinal condition that is becoming more common and killing more people each year. In its early stages, renal irregularities are curable, but it can progress irreversibly and result in renal failure. Cyst development, kidney tumours, and stone are the three predominant kidney irregularities that impair renal function among numerous diseases. The prompt detection and treatment of renal disease is a major challenge to the medical community. If renal problems like stones, cysts and tumours are not detected at an early stage, renal failure may ensue. Computer-assisted diagnostics is necessary to complement medical assessments made by clinicians and specialists as renal disease is more spread, there are less clinicians accessible, assessment and monitoring rates are rising, especially in developing nations. Though they still don't perform well, artificial intelligence methods like machine and deep learning have been utilized in literature to identify illness. This study uses CNN model for renal disease categorization and prognosis that is based on deep learning. For exploration, we use a benchmark CT kidney dataset from Computed Tomography. CNN first preprocesses the data before extracting the features from the pictures. The suggested method successfully classifies renal illness, with a notable accuracy of 99.3%, 99.5% precision, 95.3% recall, and 9.88% F1-score.

Keywords: Computed Tomography · Convolutional Neural Network · Feature extraction

1 Introduction

Renal abnormalities are still a major public health concern even though treatment efforts are still being made for them [5]. More than 10% of people worldwide suffer from CKD [19], which was the sixteenth leading cause of death in 2016. By 2040, forecasts indicate that it will come in sixth [9]. Around 79,000 Americans were given a kidney cancer diagnosis in 2020; 28,710 of those instances were in women and 50,290 were in men [7]. An approximate total of 431,288 cases of kidney cancer were reported globally

Published by Springer Nature Switzerland AG 2025
A. Chandrabose et al. (Eds.): ICCCSP 2024, IFIP AICT 723, pp. 144–156, 2025.
https://doi.org/10.1007/978-3-031-73617-9_12

[20]. It is significant to remember that kidney cancer ranks sixth among cancers that affect men in the US. Renal cell carcinoma and cyst development [14] are examples of primary kidney diseases that impact renal function (kidney tumor). Furthermore, persons who have a history of kidney stones typically experience recurring episodes. Dehydration is also a way of getting affected by kidney stone. Kidney disorders [6] are frequent among people of all ages. Manually detecting these anomalies, on the other hand, can be time-consuming, complicated and costly. Thus, the focus of medical research has been on creating a reliable and quick method for identifying kidney issues.

Roughly 12% of people worldwide suffer with kidney stone disease [2], which is characterized by the formation of crystalline deposits within the kidneys. Renal cell carcinoma (RCC), sometimes referred to as a kidney tumor, ranks among the top 10 cancers with the highest incidence rates worldwide [16]. Renal cell carcinoma (RCC) is the result of unchecked development and abnormal changes of kidney cells. Diseases affecting blood and kidney function have been linked to these cysts. To identify kidney problems, pathology tests are typically utilized in conjunction with other imaging modalities, such as MRIs, B-ultrasound devices [15], CT scans, and X-rays. X-ray beams are utilized by CT scanners to provide thorough cross-sectional images of the target anatomy, which produce accurate slice-by-slice images and three-dimensional data for kidney research [4]. Renal failure can be prevented in large part by treating kidney problems such as cysts, tumors, and stones early on [21]. Therefore, it is believed that detecting kidney issues early on, such as cysts, stones, and tumors, is crucial to preventing renal failure [3]. Despite recent studies, public datasets are still rather scarce. Previously, standard machine learning methods were employed to classify disorders such as cysts, tumours, and stones. In various studies, ultrasonography images were in the study. This study has made a number of benefaction like:

1. The "CT Kidney Dataset: Normal-Cyst-Tumour and Stone" collection is used, which includes 12,446 full-body urogram images of the abdomen.
2. The use of a CNN model to identify renal diseases. The study paper includes both a complete performance analysis and a full description of the mechanics of the suggested technique.
3. Accuracy, recall, F1 score, precision, and other metrics derived from the confusion matrix are used to assess the CNN model's performance. These outcomes unequivocally demonstrate the model's ability to identify and classify kidney issues.

2 Literature Survey

The report provides an extensive overview of early renal research from multiple angles. Numerous studies have been produced as a result of applying deep learning to image processing and classification, most notably in the area of radiological self-diagnosis. Several image classification techniques have been studied for the classification of renal diseases. In a research, CNNs were compared against typical algorithms such as Random Forest, MultiLayer Perceptrons, Support Vector Machines Decision Trees (DTs), K-Nearest Neighbours (KNNs), Naive Bayes, and so on [8]. The authors' methodology proved to be beneficial as evidenced by their highest F1 score of 0.853 among the several approaches used.

To extract information from renal ultrasound photos, the authors of [1] used pre-trained Deep Neural Network (DNN) models, such as ResNet-101, Shuffle Net, and MobileNetv2. Following the gathering of attributes, Support Vector Machines (SVM) were used to categorize them [8]. The majority vote technique was then used to generate the final forecasts. The study's main focus was the classification of ultrasound images, which had an amazing accuracy of 95.58. The authors of [18] used a mix of deep and conventional transfer learning techniques in a second investigation. The scientists reported a technique that uses coronal CT scans and deep learning algorithms to automatically diagnose kidney stones [11]. Their suggested method boasts a remarkable 96.82percent detection accuracy. To train and evaluate the model, 1,799 photos were used in the dataset. Similar to this, the authors of [17] developed a method for recognizing images of kidney cysts using CT scan data from the abdomen. For this challenge, they employed a fully linked CNN, and their true positive rate came out at 84.3. In order to enable classification into five distinct classes, the authors of [22] altered the ResNet-101 model by adding a $1 \times 1 \times 1$ convolution layer with initialized weights and changing the final dense layer.

The integration of machine learning [12] in healthcare promises earlier diagnoses and personalized treatments, despite challenges like data privacy and model robustness. Future advancements aim to refine prognosis prediction and enhance health policy-making through data-driven insights. The model's accuracy rating was 0.72. Five categories are used to classify the renal ultrasonography images [10]: tumor, cyst, normal, stone, and failure. Principal Component Analysis [13] was used by the scientists to identify the most important characteristics from a limited amount of data. In conclusion, earlier attempts to use machine learning and deep learning models to identify particular renal radiographic abnormalities yielded promising outcomes. But most of these efforts have focused on the analysis of ultrasound or X-ray images. Few studies have focused on dual-class categorization, especially when it comes to CT scan images. This study uses four distinct groupings to categorize CT scans in an attempt to close this disparity.

3 Existing System

Prior studies have demonstrated encouraging outcomes when utilizing various algorithms to detect anomalies in renal radiography. Also dataset consisted numerical data where machine learning algorithms were deployed which might not always be the case. In image classification, the deep learning models were used but it didn't return the result with good accuracy. Nevertheless, most of study focusses on analyzing the ultrasound or X-ray pictures. There has been little research on dual-class categorization, particularly when it comes to CT scan images.

4 Objective

To develop an efficient system for kidney abnormality detection using CNN with the primary goals of improving the speed, precision, and consistency of kidney irregularity analysis. Deep learning models accurately classify kidney diseases by analyzing large data sets, identifying patterns not easily recognizable by humans. Early detection is crucial for timely treatment and better outcomes.

5 Proposed System

The proposed system describes a method to classify CT images by using several measures. This study focuses on the accuracy of the suggested model as the dependent variable and analyses its impact on independent factors. The proposed model is divided into four steps, the first of which involves selecting the CT kidney dataset as shown in the Fig. 1. The second stage involves data preprocessing such as grayscale conversion, image scaling, and bilinear interpolation. The third stage involves feature extraction. In the final phase, CNN determines whether a kidney is affected by stone, tumour, cyst or it is normal. At last, a webpage is created where the user uploads the CT scan image as the input. The image is sent to the model and the result is displayed as the output in the webpage as shown in the Fig. 1.

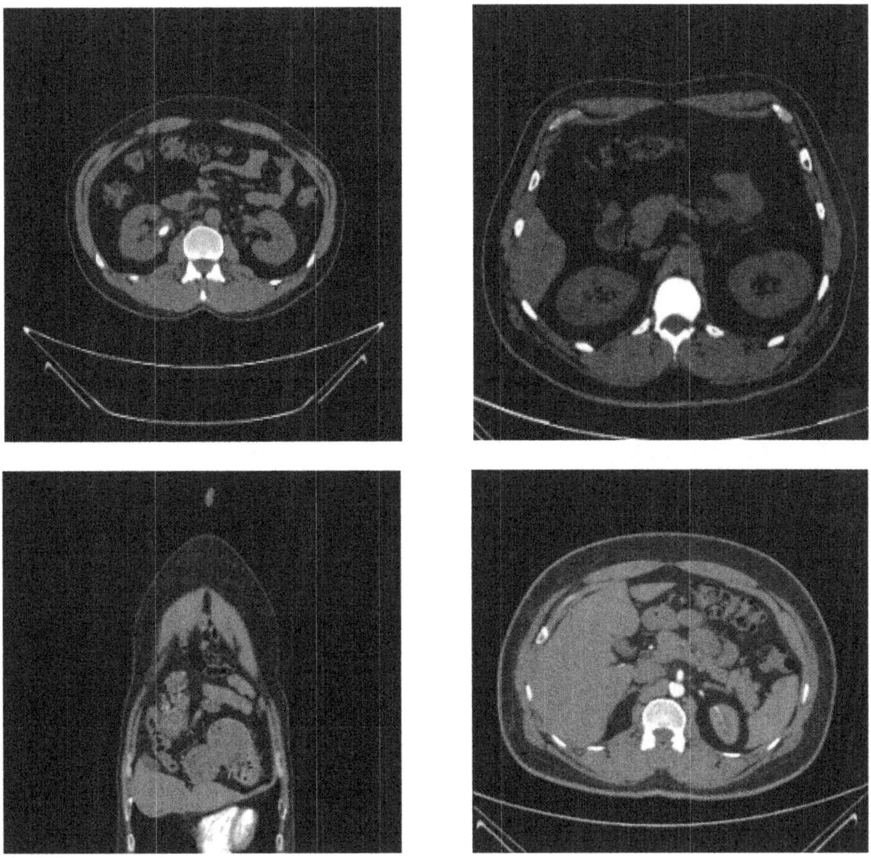

Fig. 1. Sample dataset images of cyst, stone, tumor and normal are in order (left to right)

The algorithm is educated on the data and the model with the highest accuracy and the lower training time is selected. Then the app file is running so that the webpage opens where the user has to upload the CT scan image and then click submit. The webpage

page is connected to the model where the image is sent as input and then the image is processed through all the layers and at the last the image is classified and then the result is displayed to the user of their abnormality.

6 Methodology

This section describes the algorithm to categorize CT renal disease using multiple metrics. The correctness of the developed model is the dependent variable in this study, and the effects of independent factors are examined. The CT kidney dataset is selected in the first phase of the developed model, which contains four stages. Additionally, the second stage involves pre-processing of data, which involves actions such as bilinear interpolation, scaling of image and grayscale conversion. The final step involves feature extraction. CNN is utilized in the last stage to determine whether a kidney is affected by stone, tumour, cyst, or it is normal.

6.1 Dataset Description

Using Picture Archiving and Communication Systems (PACS), the dataset was assembled. Patients with kidney cysts, tumours, and normal or stone results were identified. The urogram and whole abdomen protocols are used to choose the radial and coronal slices from non-contrast and chromatic examinations. Subsequently, a single evaluation at a time, researchers assembled a set of photos for each diagnostic result from the meticulously selected Dicom study. To ensure the quality of the data each image was assessed twice of their quality. The generated dataset contains 12,446 distinct data points, 3,709 are cysts, 5,077 are normal data, 1,377 are stones, and 2,283 are tumours. A sample dataset image of the renal irregularities is shown in Fig. 1.

6.2 Data Pre-processing

To improve the model's performance, this phase completed data preparation stage. By rescaling through the created picture data, the dataset is examined for identifying 11200 photos that belong to 4 different classes. The Dicom picture dataset for kidney disease contains images of different sizes, shapes, and widths. In this work, bilinear interpolation is used to resize each image to 227 by 227 pixels. When interpolation is used, image with same pixels is transformed, each pixel is given the appropriate intensity distribution, and the result is an image that seems smoother. Using the 9957 files for training, we were able to find 12446 files that belonged to the four classifications cyst, normal, stone, and tumour.

6.3 Feature Extraction

The Dicom picture dataset is then trained using the preprocessed data. Features that signify a kidney cyst, stone, tumor, or normal are removed. Without requiring human intervention, the CNN-based models automatically extract the crucial information. In this study, the CNN model is used to extract comprehensive information from a picture and identify the different types of CT renal ailment. The collected features are then given as input to the models.

6.4 Convolutional Neural Network (CNN)

Extraction of the spatial and temporal aspects of an image is useful. CNN evaluate inputs for relevant information using a variety of CNN layers and apply convolutional filters on the input to figure out the result of the connected neurons to the various input areas. The CNN model has three basic layers: fully connected, max-pooling, and convolutional. The CNN has three crucial parameters: pitch, padding, and filter size. Several filters are used to each layer in order to precisely extract characteristics. The filters are positioned inside the pictures according on stride. CNN performs poorly if the stride size exceeds two; it can only be one or two. When each input picture in the convolutional layer is not completely protected by the filter, zero padding is needed to preserve the structural evaluation. The ReLU layer transmits positive values while suppressing and setting negative values to zero. The two utilised max-pooling layer approaches are average and max. The image is divided into categories by the completely connected layer, which has 128 units. The feature map normalization process makes use of the batch normalization layer. These tiers enhance network training and regulation. The CNN model's design is shown in Fig. 2. Every convolutional block incorporates both max-pooling and 2D CNN. There are 15 layers in the network: six convolutional layers, two dense layers, six max pooling layers and 1 flattened layer.

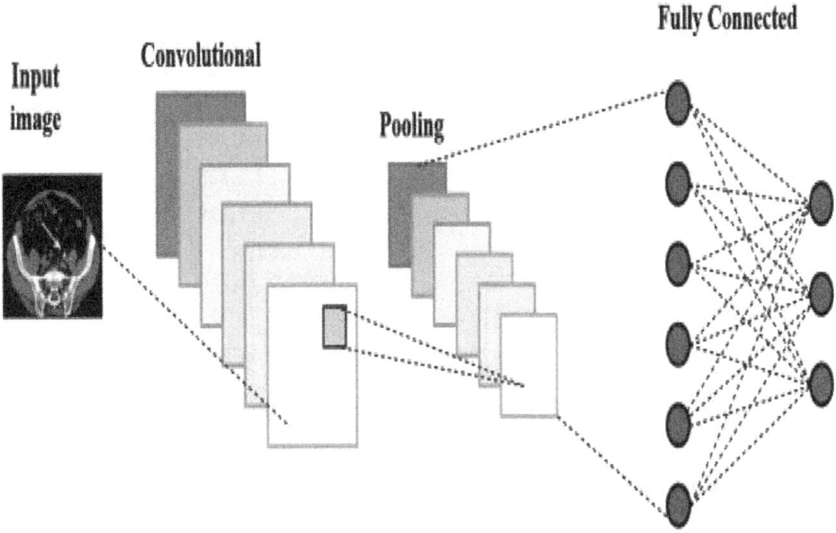

Fig. 2. Architecture of the proposed CNN model

The ReLU function activates the convolutional layer, which uses a 3×3 kernel size to extract features from the images. A 3×3 kernel size max-pooling layer reduces an input image's dimensionality. The input sizes of each of the six convolutional layers vary: The first and the second has input size of 32 followed by 64 of third and the fourth and the last two has their input size as 128. The two dense layers' employ ReLU activation and the softmax function, with input size of 512 and 4. Less shrinkage results in less distortion of the image's internal features and structures. The summary of the CNN architecture is shown in Table 1. The layer types, input size, and kernel size are provided in detail. The dense layer has input and output dimensions of 512 and 4, respectively. With different input sizes, the max-pooling and convolutional layers reduce the image. Less contraction results in less distortion of the image's internal features and patterns. The architecture uses a fully connected layer to classify the Dicom image into stone, tumour or cyst after looking at the time-related properties. Ten training epochs of the rmsprop optimizer are used to train the suggested model is used to losses and metrics.

Table 1. CNN Network Summary

Types	Input Size	Output
Conv2d	32	198, 198, 32
MaxPool2D	2	99,99,32
Conv2D	32	97,97,32
MaxPool2D	2	48,48,32
Conv2D	64	46,46,64
MaxPool2D	2	23,23,64
Conv2D	64	21,21,64
MaxPool2D	2	10,10,64
Conv2D	128	8,8,128
MaxPool2D	2	4,4,128
Conv2D	128	2,2,128
MaxPool2D	2	1,1,128
Flatten	-	128
Dense	512	512
Dense	4	4

7 System Requirements

System requirements refer to the specifications and capabilities that a software or hardware product must possess in order to operate effectively on a particular system or platform. Software requirements are shown in the Table 2.

The languages that are used for the frontend and backend are listed in the Table 3.

Table 2. Software Tool Requirements

Code Editors	• Pycharm • Anaconda
Output Software[Browser]	• Google Chrome • Firefox

Table 3. Frontend and Backend Languages

Webpage Creating	*Styling*	*Framework*
HTML	*CSS*	*Flask*

8 Implementation Details

Many metrics are used to evaluate the prediction and classification problems, including precision, accuracy, and recall. Following measures are deployed to determine effectiveness of the proposed system. It determines the percentage of True Positives (TP), False Positives (FP), False Negative (FN), True Negatives (TN) to assess success of the developed algorithm. Accuracy is calculated as given in the Eq. 1:

$$\text{Accuracy} = ((\text{TP} + \text{TN})/((\text{TP} + \text{TN} + \text{FP} + \text{FN})) \quad (1)$$

Precision is defined as the ratio of true positives among all positive predictions as given in the Eq. 2:

$$\text{Precision} = (\text{TP}/(\text{TP} + \text{FP})) \quad (2)$$

Recall measures percentage of true positives correctly identified among all actual values as given in the Eq. 3:

$$\text{Recall} = (\text{TP}/(\text{TN} + \text{FN})) \quad (3)$$

The weighted average of precision and recall is given in the Eq. 4 as F1-score.

$$\text{F1 - Score} = (2 * ((\text{Precision} + \text{Recall})/(\text{Precision} + \text{Recall}))) \quad (4)$$

Categorical Cross-Entropy Loss measures dissimilarity shown between the predicted probabilities (y) and actual labels (p) as given in the Eq. 5.

$$\text{L}(\text{y}, \text{p})_{\text{i}} = 14\text{y}_{\text{i}}\log(\text{p}_{\text{i}}) \quad (5)$$

9 Performance Analysis

The CNN model achieves 99.3% accuracy, 99.5% precision, 98.3% recall, and 98.8% F1-score, which implies that it can accurately diagnose kidney ailment, be it cyst, normal, stone, or tumour. Figure 3 presents a graphic representation of the convolutional neural network's precision, recall, accuracy and loss.

Suggested improved CNN model should be used for renal disease diagnosis, according to this study. The result is an image that seems smoother. Using the 9957 files for training, we were able to find 12446 files that belonged to the four classifications cyst, normal, stone, and tumor. Research report provides a comprehensive analysis and fundamentals of proposed technique. Confusion matrix of the suggested approach is graphically displayed in Fig. 4. Kidney disease is classified by the CNN model into four categories: cysts, normal, stones and tumours.

Table 4 shows the comparison between the existing and the proposed approach and Fig. 5 displays the recall, accuracy and precision of the existing and the proposed approaches.

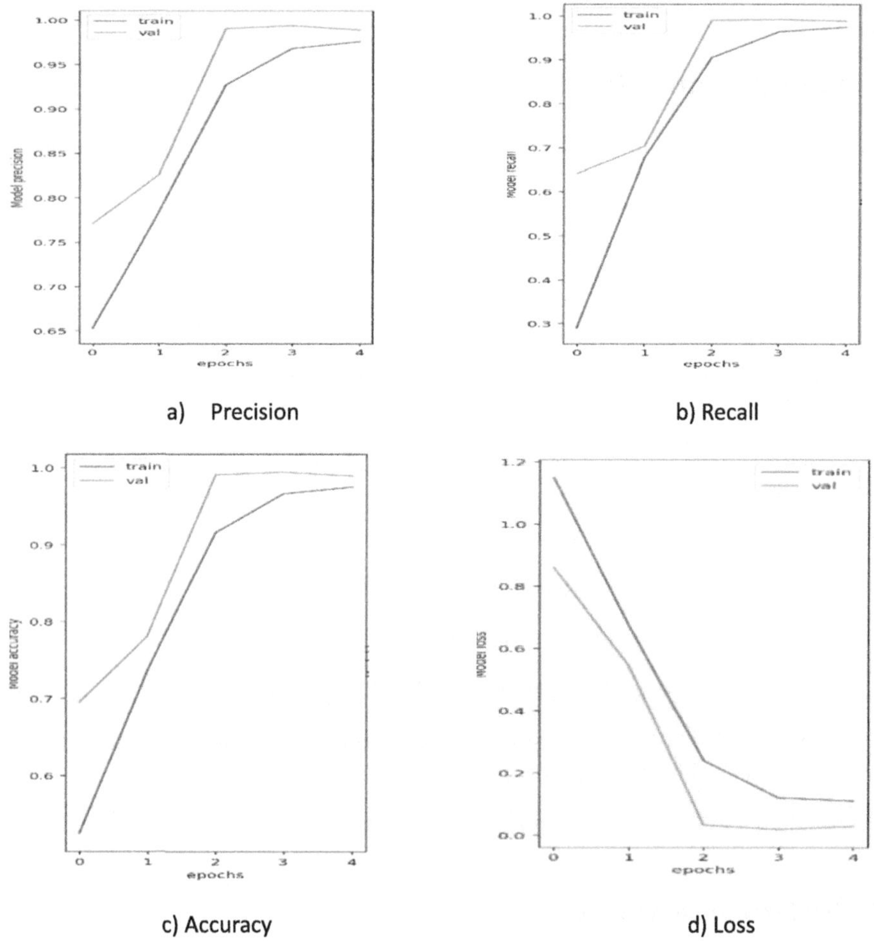

Fig. 3. Results of various metrics

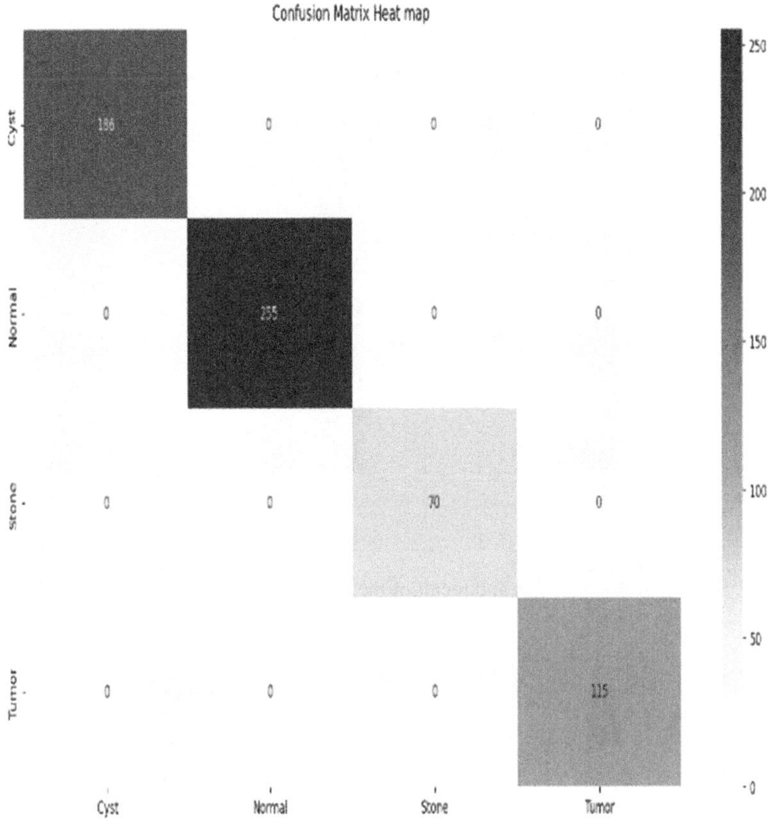

Fig. 4. Contingency Table of the CNN model

Table 4. Comparison between the existing and the proposed approach

Reference	Model	Acc	Precision	Recall
[19]	Yolov8	82.5%	85.7%	75.2%
[8]	VGG16	95.2%	95.4%	89.3%
Proposed Approach	CNN	99.3%	99.5%	95.3%

10 Results

After the model displays the evaluation metrics, the webpage opens and the user can upload the CT scan image in the flask framework. The result will be displayed depending upon the irregularity found. Result is overwritten in the image itself as shown in the Fig. 6. The page has a submit option to upload the image to the flask framework and clear button to clear and reupload image.

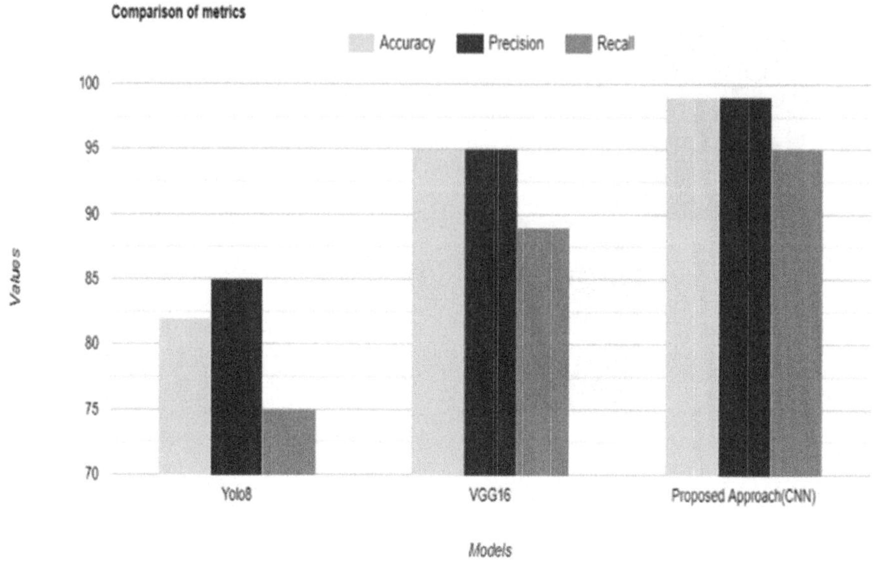

Fig. 5. Accuracy, precision and recall of the existing and the proposed approaches

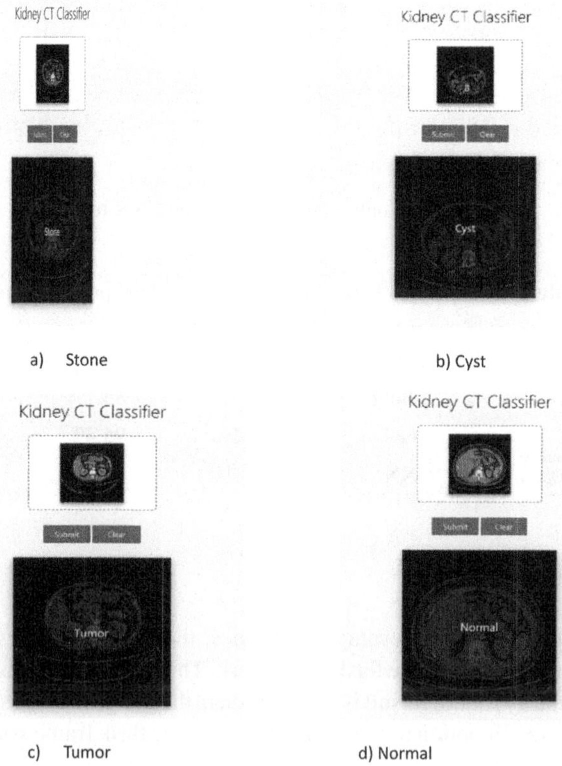

Fig. 6. User Interface of the Webpage

11 Conclusion and Further Research

Kidney disease is a serious medical condition that significantly raises the risk of death and morbidity around the globe. Kidney damage may lead to renal failure if it is not identified and treated on a regular basis. Because diagnosis and therapy for chronic renal disease are expensive, there are fewer experts available, and the condition is growing more common, computer-assisted diagnostics is essential to support doctors' and experts' diagnostic decisions. In the early stages of illness identification and prediction, a number of techniques are deployed to process images in the domain. Second, a CNN is used by the suggested model to retrieve the features. The best results are obtained by the developed model, which has a F1-score of 98.8%. Future studies would examine the effectiveness of the developed method using an ensemble deep learning model, optimization model, and extraction model. Furthermore, the model's generalizability will be tested with additional datasets. The findings show that the CNN algorithm accurately and efficiently detects renal diseases. The models accuracy in the study proves its effectiveness. Further advancements might incorporate newer kinds of CNN to enhance the existing design. Xploring explainable AI approaches for interpreting CNN decisions will increase diagnostic transparency, merging real-time monitoring and patient-specific data may lead to personalized medicine applications, improving the overall efficiency and effectiveness of renal abnormality detection systems.

References

1. Aksakalli, I., Kac Dioglu, S., Hanay, Y.S.: Kidney x-ray images classification using machine learning and deep learning methods. Balkan J. Electr. Comput. Eng. **9**(2), 144–151 (2021). https://doi.org/10.17694/bajece.878116
2. Castiglioni, I., et al.: AI applications to medical images: from machine learning to deep learning. Physica Med. **83**, 9–24 (2021)
3. Gunasekara, T., et al.: Urinary biomarkers indicate paediatric renal injury among rural farming communities in Sri lanka. Sci. Rep. **12**(1), 1–13 (2022)
4. Guo, J., Zeng, W., Yu S., Xiao, J.: RAU-Net: U-Net Model Based on Residual and Kidney Tumour Segmentation. In: IEEE International Conference on Consumer Electronics and Computer Engineering (ICCECE), p. 353356 (2021)
5. Hadjiyski, N.: Kidney cancer staging: deep learning neural network based approach. In: International Conference on e-Health and Bioengineering (EHB), pp. 1–4 (2020)
6. Mardison, Y.: Detection of kidney cysts of kidney ultrasound image using hybrid method: KNN, GLCM, and ANN backpropagation. In: International Conference on Computer Science, Information Technology and Engineering, pp. 222–227 (2023)
7. Mehedi, M.H.K., Haque, E., Radin, S.Y., Ur Rahman, M.A., Reza, M.T., Alam, M.G.R.: Kidney tumour segmentation and classification using deep neural network CT images. In: International Conference Digital Image Computing: Techniques and Applications (DICTA), pp. 1–7 (2022)
8. Monaco S., et al.: Cyst segmentation on kidney tubules by means of U-Net deep-learning models. In: IEEE International Conference Big Data, pp. 3923–3926 (2021)
9. Pande, S.D., Agarwal, R.: Multi-class kidney abnormalities detecting novel system through computed tomography. IEEE Access **12**, 21147–21155 (2024)

10. Patil, S., Choudhary, S.: Prediction of ultrasound kidney imaging using convolution neural networks. In: IEEE 12th International Conference on Communication Systems and Network Technologies (CSNT). pp. 451–455 (2023)
11. Rosy Salomi Victoria, D., Ramalakshmi, N.R, Mayuri, K, Meghna, G.K.: An ensemble stacking methodology for identifying heart disease. In: IEEE International Conference on Smart Electronics and Communication (ICOSEC), pp. 1138-1142 (2023)
12. Rosy Salomi Victoria, D., Subhishwaran, T., Velan, P.: Comprehensive analysis of multiple diseases using machine learning, In: 7th International Conference on Inventive Computation Technologies ICICT, pp. 1327–1333 (2024)
13. Sadeghi, M.H., Zadeh, H.M., Behroozi, H., Royat, A.: Accurate kidney tumour segmentation using weakly-supervised kidney volume segmentation in CT images. In: 28th National and 6th International Iranian Conference on Biomedical Engineering (ICBME), pp. 38–43 (2021)
14. Shaikh Abdul, H., Pushparaj, P.: Detection and Classification of Kidney Disease Using Convolutional Neural Networks. J. Neurol. Neuro Rehabil. Res. **8**(2), 136 (2023)
15. Sitanaboina, S.L.P., et al.: Attention 3D-CU-Net: enhancing kidney tumour segmentation accuracy through selective feature emphasis. IEEE Access **11**, 139798–139810 (2023)
16. Soni, A., Rai, A.: Kidney stone recognition and extraction using directional emboss svm from computed tomography images. In: Third International Conference Multimedia Processing. Communication Information Technology, pp. 57–62 (2020)
17. Subramanian, R.R., et al.: Design and evaluation of a deep learning aided approach for kidney stone detection in CT scan images. In: International Conference on Applied Intelligence and Sustainable Computing (ICAISC), pp. 1–6 (2023)
18. Sudharson, S., Kokil, P.: An ensemble of deep neural networks for kidney ultrasound image classification. Comput. Methods Programs Biomed. **197**, 105709 (2020)
19. Sudharson, S., Kokil, P.: Computer-aided diagnosis system for classification of multi-class kidney abnormalities in noisy ultrasound images. Comput. Methods Programs Biomed. **205**, 106071 (2021)
20. Wasi, S., Alam, S.B., Rahman, R., Amin, M.A., Kobashi, S.: Kidney tumor recognition from the abdominal CT images using transfer learning. In: IEEE 53rd International Symposium Multiple Valued Logic (ISMVL), pp. 54–58 (2023)
21. Yan, X., et al.: An efficient hybrid model for kidney tumour segmentation in CT images. In: IEEE 17th International Symposium on Biomedical Imaging (ISBI), pp. 333–336 (2020)
22. Wu, Y., Yi, Z.: Automated detection of kidney abnormalities using multi-feature fusion convolutional neural networks. Knowl.-Based Syst. **200**, 105873 (2020)

Surveillance and Mitigation of External Stimuli-Induced Sensory Overload in Autism with IoMT: Communicating Insights to Caregivers

S. Chithra[1(✉)], Shri Janani Muruganantham[1], and V. Kiruthika[2]

[1] Department of Computer Technology, Madras Institute of Technology, Anna University, Chennai, India
chithras@annauniv.edu

[2] Department of Computer Science, Shrimati Indira Gandhi College, Trichy, India
kiruthy.janani@gmail.com

Abstract. Autism Spectrum Disorder (ASD) poses a notable developmental obstacle linked to neural abnormalities, characterized by repetitive and non-functional behaviour. The sensory overloads lead to elevated aggression, social phobia, tantrums, hypervigilance, and heightened sensitivity to external stimuli, necessitating heightened awareness. Caregivers encounter challenges in ensuring constant monitoring and surveillance. In response to these difficulties, a project has been devised, integrating diverse sensors on a wearable device to identify the environmental disturbances through PGP for heart rate, MEMS for stereotypic sensing,GSR to analyse the sweat, also external stimuli as for over loudness and suspicious gas, an IoT module with Raspberry pi, and machine learning methodologies for classifying and categorisation exact situation by analysing data using Convolution Neural Network CNN with better 97.6% accuracy. This helps to give immediate alert to caregivers by GSM module also with self-assistance. The central control of the project is facilitated by a PIC microcontroller and driving relays. Through the monitoring of IoT-collected data, a detailed analysis illustrates the frequency of incidents, including aggressiveness detected by the accelerometer sensor, heightened gas levels, along with increased occurrences of loud noise noted along with the heartbeat and sweat sensor. This analytical method empowers caregivers and doctors with a comprehensive understanding of the patient's medical condition.

Keywords: Autism · Sensory Overload · External Stimuli · IoT · Wearable Device · Machine Learning

1 Introduction

Autism Spectrum Disorder (ASD) is a complex condition marked by diverse symptoms that vary significantly among individuals. Challenges in social interaction, difficulties in verbal and non-verbal communication, and repetitive behaviours are widespread manifestations [1]. The worldwide incidence of ASD is approximately 1 in 160 children,

Published by Springer Nature Switzerland AG 2025
A. Chandrabose et al. (Eds.): ICCCSP 2024, IFIP AICT 723, pp. 157–166, 2025.
https://doi.org/10.1007/978-3-031-73617-9_13

with prevalence rates differing among regions and populations. Socially, individuals with ASD may encounter obstacles in making eye contact, interpreting social cues, and forming lasting friendships. Communication hurdles may involve delayed speech development, limited use of gestures, and struggles in engaging in reciprocal conversations. Repetitive behaviours include distinctive movements or adherence to specific routines, while sensory sensitivities can result in heightened or reduced reactions to stimuli such as lights or sounds [2]. Those with ASD might also display intense, focused interests and be resistant to engaging in activities outside their preferences [18].

Communication challenges arise for individuals with ASD, posing hurdles for caregivers striving to understand their needs and preferences. Managing repetitive actions, meltdowns, and navigating social interactions presents ongoing dilemmas for caregivers [11]. The demands of caring for someone with ASD can escalate stress, anxiety, and fatigue levels, especially when support and resources are insufficient. The financial strain emerges from the substantial costs associated with specialized therapies, interventions, and tailored educational programs [10]. Caregivers often find themselves socially isolated due to the distinctive needs and behaviours of individuals with ASD, limiting participation in typical social activities.

Leveraging the combined capabilities of IoT, Raspberry Pi, and machine learning holds great promise in enhancing support for individuals with autism [3]. Continuous monitoring facilitates long-term data collection, refining interventions over time by a wearable compact device can escalate the continuous surveillance [7]. This comprehensive approach provides a comprehensive and adaptive solution to understand, monitor, and assist individuals with autism effectively [9].

2 Novel Contribution

The distinctive contributions of this current paper in the continuous monitoring collectively signify a noteworthy advancement in autism assistance methodologies, offering a more nuanced and comprehensive understanding of physiological indicators and can be elaborated as follows,

i. **Comprehensive Sensor:** The paper introduces a novel sensor designed to quantifiably measure the external noise, irritative light beam sensors and odour sensors collaborate with rate of heartbeat, rate of motion and body sweat. This sensor provides an accurate means of assessing sensory overload.
ii. **Multifactorial Analysis:** Unlike conventional approaches, the proposed method combines multiple factors, by understanding the sensed values. This multifactorial analysis enhances the accuracy and speed of categorizing the external factor and reciprocates based on the result from highly trained convolutional neural network model to categorise the existence of the sensory overload.
iii. **Self Pacing Techniques:** The paper introduces a pioneering methodology to divert the autistic child by music, voice instruction based on the highly predominant external factors to reduce the sensory overload. This act as an additional feature enhancing solution based approach for certain situations (Fig. 1).

Fig. 1. Range of sensors to sense various stimuli.

3 Proposed Methodology

The collaborative capabilities of IoT, Raspberry Pi, wireless sensor network (WSN)-based systems and machine learning shows great potential in improving assistance for individuals with autism. Through the integration of diverse sensors and devices via IoT, including motion sensors, heart rate monitors, and environmental sensors, real-time data about the patient's activities and responses can be gathered. This information undergoes processing and analysis using machine learning algorithms executed on the Raspberry Pi, providing personalized insights into the patient's behavioural patterns and triggers.

For instance, machine learning algorithms such as Convolutional Neural Network Algorithm can be utilized to identify and predict patterns linked to aggressive or anxious behaviour. The Raspberry Pi acts as a central controller, streamlining communication among the sensors, the IoT network, and the machine learning models. This cohesive system allows for the timely identification of potential challenges, such as sensory overload or aggressive tendencies, enabling proactive interaction and support.

3.1 Data Collection

1. **Sensory Monitoring:** Implement sensors such as accelerometers, heart rate monitors, and environmental sensors to detect changes in the individual's physiological and environmental conditions, providing insights into potential triggers for aggression.
   i. **Heart Rate Sensor:** The MAX30102 heart rate sensor utilizes photoplethysmography (PPG) to measure blood volume changes in the microvascular bed of tissue. This sensor emits light into the skin using LEDs, and a photodetector gauges the amount of light absorbed, enabling the calculation of heart rate [10]. The output data from MAX30102 is subsequently processed and read by Node MCU if the light is absorbed by the oxygenated blood. The pulse rate should be between 60–100 bpm for a normal functioning of the heart.
   ii. **Accelerometer Sensor:** The ADXL345 accelerometer is a widely utilized device for gauging acceleration and movement [11]. It utilizes microelectromechanical systems (MEMS) technology to detect changes in capacitance, brought about by the motion of minuscule internal structures [12]. The measurement range from ADXL345 can be set to operate within ± 2 g, $\pm$ 4 g, ± 8 g, or ± 16 g, providing adaptability to sense various levels of acceleration (Fig. 2).

iii. **Galvanic Skin Response (GSR) Sensor:** Emotional responses, particularly strong emotions experienced during stress, can activate the sympathetic nervous system [13]. This activation often leads to increased sweating in the sweat glands, subsequently causing a rise in skin resistance. In the envisioned system, the Grove – GSR Sensor plays a crucial role in gauging the stress levels of individuals with ASD by measuring the skin's conductive voltage (CV) with range of values from 0.95 V to at most 0.43 V, which varies proportionally with changes in skin resistance.

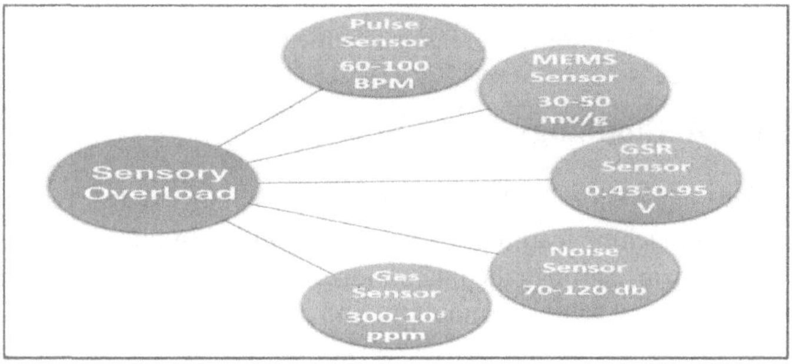

Fig. 2. Feasible Range of values for the sensor.

iv. **Noise Sensor:** The loudness sensor functions as a tool to identify sounds surpassing normal levels or disruptions that may trigger aggression. It achieves this by incorporating an LM2904 amplifier and an integrated microphone. The microphone captures environmental sounds and the LM2904 amplifier, in turn, amplifies variations in air pressure caused by sound into electrical signals and filters the high-frequency elements of these signals. The resulting positive envelope, indicative of the sound's loudness when ranging exceeding 70–120 db. To ensure precision and filter out unwanted signal disturbances, the input signal undergoes dual filtering stages within the module.

v. **Gas Sensor:** Gas Sensor, designed for measuring air quality and detecting any exposure to irritants that can cause sensory overload, Gas sensors are available in different types, including MQ series gas sensors, MiCS-5524, or MiCS-5524/5529 which helps to sense the normal range of 300 to 10^3 ppm feasible gas values. These sensors utilize diverse technologies like metal oxide or electrochemical sensors to sense carbon monoxide and natural gas leakage detection and other specific elements to analyse the indoor air quality to avoid the melt downs.

2. **IoT Integration:** Connect sensors through the Internet of Things (IoT) to enable real-time data collection and communication. This allows for continuous monitoring of the individual's behaviour and immediate transmission of information to caregivers. Integrating IoT for sensor connectivity involves several technical elements to facilitate real-time data collection and transmission. Initially, sensors are outfitted with IoT-compatible hardware modules for internet connectivity. These sensors then send data to a central gateway device, which consolidates and relays the data to a cloud-based platform. Within the cloud, real-time data processing and analysis take place, utilizing

either edge computing or cloud-based analytics. Communication between the IoT platform and caregiver devices is facilitated by application programming interfaces (APIs), ensuring smooth data transmission. Security measures such as encryption, authentication, and access control are implemented at multiple levels to safeguard sensitive data. Moreover, a scalable infrastructure is essential to efficiently manage the large volume of data from various sensors. Thus, successful IoT integration for continuous monitoring necessitates a robust architecture encompassing hardware, connectivity, data processing, and security components.

3. **Raspberry Pi Controller:** Employ a central control unit, like Raspberry Pi, to manage the communication between sensors, IoT devices, and machine learning models. This facilitates efficient data processing and analysis [16]. It functions by receiving data streams from sensors connected via various interfaces such as Wi-Fi, Bluetooth, or GPIO pins. The Raspberry Pi processes and aggregates this data before transmitting it to the cloud or local storage for further analysis. Additionally, it coordinates the execution of machine learning algorithms for real-time data analysis and decision-making. Overall, the Raspberry Pi plays a crucial role in ensuring efficient data processing and analysis in an IoT ecosystem.

3.2 Data Processing and Categorization

Machine Learning Algorithm: Utilize machine learning algorithms, such as Convolutional Neural Networks (CNNs), to analyse patterns in the collected data. Train the algorithm to recognize signs of aggression, stress, or sensory overload based on individualized characteristics of each multifactor combination of sensors. Analyzing behavioral and sensory overload through Convolutional Neural Networks (CNN) in conjunction with various sensors involves several key steps and mathematical operations [18]. The process begins with data preprocessing, where sensor data is normalized or standardized to a common scale and converted into 2D arrays suitable for CNN input.

For classification with numeric data comprising five attributes, the dataset is normalised to have a mean of zero and a standard deviation of one to facilitate quicker convergence during training. The CNN architecture constructed with an input layer shaped according to the data dimensions, followed by convolutional layers for feature extraction, pooling layers such as MaxPooling for dimensionality reduction, and a flatten layer to prepare the output for the fully connected layers. The fully connected layers process the flattened output for final classification, with a single neuron in the output layer utilizing a sigmoid activation function for binary classification.

An input sequence X and a filter (kernel) W, the convolution operation computes the dot product between the filter and segments of the input sequence.

$$(X * W)[i] = \sum_{j=0}^{F-1} X[i+j] \cdot W[j] + b$$

where F is the filter size, and b is the bias.

In forward pass, input data traverses through the layers, applying convolution and pooling operations, with Rectified Linear Unit ReLU activation ReLU(x) = max(0,x) typically applied except for the output layer. Backpropagation is then employed to adjust weights using optimization algorithms like stochastic gradient descent or Adam after computing the loss between predicted and actual labels. Training involves dividing the dataset into training and validation subsets, adjusting hyperparameters to prevent overfitting, and monitoring performance on the validation set for model refinement. Finally, evaluate the trained model's performance on a separate test set to assess its efficacy in classification tasks (Fig. 3).

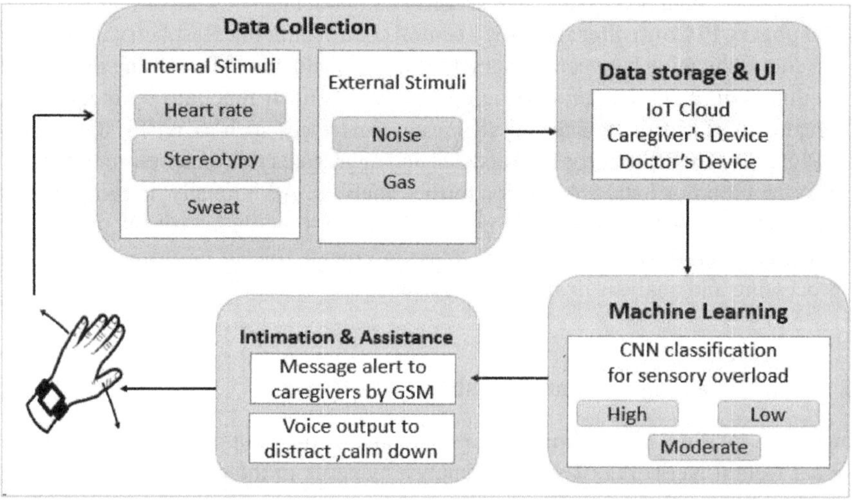

Fig. 3. Proposed Architecture of the System.

Data Storage and Analysis

Establishing a secure data storage system for preserving historical data to facilitate future medical analyses is achieved through the utilization of Sensor Cloud in this implementation. This data repository serves as a valuable resource for caregivers, therapists, and healthcare professionals, enabling them to discern patterns over time and tailor interventions more effectively (Table 1).

The integration involves connecting medical databases, servers, and storage within the cloud module. This cloud module is intricately linked to the IoT module, which generates real-time observational results for individuals with autism. The Cloud Module, functioning as web-based software, empowers clinicians to monitor the daily activities of autistic patients and analyse repetitive behaviors based on the acquired data. Clinicians can then offer insights to caregivers during subsequent medical checkups and devise therapeutic approaches for autistic individuals by extrapolating trends from the data.

Table 1. Sensory Overload Analysis.

Sensors	PPG MAX30102	MEMS ADXL345	SKIN GSR	NOISE LM2904	GAS MiCS-5524
Metrics	60-100 bpm	50-150 Hz	0.45-1.90 v (x100)	70-120 dB	300-1000 ppm (/ 10)
Instance #1	67	58	73	86	40
Instance #2	85	74	164	95	57
Instance #3	79	88	159	83	68
Instance #4	62	59	140	72	98
Instance #5	54	65	120	113	85
Instance #6	62	74	97	65	74
Instance #7	75	98	115	108	89
Instance #8	99	149	189	119	98
Instance #9	90	105	175	109	63
Instance #10	86	123	129	93	54
Instance #11	75	94	86	84	49
Instance #12	62	86	75	79	36

3.3 Intimation and Mediation

Notification alerts via GSM messaging are triggered when the sensory load reaches a critical level, determined by a multifaceted assessment involving heart rate, gas concentration, ambient noise, sweat levels, and accelerometer readings. Simultaneously, soothing music is initiated as part of the intervention strategy (Fig. 4).

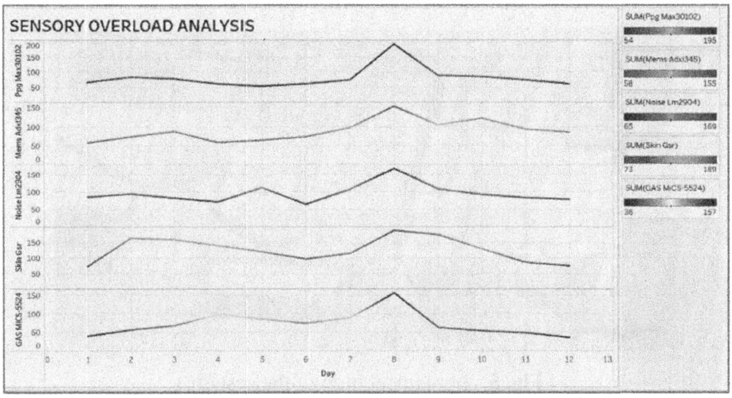

Fig. 4. Analysis of Sensory Overload

The various analysis can be seen through analysis to mark the exceed values of threshold, to trigger the event of alert to the care givers. The collected values from sensor with different ranges are made to be normalised using the decimal scaling method. A set of predefined statements is conveyed through the GSM messages, strategically designed to distract the individual and facilitate a calming effect, mitigating the potential for aggressive behaviors [9]. This comprehensive approach utilizes a combination of sensory data, communication technology, and music to proactively address heightened stress levels in individuals, especially children, with autism.

4 Results and Discussions

The usage of IOT can help us to get notification of the autistic person's data and various health conditions by continuous monitoring. This device exclusively provides a greater solution at uncontrollable situations through various ideas. They are provided by the regular capturing of values in the sensor and take curative measures. The gas sensor helps in the detection of autistic person's hyper-sensitivity to unwanted odour that can be intimated and buzzer will give alert sound.

Next to this when the autistic people behave arrogantly and aggressive in their unwanted situations, the accelerometer senses repetitive movement which can suddenly acknowledge care giver and the vibrator helps the autist for immediate distraction from their aggression, preceded by the soothing melodies can be played by the voice board to reduce their irritation. In addition to them, the frequent occurrence of epilepsy can be monitored by abnormal values observed by the combination of the heartbeat, accelerometer and tilt sensor values.

When they exceed the threshold value an instantaneously an iron rod is provided for the autistic person. All these monitored data are continuously collected in IOT and help to know the complete history of the autistic person. Thus, the impersonation of this past data can help us to analyse the patient's physical ailment systems and rehabilitation engineering (Fig. 5).

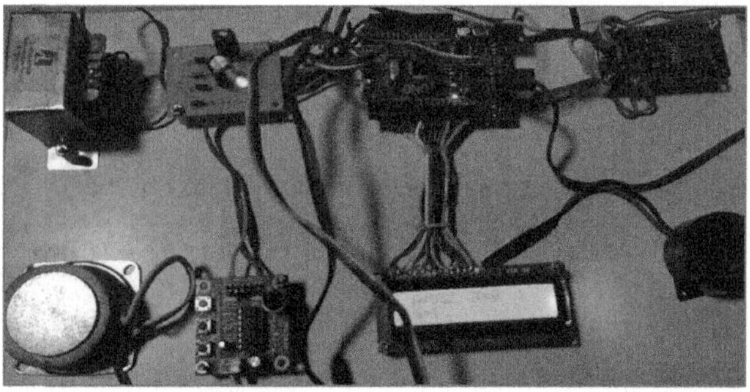

Fig. 5. Implementation of the system.

By using the various monitored data of the patient from the IoT, a complete data analysis can be made for the autistic patient as a linear graph representation with the X axis denoting the timeline of occurrences and Y axis is provided to show the frequency of contact with the high intensity of gas, high aggressiveness through accelerometer sensor, and the event of epilepsy through the heartbeat and the tilt sensor. This analysis helps the caregivers and doctors to completely know about the patient's medical condition.

5 Conclusion

The use of technology-assisted systems can offer a personalized and measurable rehabilitation platform. However, the current systems available in the market tend to emphasize connecting learning with a user's success, which may restrict the degree of personalization that can be achieved. By leveraging advanced technologies like IoT, sensors, and data analytics, we can create a powerful solution for monitoring individuals with autism. This approach offers crucial alerts to caregivers and guardians when unexpected events occur while they are away, as continuous monitoring is often not possible. This innovative idea provides a means for constructing a new device that can continuously survey individuals with autism, helping to ensure their safety and wellbeing.

Declarations.

Conflict of Interest. On behalf of all authors, the corresponding author states that there is no conflict of interest.

References

1. Khaledi, H., Aghaz, A., Mohammadi, A., et al.: The relationship between communication skills, sensory difficulties, and anxiety in children with autism spectrum disorder. Middle East Curr. Psychiatry **29**(1), 69 (2022). https://doi.org/10.1186/s43045-022-00236-7
2. National Institute of Mental Health. Autism SpectrumDisorder. https://www.nimh.nih.gov/health/topics/autism-spectrum-disorders-asd/index.shtml (2018). Accessed on 10 Dec 2020
3. Iqbal, A., et al.: Wearable internet-of-things platform for human activity recognition and health care. Int. J. Distrib. Sensor Netw. **16**(6), 155014772091156 (2020)
4. Koo, S.H., Gaul, K., Rivera, S., Pan, T., Fong, D.: Wearable technology design for autism spectrum disorders. Archiv. Des. Res. **31**(1), 37–55 (2018). https://doi.org/10.15187/adr.2018.02.31.1.37
5. Alwakeel, S.S., Alhalabi, .B, Aggoune, H., Alwakeel, M.: A machine learning based WSN system for autism activity recognition. In: Proceedings of the 2015 IEEE 14th International Conference on Machine Learning ICMLA 2015, Miami, FL, USA, 9–11 Dec 2015
6. Amiri, A., et al.: WearSense: detecting autism stereotypic behaviors through smartwatches. Healthcare **5**(1), 11 (2017). https://doi.org/10.3390/healthcare5010011
7. Abdel Hameed, M., Hassaballah, M., Hosney, M.E., Alqahtani, A.: An AI-enabled internet of things based autism care system for improving cognitive ability of children with autism spectrum disorders. Comput. Intell. Neurosci. (2022). https://doi.org/10.1155/2022/2247675
8. Samadi, S.A., Rashid, H.M.: Impacts of caregiving for individuals with autism in low-resource settings, a report from the kurdistan region of Iraq. J. Autism Dev. Disord. (2023). https://doi.org/10.1007/s10803-023-06165-6
9. Bradshaw, J., et al.: Predictors of caregiver strain for parents of children with autism spectrum disorder. J. Autism Dev. Disord. **51**(9), 3039–3049 (2021). https://doi.org/10.1007/s10803-020-04625-x
10. Wójcikowski, M., Pankiewicz, B.: Photoplethysmographic time-domain heart rate measurement algorithm for resource-constrained wearable devices and its implementation. Sensors **20**(6), 1783 (2020)

11. Yang, W., Li, M.H., Yu, J.J., et al.: The associations between accelerometer-measured physical activity levels and mental health in children and adolescents with intellectual disabilities during the COVID-19 pandemic. J. Autism Dev. Disord. **53**, 4809–4821 (2023). https://doi.org/10.1007/s10803-022-05777-8
12. Mannini, A., Rosenberger, M., Haskell, W.L., Sabatini, A.M., Intille, S.S.: Activity recognition in youth using single accelerometer placed at wrist or ankle. Med. Sci. Sports Exerc. **49**(4), 801–812 (2017). https://doi.org/10.1249/MSS.0000000000001144
13. Rizwan, A., Ali, N.A., et al.: Non-invasive hydration level estimation in human body using galvanic skin response. IEEE Sens. J. **20**(9), 4891–4900 (2020)
14. Guha, P.K., Santra, S., Gardner, J.W.: Integrated CMOS-Based Sensors for Gas and Odor Detection. In: Semiconductor Gas Sensors, pp. 465–487. Elsevier (2020). https://doi.org/10.1016/B978-0-08-102559-8.00014-8
15. Di Palma, S., Tonacci, A., Narzisi, A., Domenici, C., Pioggia, G., Muratori, F., et al.: Monitoring of autonomic response to sociocognitive tasks during treatment in children with autism spectrum disorders by wearable technologies: A feasibility study. Comput. Biol. Med. **85**, 143–152 (2017)
16. Norris, D.J.: Machine Learning with the Raspberry Pi-Experiments with Data and Computer Vision (2019). https://doi.org/10.1007/978-1-4842-5174-4
17. Ahmed, I.U., Hassan, N., Rashid, H.: Solar powered smart wearable health monitoring and tracking device based on GPS and GSM technology for children with autism (2017)
18. Rad, N.M, Bizzego, A., Kia, S.M, Jurman, G., Venuti, P., Furlanello, C.: Convolutional Neural Network for Stereotypical Motor Movement Detection in Autism (2015). arXiv:1511.01865

SDG 4 Quality Education

A New Innovative Initialization Strategy in Population-Based Evolutionary Optimization Algorithms

A. Baskar(✉)

Panimalar Institute of Technology, Poonamallee, Tamil Nadu 600123, India
a.baaskar@gmail.com

Abstract. Population-based optimization algorithms start with initializing a random population and iteratively move towards the optimal solution. Most of these algorithms use the expression, "Lower Bound + random*(Upper Bound – Lower Bound)" to initialize the random solutions. This paper analyses four initialization strategies; the widely used one, the strategy used by "Jellfish Optimizer" and two newly proposed strategies. Among the newly proposed strategies, the first one is a modified version of the strategy used in the "Jelly Fish Optimizer" and the other one is based on a larger initial population combined with the concept of "Opposite Number". Fifty-five benchmark functions including real-world industrial problems are considered in this work for the performance analyses. The obtained results demonstrate the better performance of the larger initial population-based strategy that uses the "Opposite Number" concept in both constrained and unconstrained benchmark instances. For fair analysis, the number of function evaluations and population size are kept the same.

Keywords: Initialization · Optimization · Benchmarks · Metaheuristics · Opposite Number · Industry · Innovation & Infrastructure

1 Introduction

Optimization sometimes may also be referred to by researchers as "mathematical programming" is a collection of "mathematical principles and methods" used for solving numerical problems in different disciplines including business, economics, engineering and science. Mathematical optimization selects the best one from a set of possible options based on a specific criterion. Engineering Optimization, a sub-set of optimization, is considered a key sphere of Operations Research that finds wide applications in real-world problems. Engineering optimization essentially uses suitable optimization techniques to achieve the required design goals.

Optimization problems may be categorized into several classes:

- Unconstrained or Constrained
- Single-Objective or Multi-Objective

Published by Springer Nature Switzerland AG 2025
A. Chandrabose et al. (Eds.): ICCCSP 2024, IFIP AICT 723, pp. 169–185, 2025.
https://doi.org/10.1007/978-3-031-73617-9_14

- Continuous or Discrete
- Local or Global
- Deterministic or Stochastic

For solving optimization problems, researchers have proposed several algorithms over the past decades that are available for the research community. Optimization algorithms are broadly classified into deterministic and stochastic algorithms (Yang, 2010a). Linear, non-linear programming and gradient-based algorithms fall under the deterministic category whereas, heuristic algorithms as well as other related metaheuristics are part of stochastic algorithms. Population-based algorithms are an important subset of metaheuristics and are popular nowadays.

Modelling and analysis are the two key elements of any optimization process. Modelling involves converting a problem into a mathematical expression with or without constraints as applicable. This is generally referred to as the "Objective Function". The analysis using a suitable algorithm is responsible for evaluating the best possible alternative under the specified conditions.

Metaheuristic algorithms are capable of yielding results, in many cases, with acceptable accuracy levels in a reasonable period. Several such algorithms mimic natural processes; may be a physical system, chemical process or biological activity (Gandomi et al., 2013). This feature may be one of the several factors for the success as well as the growing popularity of metaheuristics and hence, their applications increase in all areas of science and engineering.

Population-based stochastic algorithms fall under metaheuristics and have been widely studied by researchers in recent times. Genetic Algorithm (GA) (Holland, 1992) invented using the principle of natural selection of genetics, further development of GA, the Differential Evolution (Storn and Price, 1997) algorithm, Ant Colony Optimization (ACO), an algorithm that imitates the foraging conduct of ant colonies (Dorigo, 1992), Particle swarm optimization (PSO) algorithm that is simulated by the behaviour of swarms (Kennedy and Eberhart, 1995), music-inspired Harmony search (HS) algorithm (Geem et al. 2001) are some of the better performing algorithm of earlier days.

Karaboga's (2005) artificial bee colony (ABC) algorithm, firefly algorithm (FA) developed based on the flashing patterns of (Yang, 2009), Cuckoo Search (CS) algorithm originated from the "brood parasitism" of specific cuckoo species (Yang and Deb, 2009), Bat algorithm (BA) inspired by the concept of echoing of micro bats (Yang, 2010b), Teaching–learning-based optimization (TLBO) that works on the influence of a teacher on students (Rao et al., 2011), Grey wolf optimizer (GWO) motivated by the hunting nature of grey wolves (Mirjalili et al., 2014), humpback whales inspired Whale Optimization Algorithm (WOA) (Mirjalili and Lewis, 2016), Arithmetic optimization Algorithm (AOA) that utilizes the arithmetic operators used in mathematics (Abualigah et al., 2021), Social Network Search (SNS) algorithm (Bayzidi et. al., 2021) that models the decision moods, including imitation, conversation, disputation, and innovation, of social network users, the trigonometric algorithms, Sine(B), Sine(AB) and Cosine(AB) (Baskar, 2022a, 2022b) and the four-point direction search algorithms (Baskar and Xavior, 2021, 2023) are a few population-based algorithms proposed in the past two decades.

For effective simulation of any metaheuristic algorithm, intensification (exploitation) and diversification (exploration) are the two most critical features (Gandomi and Alavi 2012). The exploitation phase explores the current best locations to improve the solutions whereas new search spaces are ensured by the exploration phase. Proper balancing between these two essentials is required for better performance of any algorithm.

According to one of the "No Free Lunch Theorems" (Wolpert and Macready, 1997), it is impossible to have a single optimization algorithm that is capable of handling all types of optimization problems and yield better results. This makes a space for every algorithm in the optimization domain.

This paper proposes two new initialization strategies that could be used in a population-based metaheuristic algorithm and analyses the same along with two other existing strategies. Fifty-five single objective benchmark instances which include unconstrained and constrained functions are used for the analyses.

2 New Initialization Strategies

A general expression for an optimization problem could be:

$$\boldsymbol{Minimize}, \boldsymbol{f}_i(\boldsymbol{x}); \boldsymbol{x} \in \mathbb{R}^n, \boldsymbol{i} = \mathbf{1} \; \boldsymbol{to} \; \boldsymbol{M} \quad (1)$$

M = Number of objectives, n = Number of dimensions.

Subject to,

$\boldsymbol{h_j = 0, j = 1 \; to \; J}$ (Equality Constraints).

$\boldsymbol{g_k \leq 0, k = 1 \; to \; K}$ (Inequality Constraints).

A maximization problem can be tackled by negating the objective function.

The important steps in a population-based algorithm applied for solving any optimization problems essentially include; fixing the user-defined parameters, initialization of the approximate solutions, improving the approximate solutions through a set of well-designed strategies, bounding the solutions if required and reporting the best cost and solution. The user-defined parameters include the population size, number of iterations, tuning parameters if any and other parameters required to increase the efficiency of a particular algorithm.

In most of the metaheuristic algorithms, for generating initial approximate solutions (initialization) the expression used is,

$$\boldsymbol{Initial\ Approximate\ Solutions} = \boldsymbol{LB} + \boldsymbol{R} * (\boldsymbol{UB} - \boldsymbol{LB}). \quad (2)$$

"***R***" is the "random" function used to generate uniformly distributed random numbers between [0, 1], LB refers to the lower bound and, UB the upper bound.

In addition, other expressions also could generate random numbers between 0 and 1 few of which are presented in Table 1 from 2 to 5.

Jelly Fish Optimizer (Chou and Truong, 2021) uses a different initialization strategy that also uses the "random" function but, for generating the first random approximate solution only. That is, if the population size is 10, the first population will be generated using the "random" function, the second population will be computed from this first population, the third one from the second solution and so on.

Table 1. Different Possible Expressions for Generating Random Numbers from 0 to 1

S. No	Expression, R	Result Range
1	random	0 to 1
2	Sin(random*pi/2)	0 to 1
3	Sin(random*pi)	0 to 1 to 0
4	Cos(random*pi/2)	1 to 0
5	Cos(random*pi) if random <= 0.5; Cos(pi + random*pi) otherwise	1 to 0 to 1

In this work, four initialization strategies are analysed all of them use the "random" function in some way. The "random" function generates an array(s) of uniformly distributed random numbers in the span [0, 1]. Other expressions presented in Table 1 are not considered in this paper.

The four strategies are implanted in four algorithms and named Algorithm 1, Algorithm 2, Algorithm 3 and Algorithm 4. Only the initialization strategy is different in each algorithm and all other things remain the same. The strategies are discussed below:

Algorithm 1 (widely used): The initialization process is the usual one that is being used by most of the population-based metaheuristic algorithms.

$$\boldsymbol{Initial\ Population} = \boldsymbol{LB} + \boldsymbol{random} * (\boldsymbol{UB} - \boldsymbol{LB}). \tag{3}$$

The computational complexity of initialization process equals O(N*D), where N is the population size and, D is the dimension of the problem.

Algorithm 2: This is the strategy that is used in the "Jellyfish Optimization algorithm" and, is different from the regular strategy. This has the following steps:

- Generation of a row of random numbers, xT = random(1, dimension).
- Generation of a set of random numbers equal to (population size*dimensions),

```
For i=1 to (population size-1)
   xT(i+1) = 4*xT(i).*(1-xT(i))
End
• Initial population,
For i=1 to (population size)
   X(i) = Lower Bound + xT(i).*(Upper Bound – Lower Bound).
End
```

The computational complexity of initialization remains the same and equals O(N*D).

Algorithm 3 (new): This is a slightly modified version of Alg.2.

- Generation of a row of numbers [0, 1],

```
del=0.45/dimension
For j=1 to dimension
 x0(1,j)=del*j;
End
```

- Generation of a set of random numbers equal to (population size*dimensions),

```
For j=1 to dimension
 xT(1,j)=x0(1,j)*(1-x0(1,j));
End
For i=1 to (population size-1)
  xT(i+1)=4*xT(i).*(1-xT(i))
End
```

- Initial population,

```
For i=1 to (population size)
 X(i) = Lower Bound + xT(i).*(Upper Bound – Lower Bound).*(0.9+(-
1+2*rand).*0.1)
End
```

The computational complexity of initialization remains the same and equals O(N*D).

Algorithm 4 (new): This uses a larger initial population and the concept of "Opposite Numbers".

The "Opposite Number" concept was first proposed by Tizhoosh (2005) and is applied as a part of the new strategy used in Algorithm 4.

The initial larger population, XT is taken as (7*population size).

Since the number of function evaluations (FEs) will be 6 times more than that of the usual FEs in the initialization stage, the number of iterations is reduced accordingly to keep the FEs the same in line with the other 3 algorithms.

The cost is evaluated for this larger initial population.

The "Opposite Populations (OP)" are calculated using the expression, OP = Lower Bound + (Upper Bound – XT).

The "Opposite Cost" is evaluated for this set of "Opposite Population".

If the "Opposite Cost" is better than the original cost, the corresponding "Opposite Population" is selected else, the original population itself is retained.

From this temporary initial population (70 in this case) that contains better "Opposite Population Members" also, the initial population (10 in this case) is selected that has the better costs. The computational complexity of initialization process is different for this strategy and equals O(C*N*D), where C*N is the initial population size and, D is the dimension of the problem. "C" is an integer which can be taken as 3, 5, 7 or any suitable value.

Apart from the initialization stage, all four algorithms are the same in all other features including:

Two-phase algorithms,
Two FEs per iteration,
Population Size: 10,
Number of Iterations: 1000 for Alg.1 to Alg.3 and 997 for Alg.4 (to keep the FEs same),
Number of Trials: 300,
Updating Expression in Phase I: ***newX = X + (-1+2*rand)*X,*** (4)
Greedy selection and updation,
Updating Expression in Phase II:
newX = X + (-1+2*rand)* (Mean Solution-Best Solution), (5)
Greedy Selection and updation.
Four counters are introduced into the algorithms; Count1, Count2, Count3 and Count4, the purpose of which are described below:
Count1: Records the number of better "Opposition Costs" in the initialization stage (applicable only for Algorithm 4).
Count2: Counts the "Best Cost" updates during the initialization stage of all the algorithms.
Count3: Keeps track of the "Best Cost" updates in Phase-I of all the algorithms.
Count4: Tracks the number of "Best Cost" updates in Phase II of all the algorithms.

The objective of this specific work is to analyse and compare the performance of the initialization strategies keeping other things the same. The expressions used in Phase-I (line 23 in Fig. 1) and Phase-II (lines 29 to 31 in Fig. 1) for improving the solution are the same for all algorithms and they are devised by the author for the analyses of the initialization strategies and not a part of any other algorithm from the published literature. Comparing the algorithms implicitly compares the initialization strategies only.

3 Benchmark Used

The mathematical models and their optimal values of several benchmarks including many real-world engineering problems are available nowadays. They are widely used by researchers for validation of their results and comparison with other popular algorithms. In this work, for analyzing the performance of different initialization strategies, 55 such single objective benchmark functions are used. They include 15 constrained real-world engineering problems, 5 constrained special functions, 15 unconstrained functions with zero optimal, 10 unconstrained functions with negative optimal values and 10 instances of CEC2019.

```
% Random Initialization
"Best Cost"
"Best Solution"
For i = 1 to (C*N)                                  % C = an Integer; N = Population Size
    Random Solution: X(i) = LB + rand.*(UB - LB)
    Opposition Solution: X1(i) = LB + (UB - X(i))
    Corresponding Costs: Cost(X(i)) and Cost(X1(i))
    If Cost(X1(i)) < Cost(X(i))              % Greedy Selection
        Cost(X(i)) = Cost(X1(i))
        X(i) = X1(i)
        If Cost(X(i)) < Best Cost         % Updation
            Best Cost = Cost(X(i))
            Best Solution = X(i)
        End If
    End If
End For
Sorting the Cost
Selecting the best "N" Solutions
% Iteration Loop
While (Current_Iteration < (Maximum_Iteration - (C-1)/2)) do    % while loop starts
% Phase-I
For i = 1 to N
    New Solution: newX(i) = X(i) + (-1+2*rand).*X(i)
    New Cost: Cost(newX(i))
    Greedy Selection and Updation
End For
% Phase-II
For i = 1 to N
    Mean Solution = mean(newX)
    Step = (Mean Solution - Best Solution)
    Improved Solution: newX1(i) = newX(i) + (-1+2*rand).*Step
    Improved Cost: Cost(newX1(i))
    Greedy Selection and Updation
End For
  Memorizing the "Best Cost"; "Best Solution"
  Current_Iteration = (Current_Iteration + 1)
End While                                                   % while loop ends
Returning the "Best Cost"; "Best Solution"
```

Fig. 1. Pseudo code of Algorithm 4

UN's Sustainable Development Goal No. 9 talks about "building resilient infrastructure, promoting sustainable industrialization and fostering innovation". Engineering optimization helps in reducing resources, ensures economic development and improves comfort in the work place resulting in sustainable industrialization. Solving real-world problems which involve several constraints is being given more preference nowadays. Hence, the proposed new initialization strategy is applied to a few constrained real-world engineering problems, constrained special functions and the improvements analyzed.

The constrained engineering problems considered here are 15 in number with the number of variables from 2 to 11 and constraints from nil to 11. They reflect many real-world engineering problems the details of which are available in the paper of Bayzidi et al. (2021) except the Himmelblau's Function (Himmelblau, 1972), Tension/Compression Spring (Discrete) (Deb and Goyal, 1997) and Cantilever Stepped Beam (Continuous) [MathWorks Help Center] problems.

The unconstrained benchmarks, corresponding known optimal values and MATLAB codes are extracted from Simon Fraser University's official portal and, Al-Roomi Web Portal.

Another important benchmark used in this paper is the "100 digit challenge of CEC2019", the details are available in Price et al., 2018. This is a 10 problems dataset the optimal value of which is 1 for each instance. The number of variables is 9, 16 and 18 respectively for the first three problems and 10 for the remaining. The bounds of problem number 2 are widely separated [−16384, 16384] whereas, the third problem has the narrowest search span [−4, 4].

The search space, optimal values, dimensions and the number of constraints are presented in the Results and Discussions section.

4 Results and Discussion

Codes are written in MATLAB for these new strategies and run on an i5 desktop PC with 4 GB RAM.

The computing environment is maintained as the same and uniformly a population size of 10 is taken. 300 trials are conducted in each case to compute the statistical metrics; "minimum", "mean" and "standard deviation". The maximum number of iterations is 1000 for Algorithm 1, Algorithm 2 and Algorithm 3 whereas for Algorithm 4 it is 1000 − (C − 1)/2 to have the same function evaluations (FEs). Total computation time is also computed and recorded for each function and algorithm.

In Algorithm 4, "C" is taken as 7 which means, during the initialization process, 7 times the population size is generated. That is, the initial temporary population size is 70 instead of 10 taken in the other 3 algorithms. Hence, Algorithm 4 will be run for 1000 − (7–1)/2 = 997 iterations only whereas the other 3 algorithms are run for 1000 iterations.

Total number of FEs = 10 + 1000*(2*10) = 20010 for Algorithm 1, Algorithm 2 and Algorithm 3 and, Total number of FEs = 70 + 997 * (2 * 10) = 20010 for Algorithm 4 making it at par with the other three algorithms. The best results are obtained for the statistical metrics "minimum", "mean" and "standard deviation" for the respective initialization strategy for each dataset. The important results are presented for all the datasets including the important real-world engineering problems in Tables 2, 3, 4 and 5 and CEC2019 in Table 6.

Table 2. Unconstrained Benchmark Functions with Zero Optimal, Best Results

S. No	Function	Results (Algorithm)	Search Range	No. of Variables
1	Ackley	4.4409e−16 [ALL]	[−32 32]	30
2	Brown	1.4146e−128 [A4]	[−1 4]	30
3	Cigar	1.1343e−118 [A4]	[−100 100]	30
4	Csendes	1.8511e−271 [A2]	[−1 1]	30
5	Damavandi	0.0007287 [A1]	[0 14]	2
6	DeVilliers Glasser2	2.3613 [A4]	[0 60]	5
7	Dixon Price	0.6667 [A1]	[−10 10]	30
8	Levy	0.1547 [A1]	[−10 10]	30
9	Rastrigin	0 [ALL]	[−5.12 5.12]	30
10	Rosenbrock	25.5145 [A2]	[−30 30]	30
11	Rotated Hyper Ellipsoid	1.8511e−124 [A2]	[−65.536 65.536]	30
12	Salomon	2.6515e−22 [A1]	−100 to 100	30
13	Sum Squares	2.5020e−130 [A1]	[−10 10]	30
14	Whitley	5931.8087 [A2]	−10.24 to 10.24	30
15	Zakarov	4.7202e−25 [A4]	[−5 10]	30

Table 3. Unconstrained Benchmark Functions with Negative Optimal Values, Best Results

S. No.	Problem	Results (Algorithm)	Optimal	Search Space	Variables
1	Dolan	−529.8260 [A4]	−529.8714	[−100 100]	5
2	Easom	−1.0 [ALL]	−1	[−100 100]	2
3	Egg Holder	−959.6407 [A2]	−959.6407	[−512 512]	2
4	Hartmann 6	−3.0424 [A1]	−3.0425	[0 1]	6
5	Michalewicz 2	−1.8013 [A4]	−1.8013	[0 pi]	2
6	Shekel	−10.5364 [A3]	−10.5364	[0 10]	4
7	Shubert	−186.7308 [A1]	−186.7309	[−5.12 5.12]	2
8	Trid 30	−577.4190 [A2]	−4930	[−900 900]	30
9	Vincent	−19.8388 [A3]	−30	[0.25 10]	30
10	Xin She Yang 3	2.3551e−64 [A1]	−1	[−20 20]	30

Table 7 shows the summary of the simulations carried out to evaluate the performance of all 4 initialization strategies. Both unconstrained and constrained functions are grouped into 2 categories each and CEC2019 separately. The "minimum", "mean" and

Table 4. Constrained Engineering Problems, Best Results

S. No	Problem	Constraints	Results (Algorithm)	Optimal Value
1	Cantilever Beam	1	1.3399674 [A3]	1.3399576
2	Car Side Impact	10	22.8601295 [A2]	22.8429695
3	Corrugated Bulkhead	6	6.8430989 [A3]	6.8429580
4	Gear Train	0	2.7008571e−12 [ALL]	2.7008571e−12
5	Himmelblau's Function	6	−30665.5 [A1]	− 30665.5
6	I-shaped Beam	2	0.0130741 [A2]	0.0130741
7	Pressure Vessel	4	6063.5667598 [A3]	6059.7143350
8	Reinforced Concrete Beam	2	359.2080 [ALL]	359.2080
9	Speed Reducer	11	2994.432999 [A2]	2994.424466
10	Tension/Compression Spring (Continuous)	4	0.01267555 [A3]	0.01266051
11	Tension/Compression Spring (Discrete)	8	2.6585607 [A4]	2.6585591
12	Cantilever Stepped Beam (Continuous)	11	63621.6 [A4]	63408.9
13	Three-Bar Truss	3	263.8958589 [A3]	263.8958434
14	Tubular Column	6	26.4863705 [A1]	26.4863615
15	Welded Beam	7	1.7260293 [A1]	1.7248523

Table 5. Constrained Special Functions, Best Results

S. No.	Problem	Constraints	Results (Algorithm)	Optimal
1	Function, D1 (Deb, 2000)	2	13.59084 [A3]	13:59085
2	Function, D4 (Deb, 2000)	6	7784.411303 [A4]	7049:330923
3	Function, D5 (Deb, 2000)	4	680.6652528 [A4]	680.6300573
4	Function, D8 (Deb, 2000)	8	25.878610 [A4]	24.306209
5	Function, P8 (Mehta and Dasgupta, 2012)	2	−6961.79118 [A3]	− 6961.81388

"standard deviation" metrics are used for comparison purposes. A total of 55 functions are used and hence the total equals 55 * 3 = 165 evaluation cases. The performance is similar in both unconstrained and constrained functions wherein Algorithm 4 is the better performer followed by Algorithm 1, Algorithm 2 and finally Algorithm 3. For the CEC2019 test bed, the case is slightly different. Algorithm 4 is the better performer with

Table 6. 100 Digit Challenge: Basic Test Functions (CEC2019) [Optimal Value: 1]

S. No.	Function	Minimum (Algorithm)	Mean (Algorithm)
1	Storn's Chebyshev Polynomial Fitting Problem	41744.8647 [A1]	6247187.3141 [A3]
2	Inverse Hilbert Matrix Problem	18.3429[A2]	18.3429[A4]
3	Lennard-Jones Minimum Energy Cluster	13.7024 [A1]	13.7024 [A1]
4	Rastrigin's Function	21.3497 [A4]	149.8591 [A4]
5	Griewangk's Function	2.1828 [A2]	2.6363 [A3]
6	Weierstrass Function	8.5964 [A4]	11.7777 [A3]
7	Modified Schwefel's Function	148.4252 [A4]	676.8304 [A3]
8	Expanded Schaffer's F6 Function	3.9974 [A1]	5.6853 [A4]
9	Happy Cat Function	3.3813 [A2]	3.8572 [A4]
10	Ackley Function	16.0390 [A2]	21.2898 [A4]

12 cases followed by Algorithm 3 which reports better results in 7 instances followed by Algorithm 2 (6 cases) and Algorithm 1 (5 cases).

The new initialization strategy applied in Algorithm 4 outperforms others in 71 instances overall, performing well in both constrained and unconstrained functions followed by 41 of Algorithm 1. The initialization strategy used in "Jellyfish Optimizer" comes third with 39.

When the "minimum" is considered, both Alg4 and Algorithm 1 perform well in 19 problems each followed by Algorithm 2 and Algorithm 3 with 18 and 14 cases respectively. However, for the important "mean" metric, Algorithm 4 outperforms the other three strategies performing well in 26 cases followed by Algorithm 1 in 12 cases. Here, Algorithm 3 performs better than Algorithm 2 with 11 cases against 9 of Algorithm 2. The performance of Algorithm 4 is better for "standard deviation" also with 26 cases followed by Algorithm 2 in 12 cases. Both Algorithm 1 and Algorithm 3 report better SD in 10 problems each.

Count1 is reported by Algorithm 4 for all 20 constrained, 18 out of 25 unconstrained problems (Table 8) and all 10 CEC2019 problems. However, in the case of Xin She Yang3, Acklay, Cigar, Rastrigin, Sum Squares, Damavandi and Salomon unconstrained functions; it does not report improved costs due to the nature of the functions.

Table 7. Summary of Simulations

Functions	Metric	Algorithm 1	Algorithm 2	Algorithm 3	Algorithm 4
Unconstrained					
Zero Optimal	Min	**7**	6	2	6
	Mean	5	**6**	2	5
	SD	3	4	3	**8**
Negative Optimal	Min	**4**	3	3	3
	Mean	2	0	2	**6**
	SD	2	1	3	**4**
	Best in	23	20	15	**32**
	Time Taken, s	814.8	804.0	809.0	808.3
Constrained					
Real-World	Min	5	5	**7**	4
	Mean	3	2	2	**8**
	SD	3	4	1	**7**
Special Functions	Min	0	0	2	**3**
	Mean	1	1	1	**2**
	SD	1	1	0	**3**
	Best in	13	13	13	**27**
	Time Taken, s	891.9	879.1	882.0	881.6
CEC2019	Min	3	**4**	0	3
	Mean	1	0	4	**5**
	SD	1	2	3	**4**
	Best in	5	6	7	**12**
	Time Taken, s	1503.6	1491.5	1537.8	1523.1
Overall	**Best in**	41	39	35	**71**

Count4 > Count3 in all 20 constrained functions and nine functions with negative optimal except the Shubert function. Whereas for the functions with zero optimal, Count3 > Count4 in 12 out of 15 functions and, for the Dixon Price, Rosenbrock and Damavandi functions; Count4 > Count3. (Note: In the case of Trid30 function with negative optimal value and Dixon Price function with zero optimal value, Count3 > Count4 for Algorithm 3 whereas, Count4 > Count3 for the other 3 algorithms).

For the CEC2019 dataset; Count3 > Count4 in 5 cases and in the remaining 5 cases, Count4 > Count3. The performance of the new strategy in different datasets and "Best Updations" in Phase-I and Phase-II are presented in Figs. 2, 3, 4, and 5 graphically.

From Table 8, the following inferences could be made for the considered benchmarks,

Table 8. Summary of Best Updations

Functions	Count1 reported by Algorithm 4 in	Count3 > Count4 in	Count4 > Count3 in
Unconstrained			
Zero Optimal	9 Functions	12 Functions	3 Functions
Negative Optimal	9 Functions	1 Functions	9 Functions
Constrained			
Real-World	15 Functions	0	15 Functions
Special	5 Functions	0	5 Functions
CEC2019	10 Functions	5 Functions	5 Functions
Total: 55	**48 Functions**	**18 Functions**	**37 Functions**

- The larger initial population combined with the "Opposite Number" concept does well in all constrained problems, most of the unconstrained functions with negative optimal (9 out of 10) and in all 10 problems of CEC2019. Its performance is moderate in the case of unconstrained functions with zero optimal (only 9 out of 15 problems).
- The "Best Cost" updation is good in Phase II for all constrained problems and for the functions with negative optimal (9 out of 10 functions). The "Best Cost" updation is below average in Phase II in the case of functions with zero optimal values (only in 3 problems out of 15).
- The "Best Cost" updation is good in Phase I only for unconstrained functions with zero optimal. That is, in 12 of the 15 cases, the "Best Cost" updation is better than Phase II. In other cases, the updation is below average.
- •For the CEC2019 dataset, the "Best Cost" updates are equal in both Phase I and Phase II.

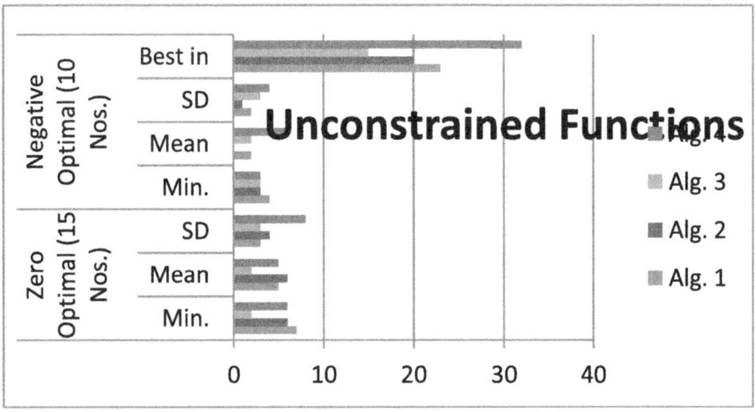

Fig. 2. Performance in Unconstrained Functions

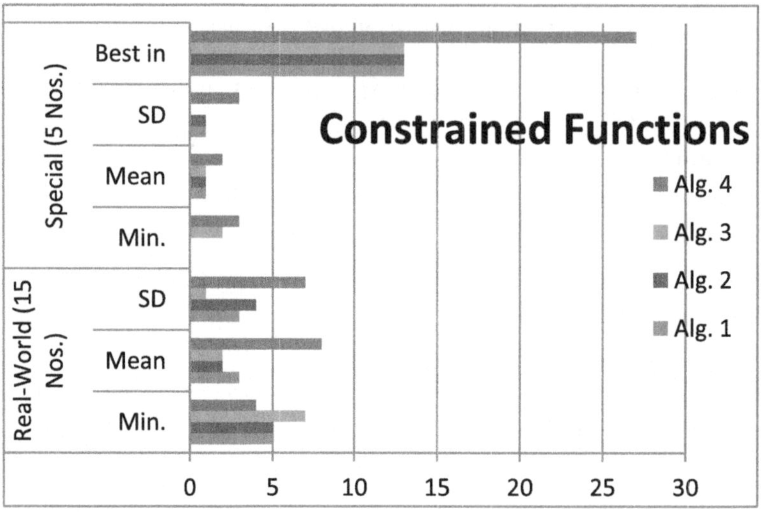

Fig. 3. Performance in Constrained Functions

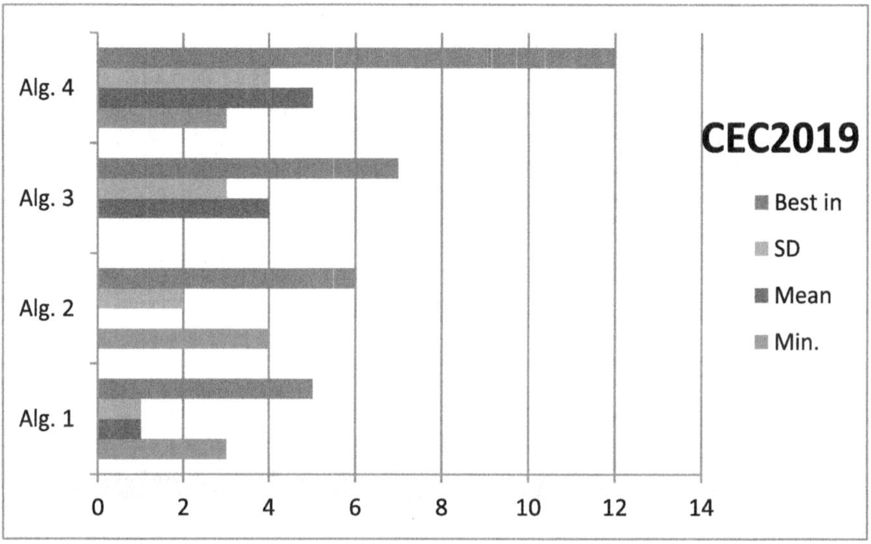

Fig. 4. Performance in CEC2019 Dataset

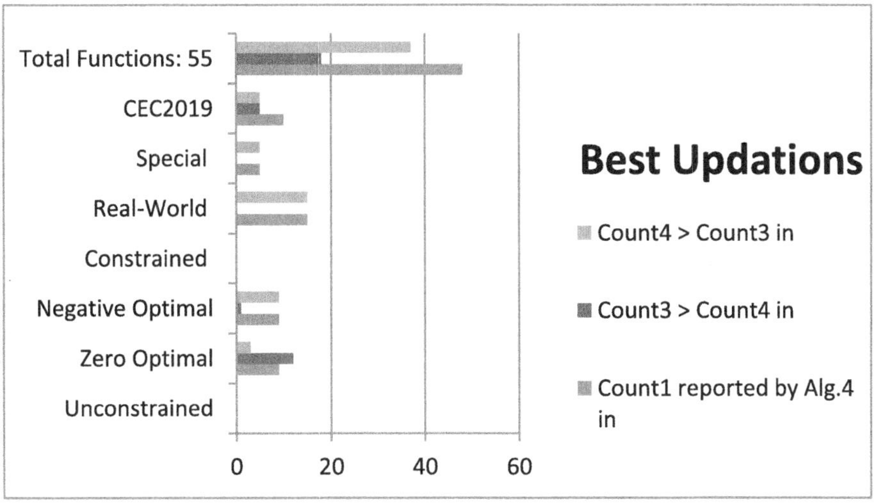

Fig. 5. Best Updations in Phase-I and Phase-II

5 Conclusions and Future Work

Initialization is the first and most important step in any population-based evolutionary algorithm for dealing with any optimization problem. The initial population is generated using the Lower Bound + random*(Upper Bound – Lower Bound) expression by most of the algorithms available in the literature. One different strategy is applied by the "Jelly Fish Optimizer" which also uses one "random" function for generating the first population and the remaining are generated from the previous one. Two new strategies are proposed in this paper, one is a modified version of the strategy used in "Jellyfish Optimizer" and the other one is based on a larger initial population size and the concept of "Opposite Number". 55 popular benchmarks available in the literature, unconstrained and constrained, are coded in MATLAB and used for the simulation. The results show that the new strategy based on a larger initial population combined with the "Opposite Number" concept performs well in both unconstrained and constrained problems followed by the regular strategy. However, as the search space is narrowed down during the initialization process itself, a bit of randomness is lost. As a result, though the performance is good for the "mean" and "standard deviation" metrics, it is moderate when the "minimum" metric is considered. The strategy used by the "Jellyfish Optimizer" comes next. In all strategies, the "random" function is used in some way. Proposed future work includes analyzing more instances by applying other "random" number-generating methods.

References

Abualigah, L., Diabat, A., Mirjalili, S., Abd Elaziz, M., Gandomi, A.H.: The arithmetic optimization algorithm. Comput. Methods Appl. Mech. Eng. **376**, 113609 (2021)

Baskar, A.: Sine (B): a single randomized Population-based algorithm for solving optimization problems. Mater. Today: Proc. **62**, 4745–4751 (2022)

Baskar, A.: New simple trigonometric algorithms for solving optimization problems. J. Appl. Sci. Eng. **25**(6), 1257–1272 (2022)

Baskar, A., Anthony Xavior, M.: A four-point direction search heuristic algorithm applied to facility location on plane, sphere, and ellipsoid surfaces. J. Operat. Res. Soc. **73**(11), 2385–2394 (2021)

Baskar, A., Anthony Xavior, M.: A Simple Hybrid Local Search Algorithm for Solving Optimization Problems. In: Mercier-Laurent, E., Fernando, X., Chandrabose, A. (eds.) Computer, Communication, and Signal Processing. AI, Knowledge Engineering and IoT for Smart Systems: 7th IFIP TC 12 International Conference, ICCCSP 2023, Chennai, India, 4–6 Jan 2023, Revised Selected Papers, pp. 246–259. Springer Nature Switzerland, Cham (2023). https://doi.org/10.1007/978-3-031-39811-7_20

Bayzidi, H., Talatahari, S., Saraee, M., Lamarche, C.P.: Social network search for solving engineering optimization problems. Comput. Intell. Neurosci. **2021**, 1–32 (2021)

Chou, J.S., Truong, D.N.: A novel metaheuristic optimizer inspired by behavior of jellyfish in ocean. Appl. Math. Comput. **389**, 125535 (2021)

Deb, K.: An efficient constraint handling method for genetic algorithms. Comput. Methods Appl. Mech. Eng. **186**(2–4), 311–338 (2000)

Deb, K., Goyal, M.: Optimizing engineering designs using a combined genetic search. In: ICGA, pp. 521–528 (1997)

Dorigo, M.: Optimization, learning and natural algorithms. Ph. D. Thesis, Politecnico di Milano (1992)

Gandomi, A.H., Alavi, A.H.: Krill herd: a new bio-inspired optimization algorithm. Commun. Nonlinear Sci. Numer. Simul. **17**(12), 4831–4845 (2012)

Gandomi, A.H., Yang, X.S., Talatahari, S., Alavi, A.H.: Metaheuristic algorithms in modeling and optimization. Metaheuristic Appl. Struct. Infrastruct. **1**, 1–24 (2013)

Geem, Z.W., Kim, J.H., Loganathan, G.V.: A new heuristic optimization algorithm: harmony search. SIMULATION **76**(2), 60–68 (2001). https://doi.org/10.1177/003754970107600201

Himmelblau, D.M.: Applied Nonlinear Programming McGraw-Hill Book Company. New York (1972)

Holland, J.H.: Genetic algorithms. Sci. Am. **267**(1), 66–73 (1992)

Karaboga, D.: An idea based on honey bee swarm for numerical optimization, vol. 200, pp. 1–10. Technical report-tr06, Erciyes university, engineering faculty, computer engineering department (2005)

Kennedy, J., Eberhart, R.: Particle swarm optimization. In Proceedings of ICNN'95-International Conference on Neural Networks, vol. 4, pp. 1942–1948. IEEE (1995)

Mehta, V.K., Dasgupta, B.: A constrained optimization algorithm based on the simplex search method. Eng. Optim. **44**(5), 537–550 (2012)

Mirjalili, S., Lewis, A.: The whale optimization algorithm. Adv. Eng. Softw. **95**, 51–67 (2016)

Mirjalili, S., Mirjalili, S.M., Lewis, A.: Grey wolf optimizer. Adv. Eng. Softw. **69**, 46–61 (2014)

Price, K.V., Awad, N.H., Ali, M.Z., Suganthan, P.N.: The 100-digit challenge: Problem definitions and evaluation criteria for the 100-digit challenge special session and competition on single objective numerical optimization. Nanyang Technological University (2018)

Rao, R.V., Savsani, V.J., Vakharia, D.P.: Teaching–learning-based optimization: a novel method for constrained mechanical design optimization problems. Comput. Aided Des. **43**(3), 303–315 (2011)

Storn, R., Price, K.: Differential evolution–a simple and efficient heuristic for global optimization over continuous spaces. J. Global Optim. **11**, 341–359 (1997)

Tizhoosh, H.R.: Opposition-based learning: a new scheme for machine intelligence. In International conference on computational intelligence for modelling, control and automation and international conference on intelligent agents, web technologies and internet commerce (CIMCA-IAWTIC'06), vol. 1, pp. 695–701. IEEE (2005)

Wolpert, D.H., Macready, W.G.: No free lunch theorems for optimization. IEEE Trans. Evol. Comput. **1**(1), 67–82 (1997)

Yang, X.-S.: Firefly algorithms for multimodal optimization. In: Watanabe, O., Zeugmann, T. (eds.) Stochastic Algorithms: Foundations and Applications, pp. 169–178. Springer Berlin Heidelberg, Berlin, Heidelberg (2009). https://doi.org/10.1007/978-3-642-04944-6_14

Yang, X.S.: Engineering Optimization: An Introduction with Metaheuristic Applications. John Wiley & Sons (2010)

Yang, X.S.: A new metaheuristic bat-inspired algorithm. In Nature inspired cooperative strategies for optimization (NICSO 2010), pp. 65–74. Springer Berlin Heidelberg, Berlin, Heidelberg (2010b)

Yang, X.S., Deb, S.: Cuckoo search via Lévy flights. In: 2009 World congress on nature & biologically inspired computing (NaBIC), pp. 210–214. IEEE (2009)

https://www.al-roomi.org/benchmarks/unconstrained. Last accessed 12 Feb 2021

https://in.mathworks.com/help/gads/solving-a-mixed-integer-engineering-design-problem-using-the-genetic-algorithm.html. Last accessed 16 Jan 2021

https://www.sfu.ca/~ssurjano/optimization.html, last accessed 2 Nov 2021

AI-Enhanced Sign Language Interpreter

Vasanth Kumar CH[1](✉) and A. Fawziya[2]

[1] Department of EIE, SCOFT, Saveetha Engineering College, Chennai 602105, India
sreevasanthkumarchoda@gmail.com

[2] Department of AI and DS, Saveetha Engineering College, Chennai 602105, India

Abstract. Communication is a basic human right, yet people with hearing impairments often face great challenges when trying to interact with the world. This project addresses the communication-demanding situations confronted with the aid of individuals with listening impairments by proposing a complete answer for hand signal gesture detection and translation into text and speech. Leveraging present-day technologies such as MediaPipe, OpenCV, and neural networks, the gadget captures actual hand gestures via a webcam. The neural community is designed and skilled for strong key point detection, as it should identify and classify the hand symptoms. The integration of OpenCV enables seamless interplay with the webcam, ensuring efficient gesture recognition. Upon successful detection, the corresponding gestures are translated into each text and speech, presenting a dual-mode communication interface. The utilization of neural networks complements the gadget's ability to evolve to a wide variety of gestures, selling inclusivity for customers using distinct sign languages. Upon successful detection, the system translates the identified gestures into both textual and spoken output, offering a dual mode communication interface. The utilization of neural networks enhances the system's adaptability to a diverse range of gestures, promoting inclusivity for users employing various sign languages. Notably, the proposed solution demonstrates an impressive accuracy of 97%, underscoring its efficacy in accurately interpreting and translating hand signals. The proposed solution now not simplest serves as a useful resource for the deaf and listening-to-impaired network but also establishes a basis for destiny advancements in assistive technology. This project contributes to the intersection of computer vision, system mastering, and accessibility, fostering innovation in the pursuit of an inclusive digital society.

Keywords: Media Pipe · OpenCV · Neural Networks · Sign Language

Abbreviations

SLR	Sign Language Recognition
ASL	American Sign Language
HMM	Hidden Markov Model
CNN	Convolutional Neural Network
3D-CNN	3-Dimensional Convolutional Neural Network
BSL	British Sign Language

Published by Springer Nature Switzerland AG 2025
A. Chandrabose et al. (Eds.): ICCCSP 2024, IFIP AICT 723, pp. 186–198, 2025.
https://doi.org/10.1007/978-3-031-73617-9_15

GPU	Graphics Processing Unit
RAM	Random Access Memory
SSD	Solid State Drive
IDE	Integrated Development Environment
UI	User Interface
HCI	Human-Computer Inter-action
FPS	Frames Per Second
IoT	Internet of Things
SDK	Software Development Kit
GUI	Graphical User Interface
ML	Machine Learning
DL	Deep Learning
CV	Computer Vision

1 Introduction

In a world that increasingly relies on digital communication, individuals with hearing loss face unique challenges in expressing themselves and communicating with others. Addressing this gap, our work calls for the power of state-of-the-art technology will be used to empower Deaf and Deaf communities. Using the combination of Media Pipe, OpenCV, and neural networks, we provide a comprehensive solution for real-time handwriting and handwriting recognition. The project aims to bridge the communication divide not only by accurately recognizing various gestures through the installation of a webcam but also by translating these gestures into written language. This combination of advanced technologies, specially designed for complex key point detection, ensures a reliable and efficient system. OpenCV provides seamless integration of the application with web browsers, enabling better gesture recognition in different environments. A carefully trained neural network for gesture segmentation lays the foundation for a multifunctional system capable of understanding and interpreting a wide variety of sign language input. In addition to the immediate goal of supporting the deaf and hard-of-hearing community, this project aligns with the broader vision of creating an inclusive digital society through computer vision, device learning and exploring the means of communication so our program contributes to the ongoing development of assistive technology. This introduction sets the stage for an in-depth analysis of our processes, applications, and potential social impacts of our innovative solutions.

A comprehensive survey on recognizing sign language provides an in-depth examination of the challenges and methodologies associated with Sign Language Recognition (SLR) [11]. The primary focus of SLR is to automatically interpret the gestures and expressions employed by users of sign language. Ethical and social concerns related to SLR are also highlighted. The paper suggests future directions for improvement, such as the development of multimodal and multi-lingual SLR systems, integration of natural language processing and speech synthesis techniques, enhancement of user feedback mechanisms, utilization of deep learning and transfer learning approaches, and addressing ethical and social aspects of SLR. In the exploration of recognizing real-time American Sign Language (ASL) from video, a system leveraging Hidden Markov Models

(HMMs) and video images is introduced [22]. The focus is on instantaneous recognition of ASL through the application of HMMs to video data. The paper underscores the structured nature of sign language and the efficacy of HMMs in deciphering intricate hand gestures. The document provides an overview of previous work in sign language recognition and the application of HMMs in gesture recognition. The scalability and feasibility of employing HMMs for sign language recognition are highlighted, emphasizing the system's potential. In essence, the paper presents a promising approach to ASL recognition using HMMs and points to avenues for further research and development in this domain. In the exploration of recognizing automatic hand gesture, the system introduced a 3D CNN model, showcasing efficiency through deep learning methodologies [5].

To address communication challenges between individuals with hearing abilities and those who are hearing-impaired, the proposed system distinguishes itself through its absence of hardware requirements. Leveraging a motion segmentation algorithm, this study explores the capture and utilization of 2D motion trajectories to recognize hand gestures within image sequences [18]. The algorithm employs a multiscale approach, identifying regions characterized by uniform motion, establishing matches across frames, computing affine transformations, and ultimately segmenting the motion field into areas displaying consistent motion. To improves the recognition process; the acquired motion patterns undergo learning via a time-delay neural network. This approach is practically demonstrated within the domain of hand gesture recognition, with a specific emphasis on identifying different hand gestures in American Sign Language. The experimental outcomes highlight the achieved accuracy in recognizing hand gestures through the integration of motion trajectories. Deep Gesture Recognition introduces a groundbreaking methodology for achieving precise recognition of static hand gestures through the utilization of convolutional neural networks (CNN). The system is designed to enhance the accuracy and efficiency of recognizing static hand gestures, contributing to advancements in the field of gesture recognition technology [8]. In response to the challenges posed by cluttered back-grounds in existing methods, the paper introduces a CNN-based framework that obviates the need for explicit feature extraction or foreground segmentation. Through rigorous experimentation on various datasets, the proposed approach demonstrates superior performance. The study delves into additional strategies, including data augmentation, activation functions, and dropout techniques, employed to further enhance the CNN's efficacy. Emphasizing its versatility, the paper concludes by underlining the proposed framework's effectiveness in recognizing static hand gestures across diverse backgrounds, with anticipated applications in sign language recognition and human computer interaction.

2 Problem Statement

The Deaf and hard-of-hearing communities encounter formidable obstacles in a world increasingly dominated by spoken language and digital communication. Although traditional sign language methods are proven, they grapple with limitations concerning comprehensibility and broad interpretation. This project con-fronts the challenge head-on by embarking on the development of a real-time gesture and gesture recognition system capable of accurately deciphering a diverse spectrum of sign language words. The prevailing assistive technologies often lack the precision and adaptability required to effectively translate intricate sign languages across diverse settings. Moreover, the absence of a cohesive solution that seamlessly integrates gesture recognition with text and spoken language interpretation leaves deaf and hard-of-hearing individuals with limited communication options.

3 Technology Stack Used for The Implementation of the Model

3.1 Graphics Processing Unit (GPU)

The computational power of a graphics processing unit (GPU), specifically the NVIDIA GeForce GTX series GPU Max-Q Design with a focus on the GTX 1650 model. This GPU is chosen for its advanced capabilities, making it well-suited for the demands of the hand sign recognition system.

3.2 Operating System

The computational power of a graphics processing unit (GPU), specifically the NVIDIA GeForce GTX series GPU Max-Q Design with a focus on the GTX 1650 model. This GPU is chosen for its advanced capabilities, making it well-suited for the demands of the hand sign recognition system.

3.3 Development Environment

The computational power of a graphics processing unit (GPU), specifically the NVIDIA GeForce GTX series GPU Max-Q Design with a focus on the GTX 1650 model. This GPU is chosen for its advanced capabilities, making it well-suited for the demands of the hand sign recognition system.

3.4 Deep Learning Frameworks

The computational power of a graphics processing unit (GPU), specifically the NVIDIA GeForce GTX series GPU Max-Q Design with a focus on the GTX 1650 model. This GPU is chosen for its advanced capabilities, making it well-suited for the demands of the hand sign recognition system.

3.5 Computer Vision Libraries

The computational power of a graphics processing unit (GPU), specifically the NVIDIA GeForce GTX series GPU Max-Q Design with a focus on the GTX 1650 model. This GPU is chosen for its advanced capabilities, making it well-suited for the demands of the hand sign recognition system.

3.6 Integrated Development Environment (IDE)

The computational power of a graphics processing unit (GPU), specifically the NVIDIA GeForce GTX series GPU Max-Q Design with a focus on the GTX 1650 model. This GPU is chosen for its advanced capabilities, making it well-suited for the demands of the hand sign recognition system.

4 System Methodology

The development of the Hand Sign Recognition System involves a detailed and systematic methodology, commencing with the project definition and planning phase. This phase establishes specific, measurable goals for the system, providing a clear direction for subsequent development. The conception and execution phase intricately designs the project architecture, relying on OpenCV for video frame capture and MediaPipe for precise hand landmark detection. OpenCV facilitates the real-time capture of video frames from a webcam, forming the basis for subsequent processing, while MediaPipe specializes in accurate hand landmark detection, mapping key points on the detected hand. Dataset acquisition is a pivotal step, ensuring the model is trained on a diverse and representative set of hand gestures. Leveraging the capabilities of the MediaPipe library, the dataset encompasses a variety of hand signs, optimizing the system's ability to generalize effectively. In the subsequent preprocessing phase, a series of essential techniques are seamlessly integrated to enhance the quality and relevance of input data for robust hand gesture recognition. This process begins with normalization, ensuring that landmark coordinates fall within a consistent range of 0 to 1, stabilizing and expediting the training of machine learning models. Subsequently, converting landmark coordinates to relative coordinates mitigates the impact of variations in hand size and position. This is achieved by subtracting base coordinates from a reference point, typically the wrist or palm. Additionally, a bounding box is calculated around the detected hand, emphasizing the region of interest and removing potentially irrelevant background information to streamline the input data and improve model efficiency. Lastly, the methodology incorporates a history length mechanism, maintaining a temporal record of previous hand positions to capture motion-related nuances in gestures, while managing memory usage by limiting the history length. This holistic approach ensures the system's accuracy and robustness in recognizing diverse and intricate hand gestures. The coding phase unfolds through two meticulously crafted modules. The initial module utilizes OpenCV to capture video frames, feeding them into the MediaPipe Hand module for landmark detection, establishing the foundational key point classification.

The second module represents a significant advancement, introducing point history analysis and finger gesture identification. This sophisticated module enhances the system's capabilities, allowing for nuanced recognition of intricate hand gestures. The integration of these modules ensures a cohesive and robust hand gesture recognition system. TensorFlow and Keras play a pivotal role in the model training process. The dataset is prepared and utilized to configure the model, incorporating layers for input, dropout regularization, dense hidden layers, and an output layer with softmax activation for multiclass classification.

Crafting a User Interface (UI) tailored for intuitive user interaction becomes paramount, and this is achieved through the implementation of the Streamlit framework. The UI serves as the face of the Hand Sign Recognition System, offering an accessible and seamless experience for users with varying levels of technical proficiency. The Interaction Flow commences with Video Input Processing using OpenCV (Version 4.8.1), where each frame of the video input undergoes systematic capture and processing. This enhances the visibility of gestures, preparing the input for subsequent stages. Media Pipe Hand Landmark Detection (Version 0.10.7) is then applied to the preprocessed frames, extracting intricate details such as finger positions and palm features.

The pinnacle of the Interaction Flow is reached with the Gesture Recognition Model, a pre-trained deep learning model. This model meticulously analyzes the extracted hand landmarks, employing its learned patterns to classify gestures with a high degree of accuracy. The entire process, from real-time data capture to deep learning-based recognition, ensures the system's proficiency in accurate and efficient sign language detection. Each component seamlessly contributes to the overall success of the Hand Sign Recognition System, embodying a streamlined and cohesive methodology.

Rigorous testing follows, evaluating the system's accuracy. The implementation of the Model Checkpoint callback in TensorFlow ensures the preservation of the best model during training, contributing to optimal performance. The project concludes with a comprehensive analysis, including the confusion matrix, ROC-AUC curve, and a detailed classification report. The documentation encompasses the model architecture, training

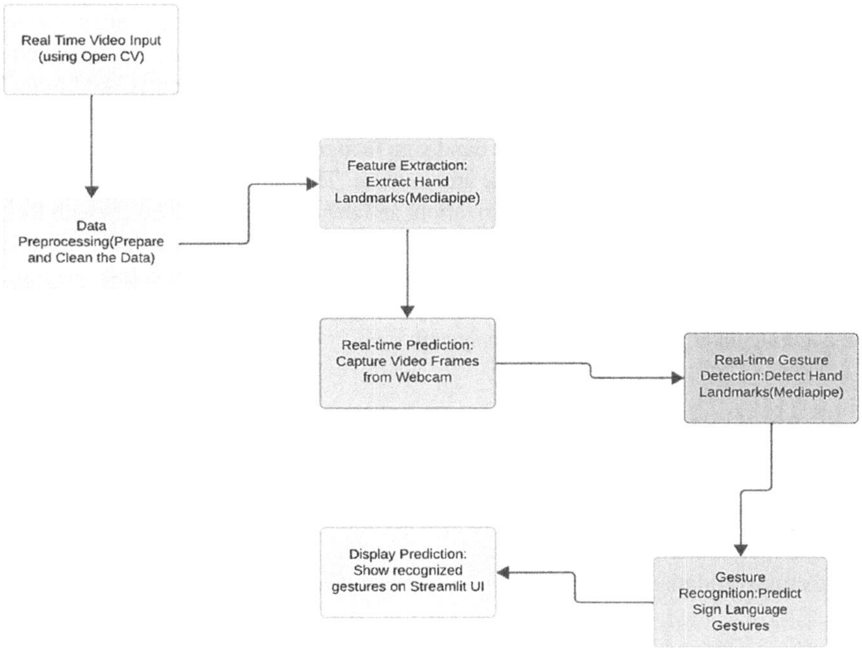

Fig. 1. System Architecture

details, and instructions for deployment. The Hand Sign Recognition System, thus developed, stands as a testament to a meticulous and systematic methodology, poised for real world applications across diverse domains (Fig. 1).

5 Algorithm

Embarking on the algorithmic journey for the Hand Sign Recognition System, the process unfolds with the initial phase dedicated to capturing relevant data using a webcam. OpenCV, a computer vision library, is employed to facilitate video frame capture, laying the foundation for subsequent analysis. The focal point shifts to hand landmark detection, a critical step accomplished through the integration of Media Pipe, a popular library for hand tracking. Media Pipe not only identifies key hand landmarks but also provides their spatial coordinates, offering a comprehensive understanding of hand gestures.

Following landmark detection, the system transitions into the realm of key-point classification. The captured hand landmarks are meticulously processed and fed into a Dense Neural Network (DNN). This DNN, constructed using Ten-sorFlow and Keras, is designed to classify the keypoints, enabling the system to discern intricate details of hand gestures. The model undergoes rigorous training and testing using a dataset specifically curated for diverse and representative hand gestures. Simultaneously, the project delves into the integration of point history analysis, enhancing the system's temporal understanding of gestures. The intricate dance of fingers and hands over successive frames is scrutinized to infer dynamic gestures, elevating the recognition capabilities.

The methodology encompasses meticulous testing procedures to validate the system's accuracy and reliability. The model's performance is evaluated through metrics such as ROC-AUC curves, confusion matrices, and classification reports. Additionally, the project incorporates model checkpointing and early stopping mechanisms to preserve the best-performing model. The hand sign recognition system culminates with the deployment of Dense Neural Network architecture. This architecture, characterized by input layers, dropout layers for regularization, and densely connected layers with ReLU activation, encapsulates the essence of the trained model. The final model is saved and can be utilized for real-time hand sign recognition, showcasing the seamless integration of computer vision, machine learning, and neural networks to accomplish a sophisticated and accurate hand gesture recognition system.

6 Evaluation

To rigorously assess the performance of the hand sign recognition system, a meticulous evaluation methodology was employed. Recognizing the importance of mitigating potential biases and ensuring the model's robustness, a more sophisticated approach, 5-fold cross-validation, was subsequently implemented (Fig. 2).

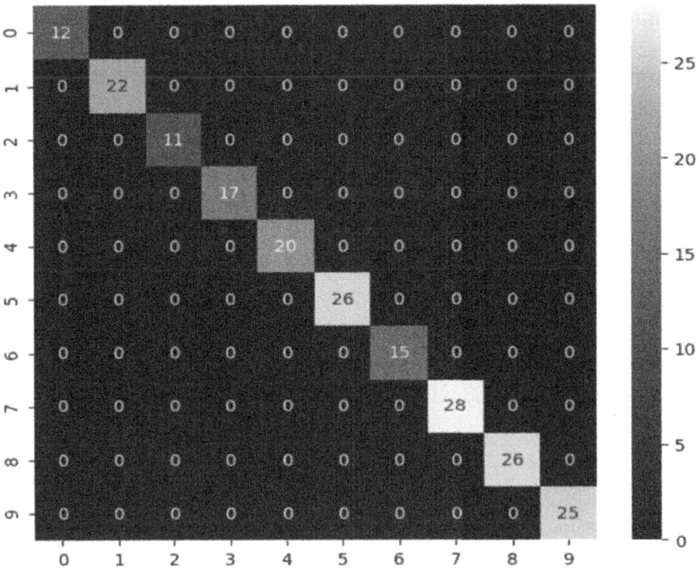

Fig. 2. Confusion Matrix

This is the Confusion Matrix with a detection accuracy of 97% for the classification model which demonstrates a high overall performance (Fig. 3).

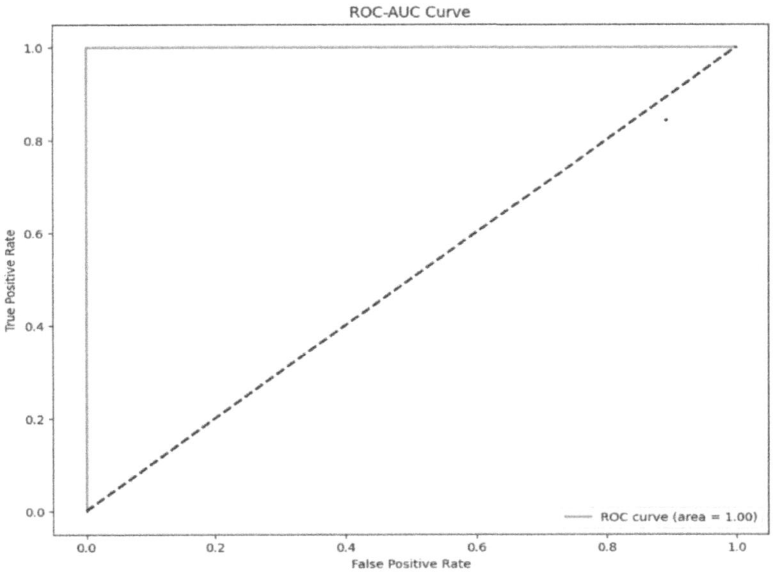

Fig. 3. True Positive Rate vs. False Positive Rate

The validation results at a threshold of 0.98 for the hand sign recognition system suggest that the model demonstrates a notable inclination toward predicting the positive class.

Table 1. Comparison Table between the original model and other models

Aspect	Dense Neural Network	Convolutional Neural Network	Recurrent Neural Network	Faster R-CNN
Model Architecture	Dense Layers	Convolutional Layers	Recurrent Layers	Fewer Dense Layers
Model Complexity	Moderate	Higher (Due to CNN layers)	Moderate	High
Training Accuracy	82.48%	85%	80%	70%
Validation Accuracy	97.41%	96.83%	93%	95.31%
Inference Time	0.23 Seconds	0.3 Seconds	0.5 Seconds	2 Seconds
Memory Utilization	7.31 GB	9 GB	8 GB	10 GB
Real-Time Capability	Fast, Suitable for real-time	Suitable for real-time	May Introduce Latency Issue	May have a latency issue

The comprehensive analysis of AI-enhanced sign language interpreter models sheds light on their distinctive characteristics crucial for operational effectiveness. The original model, distinguished by densely connected layers, skillfully navigates the delicate balance between precision and computational efficiency. Conversely, the Convolutional Neural Network (CNN) excels in intricate feature extraction, albeit at the cost of heightened complexity and increased memory requirements. The Recurrent Neural Network (RNN) strategically prioritizes temporal understanding, maintaining a moderate level of complexity. In contrast, the Faster R-CNN, integrating object detection, showcases elevated complexity and augmented memory demands. Key evaluation metrics, spanning training and validation accuracies, underscore the exceptional capabilities of each model, with the original model particularly standing out in both domains. In the context of inference time, the original model and CNN demonstrate commendable real-time processing efficiency, while the RNN and Faster R-CNN introduce marginal delays attributable to sequential processing and intricate object detection, respectively. Memory utilization intricately aligns with model complexity, and the nuanced discussion of real-time capability underscores the delicate equilibrium between accuracy and responsiveness across diverse sign language interpretation scenarios. This elucidation aims to provide a comprehensive understanding of the insights presented in Table 1.

Table 2 outlines the key hyper parameters employed for training each model in the Hand Sign Recognition System. Parameters include learning rate, batch size, epochs, and

Table 2. Hyperparameters of Different NN Models

Model	Learning Rate	Batch Size	Epochs	Optimizer
DNN	0.001	64	50	Adam
CNN	0.0005	128	40	SGD
RNN	0.0008	32	60	RMSprop
Faster R-CNN	0.002	16	30	Adam

optimizer choice, providing insights into the configuration specifics that govern the training process. The Dense Neural Network utilizes a learning rate of 0.001, batch size of 64, trains for 50 epochs using the Adam optimizer, while the Convolutional NN, Recurrent NN, and Faster R-CNN employ distinct hyper parameter settings, tailoring their training characteristics for optimal performance. The table serves as a comprehensive reference for the model training setup (Figs. 4 and 5).

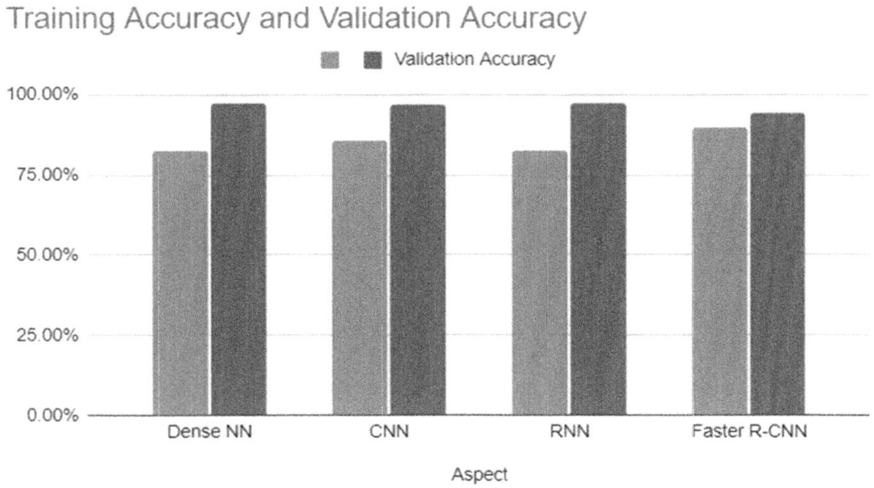

Fig. 4. Comparison Column Graph between training accuracy and validation accuracy of dense NN and other neural network models

In summary, The Dense Neural Network (Dense NN) excels in hand sign recognition with impressive accuracy during training and validation. It ensures rapid real-time processing and maintains efficient memory utilization, crucial for effective communication. In contrast to more complex models like RNN or Faster R-CNN, Dense NN's simplicity proves advantageous, providing reliable accuracy without unnecessary computational overhead (Figs. 6 and 7).

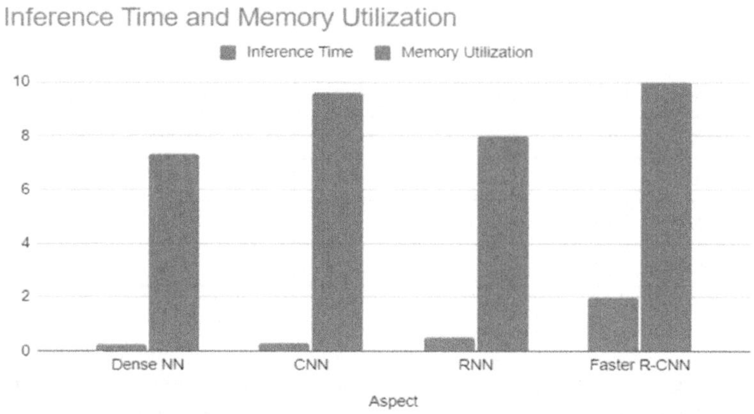

Fig. 5. Comparison Column Graph between Inference time and Memory utilization of dense NN and other neural network models

7 Result

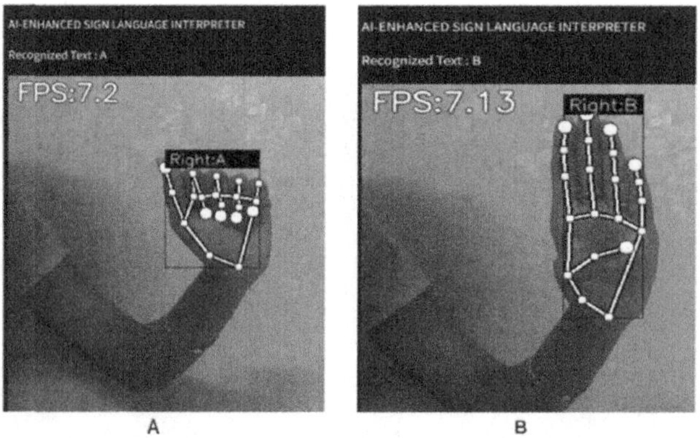

Fig. 6. (A) Recognized Hand Sign gesture of Alphabet A, (B) Recognized Hand sign gesture of Alphabet B

Fig. 7. Example of Recognized Text

8 Conclusion

In conclusion, the Hand Sign Recognition System represents a significant stride in harnessing the capabilities of computer vision and machine learning to interpret and comprehend sign language. Through the integration of cutting-edge models and innovative techniques, the system has exhibited commendable achievements in accurately detecting and recognizing a diverse array of hand signs. The key accomplishments include its robustness across different gestures and hand positions, ensuring accurate interpretation. Moreover, the implementation's real-time processing capability enhances its practicality and responsiveness in dynamic communication scenarios. The development of a user-friendly interface further contributes to a seamless user experience, allowing intuitive interaction with the system. Looking towards future enhancements, there are promising avenues for improvement and expansion. The integration of multi-language support would make the system more inclusive and globally applicable by recognizing and interpreting signs from various sign languages. Additionally, introducing a gesture customization feature would enhance adaptability, catering to individual preferences. The prospect of mobile application integration opens opportunities for on-the-go accessibility, extending the reach of the Hand Sign Recognition System beyond traditional computing platforms.

References

1. Kothadiya, D.R., et al.: SignExplainer: An Explainable AI-Enabled Framework for Sign Language Recognition with Ensemble Learning. IEEE Access (2023)
2. Lipisha, C., Tejaswini, A., Enjamamul, H., IfeomaNwogu, O.: SignNet II: a transformer-based two-way sign language translation model. IEEE Trans. Pattern Anal. Mach. Intell. (2022). https://doi.org/10.1109/tpami.2022.3232389
3. Niranjan, P.: Artificial Intelligence based Indian Sign Language Recognition with Accelerated Performance under HPC Environment (2022). https://doi.org/10.1109/OCIT56763.2022.00051
4. Feng, W., Zixuan, Z., Tianyiyi, H., Chengkuo, L.: AI enabled sign language recognition and VR space bidirectional communication using triboelectric smart glove. Nat. Commun. (2021). https://doi.org/10.1038/S41467-021-25637-W
5. Al-Hammadi, M., et al.: Hand gesture recognition for sign language using 3DCNN. IEEE access **8**, 79491–79509 (2020)
6. Rastgoo, R., Kiani, K., Escalera, S.: Hand sign language recognition using multi-view hand skeleton. Expert Syst. Appl. **150**, 113336 (2020)
7. Chou, J.S., Truong, D.N.: A novel metaheuristic optimizer inspired by behavior of jellyfish in ocean. Appl. Math. Comput. **389**, 125535 (2021)
8. Lim, K.M., et al.: Isolated sign language recognition using convolutional neural network hand modelling and hand energy image. Multimedia Tools and Applications **78**, 19917–19944 (2019)
9. Mohanty, S.S.R., Sahay, R.R.: Deep gesture: Static hand gesture recognition using CNN. Proc. Comput. Vis. Image Process. 449–461 (2017)
10. Pisharady, P.K., Vadakkepat, P., Loh, A.P.: Attention based detection and recognition of hand postures against complex backgrounds. Int. J. Comp. Vision **101**, 403–419 (2013)

11. Dardas, N.H., Georganas, N.D.: Real-time hand gesture detection and recognition using bag-of-features and support vector machine techniques. IEEE Trans. Instrum. Meas. **60**(11), 3592–3607 (2011)
12. Kausar, S., Younus Javed, M.: A survey on sign language recognition. 2011 Frontiers of Information Technology. IEEE (2011)
13. Li, H., Greenspan, M.: Model-based segmentation and recognition of dynamic gestures in continuous video streams. Pattern Recogn. **44**(8), 1614–1628 (2011)
14. Murthy, G.R.S., Jadon, R.S.: Hand gesture recognition using neural networks. 2010 IEEE 2nd international advance computing conference (IACC). IEEE (2010)
15. Suryanarayan, P., Subramanian, A., Mandalapu, D.: Dynamic hand pose recognition using depth data. In: 2010 20th International Conference on Pattern Recognition. IEEE (2010)
16. Zhou, H., Lin, D.J., Huang, T.S.: Static hand gesture recognition based on local orientation histogram feature distribution model. In: 2004 Conference on computer vision and pattern recognition workshop. IEEE (2004)
17. Huang, T.S., Wu, Y., Lin, J.: 3D model-based visual hand tracking. Proceedings. IEEE International Conference on Multimedia and Expo. Vol. 1. IEEE (2002)
18. Bretzner, L., Laptev, I., Lindeberg, T.: Hand gesture recognition using multiscale color features, hierarchical models and particle filtering. In: Automatic Face and Gesture Recognition, 2002. Proceedings. Fifth IEEE International Conference on, pp. 423–428. IEEE (2002)
19. Yang, M.-H., Ahuja, N., Tabb, M.: Extraction of 2D motion trajectories and its application to hand gesture recognition. IEEE Trans. Pattern Anal. Mach. Intell. **24**(8), 1061–1074 (2002)
20. Zhu, Y., Guangyou, X., Kriegman, D.J.: A real-time approach to the spotting, representation, and recognition of hand gestures for human–computer interaction. Comput. Vis. Image Underst. **85**(3), 189–208 (2002)
21. Viola, P., Jones, M.: Robust real-time object detection. Int. J. Comput. Vision **4**(34–47), 4 (2001)
22. Marcel, S., et al.: Hand gesture recognition using input-output hidden Markov models. Proceedings fourth IEEE international conference on automatic face and gesture recognition (Cat. No. PR00580). IEEE (2000)
23. Starner, T., Pentland, A.: Real-time American sign language recognition from video using Hidden Markov Models. Proceedings of International Symposium on Computer Vision-ISCV. IEEE (1995)
24. Dorner: Hand shape identification and tracking for sign language interpretation. IJCAI Workshop on Looking at People (1993)
25. Poizner, H., Bellugi, U., Lutes-Driscoll, V.: Perception of American sign language in dynamic point-light displays. J. Exp. Psychol. Hum. Percept. Perform. **7**(2), 430 (1981)

An NLP Based Approach to Automate and Enhance the Systematic Review Within PRISMA Format

Jeena A. Thankachan(✉) and Bama Srinivasan

Department of Information Science and Technology, College of Engineering, Anna University, Guindy, Chennai 600025, Tamilnadu, India
{jeena,bama}@auist.net

Abstract. Systematic Literature Review (SLR) is an integral part of research; however, to conduct an SLR, the manual review process would be time-consuming due to the high volume of literature involved. This paper presents a method that uses Natural Language Processing (NLP) and Machine Learning (ML) techniques to automate the systematic review process at two key stages: screening and eligibility assessment. The approach utilizes BERT (Bidirectional Encoder Representations from Transformers) embeddings and cosine similarity for automated label assignment and categorization of research articles. The proposed approach aligns to the principles of PRISMA (Preferred Reporting Items for Systematic Reviews and Meta-Analyses) in the automation of the domain based categorization of articles, and resolves the challenges posed by the state of art techniques. The proposed work considers three datasets with total 2164 records, collected based on identification criteria of PRISMA, to be classified into three categories. The proposed method based on BERT gives good results on categorization of article with an accuracy of 99% , 98% and 96% for each dataset.

Keywords: Systematic Literature Review (SLR) · PRISMA format · BERT embeddings · automate · label assignment · categorization

1 Introduction

Systematic literature reviews (SLR) are essential for evidence-based research as they help synthesize and summarize existing knowledge on specific research questions or topics. An SLR process includes search, screen, categorize, and synthesize the research articles. The traditional systematic review process involves manual classification of research articles into categories, which are prone to human errors with more time consumption. However, for more intricate subjects, the rate of errors and time consumption may rise for an SLR process. Similarly, reviewers might need to examine hundreds or even thousands of abstracts to choose the ones that are relevant. Therefore, SLR facilitates with the steps to reduce human bias and uncover hidden insights in the literature.

Published by Springer Nature Switzerland AG 2025
A. Chandrabose et al. (Eds.): ICCCSP 2024, IFIP AICT 723, pp. 199–212, 2025.
https://doi.org/10.1007/978-3-031-73617-9_16

Existing standards for SLRs can serve as guiding principles to execute the processes involved within the workflow. Two common standards employed for conducting SLRs include PRISMA (Preferred Reporting Items for Systematic Reviews and Meta-Analyses) and the PICO (Patient, Intervention, Comparison, and Outcome) framework. PRISMA primarily serves as a framework for systematic reviews with different objectives and emphasizes reporting reviews that assess intervention effects [19]. Meanwhile, the PICO tool helps identify distinct elements of clinical evidence for systematic analysis, and it is acknowledged by the Cochrane Collaboration [2]. The paper focus on the PRISMA elements to automate the process of certain items described for an SLR.

Recent progress in natural language processing (NLP), can leverage the transfer learning technique to automate the elements of literature review process [9]. As the PRISMA format includes detailed text data extraction from research databases, it is essential to automate the process of selection, collection, screening, and classification of data to create information through synthesis [22].

The paper introduces a novel approach that uses the NLP techniques to automate the label assignment and classification of articles within the PRISMA framework. The proposed approach uses BERT (Bidirectional Encoder Representations from Transformers) embeddings, followed with label assignment based on cosine similarity and the BERT-based text classification [11,15].The goal is to assign labels and categorize text documents into multiple labels to automate the categorization of articles and help researchers speed up the review process.

The contents in the paper are structured as follows: related works in Sect. 2 and problem formulation in Sect. 3, followed with methodology part in Sect. 4 and experimental settings in Sect. 5. Finally the results, discussion and conclusion are presented in Sects. 6 and 7 respectively.

2 Related Works

This section describes the state of art techniques in two subsections: "Automating the Systematic Review Process" in Sect. 2.1 and "The PRISMA " in Sect. 2.2.

2.1 Automate the Systematic Review Process

In the systematic literature review (SLR), several significant advancements and tools have emerged to enhance the process. The use of natural language processing (NLP) and machine learning (ML) has gained attention as a means to automate the identification of specific data elements in research publications, reducing the need for labour-intensive manual annotation.

Tanmay Basu et al. [4], combines Jaccard similarity for training corpus generation from references with an SVM classifier for data extraction. This technique pose challenges as the process relies solely on references from related papers that may lead to an incomplete representation of the depth of the literature on the topic of interest. Additionally, the quality of references can vary across different papers, that introduces noise into the training corpus. Some studies may cite a wide range of related works, while others may focus on a narrower set, further complicates the corpus generation process. Extraction of meaningful relationships between words and phrases from the text requires careful preprocessing and feature selection to avoid introducing noise into the SVM classifier. Moreover, constructing a training corpus solely from references may limit the model's ability to generalize to new studies that are not explicitly referenced in existing literature, that hinders its effectiveness in data extraction.

Shemilt et al. [20], adopts text mining techniques to reduce the screening load in systematic reviews. The technical language commonly found in research articles poses a significant obstacle for text mining algorithms, that limit their ability to accurately identify relevant studies. Ambiguity and synonymy in terminology further compound these challenges, as different terms may be used interchangeably to denote the same concept, or a single term may carry multiple meanings contingent on context. These inherent linguistic nuances make it challenging for text mining algorithms to effectively discern the true relevance of studies.

Choong et al. [5], uses automatic citation snowballing, a technique that aims at evidence retrieval in systematic reviews, encounters several challenges when integrated into PRISMA-based literature reviews. The process, which relies on recursively tracing citations from a seed set of articles, faces the risk of recursive bias towards well-cited works, potentially neglecting lesser-known yet pertinent studies. Incompleteness within citation networks, especially prevalent in emerging fields, can hinder the thorough retrieval of relevant evidence.

Wallace et al. [24], uses machine learning techniques, particularly active learning for ML-assisted citation screening. This technique presents challenges including bias in training data, scalability, heterogeneity in literature, interpretability issues, human-in-the-loop challenges, quality assurance, and ethical considerations.

Yu et al. [27], utilizes a Fastread tool for classification of relevant and non-relevant papers. It presents challenges when domain based or multi classification of articles is a need.

The development of ExaCT represents a significant advancement in automatic information extraction from full-text journal articles [1]. The system's two components, an information extraction (IE) engine and a user interface for manual review and modification, showcase how statistical text classifiers and simple rules can efficiently extract crucial trial characteristics.

Cohen et al. [6], introduces machine learning and text mining, particularly supervised learning, into citation screening that offers significant contributions but also presents challenges. These include the quality and representation of training data, annotation effort and expertise, generalised models, algorithmic bias, interpretation and transparency of predictions, scalability of algorithms, and integration with existing workflows.

Cormack et al. [7], uses Technology-assisted review (TAR) for legal electronic discovery to find as many relevant documents as possible. It includes uncertainties regarding the suitability of Technology-assisted review (TAR) for low-prevalence collections, as traditional methods may not be as effective. The study did not include high-prevalence collections, that hinders the understanding of TAR's comparative advantage. Further, there are unexplored design choices in the evaluation toolkit, leaving room for investigation.

Application of text classification methods to streamline the screening process in systematic reviews has yielded notable results. Various machine learning algorithms and feature selection techniques have been employed in experiments, with precision and recall measurements reaching up to 84% [21]. It is to be noted that using article titles alone can yield similar results as incorporating abstracts, emphasizing the importance of selecting appropriate machine learning algorithms and text sections for effective outcomes in systematic reviews.

These advancements collectively contribute to a more efficient and effective landscape for literature surveys and systematic reviews across various domains. The challenges posed by these techniques need to be addressed for the precision of systematic literature reviews, to enhance the reliability and validity of research findings.

2.2 The PRISMA

The PRISMA (Preferred Reporting Items for Systematic Reviews and Meta-Analyses) provides guidelines to conduct and report transparent and consistent systematic reviews [19].

The PRISMA protocol was developed in 2009, to address issues commonly associated with review-type articles [8]. In 2020, it was updated to reflect advances in systematic review methodology and terminology, resulting in the PRISMA 2020 statement [16]. This revised statement includes a 27-item checklist, an abstract checklist, and modified flow diagrams, all designed to help systematic reviewers transparently report the rationale, methodology, and findings of their reviews [14].

The PRISMA 2020 checklist comprises 27 essential items that guide authors in systematically reporting their systematic reviews. These 27 essential items cover the review's fundamental components, including the title, rationale, objectives, eligibility criteria, information sources, search methodology, study selection, data collection processes, data items, assessment of risk of bias in individual studies, summary measures, synthesis of results, evaluation of risk of bias across studies, additional analyses, study characteristics, results of individual studies, summary of evidence, and funding sources [17]. The key elements in the systematic review process that emphasize PRISMA checklist are: Selection Process (Item 8), Data Collection Process (Item 9), Data Items (Items 10a and 10b), Effect Measures (Item 12), and Synthesis Methods (Item 13a) [17].

Figure 1 shows the process flow within the PRISMA framework that involves identification, screening, eligibility assessment, and inclusion.

Identification: The identification stage involves systematically searching various databases, such as PubMed, Scopus, or Web of Science, using predefined

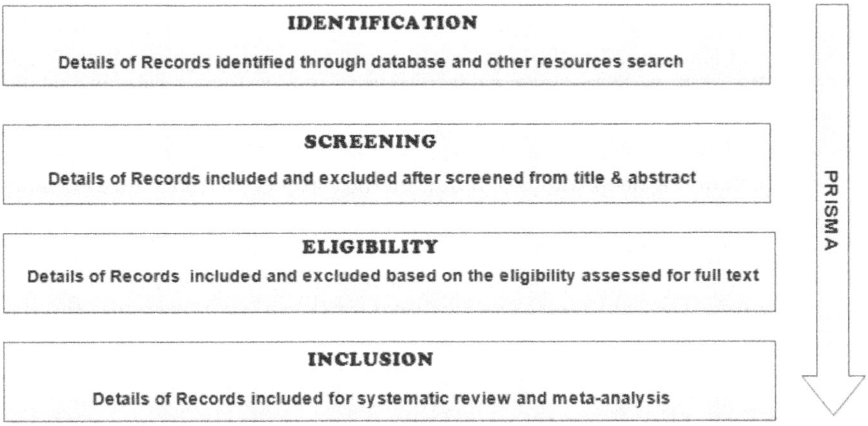

Fig. 1. PRISMA work flow

search terms and criteria. The goal is to identify all potentially relevant studies related to the research question or topic of interest [16,18].

Screening: During the screening stage, researchers evaluate the titles and abstracts of the identified studies to determine their relevance to the research question and predefined inclusion/exclusion criteria. Studies that clearly do not meet the criteria are excluded, while potentially relevant studies proceed to the next phase for full-text assessment [16,18].

Eligibility Assessment: In the eligibility assessment stage, researchers obtain and assess the full texts of the studies that passed the initial screening phase. Each study is carefully evaluated against the predefined inclusion/exclusion criteria outlined in the review protocol to determine whether it meets the eligibility criteria for inclusion in the systematic review. Studies that meet the criteria are included in the final analysis, while those that do not are excluded [16,18].

Inclusion: The inclusion stage finalizes the selection of studies that meet the eligibility criteria and will be included in the systematic review. These included studies undergo further analysis, data extraction, and synthesis as part of the systematic review process. The inclusion stage ensures that only high-quality, relevant studies are included in the systematic review, contributing to the reliability and validity of the review's findings [16,18].

Henceforth, PRISMA ensures that systematic reviews are conducted in a transparent and reproducible manner, that enhances the quality and credibility of the research findings.

2.3 Challenges

The sheer volume of data available from multiple databases such as SCOPUS, Web of Science, ACM, IEEE, and Google Scholar presents a significant challenge for researchers and professionals. The extensive amount of downloaded data necessitates rigorous manual review to ensure accuracy and relevance. This manual review and classification process involves handling large volumes of data, which can be overwhelming and labor-intensive. Furthermore, classifying data based on various criteria such as theory, technology, concept, and relationships adds an additional layer of complexity to the review process. This intricacy not only demands a deep understanding of the subject matter but also makes the task time-consuming. Additionally, the constant influx of new publications exacerbates the situation, making it essential to develop and implement efficient review strategies to keep up with the continuous flow of information. Consequently, finding ways to streamline this process is critical to manage the data efficiently and effectively.

3 Scope of the Proposed Work

The challenges posed by various techniques, including machine learning, text mining, automatic citation snowballing, and ML-assisted citation screening, necessitate comprehensive solutions to enhance the precision of systematic literature reviews and ensure the reliability and validity of research findings. To address these challenges, this study proposes the integration of Natural Language Processing (NLP) and Machine Learning (ML) techniques.

The paper introduces a novel approach that uses NLP and ML technique to enhance the systematic review process. To automate the classification of research articles, the proposed methodology aims to address the principles outlined in PRISMA's selection criteria (Item 8), Data Collection Process (Item 9), Data Items (Items 10a and 10b), Effect Measures (Item 12), and Synthesis Methods (Item 13a) [17]. By the use of NLP methodologies, such as customised category creation, tokenization, and BERT-based embedding generation, coupled with ML algorithms, the proposed approach aims to mitigate the limitations associated with each technique. Through careful preprocessing, feature selection, and algorithmic refinement, the effectiveness and efficiency of evidence retrieval and data extraction in systematic reviews is optimised. This approach seeks to streamline the systematic review process aligned with PRISMA's principles for evidence synthesis.

The following sections delve into the methodology, implementation, and results of NLP-based techniques, shedding light on its potential to revolutionize evidence synthesis in an era of information abundance.

4 Methodology

In this section, we outline the methodology used for the classification of unlabeled text data using BERT (Bidirectional Encoder Representations from Transformers). Text classification is a natural language processing (NLP) task, and BERT represents a state-of-the-art model for various NLP tasks [10,13].

A scientific research begins with data review and collection, where data is searched on databases like SCOPUS, Web of Science, PsychINFO, ACM, IEEE, and Google Scholar. The required data are screened using various options of selection criteria and are downloaded. Most of the time, the downloaded data would be large enough for manual review and content classification based on theory, technology, concept, relationship, and so on.

In the proposed method, a case scenario of SLR on "Intelligent Tutoring Systems (ITS)" is considered. The data collection and screening from the databases were specific towards ITS with keywords like online learning or blended learning or LMS (Learning Management Systems). After the screening process, an unlabeled textual dataset (with dimensions m rows $\times$ n columns) is obtained from the scientific digital libraries. The dataset comprises various attributes, that includes article titles, abstracts, author keywords, journal details, author details and index terms.

In the proposed work, the attributes that contain textual information relevant to the study are combined to create a text data corpus. Based on the initial (a broader) review study and understanding by a researcher, a manual categorical labels are listed. The labels are defined with standard references and embedded using BERT to facilitate text corpus labeling. The case scenario considered introduces customised categories to label the text data. The customised categories are "pedagogy", "learner", and "user-interface (UI)", that are the main components of an ITS. The categories are defined with two standard or example sentences that represents each of these categories.

The core of the methodology relies on the use of the BERT model to generate BERT embeddings for the textual data and the custom categories, as in Fig. 2. First, a pre-trained BERT model is loaded; a 'bert-base-uncased' model with 12 layers of transformer block, 768 hidden size and 12 self attention heads. This transformer model generates BERT embeddings for both the textual data and the defined categories. A BERT tokenizer is used to tokenize the text within the 512-token limit. The tokenized output is then passed through the BERT model to compute word embeddings. BERT embeddings result in a 3D tensor output. The shape of the embedded 3D tensor output is a tuple with dimensions representing the number of input sentences (m), the maximum sequence length (or the maximum number of tokens in the input sentences), and the hidden units of the model (768) [3,23,26].

The 3D tensor output is sliced at the CLS token, along with the hidden units, to obtain the 2D tensor output. Since CLS and the final hidden state of BERT associated with this token function as a unique classification token. The 2D tensor outputs for text and categories are compared using the cosine similarity metric. Cosine similarity scores measure the similarity between example sentences within each category [12]. This allows us to assess how well BERT captures the essence of each category based on the provided exemplars. The next step involves associating labels with the text data sentences based on the highest cosine similarity score. For each sentence embedding in the dataset, a category label that yields the maximum similarity score is assigned as the label [25].

The data frame with labels is hence prepared for BERT-based text classification. A binary label (0 or 1) is assigned to each sentence based on the pres-

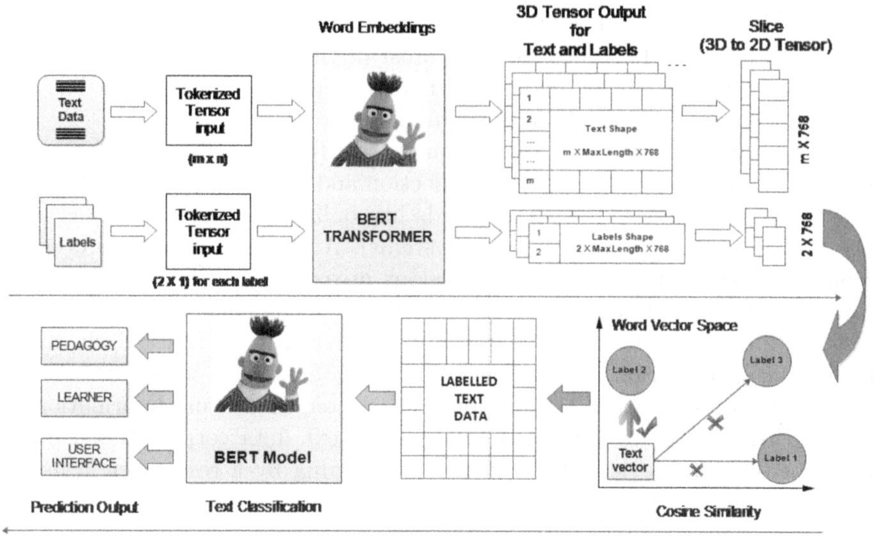

Fig. 2. Proposed work flow

ence of specific categories. A multi-target classification model, which includes three branches, each corresponding to one of the three categories: "pedagogy", "learner," and "UI" is developed.

Text data is encoded to be compatible with the BERT model. The encoder generates input IDs, attention masks, and token type IDs for each sentence in the dataset. These encoding are crucial for feeding the data into the BERT-based classification model. The model is compiled with binary cross-entropy loss and trained using the encoded text data and the associated target labels.

Finally, a prediction function is developed to compute predictions for each of the categories, based on the BERT embeddings of the input text. Further, the labeled dataset is saved for further analysis and reference.

The proposed methodology encompasses data preprocessing, BERT-based embeddings, custom category analysis, labeling, and the construction of a multi-classification model. This approach allows us to effectively classify scientific literature text data into relevant categories for a systematic review. This helps identify research gaps with less explored and high explored, categorized data for further exploration. The proposed approach is used in the screening and decision of eligible records for the systematic review process.

The following section provides an overview of the primary stage, namely, the 'identification of records,' in the context of Systematic Literature Review (SLR).

5 Experimental Settings

In this paper, three set of records are extracted from full-text databases of ACM digital library, IEEE Xplore and Scopus, as shown in Table 1. These databases archive the full texts or abstracts of most of the articles. These records are the data identified based on the advanced search options with inclusion and exclusion criteria provided within the database search systems. The data collected is based on the article keywords 'cognitive evaluation' and 'personalization' and 'online learning' or 'LMS', published during the year range of 2015–2023, in the language medium of 'English'. Henceforth, around 2164 records of data are identified as per the protocol of PRISMA for further steps of screening and eligibility assessment.

Table 1. Number of Records

IEEE	Scopus	ACM
659	505	1000

The keywords used by a researcher in the identification stage are decided based on the prior art of search. Similarly the further inclusion and exclusion of articles in the screening stage would be based on the methods of theory, technology, technique, concept or experiment type would be decided by the researcher. According to the proposed method, this stage is automated by the customised categorisation of records.

In this case study of data collection and identification, the researcher understands the need to classify the record based on the three possible categories, that are relevant to narrow down the research gaps or the findings. The three categories considered are 'pedagogy', 'learner' and 'UI' (user-interface). In order to customise the records with these categories, each of the category is defined with evidence based standard keywords or sentences within the token limit of 512.

This method is implemented over an end to end open source of machine learning, the Tensorflow. It uses a pretrained BERT model (bert-base-uncased). Hyperparameters used are batch size = 4, epochs = 5, and lr = 0.001.

6 Results and Discussions

In this section, we present the results of our research, which involves the use of cosine similarity scores and BERT classification. We discuss the cosine similarity values between label and sentence embedding in three different databases. Following this, we showcase samples of labels assigned based on the highest cosine scores, and provide insights into the number of labels assigned through cosine similarity. Finally, we use BERT model for classification that evaluates the performance of the BERT model.

6.1 Cosine Similarity for Label Assignment

In the analysis of label-text relationships using cosine similarity, we first present cosine similarity values for each databases, highlighting label-text associations.

Subsequently, we showcase assigned labels and explore the distribution of labels in our dataset.

Table 2. Table with a sample of Cosine Similarity Values

Data Source	ID	Pedagogy	Learner	UI	Label
IEEE Data	1	0.714	0.764	0.709	Learner
	2	0.730	0.750	0.715	Learner
	3	0.727	0.775	0.726	Learner
	4	0.728	0.726	0.659	Pedagogy
Scopus Data	1	0.719	0.770	0.706	Pedagogy
	2	0.674	0.630	0.676	UI
	3	0.677	0.778	0.671	Learner
	4	0.785	0.712	0.709	Pedagogy
ACM Data	1	0.643	0.734	0.701	Learner
	2	0.766	0.819	0.737	Learner
	3	0.764	0.790	0.793	UI
	4	0.808	0.809	0.739	Learner

Cosine similarity measures the similarity between the corpus vectors and the customised categorical vectors. The range of values it can take is from -1 to 1: a value of 1 indicates perfect similarity, a value of 0 indicates no similarity, and value of -1 implies maximal dissimilarity or negative correlation.

In the context of text similarity, cosine similarity is employed to assess how similar or dissimilar labels and text data are by comparing their vector representations in a high-dimensional space.

As shown in Table 2, corresponding to each database: IEEE, ACM, and Scopus, it reveals the cosine similarity scores, illustrating how closely related the labels are to the content (ID) in each database.

6.2 Performance Analysis of the BERT Model

The evaluation performance of the BERT model based on the metrics such as precision, recall, and F1-score for each label, are discussed in the following subsection.

Tables 3, 4, and 5 show the categorised classification of the selected records. Though the accuracy metric for each category shows a good result of classification, the performance of other metrics like precision, recall and f1 score gives biased range of values due to the imbalance in the distribution of labelled records. The "support" column indicates the distribution of predicted records under each category, which indicates the imbalance in the data.

Table 3. Classification Report for Scopus Data

Category	Class	Precision	Recall	F1-Score	Support
Pedagogy	0	0.99	1.00	1.00	502
	1	0.00	0.00	0.00	3
Accuracy				0.99	505
Learner	0	0.00	0.00	0.00	23
	1	0.95	1.00	0.98	482
Accuracy				0.95	505
UI	0	0.96	1.00	0.98	485
	1	0.00	0.00	0.00	20
Accuracy				0.96	505

Table 4. Classification Report for ACM data

Category	Class	Precision	Recall	F1-Score	Support
Pedagogy	0	0.98	1.00	0.99	977
	1	0.00	0.00	0.00	23
Accuracy				0.98	1000
Learner	0	0.00	0.00	0.00	443
	1	0.86	1.00	0.72	557
Accuracy				0.86	1000
UI	0	0.88	1.00	0.73	580
	1	0.00	0.00	0.00	420
Accuracy				0.88	1000

Table 5. Classification Report for IEEE data

Category	Class	Precision	Recall	F1-Score	Support
Pedagogy	0	0.97	1.00	0.98	639
	1	0.00	0.00	0.00	20
Accuracy				0.97	659
Learner	0	0.00	0.00	0.00	74
	1	0.89	1.00	0.94	585
Accuracy				0.89	659
UI	0	0.92	1.00	0.96	605
	1	0.00	0.00	0.00	54
Accuracy				0.92	659

The proposed work developed a prediction function based on BERT embeddings to predict the future influx of research articles in the customised categories. The predicted and labeled dataset is saved for further analysis and reference.

The label assignment and categorisation of each identified record using BERT embeddings, cosine similarity and BERT classification model are the significant contribution to automated the distribution of records within each category. The proposed method can be further repeated with screened records for next set of categories in order to further screen the records.

This approach aligns with the checklist items of 'Methods' of a systematic review manuscript, especially in selection process, data collection process, data items, effect measures and synthesis methods.

The classification results for Scopus, ACM, and IEEE datasets reveals the class imbalance it suffers across all categories. The model's ability to balance precision and recall varies, that emphasize the need for class-specific fine-tuning and address the class distribution challenges. The following section discusses the reliability of the proposed approach in case of imbalanced datasets and multi-class classification.

6.3 Discussion

The section highlights the reliability of the classification model in handling imbalanced datasets utilising Cohen's Kappa coefficient. It is a measure that considers agreement between observed and predicted labels that accounts for chance agreement. In this paper, the performance of a classification model for an identified set of articles is analysed, that can be assigned customised labels on pedagogy, learner, and User Interface (UI). A sample of 100 articles from the collected and the identified dataset is annotated.

The results of the evaluation indicate that the model achieves an overall accuracy of 86%, meaning that 86 out of 100 records are correctly predicted. Specifically, the model predicts pedagogy, learner, and UI labels 32, 23, and 45 times, respectively. Comparing these predictions to the true occurrences of these labels, which are 28, 25, and 47, respectively, gives an evaluation of kappa value as 0.779.

The kappa coefficient value of 0.779 demonstrates a substantially strong agreement between predicted and observed labels. This suggests that the model is proficient in capturing key features within the defined categories. While the model performs well across all categories, there are opportunities for further optimization, particularly in identifying individual differences within learner characteristics.

7 Conclusion

This paper focuses on the need to automate the certain elements of systematic literature review (SLR) to support an evidence-based research. The paper attempts to address the challenges associated with the manual processes involved in the same. It underscores the increasing volume of scientific literature, which necessitates approaches to streamline the review process.

The article introduces an approach that leverages Natural Language Processing (NLP) and Machine Learning (ML) techniques to automate the classification of research articles based on the PRISMA framework, which includes study selection criteria, data collection, and synthesis methods.

By employing NLP techniques, such as BERT embedding along with cosine similarity, this methodology offers a solution to automate the categorization of articles into labels grounded in theory, technology, concept, relationship, and more. The approach not only speeds up the review process but also helps maintain the transparency of systematic reviews, as advocated by PRISMA.

Overall, this article presents a significant contribution to the field of evidence synthesis, offering a path to harness the power of NLP and ML to enhance the systematic review process and cope with the ever-expanding landscape of scientific literature. It highlights the potential of automation to revolutionize the way researchers conduct systematic reviews.

References

1. Adeva, J.G., Atxa, J.P., Carrillo, M.U., Zengotitabengoa, E.A.: Automatic text classification to support systematic reviews in medicine. Expert Syst. Appl. **41**(4), 1498–1508 (2014)
2. Armstrong, R., Hall, B.J., Doyle, J., Waters, E.: 'Scoping the scope' of a cochrane review. J. Public Health **33**(1), 147–150 (2011)
3. Aum, S., Choe, S.: srBERT: automatic article classification model for systematic review using BERT. Syst. Control Found. Appl. **10**(1), 1–8 (2021)
4. Basu, T., Kumar, S., Kalyan, A., Jayaswal, P., Goyal, P., Pettifer, S., Jonnalagadda, S.R.: A Novel Framework to Expedite Systematic Reviews by Automatically Building Information Extraction Training Corpora (2016). arXiv preprint arXiv:1606.06424
5. Choong, M.K., Galgani, F., Dunn, A.G., Tsafnat, G.: Automatic evidence retrieval for systematic reviews. J. Med. Internet Res. **16**(10), e223 (2014)
6. Cohen, A.M., Hersh, W.R., Peterson, K., Yen, P.Y.: Reducing workload in systematic review preparation using automated citation classification. J. Am. Med. Inform. Assoc. **13**(2), 206–219 (2006)
7. Cormack, G.V., Grossman, M.R.: Evaluation of machine-learning protocols for technology-assisted review in electronic discovery. In: Proceedings of the 37th International ACM SIGIR Conference on Research & Development in Information Retrieval, pp. 153–162 (2014)
8. Cumpston, M., et al.: Updated guidance for trusted systematic reviews: a new edition of the cochrane handbook for systematic reviews of interventions. Cochrane Database Syst. Rev. **2019**(10), (2019)
9. Jusoh, S.: A study on NLP applications and ambiguity problems. J. Theor. Appl. Inf. Technol. **96**(6), (2018)
10. Kici, D., Malik, G., Cevik, M., Parikh, D., Basar, A.: A BERT-based transfer learning approach to text classification on software requirements specifications. In: Canadian Conference on AI, vol. 1, p. 042077 (2021)

11. Lahitani, A.R., Permanasari, A.E., Setiawan, N.A.: Cosine similarity to determine similarity measure: study case in online essay assessment. In: 2016 4th International Conference on Cyber and IT Service Management, pp. 1–6. IEEE (2016)
12. Li, B., Han, L.: Distance weighted cosine similarity measure for text classification. In: Intelligent Data Engineering and Automated Learning–IDEAL 2013: 14th International Conference, IDEAL 2013, Hefei, China, October 20–23, 2013. Proceedings 14, pp. 611–618. Springer (2013)
13. Liu, S., Tao, H., Feng, S.: Text classification research based on BERT model and Bayesian network. In: 2019 Chinese Automation Congress (CAC), pp. 5842–5846. IEEE (2019)
14. Moher, D., Liberati, A., Tetzlaff, J., Altman, D.G., Group*, P.: Preferred reporting items for systematic reviews and meta-analyses: the Prisma statement. Ann. Inter. Med. **151**(4), 264–269 (2009)
15. Nugroho, K.S., Sukmadewa, A.Y., Yudistira, N.: Large-scale news classification using BERT language model: spark NLP approach. In: Proceedings of the 6th International Conference on Sustainable Information Engineering and Technology, pp. 240–246 (2021)
16. Page, M.J., McKenzie, J.E., Bossuyt, P.M., Boutron, I., Hoffmann, T.C., Mulrow, C.D., Shamseer, L., Tetzlaff, J.M., Akl, E.A., Brennan, S.E., et al.: The Prisma 2020 statement: an updated guideline for reporting systematic reviews. Int. J. Surg. **88**, 105906 (2021)
17. Page, M.J., et al.: Prisma 2020 explanation and elaboration: updated guidance and exemplars for reporting systematic reviews. BMJ **372**, (2021)
18. Pahlevan-Sharif, S., Mura, P., Wijesinghe, S.N.: A systematic review of systematic reviews in tourism. J. Hosp. Tour. Manag. **39**, 158–165 (2019)
19. Selçuk, A.A.: A guide for systematic reviews: Prisma. Turk. Arch. Otorhinolaryngol. **57**(1), 57 (2019)
20. Shemilt, I., et al.: Pinpointing needles in giant haystacks: use of text mining to reduce impractical screening workload in extremely large scoping reviews. Res. Synth. Methods **5**(1), 31–49 (2014)
21. da Silva Júnior, E.M., Dutra, M.L.: A roadmap toward the automatic composition of systematic literature reviews. Iberoamerican J. Sci. Measur. Commun. **1**(2), 1–22 (2021)
22. Silva Júnior, E.M.d., Dutra, M.L.: A roadmap for composing automatic literature reviews: a text mining approach. In: International Conference on Data and Information in Online, pp. 229–239. Springer (2021)
23. Vaswani, A., et al.: Attention is all you need. Adv. Neural Inf. Process. Syst. **30**, (2017)
24. Wallace, B.C., Trikalinos, T.A., Lau, J., Brodley, C., Schmid, C.H.: Semi-automated screening of biomedical citations for systematic reviews. BMC Bioinform. **11**(1), 1–11 (2010)
25. Xia, P., Zhang, L., Li, F.: Learning similarity with cosine similarity ensemble. Inf. Sci. **307**, 39–52 (2015)
26. Yu, S., Su, J., Luo, D.: Improving BERT-based text classification with auxiliary sentence and domain knowledge. IEEE Access **7**, 176600–176612 (2019)
27. Yu, Z., Kraft, N.A., Menzies, T.: Finding better active learners for faster literature reviews. Empir. Softw. Eng. **23**, 3161–3186 (2018)

Closing the Communication Divide: Enhancing Sign Language Recognition with Gesture-to-Text Conversion Through Computer Vision

R. Krishnakumar(✉), M. Kapil, and V. Muthu Lakshmi

Department of Information Technology, St. Joseph's College of Engineering, OMR, Chennai, Tamil Nadu, India
Kichu19062003@gmail.com, computercoordinator@stjosephs.ac.in

Abstract. This paper introduces an innovative method specifically created for identifying and understanding fixed hand movements that represent symbols in American Sign Language (ASL). With the goal of improving communication and learning for those with hearing and speaking difficulties, this system is exceptionally useful for the deaf community to interact with technology. Utilizing the widespread use of ASL as a widely accepted form of communication, the system primarily concentrates on recognizing and converting static hand gestures that correspond to ASL letters into written output. Furthermore, it also includes the ability to convert text to speech, adding to its functionality. At the heart of our groundbreaking approach is the use of Principal Component Analysis (PCA) on still images of the ASL alphabet to accurately detect gestures. By utilizing the power of PCA to identify crucial elements, our system can effectively classify input images and provide accurate recognition of the corresponding ASL alphabet. This output is then presented as text, and can even be transformed into speech, making it a comprehensive tool for individuals with hearing and speech impairments to seamlessly communicate through computer technology. Significantly, this system eliminates the requirement for extra data collecting tools, making it more convenient for users. The strong recognition of ASL gestures, along with the ability to convert those gestures into text and sound, empowers those who are deaf or hard of hearing to effectively communicate through technology.

Keywords: American Sign Language (ASL) · Hand movements · Principal Component Analysis (PCA) · Gesture recognition · Text-to-speech · Communication · Deaf community

1 Introduction

In contemporary times, the sign language domain has made remarkable progress, especially in the area of gesture and facial recognition technologies. These groundbreaking developments have immense potential for individuals with hearing disabilities, providing them with a means to engage in seamless communication through the intricacies of gestures. Whether expressed through hand movements or body language, gestures serve as

Published by Springer Nature Switzerland AG 2025
A. Chandrabose et al. (Eds.): ICCCSP 2024, IFIP AICT 723, pp. 213–224, 2025.
https://doi.org/10.1007/978-3-031-73617-9_17

the building blocks of sign language, encapsulating complex patterns that communicate deep layers of significance. Internationally, an estimated 4.94 billion individuals face difficulties with hearing, highlighting the pressing need for technological advancements in the realm of sign language. Current solutions for sign language translation often focus on factors such as hand positioning, shape, and motion. Each sign in the lexicon carries a unique significance, adding to the intricacy and depth of communication for those with hearing impairments. The world is filled with a vast array of linguistic landscapes, each one giving rise to its own distinct and unparalleled sign language.

These languages are a reflection of the unique fusion of local dialects and cultural influences. While sign language is a universal mode of communication, its true universality is still difficult to attain as different cultural contexts employ their own distinctive forms of sign language. The focus of our study is the examination of hand gestures and positioning in the context of American Sign Language (ASL). Unique from other sign languages, ASL primarily uses one hand, making it ideal for our proposed approach. As an independent and ever-evolving language, ASL breaks away from reliance on spoken languages, paving its own distinctive path of growth. The proposed system begins with capturing images using a camera and involves multiple stages. The first step is preprocessing, which converts RGB images to grayscale for smooth processing. Principal Component Analysis (PCA) is a tried-and-true method in statistics and data science for dimensionality reduction and data representation. Transformation is the manner by which the original high-dimensional inputted data becomes new set of orthogonal variables, also called principal components accounting for the maximum variance in the data. The first principal component is the one describing the largest variance, the second principal component indeed the one corresponding to the second largest variance, and so on. PCA carries out this operation by keeping the k principal components that explain the highest proportion of data variance, therefore lowers the dimensionality of the dataset while the resulting output retains precious information in the data. To emphasize the usefulness of PCA, it reduces the task of the computation and the repeated or meaningless features, which in turn increases the performance and prevents other models from overfitting. Moreover, PCA may be a good tool that allows for detecting the hidden patterns and relations in the data and thus it is easier to make credible conclusions from the analysis. Different from that, PCA has other uses, such as those for data visualization which projects high-dimensional data into a lower-dimensional space that can be visualized and understood easily. In a nutshell, PCA is a very versatile technique for dimensional reduction, preparing data, and exploratory data analysis which could be useful in many fields such as image processing, bio-informatics, finance, and many others. Next, the Canny edge detection algorithm is applied to track edges. This leads to the final stage of identifying patterns through a template-matching algorithm, producing a text-based output. By bridging the communication gap between the deaf community and society, this ground-breaking solution intends to eliminate the need for middle-man interpreters. The main aim is to convert sign language gestures into text, providing a new and inclusive way of communicating for those with hearing impairments. Prior to discussing the methodology, a thorough analysis of previous research offers valuable understanding of the progress and improvements in sign language recognition.

2 Related Works

[1] This paper emphasises that the move to standardize Indian Sign Language has created an opportunity for researchers to focus on solving local problems, thereby increasing its reach. In this paper, a survey and assessment of the techniques applied to the recognition and conversion of Indian Sign Language are conducted. An overview of the techniques used in sign language recognition for Indian Sign Language is provided to comprehend the status of research in this field. Subsequently, a comparison of techniques is presented to offer a more detailed understanding of the research outcomes. The challenges encountered by researchers, the limitations of current techniques, and the imperative for enhanced research in this domain are underscored. With the aim of catalyzing more comprehensive research, key areas within the approaches and techniques requiring refinement are summarized.

[2] Its miles elucidated that signs and symptoms and gestures constitute a method of communique relying on moves and hand gestures, followed through adjustments in facial expression and bodily moves, in lieu of spoken phrases. Similar to spoken languages, there exist numerous distinct sign languages globally. Predominantly utilized by individuals with listening to impairments, signs and gestures serve as a method to express emotions and facilitate interplay. In ancient instances, previous to the appearance of spoken languages, gestures and symptoms were the primary mode of communication, taken into consideration innate and simple. However, with the passage of time, signal language adoption became extra regular among individuals with hearing impairments. Presently, over eighty million human beings global depend upon hand gestures and symbols for communique, constituting a fraction of the worldwide population of seven.8 billion as of 2020. Despite its importance for learning, getting access to offerings, and network integration, limited availability of signal interpreters hinders the supply of vital offerings. To deal with the challenges arising from insufficient records and guide for signal languages, there is a pressing need to sell their utilization amongst the overall populace. However, this enterprise demands good sized effort and won't yield commensurate results. Recognizing correct signs and symptoms in pix poses a complicated assignment, regularly regarding diverse preprocessing strategies. In this venture, pix depicting American Sign Language symptoms are processed and applied to put into effect a Convolutional Neural Network (CNN) version for classifying these images in keeping with their alphabetical equivalents.

[3] Many people, especially the deaf and hard of hearing, depend on sign language as their main way of communicating, but there is a lack of access to information because of differences in proficiency. Systems that translate sign language into text or audio, and the other way around, are very important. Deep learning models have gotten a lot better at recognizing and translating sign language, but there are still problems, such as the need for more accurate models and the need to take into account differences in dialects and cultures. This article reviews the latest sign language translation technologies, including recognition, text, and audio translation.

[4] A study in this paper emphasizes the importance of realistic gestures for virtual agents and robots. They developed a model that uses deep learning to create gestures from spoken text. This model translates words into joint coordinates describing the gesture's movement. The researchers extended an existing dataset with text and speaker

information and trained the model on it.Research involving multiple users has indicated that the suggested model performs as well as or better than existing models that translate speech into gestures. Additionally, the study investigated data optimization, loss function selection, and how to move the model between different speakers. The results showed that the model could be transferred successfully and generate high-quality gestures, even when using a transformer architecture.

[5] In a previous study, researchers emphasized the importance of hand gesture recognition systems for helping people with disabilities and improving communication between humans and computers. These systems are easy to use and cost-effective, but making them fast, accurate, and reliable is still a problem. This research aims to fill this gap by proposing a new approach that uses native OpenCV functions to speed things up and be more accurate. The new system is faster because it uses optimized functions instead of histograms to do calculations. The system that was built can recognize 37 different gestures with 98% accuracy and has a calculator mode for doing math problems.This study uses computer vision technology to develop recognition systems that require less memory and computing power. These systems have the potential to be used in commercial applications and could be deployed in app stores in the future.

[6] A previous study highlighted the importance of overcoming communication challenges for those with speech disabilities, suggesting sign language as a solution. This paper aims to connect individuals with disabilities, such as the deaf and mute, with others by developing a system that recognizes sign language gestures. Using methods from image processing and machine learning, a real-time system was created. Image processing is utilized to extract hand gestures from the background, which are then used to create a dataset of 24 English alphabet gestures.The Convolutional Neural Network (CNN) model developed has been tested on a custom dataset and on live hand gestures made by people with various skin tones. The model achieved an accuracy of 83% in this testing.

[7] Deep learning in computer vision has advanced technologies in target detection, recognition, and tracking. Sign language recognition, a growing field in machine learning, aims to overcome communication barriers for the deaf. This project uses computer vision techniques for sign language recognition to improve everyday communication for deaf people. It investigates two algorithm models: a CNN + LSTM network structure and YOLOv5 target detection.Sign language recognition depends on algorithms, which have been compared for effectiveness. YOLOv5, which recognizes hand motions, detects signals faster. This speed advantage makes YOLOv5 ideal for real-time translation of sign language, enabling its practical use.

[8] This paper describes the importance of signal language as a awesome shape of verbal exchange is emphasized, catering to various segments of society. Visual signal language reputation, characterized by using variations in hand shape, motion profile, and positioning of hand, face, and frame parts, presents a complicated studies area inside pc imaginative and prescient. Recent years have witnessed extensive advancements, mainly via deep learning techniques, in proposed models for signal language reputation. This survey comprehensively evaluations imaginative and prescient-based totally fashions using deep getting to know strategies for signal language reputation over the past five years. While these models showcase great enhancements in reputation accuracy, several

challenges persist. A taxonomy is supplied to categorize the proposed fashions, distinguishing between remoted and non-stop signal language popularity, while discussing packages, datasets, hybrid models, complexity, and future research guidelines in the discipline.

[9] This paper considers the difficulties that deaf and dumb people run into when they want to communicate with general public, as typical population know little of sign language. It describes the development of an artificial neural network converter in Indian sign language. It uses the convolutional neural network algorithm. The goal is to create an Indian Sign Language (ISL) speech recognition system by mapping the 26 letters in ISL to their corresponding alphabet letters from the images captured and text translated. First of all, a voluminous database containing various professions is presented, and multiple image processing techniques are used to streamline the process of feature extraction. Thereafter, the convolutional neural network (CNN) algorithm in a Python environment is employed to extract features from the images. Systematic checking of both with and without live images provides 96 % false positives for imaging samples and 87.69 % classifier for no live images.

[10] People tackle the task of recognizing sign language from videos, specifically focusing on the sign language used in Morocco. While traditional methods rely on manually selecting important features for each sequence of signs, our approach leverages deep learning models. This paper introduces two such models: 2D Convolutional Recurring Neural Network (2DCRNN) and 3D Convolutional Neural Network (3DCNN). These models automatically extract significant features from video sequences, leading to impressive accuracy levels. Using a dataset of 224 videos and a validation technique called fourfold cross-validation, we achieved an accuracy of 92% with the 2DCRNN model and a remarkable 99% accuracy with the 3DCNN model.

3 System Structure

The initial stage in the image processing process is extracting the image from a hardware-based source. Web cameras are used as the source in this project. This initial step is essential because without an image, no further processing can take place. The obtained picture is in its raw, unprocessed form. Segmentation refers to the technique of isolating objects or signs from the captured image. Our proposed methodology utilizes various methods such as text subtraction, skin-color detection, and edge detection to achieve segmentation. Detecting and segmenting the hand's motion and location is crucial for accurately identifying gestures (Fig. 1).

The pre-processed images are scanned for predefined features such as form, contour, geometrical parameters (position, angle, distance, etc.), color, histogram, and other characteristics. These features are then extracted and utilized in the classification and recognition of signs. By doing so, we are able to reduce the dimensions of the data, making the processing easier and more manageable. The vast number of variables in these data sets is the key factor, requiring a significant amount of computational power for proper processing. Function extraction is a valuable tool for extracting the most relevant feature from extensive data sets. It involves the combination of variables into functions, resulting in a smaller and more manageable data size. These functions are both user-friendly and accurately describe the data being analysed. Before undergoing function

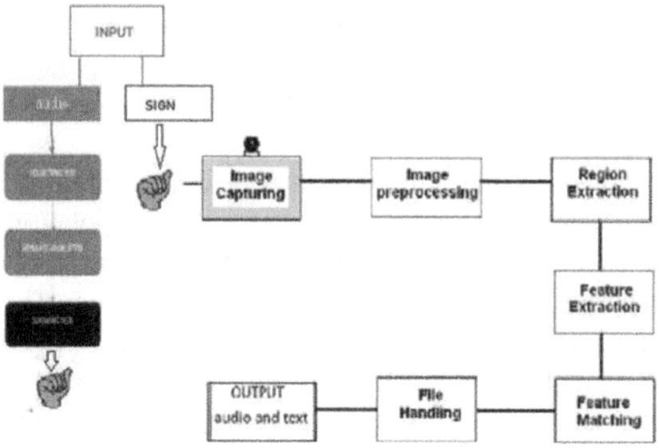

Fig. 1. System Framework

extraction, each image is first refined through various filters such as erosion, dilation, and Gaussian smoothing. This helps to remove any unwanted noise. Additionally, when dealing with color images, they are converted to grayscale to reduce the data size. Such methods greatly aid in minimizing the data being processed. The choice of classifiers is essential for our project's success. These algorithms are crucial as they help us make sense of the data signals. Among the popular classifiers utilized like Hidden Markov Model, K-Nearest Neighbour classifiers, Support Vector Machines, and Artificial Neural Networks are among the tools used for sign language interpretation, and Principal Component Analysis. However, for our specific project, we have selected the Convolutional Neural Network (CNN) as our classifier of choice. This is due to its exceptional accuracy in image classification and recognition tasks.

Principal Component Analysis (PCA) is a statistical approach used for dimensionality discount and data visualization. In this paper, PCA is used for extracting the maximum important records from your dataset at the same time as reducing its complexity. PCA offers a effective tool for reducing the dimensionality of the dataset, extracting meaningful functions, visualizing complex facts, decreasing noise, and enhancing interpretability. Incorporating PCA into this paper can enhance the capability to investigate and derive insights from the facts efficiently (Fig. 2).

The CNN's hierarchical structure resembles a funnel, ultimately leading to a fully-connected layer where all neurons are interlinked and data is processed efficiently. By comprehending human actions and recognizing a range of bodily positions and gestures, this technique translates them into written words. A convolutional neural network (CNN) utilizes a specialized architecture, similar to a multilayer perceptron, specifically created for lower processing demands. Its layers are an input layer, an output layer, and a hidden layer that contains numerous fully connected, convolutional, pooling, and normalizing layers. Eliminating constraints and enhancing efficiency in processing visual information leads to a highly effective system that is easier to train, enabling it to handle both image and natural language processing tasks with greater proficiency.

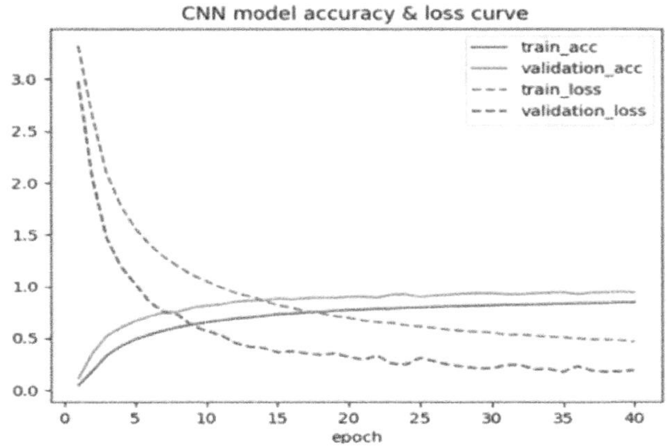

Fig. 2. Loss and Accuracy Curve

4 Module Outline

Sign to Audio

Image Procurement

Image Procurement is the first stage of every image processing system. This important step is transforming an optical image or actual data into computer-manageable numerical values. To capture the gestures, a web camera is utilized, while an OpenCV video stream is employed to record the entire signing process. Each frame of the stream is then extracted and converted into a grayscale image with a standardized dimension of 50*50. This uniform size is maintained throughout the project, ensuring consistency throughout the dataset (Figs. 3 and 4).

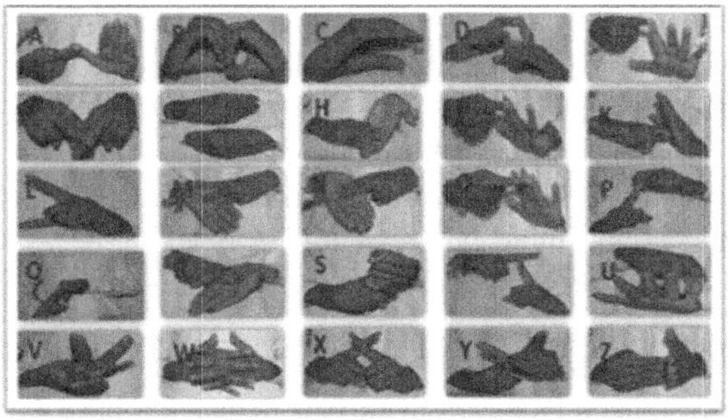

Fig. 3. Double Handed Sign Language

Hand Region Segmentation and Hand Region Tracking

The collected images go through preprocessing to check for hand motions before being placed into the model for prediction. By enhancing the segments that contain gestures, the chances of accurate prediction are greatly amplified.

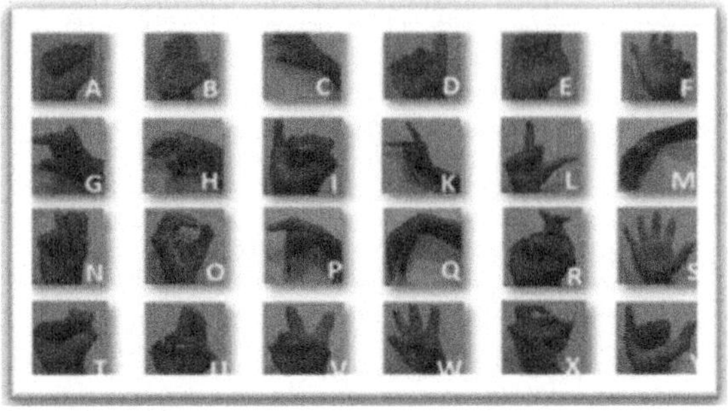

Fig. 4. Single Handed Sign Language

Hand Posture Recognition

The keras CNN model is fed pre-processed images, allowing it to generate a predicted label based on its previous training. Each gesture label is assigned a probability, and the label with the highest probability is ultimately considered to be the predicted label. This approach ensures maximum accuracy in prediction (Fig. 5).

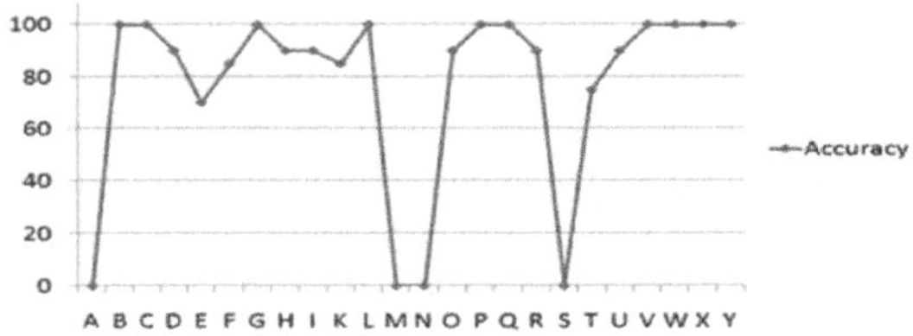

Fig. 5. Accuracy Rate of the System

Display as Text and Speech

The model collects and incorporates the identified gesture into spoken words. Utilizing the pyttsx3 library, the recognized words are transformed into speech. This text-to-speech function may seem simple, but it is a crucial aspect of the project as it creates an immersive verbal interaction experience.

Convolutional Neural Network

CNNs are surpassing other methods from the benefit that they have the power to work out hierarchical information from raw input data themselves. With the convolutional layers, edge and texture features of the lower order are extracted progressively and developed to make up classes in accordance with the higher order representation. The hierarchy characteristic of CNNs formulates internal feature learning and provide the ability to exploit complex relationships and spatial dependencies, especially in cases of image, video and spatial data generation. Furthermore, pooling layers introduce downsampling while nonlinearity. This results in a more stable and descriptive performance. Moreover, the existence of pre-trained models and transfer learning makes the task-specific dataset fine-tuning easier feeding with knowledge from large-scale datasets. On the whole, CNNs' hierarchical feature learning, spacial consciousness, non-linear activation functions and transfer learning is indeed the reason for their superior precision in a wide range of machine learning and computer vision tasks.

Audio To Sign Language:

Forms of Input

Our project aims to collect inputs in various formats, such as •Live Speech •Recorded Audio Files.

Speech Recognition

Our system utilizes the Python package PyAudio to receive live speech from the microphone. This package allows for audio recording on various platforms. Once the audio is received, it undergoes conversion to text using the Google Speech Recognizer API. This API uses neural network models to accurately translate spoken words into written text. The audio file can also be inputted directly for conversion, with the Google Speech Recognizer breaking it into smaller, more manageable chunks to ensure efficient and accurate transcription.

Pre-processing of Text

Image preprocessing is a critical process that preps images for successful model training and inference. Its tasks encompass a wide range of actions, such as resizing, orienting, and color corrections, among others (Figs. 6 and 7).

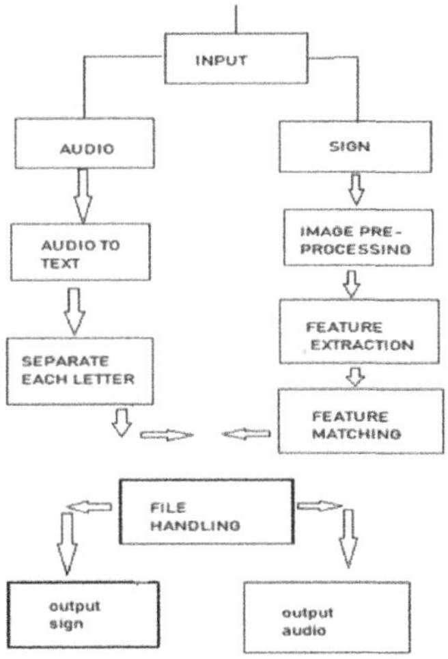

Fig. 6. Data Flow Diagram

Text to Sign Language

As the system progresses through each word in the processed text sentence, it diligently

Classification Report

	precision	recall	f1-score	support
0	1.00	0.99	0.99	410
1	0.98	0.92	0.95	385
2	0.91	0.99	0.95	318
accuracy			0.96	1113
macro avg	0.96	0.96	0.96	1113
weighted avg	0.96	0.96	0.96	1113

Fig. 7. Classification Report of the Proposed System.

searches for the matching sign language video sequences in its local database. If a match is found, the result is presented as a video sequence using the power of Python's OpenCV module. This versatile and open-source library excels in image processing, video analysis, and various other computer vision tasks. By passing the video sequence's location to OpenCV, the system beautifully showcases the video frame by frame (Fig. 8).

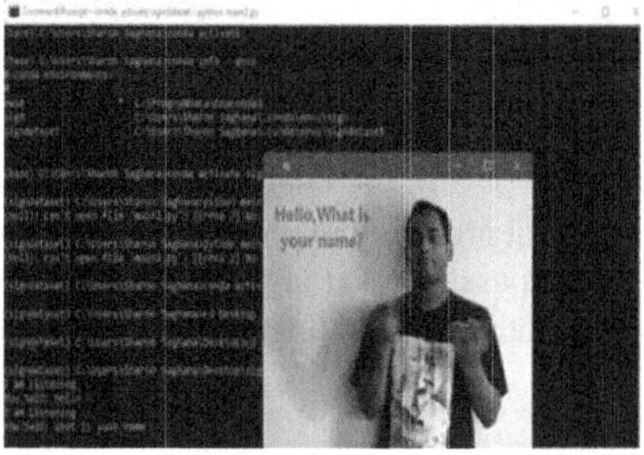

Fig. 8. Expected Terminal Output

Web scraping is the ultimate technique for gathering content from websites. It's a nifty automated method that yields large volumes of data from all sorts of websites. While most of this data is untamed and unorganized in HTML, it can easily be transformed into a structured format like a spreadsheet or database. This transformed data is highly versatile and can be applied in various applications. With numerous methods available, web scraping can be done through online services, specific APIs, or even via personalized code. Numerous prominent websites, including Google, Twitter, Facebook, and Stack Overflow, have API's that permit users to retrieve their data in an organized manner (Fig. 9).

While this is typically the most efficient and user-friendly approach, there are other websites that lack the technological means or the option to access large quantities of data in a structured format. For these cases, Web Scraping is a valuable tool for extracting data from these websites. The process involves utilizing the Beautiful Soup module, specifically designed for working with HTML files in Python, to search, manipulate, and extract desired data.

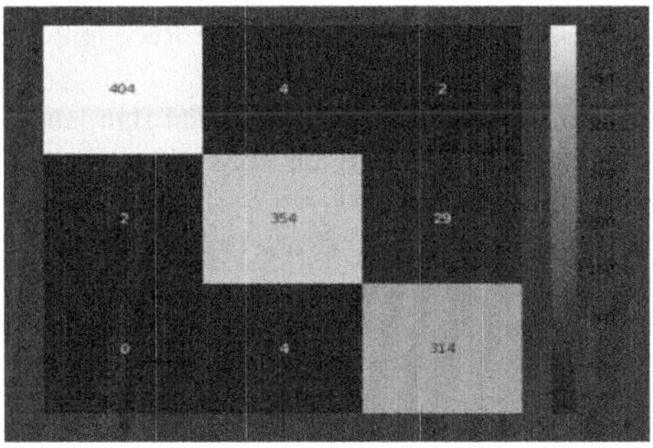

Fig. 9. Confusion Matrix.

5 Conclusion

The papers reviewed have consistently highlighted the ever-changing landscape of sign language recognition systems, with a specific emphasis on meeting the unique needs of those with hearing impairments. This innovative progress is exemplified by the incorporation of cutting-edge technologies such as smart gloves, computer vision, and advanced sensors, all aimed at breaking down communication barriers for the deaf community. The accuracy of these systems in comprehending both static and dynamic hand gestures is crucial in facilitating the fluent translation of sign language into written or spoken words. Additionally, the emphasis on minimizing the use of extra data collection devices further improves the convenience and accessibility of these systems within the larger scope of their impact on the community.

References

1. Bhat, A., Yadav, V., Dargan, V., Yash: Sign language to text conversion using deep learning. In: 2022 3rd International Conference for Emerging Technology (INCET). Belgaum, India (2022)
2. Rao Mangalore, K.K., Pradeep, N., Rajpal, B., Prasad, N., Shastri, R.: A survey on the techniques applied to the recognition and conversion of Indian sign language. J. Appl. Res. Indus. Eng. (2021)
3. Betsy Angelin, S., Nithya, E., Devianugraga, M.S.: A survey on conversion of audio and text to sign language and vice versa using deep learning. In: 2023 9th International Conference on Smart Structures and Systems (ICSSS). CHENNAI, India (2023)
4. Asakawa, E., Kaneko, N., Hasegawa, D., Shirakawa, S.: Evaluation of text-to-gesture generation model using convolutional neural network. Neural Networks **151** (2022)
5. Khati, U., Singh, P., Shankar, A.: Text Generation through Hand Gesture Recognition (June 23, 2020). Proceedings of the International Conference on Innovative Computing & Communications (ICICC) (2020)
6. Raval, J.J., Gajjar, R.: Real-time sign language recognition using computer vision. In: 2021 3rd International Conference on Signal Processing and Communication (ICPSC). Coimbatore, India (2021)
7. Li, T., Yan, Y., Du, W.: Sign language recognition based on computer vision. In: 2022 IEEE International Conference on Artificial Intelligence and Computer Applications (ICAICA). Dalian, China (2022)

8. Rastgoo, R., Kiani, K., Escalera, S.: Sign Language Recognition: A Deep Survey. Expert Systems with Applications **164** (2021)
9. Intwala, N., Banerjee, A., Meenakshi, Gala, N.: Indian sign language converter using convolutional neural networks. In: 2019 IEEE 5th International Conference for Convergence in Technology (I2CT). Bombay, India (2019)
10. Boukdir, A., Benaddy, M., Ellahyani, A., et al.: Isolated video-based arabic sign language recognition using convolutional and recursive neural networks. Arab. J. Sci. Eng. **47**, 2187–2199 (2022)

Evolving GAN-BERT Architecture for Efficient Text Categorization with Minimal Labeled Data

C. Bagavathi(✉), M. Raakesh, Chanamala Vipasyana Bhanu, Katheram Venkata Sai Ram Reddy, and Kancharla Rupesh Sai Sathwik

Department of Computer Science and Engineering, Amrita School of Computing, Amrita Vishwa Vidyapeetham, Coimbatore, India
c_bagavathi@cb.amrita.edu,
{cb.en.u4cse20152,cb.en.u4cse20114,cb.en.u4cse20131,
cb.en.u4cse20030}@cb.students.amrita.edu

Abstract. Categorical text generation is an upcoming field within natural language processing focusing on producing text tailored to specific categories or domains. The goal of categorical text production is to produce text that complies with the requirements and characteristics of the chosen category while also adhering to the grammatical and structural conventions of the language. Text classification works across multiple data categories, and the synthetic data generated usually adheres to a preset pattern and ignores the text's nuanced emotional content. The proposed approach begins with using BERT to get the text's deep contextual embeddings. Using these text embeddings, the underlying semantics of the target category can be better understood by adding a task-specific layer that places the sentences in the closest corresponding class. After that, the architecture and settings of the GAN are optimized through evolutionary computing techniques to guarantee that the generated text conforms to the constraints and characteristics specific to each category.

Keywords: Text Categorization · Evolutionary Computation · BERT · Generative Adversarial Networks

1 Introduction

Text categorization, sometimes called Text Classification, is a Natural Language Processing (NLP) task in which a text is given one or more predetermined labels or categories [1]. The objective is to automatically evaluate text documents according to their content and classify them into predetermined groups or classes. To generate predictions on new, unseen text, a machine learning model is trained on a labeled dataset, which is an example of supervised learning [2].

Several processes are involved in the text categorization process, including data collection, pre-processing, feature extraction, model training, and evaluation. Various text categorization applications include topic classification in news

Published by Springer Nature Switzerland AG 2025
A. Chandrabose et al. (Eds.): ICCCSP 2024, IFIP AICT 723, pp. 225–238, 2025.
https://doi.org/10.1007/978-3-031-73617-9_18

articles [3], text classification [4], sentiment analysis in social media [5], recommendation systems in e-commerce [6], Language identification [7], Named Entity Recognition [8], and spam detection in emails, among many more [1]. Automating the processing and arrangement of massive amounts of textual material is essential for efficient text categorization. Various methods can be used to categorize text, ranging from traditional machine learning approaches to more advanced deep learning techniques [9].

The difficulty of text categorization can be attributed primarily to traditional machine learning techniques, such as supervised, semi-supervised, and unsupervised approaches that rely on feature engineering techniques. Techniques like the bag-of-words (BoW) model or bag-of-n-gram vectors, where features include punctuation, stop words, emoticons, negation words, lexicons, elongated words, and other delineated patterns, are frequently used for categorization [29]. Another roadblock in text categorization is that the number of labeled samples is difficult to process for a new dataset. Also, many datasets have few labeled data points, affecting the categorization models' metrics [10].

Category-aware text generation is receiving attention nowadays due to the current level of information overload, the number of applications depending on text, and the personalized information expected from users to easily use a platform [2].

The proposed study uses GAN models with BERT encoders for dataset pretraining and hierarchical evolutionary computing to generate and categorize text. With less labeled datasets, it develops a novel method for optimizing text categorization using evolutionary algorithms and BERT. The ability to increase the efficacy and efficiency of activities connected to text production and comprehension adds a feather to the crown of combining the capabilities of BERT with category-aware GAN. BERT can be used to supplement CatGAN, which is well-known for its category-specific text creation and excellent contextual comprehension. When coupled, these methods can produce content that not only falls into predefined categories but also demonstrates a deeper comprehension of contextual nuances, leading to the creation of a language model of better caliber. Furthermore, the generated content may be contextually adjusted using BERT to ensure coherence and linguistic accuracy.

2 Text Categorization and GAN

Generative Adversarial Networks (GANs) have recently demonstrated promising text generation performance. A class of machine learning models, Generative Adversarial Networks (GANs) [11], was first presented in 2014. Generative tasks involve creating new data samples that bear similarities to a given dataset. An adversarial training process between two neural networks—a generator and a discriminator-is the fundamental concept underlying GANs. There has been development in using Generative Adversarial Networks (GANs) for text production and, consequently, text categorization, even though GANs are mostly known for their efficiency in image generation tasks. However, text GANs suffer from several issues, including discreteness, training instability, mode collapse, lack of variety, and the ability to control [12].

Text generation is the first step in text categorization. Text generation is the process of producing text without any constraints or preconditions. The model receives no particular context, subject, or category during generating content. The aim is to produce writing that, without restricting the content to a predefined category or theme, is both cohesive and meaningful in the context of the content. Several Text Generation GANs exist in literature ans some of them are SeqGAN [13], LeakGAN [14], MaliGAN [15], RankGAN [16], RelGAN [17], and DPGAN [18] are a few of them.

Category-based text generation [19] is the process of creating text content within categories or subjects. The text generated by the model fits inside a predefined framework, since it was trained on a certain category or theme. The objective is to produce relevant text to a designated category or subject while ensuring that the information generated adheres to the established standards. Category-aware text generation is the process of creating news stories containing content that falls into predefined categories, like "Sports", "Technology", or "Politics". For Category Text Generation, GANs mostly come in two varieties. SentiGAN and CatGAN are their names.

A particular kind of Generative Adversarial Network (GAN) called SentiGAN [20] is intended to produce sentimental texts with modifiable sentiment labels. With many generators and a single multi-class discriminator, it uses a special framework to address the shortcomings of traditional GANs for sentiment management. SentiGAN offers fine-grained control over the mood of the generated text, enabling the creation of sentences with the right emotional overtones. Using many generators and a multi-class discriminator generates more realistic and relevant text than typical GANs. Since SentiGAN does not require labeled data for training, it is more efficient and versatile than existing sentiment analysis models. SentiGAN has certain restrictions. It can require more processing resources to train than simpler GAN models because it uses several generators and has an intricate training procedure.

Category-aware Generative Adversarial Networks, or CatGANs [19], are a particular kind of GAN that can produce text aligned in several categories. It tackles the drawback of conventional GANs, which frequently produce homogeneous text that lacks diversity. CatGAN incorporates an efficient model that quantifies the variation between generated and actual samples for every category. This allows the model to focus on generating high-quality text that falls within the assigned category. To improve training stability and avoid utilizing sophisticated learning mechanisms, CatGAN employs the Gumbel-SoftMax relaxing approach [21]. This expedites the learning process and makes training on discrete data more smooth. To address the mode collapse issue and encourage variation in generated text, CatGAN employs a hierarchical evolutionary learning technique. This algorithm helps the model balance diversity and quality during training. CatGAN requires a large amount of category-specific data for training, which may not be readily available for all domains. Another drawback of CatGAN is that its hierarchical evolutionary learning approach may be computationally expensive for large datasets. It can be challenging and expert to fine-tune the many CatGAN parameters to achieve the best results [22].

BERT stands for Bidirectional Encoder Representations from Transformers. It is a natural language processing model that can learn from both directions of the text. BERT can be fine-tuned for various tasks, such as question answering, sentiment analysis, and named entity recognition. The transformer based BERT uses self-attention to encode the input sequence.

Bert base case is a transformer model that was trained in a self-supervised manner using an enormous corpus of English data. This model distinguishes between English and English and is case-sensitive. It is primarily meant to be refined for use in downstream tasks like sequence classification, token classification, and question answering, where judgments are made using the entire sentence—possibly hidden [23].

Bert base uncased model is uncased, meaning that it is insensitive to the distinction between English and English. It is primarily meant to be refined on downstream tasks like sequence classification, token classification, and question answering, where judgments are made using the entire phrase (perhaps disguised). Cased and uncased versions were developed for BERT models connected to batteries. While the uncased models only use lowercase words, the cased model retains the entire text from the original papers as input, including both uppercase and lowercase terms [23].

RoBERTa-based model is a transformer-based model that is pre-trained on a huge corpus of English content in a self-supervised manner. The model was already trained with raw text content. The Masked Language Modeling (MLM) was used during pre-trained training. The model works on a sentence and randomly masks 15% of the words in the input sentence. The model then runs the complete masked sentence through the model and must predict the hidden words. It is employed in decision-making processes like sequence categorization [24].

ALBERT-based-v2 was pre-trained with Masked language modeling (MLM) and Sentence Ordering Prediction (SOP). There are 12 repeating layers and 11M parameters in this model. The primary goal of this model's refinement is tasks like token and sequence classification, where decisions are made using the entire sentence [25].

XLM-RoBERTa is a multilingual version of RoBERTa. It is pre-trained model with 2.5 TB of filtered data spanning over 100 languages. The XLM-RoBERTa model's characteristics can be used as inputs to train a conventional classifier. This is used for question-answering tasks [25].

BORT is a highly compressed version of BERT-large that can infer up to ten times faster. The model is an ideal BERT-large sub-architecture that has been discovered by neural architecture search. It is also 7.9× quicker on a CPU and outperforms other compressed implementations of the architecture as well as some non-compressed ones [26].

Finding accurate and efficient text classification models is a top priority in natural language processing. Although BERT and other pre-trained language models have demonstrated outstanding outcomes, their substantial reliance on massive volumes of labeled data may limit their application in real-world circumstances. Herein lies the unique method called GAN-BERT [27], which uses BERT for dependable and efficient semi-supervised learning by leveraging the power of Generative Adversarial Networks (GANs). GAN-BERT addresses the drawbacks of traditional supervised learning methods by integrating labeled and unlabelled data throughout its training process. The GAN framework works as a dynamic engine producing synthetic text to improve the model's comprehension of linguistic patterns and supplement the tagged data. This significantly improves representation learning, allowing GAN-BERT to achieve performance on par with or better than standard BERT models using a substantially smaller amount of labeled data. Apart from its remarkable efficacy, GAN-BERT offers other significant advantages. Its robustness and stability ensure constant performance even with weakly labeled data, and its adaptability allows it to be easily adjusted to a wide range of text classification tasks and domains. Furthermore, GAN-BERT may employ unlabeled data, reducing computational costs and speeding up training duration, making it a viable solution for real-world applications.

3 Proposed Methodology

Bidirectional Encoder Representations from Transformers (BERT) provides contextual embeddings for words in sentences and sentence-level semantics, allowing it to encode individual words, entire sentences, and pairs of sentences. These embeddings can be adapted for tasks like sentence classification or sequence labeling by appending layers which are specific to a task and fine-tuning the labeled data.

In this study, BERT's fine-tuning process is enhanced by incorporating Evolutionary Computing and custom layers. Fine-tuning a pre-trained BERT model involves two main additions: (i) task-specific layers for BERT fine-tuning and (ii) modified-GAN layers to implement semi-supervised learning. On the generator, an evolutionary algorithm is incorporated to enable hierarchical evolutionary learning and the generation of diverse synthetic samples (fake samples).

As shown in Fig. 1, modified GAN architecture is added with of BERT through a discriminator D for classifying fake and real examples, and a generator G that acts adversarially. The Generator G is a Multi-Layer Perceptron (MLP) that input with 100 dimensions which is a noise vector and produces an output vector h_fake. The discriminator obtains a vector h* as input. The discriminator input can either be a fake data from generator or a real data. The final layer of the discriminator is a softmax activation layer, which gives an output of k + 1 vector of logical digits.

The input dataset consists of both labeled and unlabeled cases. As a pre-trained transformer-based language model, BERT is particularly good at identifying the subtle contextual details between words in a phrase. The contextual

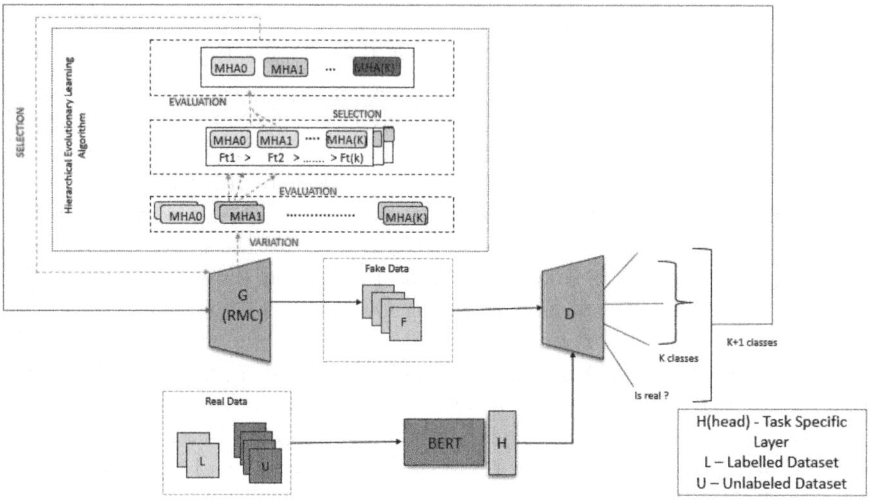

Fig. 1. Proposed Model Architecture

embeddings that BERT generates for each word in a sequence capture the complex relationships and meanings that are inherent to the language; these embeddings might be useful as rich features for downstream applications like text classification or sentiment analysis for labeled samples. The BERT embeddings also provide a way to extract contextual information from unlabeled samples too, which is useful for semi-supervised learning, clustering, and other context-dependent tasks that need a reliable representation of the input.

The Evolutionary Computation (EC) framework, depicted in Fig. 1 has a category-aware model incorporated with hierarchical evolutionary learning algorithm. BERT supplies pre-trained real data; the evolved generator generates synthetic samples using an evolutionary learning process. This process evolves a group of generators through various environmental mutation strategies. The best generator of the selected group is identified as the final choice to produce meaningful sentences with the specified text category.

3.1 Hierarchical Evolutionary Algorithm

This hierarchical evolutionary learning algorithm evolves the generator by varying the internal neural architecture of generators to compete with the discriminators adversarially.

Variation: During the variation step, the generator is mutated based on mutation probability strategies, i.e., mutating the Multi-Head Attention module (MHA) by changing the number of parameters incorporated. The mutation rate is chosen as 0.3, which is responsible for changing the weightage of the MHA parameter.

Evaluation: During the evaluation procedure, the generated fake samples of the current generator Gi are forwarded to the discriminator to compete in the adversarial game, thus identifying whether the generated sample is fake or not. During the forward step, when real instances are sampled, the discriminator should classify the real instance of the samples in one of the k categories. When $h^* = h\_fake$, it should classify each example in the $k + 1$ category. This $k + 1$ vector is sent again to the generator for future hierarchical evolution.

Selection: Each iteration stage's evaluation process is equivalent to a selection process that chooses the individuals with higher evaluation scores. First, the most accurate individual is kept. Next, the individuals that make it are further filtered according to Fobj to identify the better generators as the new parents, which will take part in the subsequent adversarial training iteration. By applying the "survival of the fittest" principle, the generator's ideal temperature and training objective are chosen, enabling the model as a whole to be trained more effectively.

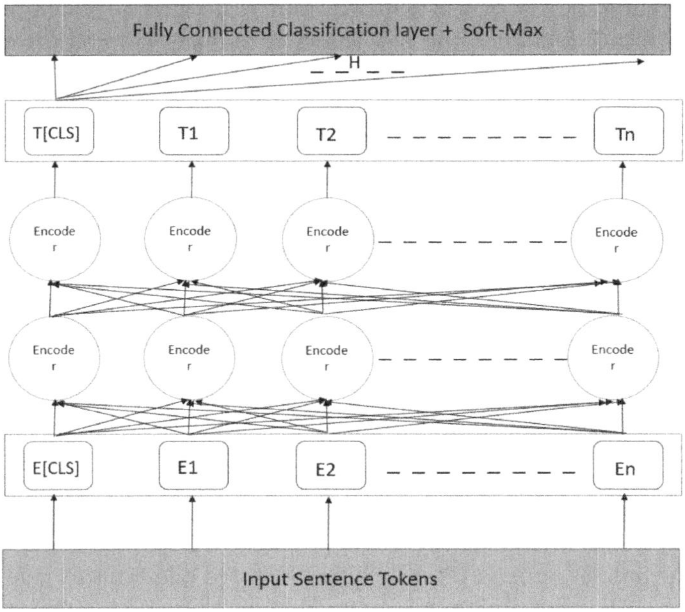

Fig. 2. Token passing mechanism is the proposed model

The discriminator class is a neural network model for binary classification (real or fake). This method has a single hidden layer along with two output classes and a dropout layer that will be applied to the input representation before passing it through the neural network, which helps prevent overfitting during training. The discriminator has a list of layers for the neural network.

It iterates over the hidden layer sizes and creates a sequence of linear layers, leaky ReLU activation functions, and dropout layers. By creating a linear (fully connected) layer connecting the current layer i to the next layer i + 1. It takes the input size hidden_sizes[i] and produces an output size hidden_sizes[i + 1].

The LeakyReLU introduces a small negative slope during the forward pass to allow a small gradient when the unit is inactive. The SoftMax activation function along the last dimension converts the raw logits into class probabilities.

During the forward pass, the discriminator applies dropout to the input representation and then passes it through the hidden layers. Further, it calculates logits using the final linear layer and computes probabilities using the SoftMax activation, which returns the last hidden representation, logits, and probabilities as explained in Fig. 2.

By learning to differentiate between the two, the discriminator can discern subtle nuances and characteristics that distinguish authentic from generated content. The core of the GAN system is this adversarial training process, in which the discriminator hones its discriminating skills while the generator tries to provide ever more realistic data. When these two neural networks interact, a dynamic equilibrium is reached that, in theory, produces a generator that can produce artificial data that the discriminator cannot tell apart from genuine data.

4 Experimental Results

The impact of our proposed model over text classification tasks characterized by different training conditions, i.e., number of examples and number of categories, is evaluated in this section.

4.1 Datasets

The Text REtrieval Conference (TREC) Question Classification dataset contains 5390 unlabeled questions, 110 labeled questions in the training set, and another 500 for the test set. The dataset has 6 labels and 47 level-2 labels. The average length of each sentence is 10, and the vocabulary size is 8700. Four sources provide the data: 894 TREC 8 and TREC 9 questions, 500 questions from TREC 10, which is the test set, around 500 manually generated questions for a few unusual classes, and 4,500 English questions provided by USC. Also, other benchmark datasets, like Topic Classification on the 20News (20N) dataset and Sentiment Analysis on the SST dataset (SST-5) are used as datasets for this problem.

The IMDb Movie Reviews dataset related to sentiment analysis with 50,000 binary reviews from the Internet Movie Database (IMDb). It has sentiment labels indicating whether the review expresses a positive or negative sentiment. Only 1/5th of the dataset has been used, 5000 as labeled, 5000 as unlabeled, and 500 as test datasets to check the efficiency of the model to work on small set of labelled data.

Table 1. Experimental aspects performed with Proposed method

Type of Classification	Task Performed	Dataset
Binary classification	Sentiment classification	Movie Review dataset [30]
	Analysis of Labelled data size	Movie Review dataset [30]
Multi-class classification	Question Classification	TREC dataset [31]

As a comparison, the BERT-base model and GAN-BERT model are fine-tuned on the same dataset and the performance comparison has been reported. BERT-base has been used as the initial model for analysis.

The proposed model, with various pre-trained language model classification results, is shown in Table 2, with 5000 rows in the labeled dataset in this configuration, the model had clear instances to train from. In addition, a 5000-row unlabeled dataset was included simultaneously, enabling the model to identify latent patterns in unannotated text. The 2500-row test dataset was used as an external benchmark to assess the model's performance. Remarkably, just 10% of the 50000 rows in the entire dataset were used for training, demonstrating the effectiveness of the model in learning from a comparatively small quantity of labeled data.

Table 2. Test Accuracy and Loss for Movie Review Dataset [30] applied to BERT variations through GAN-BERT [27] and the proposed technique for binary classification

Sl. No	Model	Test accuracy	Test loss
1	BERT-base-cased	0.768	1.326
2	BERT-base-uncased	0.794	1.297
3	Roberta-base	0.774	1.926
4	Albert-base-v2	0.778	0.965
5	Xlm-roberta-base	0.478	0.699
6	Amazon-bort	0.702	1.809

Results in Table 2 show that less than 10% of the 50,000 rows in the full dataset were utilized for training, indicating how well the model learned with a very small amount of labeled data. The highest accuracy (0.794) was obtained for the model "BERT base-uncased".

In comparison to Senti-Gan [20], which has an accuracy of 0.885 and uses the full dataset for training. The proposed work extends to reducing the use of labeled datasets, as the collection of labeled datasets is costly and computationally taxing in the real world. Thus, the proposed model guarantees a better trade-off between labeled data and accuracy.

This simplified method is especially useful when there is a dearth of labeled data, since the model may use many unlabeled data to improve its comprehension of various textual patterns. Six distinct transformer-based pre-trained models were also used, adding a multi-modal element to the learning process and allowing the model to incorporate a variety of contextual subtleties and characteristics found in the input text.

As part of the experiments mentioned in Table 1, the next experiment has ventured into multi-class classification, augmenting the versatility of our methodology. Six different pre-trained models, each reflecting a unique transformer-based architecture, were used in our experiments. These models were carefully chosen to evaluate their efficacy in various categorization settings.

Table 3. Test Accuracy and Loss for QC TREC Dataset [31] applied to BERT variations through GAN-BERT [27] and the proposed technique for multi-class classification.

Metrics		Test accuracy		Test loss	
Sl. No	Model	GAN-BERT [1]	Proposed	GAN-BERT [1]	Proposed
1	BERT-base-cased	0.626	0.652	2.339	2.302
2	BERT-base-uncased	–	0.620	–	2.758
3	Roberta-base	–	0.110	–	3.767
4	Albert-base-v2	–	0.406	–	3.864
5	Xlm-roberta-base	–	0.110	–	3.657
6	Amazon-bort	–	0.246	–	5.228

Table 3 shows that the accuracy of the proposed model is 2.6% higher than the GAN-BERT's accuracy for the "BERT base-cased" model, making the proposed method more accurate in categorizing the texts. This marginal improvement in accuracy can even be improved by using a large BERT-based pre-trained model but with the catch of computational cost. The proposed model is also extended by incorporating Evolutionary Algorithm in Generators for improved adversarial learning of data.

Table 4. Proposed method for Binary classification with varying the labeled dataset size of Movie Review dataset

Sl. No	Labeled Dataset	Test Accuracy	Test Loss
1	150	0.663	2.668
2	500	0.726	1.990
3	1000	0.744	1.415
4	5000	0.761	1.063
5	10000	0.818	0.859

Table 4 shows the trade-off between the labeled dataset and accuracy; as the labeled dataset size is increased, the accuracy improves, and our experiments predict that with only 50% of the total dataset, it is pliable to achieve better results than the existing state-of-art methods.

Table 5. Result comparison of our proposed model with BERT base cased, GAN-BERT [27] of QC on TREC dataset

Sl. No	Annotated percentage	BERT	GAN-BERT	Proposed
1	1	0.020	0.24	0.466
2	2	0.04	0.49	0.564
3	5	0.17	0.66	0.662
4	10	0.30	0.70	0.762
5	20	0.56	0.78	0.824
6	30	0.64	0.775	0.825
7	40	0.71	0.79	0.840
8	50	0.76	0.80	0.870

Table 5 shows that the proposed model significantly improves accuracy compared to the other two state-of-the-art models. 1% annotated BERT and GAN-BERT have very little accuracy compared to the proposed model, as the main motive of this research work is to reduce the inclination towards the labeled dataset and to develop a model that procures a less annotated dataset, yet gives better results. With only 50% of the annotated dataset, it is shown that 0.87% accuracy has been achieved on the QC fine-grained dataset. Figure 3 shows that our proposed model's graph monotonically increases as the annotated datasets' percentage increases.

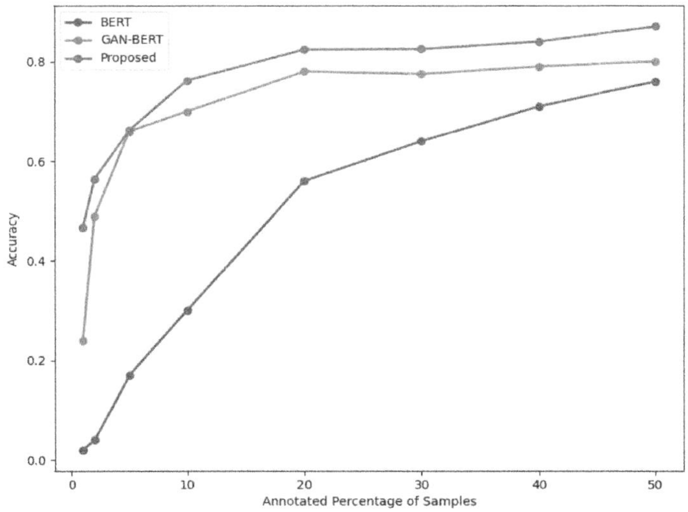

Fig. 3. Comparison of various models and the accuracy

5 Conclusion and Future Work

In this article, a modified GAN-BERT architecture for efficient text categorization augmented with Evolutionary Computing has been proposed. The experimented approach leverages the power of Generative Adversarial Networks (GANs) and bidirectional encoder representations from transformers (BERT) to learn robust and discriminate features from unlabeled text data. The proposed model can achieve competitive results on text categorization tasks with only a few labeled examples per task for both binary and multi-class datasets. The model generated an accuracy of 87% when the number of labeled samples used for training was only half the original model. This proves that the proposed model is well-suited for low-labeled dataset environments.

The work can be extended in the future, where this model can be used to define semi-supervised learning architectures in natural language processing. The accuracy obtained with minimally labeled samples can be improved through techniques such as augmentation and better GAN architectures with proper pre-training. Few-shot or zero-shot methods on GAN-BERT structures can also be explored for text categorization.

References

1. Dhar, A., Mukherjee, H., Dash, N.S., Roy, K.: Text categorization: past and present. Artif. Intell. Rev. **54**, 3007–3054 (2021)
2. Yadav, B.P., Ghate, S., Harshavardhan, A., Jhansi, G., Kumar, K.S., Sudarshan, E.: Text categorization performance examination using machine learning algorithms. In: IOP Conference Series: Materials Science and Engineering, vol. 981, no. (2), pp. 022044. IOP Publishing (2020)
3. Kim, S.E., Kaibalina, N., Park, S.B.: A topical category-aware neural text summarizer. Appl. Sci. **10**(16), 5422 (2020)
4. Vijayan, V.K., Bindu, K.R., Parameswaran, L.: A comprehensive study of text classification algorithms. In: 2017 International Conference on Advances in Computing, Communications and Informatics (ICACCI), pp. 1109–1113. IEEE (2017)
5. Naveenkumar, K.S., Vinayakumar, R., Soman, K.P.: Amrita-cen-sentidb 1: improved twitter dataset for sentimental analysis and application of deep learning. In: 2019 10th International Conference on Computing, Communication and Networking Technologies (ICCCNT), pp. 1–5. IEEE (2019)
6. Yu, W., Sun, Z., Liu, H., Li, Z., Zheng, Z.: Multi-level deep learning based e-commerce product categorization. In: eCOM@ SIGIR (2018)
7. Kumar, R.V., Kumar, M.A., Soman, K.P.: AmritaCEN_NLP@ FIRE 2015 language identification for indian languages in social media text. In: FIRE workshops, pp. 26–28 (2015)
8. Sharma, A., Amrita, Chakraborty, S., and Kumar, S.: Named entity recognition in natural language processing: A systematic review. In: Proceedings of Second Doctoral Symposium on Computational Intelligence: DoSCI 2021, pp. 817–828, Springer Singapore (2022)
9. Winata, G.I., Khodra, M.L.: Handling imbalanced dataset in multi-label text categorization using Bagging and Adaptive Boosting. In 2015 International Conference on Electrical Engineering and Informatics (ICEEI), pp. 500–505. IEEE (2015)

10. Harikrishnan, C., Dhanya, N.M.: Improving text classifiers through controlled text generation using transformer wasserstein autoencoder. In Inventive Communication and Computational Technologies: Proceedings of ICICCT 2021, pp. 97–105. Springer Singapore (2022)
11. Creswell, A., White, T., Dumoulin, V., Arulkumaran, K., Sengupta, B., Bharath, A.A.: Generative adversarial networks: an overview. IEEE Signal Process. Mag. **35**(1), 53–65 (2018)
12. Zhang, H., et al.: Text feature adversarial learning for text generation with knowledge transfer from GPT2. IEEE Trans. Neural Netw. Learn. Syst. (2022)
13. Yu, L., Zhang, W., Wang, J., Yu, Y.: Seqgan: Sequence generative adversarial nets with policy gradient. In: Proceedings of the AAAI conference on artificial intelligence, vol. 31, no. (1) (2017)
14. Guo, J., Lu, S., Cai, H., Zhang, W., Yu, Y., Wang, J.: Long text generation via adversarial training with leaked information. In: Proceedings of the AAAI Conference on Artificial Intelligence, vol. 32, no. 1 (2018)
15. Che, T., et al.: Maximum-Likelihood Augmented Discrete Generative Adversarial Networks (2017). arXiv preprint arXiv:1702.07983
16. Lin, K., Li, D., He, X., Zhang, Z., Sun, M.T.: Adversarial ranking for language generation. Adv. Neural Inf. Process. Syst. **30**, (2017)
17. Nie, W., Narodytska, N., Patel, A.: Relgan: relational generative adversarial networks for text generation. In: International Conference on Learning Representations (2018)
18. Xu, J., Ren, X., Lin, J., Sun, X.: DP-GAN: Diversity-Promoting Generative Adversarial Network for Generating Informative and Diversified Text (2018). arXiv preprint arXiv:1802.01345
19. Liu, Z., Wang, J., Liang, Z.: Catgan: category-aware generative adversarial networks with hierarchical evolutionary learning for category text generation. Proc. AAAI Conf. Artif. Intell. **34**(05), 8425–8432 (2020)
20. Wang, K., Wan, X.: Sentigan: Generating Sentimental Texts Via Mixture Adversarial Networks. IJCAI, pp. 4446–4452 (2018)
21. Potapczynski, A., Loaiza-Ganem, G., Cunningham, J.P.: Invertible gaussian reparameterization: revisiting the gumbel-softmax. Adv. Neural. Inf. Process. Syst. **33**, 12311–12321 (2020)
22. Sheng, X., Xu, L., Xu, Y., Bao, C., Chen, H., Ren, B.: CoCGAN: contrastive learning for adversarial category text generation. In: Proceedings of the 29th International Conference on Computational Linguistics, pp. 6403–6414 (2022)
23. Devlin, J., Chang, M.-W., Lee, K., Toutanova, K.: BERT: Pre-training of Deep Bidirectional Transformers for Language Understanding. arXiv:1810.04805 [cs.CL]
24. Liu, Y., et al.: RoBERTa: A Robustly Optimized BERT Pretraining Approach. arXiv:1907.11692 [cs.CL]
25. Lan, Z., Chen, M., Goodman, S., Gimpel, K., Sharma, P., Soricut, R.: ALBERT: a Lite BERT for Self-supervised Learning of Language Representations. arXiv:1909.11942 [cs.CL]
26. Conneau, A., et al.: Unsupervised Cross-lingual Representation Learning at Scale. arXiv:1911.02116 [cs.CL]
27. Croce, D., Castellucci, G., Basili, R.: GAN-BERT: Generative Adversarial Learning for Robust Text Classification with a Bunch of Labeled Examples. ACL (2020)
28. de Wynter, A., Perry, D.J.: Optimal Subarchitecture Extraction For BERT. arXiv:2010.10499 [cs.CL]

29. Vinayakumar, R., Soman, K. P., Poornachandran, P.: Deep encrypted text categorization. In 2017 International Conference on Advances in Computing, Communications and Informatics (ICACCI), pp. 364–370. IEEE (2017)
30. Maas, A.L., Daly, R.E., Pham, P.T., Huang, D., Ng, A.Y., Potts, C.: Learning word vectors for sentiment analysis. In: Proceedings of the 49th Annual Meeting of the Association for Computational Linguistics: Human Language Technologies, pp. 142–150, Portland, Oregon, USA. Association for Computational Linguistics (2011)
31. Li, X., Roth, D.: Learning question classifiers. In: COLING 2002: The 19th International Conference on Computational Linguistics (2002)
32. Shyju, S., Murali, R.: ATLAS-A co-evolutionary framework for automatic tuning of adversarial neural networks. In: Proceedings of the Companion Conference on Genetic and Evolutionary Computation, pp. 2398–2401 (2023)

Assessing Degradation Levels of Palm Leaf Manuscripts with Random Forest Using Gabor Features

Achyuta Siva Sai Kowshik, Ambati Sai Sindhur, Annem Gnaneswara Reddy, Manasa Ganesh, Remya Sivan, and Peeta Basa Pati(✉)

Department of Computer Science and Engineering, Amrita School of Computing Bengaluru, Amrita Vishwa Vidyapeetham, Bengaluru, India
bp_peeta@blr.amrita.edu

Abstract. This experiment focuses on employing machine learning techniques to create an automated system for classifying palm leaf manuscripts into three distinct categories based on their degradation levels: good, bad, and medium. The study collects a wide range of palm leaf samples at different degradation levels. Using advanced machine learning algorithms and an efficient feature extraction method, a model is created that accurately classifies palm leaves by level of degradation. The research incorporates Gabor feature extraction and statistical classifiers to train the extracted features. The classifiers used are k-Nearest Neighbor (k-NN), Support Vector Machine (SVM), Multi-Layer Perceptron (MLP), Logistic Regression (LR), Random Forest (RF), Decision Tree (DT), Naive Bayes (NB), XG Boost (XGB), and Ada Boost (AB). After employing SMOTE, normalization, and feature selection, RF obtained the highest mean accuracy of 87.25% and a standard deviation of 0.08 in comparison with the other classifiers.

Keywords: palm leaves · machine learning · palm leaf degradation level · Classification · Gabor feature extraction · SDG 4

1 Introduction

In the past, people treasured palm leaf manuscripts as repositories of knowledge, customs, and history in various world regions, from Southeast Asia to the Indian subcontinent. Palm leaf manuscripts are made by writing text on dried palm leaves using a specialized iron stylus. It reflects different cultural traditions, knowledge, and the richness of different regions of the world. Hence, it is considered as a rich cultural, historical, and traditional records. These manuscripts connect many nations' cultural legacy through inscriptions on dried palm leaves. These historical records reveal past practices, events, and changes in society. Palm leaf manuscripts contain ancient wisdom, including medical and agricultural traditions, illuminating cultures' intellectual and practical talents beyond history. Religious texts and rites are also preserved in these documents. Calligraphy and various scripts enrich its artistic and linguistic value. Thus, these cultural items must be preserved for future generations.

Published by Springer Nature Switzerland AG 2025
A. Chandrabose et al. (Eds.): ICCCSP 2024, IFIP AICT 723, pp. 239–249, 2025.
https://doi.org/10.1007/978-3-031-73617-9_19

Palm leaf manuscripts play an important role in both cultural and historical aspects. But unfortunately, they are subjected to vulnerable environmental causes. Since it is made from dried palm leaves it degrades with humidity, temperature variations, insect bites, and sunlight. Due to poor storage conditions deterioration intensity enhances. Figure 1 shows different degradations present on the palm leaf manuscripts. These challenges make palm leaf preservation difficult.

Digitization is one of the possible solutions to preserve these valuable documents. Digitization starts with a preprocessing stage like document enhancement and binarization. Since the degradation level of these documents varies across the documents, different types of preprocessing steps are required for these documents based on the degradation level. Researchers often use visual inspection and subjective evaluation to classify palm documents according to their level of degradation. Even though this method has produced meaningful data, it is time-consuming with cumbersome steps, and a reliance on the individual examiners' expertise. Given the growing demand for digitization and increased access to these manuscripts, systems are required for automated, impartial, and scalable classification.

Fig. 1. Different types of degradations present on the palm leaf images

The in-depth analysis of the research environment in this work focuses on the classification of palm leaf manuscripts according to the degree of degradation they have suffered. We explore and investigate a wide range of techniques, methodologies, and computation-based technologies for the autonomous deterioration classification of palm leaf manuscripts. The approaches used in the study, include Gabor feature extraction and selection, and machine learning algorithms. This research aims to provide scholars, preservation of cultural heritage, and the historians with a comprehensive review of the state of the art in palm leaf document classification. By promoting a broader awareness of current approaches and issues, the aim is to stimulate more study and innovation in this crucial area, ultimately contributing to the protection and accessibility of this irreplaceable cultural heritage.

The novelty of this work is to classify the historical palm leaf documents based on their degradation level by incorporating Gabor features and statistical classifiers. Additionally, our dedication to preserving knowledge for future generations and improving historical document digitalization aligns with the United Nations Sustainable Development Goals (SDG), specifically, SDG 4.

The paper is organized as follows: Section 2 presents a comprehensive literature survey on document analysis and classification. Section 3 describes the dataset used in this study, whereas Sect. 4 outlines the methodology employed. The obtained results and the subsequent analysis are presented in Sect. 5. Section 6 concludes the paper and outlines its future scope.

2 Literature Survey

Limited research has been conducted on the classification of palm leaf deterioration levels. However, two studies have been reported focusing on palm leaves, although their methodologies diverge from ours. Wang et al. [1] introduce a model for identifying damage in Sanskrit palm leaf manuscripts using Segformer. Bipin et al. [2] propose document image classification to categorize deteriorated Malayalam handwritten palm leaf manuscripts, employing a Bag of Words approach to classify manuscripts based on textual components recognized by OCR. Furthermore, several works have addressed quality assessment and degraded document classification in historical documents. Shahkolaei et al. [3] propose a Multi-distortion Document Quality Measure for evaluating physically degraded document images. Saddami et al. [4] utilize pre-trained models like ResNet101, MobileNet V2, and ShuffleNet for image classification. Chen et al. [5] propose image classification for historical documents using Dual Attention Vision Transformers.

Raju et al. [6] employ Gabor filters and block energy analysis in their document image analysis for libraries, demonstrating advancements in text extraction from digital documents and offering valuable insights for improving methods in this context. Pati et al. [7] utilize Gabor filters for processing Indian bilingual documents, showcasing its applicability and relevance in the domain of bilingual document understanding.

Nourbakhsh et al. [8] leverage Harris corner points for document page layout analysis, incorporating the Harris corner detection algorithm to enhance accuracy and efficiency. Sarkar et al. [9] propose a method for learning image anchor templates to enhance document classification and data extraction from images. Usilin et al. [10] present a document image classification method based on visual appearance, contributing to the evolving field of visual document analysis. Khare et al. [11] tackle graphical document image classification using content-based methods, providing insights into handling complex document formats. Bukhari et al. [12] conduct a comprehensive evaluation and benchmarking of visual appearance-based document classification methods, contributing to performance assessment in the field.

Jayant et al. [13] present a method for unsupervised classification, focusing on structurally similar document images to address challenges in document organization. Kumar et al. [14] leverage structural similarity measures for document image classification and retrieval, enhancing the understanding of document content. Tian et al. [15] explore the synergy of text and visual features for image classification, offering a comprehensive approach to multimedia data.

Augereau et al. [16] propose an enhanced classification approach by combining visual and textual features, with a focus on industrial document databases. Kang et al. [17] explore the application of Convolutional Neural Networks (CNNs) for document image classification, showcasing the potential of deep learning in this domain. Noce et al. [18] introduce a method that utilizes embedded textual content for document image classification, integrating CNNs. Kölsch et al. [19] present a real-time document image classification system employing Deep CNNs and Extreme Learning Machines, highlighting the importance of efficiency in classification tasks. Asim et al. [20] propose a two-stream deep network for document image classification, showcasing advancements in deep learning architectures for this application.

Sidère et al. [21] propose a compliant document image classification system based on a one-class classifier, offering a specialized approach for certain document types. Rajesh et al. [22] address document classification challenges using hierarchically structured dictionaries, enhancing efficiency and accuracy in classification algorithms. Shahira et al. [23] focus on document image classification to assist visually impaired individuals, emphasizing the potential societal impact of classification technologies. Xu et al. [24] introduce Layoutlm, a pre-training approach that incorporates both text and layout information for enhanced document image understanding. Jadli et al. [25] present an improved document image classification method using deep transfer learning and feature reduction, emphasizing advancements in classification techniques. Sevim et al. [26] explore the application of vision transformers for document image classification, contributing to the evolving landscape of transformer-based approaches.

As part of historical document digitization, Sivan et al. [27, 28] employ deep learning techniques for Malayalam character recognition from palm leaves, offering advancements in optical character recognition for historical artifacts. Nair et al. [29] utilized the Resnet model to binarize the palm leaf document. Jayakumari et al. [30] focus on the classification of heterogeneous Malayalam documents, leveraging deep learning models and structural features for improved accuracy. Gabor filters, like textual features derived from T5-generated summaries Prabhakar et al. [31], can extract textual features, thus fulfilling a similar role in capturing textual information. Sastry et al. [32] present a comprehensive system for Telugu palm leaf document acquisition and analysis, contributing to document digitization and cultural heritage preservation. Sastry et al. [33] introduce a Radon Transform-based method tailored for Telugu palm leaf character recognition, addressing challenges in cultural heritage preservation.

The literature surveys presented cover a wide spectrum of document image analysis techniques, ranging from traditional methods like Gabor filters and Harris corner points to advanced approaches such as CNNs, transformers, and deep learning architectures. While significant progress has been made in individual methods, there is a noticeable gap in integrating these diverse techniques into a unified framework. A comprehensive and cohesive approach that combines traditional image processing with state-of-the-art deep learning methodologies is essential to address the complexities of document understanding and classification across various cultural and linguistic contexts. The existing literature indicates a noticeable absence of substantial research focused on classifying palm leaf documents according to their degradation levels. All reported attempts in this subject focus on historical paper records or other mediums, with no evident work addressing palm leaf document degradation levels.

3 Dataset

In this experiment, dataset D is considered, consisting of 3253 palm leaf manuscripts. The feature extraction process uses the Gabor method with parameters from Table 1, resulting in a 50-dimensional feature space for each image. The target column in the dataset is 'label' and the classes are medium, good, and bad each having 1634,1055, 564 respectively. The dataset's target column is Y, and y^i represents the ith sample's label, where i = 1,2,...3253. Label $y^i \in$ { 'good','medium','bad'} with $n_{(medium)} = 1634$, $n_{(good)} = 1055$, $n_{(bad)} = 564$.

Table 1. Parameters for the Gabor Feature extraction

Parameter	Value
Gamma	0.5
Sigma	0.56
Theta list	[0, π, π /2, π /4, 3* π /4]
Phi	0
Lambda list	[2*π/1,2*π/2,2*π/3,2*π/4,2 π /5]

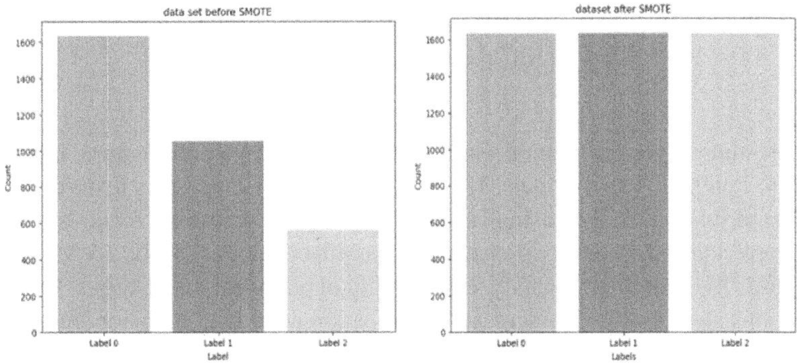

Fig. 2. Before(left) and after(right) implementing SMOTE

A two-step pre-processing method is utilized to improve the dataset's efficiency. First, min-max normalization is used to scale all features within [0,1]. This normalization maintains feature magnitude consistency, preventing a large number of features from dominating the study. SMOTE is used to correct the initial class imbalance. This method corrects class distribution by systematically generating minority-class synthetic instances. Figure 2 shows the dataset's balance after these pre-processing procedures with the number of instances before and after SMOTE for each class.

4 Methodology

The proposed method has utilized statistical classifiers to analyze the quality of the palm-leaf manuscripts, and these statistical classifiers are trained on Gabor features. To enhance the performance of the classifiers, normalization, and dimensionality reduction techniques are also utilized. The process flow is illustrated in Fig. 3. It comprises of four main steps: I. Collection of images and Feature extraction II. Preprocessing III. Feature selection IV. Training.

The Gabor method is utilized to extract the features from the manuscripts. Preprocessing methods, SMOTE, and min-max are employed to improve the dataset's efficiency. After dataset refining, informative characteristics are carefully selected. Retaining only the important features in the updated dataset, optimizes model performance and computational efficiency. SMOTE, normalization, and feature selection create a more robust and balanced dataset for analysis and model development.

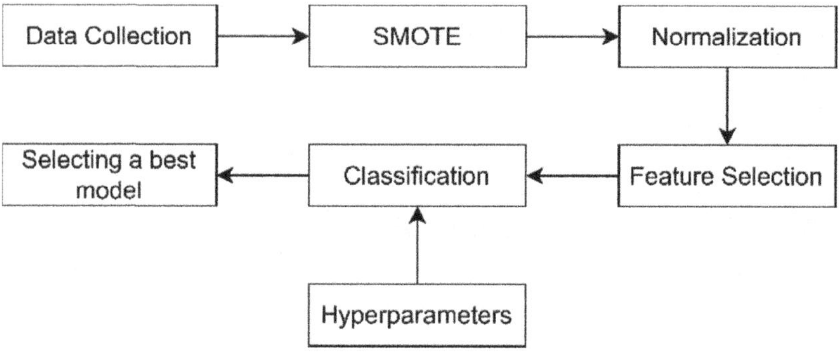

Fig. 3. Work Flow of the Proposed System

The feature selection method employed is the "Tree-based Feature Importance," intrinsic to Random Forest models. This approach assesses and ranks features according to their contribution to decreasing order of importance across all features. Employed seven simple classifiers and two ensemble classifiers such as k-NN, SVM, MLP, LR, RF, DT, NB, XGB, and AB to analyze the quality of palm leaf manuscripts. By carefully handling this step, we aim to increase classification accuracy, precision, recall, and F1 score.

5 Results and Analysis

The experiment is started with statistical classifiers on raw data. The mean accuracy after applying 10-fold cross-validation of each classifier has been determined and reported as shown in Fig. 4. The k-NN classifier reported the highest mean accuracy of 81.67% and a standard deviation of 0.15.

Subsequently, to tackle the data imbalance, SMOTE is employed, and min-max normalization is implemented to improve the classifier performance. The reported results indicated significant increases in mean accuracies. The mean accuracy after applying 10-fold cross-validation of each classifier has been determined and reported as shown in Fig. 4. The RF classifier has reported with highest mean accuracy of 88.84%.

Table 2. Hyperparameters used for classification

Classifier	Hyperparameters
k-NN	'n_neighbors': 7, 'weights': 'distance'
RF	'max_depth': 20, 'min_samples_split': 2, 'n_estimators': 200
DT	'max_depth': None, 'min_samples_split': 2
MLP	'alpha': 0.001, 'hidden_layer_sizes': (50,)
SVM	'C': 1, 'gamma': 'scale', 'kernel': 'linear'
NB	Alpha = 1
LR	'C': 0.1, 'penalty': 'l2'
XGB	'learning_rate': 0.2, 'n_estimators': 100
AB	'learning_rate': 0.1, 'n_estimators': 200

To make the models more efficient the feature selection is done and the features that have less importance have been removed. The remaining features form a new efficient feature set. 30 of 50 features are removed after feature selection. Despite this large dimensionality reduction, the model performed well, demonstrating the selected features' robustness and efficiency. This shows that the feature selection procedure retains important information while eliminating irrelevant variables. The feature selection technique has increased system performance by streamlining the model's computational efficiency and predictive abilities. The mean accuracy after applying 10-fold cross-validation of each classifier has been determined and reported as shown in Fig. 4. Even after feature selection the RF classifier shows the highest accuracy mean of 87.25% and a standard deviation of 0.08.

The results of 9 classifiers' performance, showcase diverse accuracies. SVM lags indicating a need for exploration beyond hyperparameter fine-tuning. RF emerges as the top performer with an accuracy mean of 87.25%, underlining its robust classification capabilities. MLP exhibits commendable accuracy at 84.33%, suggesting the potential benefits of exploring different architectures or activation functions. Naïve Bayes, with a mean accuracy of 45.92%, prompts consideration of alternative feature engineering techniques to enhance its performance. LR, despite moderate accuracy, may benefit from feature selection methods to improve its predictive power. XGB shows a good performance with an accuracy mean of 86.56%, proving to be reliable in classification tasks. AB with the hyperparameter fine-tuning achieves a moderate mean accuracy of 67.19%. This signifies that even though certain readjustments have been done, other considerations such as alternative hyperparameters, or ensemble methods are essential to reach optimal outcomes. The classifier utilizes optimized hyperparameters listed in

Table 2. to classify the palm leaf documents. These hyperparameters undergo evaluation through the implementation of the grid search method.

To the best of our knowledge, there is a lack of research addressing the classification of palm leaf documents according to their deterioration level. Wang et al. [1] reported on an optimized segmentation model that achieved a 51.2% mIoU for detecting damaged areas on palm leaf documents. Additionally, Bipin et al. [2] conducted a study classifying palm leaf documents into six distinct groups based on their content. Their approach achieved an overall accuracy of 83% without voting and 84.5% with voting. In this study, an F-score of 0.90 in both scenarios using Tesseract OCR for text recognition was obtained. Therefore, our proposed work is novel and achieved an mean accuracy of 87.25% for classifying palm leaf documents.

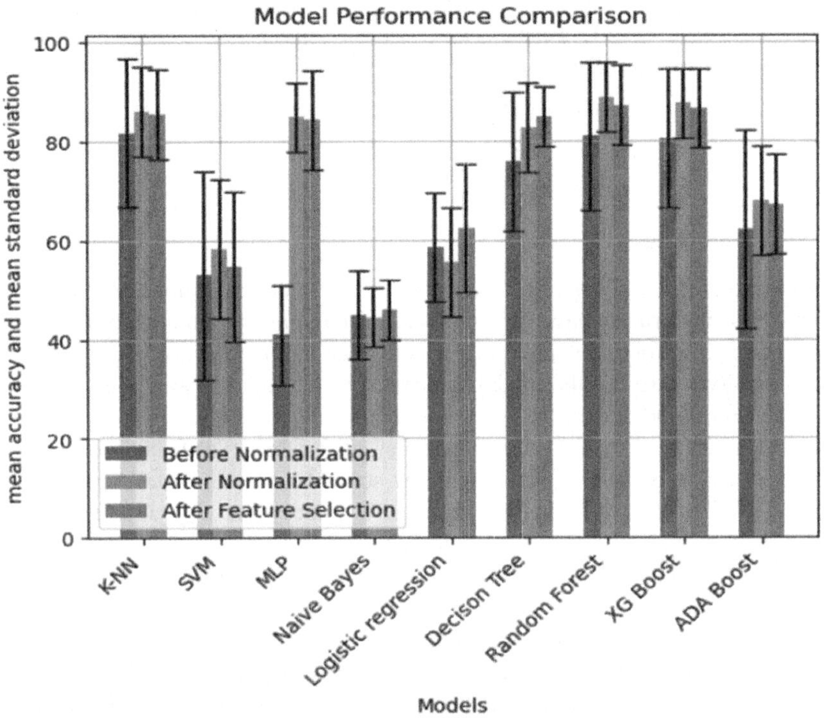

Fig. 4. Cross-validation mean accuracy and mean standard deviation for all the models.

6 Conclusion

In conclusion, the importance of a thorough classifier evaluation process stands out. Classifiers like k-NN, RF, and XGB exhibit impressive performances, but the diverse outcomes across various algorithms highlight the task's complexity. It becomes evident that it is important to delve into precise methods beyond adjusting hyperparameters when seeking optimal results.

As the project transitions to classifying data into labels good, bad, and medium future work could benefit from employing tailored preprocessing techniques for each label, refining feature engineering, and data transformations to boost classification accuracy.

Acknowledgement. We would like to express our sincere gratitude to Amrita Vishwa Vidyapeetham for the infrastructure and support provided towards the completion of this project. We acknowledge that we used ChatGPT to paraphrase some sentences in this article.

References

1. Wang, Y., et al.: Automatic damage identification of Sanskrit palm leaf manuscripts with SegFormer. Heritage Science. **12**(1), 8 (2024)
2. Nair, B.J., Rani, N.S., Khan, M.: Deteriorated image classification model for malayalam palm leaf manuscripts. Journal of Intelligent & Fuzzy Systems, 4031–4049 (2023)
3. Shahkolaei, A., Beghdadi, A., Cheriet, M.: Blind quality assessment metric and degradation classification for degraded document images. Signal Processing: Image Communication **76**, 11–21 (2019)
4. Saddami, K., Munadi, K., Arnia, F.: Degradation classification on ancient document image based on deep neural networks. In: 2020 3rd International Conference on Information and Communications Technology (ICOIACT), pp. 405–410. IEEE (2020)
5. Chen, J.A., Hou, J.C., Tsai, R.T., Liao, H.M., Chen, S.P., Chang, M.C.: Image classification for historical documents: a study on Chinese local gazetteers. Digital Scholarship in the Humanities **39**(1), 61–73 (2024)
6. Raju, S.S., Pati, P.B., Ramakrishnan, A.G.: Gabor filter based block energy analysis for text extraction from digital document images. In: First International Workshop on Document Image Analysis for Libraries, pp. 233–243. IEEE (2004)
7. Pati, P.B., Raju, S.S., Pati, N., Ramakrishnan, A.G.: Gabor filters for document analysis in Indian bilingual documents. In: International Conference on Intelligent Sensing and Information Processing, pp. 123–126. IEEE (2004)
8. Nourbakhsh, F., Pati, P.B., Ramakrishnan, A.G.: Document page layout analysis using harris corner points. In: 2006 Fourth International Conference on Intelligent Sensing and Information Processing, pp. 149–152. IEEE (2006)
9. Sarkar, P.: Learning image anchor templates for document classification and data extraction. In: 2010 20th International Conference on Pattern Recognition, pp. 3428–3431. IEEE (2006)
10. Usilin, S., Nikolaev, D., Postnikov, V., Schaefer, G.: Visual appearance based document image classification. In: 2010 IEEE International Conference on Image Processing, pp. 2133–2136. IEEE (2010)
11. Khare, A., Jeph, P., Ghosh, H.: Content-based classification of graphical document images. In: 2010 2nd European Workshop on Visual Information Processing (EUVIP), pp. 241–246. IEEE (2010)
12. Bukhari, S.S., Dengel, A.: Visual appearance based document classification methods: Performance evaluation and benchmarking. In: 2015 13th International Conference on Document Analysis and Recognition (ICDAR), pp. 981–985. IEEE (2015)
13. Kumar, J., Ye, P., Doermann, D.: Structural similarity for document image classification and retrieval. Pattern Recogn. Lett. **43**, 119–126 (2014)
14. Kumar, J., Doermann, D.: Unsupervised classification of structurally similar document images. In: 2013 12th International Conference on Document Analysis and Recognition, pp. 1225–1229. IEEE (2013)

15. Tian, L., Zheng, D., Zhu, C.: Research on image classification based on a combination of text and visual features. In: 2011 Eighth International Conference on Fuzzy Systems and Knowledge Discovery (FSKD), Vol. 3, pp. 1869–1873. IEEE (2011)
16. Augereau, O., Journet, N., Vialard, A., Domenger, J.P.: Improving classification of an industrial document image database by combining visual and textual features. In: 2014 11th IAPR International Workshop on Document Analysis Systems, pp. 314–318. IEEE (2014)
17. Kang, L., Kumar, J., Ye, P., Li, Y., Doermann, D.: Convolutional neural networks for document image classification. In: 2014 22nd International Conference on Pattern Recognition, pp. 3168–3172. IEEE (2014)
18. Noce, L., Gallo, I., Zamberletti, A., Calefati, A.: Embedded textual content for document image classification with convolutional neural networks. In: Proceedings of the 2016 ACM Symposium on Document Engineering, pp. 165–173 (2016)
19. Asim, M.N., et al.: Two stream deep network for document image classification. In: 2019 International Conference on Document Analysis and Recognition (ICDAR), pp. 1410–1416. IEEE (2019)
20. Kölsch, A., Afzal, M.Z., Ebbecke, M., Liwicki, M.: Real-time document image classification using deep CNN and extreme learning machines. In: 2017 14th IAPR International Conference on Document Analysis and Recognition (ICDAR), Vol. 1, pp. 1318–1323. IEEE (2017)
21. Sidère, N., Ramel, J.Y., Barrat, S., D'Andecy, V.P., Kebairi, S.: A compliant document image classification system based on one-class classifier. In: 2016 12th IAPR Workshop on Document Analysis Systems (DAS), pp. 96–101. IEEE (2016)
22. Menon, R.R., Aswathi, P.: Document classification with hierarchically structured dictionaries. In: Intelligent Systems Technologies and Applications, Vol 2, pp. 387–397. Springer International Publishing (2015)
23. Shahira, K.C., Lijiya, A.: Document image classification: towards assisting visually impaired. In: TENCON 2019–2019 IEEE Region 10 Conference (TENCON), pp. 852–857. IEEE (2019)
24. Xu, Y., Li, M., Cui, L., Huang, S., Wei, F., Zhou, M.: LayoutLM: Pre-training of text and layout for document image understanding. In: Proceedings of the 26th ACM SIGKDD International Conference on Knowledge Discovery & Data Mining, pp. 1192–1200 (2020)
25. Jadli, A., Hain, M., Habaoui, A.: An improved document image classification using deep transfer learning and feature reduction. Int. J. **10**(2), 549–557 (2021)
26. Sevim, S., Omurca, S.İ., Ekinci, E.: Document image classification with vision transformers. In: International Congress of Electrical and Computer Engineering, pp. 68–81. Springer International Publishing, Cham (2022)
27. Sivan, R., Singh, T., Pati, P.B.: Malayalam character recognition from palm leaves using deep-learning. In: 2022 OITS International Conference on Information Technology (OCIT), pp. 134–139. IEEE (2022)
28. Sivan, R., Palaniswamy, S., Pati, P.B.: Comparative study of deep learning models to recognize palm leaf malayalam characters. In: 2022 6th International Conference on Computation System and Information Technology for Sustainable Solutions (CSITSS), pp. 1–6. IEEE (2022)
29. Nair, B.J., Nair, A.S.: Ancient horoscopic palm leaf binarization using a deep binarization model-RESNET. In: 2021 5th International Conference on Computing Methodologies and Communication (ICCMC), pp. 1524–1529. IEEE (2021)
30. Balakrishnan Jayakumari, B.N., Kavana, A.T.: Classification of heterogeneous malayalam documents based on structural features using deep learning models. Int. J. Electr. Comp. Eng. **13**(1), 894 (2023)
31. Prabhakar, P., Gupta, D., Pati, P.B.: Abstractive summarization of Indian legal judgments. In: 2022 OITS International Conference on Information Technology (OCIT), pp. 256–261. IEEE (2022)

32. Sastry, P.N., Krishnan, R.: A data acquisition and analysis system for palm leaf documents in Telugu. In: Proceedings of the Workshop on Document Analysis and Recognition, pp. 139–146 (2012)
33. Sastry, P.N., Krishnan, R.: Isolated Telugu palm leaf character recognition using Radon Transform—A novel approach. In: 2012 World Congress on Information and Communication Technologies, pp. 795–802. IEEE (2012)

Sign Language Recognition System – A Review

Jovitha Sahayaraj, K. Kaviyapriya, and P. Vasuki(✉)

Sri Sivasubramaniya Nadar College of Engineering, Kalavakkam 603110, India
vasukip@ssn.edu.in

Abstract. Speech is the easiest and the most basic mode of communication in our day-to-day life. Hence, speech impaired people are at a major disadvantage in this concern. The staple mode of communication for the speech impaired is Sign Language which in turn isolates them from the rest of the world in more ways than one. The Sign Language Recognition (SLR) System is an attempt to compress this isolation by recognizing the gestures of the Sign Language. The application may be used to map the sign into their corresponding text or speech in the given spoken language. In general, the system has been realized either using image processing techniques or with sensor signals employed in smart gloves. The system based on image processing captures the hand gestures made by an individual and maps it to their corresponding alphabets, words or phrases pre-defined in the existing dataset. Although this system proves to be useful, the dwindling accuracy of the image capturing process is a major drawback. The sensor-based system, on the other hand, works using a number of sensors attached to a glove which detects the hand gestures and computes it to its corresponding meaning. The performance of these systems is relatively higher but they also have a few setbacks, one of which is its high price due to the involvement of sensors making it unattainable to people of all economic strata. In addition to this, the extensive usage of wires and other electronic devices increases the weight of the glove making it inconvenient to be worn for long hours. There are a number of Sign languages existing from various parts of the world, each of which have their own recognition systems individually. This comes out as another drawback of the Sign Language Recognition Systems as they aren't adaptable to all Sign Languages and are restricted to a specific Sign Language as per its dataset. This paper illustrates the state of art of SLR with the detailed descriptions on various Sign Languages, dataset and recognition methodology and the mode of output, accuracy and application.

Keywords: Sign Language Recognition · Image Detection · Hand Gesture Recognition · Machine Learning Models

1 Introduction

In today's time, the lack of accessibility of technology by the speech impaired has caused various complications in the communication between the people of all domains of the society. It's as good as two parties trying to communicate with each other in two different languages, in turn requiring a third-party mediator, preventing them yet again from being self-sufficient.

Published by Springer Nature Switzerland AG 2025
A. Chandrabose et al. (Eds.): ICCCSP 2024, IFIP AICT 723, pp. 250–261, 2025.
https://doi.org/10.1007/978-3-031-73617-9_20

Although in this era of information, the rapid evolution of technology is no big deal, Sign language still remains the primary mode of communication for the speech impaired. For the people well-versed in Sign Language, its usage for communication is not an issue but it results in a clear classification of the society based on the knowledge on Sign Language. Thus, the Sign Language Translator is an essential tool that integrates all parts of the society by enabling everyone to communicate with each other.

2 Recent Developments

Sign language is a mode of communication that employs hand gestures to enable communication between the speech impaired and the rest of the society. Most of the developing projects use glove-based hand gesture recognition systems for the understanding of gestural languages. Various systems are developed to solve this issue and each system differs in their number of signs trained to their dataset which ranges from a single word to several million words and the percentage of accuracy in their classified signs. Simple systems are developed with the aim of understanding only the manual alphabets of a particular sign language.

A data glove is a glove made with flex sensors and accelerometer to translate the hand gestures made by the speech impaired people into speech or text. Acceleglove was developed by J. L. Hernandez Rebollar, R. W. Lindeman, and N. Kyriakopoulos [19] for recognizing the American sign language. It is a nylon glove that uses six sensors that are integrated to measure the orientation of the fingers. These complex systems are developed with a motive of understanding a series of hand gestures that indicate the words and sentences. A system was developed by Kim to recognize the Korean sign language [20], cyber glove for recognizing Chinese Sign Language by Gao [21]. Cyber gloves are a kind of data glove that contain 22 sensors, four abduction sensors, three flexion sensors and a palm arch sensor that measures the wrist flexion accurately.

3 Existing Systems

A taxonomy to categorize the existing systems is given in Table 1 which discusses the data sets, applications and so on of these systems.

4 Challenges and Solutions

Although Sign Language is the ultimate communication tool for the especially abled, it has to be acknowledged that it also alienates them from the larger population who aren't educated in it. This gap of alienation between these two islands of people has been attempted to be met via many research attempts which have been fairly successful. Numerous software and devices have been carved to help these differently abled people of our society lead a normal life. These software and devices mainly work on the principle of either Image Processing or Sensor Based Gloves. Both these principles basically involve the signs and gestures as input which are processed by a processing unit which are then converted into text/audio as per requirement and sent out as output.

Figure 1 depicts the basic processing of Sign Language Recognition System.

Table 1. Taxonomy of Existing Systems

Sunoo	Corpus Name	Author	Year of Publication	Description	Accuracy
A	Sign Language Identification using Skeletal Point-based Patio-Temporal Recurrent Neural Network	J. Johnson, J. Joseph, M. Reji, M. E. George and T. D. Sajanraj	2023	Conversion of ISL into corresponding words using a skeletal-point feature extraction framework to identify hand landmarks and use them to build a model for recognizing hand gestures using various LSTM Networks. [1]	99%
B	Sign language recognition system using tensor flow object detection API	Sharvani Srivastava, Amisha Gangwar, Richa Mishra, Sudhakar Singh	2022	Development of webcam-based sign language recognition dataset to build a model. [2]	85%
C	Real time sign language recognition system: wearable sensor-based 3D printed humanoid	M.A. Ahmed, B.B. Zaidan, A.A. Zaidan, Mahmood M. Salih,	2021	This wearable data glove uses 17 sensors with 65 channels to recognize the Malaysian sign language. A 3D printed humanoid arm is employed for validating the finger flexion measured by the sensors [3]	93.4%
D	Sign language detection and recognition using deep learning	Deep Kothadiya, Chintan Bhatt, Krenil Sapariya, Kevin Patel, Ana-Belen, Juan M Corchado	2022	It detects and recognizes sign language using deep learning methods like LSTM [4]	97%
E	Vernacular sign language using media-pipe and machine learning	Arpita Haldera, Akshit Tayade	2021	This system proposed a methodology using Media-pipe framework and Machine Learning Algorithm for recognizing hand gestures. ASL, ISL and TSL are employed for analysing the efficiency of this framework. [5]	99%

(*continued*)

Table 1. (*continued*)

Sunoo	Corpus Name	Author	Year of Publication	Description	Accuracy
F	AI enabled sign language recognition and VR space bidirectional communication using triboelectric smart glove	Feng Wen, Zixuan Zhang, Tianyiyi He & Chengkuo Lee	2021	An AI-driven Sign Language Recognition (SLR) system, integrating sensing gloves, deep learning, and virtual reality, recognizes 50 words and 20 sentences. It employs segmentation-assisted deep learning to accurately interpret sign language, projecting results into virtual space for remote communication between signers and non-signers. [6]	95%
G	Sign Language Detection using Convolutional Neural Network (CNN)	Nipun Jindal, Nilesh Yadav, Nishant Nirvan, Dinesh Kumar	2022	The system works on two models to convert sign gestures to text using Convolutional Neural Network (CNN) in Python and Alex Net in MATLAB. [7]	94%
H	American Sign Language Recognition using Video Vision Transformers	Nishant Singh, Vinayak Shinde, Pratik Kanani	2023	This paper describes a system that makes use of video vision transformers (ViViT) to leverage the power of multi head attention in a temporal and spatial setting and experiment with two feature extraction models like Truncated Resnet50 and Move Net-thunder which act as a precursor to the ViViT. [8]	59.44%

(*continued*)

Table 1. (*continued*)

Sunoo	Corpus Name	Author	Year of Publication	Description	Accuracy
I	Sign language recognition from digital videos using feature pyramid network with detection transformer	Yu Liu, Parma Nand, Md Akbar Hossain, Minh Nguyen, Wei Qi Yan	2023	This paper, proposes a Vision Transformer-based sign language recognition method called DETR (Detection Transformer), aiming to improve the current state-of-the-art sign language recognition accuracy. The DETR method is able to recognize sign language from digital videos with a high accuracy using a new deep learning model ResNet152 + FPN (i.e., Feature Pyramid Network), which is based on Detection Transformer. [9]	96.45%
J	Regional-CNN-based enhanced Turkish sign language recognition	Yirtici, T., Yurtkan	2022	This paper proposes a novel method for the recognition of Turkish Sign Language. It's tested on captured images containing signs. R-CNN is used to train the new model while Alex net is employees as a pre-trained network. [10]	99.7%
K	Hybrid Sign Language Learning Approach Using Multi-Scale Hierarchical Deep Convolutional Neural Network (MDCnn)	Sharma, S., Saxena, V.P	2023	This paper presents convolutional neural network model approach with multi-scale layers and various filters that serve as an additional layer in the design. This model could be used on a variety of data sets and is also useful for real-time picture streaming. [11]	98% on ISL + 95% on ASL dataset

(*continued*)

Table 1. (*continued*)

Sunoo	Corpus Name	Author	Year of Publication	Description	Accuracy
L	Sign language recognition using the fusion of image and hand landmarks through multi-headed convolutional neural network	Pathan, R.K., Biswas, M., Yasmin, S. et al.	2023	A multi-headed convolutional neural network (CNN) model has been proposed and tested with 30% of the dataset to train these two layers. To avoid the overfitting problem, data augmentation and dynamic learning rate reduction have been used. [12]	98.98%

Fig. 1. Basic processing of Sign Language Recognition System

4.1 Existing System Based on Image Processing

Image processing-based Sign Recognition System, the image is captured through a webcam attached to the system. The input image is pre-processed and undergoes noise removal and smoothening. After the preprocessing of the image is complete, it is then passed on to the feature extraction phase. The test image is classified in the nearest neighbour's class in the training set. The classification results then undergo text to speech conversion and are then produced to the user as per discretion (Fig. 2).

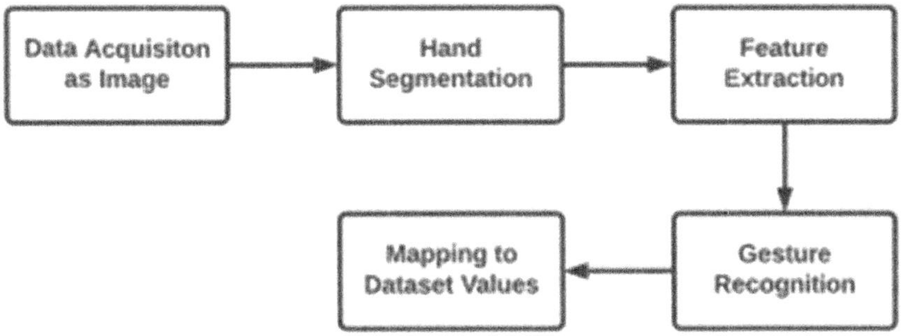

Fig. 2. Phases of Image based Sign Language Recognition System

CNN is one of the widely used Machine Learning algorithms in this field of research lately due to its ability to learn to detect features like edges and corners in the lower layers itself and then gradually combine them to detect more complex features like handshapes and gestures in higher layers. [7] describes how the raw data acquired as frames of images is segmented and put through feature extraction before it is pre-processed to remove noise and bring in uniformity in the data. This data is now passed to a CNN model which is a hierarchical model built in the form of a network using a group of learnable filters. This model then classifies the given images into its respective Sign Language meaning.

Transformers are state of the art tools for sequence modelling. The research on Sign Language Recognition has lately escalated from processing static image signs to now processing on videos using Video Vision Transformers [22]. The video frames containing the gestures are treated as a sequence of images which are then tokenised. Then the position of each token in the sequence is learned by the transformer via positional encoding. Self-Attention Mechanism forms the core of any transformer model which allows the model to weigh the importance of each token while making predictions. This mechanism runs in layers which helps in efficient classification. The model is further trained using labelled datasets.

4.2 Existing System Based on Smart Gloves

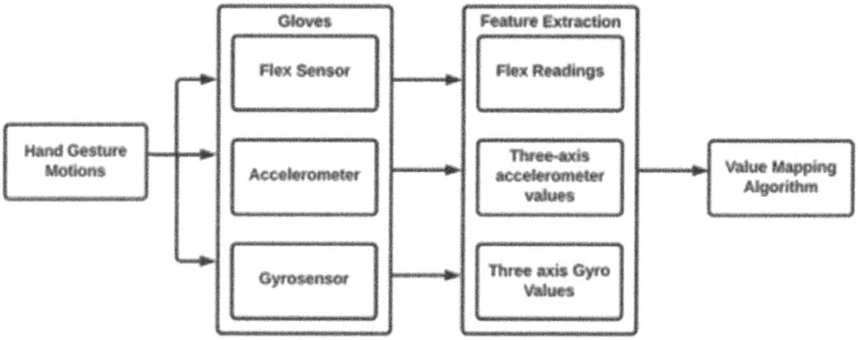

Fig. 3. Feature extraction mechanism of glove-based sign recognition system

Figure 3 depicts the working of a sample Glove based Sign Recognition System. In this prototype, the glove contains flex sensors, gyro sensors and accelerometers whose three-dimensional readings are taken and passed to the Arduino. From here, data acquisition, feature extraction, and customized machine learning algorithms are implemented to obtain the required output in the form of speech.

[23] discusses one such innovation wherein a wearable organohydrogel-based e-skin is used to construct smart gloves which carries out large-scale data collection of common gestures and sign languages. This in collaboration with deep learning methods, recognition and translation of various gestures could be achieved with an accuracy of 93.5%.

Similarly, [24] describes a Smart Glove that utilizes only flex sensors to capture hand gestures whose readings are processed and sent as input to a machine learning model trained on a comprehensive sign language dataset with an average recognition rate of 90%.

5 Challenges Faced in Current System

The existing sign language recognition systems face a number of challenges including lack of availability of downloadable datasets, continuous and accurate tracking of hand gestures and also challenges related to hardware, processing techniques and limited signs for communication.

5.1 Sensor based Challenges

It is found that there are several factors that cause challenges in the glove-based system. Firstly, the probability of error in the synchronization of two gloves while using a pair of gloves can lead to mismatched results because of unsynchronized processing. In addition to this, the computational cost of processing data is expensive, hence processing and recognizing thousands of gestures is quite challenging. The last but not the least are the accuracy issues. The finger flexions are affected by the force involved in opening and closing of fingers. All of these challenges are being handled to provide accuracy only up to 90% in average in the existing systems but they still continue to prevail and cause inconsistency under some circumstances.

5.2 Corpus Based Challenges

Sign language being not universal is one of the major challenges faced by the Sign Language Recognition Systems. There are somewhere between 100 to 300 different sign languages used throughout the world today. There are many sign languages used in a country but it is a fact that each country uses only one sign language predominantly. The Chinese Sign Language is one of the most predominantly used sign language with about 20 million users. Each language differs in their vocabulary sets. Some languages may have only alphabets in their available datasets and the other may have various vocabularies for certain circumstances. The other challenges include computational cost to recognize the gestures accurately which make it difficult to use it commercially. The sign language recognition system differs from each researcher as they build their models by their own analysis of the existing models.

6 Available Datasets

Sunoo	Title	Description
1	Indian Sign Language Skeletal-Point NumPy Array Using Media pipe	The dataset comprises NumPy arrays of ISL alphabets, excluding 'R', with (x,y,z) coordinates of 21 skeletal points for each hand across 120 sequences divided into 30 frames each, yielding 3600 .np files per alphabet, utilizing MediaPipe [13]
2	Indian Sign Language Dataset for Continuous Sign Language Translation and Recognition	The dataset contains 700 annotated videos, including 18863 sentence-level frames and 1036 word-level images, covering 100 spoken language sentences by 7 signers. It aims to advance Sign Language Translation and Recognition research [14]
3	Word-level Deep Sign Language Recognition from Video	The Video dataset has been introduced, featuring over 2000 words performed by more than 100 [15]
4	American Sign Language Lexicon Video Dataset (ASLLVD)	The dataset contains over 3,300 ASL signs in citation form, with contributions from 1–6 native ASL signers, totalling nearly 9,800 tokens. This dataset provides gloss labels, sign timings, handshape labels, and morphological classifications [16]
5	N-WLASL (Word-Level American Sign Language dataset)	This is a synthetic event-based collection comprising 21,093 samples representing 2,000 glosses. Using an event camera directed at an LCD monitor displaying video frames from WLASL, it was recorded with a resolution of 346×260, while WLASL frames have a resolution of 256×256 and a frame rate of 25 Hz [17]
6	Static Hand Gesture ASL Dataset	The dataset consists of static gestures representing the American Sign Language alphabet, captured from 8 individuals, excluding dynamic gestures for letters J and Z. Utilizing a Logitech Brio webcam with a resolution of 1920×1080 pixels in a university laboratory environment with artificial lighting, images were extracted with a defined hand region of 400×400 pixels for each gesture [18]

7 Performance

Indian sign language uses gestures to represent the words and phrases for speech impaired people. It contains 33 poses including 10 digits and 23 alphabets. The speech impaired community in India uses this ISL to communicate with people. The Hidden Markov Model is fed with hand gestures for classifying the gestures corresponding to the 12 pre-selected gestures defined in ISL. It was observed that it is able to achieve 95% of accuracy for static hand poses, and 97% for gesture recognition. The orientation-sensitive feature is used for the feature extraction process for Chinese sign language. This method calculates the distance between the center of the palm and the tip of the finger and these features are transformed in a better representation format by dynamic time warping- (DTW) based feature mapping approach. The American sign language have 2520 gesture images that shows an accuracy of 99.92% It is concluded that the performance depends on complexity of the sign language and the accuracy of the sensor or cameras used.

8 Conclusion

This study on the emerging development in the field of Sign Language Recognition has led to the realization of how impactful it is to the society with respect to bridging the gap between the differently abled and the rest of the world. Though the SLR systems are already sophisticated there is always scope for future development especially when integrated with emerging technologies like Artificial Intelligence, Virtual Reality, Deep Learning develop products that assist the especially abled communities. Hence, this discipline of study and research is an open field with no boundaries with new innovations always welcome and useful.

References

1. Johnson, J., Joseph, J., Reji, M., George, M.E., Sajanraj, T.D.: Sign Language Identification using Skeletal Point-based Spatio-Temporal Recurrent Neural Network. In: 2023 9th International Conference on Smart Computing and Communications (ICSCC), pp. 465–470. Kochi, Kerala, India (2023). https://doi.org/10.1109/ICSCC59169.2023.10334974
2. Srivastava, S., Gangwar, A., Mishra, R., Singh, S.: Sign Language Recognition System Using TensorFlow Object Detection API. In: Woungang, I., Dhurandher, S.K., Pattanaik, K.K., Verma, A., Verma, P. (eds.) Advanced Network Technologies and Intelligent Computing. ANTIC 2021. Communications in Computer and Information Science, vol 1534. Springer, Cham (2022). https://doi.org/10.1007/978-3-030-96040-7_48
3. Ahmed, M.A., Zaidan, B.B., Zaidan, A.A., Salih, M.M.: Real time sign language recognition system: wearable sensor-based 3D printed humanoid. published in (2021). https://doi.org/10.1016/j.measurement.2020.108431
4. Kothadiya, D., et al.: Sign language detection and recognition using deep learning. Published in Measurement (2023). https://doi.org/10.3390/electronics11111780
5. Haldera, A., Tayade, A.: Vernacular sign language using media-pipe and machine learning. Published in International Journal of Research Publication and Reviews (2021)

6. Wen, F., Zhang, Z., He, T., et al.: AI enabled sign language recognition and VR space bidirectional communication using triboelectric smart glove. Published in Nature Communications (2021). https://doi.org/10.1038/s41467-021-25637-w
7. Jindal, N., Yadav, N., Nirvan, N., Kumar, D.: Sign language detection using convolutional neural network (CNN). In: 2022 IEEE World Conference on Applied Intelligence and Computing (AIC), pp. 354–360. Sonbhadra, India (2022). https://doi.org/10.1109/AIC55036.2022.9848844
8. Singh, N., Shinde, V., Kanani, P.: American sign language recognition using video vision transformers. In: 2023 International Conference on Advanced Computing Technologies and Applications (ICACTA), pp. 1–6. Mumbai, India (2023). https://doi.org/10.1109/ICACTA58201.2023.10392991
9. Liu, Y., Nand, P., Hossain, M.A., et al.: Sign language recognition from digital videos using feature pyramid network with detection transformer. Multimed Tools Appl **82**, 21673–21685 (2023). https://doi.org/10.1007/s11042-023-14646-0
10. Yirtici, T., Yurtkan, K.: Regional-CNN-based enhanced Turkish sign language recognition. SIViP **16**, 1305–1311 (2022). https://doi.org/10.1007/s11760-021-02082-2
11. Sharma, S., Saxena, V.P.: Hybrid sign language learning approach using multi-scale hierarchical deep convolutional neural network (MDCnn). In: Shakya, S., Du, K.L., Ntalianis, K. (eds.) Sentiment Analysis and Deep Learning. Advances in Intelligent Systems and Computing, vol 1432. Springer, Singapore (2023). https://doi.org/10.1007/978-981-19-5443-6_51
12. Pathan, R.K., Biswas, M., Yasmin, S., et al.: Sign language recognition using the fusion of image and hand landmarks through multi-headed convolutional neural network. Sci. Rep. **13**, 16975 (2023). https://doi.org/10.1038/s41598-023-43852-x
13. Johnson, J., Joseph, J., Reji, M., George, M.: Indian Sign Language Skeletal-point NumPy array using MediaPipe. IEEE Dataport (2023). https://doi.org/10.21227/6emn-2r12
14. Elakkiya, R., Natarajan, B.: ISL-CSLTR: Indian Sign Language Dataset for Continuous Sign Language Translation and Recognition. Mendeley Data, V1 (2021). https://doi.org/10.17632/kcmpdxky7p.1
15. Li, D., Opazo, C.R., Yu, X., Li, H.: Word-level Deep Sign Language Recognition from Video: A New Large-scale Dataset and Methods Comparison. https://doi.org/10.48550/arXiv.1910.11006
16. Neidle, C., Thangali, A., Sclaroff, S.: Challenges in Development of the American Sign Language Lexicon Video Dataset (ASLLVD) Corpus. In: 5th Workshop on the Representation and Processing of Sign Languages: Interactions between Corpus and Lexicon, Language Resources and Evaluation Conference (LREC) 2012. Istanbul, Turkey (2012)
17. Shi, Q.: N-WLASL. IEEE Dataport (2023). https://doi.org/10.21227/x23b-d084
18. Farrapo Pinto Junior, R., Cavalvante de Paula Junior, I.: Static Hand Gesture ASL Dataset. IEEE Dataport (2019). https://doi.org/10.21227/gzpc-k936
19. Hernandez-Rebollar, J.L., Kyriakopoulos, N., Lindeman, R.W.: The acceleglove: a whole-hand input device for virtual reality, (Technical Sketch). Conference Abstracts and Applications, ACM SIGGRAPH **2002**, 259 (2002)
20. Shin, H., Kim, W.J., Jang, K.: Korean sign language recognition based on image and convolution neural network. In: Proceedings of the 2nd International Conference on Image and Graphics Processing (ICIGP '19), pp. 52–55. Association for Computing Machinery, New York, NY, USA (2019). https://doi.org/10.1145/3313950.3313967
21. Ma, J., Gao, W., Wu, J., Wang, C.: A continuous Chinese sign language recognition system. In: 2013 10th IEEE International Conference and Workshops on Automatic Face and Gesture Recognition (FG), 9, pp. 428–433. Grenoble, France (2000). https://doi.org/10.1109/AFGR.2000.840670
22. Singha, J.D.: Hand gesture recognition based on Karhunen – Loeve transform. Published in Mobile and Embedded Technology International conference (2013)

23. Song, B., Dai, X., Fan, X., Gu, H.: Wearable multifunctional organohydrogel-based electronic skin for sign language recognition under complex environments. J. Mat. Sci. Technol. **181**, 91–103 (2024). ISSN 1005-0302, https://doi.org/10.1016/j.jmst.2023.10.008
24. Abougarair, A., Arebi, W.: Smart glove for sign language translation. Int. J. Robot. Auto. **8**, 109–117 (2022). https://doi.org/10.15406/iratj.2022.08.00253

SDG 9 Industry, Innovation and Infrastructure

Implementing a NFT Based Album Purchasing Web Application Using ReactJs by Integrating with Ethereum Blockchain

D. Thamizhselvi(✉), M. Shabika Fathima, M. Dhivya, and M. Srinidhi

Sri Sairam Engineering College, Sai Leo Nagar, Poonthandalam Village, West Tambaram, Chennai 600044, India
thamizhselvi.it@sairam.edu.in, {sec20it074,sec20it034, sec20it0104}@sairamtap.edu.in

Abstract. Blockchain is one of the emerging technologies, which is trustless, decentralized and secure. In today's world blockchain can be almost applicable anywhere. Using blockchain technology in the music industry, where many artists lose their music ownership and revenue to streaming platforms and production houses. Blockchain can be utilized to overcome this problem faced by artists, by using the concept of Non Fungible Token (NFTs). A dynamic web application built using ReactJs for the artist to mint their NFTs and store the metadata in off-chain using IPFS protocol and an ERC721 smart contract built using Solidity is deployed to Ethereum Blockchain and the IPFS CID along with the contract address is stored in MySql database using SpringBoot data Jpa and RESTful API for rendering data in webpage. Graph protocol is used for indexing and querying smart contract transactions and it is visualized using ChartJs.

Keywords: Ethereum Blockchain · ReactJs · Non Fungible Tokens (NFTs) · Interplanetary File System (IPFS) · Graph Protocol · Infrastructure · industrialization

1 Introduction

In today's music industry, streaming platforms like Spotify and Gaana have redefined the way we consume and access music. These platforms have opened up unprecedented opportunities for artists to share their work with a global audience. However, the current landscape poses a significant challenge for individual musicians: a substantial portion of the revenue generated from streaming their music goes to the platforms themselves, leaving artists with a relatively small share. To address this issue and ensure that more of the earnings find their way into the hands of the rightful creators, we propose the development of a mobile application for trading music albums as non-fungible tokens (NFTs). This innovative approach aims to redirect 90% of the profits back to the artists while allocating only 10% for transaction fees. In this paper, we explore the concept of NFTs in the music industry and the potential of NFT-based album trading platforms to revolutionize the revenue distribution model for artists.

Published by Springer Nature Switzerland AG 2025
A. Chandrabose et al. (Eds.): ICCCSP 2024, IFIP AICT 723, pp. 265–275, 2025.
https://doi.org/10.1007/978-3-031-73617-9_21

Objective and Motivation of This Project
The ultimate motivation of this project is to build a website integrated with blockchain to provide artists a secure, decentralized platform for authentic digital music ownership. This project aims to reduce piracy and counterfeiting by utilizing blockchain technology and smart contracts while empowering artists to receive fair royalties directly. By enhancing transparency, trust, and user privacy, this application promotes innovation in the music industry, encouraging early adoption and providing a user-friendly experience. Additionally, it positions itself to adapt and scale as the market for NFT-based music albums grows.

2 Review of Literature

In [1], the authors proposed that NFTs on the blockchain represent unique digital assets, with smart contract metadata ensuring their authenticity and blockchain transparency building trust in the NFT ecosystem.

In [2], the authors proposed the rapid growth of decentralized finance has led to the tokenization of assets, with non-fungible tokens (NFTs) gaining attention. NFTs offer unique, non-substitutable properties and have found success in digital art, gaming, and collectibles. This paper explores the under-researched use of NFTs in Intellectual Property (IP), specifically patents, aiming to streamline and enhance the patenting process. The proposed NFT-based patent framework provides guidance for businesses and highlights open challenges and future directions in this innovative application.

In [3], the authors illustrated a systematic review of blockchain's impact in the sector, revealing significant contributions to cross-border e-commerce platforms, supply chain operations, and data governance. It offers valuable insights for researchers and industry professionals seeking to enhance supply chain management in this context.

In [4], the authors proposed a NFTs represent digital assets like art and in-game items, with significant growth in their markets. Research shows that Bitcoin price shocks boost NFT sales, while Ether price shocks decrease active NFT wallets, indicating cryptocurrency markets' influence on NFT.

In [5], the authors proposed tokens, seen as blockchain's killer application, offer digital representations of various assets. They're managed by smart contracts, mainly on Ethereum, and can be broadly categorized into payment, security, and utility tokens.

In [6], the authors proposed the study delves into maintenance challenges unique to Ethereum smart contracts, addressing issues faced by developers in various maintenance categories. By conducting a literature review and surveying 165 smart contract developers, it offers insights into current maintenance methods and future strategies for enhancing smart contract maintainability.

In [7], the authors illustrated that Blockchain, a decentralized and tamper-proof technology, is poised to revolutionize various sectors beyond cryptocurrency. Its potential spans government, finance, accounting, and business processes, with research focusing on uncovering opportunities and addressing challenges in diverse applications, making it a significant force for the future.

In [8], the authors proposed a complex networks modeling framework to analyze the Ethereum blockchain. We depict blockchain accounts as nodes and the interactions between them as links in the network. This approach allows us to uncover valuable mathematical insights into the dynamics of blockchain interactions. Furthermore, it enables us to identify significant shifts in the blockchain's evolution by studying its historical data.

In [9], the authors asserts that blockchain, similar to past network revolutions, is set to disrupt urban settings. It introduces the "Future Living Framework" within the "Blockchain4Cities" research, demonstrating the advantages of employing blockchain technology in urban environments contexts through the lens of the UN's New Urban Agenda. By applying blockchain to urban policies and standards, the paper underscores its potential as the next transformative network for cities, akin to past paradigms like Cybernetics and Ubiquitous Computing.

3 System Implementation

We have proposed an off-chain album/music trading application which conceptualize the use of blockchain technology, Non Fungible Tokens (NFTs) and Graph Protocol for decentralized storage and to index data from Ethereum blockchain and ReactJs for building a dynamic web application. Our proposed solution involves 4 modules for our idea implementation.

They are as listed below:

1. Designing and developing Smart Contract for our NFTs using ERC721 standards.
2. Designing and building a music trading web application.
3. Integrating Smart contract and wallet connection for users.
4. Querying and indexing transactions of users.

Each module is developed separately and tested, later it is integrated with other modules and finally it is deployed.

3.1 Conceptual Flow of the Project

(See Fig. 1).

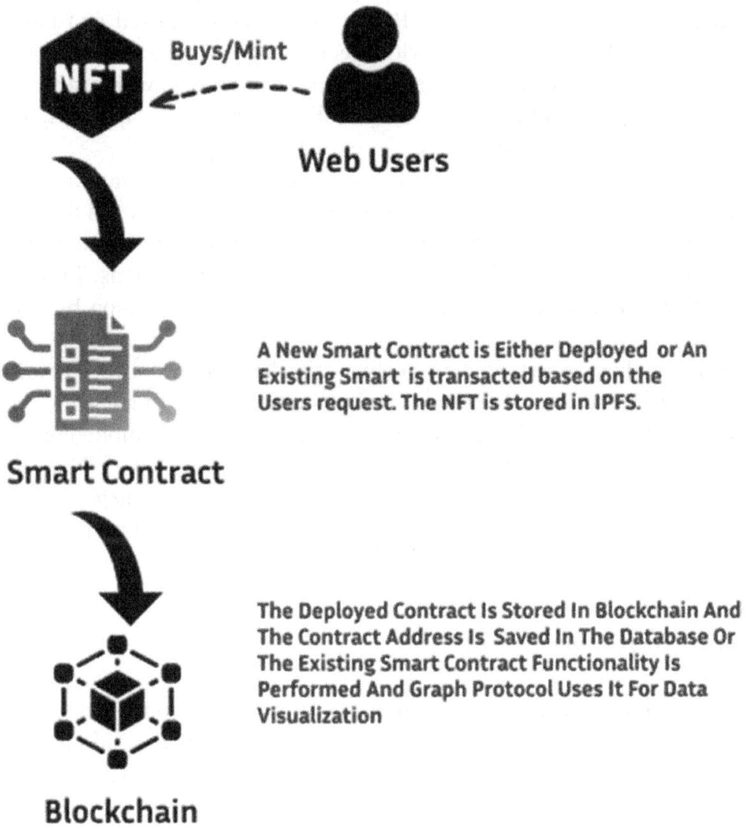

Fig. 1. Conceptual flow of the project

3.2 First Module

The initial module focuses on the creation and development of our Smart Contract through the utilization of the Solidity programming language and we are using the ERC721 standards developed by OpenZeppelin. Non Fungible token also known as NFTs are considered as assets in the blockchain world, here NFTs are treated as digital assets, which can be any media files ranging from images, audio, videos and even svg. These assets' value is defined by the NFT owner, who can set the limit for how many copies these NFTs can be generated or distributed among others.

ERC721 contains functionalities which defines the owner, token count, transfer and other functionalities which performs the basic operation of buying and selling of NFTs. Here the NFTs are considered as the albums/music that are created by music artists. Using external Smart contracts these music artists can transfer the cryptocurrency collected by the NFTs purchase done by other users.

The smart contract is tested using HardHat a Smart contract testing tool, we are using test ether such as Goerli ETH or Sepolia ETH as our cryptocurrency for development purposes.

3.3 Second Module

The second module involves the creation and implementation of a user-friendly web application using ReactJs and SpringBoot, emphasizing design and development aspects. Here Reactjs is used for building a single page application (SPA) along with CSS to style the web pages. ReactJs is a JavaScript library which helps in building dynamic web pages using components and this leads to less code lines and more code reuse.

Multiple web pages are built and all are routed using React-Router-Dom. Using React-Router-Dom helps in reducing traffic given to the server, instead of fetching web pages from the server, React-Router-Dom helps the browser in taking care of navigating to different web pages.

SpringBoot is used for building RESTful web services and it is mainly used for fetching the contract address, the URL of our NFT and other metadata which are mapped and stored to our MySql database using SpringDataJpa. Applications such as Postman are used for testing our API connectivity and working (Figs. 2, 3, 4 and 5).

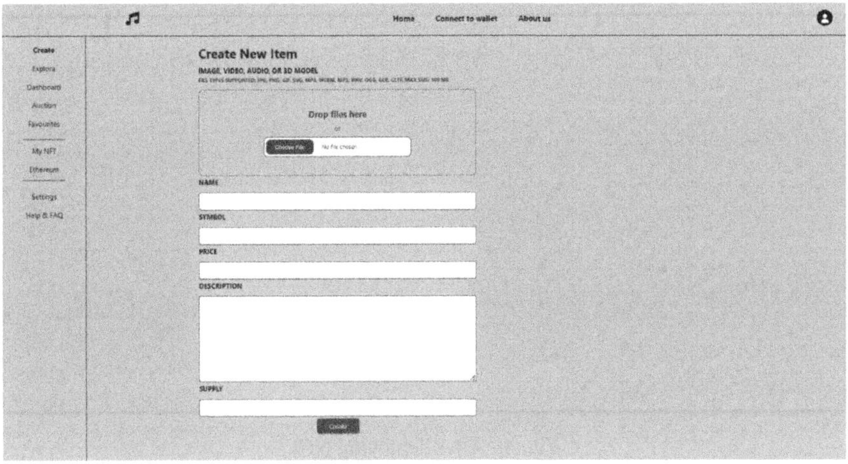

Fig. 2. Creating NFT

3.4 Third Module

Our third module deals with the integration of our smart contract along with the connection of any crypto wallet to our webpage. In our case we are using MetaMask wallet and Smart Contract integration is done using EthersJs, a JavaScript library used for integrating smart contracts to our page.

By getting the Application Binary Interface (ABI) and Bytecode of our Smart Contract, which is easily generated after compiling our Smart Contract in HardHat and using these both ABI and Bytecode we can easily deploy the Smart Contract with the help of EthersJs. The Artist fills the form in the web page which gathers all the metadata needed

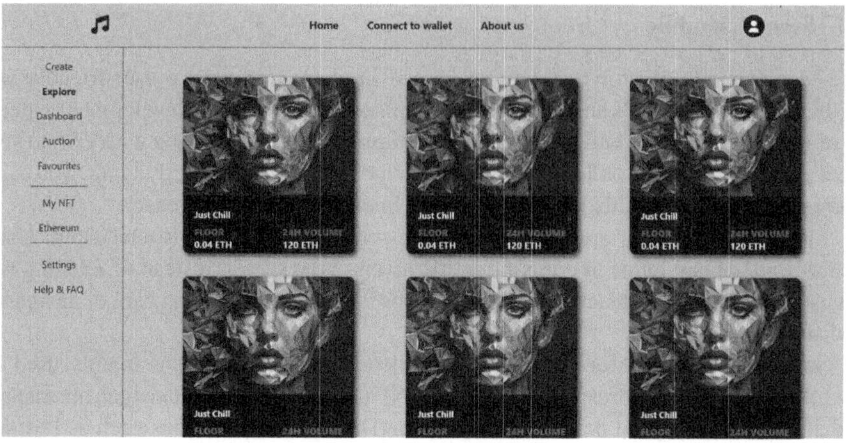

Fig. 3. Explore page

Fig. 4. After deploying NFT

for deploying the Smart Contract and the album/music created by the artist is stored in IPFS which is a decentralized protocol for storing data.

Interplanetary File System (IPFS) is a peer-to-peer file sharing protocol, all the data stored in IPFS are identified by its unique hash value generated by IPFS. These unique hash values are called CID (Content Identifier). if a duplicate copy of an already existing data in IPFS is uploaded again, The IPFS regenerates the same CID of original image to the duplicate copy.

Since storing even a small 1 MB of file in Ethereum blockchain (On-chain) can cost a fortune to the Artist, hence we decided to save the data in a decentralized platform such as IPFS, resulting in off-chain storage of our NTFs. On submitting the form in the web page results in deployment of a new Smart Contract with the Owner as the artist who created the NFT. The Artist pays some cryptocurrency for deployment and

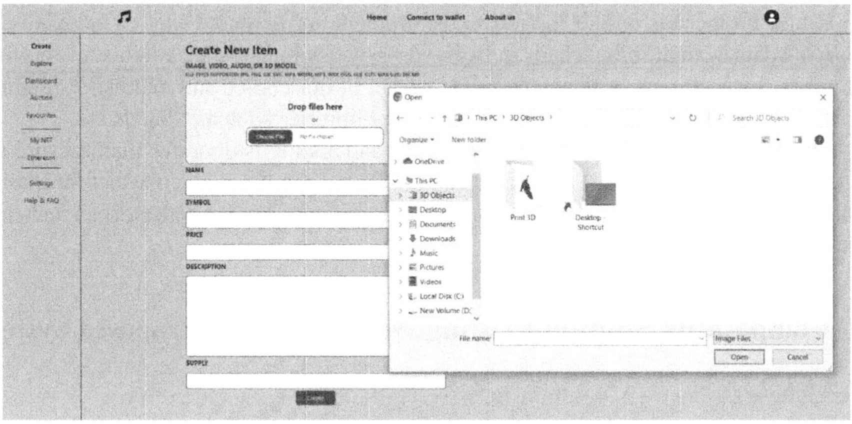

Fig. 5. Uploading File

the Smart Contract address along with the artist MetaMask wallet address and the IPFS link generated is stored in our database (Fig. 6).

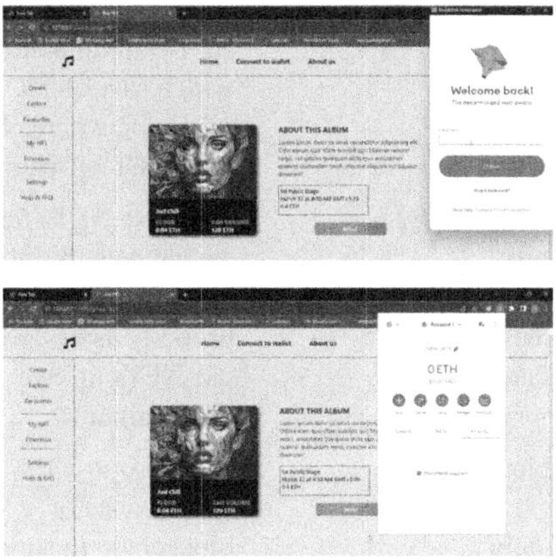

Fig. 6. Integrating with metamask

3.5 Fourth Module

Our fourth module deals with the use of Graph Protocol for indexing and querying the smart contract deployed by NFT creators, with the help of Graph we can collect all the metadata such as transaction history, NFT purchases which can be found in the blockchain. This can be used to visualize data and give the end users real-time updates and number of NFT ownership transfers.

Graph Protocol is one of the most cost efficient and scalable way of indexing and querying data from the blockchain and this works by listening to the particular event emitted when transacting a particular Smart Contract of our choice and making a subgraph of our finding and visualizing it using JavaScript libraries such as ChartJs etc.

Finally all modules are integrated together and testing is done for making sure the right working of our website and at the end finally we can use it as a product for trading albums/music. After the development phase, the application is ready to work in real-time with Ethereum blockchain.

4 Comparative Study of Existing Works with Our Proposed System

(See Table 1).

Table 1. Classification of research works and comparative study with our proposed solution.

S. NO.	Title of the paper	Published Year	Comparative study with our proposed system	Publication
01	NFT Trading Platform: A Decentralized Application using the Ethereum Blockchain	2023	They have built an NFT trading platform which saves NFT on-chain, whereas we save NFT off-chain	International Conference on Blockchain Technology (ICBT)
02	Patents and intellectual property assets as non-fungible tokens: key technologies and challenges	2023	They use NFTs for saving patents and other intellectual property assets, we use NFTs to save music albums	Research Gate Online Library
03	Blockchain-Enabled Cross-Border E-Commerce Supply Chain Management: A Bibliometric Systematic Review	2022	They propose the significance of blockchain in supply chain and E-commerce platform, whereas we propose about the significance of applying blockchain in music streaming platform	IEEE Xplore

(*continued*)

Table 1. (*continued*)

S. NO.	Title of the paper	Published Year	Comparative study with our proposed system	Publication
04	The non-fungible token (NFT) market and its relationship with Bitcoin and Ethereum	2021	The increase of sales in web3 industry after implementation NFTs in blockchain such as bitcoin and ethereum, we have proposed how with the use of NFTs music artist get high revenue	Social Science Research Network (SSRN)
05	Tokens, Types, and Standards: Identification and Utilization in Ethereum	2020	A deep study of different types of tokens and standards used in Ethereum such as ERC721, ERC20 etc. We mention the use of ERC721 standard for our NFT implementation	IEEE International Conference on Decentralized Applications and Infrastructures
06	Maintaining Smart Contracts on Ethereum: Issues, Techniques, and Future Challenges	2020	They mention the different ways to maintain a smart contract, whereas we focus on how to index and query a smart contract using Graph protocol	Research Gate Online Library
07	A Review of Blockchain Technology and Its Applications in the Business Environment	2019	A review of how blockchain can shape the business world is made and we mention on how the use of blockchain can shape the music industry	Research Gate Online Library

5 Architectural Model

5.1 System Requirements

The hardware requirements for the system are minimal, the system involves a working personal computer or laptop with minimum 4 GB RAM and a good processor such as I3 and enough storage space.

The software requirements are Integrated Development Environment (IDE) such as Visual Studio Code, Intelliji and Node Package Manager (NPM) for installing Node modules and other third party modules including EthersJs, Graph, ReactJs, IPFS, ChartJs, Hardhat and Solidity used for the frontend and Smart Contract testing. Meanwhile Postman is used for API testing and MySQL database for storing non-blockchain related information. A web browser such as Google Chrome, Microsoft Edge or Brave needed to be installed for hosting the website using localhost (Fig. 7).

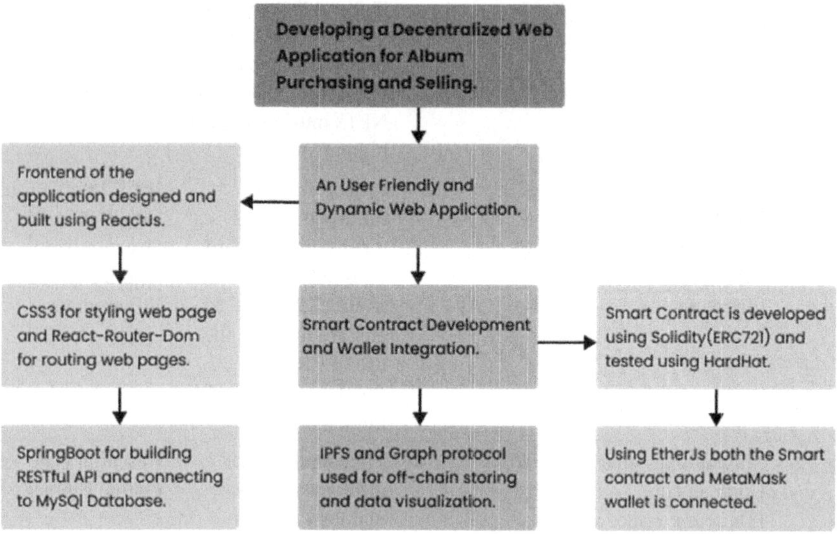

Fig. 7. Illustrates the comprehensive flow model of the project, detailing each module and its respective sub-modules.

6 Result and Discussion

A decentralized music trading platform is built which is dynamic and user friendly, here the saved data is tampered proof since all the data is stored in blockchain, which is known for its decentralization and trustlessness. Easy buying and minting of NFTs leading to the rightful revenue generation of artist. With the use of protocol such as Graph has helped in visualizing transaction rate and history leading to the improvement of user experience. Overall the ownership of album/music remains safe from exploitation and gives the rightful revenue back to the NFTs creator.

7 Conclusion

Although Ethereum blockchain is decentralized and secure technology which is unhackable till now, but the smart contract that lives in Ethereum Virtual Machine (EVM) is hackable. A proper auditing of Smart Contract needs to be done for the secure transaction of Smart Contract. IPFS is a decentralized protocol which saves data and provides a Content Identifier (CID) which remains the same for each of copy of the same data stored in IPFS. If all the nodes in the IPFS remove a particular NFT stored. This could lead to the permanent removal of that particular NFT in IPFS. The music trading platform should be made compatible with different cross chain technologies such as Solana, Polygon, BitCoin etc. Even though the application offers rightful ownership and revenue for NFT creators, still the cost of creating and deploying a NFT to blockchain cost a lot and even if the NFT is stored off-chain.

References

1. Pawar, M., Balkar, R., Pawar, V., Roy, S.: NFT Trading Platform: A Decentralized Application using the Ethereum Blockchain, 19 May 2023. https://doi.org/10.2139/ssrn.4453987. https://ssrn.com/abstract=4453987
2. Hosseini BamakanBamakan, S.M.H., Nezhadsistani, N., Bodaghi, O., Qu, Q.: Patents and intellectual property assets as non-fungible tokens: key technologies and challenges (2023)
3. Zhou, F., Liu, Y.: Blockchain-enabled cross-border e-commerce supply chain management: a bibliometric systematic review. Sustainability **14**, 15918 (2022). https://doi.org/10.3390/su142315918
4. Ante, L.: The non-fungible token (NFT) market and its relationship with Bitcoin and Ethereum, 6 June 2021. https://doi.org/10.2139/ssrn.3861106. https://ssrn.com/abstract=3861106
5. Di Angelo, M., Salzer, G.: Tokens, Types, and Standards: Identification and Utilization in Ethereum (2020). https://doi.org/10.1109/DAPPS49028.2020.00001
6. Chen, J., Xia, X., Lo, D., Grundy, J., Yang, X.: Maintaining Smart Contracts on Ethereum: Issues, Techniques, and Future Challenges (2020)
7. Kitsantas, T., Vazakidis, A., Chytis, E.: A Review of Blockchain Technology and Its Applications in the Business Environment (2019)
8. Ferretti, S., D'Angelo, G.: On the Ethereum blockchain structure: a complex networks theory perspective. Concurr. Comput.: Pract. Exp. **32** (2019). https://doi.org/10.1002/cpe.5493
9. Marsal, L.: Future living framework: is blockchain the next enabling network? Technol. Forecast. Soc. Change **128** (2017). https://doi.org/10.1016/j.techfore.2017.12.005

A Deep Learning-Based Algorithm for Predicting the Turning Point of Cloud Workload

Anmol Jain and Sanjaya Kumar Panda(✉)

National Institute of Technology Warangal, Warangal 506004, Telangana, India
aj22csm1r04@student.nitw.ac.in, sanjaya@nitw.ac.in

Abstract. Cloud workload data is time series data that consists of the logs of the resource consumption, such as central processing unit (CPU) utilization, memory utilization and bandwidth consumption, on a particular machine in a cloud environment. These logs are essential for analyzing the machine's performance and debugging purposes at fault time. It is worth noting that the utilization fluctuates due to changes in load over time. Moreover, there are some peaks and valleys in the utilization pattern, and predicting such points in the cloud workload is challenging and not well-studied. The prediction can be helpful in saving the waste of resources and providing quality services to the customers. Recently, researchers have used deep learning algorithms to predict the turning points using basic and fluctuating features. However, the prediction can be improved by taking the extreme points of the adjacent segments, and it is effective for high-variance time series data. This paper presents a turning point prediction (TPP) algorithm on cloud workload data using deep learning models, namely long short-term memory (LSTM), bidirectional LSTM (BiLSTM) and gated recurrent unit (GRU) networks, that use some novel features. TPP uses a piece-wise linear segmentation (PLS) algorithm to generate the segments. Then, it determines the potential turning points and labels them into two classes. Finally, the LSTM, BiLSTM, and GRU are applied to classify the turning points. We simulated the TPP on two datasets, Google cloud and Alibaba, and compared its three variants in terms of precision, recall and F1-score to show its effectiveness.

Keywords: Cloud Computing · Deep Learning · Turning Point Prediction · Long Short-Term Memory · Piece-Wise Linear Segmentation · Time Series Data · Resource Utilization

1 Introduction

In today's digital world, cloud computing has emerged as a solution capable of fulfilling the dynamic resource demands of customers from anywhere at anytime [1–3]. It has revolutionized companies' business processes by storing and managing data and applications. It can handle a few to large numbers of company customers and efficiently manage their required resources [4,5]. It provides enormous

Published by Springer Nature Switzerland AG 2025
A. Chandrabose et al. (Eds.): ICCCSP 2024, IFIP AICT 723, pp. 276–287, 2025.
https://doi.org/10.1007/978-3-031-73617-9_22

resource flexibility to customers and charges based on usage basis [6]. Cloud service providers (CSPs), namely Amazon web services (AWS), Microsoft Azure and Google cloud platform (GCP), offer software, platform, and infrastructure services with varying levels of abstraction and management responsibilities [2,7]. These CSPs must continuously analyze the resource requirements and their utilization to fulfil the business requirements. For this, these CSPs maintain the logs (referred to as cloud workload data) of resource consumption, including central processing unit (CPU) and graphical processing unit (GPU) cores utilization, CPU and GPU memory utilization, average and maximum memory utilization and bandwidth utilization [8–13]. These logs are time series data on various machines in a cloud environment and show the machine's state at any particular point.

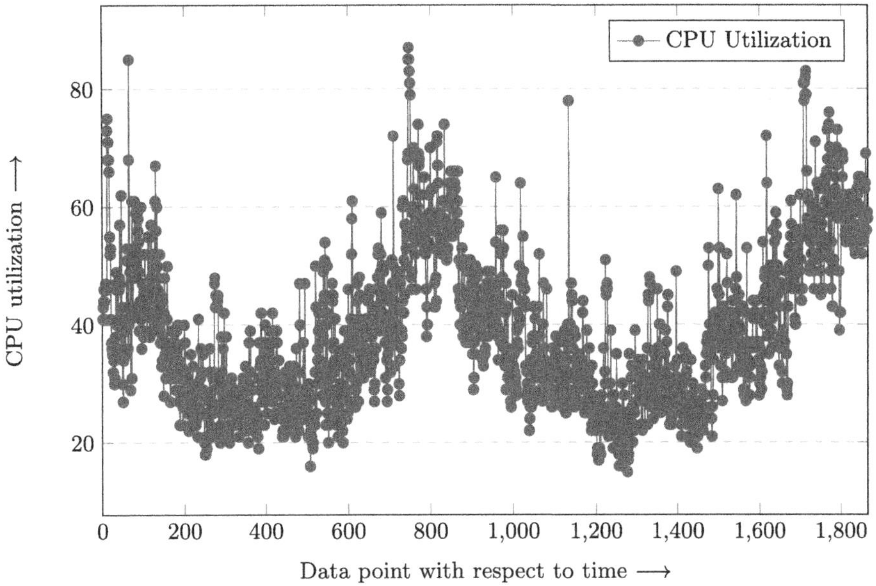

Fig. 1. Fluctuation of Alibaba cloud workload data for machine id $m1932$.

Logs can help the CSPs to monitor the machine's performance, debug at fault time, determine the resource demand patterns, and maintain the quality of services for customers. Moreover, CSPs can predict the trends in cloud workload data and make wise decisions accordingly [9]. For instance, the cloud workload data has some peaks and valleys in resource utilization. Note that the peak is a point above all of its local neighbours, and the valley is below all of its neighbours. Figure 1 represents the cloud workload of the Alibaba dataset on machine id $m1932$, which is very fluctuating. Moreover, there are many local peak and valley points. These points are referred to as turning points. Note that the x-axis represents the time, and the y-axis represents the CPU utilization. It is worth noting that finding and predicting peak and valley points in the cloud workload data is quite challenging and not widely covered in the literature. The workload prediction can be viewed from three perspectives [1]. 1) To determine the value of the future state based on the current state. 2) To determine the slope trend and its time interval. 3) To determine the turning point (i.e., peak or valley). This paper aims to address the third perspective to save resource waste and provide quality services to the customers. Recently, Ruan et al. [1] have addressed the above perspectives using basic and fluctuating features. However, the prediction can be further improved by considering the extreme points of the adjacent segments.

This paper addresses the problem of identifying and predicting a turning point and presents a turning point prediction (TPP) algorithm. This algorithm uses well-known deep learning models, namely long short-term memory (LSTM), bidirectional LSTM (BiLSTM) and gated recurrent unit (GRU) networks. It predicts the turning points in cloud workload data using novel features. TPP works for high-variance time series data. It first generates the segments using a bottom-up piece-wise linear segmentation (PLS) algorithm, which is a recursive algorithm. This segmentation algorithm iterates through all the data and finds the line segment using the regression technique with an error parameter. Then, TPP generates the label for each turning point. Finally, it uses the LSTM, BiLSTM and GRU models to classify the turning points. We consider two datasets, Google cloud and Alibaba, and simulate the three variants of TPP, namely LSTM-TPP, BiLSTM-TPP and GRU-TPP. The three variants are compared in terms of precision, recall and F1-score.

The rest of the sections are described as follows. Section 2 describes the allied literature for the workload prediction problem. Section 3 presents the problem description. Section 4 introduces the overall framework and three variants of TPP. Section 5 discusses the dataset, simulation results and analysis. Finally, Sect. 6 summarizes the work.

2 Related Work

This section briefly discusses recent works used to solve the workload prediction problem. These works are based on statistical, machine and deep learning techniques. Kumar et al. [9] have proposed a differential evolution algorithm that is self-adapting and predicts workload using neural networks. Alternatively, they have used a self-adaptive neural network for workload prediction. Hsu et al. [10] have used recurrent neural network (RNN), GRU and time series analysis for future workload prediction. Kim et al. [11] and Bi et al. [12] have built an integrated method using deep learning for time series analysis.

Gupta et al. [13] have used the BiLSTM model to find out the position of the virtual machine (VM). Duggan et al. [14] have proposed an RNN-based model to help in VM migration by predicting CPU and network bandwidth. Di et al. [15] have proposed a server CPU usage prediction algorithm based on the Bayesian model. Gao et al. [16] have used the graph neural network (GNN) architecture to predict the cloud workload. Note that GNN works well on graph-like data. Xia et al. [17] have proposed a weighted support vector machine (SVM) model for turning point prediction. Here, SVM is a classifier that tries to generate a hyperplane and separates two classes.

The above works aim to perform a point value prediction in which the researchers have predicted a future point based on past data for the observation window as their training features. They have implemented machine and deep learning models for future prediction. However, this paper aims to perform beyond the point value analysis as there are peak and valley points. On the other hand, the statistical features used in the literature do not adequately capture the fluctuating cloud workload trends. It leads to the wastage of resources in the peak and valley points. This phenomenon inspires us to develop novel features capable of capturing the cloud workload trends and determining the turning points to manage the resources accordingly.

3 Problem Description

Consider a set of $(t-1)$ points, $\{x_1, x_2, \ldots, x_{t-1}\}$, where x_t is any point at time instance t, in a cloud workload. The problem is predicting an arbitrary point x_t and determining whether that point is a turning point or not. Note that we consider $(t-1)$ points (i.e., $\{x_1, x_2, \ldots, x_{t-1}\}$) and determine the next point x_t for its possible inclusion in turning point. Moreover, we determine whether the point is a peak (i.e., a point above all of its local neighbors) or a valley (i.e., a point below all of its local neighbors) point. Mathematically,

$$x_t = \begin{cases} \text{Peak point, if } x_t > x_{t-1} \text{ and } x_t > x_{t+1} \\ \text{Valley point, if } x_t < x_{t-1} \text{ and } x_t < x_{t+1} \end{cases} \quad (1)$$

4 Proposed Algorithm

This section introduces a TPP algorithm for cloud workload data using LSTM, BiLSTM and GRU deep learning models. This algorithm aims to determine the turning points and peak and valley points. The overall framework of the proposed algorithm, TPP, is shown in Fig. 2. The framework consists of two main parts, namely pre-processing and prediction, which are described as follows.

4.1 Pre-processing of Workload

In this subsection, we define the formal definition of the turning points and the features used to train the model for prediction. Let $S = \{s_1, s_2, \ldots, s_m\}$ be the set of segment points, and s_j and s_{j+1} are the jth and $j+1^{th}$ line segments with boundary points $x_{i_{j-1}}$, x_{i_j} and $x_{i_{j+1}}$, then these points can form a turning point. Further, these points can be a peak or valley point. Figure 3 shows the consecutive line segments with boundary points to illustrate a valley turning point.

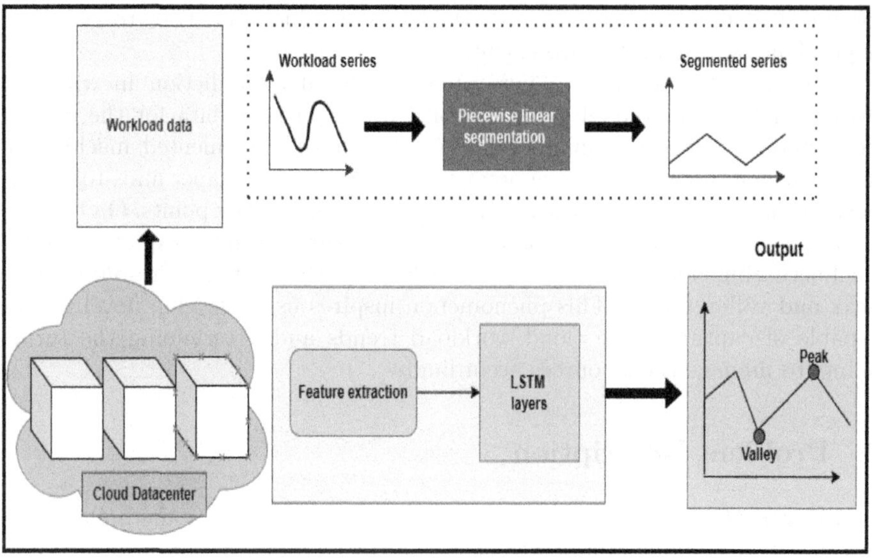

Fig. 2. The overall framework of the proposed algorithm.

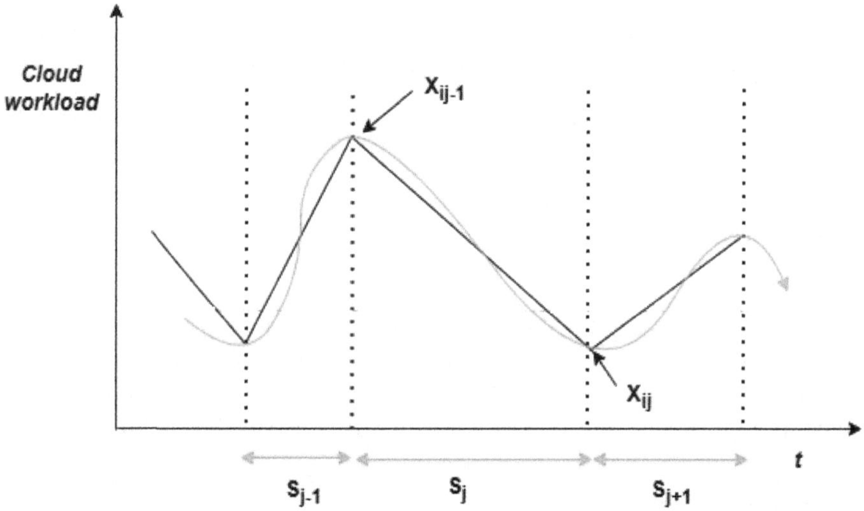

Fig. 3. An example of a turning point.

TPP takes the cloud workload data as input. Note that this data is a time series data. Let us consider a time series data with n points, i.e., $\{x_1, x_2, \ldots, x_n\}$. First, we divide the time series data into line segments. For this, we use the PLS algorithm. Note that there are some variations of the PLS algorithm, namely bottom-up, top-down and sliding window. However, we use bottom-up variation for our implementation. This variation is a recursive algorithm, which tries to fit a set of points into a straight line using regression technique and error as a parameter. We present a general overview of the PLS algorithm for the sake of completion of this paper as follows.

1. Input: It takes a time series of data points and represents a one-dimension vector.
2. Segmentation process: Each iteration finds the breakpoints where the linear relationship between the data points changes significantly and computes the error for linear fitting. Then, the breakpoints are selected to reduce total error throughout the segments.
3. Linear fitting: A linear model, typically a straight line, is fitted to the data points within each determined segment.
4. Optimization: The fitness of the piece-wise linear model depends on the cost function. Examples of such functions are the sum of squared residuals and mean squared error.
5. Output: A set of consecutive line segments is produced as output.

As TPP uses a supervised learning technique for prediction, we need labelled data. The labels are generated using line segments following the conditions below.

$$y_i = \begin{cases} 1 & \text{if } (x_{i_{j-1}} - x_{i_{j-2}}) \times (x_{i_{j-1}} - x_{i_j}) > 0 \\ 0 & \text{Otherwise} \end{cases} \tag{2}$$

where y_i represents the label, i.e., either 1 or 0. Algorithm 1 describes the filtering of turning points, which will help generate the labels and help in the training phase.

4.2 Prediction

The second part is to apply LSTM, Bi-LSTM and GRU [18] models, which will take the features extracted from the first part and predict the output. LSTM is a particular type of RNN. The main breakthrough of LSTM is its capacity to record and retrieve data across extended sequences, which lessens the difficulties caused by vanishing gradients. A memory cell and a group of gates, an input gate (I_t), an output gate (O_t), and a forget gate (F_t), are used to do this shown in Fig. 4. These gates enable LSTM to store and delete data as needed by controlling the information flow into, out of, and within the memory cell. Moreover, the LSTM model suits problems like time series analyses, natural language processing and speech recognition. Bi-LSTM is an extension of the LSTM. It is a sequence processing model, which is made up of two LSTMs, one of which takes

Algorithm 1. Filtering of turning points

Inputs: A set of m segmented workloads, $x_{seg} = \{(x_1, x_{i_1}),\ldots, (x_{i_{j-1}}, x_{i_j}),\ldots, (x_{i_{m-1}}, x_{i_m})\}$

Outputs: A set of turning points labels, $y_{label} = \{y_1,\ldots, y_2,\ldots, y_m\}$

$temp \leftarrow [\,]$ ▷ [ ] represents an empty array.
for $j = 2$ to $len(x_{seg} + 1)$ **do** ▷ len is a function that determines the length.
  $(x_1, x_2) = x_{seg_j}$
  $(x_0, x_1) = x_{seg_{j-1}}$
  if $x_1 < x_0$ and $x_1 < x_2$ **then**
    temp.append(1);
  else if $x_1 > x_0$ and $x_1 > x_2$ **then**
    temp.append(1);
  else
    temp.append(0);
  end if
end for
$y_{label} = temp$

input in a forward manner and the other in a backward manner. Bi-LSTM efficiently expands the network's information pool, enhancing the context. On the contrary, GRU uses two gates, reset (R_t) and update (Z_t), shown in Fig. 5. The update gate defines how much of the new input should be used to update the hidden state, while the reset gate determines how much of the prior hidden state should be forgotten. The updated hidden state is the basis for calculating the GRU's output. Therefore, it has fewer parameters than LSTM and Bi-LSTM.

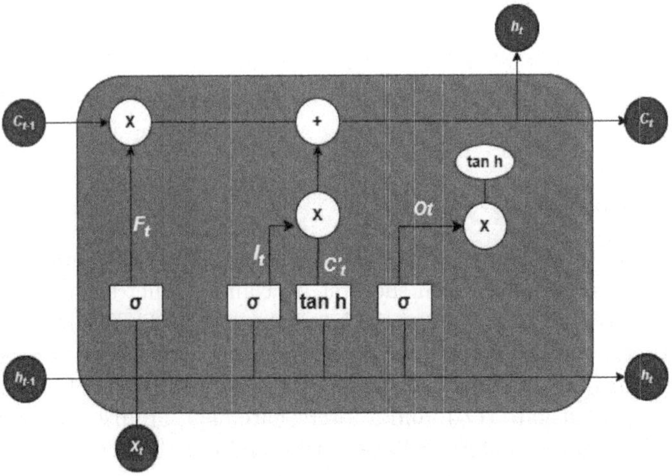

Fig. 4. A LSTM gate unit [19].

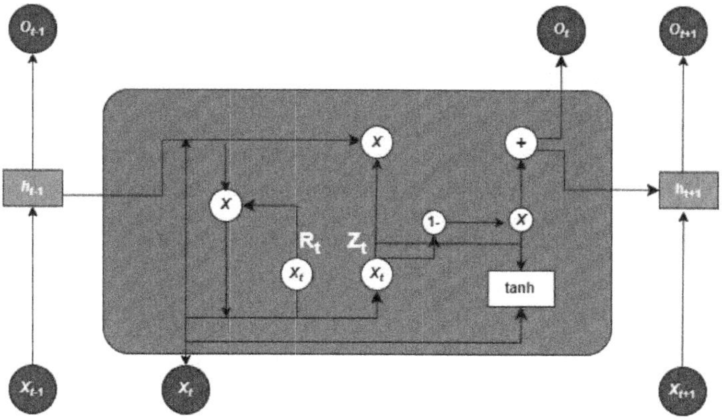

Fig. 5. A GRU gate unit [20].

4.3 Feature Generation

We found that the previous algorithms used the sliding window technique. In this technique, such algorithms took a window of size n. Then, the algorithms try to calculate different statistical features, such as mean, variance, and other complex features like slope, by looking at the past n data points. Now, the algorithms find the features and assign the corresponding output labels for the selected window size. Then, a window is shifted by one, and these features are fed to some deep learning model capable of handling the data sequence, like the LSTM or the RNN model, to predict the turning points. Our algorithm found that turning points directly depend on the consecutive line segments generated by the PLS algorithm. Therefore, the algorithm used endpoints of the consecutive line segments as features. If we have two line segments, $S_{i-1} = (x_{i-1}, x_i)$ and $S_i = (x_i, x_{i+1})$, then our features would be (x_{i-1}, x_i, x_{i+1}). We consider these features in various models for turning point prediction. Algorithm 2 shows the proposed TPP algorithm.

5 Dataset Description, Results and Analysis

The simulation process requires actual cloud workload data to predict the turning points. For this, we use two real-world cloud workload datasets, which are publicly available [21]. We use the first dataset, the Google cloud dataset, released by Google in 2011. This dataset consists of massive data with a total size of 40 gigabytes. Note that it is a log of different machines. We randomly use a dataset with machine ID 85515092 comprising 8352 records. This dataset consists of many features in which we use CPU usage as our training attribute. The second one is named the Alibaba cloud workload dataset, which consists of the workload traces of different machines on the cloud servers. The log contains various parameters: CPU load, bandwidth utilization, disk usage and many more.

Algorithm 2. TPP

Inputs: A set of n points $(x_1, x_2, \ldots, x_{t-1}, x_t, x_{t+1}, \ldots, x_n)$
Outputs: Whether a point is a turning point or not

Determine n future points $(x_t, x_{t+1}, \ldots, x_{t+n}) \leftarrow model(x_{t-1}, x_{t-2}, \ldots, x_{t-n})$ ▷ model is a function that represents either LSTM, Bi-LSTM or GRU.
$x_{seg} \leftarrow PLS((x_1, x_2, \ldots, x_i, \ldots, x_n), \text{error})$ ▷ $x_{seg} = s_1, s_2, \ldots, s_n$
$y_{label} \leftarrow label\_generator(x_{seg})$ ▷ $y_{label} = y_1, y_2, \ldots, y_n$
for $j = 2$ to $len(x_{seg} + 1)$ **do**
    $(x_1, x_2) = x_{seg_j}$
    $(x_0, x_1) = x_{seg_{j-1}}$
    $features \leftarrow (x_0, x_1, x_2)$
end for
$z \leftarrow model(features, y_{label})$
if z is a turning point **then**
    $output \leftarrow true$
else
    $output \leftarrow false$
end if

We use CPU load as our parameter to predict turning points from different features. We use data from three machines, which consists of approximately 17000 records, for our simulation. Subsequently, we pre-processed our dataset and generated the labels. Then, we pass the data to an LSTM model. It is noteworthy that we use a stacked LSTM model with a three-layer LSTM architecture with Adam optimizer and a learning rate of 0.1 for our implementation. The dataset is divided 70% for training, 10% for validation, and the rest 20% for testing. Moreover, we use cross-entropy loss function, i.e., $l(y, p)$. Mathematically [22],

$$l(y, p) = -\frac{1}{N} \sum_{i=1}^{N} (y_i \times \log(p_i) + (1 - y_i) \times \log(1 - p_i)) \tag{3}$$

where N is the total number of samples, y_i is the ith element of true label and p_i is the ith element of predicted probability.

We train the model for fifty iterations. We use three different performance matrices, precision, recall, and F1-score, to evaluate and compare the proposed algorithm with other algorithms. These matrices are defined as follows.

$$\text{Precision} = \frac{\text{True Positive}}{\text{True Positive} + \text{False Positive}} \tag{4}$$

$$\text{Recall} = \frac{\text{True Positive}}{\text{True Positive} + \text{False Negative}} \tag{5}$$

$$\text{F1-score} = 2 \times \frac{\text{Precision} \times \text{Recall}}{\text{Precision} + \text{Recall}} \tag{6}$$

Table 1 shows the simulation results of the proposed and existing algorithms using two datasets, namely Alibaba and Google cloud. We found that GRU-TPP performs better than other models, namely LSTM-TPP and BiLSTM-TPP (Figs. 6, 7, 8).

Table 1. Comparison of precision, recall and F1-score for LSTM-TPP, BiLSTM-TPP and GRU-TPP

Dataset	Precision			Recall			F1-Score		
	LSTM-TPP	BiLSTM-TPP	GRU-TPP	LSTM-TPP	BiLSTM-TPP	GRU-TPP	LSTM-TPP	BiLSTM-TPP	GRU-TPP
Alibaba	0.99	0.99	0.98	0.95	0.95	0.96	0.97	0.97	0.98
Google Cloud	0.93	0.92	0.93	0.87	0.90	0.92	0.89	0.87	0.90

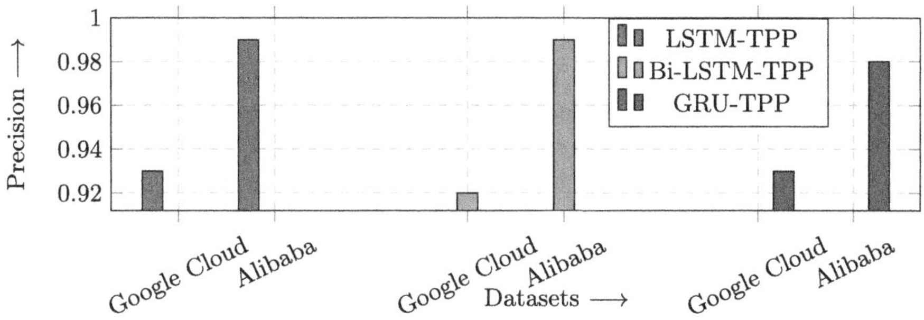

Fig. 6. Graphical representation of the precision for the Google cloud and Alibaba datasets.

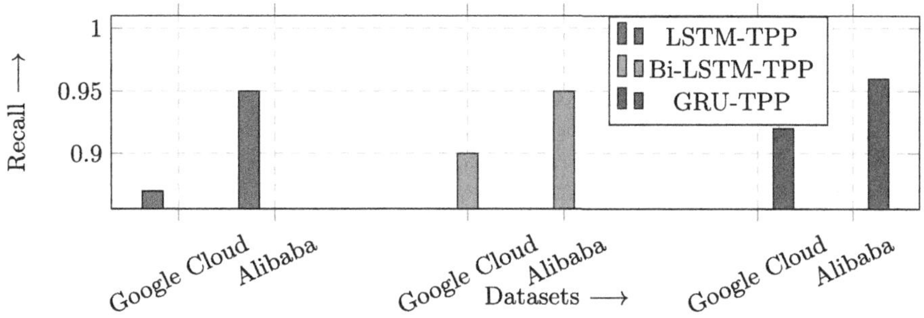

Fig. 7. Graphical representation of the recall for the Google cloud and Alibaba datasets.

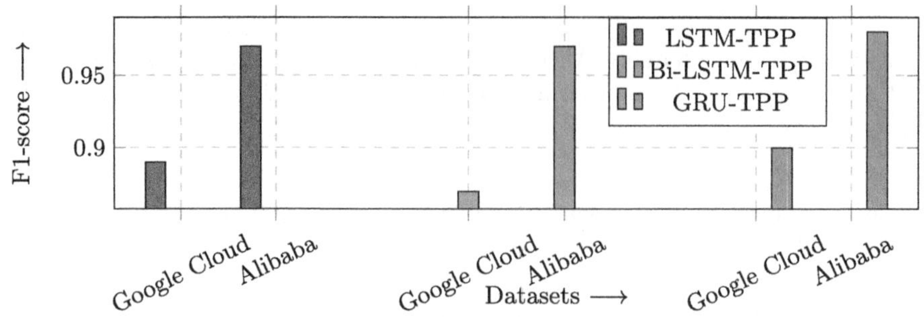

Fig. 8. Graphical representation of the F1-score for the Google cloud and Alibaba datasets.

6 Conclusion

In this paper, we have described an algorithm called TPP for cloud workload. TPP can predict the trend in the cloud workload data. For this, TPP has segmented the time series data using the PLS algorithm to get the smaller chunks of the workload data. Subsequently, TPP has used different deep learning models (i.e., LSTM, BiLSTM, and GRU) for turning point prediction. We have evaluated our work on two real-world datasets (i.e., Google cloud and Alibaba) using well-known evaluation metrics (i.e., precision, recall and F1-score). We have found out that GRU-TPP works well compared to all its variants and makes a good prediction.

References

1. Ruan, L., et al.: Cloud workload turning points prediction via cloud feature-enhanced deep learning. IEEE Trans. Cloud Comput. **11**, 1719 (2022)
2. Panda, S.K., Gupta, I., Jana, P.K.: Task scheduling algorithms for multi-cloud systems: allocation-aware approach. Inf. Syst. Front **21**, 241–259 (2019)
3. Panda, S.K., Jana, P.K.: An efficient resource allocation algorithm for IAAS cloud. In: Distributed Computing and Internet Technology: 11th International Conference, ICDCIT 2015, Bhubaneswar, India, February 5–8, 2015. Proceedings 11, pp. 351–355. Springer (2015)
4. Panda, S.K., Jana, P.K.: An efficient request-based virtual machine placement algorithm for cloud computing. In: Distributed Computing and Internet Technology: 13th International Conference, ICDCIT 2017, Bhubaneswar, India, January 13–16, 2017, Proceedings 13, pp. 129–143. Springer (2017)
5. Panda, S.K., Jana, P.K.: An efficient energy saving task consolidation algorithm for cloud computing systems. In: 2014 International Conference on Parallel, Distributed and Grid Computing, pp. 262–267. IEEE (2014)
6. Pande, S.K., et al.: A smart cloud service management algorithm for vehicular clouds. IEEE Trans. Intell. Transp. Syst. **22**(8), 5329–5340 (2020)
7. Panda, S.K., Jana, P.K.: Uncertainty-based QOS min-min algorithm for heterogeneous multi-cloud environment. Arab. J. Sci. Eng. **41**, 3003–3025 (2016)

8. Hussain, A., Aleem, M.: GoCJ: Google cloud jobs dataset for distributed and cloud computing infrastructures. Data **3**(4), 38 (2018)
9. Jitendra Kumar and Ashutosh Kumar Singh: Workload prediction in cloud using artificial neural network and adaptive differential evolution. Future Gener. Comput. Syst. **81**, 41–52 (2018)
10. Hsu, Y.-F., Matsuda, K., Matsuoka, M.: Self-aware workload forecasting in data center power prediction. In: 2018 18th IEEE/ACM International Symposium on Cluster, Cloud and Grid Computing (CCGRID), pp. 321–330. IEEE (2018)
11. Kim, I.K., Wang, W., Qi, Y., Humphrey, M.: Forecasting cloud application workloads with cloudinsight for predictive resource management. IEEE Trans. Cloud Comput. **10**(3), 1848–1863 (2020)
12. Bi, J., Li, S., Yuan, H., Zhou, M.C.: Integrated deep learning method for workload and resource prediction in cloud systems. Neurocomputing **424**, 35–48 (2021)
13. Gupta, S., Dileep, A.D., Gonsalves, T.A.: Online sparse BLSTM models for resource usage prediction in cloud datacentres. IEEE Trans. Netw. Serv. Manag. **17**(4), 2335–2349 (2020)
14. Duggan, M., Shaw, R., Duggan, J., Howley, E., Barrett, E.: A multitime-steps-ahead prediction approach for scheduling live migration in cloud data centers. Softw. Pract. Exp. **49**(4), 617–639 (2019)
15. Di, S., Kondo, D., Cirne, W.: Host load prediction in a google compute cloud with a Bayesian model. In: SC'12: Proceedings of the International Conference on High Performance Computing, Networking, Storage and Analysis, pp. 1–11. IEEE (2012)
16. Gao, M., Li, Y., Yu, J.: Workload prediction of cloud workflow based on graph neural network. In: Web Information Systems and Applications: 18th International Conference, WISA 2021, Kaifeng, China, September 24–26, 2021, Proceedings 18, pp. 169–189. Springer (2021)
17. Xia, B., Li, T., Zhou, Q., Li, Q., Zhang, H.: An effective classification-based framework for predicting cloud capacity demand in cloud services. IEEE Trans. Serv. Comput. **14**(4), 944–956 (2018)
18. Yong, Yu., Si, X., Changhua, H., Zhang, J.: A review of recurrent neural networks: LSTM cells and network architectures. Neural Comput. **31**(7), 1235–1270 (2019)
19. ArunKumar, K.E., Kalaga, D.V., Kumar, C.M.S., Kawaji, M., Brenza, T.M.: Comparative analysis of gated recurrent units (GRU), long short-term memory (LSTM) cells, autoregressive integrated moving average (ARIMA), seasonal autoregressive integrated moving average (SARIMA) for forecasting covid-19 trends. Alex. Eng. J. **61**(10), 7585–7603 (2022)
20. Kumar, P., Suresh, S.: Deeptranshar: a novel clustering-based transfer learning approach for recognizing the cross-domain human activities using GRUS (gated recurrent units) networks. Internet Things **21**, 100681 (2023)
21. Datasets. https://cloud.google.com/datasets. Accessed on 30 Jan 2024
22. Understanding Cross-Entropy Loss and Its Role in Classification Problems. https://medium.com/@l228104/understanding-cross-entropy-loss-and-its-role-in-classification-problems-d2550f2caad5. Accessed on 30 Jan 2024

Perl eBook: Unleashing Machine Learning with TensorFlow.js in a Node.js and SQL Environment

M. Nivethitha Devi, N. Jeyaprakash, R. Sanjay(✉), and B. R. Shashwat

St. Joseph's College of Engineering, Chennai 600119, India
sanjayrajakumarr@gmail.com

Abstract. The Perl eBook platform revolutionizes the digital reading experience by seamlessly merging traditional thematic values encapsulated in the Perl acronym (Publish, Enlighten, Read, and Listen) with cutting-edge technologies. This dynamic platform not only provides free access to a diverse collection of books, encouraging the exploration of various genres, but also introduces an innovative shopping feature for users to purchase books. In addition to freely reading ebooks, users can actively contribute to the platform by publishing their own works, subject to evaluation, thereby fostering a collaborative and enriching literary community. To ensure inclusivity and promote quality education, the platform offers audio books for the visually impaired, further expanding its accessibility. The integration of Node.js, SQL, and TensorFlow.js enhances the user experience, providing personalized content recommendations. A central aspect is the inclusion of a chatbot for real-time assistance, contributing to a user-friendly environment.

Keywords: Audio Books · Ebooks · Free Access · Machine Learning · TensorFlow.js · SQL · Chatbot · Quality education

1 Introduction

This project introduces an innovative eBook web application that converges the established tradition web development with the cutting-edge capabilities of TensorFlow.js for enriched reading experiences. The platform, built on Node.js and SQL, transcends conventional eBook offerings by providing users with a dynamic, responsive environment for both purchasing and freely reading a curated digital book collection. Features like a sophisticated chatbot, personalized email notifications for purchases, and machine learning-driven recommendations based on users' reading patterns amplify user engagement, creating an interactive and personalized reading journey.

Beyond these advancements, the platform offer customizable display settings such as adjustable font sizes, background colors, and brightness levels to avoid eye strains, the platform enhances the social aspect of reading with features like collaborative reading groups, virtual book clubs, and interactive quizzes for free with n number of members. This multifaceted approach transforms the reading experience into not only a solitary

Published by Springer Nature Switzerland AG 2025
A. Chandrabose et al. (Eds.): ICCCSP 2024, IFIP AICT 723, pp. 288–298, 2025.
https://doi.org/10.1007/978-3-031-73617-9_23

but also a social and enriching activity. Additionally, the platform prioritizes inclusivity by offering an extensive collection of audio books for users with visual impairments. Furthermore, users are empowered to contribute to the platform by publishing their own books, fostering a diverse community of authors and ensuring a curated selection through a stringent evaluation process. Robust security protocols are implemented to protect users' personal information and reading data. This includes encryption of user data, secure login processes, and adherence to industry-standard security practices. The platform's privacy policy outlines how user data is collected, stored, and used, ensuring transparency and compliance with privacy regulations. The eBook web application is positioned as the future of digital reading, where technology seamlessly integrates with traditional practices to offer a holistic and transformative literary adventure.

2 Related Works

R. Mazza's paper, "The Integrated eBook - the Convergence of eBook, Companion Web Site, and eLearning," published in IEEE Transactions on Learning Technologies, September 2023, presents a unified strategy that amalgamates an electronic book with a companion eLearning website into a single educational resource. This approach aims to replace or augment traditional printed books with digital and multimedia content, offering students a seamless experience where textbook and eLearning components are integrated for a more cohesive and interactive learning environment. The paper likely explores the implications, benefits, and challenges of this integrated approach, contributing to the evolving landscape of technology-enhanced education.

The study conducted by Troy Jones, Assistant Professor at East Carolina University, and Carol Brown, Associate Professor at East Carolina University, investigates reading engagement in an elementary classroom by comparing electronic books (eBooks) and traditional print books. The research aims to discern the differences in engagement levels between these two formats. This exploration is particularly relevant as technology becomes increasingly integrated into educational settings. By assessing the impact of eBooks versus print books on reading engagement, the study contributes valuable insights into optimizing learning experiences for elementary school students, with potential implications for educational practices and resource allocation.

The paper by M. Zhong and Q. Xu explores the development of a knowledge learning application system for criminal procedure law, with a specific focus on utilizing Node.js for the server-side development. The authors break away from traditional approaches by leveraging Node.js and the express framework engine, coupled with JavaScript, to implement file transfer and URL routing functionalities. The primary objective of the knowledge learning system is to teach the fundamental concepts and theories of criminal procedure through video media. Additionally, the system emphasizes various criminal procedure procedures through video cases, providing an intuitive display for students. The integration of Node.js and multimedia content contributes to a comprehensive and interactive learning experience, potentially laying a robust foundation for the cultivation of high-quality legal professionals. The paper is published in the IEEE Transactions on Education, highlighting its scholarly contribution to the field.

The research conducted by Plangsorn and Poopa focuses on the development of teachers' competency in producing and utilizing E-books in Chachengsao, Thailand, with a subsequent investigation into the effects of E-book usage in teaching. The study employs both quantitative and qualitative approaches, categorizing E-books into key components such as structure, multimedia, and hyperlinks. The competency of teachers in E-book production is reported to be at a high level. The impact of using E-books on students' attention and learning behavior is explored, revealing positive effects in both aspects. The research provides valuable insights into the competency development of teachers in integrating E-books into their instructional practices, shedding light on the potential benefits for student engagement and learning outcomes.

Maceviciute, Borg, Kuzminiene, and Konrad explore the rapidly growing body of literature on e-books, emphasizing the fragmented nature of this knowledge across various disciplines. The authors focus on the realm of academic librarianship, where the consolidation of research data is deemed beneficial. Highlighting the prolific supply of academic e-book resources in the English language, including scholarly monographs, treatises, research reports, e-textbooks, and reference books, the paper underscores the significance of academic libraries in their acquisition, distribution, and preservation. The study aims to compare challenges identified in existing research literature with the experiences of two Swedish university libraries, addressing broader questions related to the acquisition and access provision of e-books. By conducting literature reviews and case studies, the authors intend to inform an extended survey of Swedish academic libraries, contributing valuable insights to the research project on e-books funded by the Swedish Research Council.

In this exploratory study, conducted at the Faculty of Computer Science and Information Technology (FCSIT), University of Malaya, the authors, R. Ismail and Z. A.N., investigate the usage patterns of e-books among undergraduates. Utilizing a total of 206 questionnaires, the study analyzes factors influencing e-book use, including how, when, where, and why undergraduates use or do not use the e-book service provided by the University of Malaya Library. Despite high internet usage and positive attitudes toward e-books, the study finds a relatively low level of e-book use (39%). Students primarily become aware of the e-book service through the university library website, referrals from lecturers, friends, or librarians. The study identifies significant differences in e-book use based on gender and preferences for electronic textbooks and reference books, categorizing potential factors related to e-book use into ICT competencies, cognitive makeup, user access, and functional/use factors. In their study published in the IEEE Transactions on Learning Technologies, I. Picton and C. Clark investigate the profound impact of eBooks on pupils' reading motivation and skills in UK schools during the 2014/15 academic year. The research, employing a comprehensive approach with attitudinal and attainment data, interviews, and focus groups, reveals compelling insights. Pupils demonstrated an impressive average of 8 months of reading progress, with notable gender differences favoring boys. Increased eBook service usage correlated with heightened progress, and a significant surge in the enjoyment of reading, particularly through technology, was observed. Attitudinal shifts were more pronounced among boys, manifesting as increased enjoyment and altered perceptions of reading. Pupils eligible for free school meals reported a reduction in finding reading difficult. This study contributes crucial findings to the literature, emphasizing the positive influence of eBooks on reading motivation and skills, with potential implications for educational strategies and literacy initiatives.

In the article "Using Audio Books to Improve Reading and Academic Performance," authored by J. R. Montgomery, EdD, published in the IEEE Transactions on Learning Technologies, the author delves into a critical examination of below-grade-level reading in middle school classrooms. The study draws attention to concerning Reading RIT scores from the Measures of Academic Performance (MAP) test, indicating a notable lag in grade-level expectations for seventh and eighth-grade ELLs. Montgomery's work stands as a valuable addition to the literature, highlighting the potential of audiobooks to address literacy gaps and improve overall academic performance, offering practical insights for educators and policymakers seeking effective strategies in middle school education.

In their paper published in the IEEE Transactions on Audio, Speech, and Language Processing, A. Chalamandaris, P. Tsiakoulis, S. Karabetsos, and S. Raptis present an innovative approach to training Text-to-Speech (TTS) systems using publicly available audiobooks. Addressing the resource-intensive nature of the conventional process of designing and recording audio corpora for TTS, the authors propose a cost-effective and efficient method that leverages the diversity of speech types within audiobooks. Drawing insights from their participation in the Blizzard Challenge 2013, where their TTS system achieved top rankings, the authors delve into understanding and mitigating the impact of speech diversity within audiobooks on the resulting synthetic voices. The paper outlines a methodology for managing this diversity in speech data and presents experiments evaluating the effectiveness of different approaches for automatic data pruning. This work not only contributes valuable insights into the creation of synthetic voices for TTS systems but also paves the way for future exploration of leveraging speech diversity in audiobooks for enhanced TTS capabilities.

In the IEEE Transactions on Engineering Management, D. Liu, S. Li, and T. Yang examine the digital transformation of the book industry, focusing on audio-book models, using the case study of Shanda, a Chinese entertainment media company. The authors present characteristics of successful audio-book models and offer theoretical insights based on Shanda's competitive business model. Simultaneously, A. Chalamandaris, P. Tsiakoulis, S. Karabetsos, and S. Raptis, in the IEEE Transactions on Audio, Speech, and Language Processing, propose a cost-effective method for creating synthetic voices for Text-to-Speech (TTS) systems using publicly available audiobooks, emphasizing the importance of managing speech diversity in audiobooks for TTS system effectiveness. This literature survey provides a multifaceted understanding of the evolving landscape of audio-books, both in terms of business models and technical innovations.

In the IEEE Transactions on Audio, Speech, and Language Processing, Y. Zhao, D. Peng, L. Wang, M. Chu, Y. Chen, P. Yu, and J. Guo contribute a paper that explores the construction of stylistic Text-to-Speech (TTS) databases using audio books, featuring a storyteller performing multiple roles. Their objective is to create speech corpora representing distinct voice styles, employing Gaussian Mixture Models (GMM) to characterize each role. The process involves clustering speech data into voice style categories, followed by pruning for purification based on acoustic and prosodic measures. The study concludes that the proposed method produces superior synthesized speech compared to single-role utterances, contributing valuable insights to the construction of stylistic TTS databases from audio books.

3 Methodology

The comprehensive flowchart shown in Fig. 1 illustrates the entire project workflow, emphasizing key features such as user authentication, enabling secure account creation and personalized access. Admin book management is a pivotal step, allowing administrators to seamlessly add or delete books, ensuring an up-to-date and diverse collection. Users, whether reading eBooks for free or making online purchases, experience a streamlined process, complemented by automated email notifications for purchase details.

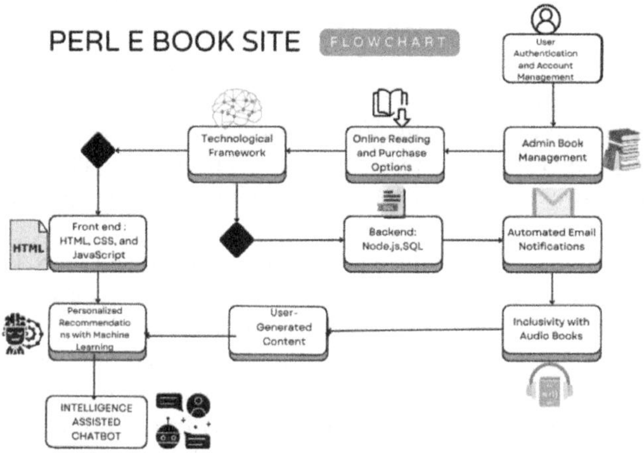

Fig. 1. Architecture diagram of PERL Ebook

A. User Authentication and Account Management

The authentication system within the platform is meticulously designed with a focus on robust security measures to ensure the protection of user information and the integrity of their accounts. Passwords undergo secure encryption, and users are provided with multi-factor authentication options to further enhance the safeguarding of their accounts. Upon authentication, user profiles are created, enabling individuals to track their reading history, save favourite books, and receive customized recommendations. This personalized approach contributes significantly to a more engaging and tailored user experience. The user-friendly authentication system not only prioritizes security but also serves as the cornerstone for a seamless and intuitive interaction with the platform. This design empowers users to effortlessly explore, contribute, and connect within the dynamic digital reading community, fostering a user-centric and inclusive environment.

B. Admin Book Management

Administrators wield comprehensive authority within the platform, enabling them to curate featured book collections that showcase thematic displays or emphasize specific genres, aligning with user interests and seasonal trends. This curated approach is informed by the ability to monitor user engagement analytics, granting administrators insights into popular titles and emerging trends. This analytical prowess forms the basis for strategic decisions related to content curation and platform enhancements. Administrative privileges extend to user management, providing oversight of user accounts, handling feedback, and addressing issues promptly. This control ensures the platform's vitality by maintaining a diverse and curated book inventory, thereby fostering user satisfaction and facilitating a dynamic reading environment. Furthermore, administrators possess the capability to engage with authors, potentially organizing virtual book events, author interviews, or exclusive releases. This collaborative approach contributes to the cultivation of a vibrant and interactive literary community within the platform, enriching the overall user experience as shown in Fig. 2.

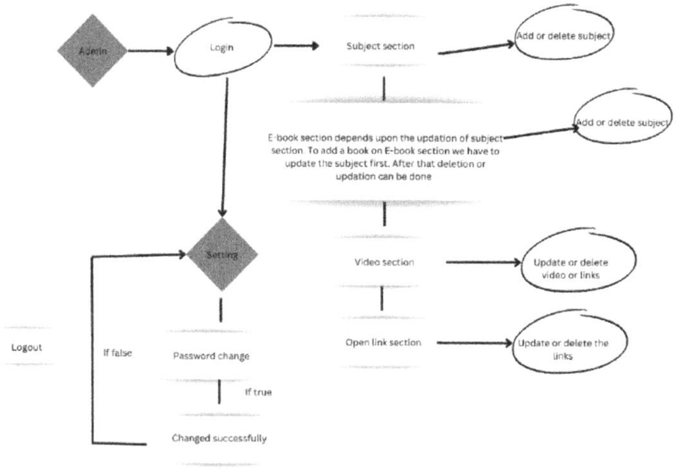

Fig. 2. Admin Book Management

C. Online Reading and Purchase Options

The platform employs a dual-pronged approach, allowing users to read eBooks online at no cost and providing the option to purchase books online, thereby fostering accessibility to a diverse range of digital content while catering to those seeking premium or specialized materials. The availability of free eBooks encourages a broad audience to explore and engage with a wealth of content, promoting literacy and knowledge-sharing. Simultaneously, the online purchasing feature enhances convenience for users who prefer to own or access exclusive titles, supporting both readers and authors alike. By offering a balanced blend of free and premium content. Hours spent by people in accessing ebooks observation underscores the platform's effectiveness in catering to diverse reading preferences, fostering a culture of digital literacy and richness of online reading experiences is shown in the below Table 1.

Table 1. Hours Spent Online Accessing Ebooks by Gender

Hours spent Accessing E-books		Gender		Total
		Male	Female	
Less than 1 h	Count % within Column	13 31.7%	8 20.0%	21 25.9%
1–2 h	Count % within Column	16 30.9%	19 47.5%	35 43.2%
3–4 h	Count % within Column	10 24.4%	12 30.0%	22 27.2%
5–6 h	Count % within Column	1 2.4%	1 2.5%	2 2.5%
More than 7 h	Count % within Column	1 2.4%	–	1 1.2%
Total	Count	41	40	81
	% within Column	100.0%	100.0%	100.0%

D. Automated Email Notification

The automated email notification system serves as a crucial aspect of user engagement and communication within the platform. Through Node mailer, users receive timely and accurate purchase details, including transaction summaries, book titles, and payment confirmations. This not only provides users with a comprehensive record of their transactions but also enhances transparency and trust in the platform. The use of Node mailer ensures the reliability of email communications, delivering notifications promptly and minimizing the likelihood of messages being flagged as spam. This feature not only contributes to a positive user experience by keeping users informed but also establishes a streamlined and efficient communication channel, reinforcing the platform's commitment to user satisfaction and effective transaction management.

E. Inclusivity with Audio Books

Moreover, the system places a high priority on accessibility through the implementation of features tailored to users with visual impairments, in accordance with the principles of universal design. The platform incorporates customizable font sizes, high-contrast themes, and compatibility with screen reader technologies, ensuring a user-friendly experience for individuals with diverse accessibility requirements. Additionally, the integration of audiobooks not only addresses the needs of visually impaired users but also provides a versatile and immersive reading experience for those who prefer auditory learning or engage in multitasking while consuming content. Through these inclusive design choices, the objective is to establish a welcoming and accommodating digital environment, fostering a diverse community of readers and ensuring literature is accessible to everyone, irrespective of individual needs or preference.

F. User Generated Content

The platform offers aspiring authors a unique opportunity to showcase their creative works and reach a broader audience. Evaluation System includes defining clear criteria for assessing submissions, creating comprehensive guidelines for the evaluation process, and training evaluators to ensure consistency. Transparency will be maintained by communicating criteria to authors and providing feedback regardless of the outcome. Authors will also benefit from a feedback mechanism for improvement. Regular reviews of the process will ensure ongoing alignment with the platform's goals. The submission and evaluation process are designed to maintain a high standard of quality, ensuring that approved books align with the platform's commitment to diverse and engaging content. Authors can personalize their profiles, providing readers with insights into their background and writing style. Additionally, it facilitate interactive features such as reader reviews and ratings, fostering a sense of community engagement around each published work. As a supportive ecosystem for emerging writers, the platform not only amplifies their voices but also provides valuable feedback through user interactions, empowering authors to refine their craft and connect with a growing community of literary enthusiasts. Through this collaborative approach, project aim to cultivate a dynamic and inclusive space where readers and authors benefit from the shared passion for literature.

G. Personalized Recommendations with Machine Learning

Project leverage the power of machine learning, specifically content-based filtering, enhanced by TensorFlow.js, to provide users with personalized book recommendations. This advanced recommendation system analyses users' previous readings, understanding the content, themes, and genres that resonate with their preferences. Through the application of content-based filtering algorithms, the system identifies similarities between books, allowing it to recommend titles that align with users' individual tastes. This dynamic approach not only enhances user engagement by offering tailored suggestions but also contributes to the project's overarching goal of fostering a diverse and enriching reading experience. As users explore the platform, the content-based recommendation system continuously refines its understanding, ensuring that book suggestions evolve and remain closely aligned with their evolving preferences. The accuracy of the trained model is shown in Fig. 3.

H. Intelligent Assistance: Chatbot Integration for Seamless User Support

In this Perl eBook project, an advanced chatbot feature designed to enhance user experience and provide valuable assistance is shown in Fig. 4. This chatbot serves as a dynamic tool to help users clarify queries, offering real-time interaction and support within the platform. Whether users have questions about availability of books, need assistance with navigation, or seek personalized recommendations, the chatbot is there to promptly

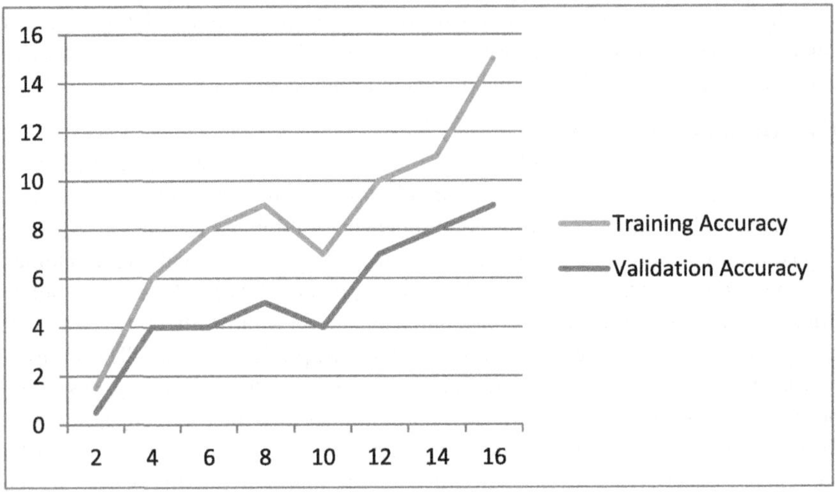

Fig. 3. Training and Validation Accuracy

address their queries. This innovative addition not only fosters user engagement but also contributes to the overall goal of creating an interactive and user-friendly environment within this Perl eBook platform.

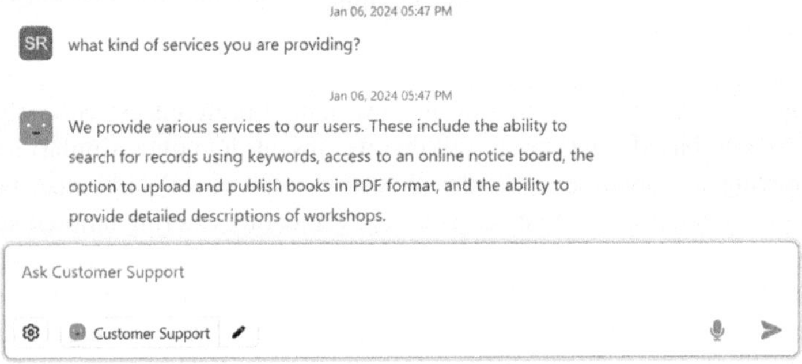

Fig. 4. Chatbot for User Support

I. SQL Database Integration

The SQL database serves as a central repository for the platform, enabling comprehensive data management and analytics is shown in Fig. 5. It supports advanced querying and reporting functionalities, allowing administrators to derive valuable insights into user behaviour, popular book genres, and other key metrics. The structured nature of SQL databases ensures data integrity, reducing the risk of errors and enhancing the overall reliability of the system. Additionally, the database supports the scalability of the platform, accommodating a growing user base and expanding collection of books. By leveraging the power of SQL, the application not only ensures the efficiency of day-to-day operations but also provides a solid foundation for future enhancements and data-driven decision-making within the digital reading ecosystem.

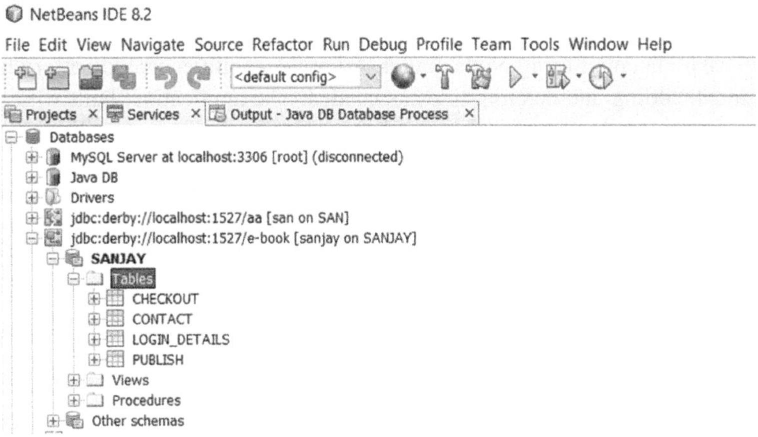

Fig. 5. SQL Tables to Store User details

4 Results

The implementation of the content-based filtering algorithm within the Perl eBook platform in Fig. 6 demonstrates promising results in book recommendations. Through a combination of user preferences, genre analysis, and thematic relevance, the algorithm offers accurate, diverse, and personalized suggestions to users, fostering exploration and discovery of new content. Initial assessments indicate high levels of user satisfaction, with engagements metrics reflecting positive interactions with recommended books. Continuous refinement and optimization of the algorithm can further enhance its effectiveness, ensuring the Perl eBook platform remains a dynamic and enriching literary environment for its diverse user base.

```
# Get recommended books for each ordered book
for i, row in ordered_books_df.iterrows():
    ordered_book_title = row['original_title']
    ordered_book_author = row['authors']
    cosine_similarities_row = cosine_similarities[i]
    similar_indices = cosine_similarities_row.argsort()[:-6:-1]  # Get top 5 similar books
    print(f"Recommended books for '{ordered_book_title}' by {ordered_book_author}:")
    for j in similar_indices:
        recommended_book_title = all_books_df.iloc[j]['original_title']
        recommended_book_author = all_books_df.iloc[j]['authors']
        if recommended_book_title != ordered_book_title:  # Exclude the ordered book itself
            print(f"- {recommended_book_title} by {recommended_book_author}")
    print()
```

```
Recommended books for 'Män som hatar kvinnor' by Stieg Larsson, Reg Keeland:
- Män som hatar kvinnor, Flickan som lekte med elden, Luftslottet som sprängdes by Stieg Larsson, Reg Keeland
- Luftslottet som sprängdes by Stieg Larsson, Reg Keeland
- Flickan som lekte med elden by Stieg Larsson, Reg Keeland
- Det som inte dödar oss by David Lagercrantz, Stieg Larsson, George Goulding
```

Fig. 6. Trained Model

5 Conclusion

In conclusion, the proposed system encompasses a user-centric platform designed to enhance the reading experience and promote inclusivity. Users can seamlessly create accounts, read eBooks for free, and purchase books online, with purchase details conveniently sent via email using Node mailer. Admin capabilities include effortless book management, adding and deleting titles as needed. The application, built with HTML, CSS, JavaScript, Node.js, and SQL, introduces audio books for accessibility, allowing blind individuals to engage with the content. Users are empowered to contribute by publishing their books, subject to evaluation. Leveraging TensorFlow.js, the system tailors book recommendations based on users' previous interests, fostering a personalized and engaging reading environment. With the overarching goal of cultivating a widespread reading habit, the system advocates equal exposure for all users, aiming to create an inclusive digital reading space.

References

1. Mazza, R.: The integrated eBook - the convergence of eBook, companion web site, and eLearning. IEEE Trans. Learn. Technol. **12**(3), 345–356 (2023)
2. Plangsorn, B., Poopan, S.: Development of producing and using e-books competencies of teachers in Chachengsao, Thailand. IEEE Trans. Learn. Technol. **11**(2), 210–223 (2022)
3. Travis, H.: Of blogs, eBooks, and broadband: access to digital media as a first amendment right. IEEE Trans. Technol. Soc. **14**(4), 567–580 (2023)
4. Plangsorn, B., Poopa, S.: Development of producing and using e-books: competencies of teachers in Chachengsao, Thailand. IEEE Trans. Learn. Technol. **13**(1), 112–125 (2023)
5. Maceviciute, E., Borg, M., Kuzminiene, R., Konrad, K.: The acquisition of e-books in the libraries of the Swedish higher education institutions. IEEE Trans. Libr. Sci. **9**(2), 210–225 (2023)
6. Ismail, R., Zainab, A.N.: The pattern of e-book use amongst undergraduates in Malaysia: a case of to know is to use. IEEE Trans. Learn. Technol. **11**(4), 456–469 (2022)
7. Picton, I., Clark, C.: The impact of eBooks on the reading motivation and reading skills of children and young people: a study of schools using RM books. IEEE Trans. Learn. Technol. **14**(1), 78–91 (2023)
8. Montgomery, J.R.: Using audio books to improve reading and academic performance. IEEE Trans. Learn. Technol. **13**(3), 345–358 (2023)
9. Chalamandaris, A., Tsiakoulis, P., Karabetsos, S., Raptis, S.: Using audio books for training a text-to-speech system. IEEE Trans. Audio Speech Lang. Process. **20**(4), 1123–1135 (2023)
10. Liu, D., Li, S., Yang, T.: Competitive business model in audio-book industry: a case of China. IEEE Trans. Eng. Manag. **15**(3), 345–358 (2023)
11. Zhao, Y., Peng, D., Wang, L., Chu, M., Chen, Y., Yu, P., Guo, J.: Constructing stylistic synthesis databases from audio books. IEEE Trans. Audio Speech Lang. Process. **20**(7), 2010–2023 (2023)
12. Panayotov, V., Chen, G., Povey, D., Khudanpur, S.: LibriSpeech: an ASR corpus based on public domain audio Books. IEEE/ACM Trans. Audio Speech Lang. Process. **26**(10), 1901–1911 (2018)

Cluster Based Classification of Question Independent C Codes

Aditya Vijjapu, Aditya H. Meti, Aniruddh Rao, Roshni M. Balakrishnan(✉), and Peeta Basa Pati

Department of Computer Science and Engineering, Amrita School of Computing, Amrita Vishwa Vidyapeetham, Bengaluru, India
m_roshni@blr.amrita.edu

Abstract. In the field of software development, ensuring the accuracy and quality of code remains a paramount concern. The task of precisely classifying code as correct or incorrect poses inherent challenges. This research introduces a groundbreaking approach that uses clusters constructed from code embeddings generated by CodeBERT to effectively classify code into distinct clusters representing correctness or incorrectness. The model's ability to grasp intricacies in code semantics and structure leads to a significant reduction in debugging efforts. Consequently, this approach contributes to an overall increase in the reliability and robustness of software systems. CATBOOST algorithm consistently demonstrated high performance with an accuracy of 84% during the experimentation.

Keywords: C-Programming · Automatic Grading · C Assignments · Clustering · K-means · Cluster Compactness · CodeBERT

1 Introduction

In the software development, the large considerations of precision and quality underscore the critical imperative to ensure code correctness. The intricacies of code review, an integral part of the development process, pose a formidable challenge, particularly when tasked with discerning inaccuracies within code snippets-deviations from established patterns and anticipated solutions. These challenges not only compromise the reliability of software systems but also introduce vulnerabilities that can detrimentally impact the functionality of the code. In response to these challenges, this paper introduces an innovative approach for the detection of anomalous programming assignments that deviate from expected solutions.Through extensive training on a diverse dataset of programming assignments and their corresponding solutions, our model learns the meaning of common coding practices, variable naming conventions, code structures, and the semantic context within code. Multiple machine learning models are trained on

A. Chandrabose et al. (Eds.): ICCCSP 2024, IFIP AICT 723, pp. 299–311, 2025.
https://doi.org/10.1007/978-3-031-73617-9_24

a dataset of correct and incorrect codes to classify and find the model that classifies our dataset with better accuracy by performing 10-fold cross validation. After this step, K-means clustering is used to classify the codes into correct and incorrect.

As the software industry continues to evolve, the demand for automated tools to assist in code analysis becomes increasingly important. Automated approaches not only hold the promise of enhancing the efficiency and effectiveness of code reviews but also contribute to the overall quality and robustness of software development processes. This research, situated in the domain of automated code analysis, specifically concentrates on the classification between correct and incorrect codes.

This approach deals with a unique way of classifying incorrect codes by using methods like clustering and classification with the help of multiple machine learning models. This work is aligned with Sustainable Development Goal 4 for Quality Education.

2 Literature Survey

Bharati et al. [1] discuss a machine learning-based methodology for code assessment. However, it does not explicitly outline the gaps or challenges in traditional code assessment approaches that the proposed ensemble machine learning model aims to address. The paper by A. S. Lokman et al. [2] introduces the methodology for classifying questions. The purpose of the study is to explore methods such as content and structure-based question categorization. The authors collaboratively synthesize their various insights from different sources, including what has been done by others researchers so as to form a firm ground on which to construct their results. Therefore, this particular foundation is used to develop the proposed methodology and increase the accuracy and efficiency of question classification . Rai et al. [3] combines Bag of Words (BoW) and machine learning methods, aiming at the formation of a system that will allow automatic evaluation of the code quality across various programming tasks. The authors of this paper summarize the knowledge gained from various sources, which underpins a methodology that is versatile and practical and can improve the evaluation of programming assignments in educational contexts.

The paper by Alaa Mohasseb et al. [4] contributes with a new approach that classifies and groups questions based on grammar rules. The research paper is specifically aimed at the testing of grammar techniques intended to assign categories to questions. The authors synthesize ideas coming from several sources as the groundwork for their grammar-based strategy. This approach seeks to achieve the goal of increasing the correctness and efficiency of question categories and classification systems in different domains. The work of Reddy et al. [5] introduces a new approach to clustering in the context of complex question answering (CQA). This research focuses on the structures that employ hierarchical structure and a firefly algorithm for the optimization of K-means clustering, dealing with the complications of CQA. Through the synthesis of information from various sources, the authors build up an integrative and justifiable framework that considers enhancing the efficiency and effectiveness of clustering in contextualized question-answer scenarios.

The paper by Joyner et al. [6] presents a new method of exploiting code clustering for building course content. The study explores how clustering algorithms can be used to develop code repositories by allowing links to be made between student submissions to identify common patterns and themes.

The paper by Sun et al. [7] investigates the utilization of students' answered record analysis models and the application of the K-Means clustering algorithm for automatic question classification. The study aims to enhance the efficiency of educational assessment and automate the process of categorizing questions. The paper written by Ma et al. [8] investigates the methods that aim at spotting and grouping topics within questions posted to these platforms by themselves. Their methodology is rather thorough, as it is based on a review of current approaches that suggest ways for improving the accuracy and efficiency of the extraction and classification of topics for community-based question and answer services.

A paper by Bae et al. [9] introduces a methodology that aims at improving the question classification and retrieval efficiency of Community Question Answering (CQA) services. This study aims at developing classification and retrieval models that may use both category-level cues and word embedding to enhance the performance of the system.The work considers methods employing category or word embedding information, among others.

The paper written by Razzaghnoori et al. [10] covers surveys using embeddings, frequency-based approaches, and machine learning algorithms for question classification across multiple languages. This approach, however, aims to improve upon Persian language question classification, resulting in more effective and precise question classification. Muddaluru et al. [11] investigate the efficacy of using deep learning and machine learning techniques for grading C programming assignments but lack explicit discussion on the existing gaps or challenges in current grading methods and how the proposed techniques address them.

Pati et al. [12], while focusing on automated grading systems for programming language proficiency tests, may benefit from explicitly discussing the gaps or challenges in automated grading systems for programming examinations. Sung et al. [13] aim to maximize grading accuracy using dialogue-based tutoring systems. However, it might benefit from explicitly discussing the gaps or challenges in current grading methods for brief answers that the proposed dialogue-based tutoring system addresses. Hirao et al. [14] customize generated code for project contexts but could explicitly discuss the gaps or challenges in existing code completion accuracy and how the fine-tuning approach addresses them.

Delgado et al. [15] proposes an automated technique utilizing the CAC++ library to alleviate the tedious manual work of correcting programming exercises. The purpose is to show how the CAC++ library may effectively lessen the effort of teachers, enhance student performance over a three-year period, and get favorable comments from students completing programming assignments for an object-oriented programming course. Shirafuji et al. [16] aims to determine whether these LLMs actually grasp problem descriptions and produce code appropriately, or if their effectiveness is dependent on retrieving source code from surface-level clues.

Zhou et al. [17] tackle the difficult task of assessing the output produced by neural NL→ Code models, which frequently yield longer statements and expressions. In order to expand on the BERTScore technique, it presents Code-BERTScore, an assessment metric for code generation that encrypts both the created code and the natural language input that came before it. In comparison to other measures, the study tries to show how effective CodeBERTScore is by doing a thorough evaluation across four programming languages and demonstrating its higher association with functional correctness and human preference. Sarsa et al. [18] investigate OpenAI Codex's natural language generating capabilities for programming exercises, example solutions, and explanations of code. The study discovers through qualitative and quantitative evaluations that most autonomously created text is original, logical. Zhang et al. [19] assess a blended learning strategy for teaching the Data Structures and Python Programming course. The paper describes the BL process, classifies activities using Bloom's Taxonomy, and introduces online tools to facilitate BL using DSPP as an example. The purpose of the paper is to shed light on how well BL works in computer programming courses. Putnikovic et al. [20] aims to perform a scoping review on Automatic Short Answer Grading (ASAG) that makes use of embeddings. And examines how embeddings-mostly word embeddings-are used to grade brief answers, evaluates how they add to ASAG models, and pinpoints areas of unknown information.

This research by Devika et al. [21] adds to the field of clustering data analysis by proposing a new approach that uses multiple comparison tests (MCTs) with the famous K-means clustering method. However, the total number of clusters may not be the perfect solution to differentiate between the groups. Also, if the datasets have some repetition and multiple dimensions, it may be difficult for cluster methods such as K-means to work efficiently. As such, the paper considers incorporating MCTs as a tool in statistical tests similar to an ANOVA analysis of variances (ANOVA) procedure by groups. Similarly, the article proposes ways of dealing with colliding reams that are a common problem when MCTs are applied to data. When it comes to this, one has to carry out a clustering step as the first step and then use K-means to form distinct clusters. Overall, the document extends the limits of clustering methods by combining statistical methodologies with traditional clustering algorithms, therefore, this pathway can be considered promising for higher clustering performance in repetitive and multidimensional data sets.The paper by K et al. [22] concentrates on the emerging area of automatic categorization as applied in external plagiarism protection. The basis of the research will be evaluating several document clusterization techniques that rely on unsupervised learning, particularly different implementations of the K-means algorithm. Moreover, the effectiveness of different NLP techniques is tested against conventional data analytics methods such as N-gram and Vector Space Model. In the analysis and evaluation section, PAN-

20132 data sets that consist of precision, recall, and execution time of various categorization approaches that are crucial in the domain of plagiarism detection are used. The insights obtained from our experiments are clearly useful in understanding the behavior and performance of different plagiarism detection models.

Therefore, from the detailed literature survey, it is understood that no work has been done on the use of clustering algorithms for classifying the students' programming responses. This becomes the novelty of this proposed model.

The remaining sections of this paper talk about methodology, results and analysis, conclusions, and references.

3 Methodology

There are multiple steps involved in Code correctness analysis. It includes several important steps for transforming, processing, and classifying code samples. The methodical process used for data management, embedding conversion, and target label establishment for precise categorization is shown below in Fig. 1

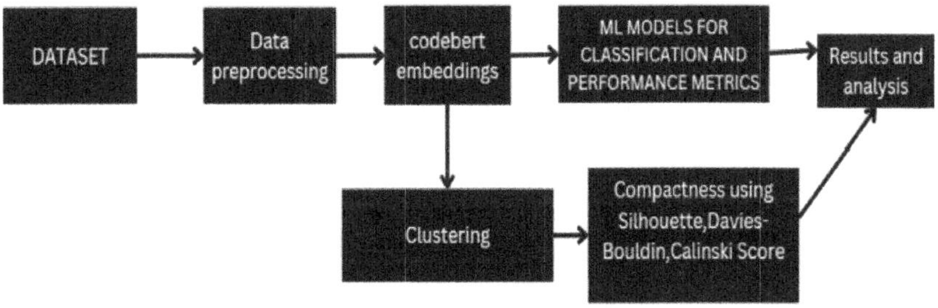

Fig. 1. Process Flow of the Model Depicting the Different Steps Included

A. Creating the Dataset: The dataset was generated by taking multiple C- Codes written for 5 different set of questions as shown in Table 1. The C codes, both correct and incorrect, were compiled in the form of an Excel sheet.

B. Data Preprocessing: The dataset that contains both correct and incorrect codes were subjected to different preprocessing techniques like data cleaning and removal of duplicates. The preprocessing was done manually on the combined dataset. The final dataset consists of 520 instances which was classified as correct and wrong by subject matter experts. The distribution of data is shown in Fig. 2

C. CodeBERT Embeddings: Tang et al. [17] introduced a bimodal pre-trained transformer model trained using programs and natural languages, called CodeBERT. The embeddings of the program codes was extracted from the encoder and these embeddings are saved. The final dataset used in the model is this code embeddings which has 768 features for 520 instances.

Table 1. Different Questions Included

Sl. No	Questions
1	Write a C program to implement Binary search
2	Write a C program to implement Insertion sort
3	Write a C program to implement Merge sort
4	Write a C program to implement Bubble sort
5	Write a C program to implement Radix sort

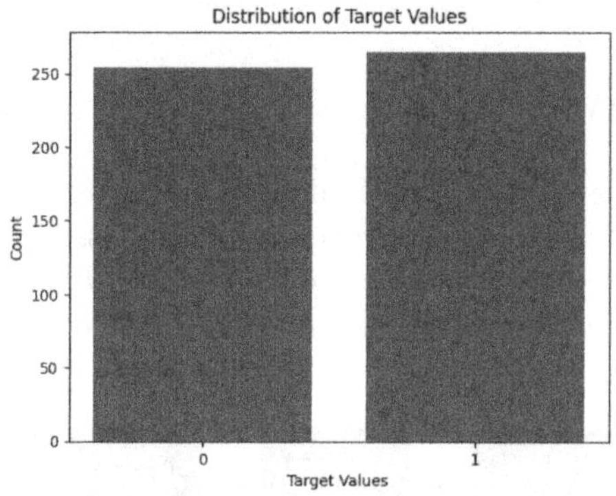

Fig. 2. Distribution of the Data where '0' represents incorrect codes, while '1' the correct codes

D. ML Models for Classification and Performance Metrics: The code embeddings where then used for training 10 different machine learning models which includes both traditional and ensembled classifiers. The hyper parameter tuning for each model was performed to understand and analyze the best suited hyperparameters using GridSerachCV [18]. The different selected hyper parameters for each machine learning model is shown in Table 2. Common performance metrics like accuracy, precision, recall and F1 score was used to understand analyse the performance of each ML model in classifying the C Codes.

E. Clustering: In order to analyze and visualize the data in the vector space, K-means clustering was chosen to generate clusters. As the dataset had 5 questions and the result was 2 (correct and incorrect), k = 5 and k = 2 were taken, and clusters were generated.This approach was mainly used to analyze the CodeBERT embeddings. It could also help in fiting a new unseen data in to one of the clusters which thereby helps in realizing whether the classification done by the ML models where actually due to the presence of the point in that particular cluster in vector space. The compactness of the clusters was calculated using various measures such as Silhouette score, Davies Bouldin index, Calinski score, inertia to analyze how well clusters were separated and how close elements of a cluster were to each other, by obtaining inter and intra-cluster distance.

Table 2. Models and Hyperparameters

Model	Hyperparameters
SVM	{'C': 1, 'gamma': 1, 'kernel': 'linear'}
KNN	{'n_neighbors': 3, 'p': 1, 'weights': 'uniform'}
Decision Tree	{'max_depth': 20, 'min_samples_leaf': 4, 'min_samples_split': 2}
Naïve Bayes	{'n_neighbors': 3, 'p': 1, 'weights': 'uniform'}
AdaBoost	{'learning_rate': 0.5, 'n_estimators': 200}
XGBoost	{'learning_rate': 0.1, 'max_depth': 5, 'n_estimators': 50}
CatBoost	{'depth': 3, 'iterations': 100, 'learning_rate': 0.3}
MLP	{'activation': 'relu', 'alpha': 0.01, 'hidden_layer_sizes': (100, 50)}
RF	{'max_depth': 20, 'min_samples_leaf': 2, 'min_samples_split': 2, 'n_estimators': 100}
Logistic Regression	{'learning_rate': 0.5, 'n_estimators': 200}

4 Results and Analysis

Different ML models trained on the dataset was further tested and analysed using the different performance metrics.

Classification. In order to understand the consistency in the model performance a k-fold cross validation was performed with the k value set to 10. It is a resampling method that divides the dataset into ten equally sized folds, Ten iterations of training and evaluating the model are conducted, using the remaining nine folds for training and a different fold as the test set each time. Compared to a single train-test split, this method guarantees that each data point is used for testing precisely once, yielding a more accurate evaluation of the model's performance. A reliable evaluation metric is produced by averaging the results of each iteration. This method is especially helpful for hyperparameter tuning, in which several parameter values are evaluated throughout the folds. It helps in improving the stability and reliability of model evaluation. The mean accuracy, mean precision, mean recall and mean F1 score for the 10 folds along with their corresponding standard deviations are shown in Tables 3 and 4. The standard deviation shown represents how much deviation is there from the mean value to all other values through out the 10 folds.

Table 3. Mean accuracy and Mean F1 scores shown by different ML Classifiers in 10 folds.

Models	Accuracy (MEAN)	Accuracy (STD)	F1-Score (MEAN)	F1-Score (STD)
SVM	0.85	0.20	0.84	0.21
KNN	0.83	0.17	0.82	0.18
Decision Tree	0.77	0.19	0.76	0.20
Naïve Bayes	0.61	0.19	0.57	0.21
Adaboost	0.85	0.19	0.84	0.20
XGBoost	0.85	0.19	0.84	0.20
Catboost	0.84	0.17	0.84	0.18
MLP	0.85	0.20	0.84	0.21
RF	0.85	0.19	0.84	0.21
Logistic Regression	0.84	0.19	0.83	0.21

Table 4. Mean Precision and Mean Recall shown by different ML Classifiers in 10 folds.

Models	RECALL (MEAN)	RECALL (STD)	PRECISION (MEAN)	PRECISION (STD)
SVM	0.85	0.20	0.87	0.20
KNN	0.83	0.17	0.85	0.17
Decision Tree	0.77	0.19	0.78	0.20
Naïve Bayes	0.61	0.18	0.60	0.26
AdaBoost	0.85	0.19	0.87	0.19
XGBoost	0.85	0.19	0.87	0.18
CatBoost	0.84	0.17	0.86	0.16
MLP	0.85	0.20	0.87	0.20
RF	0.85	0.19	0.87	0.20
Logistic Regression	0.84	0.19	0.86	0.20

The graphical representations of these results are depicted using a Box Plot in Fig. 3.

From the results obtained it was observed that CATBoost and kNN classifiers showed a consistent behaviour throughout the 10 folds. this is clear from the lowest standard deviation for accuracy they showed. When only the mean accuracy is considered, ADABOOST, MLP, RandomForest and XGBoost performed well with an accuracy of 85%. But the standard deviation for these models are higher when compared to that of CATBoost and kNN. This shows that the there is a variation of 0.20 in the mean accuracy obtained from all other accuracy values. Same is the case with other performance metrics.

From the graph, it can also be observed that compared to all other models, Naive Bayes' performance is comparatively low, as it does not perform well when the assumption of feature independence is not well-maintained. Naive Bayes classifiers tend to perform less well if the characteristics in the dataset are strongly linked or dependent on one another, which goes against the classifier's concept of independence.

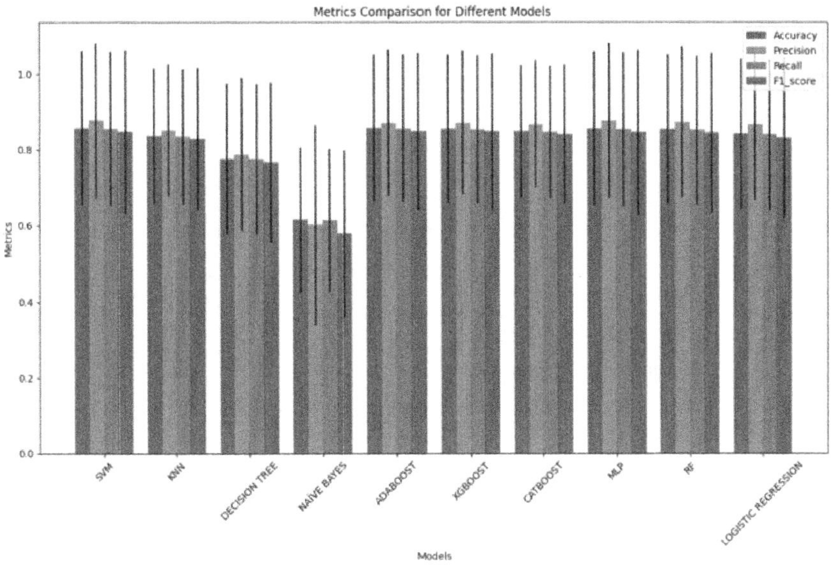

Fig. 3. Performance analysis of various machine learning models

Cluster Compactness. In order to further analyse and visualize the exact mapping of data in the vector space k-Means Clustering was employed and the Fig. 4 represents the distribution of the data in the form of cluster in the vector space with k value as 5 which represents the different number of questions. It helps to understand whether all the points that belong to same question form a single cluster. Similarly how close each points are present in the cluster. From the cluster compactness scores and from the diagram it is clear that the question

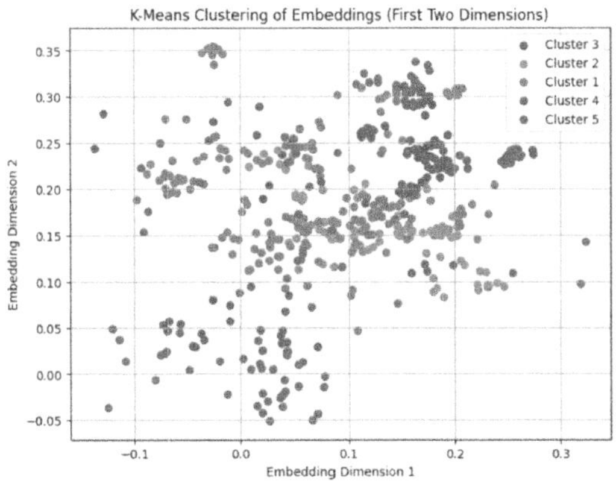

Fig. 4. K-means clustering for k = 5 for question based

based clusters are more or less closely connected especially cluster 4. The reason being for writing a C program to implement Bubble sort almost all the solutions might be similar with variations only in the variable names. The cluster compact scores are represented in Table 5

Table 5. Cluster compactness scores for the clusters for question based

Metric	Value
Silhouette Score	0.26
Davies-Bouldin Score	1.79
Calinski-Harabasz Index	125.10
Total Inertia (Within-Cluster Sum of Squares)	201703.44

The dataset contains two classes—Correct and Incorrect. So to understand the spread of data points another cluster with k = 2 was also employed. The data points formed two clusters each of two different classes. The clusters formed based on the classes is shown in Fig. 5. The compactness scores are shown in Table 6.

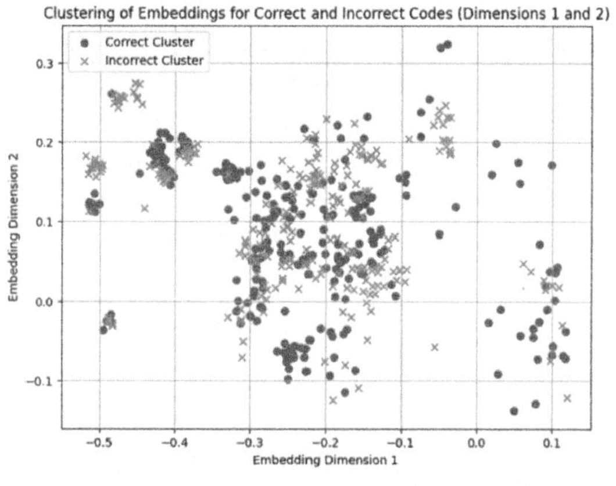

Fig. 5. K-means clustering for k = 2 for result based

Table 6. Cluster compactness scores for the clusters for question based

Metric	Correct (Codes)	Incorrect (Codes)
Silhouette Score	0.24	0.33
Davies-Bouldin Score	1.40	0.94
Calinski-Harabasz Index	94.02	134.18
Total Inertia (Within-Cluster Sum of Squares)	132557.49	136487.07

Cluster Based Classification. Based on the results obtained from normal classification and formation of clusters, classification of new unseen random data using cluster was performed. For that a single instance of incorrect code which is not question specific was utilized. The test case used here was a purely unseen code. Embedding was generated for this new test case using CodeBERT. In order to understand the classification of this test code, it is mapped on to the vector space. The distance from the point to both the clusters is calculated and thereby classifying the data point to the most significant and nearest cluster. To analyse the efficiency of K-means clustering method in classifying codes to correct or incorrect as based on clusters obtained by taking different k-values, namely 2 which was intended for correctness based clustering and 5 which was intended for question based, it was found that the correctness based cluster had a better compactness. The models behaviour for a random incorrect code is shown in Fig. 6.

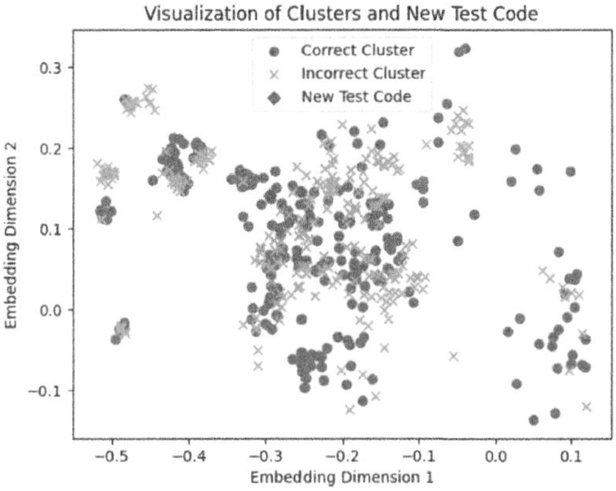

Fig. 6. Classifying Test-Code into correct or incorrect based on distance with clusters.

Table 7. Distance between the correct and incorrect cluster centroid and the test code

Cluster	Correct Cluster (Centroid)	Incorrect Cluster (Centroid)
Distance	3.38	3.32

Table 7 shows the distance from the new data point to both the clusters. When the distance is compared with correct code clusters' and incorrect code clusters' centroid, it was observed that the new test-code is nearer to incorrect code cluster, and therefore it is classified as incorrect code. This proves that the cluster based comparison holds good for binary classification of the C Codes. There are no much work done in this similar domain. Certain works that were reported on similar domain were used to compare with the current results. Automatic grading of C-programming assignments using machine learning and deep-learning techniques [11] reported a rmse of 1.89 with CodeBERT embeddings and [12] that used T5 embeddings for autograding of C Codes reported an accuracy of 78% accuracy. Though the dataset and the approach used in all these studies were unique, the learning based automatic grading of programming codes with the help of embeddings generated by pretrained models and LLMs opens a new area of research.

Conclusion

Classification based on machine learning models and clustering on the dataset was analyzed and it was found that CATBOOST out performed other traditional and ensembled machine learning models in classification with a mean accuracy of 84% and with a standard deviation of 0.17. The model also tried with creating clusters based on the number of independent questions and on the results. The compactness of these clusters was analysed. The model also tried to map unseen data into the different clusters which was successfully classifying the codes in to correct or incorrect. Therefore, for the dataset taken the result-based clustering proved to be a perfect method to classify the codes into correct or incorrect.

References

1. Ainapure, B., Pise, R., Singh,D.: Machine learning based code assessment systems. In: 2022 5th International Conference on Contemporary Computing and Informatics (IC3I). IEEE (2022)
2. Lokman, A.S., Ameedeen, M.A., Ghani, N.A.: Question classification of CoQA (QCoC) dataset. In: 2021 International Conference on Software Engineering and Computer Systems and 4th International Conference on Computational Science and Information Management (ICSECS-ICOCSIM), pp. 644–648 (2021)
3. Rai, K.K., Gupta, B., Shokeen, P., Chakraborty, P.: Question independent automated code analysis and grading using bag of words and machine learning. In: 2019 International Conference on Computing, Power and Communication Technologies (GUCON), New Delhi, India, pp. 93–98 (2019)
4. Mohasseb, A., Bader-El-Den, M.B., Haig, E.: Question categorization and classification using grammar based approach. Inf. Process. Manag. **54**, 1228–1243 (2018)
5. Reddy, A.C., Madhavi, K.: Hierarchy based firefly optimized K-means clustering for complex question answering. Indones.J. Electr. Eng. Comput. Sci. **17**, 264–272 (2020)
6. Joyner, D.A., et al.: From clusters to content: using code clustering for course improvement. In: Proceedings of the 50th ACM Technical Symposium on Computer Science Education (2019)
7. Sun, H., Shao, Z.: Research on the application of students' answered record analyze model and question automatic classify based on k-means clustering algorithm. In: 2019 10th International Conference on Information Technology in Medicine and Education (ITME), pp. 494–497 (2019)
8. Ma, Q., Murata, M.: Topic extraction and classification for questions posted in community-based question answering services. In: International Conference on Computational Science and Computational Intelligence (CSCI), 2019, pp. 1353–1358 (2019)

9. Bae, K., Ko, Y.: Efficient question classification and retrieval using category information and word embedding on cQA services. J. Intell. Inf. Syst., 1–23 (2019)
10. Razzaghnoori, M., Sajedi, H., Jazani, I.K.: Question classification in Persian using word vectors and frequencies. Cogn. Syst. Res. **47**, 16–27 (2018)
11. Muddaluru, R.V., Thoguluva, S.R., Prabha, S., Pati, P.B., Balakrishnan, R.M.: Auto-grading C programming assignments with CodeBERT and Random Forest Regressor. In: 2023 14th International Conference on Computing Communication and Networking Technologies (ICCCNT), Delhi, India, 2023, pp. 1–6. https://doi.org/10.1109/ICCCNT56998.2023.10308341
12. Narmada, N., Pati, P.B.: Autograding of programming skills. In: IEEE 8th International Conference for Convergence in Technology (I2CT), Lonavla, India, 2023, pp. 1–6 (2023). https://doi.org/10.1109/I2CT57861.2023.10126211
13. Sung, C., Dhamecha, T.I., Mukhi, N.: Improving short answer grading using transformer-based pre-training. In: Artificial Intelligence in Education: 20th International Conference, AIED 2019, Chicago, IL, USA, June 25–29, 2019, Proceedings, Part I 20, pp. 469–481. Springer International Publishing (2019)
14. Fukumoto, D., Kashiwa, Y., Hirao, T., Fujiwara, K., Iida, H.: An empirical investigation on the performance of domain adaptation for T5 code completion. In: 2023 IEEE International Conference on Software Analysis, Evolution and Reengineering (SANER), Taipa, Macao, 2023, pp. 693–697. https://doi.org/10.1109/SANER56733.2023.00073
15. Delgado-Pérez, P., Medina-Bulo, I.: Customizable and scalable automated assessment of C/C++ programming assignments. Comput. Appl. Eng. Educ. **28**(6), 1449–1466 (2020)
16. Shirafuji, A., et al.: Exploring the Robustness of Large Language Models for Solving Programming Problems (2023). arXiv preprint arXiv:2306.14583
17. Zhou, S., Alon, U., Agarwal, S., Neubig,G.: Codebertscore: Evaluating Code Generation with Pretrained Models of Code (2023). arXiv preprint arXiv:2302.05527
18. Sarsa, S., Denny, P., Hellas, A., Leinonen, J.: Automatic Generation of Programming Exercises and Code Explanations with Large Language Models (2022). arXiv preprint arXiv:2206.11861
19. Zhang, L., Chen, T., Zong, Y., Zhang, L.: Research to practice of blended learning in computer programming course. In: 2023 IEEE Frontiers in Education Conference (FIE), pp. 1–5. IEEE (2023)
20. Putnikovic, M., Jovanovic, J.: Embeddings for automatic short answer grading: a scoping review. In: IEEE Transactions on Learning Technologies (2023)
21. Devika, T.J., Ravichandran, J.: A clustering method combining multiple range tests and K-means. In: Communications in Statistics - Theory and Methods, pp. 1–56 (2021)
22. Vani, K., Gupta, D.: Using K-means cluster based techniques in external plagiarism detection. In: International Conference on Contemporary Computing and Informatics, Mysore (2014)

HyPRETo: Hybrid Pre-trained Ontology Approach for Contextual Relation Classification on Mosquito Vector Biocontrol Agents

G. Jeyakodi(✉) and P. Shanthi Bala

Department of Computer Science, School of Engineering and Technology, Pondicherry University, Puducherry, India
rjeyakodi02@gmail.com

Abstract. Pre-trained Language Model facilitates contextual relation classification by capturing contextual information, addressing word ambiguity, encoding global sentence context, enabling transfer learning, handling out-of-vocabulary words, and improving performance with limited labelled data. Existing pre-training approaches suffer in size, bias, interpretability, generalization, and the lack of domain specificity. To address this, HyPRETo, the hybrid model that combines the strength of token replacement and dynamic masking is proposed to achieve upgraded performance to increase classification accuracy. The Mosquito Vector Biocontrol Agents data is used for implementing the model for a contextual relation classification task. HyPRETo uses ontology to provide structured knowledge. HyPRETo is pre-trained by ELECTRA and fine-tuned by RoBERTa models. Feedforward and softmax activation function is used for classification. The Natural Language Processing technique and SQL database are used to develop an automated question-answering system. The HyPRETo was evaluated with state-of-art models and achieved 98.42% accuracy. As a contribution, the manually annotated input dataset on the mosquito vector control agent is prepared for the classification task. Subsequently, the enhanced model is developed. The interface for an automated question-answering system for mosquito vector biocontrol agents is developed to assist public health applications such as mosquito vector control, disease control, ecosystem management, environmental conservation, and so on.

Keywords: Pre-trained Model · Relation Classification · Contextual · HyPRETo · Mosquito Vector · Biocontrol Agents · Question-answering

1 Introduction

Contextual Relation (CR) represents the relationships between entities, events, or concepts within a given text or document, taking into account the context in which they appear. The context includes the surrounding words, phrases, or

Published by Springer Nature Switzerland AG 2025
A. Chandrabose et al. (Eds.): ICCCSP 2024, IFIP AICT 723, pp. 312–326, 2025.
https://doi.org/10.1007/978-3-031-73617-9_25

sentences that provide additional information and influence the interpretation of these relationships. CR aims to uncover the associations between the concepts in a text and how they impact each other. For example, 'The neem plant has an effect on controlling mosquito population', plants and mosquitoes are the concepts and they are associated with controlling mosquito relations. Contextual Relation Analysis (CRA) utilizes word embeddings to understand the relationships between concepts within a text based on the surrounding context [12]. CRA helps to understand the semantic structure of the text and derive meaningful insights, leading to better language understanding and more sophisticated language processing capabilities. Figure 1 shows the two different interpretations of the word "park" to represent the meaning of the word based on the context. The first use of "park" refers to finding a place to leave a car, while the second use of "park" refers to a public green space where people can go for a walk. Identifying contextual relations is essential in various Natural Language Processing (NLP) tasks such as information extraction, question answering, text summarization, text classification, machine translation, and more.

Fig. 1. Representation of Contextual Relationship

Contextual Relation Classification (CRC) categorizes the relationship between the concepts in a text based on the nearby word's contextual information. CRC assigns a categorical name to describe the relationship between the concepts [19]. For example, given the sentence "neem plant reduce mosquito population", the task would involve classifying the relationship between "neem plant" and "mosquito" as a biocontrol or lifespan. The classified relations help to extract structured information, provide accurate answers, analyze sentiment toward specific entities, populate ontologies, and improve translation quality by understanding the relationships between entities [6]. In general, to perform contextual relation classification, machine learning models including traditional algorithms and neural networks are used to train labelled datasets where the relationship between concepts is annotated. These models learn patterns and features from the data, to make predictions on unknown examples. However, these models are limited by data, interpretation, generalization, and overfitting issues [13]. Pre-trained Models (PTM) have gained significant attention for contextual relation classification due to their ability to manipulate large amounts of unlabelled data [7].

Pretrained language models offer a powerful framework for contextual relation classification by reducing training time and resources, enabling better performance, improving generalization, and efficient development of classification models with limited data compared to deep neural network models [7]. Generative Pretrained Transformer (GPT), Transformer-XL, Cross-lingual Language

Models (XLM), XLNet, and Bidirectional Encoder Representations from Transformers (BERT) are some of the different types of pre-trained language models. GPT predicts the next word in a sequence based on the preceding words and may capture global context. Transformer-XL model identifies long-range dependencies using a segment-level recurrence mechanism. XLM enables language understanding and generation in multiple languages by sharing linguistic information and facilitating knowledge transfer across different language contexts. XLNet is an auto-regressive language model that considers all possible permutations of the input sequence during training and allows bidirectional context modelling. BERT, the transformer architecture is based on the Masked Language Modeling (MLM) and Next Sentence Prediction (NSP) task [1]. In MLM, a portion of the input text is randomly masked, and the model is trained to predict the original masked words. It captures local word-context relationships effectively but struggles with long-range dependencies and global coherence [3].

BERT variants such as BERT for Biomedical Text Mining (BioBERT), A Lite BERT (ALBERT), Distilled form of BERT (DistilBERT), Robustly Optimized BERT Approach (RoBERTa), and Efficiently Learning an Encoder that Classifies Token Replacements Accurately (ELECTRA), etc. are commonly used for text classification [1]. They consider the bidirectional context of each word during training, allowing them to capture bidirectional dependencies and understand the context surrounding each word. These models capture contextual dependencies effectively and have illustrated efficient performance on various Natural Language Processing (NLP) tasks, including contextual relation classification [10]. However, each model has its specific training strategies and architectural variations to address different issues such as model size, efficiency, domain-specific adaptation, and overfitting making them personalized to specific needs and requirements. To address these issues, hybrid models can be beneficial [9].

Hybrid models combine the strengths of different architectures to overcome limitations by addressing the specific limitations of PTM, such as model size, computational resources, domain adaptation, and interpretability. The hybrid BERT model combined with a neural network has been used for multi-label text classification [2]. In addition, the ontology incorporation with the BERT model creates a more robust and domain-aware relation classification model [17]. Hence, in this paper, the HyPRETo, the ontology-based hybrid model is proposed for strengthening the complementary features of ELECTRA's token replacement and RoBERTa's dynamic masking to enhance the performance, robustness, and flexibility in capturing complex contextual dependencies. The classified relations are used for various applications such as the development of a question-answering system, knowledge graph construction, text highlighting, and so on.

2 Related works

2.1 Pre-trained Language Models for CRE

Pre-trained language models for contextual relation classification surpass early systems such as rule-based, feature-based, distant supervision, etc., by the automated learning from text. BERT captures complex patterns and contextual cues using a transformer-based neural network trained on a vast amount of unlabelled data for text classification, named entity recognition, text translation, and more [5]. Subsequently, DistilBERT, ALBERT, RoBERTa, and ELECTRA models were introduced as successive enhancements in the field of contextual relation classification [11]. The challenges encountered in each variant of BERT highlight the need for hybrid models that incorporate the strengths of different BERT variants and deep learning models to attain enhanced performance in contextual relation classification [18].

2.2 Hybrid Pre-trained Language Models for CRC

Hybrid pre-trained language models further improve the performance of contextual relation classification by combining BERT variants, and deep learning models to capture a broader range of contextual information and linguistic nuances. In 2019, BERT incorporated one-dimensional convolutional neural network (1dCNN) which has been used for extracting medical relations on three datasets BioCreative V chemical disease relation corpus, traditional Chinese medicine literature corpus, and i2b2 2012 temporal relation challenge corpus and attained significant improvement [4]. Further, various combinations of pre-training language and deep learning models have been developed for contextual relation classification. The hybrid deep learning approach that consists of BERT, Bidirectional Long Short Term Memory (Bi-LSTM), Multi-Head ATTention (MHATT), and Conditional Random Field (CRF) has been used to recognize named entities of chemicals and drugs that support entity relation extraction [15]. The hybrid model, ELECTRA-DTA which integrates ELECTRA and Convolutional Neural Network has been used to predict the drug-target binding affinity [20]. The combination of the RoBERTa and BERT ensemble model has been used to classify tweet messages and achieved enhanced results [16]. In addition, incorporating ontology into hybrid PTM for relation classification enhances their performance by providing a structured framework and semantic understanding of the domain.

2.3 Ontology-Based PTLMs

In recent years, there have been notable advancements in the field of NLP with researchers exploring integration of ontologies and deep learning-based PTM to enhance classification rates. Ilkay Yelmen et al. proposed a hybrid model that integrates ontologies and deep learning-based pre-trained models, utilizing BERT and DistilBERT, to improve classification performance on multiclass and imbalanced datasets [21]. Furthermore, Hau Liu et al. employed ontology summarization techniques and utilized the SNOMED ontology to refine the training data of BERT, focusing on identifying subsumption relationships between concepts [14].

In this paper, the ontology-incorporated hybrid pre-trained model is proposed to attain high accuracy on multi-class datasets that apply to various domains such as healthcare, finance, social media, customer service, etc. The next section explores the Hybrid Pre-Trained Ontology Approach for Contextual Relation Classification in detail.

3 HyPRETo: Hybrid PRE-Trained Ontology Approach

The proposed Hybrid PRE-Trained Ontology Approach for contextual relation classification uses the combination of ELECTRA and RoBERTa models and ontologies to classify contextual relations among the concepts in a sentence. The model consists of various components such as Input Encoding, Hybrid Learning, HyPRETo, Training, Evaluation, Classification, and Inference to classify and infer the contextual dependency among the semantic concepts in the sentence. This section further explores the formal model and the architecture of the proposed hybrid PTM for contextual relation classification.

3.1 Formal Model

The HyPRETo model combines ELECTRA and RoBERTa for learning the enriched features and contextual embeddings to capture the relationships among the concepts in the ontology-encoded input sentences. By using the strengths of both pre-training and fine-tuning, the HyPRETo gains a comprehensive understanding of the input data. The classification head identifies and predicts the most suitable relation label for new input sentences, using the knowledge acquired during training.

Representing the contextual relation classification task mathematically facilitates a clear and precise understanding of the model's capabilities in capturing complex relationships in the given text. The ontology-encoded input sentences with relation labels (S′) are represented in Eq. 1.

$$S' = S, R \tag{1}$$

The Contextual Embeddings (OE) obtained by ELECTRA and RoBERTa model is exposed in Equation in Eq. 2.

$$OE = E_e(s_i), E_r(s_i) \tag{2}$$

where, $E_e(si) = e_1, e_2, ..., e_n$ represent embeddings obtained by ELECTRA, $E_r(si) = e_1, e_2, ..., e_n$ represent embeddings obtained by RoBERTa. The embeddings obtained by ELECTRA and RoBERTa are concatenated and passed through additional layers to generate the Enriched Feature Representation ($\pounds$) as depicted in Eq. 3.

$$\pounds(s_i) = L(E_e(s_i) + E_r(s_i)) \tag{3}$$

In which L indicates the operation of additional layers. The training data $\overline{D}$ is considered as Eq. 4.

$$\overline{D} = S_i, R_i \tag{4}$$

where $i = 1, 2, 3...n$. The Inferred Results γ is exposed in the Eq. 5.

$$\gamma = p_1, p_2...p_n \tag{5}$$

where $p_1, p_2, ..., p_n$ are the probabilities assigned to each relation labels. The sum of all probabilities in the vector will be equal to 1. In general, the SoftMax activation function in the classification head is used for learning the features and relations in the given input sentence.

3.2 Architecture

The development of advanced PTM, particularly in text classification has witnessed significant progress through hybrid techniques. The ontology-based pre-trained model, HyPRETo offers a formidable approach that amalgamates various components for enhanced classification performance. The process begins with Input Encoding, where raw ontology-encoded input is transformed into tokens and relation labels are mapped for further processing. In hybrid learning, pre-training involves ELECTRA, where the model learns to distinguish real and corrupted tokens while capturing contextual information. Fine-tuning with RoBERTa refines the model for relation classification using labelled data. HyPRETo concatenates the contextual embeddings from both ELECTRA and RoBERTa to represent the enriched features. The hybrid model is fine-tuned in training to optimize the relation classification performance. The evaluation computes the model's accuracy and effectiveness, and the classification predicts the relation labels for new, unidentified sentences. Finally, in the inference phase, the predicted relation probabilities are converted into original labels for understanding. Figure 2 depicts the HyPRETo architecture.

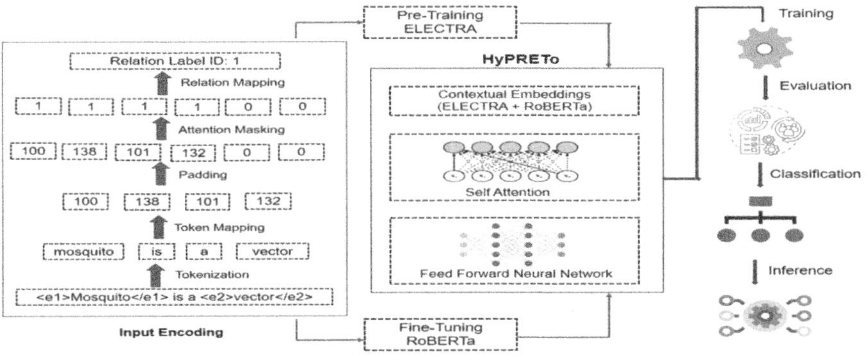

Fig. 2. HyPRETO Architecture

Input Encoding. Input encoding consists of various phases such as tokenization, mapping tokens to IDs, padding, attention masks, and relation label mapping. Tokenization converts the ontology-encoded input sentences into individual tokens and maps the token with unique token IDs using the model's vocabulary. Padding helps to fix all the sequences in the same length by adding zero. Attention mask, a binary vector indicates which tokens should be attended (1) and which should be ignored (0) for distinguishing actual and padding tokens. Finally, the relations are mapped to numerical IDs. After these, the data is ready to be used for hybrid learning.

Hybrid Learning. Hybrid learning utilizes the benefits of both pre-training and fine-tuning techniques. Pre-training by ELECTRA efficiently captures contextual information by discriminating real and fake tokens while fine-tuning by RoBERTa specialized specific downstream tasks such as relation classification. In the pre-training step with ELECTRA, the input tokens ["*Bacillus*", "*thuringiensis*", "is", "a", "common", "mosquito", "vector", "biocontrol", "agent", "."], involves token replacement and masking. A certain percentage of tokens (e.g., 15%) are randomly selected and masked (e.g., "*thuringiensis*" and "vector" might be masked as "[MASK]"). The model then generates "fake" tokens for the masked positions based on the context, and a discriminator within the ELECTRA model is trained to distinguish between real and fake tokens. The output of pre-training is an updated ELECTRA model with fine-tuned weights, capable of generating contextually rich embeddings for words and sentences as a vector representation. The pre-trained ELECTRA model is then fine-tuned for the relation classification task. Tokenized sentences and mapped relation labels obtained from the data preprocessing using RoBERTa Tokenizers are used for fine-tuning RoBERTa model. The model optimizes its parameters using gradient-based optimization techniques (stochastic gradient descent) and loss functions (cross-entropy) to minimize the prediction errors and improve its relation classification performance. The output is the trained RoBERTa model specifically adapted for relation classification, capable of predicting tokens for the masked positions in sentences. By combining these techniques in hybrid learning, the model can achieve enhanced language understanding, context awareness, and improved performance on relation classification tasks.

HyPRETo Model. The HyPRETo combines the strengths of ELECTRA and RoBERTa. The tokenized sentences and contextual embedding from both the fine-tuned RoBERTa and ELECTRA models are the input. HyPRETo concatenates the context-aware embeddings from both models for each token to create a hybrid representation to achieve higher performance in relation classification. Further, the additional layers, such as self-attention and feed-forward neural networks are incorporated to enrich the contextual embeddings. The self-attention layer allows HyPRETo to weigh the importance of different tokens within a sentence, capturing long-range dependencies and improving context awareness to provide a set of weighted contextual embeddings. The feed-forward neural network further refines the feature representations by applying non-linear transformations to generate a set of enriched feature representations as numeric vectors for capturing complex relationships and patterns within the sentence. Thus, the additional layers enhance the HyPRETo model's ability to extract meaningful features and relationships.

Training. In the training phase, the HyPRETo model is trained to optimize its performance on the relation classification task. The training involves fine-tuning the entire hybrid model on the relation classification task using labelled data. The training process helps to adapt the model's parameters to the specific characteristics of the relation classification problem by combining the advantages of both ELECTRA pre-training and RoBERTa fine-tuning. During training, the model's weights are updated using backpropagation and gradient descent, minimizing a suitable loss function to enhance model's performance in relation classification. Training outcomes the updated model with fine-tuned weights ready to make accurate predictions on relation classification for new, undetermined sentences.

Evaluation. The evaluation step assesses the performance of the trained hybrid model on relation classification. During the evaluation, the model is tested on a separate dataset containing labelled examples that were not available during training. The input sentences from this test dataset are tokenized and processed through the hybrid model, which predicts relation labels based on the enriched feature representations learned during training. The model's predicted relation labels are then compared with the true labels in the test dataset with various evaluation metrics such as accuracy, precision, recall, F-score, and Cohenś Kappa. HyPRETo predicts the relation labels from both the ELECTRA and RoBERTa models and the average of predicted probabilities from both models are considered. The evaluation results show the model's effectiveness and its generalization on relation classification tasks.

Classification. In the HyPRETo, the classification layer is added on top of the additional layers to predict the relation labels for each input sentence based on the enriched features. This layer is responsible for mapping the contextualized embeddings obtained from the pre-trained ELECTRA and fine-tuned RoBERTa models to the specific relation classification task. The classification layer consists of a feed-forward layer with a softmax activation and computes the probability distribution over different relation labels for the enriched features. The label with the highest probability is considered the predicted relation label for the input sentence.

Inference. The Inference step helps to deploy the trained HyPRETo model to make predictions on new, unnoticed sentences, enabling to use of the model to real-world data and obtain relation classification results on previously unknown examples. To perform inference, the pre-trained HyPRETo model is loaded along with the tokenizers. The new input sentences are tokenized using the tokenizers, converting them into numerical representations. The tokenized sentences are then fed into the HyPRETo, which outputs probability scores for each relation class. By selecting the class with the highest probability, the model assigns predicted relation labels to the input sentences.

4 Experimental Analysis

In the experiment phase, the HyPRETo model is implemented and evaluated on a manually annotated dataset on mosquito vector biocontrol agents collected from relevant articles. Mosquito Vector Association Ontology (MVAont) from Bioportal is used for ontology encoding [8]. The dataset contains a list of sentences that describe different relations such as "biocontrol", "cause_effect", "life_span", and others. The main objective of the experiment is to use the HyPRETo model's capability to accurately classify and predict the specific relation labels associated with each input sentence. By using pre-training and fine-tuning, the model learns to understand the contextual information and capture relevant features for relation classification. HyPRETo is implemented in Google Colab using Python libraries such as transformers for model pre-training, torch for deep learning capabilities, pandas for data handling, numpy for numerical computations, and scikit-learn for evaluation metrics. The HyPRETo model's performance is compared with other machine learning models including BERT, ALBERT, BioBERT, RoBERTa, and ELECTRA. These models are fine-tuned on the same dataset and evaluated using various evaluation metrics. Finally, the relation classification is automated and assessed the model's performance in accurately identifying diverse relations within the context of mosquito vector biocontrol agents.

4.1 Dataset

The HyPRETo uses the list of sentences related to mosquito vectors and their biocontrol agents for relation classification. This biological data is curated and annotated from abstracts downloaded from PubMed, with the assistance of domain experts. To encode the domain-specific concepts of mosquito vectors, the Mosquito Vector Association Ontology with Biocontrol Agents (MVAont)[1] is utilized to provide structured and semantically rich information, enhancing its ability to capture the intricate relationships between different entities in the context of mosquito vector biocontrol [21]. Each sentence is labelled with one of six relation classes: biocontrol, lifespan, cause_effect, is_a, repellent, and predator. The dataset consists of 630 sentences and is further divided into two subsets, comprising 504 sentences for training and 126 sentences for testing to ensure proper model evaluation. The training set helps to update the model's parameters during the fine-tuning process, while the test set remains unseen during

[1] https://bioportal.bioontology.org/ontologies/MVAONT.

training and is solely used to evaluate the model's generalization and performance on unknown data. The use of domain experts in annotating the dataset contributes to the dataset's accuracy and reliability. Domain experts provide valuable insights into the domain-specific context, ensuring that the labelled relations accurately represent the actual relationships between mosquito vectors and their biocontrol agents in the given sentences.

4.2 HyPRETo Specifications

The HyPRETo amalgamates the strengths of the ELECTRA and RoBERTa architectures, creating a robust and efficient system for relation classification. By utilizing the RoBERTa and ELECTRA tokenizers, the model efficiently encodes input sentences and captures their contextual information. With a batch size of 32 and trained over 50 epochs, the model benefits from a moderate-sized batch for efficient processing and a sufficient number of training iterations for convergence. A learning rate of 1e−5, masking probability of 0.15, and AdamW optimizer contribute to the fine-tuning process, ensuring adaptive and effective weight updates. The model's core features, such as 12 attention heads and 12 hidden layers, enable enhanced self-attention and deep representation learning. Notably, the model utilizes relative positional embeddings, enriching its ability to encode the sequential order of tokens effectively. Moreover, employing the GELU activation function in the summarization layer adds non-linearity, further enhancing the model's expressive capabilities. Table 1 explores the HyPRETo model specifications. By using this, the hybrid architecture HyPRETo offers a powerful model for relation classification in the context of mosquito vector biocontrol agents, presenting a compelling solution to extract meaningful insights and support informed decision-making in this critical domain.

4.3 Results and Discussion

In the realm of mosquito vector biocontrol agents, the hybrid pre-trained ontology-amalgamated relation classification model was meticulously developed, utilizing the mosquito vector biocontrol agent dataset containing 632 annotated sentences encoded through the MVAont context. The HyPRETo model's effectiveness is systematically evaluated through crucial metrics including accuracy, precision, recall, F-score, and Cohen's Kappa. Table 2 illustrates the model's performance over 50 epochs, capturing variations in key parameters and offering insights into its behavior and convergence patterns. There is a significant improvement in each epoch and the model reached convergence from the thirty-nine epoch, further no more changes in the performance. Indeed, the model demonstrates optimal performance with a learning rate of 1e−5, batch size 32, and dropout rate 0.25, yielding high evaluation metrics. Furthermore, an alternative effective configuration involves a learning rate of 2e−5, batch size 16, and dropout rate 0.25, displaying competitive performance across various statistical measures.

Table 1. HyPRETo Specifications

Sl. No	Component	Specification
1	Architecture	Hybrid (ELECTRA + RoBERTa)
2	Tokenizer	RoBERTa and ELECTRA Tokenizers
3	Batch Size	32
4	Number of Epochs	50
5	Learning Rate	1e−5
6	Masking Probability	0.15
7	Optimizer	AdamW
8	Loss Function	Cross Entropy Loss
9	Dropout Rate	0.25
10	Number of Attention Heads	12
11	Number of Hidden Layers	12
12	Position Embedding Type	Relative
13	Summary Activation	GELU

The performance of the HyPRETo model is assessed with traditional machine learning models and BERT variants such as BioBERT, ALBERT, RoBERTa, and ELECTRA in the given context. Table 3 offers a comprehensive comparison of the HyPRETo with other models. In addition, the model's ability to capture long-term dependencies is validated using a relation similarity metric score. The model demonstrates effective semantic relation capture without ambiguity up to a dependency length of 200. Figure 3a depicts the accuracy of HyPRETo model in fifty epochs. Figure 3b visually represents the comprehensive analysis of the model's long-term dependency capture capabilities. Figure 3c shows the comparison of HyPRETo against existing models in terms of accuracy.

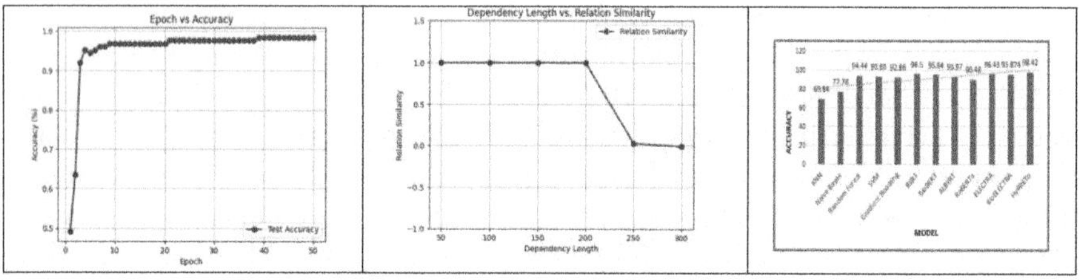

Fig. 3. a. Epoch Vs Accuracy; b. Long-term Dependency; c. HyPRETo Vs Other Models

The comparison illustrates that the hybrid model HyPRETo outperforms both machine learning and deep learning models. The performance is particularly notable in terms of accuracy and cohen's kappa, where HyPRETo attains

Table 2. HyPERTo performance

Sl. No.	Learning Rate	Batch Size	Dropout	Precision	Recall	Accuracy (%)	F-score	Cohen's Kappa
1	1e−05	16	0.2	0.954	0.952	95.24	0.951	0.926
			0.25	0.962	0.960	96.03	0.959	0.941
			0.3	0.953	0.952	95.24	0.951	0.929
2	**1e−05**	**32**	0.2	0.962	0.960	96.02	0.959	0.941
			0.25	**0.985**	**0.984**	**98.42**	**0.983**	**0.996**
			0.3	0.977	0.976	97.62	0.975	0.964
3	**2e−05**	**16**	0.2	0.977	0.976	97.62	0.975	0.964
			0.25	**0.985**	**0.984**	**98.42**	**0.983**	**0.996**
			0.3	0.955	0.952	95.24	0.952	0.929
4	**2e−05**	32	0.2	0.977	0.976	97.62	0.975	0.964
			0.25	0.953	0.952	95.24	0.951	0.928
			0.3	0.961	0.960	96.03	0.959	0.940

Table 3. HyPERTo comparison

Sl. No	Model	Precision	Recall	Accuracy(%)	F-score	Cohenś Kappa
1	KNN	0.716	0.699	69.84	0.674	0.511
2	Naïve Bayes	0.798	0.778	77.78	0.738	0.636
3	Random Forest	0.931	0.944	94.44	0.937	0.916
4	SVM	0.938	0.937	93.65	0.937	0.906
5	Gradient Boosting	0.945	0.929	92.86	0.935	0.894
6	BERT	0.962	0.965	96.50	0.963	0.951
7	BioBERT	0.958	0.956	95.64	0.954	0.949
8	ALBERT	0.942	0.94	93.97	0.938	0.914
9	RoBERTa	0.795	0.824	90.48	0.803	0.706
10	ELECTRA	0.961	0.964	96.43	0.962	0.927
11	BioELECTRA	0.955	0.956	95.874	0.955	0.941
12	**HyPRETo**	**0.985**	**0.984**	**98.42**	**0.983**	**0.996**

an accuracy value of 98.42% and cohen's kappa as 0.996. The outstanding performance highlights HyPRETo's adeptness in achieving a balance between identifying true positives and minimizing false negatives, and also signifies a substantial improvement compared to the other models, reflecting its proficiency in correctly classifying instances. The Hybrid model's accuracy and cohen's kappa exceed even the highly accurate deep learning variants like BERT, BioBERT, ALBERT, RoBERTa, ELECTRA, and BioELECTRA, which demonstrates its ability to combine the strength of the pre-trained model's variants. Therefore, the remarkable accuracy is achieved by HyPRETo, confirms its excellence in precise and comprehensive relation classification, solidifying its position as a robust solution within the realm of classification methodologies. The subsequent section explores the utilization of HyPRETo in the context of question-answering system development for mosquito vector biocontrol agents.

5 HyPRETO Application

The proposed HyPRETo relation classification model has been used for the development of a question-answering system. By accurately identifying and categorizing relations between entities, the model can comprehend the context of the input text. This enables the system to extract relevant information and generate appropriate answers for the given questions. In general, the question-answering system predicts various kinds of questions such as:

a) "What are the roles of [entity] in [relation]?"
b) "What is the significance of [relation] between [entity] and [entity]?"
c) "How does [relation] impact [entity]?"
d) "Is [entity] related to [entity] through [relation]?"

To predict "what" and "is" type questions, the system first identifies the entities in the question. For example, "What is the role of neem in *Aedes aegypti*?", the entities are neem and *Aedes aegypti.* Using the HyPRETo classified relations, the system retrieves the relation that connects the identified entities. In this case, it retrieves the relation "biocontrol". With the relation and entities, the system generates an answer as "biocontrol". For "is" type questions, such as "Is *Aedes aegypti* related to a mosquito?", by using the classified relations, the system determines the link between the entities. It may respond with a simple "Yes" or "No" based on the identified relation. The automated question-answering system for mosquito vector biocontrol agents was developed by using the insights derived from the HyPRETo model's classification capabilities. The natural language processing technique was used to effectively identify the entities for predicting "what" and "is" type questions. The SQL database was used for backend storage and Python language was used for interface design. Figure 4 illustrates the User interface and interpretation of the Mosquito vector biocontrol agents question answering system. One of the key strengths of this question-answering system lies in its capability to extract crucial information such as the vector's characteristics, the infectious pathogens, the disease it spreads, and biocontrol agents. This system facilitates timely actions that contribute to the prevention and management of vector-borne diseases, ultimately safeguarding public health.

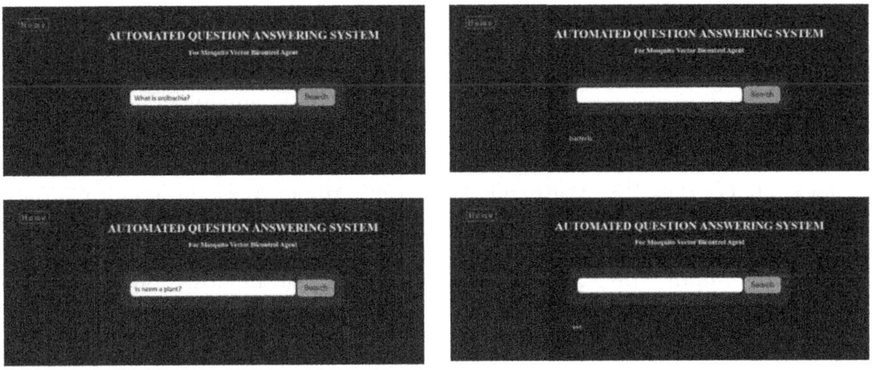

Fig. 4. Question Answering System Interface

6 Conclusion

In this paper, a novel model, HyPRETo has been developed by integrating a hybrid ontology pre-trained model with the advantages of RoBERTa and ELECTRA. This innovative model was meticulously developed to significantly enhance the accuracy of contextual relation classification. Its performance was tested using a manually annotated dataset focusing on mosquito vector biocontrol agents, revealing its superiority over established models like support vector machine and BERT variants. HyPRETo also demonstrates remarkable capabilities in capturing long-term dependencies. Furthermore, the development of a question-answering system for mosquito vector biocontrol agents signifies a remarkable advancement in the field of contextual relation classification by providing specific information about mosquito vector interactions and behaviours. In addition, this work has a great ability for applications in public health domains. The HyPRETo model's enhanced understanding of contextual relations among the mosquito vectors and biocontrol agents supports effective vector-borne disease control and improves public health strategies.

References

1. Acheampong, F.A., Nunoo-Mensah, H., Chen, W.: Transformer models for text-based emotion detection: a review of BERT-based approaches. Artif. Intell. Rev. **54**(8), 5789–5829 (2021). https://doi.org/10.1007/s10462-021-09958-2
2. Cai, L., Song, Y., Liu, T., Zhang, K.: A hybrid BERT model that incorporates label semantics via adjustive attention for multi-label text classification. IEEE Access **8**, 152183–152192 (2020). https://doi.org/10.1109/ACCESS.2020.3017382
3. Chan, J.Y.L., Bea, K.T., Leow, S.M.H., Phoong, S.W., Cheng, W.K.: State of the art: a review of sentiment analysis based on sequential transfer learning. Artif. Intell. Rev. **56**(1), 749–780 (2023). https://doi.org/10.1007/s10462-022-10183-8
4. Chen, T., Wu, M., Li, H.: A general approach for improving deep learning-based medical relation extraction using a pre-trained model and fine-tuning. Database **2019**, baz116 (2019). https://doi.org/10.1093/database/baz116

5. Devlin, J., Chang, M.W., Lee, K., Toutanova, K.: BERT: Pre-training of Deep Bidirectional Transformers for Language Understanding (2019)
6. Goyal, A., Gupta, V., Kumar, M.: Recent named entity recognition and classification techniques: a systematic review. Comput. Sci. Rev. **29**, 21–43 (2018). https://doi.org/10.1016/j.cosrev.2018.06.001
7. Han, X., et al.: Pre-trained Models: Past, Present and Future (2021)
8. Jeyakodi, G., Bala P.S., Sruthi, O., Swathi, K.: Mbors: Mosquito vector biocontrol ontology and recommendation system. J. Vector Borne Dis. (2023). https://doi.org/10.4103/0972-9062.383640. epub ahead of print
9. Kour, H., Gupta, M.K.: Ai assisted attention mechanism for hybrid neural model to assess online attitudes about covid-19. Neural Process. Lett. **55**(3), 2265–2304 (2023). https://doi.org/10.1007/s11063-022-11112-0
10. Lee, Y., Son, J., Song, M.: Bertsrc: transformer-based semantic relation classification. BMC Med. Inform. Decis. Mak. **22**(1), 234 (2022). https://doi.org/10.1186/s12911-022-01977-5
11. Li, J., Huang, Q., Ren, S., Jiang, L., Deng, B., Qin, Y.: A novel medical text classification model with Kalman filter for clinical decision making. Biomed. Signal Process. Control **82**, 104503 (2023). https://doi.org/10.1016/j.bspc.2022.104503
12. Li, S., Pan, R., Luo, H., Liu, X., Zhao, G.: Adaptive cross-contextual word embedding for word polysemy with unsupervised topic modeling. Knowl. Based Syst. **218**, 106827 (2021). https://doi.org/10.1016/j.knosys.2021.106827
13. Li, Y., Sixou, B., Peyrin, F.: A review of the deep learning methods for medical images super resolution problems. IRBM **42**(2), 120–133 (2021). https://doi.org/10.1016/j.irbm.2020.08.004
14. Liu, H., Perl, Y., Geller, J.: Concept placement using BERT trained by transforming and summarizing biomedical ontology structure. J. Biomed. Inform. **112**, 103607 (2020). https://doi.org/10.1016/j.jbi.2020.103607
15. Liu, J., et al.: A Hybrid Deep-Learning Approach for Complex Biochemical Named Entity Recognition (2020)
16. Mujahid, M., Kanwal, K., Rustam, F., Aljadani, W., Ashraf, I.: Arabic chatgpt tweets classification using ROBERTA and BERT ensemble model. ACM Trans. Asian Low Resour. Lang. Inf. Process **22**(8), 1 (2023). https://doi.org/10.1145/3605889
17. Onan, A.: Hierarchical graph-based text classification framework with contextual node embedding and BERT-based dynamic fusion. J. King Saud Univ. Comput. Inf. Sci. **35**(7), 101610 (2023). https://doi.org/10.1016/j.jksuci.2023.101610
18. Shanmugavadivel, K., Sathishkumar, V.E., Raja, S., Lingaiah, T.B., Neelakandan, S., Subramanian, M.: Deep learning based sentiment analysis and offensive language identification on multilingual code-mixed data. Sci. Rep. **12**(1), 21557 (2022). https://doi.org/10.1038/s41598-022-26092-3
19. Uzuner, O., South, B.R., Shen, S., DuVall, S.L.: 2010 i2b2/va challenge on concepts, assertions, and relations in clinical text. J. Am. Med. Inform. Assoc. **18**(5), 552–556 (2011). https://doi.org/10.1136/amiajnl-2011-000203
20. Wang, J., Wen, N., Wang, C., Zhao, L., Cheng, L.: Electra-dta: a new compound-protein binding affinity prediction model based on the contextualized sequence encoding. J. Cheminform. **14**(1), 14 (2022). https://doi.org/10.1186/s13321-022-00591-x
21. Yelmen, I., Gunes, A., Zontul, M.: Multi-class document classification using lexical ontology-based deep learning. Appl. Sci. **13**(10), 6139 (2023). https://doi.org/10.3390/app13106139

Predictive Maintenance for Hard Disk Drives Using Random Forest

Achal Baniya, Abhay Vinod, Hitesh Surya Chinta, Bhavith Manathanathu Pushakara, and Peeta Basa Pati(✉)

Department of Computer Science and Engineering, Amrita School of Computing Bengaluru, Amrita Vishwa Vidyapeetham, Bengaluru, India
bp_peeta@blr.amrita.edu

Abstract. As digital data continues to grow exponentially, the reliability of Hard Disk Drives (HDDs) becomes a critical concern for ensuring data integrity and preventing unexpected system downtimes. The research dataset contains historical SMART attribute data collected from HDDs, encompassing parameters such as spin-up time, temperature reallocated sector count and other relevant metrics. The study explored usage of various exploratory data analysis (EDA) & machine learning (ML) techniques for forecasting HDD failures. EDA techniques include Synthetic Minority Over-sampling Technique (SMOTE) algorithm for balancing class representation in training set and Principal Component Analysis (PCA) for dimensionality reduction. Diverse machine learning techniques, such as Random Forest (RF), Decision Tree (DT), K-nearest Neighbors (KNN), Gaussian Naïve Bayes (GNB), Adaptive Boosting (AdaBoost), XGBoost, Gradient Boosting (GB), Linear Discriminant Analysis (LDA), Logistic Regression (LR), are employed to predict the hard drive failure. Local Interpretable Model-agnostic Explanations (LIME) is employed to identify which features have the greatest influence on a specific prediction, providing insights into the factors driving the model's decisions. Random Forest exhibited superior performance of accuracy 99.9 and F1 score 0.98 compared to other models.

Keywords: HDDs Failure · Machine Learning · SMOTE · PCA · LIME

1 Introduction

As technology continues to advance, the reliance on digital data storage becomes more pervasive across various industries and personal spheres. Hard Disk Drives (HDDs) serve as a fundamental component for storing vast amounts of information, ranging from critical business data to personal files. However, the risk of hard disk drive failure poses a significant concern, as it can lead to data loss, system downtime, and financial implications [2].

HDD failures are expensive and costly. Data losses can have serious consequences for businesses, including compromised day-to-day operations, reputational damage and financial loss. These risks are increased when these failures are not anticipated and

Published by Springer Nature Switzerland AG 2025
A. Chandrabose et al. (Eds.): ICCCSP 2024, IFIP AICT 723, pp. 327–338, 2025.
https://doi.org/10.1007/978-3-031-73617-9_26

prevented. HDD failure can put safety and wellbeing of people in danger for healthcare, finance, and mission critical infrastructure industries [3].

In recent years, the integration of machine learning algorithms in predictive maintenance has gained traction as a proactive approach to mitigate the impact of hardware failures [4]. SMART (Self-Monitoring, Analysis, and Reporting Technology) attributes play a crucial role in predicting and monitoring the health of hard disk drives (HDDs) and solid-state drives (SSDs). These attributes provide valuable insights into the condition and potential failure risks of storage devices, allowing for proactive maintenance and risk mitigation strategies [3].

In this work, we employ ML models on the SMART attributes to significantly improve the capacity for early recognition of the HDD's failure symptoms. SMOTE is used to address the class imbalance in the dataset and PCA is used for efficient attribute selection & representation. LIME is used for interpretability of the used models. This enables system analysts and administrators to proactively identify early indicators of HDD performance degradation, enabling prompt preventive actions like maintenance or replacement. The improved interpretability and accuracy of the model lead to a more durable and dependable HDD failure prediction system, thereby, reducing the chance of data loss and system outages.

The key contributions of this work are: (i) selection of the best ML model for HDD failure prediction with a comparative analysis of the effectiveness of various ML models, and (ii) interpretability of the model's prediction behavior with LIME algorithm. This study demonstrates the effectiveness of using a system using ML algorithms as an early warning system for data centers hosting storage servers.

2 Literature Survey

We conduct a survey of literature before starting of the work. The purpose of this literature survey is aimed at identifying the existing works and their contributions along with research gaps for the proposed work. Various research articles are collected from databases such as IEE Explore and studied for their contribution in this field. These works are summarized in the following paragraphs of this section.

Cahyadi et al. [1] in their study presented the hypothesis that only smart attributes can be effective predictors, and explored the impact of class imbalance mitigation strategies. They used the LSTM model for predicting hard drive failure. They investigated the impact of different sampling methods such as partial under sampling, severe under sampling, duplicate oversampling in the accuracy of the model and they accessed these methods for the effectiveness using Matthews Correlation Coefficient as an evaluation matrix. Sobhana et al. [2] in their study used genetic algorithms for feature selection and proposed Artificial Neural Network to predict when a hard disk is likely to fail. They compared the proposed ANN model with SVM, Naïve Bayes based on accuracy and other performance metrics to demonstrate the superiority of the proposed model. Marwin et al. [3] in their study used four different machine learning model updating strategies to address the dynamic nature of the HDD failure prediction, in their research. They identified XGBoost with Hoeffding bound update trigger as achieving the overall best prediction performance.

Georgoulopoulos et al. [4] have reviewed the hardware failure prediction techniques with focus on the HDD, CPU and RAM for using ML and Deep Learning (DL) Algorithm. This survey study does a comprehensive analysis of the literature to identify these issues. Wang et al. [5] in their research proposed a two-layer classification-based feature selection scheme to improve prediction quality and modelling timeliness. They used ML an Artificial Intelligence (AI) models such as Naïve Bayesian, Random Forest, SVM, Gradient Boosting, Decision Tree, Convolutional Neural Networks, and Long Short-term Memory for predicting HDD failure. They identified Random Forest and Long Short Term Memory with proposed techniques that gives the best accuracy.

Zhang et al. [6] in their research proposed a novel framework for predicting the Remaining Useful Life (RUL) of HDD in data centers. The authors focus on leveraging machine learning and deep learning techniques, particularly the Long Short-Term Memory (LSTM) network, to analyze raw data and predict the RULE of HDD. They proposed the methods to mitigate the issue of data imbalance in the context of HDD failure prediction. Zhao et al. [7] have investigated the impact of age and workload on the annualized failure rate (AFR) of HDDs in their research. The authors explored the differences between AFR curves and Manufactures' projection using statistical modeling. They used a decision tree, XGBoost to analyze the correlation between SMART metrics and HDD health and they proposed that differences in SMART metrics over a 30-day time window can enhance prediction performance for HDD failures.

In summary, the review of the literature indicates that a wide range of approaches are used to try and anticipate hard drive (HDD) failures with accuracy. The application of genetic algorithms, smart characteristics, and machine learning models like XGBoost, ANN, and LSTM has been investigated by researchers. Proposals for strategies to deal with feature selection, dynamic model updating, and class imbalance demonstrate the many techniques used in this discipline. The research contributes to the development of HDD failure prediction by providing meaningful information and cutting-edge methods to improve the accuracy and speed of prediction.

3 Data Description

We have used a dataset taken from Hard Drive Data and Stats (Backblaze) [13, 14]. The dataset was created primarily with HDDs failure predictions in mind. The dataset has 380079 records with 49 different informative attributes. The dataset mostly consists of smart attributes which are related to the health and performance of the hard drives. The smart features are of two types: raw and normalized. The normalized value is a scaled representation of the drive health and performance for a specific smart attribute and raw value represents the actual data collected from smart attribute. The features also include failure label to predict whether the hard drive has failed (1) or not (0).

Upon further analysis, we observed that there was class imbalance in the dataset. The dataset has 367,468 records of failure and 12,594 records for non-failure as shown in Fig. 1. There is a huge difference in the number of 0's and 1's which leads to performing poorly on the minority class. To rectify this class imbalance, we used Synthetic Minority Over-sampling Technique (SMOTE). Variance threshold was applied for feature selection that eliminated the features having low variance to streamline the dataset and finally 33 features were selected for this study. 70% of the dataset randomly picked for the training set and rest 30% form the test set.

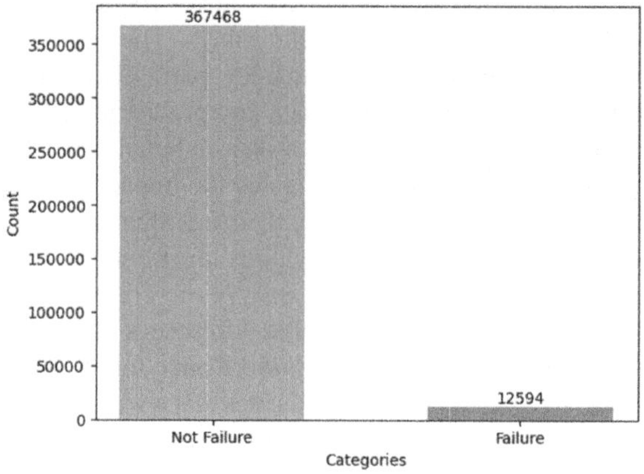

Fig. 1. Data Distribution of failure and not failure HDD

4 Methodology

We present the flow diagram of our proposed implementation in Fig. 2.

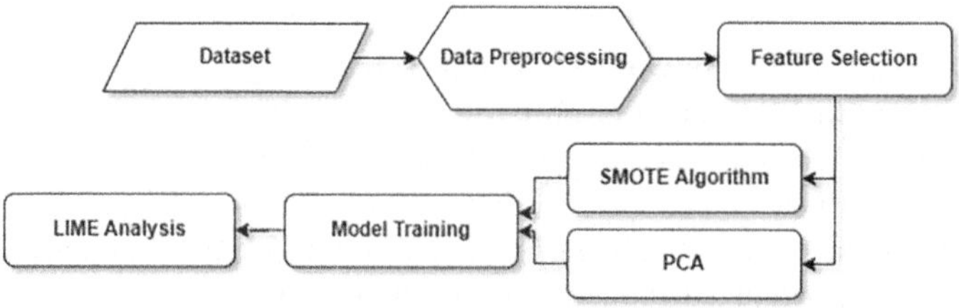

Fig. 2. Flow Diagram of proposed system

4.1 Model Training

In order to forecast HDD failure, we used nine different machine learning models, including the logistic regression, decision tree, random forest, XGBoost, gradient boosting, adaptive boosting, K-Nearest Neighbors, Gaussian Naïve Bayes, and Linear Discriminant Analysis. Decision trees examined the importance of features in a dataset and offered an interpretable approach for making decisions. Random Forest used several decision trees to increase accuracy. Random Forest was a flexible and simple technique that could be used for ascertain feature significance in supervised situations [11]. XGBoost was a classification algorithm that sets itself apart by using regularization approaches to avoid overfitting. Gradient Boosting improved predicting performance with each cycle by gradually building weak learners. Assuming normally distributed classes with comparable covariance matrices, linear discriminant analysis was used for classification and dimensionality reduction to keep class separability. Adaptive Boosting design was used to iteratively enhance the performance of weak classifiers in binary classification [12]. Logistic Regression was particularly used common in probability estimates and classification. KNNs were used as a lazy learning, non-parametric learning method for classification. Closed values are regarded by KNN as being close to one another. By determining the data's nearest value within the training data set, KNN forecasts the new data point [9]. Gaussian Naïve Bayes performed particularly well if features were considered independent especially for classification. We present the optimized hyperparameters in Table 1 for the various ML subsequent paragraphs, however, are indented.

Table 1. Hyperparameters of the ML models

Model	Hyper Parameters
Random Forest	n_estimetors = 100, min_samples_split = 2, min_samples_leaf = 1
Adaptive Boosting	Estimator = weak_learner, n_estimators = 50, random_state = 42
K Nearest Neighbors	n_neighbors = 3
Gradient Boosting	n_estimators = 100, learning_rate = 0.1, max_depth = 3, random_state = 42
XGBClassifiers	n_estimators = 2, max_depth = 2, learning_rate = 1, objective = 'binary: logistic'
Decision Tree	min_samples_split = 2,min_samples_leaf = 1
Linear Discriminant Analysis	store_covariance = False
Logistic Regression	C = 0.01, solver = 'lbfgs'

4.2 Principle Component Analysis

We employed Principal Component Analysis (PCA) as a dimensionality reduction technique to improve dataset analysis [8]. The dataset comprises 49 features providing a multidimensional representation of the observation. PCA was applied to address the challenges posed by a high dimensional dataset. It reduced the number of features from original number to selected number of principle components (19). PCA was used to improve interpretability, visualization and even the performance of machine learning models.

4.3 Model Performance

Precision, Recall, F1 score, Accuracy and Confusion metrics are key metrics for evaluating the effectiveness of machine learning models. They offer insights into the model's strengths and areas where improvement needed.

4.4 Lime Analysis

LIME helps elucidate a predictive result for a model in a consistent and understandable manner [10]. We employed LIME to improve the interpretability of model's predictions, particularly those categorized as "black box" algorithms. Rather than explaining the model as a whole, it describes the predictions made by the model for a particular case. The interpretable model's coefficients or rules serve as the foundation for LIME's explanation. This explanation helps understand which features are important in making of the decision.

5 Result and Analysis

5.1 Model Performance

In this study, we use 9 different machine learning models such as K-nearest neighbors, Gradient Boosting, Adaptive Boosting, XGBoost, Random Forest, Decision Tree, Gaussian Naïve Bayesian, and Linear Discriminant Analysis. We evaluate the performance of these models' using various performance metrics. The performance metrics used for the evaluation in this study includes: Accuracy, Precision, Recall and F1 score. We found that Random Forest performed the best outperforming other models and producing an Accuracy of 99.9 and F1 score of 0.98. The analysis has been performed on the raw data, data after SMOTE analysis and data after PCA. Table 2 shows the results of the raw data.

The low Recall in LR indicates that a notable number of positive instances were not correctly identified by the model. Similar to the Logistic Regression, a low Recall of the XGBoost and LDA suggests that the model was missing a significant number of positive instances. Precision, F1 score, Recall for both Random Forest and Decision Tree models are high, these models were performing well as compared to another model. Both were highly effective in accurately classifying instances of the positive class while minimizing false positives and false negatives. Gaussian Naïve Bayes appeared proficient

Table 2. Evaluation Result of Testing set

Model	Accuracy	Precision	Recall	F1 Score
R F	99.9	0.99	0.97	0.98
DT	99.7	0.96	0.97	0.96
KNN	98.7	0.85	0.74	0.79
AdaBoost	97.2	0.75	0.25	0.38
G B	97.4	0.92	0.26	0..41
XGBoost	96.9	0.73	0.12	0.21
GNB	40.0	0.04	0.76	0.07
LDA	96.7	0.53	0.14	0.22
LR	96.9	0.80	0.12	0.20

in identifying positive instances, the low Precision and F1 score indicated a high rate of false positives. High Precision of AdaBoost and GB indicated that they perform well in terms of correctly classifying instances, especially the positive one. However these model struggle with positive classes as they have very low Recall. The Precision and Recall of the KNN is relatively high. This model was effective at both identifying positive instances and minimizing false positives.

The bar graph of the train and test set accuracy of the different ML models are shown in Fig. 3. It shows that the balance between train and test set of accuracy. It ensure that models is learning the underlying patterns in the data rather than memorizing specific examples.

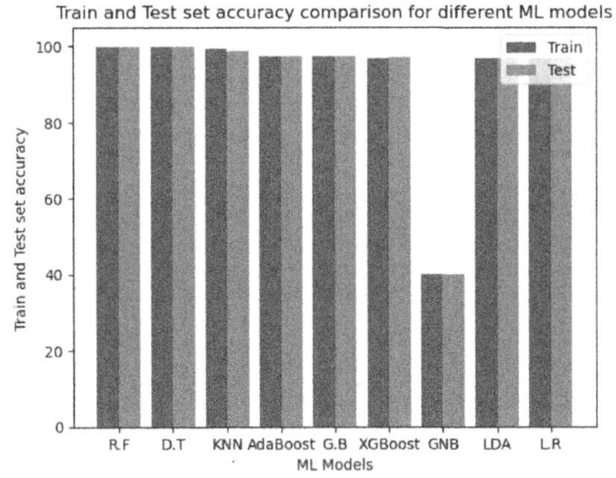

Fig. 3. Train and Test accuracy of all the model

Table 3 shows the result of the evaluation metrics of the models after applying SMOTE algorithm to the dataset.

Table 3. Evaluation Result after SMOTE

Model	Accuracy	Precision	Recall	F1score
RF	99.9	0.99	0.98	0.99
DT	99.7	0.96	0.97	0.96
KNN	97.8	0.62	0.90	0.73
AdaBoost	89.5	0.20	0.70	0.31
GB	90.5	0.21	0.67	0.32
XGBoost	81.0	0.09	0.57	0.17
GNB	15.6	0.03	0.93	0.06
LDA	73.9	0.06	0.52	0.11
LR	83.7	0.11	0.54	0.18

There hadn't been much difference in the performance of KNN, RF, DT models as they gave almost similar results even after applying the SMOTE algorithm. SMOTE addressed the issue of low Recall in AdaBoost, GB, XGBoost, LR, LDA model but led to a trade-off, resulting in lower Precision and a moderate enhancement in overall model performance. Applying SMOTE, Accuracy of GNB is reduced which indicates the decrease in overall prediction.

Table 4 shows the result of the evaluation metrics of the models after applying Principal Component Analysis.

Table 4. Evaluation result after PCA

Model	Accuracy	Precision	Recall	F1 Score
RF	99.6	0.99	0.90	0.94
DT	99.4	0.92	0.90	0.91
KNN	98.5	0.83	0.72	0.77
AdaBoost	99.4	0.92	0.90	0.91
GB	97.3	0.92	0.24	0.38
XGBoost	96.7	0.60	0.10	0.18
GNB	96.2	0.39	0.18	0.25
LDA	96.7	0.53	0.14	0.22
LR	96.9	0.77	0.11	0.19

After applying PCA, the overall performance of the AdaBoost has been improved. The Accuracy, Precision, Recall and F1 score have all shown positive changes that indicate this model is making better predictions after reducing the dimensionality of the data. The Accuracy and Precision of the GNB has been improved after applying PCA that indicates the model was now making overall correct predictions and has a reduced false positive rate. The Precision of XGBoost is reduced which indicates a high rate of false positives. LDA, LR, RF, DT, KNN yielded almost the same result even after applying PCA. After applying PCA the RF, DT, and AdaBoost exhibited superior performance compared to other models.

The Figs. 4 (a) and (b) show the bar graph of the accuracy and F1 score of the all the model. In these figs, compare the accuracy and F1 score of the model without applying SMOTE and PCA and after applying SMOTE and after PCA. It shows that after applying SMOTE the accuracy was reduced and it didn't affect much the accuracy after PCA. For GNB model after applying PCA, it shows better accuracy but F1 score was still low. F1 score of the AdaBoost increases after applying PCA.

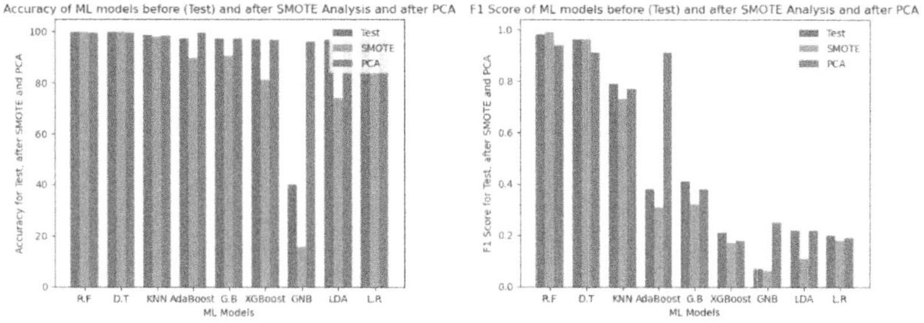

(a) **(b)**

Fig. 4. Comparative analysis of the performance of various models. Graph of: (a) Accuracy, and (b) F1 score of all the models.

5.2 LIME Analysis

Lime Analysis provides an effective means of comprehending how a machine learning model creates its predictions.

The Lime result, which is shown in Fig. 5, is essential for understanding how features contribute to HDD failure (1) and not failure (0) classes and for making inferences about the model's analysis.

LIME Analysis conducted for Random Forest as it performs better than other models. The blue line represented the probability of HDD which aren't failed (0) and orange line represented the probability of HDD which are failed (1). The blue line for the majority of the data points is significantly higher than the orange line, the model was confident for predicting the HDD which aren't failed.

The features which were important for the prediction of HDD failure are smart_192_raw, smart_189_raw, smart_7_raw, smart_242_raw, smart_4_raw, smart_189_normalized, smart_3_normalized, smart_190_raw, smart_12_raw, smart_183_raw. These features were contributed more for the class 1 which predict HDD failure.

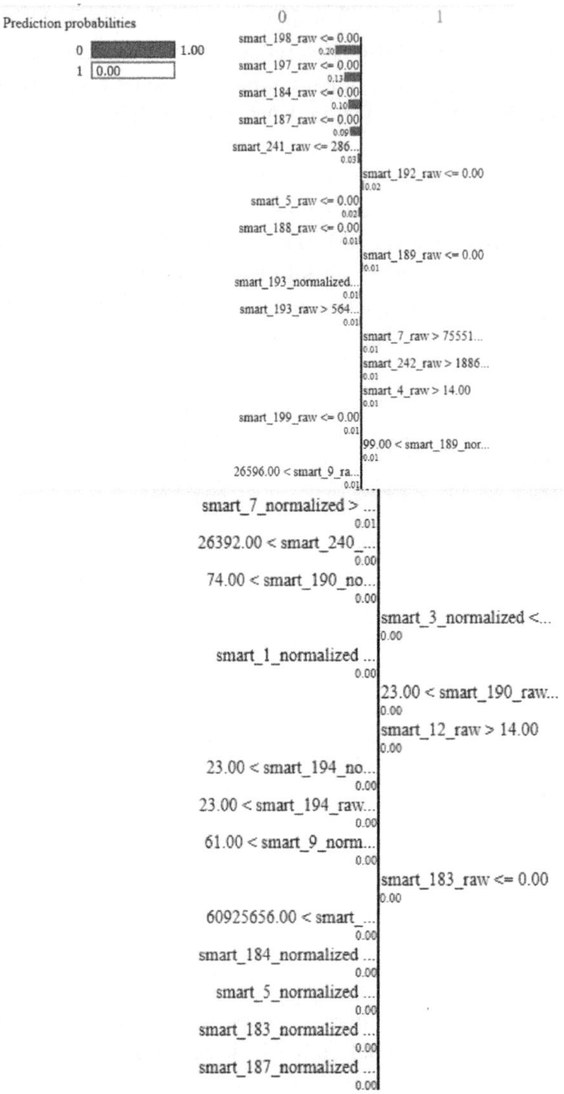

Fig. 5. LIME Analysis of Random Forest

6 Conclusion and Future Works

In conclusion, our exploration into HDD failure prediction showed the effectiveness of several models, with Random Forest outperforming the other 8 model that were taken into consideration. To address the issue of class imbalance we used SMOTE algorithm. We noticed that SMOTE enhanced Recall by effectively capturing instances of HDD failures but reduced the Accuracy and Precision of the models.

After applying Principal Component Analysis (PCA) along with the AdaBoost model, we saw a noticeable boost in predictive Accuracy. Reducing the number of features through PCA seemed to help the AdaBoost model better understand and predict patterns in the data. LIME Analysis is conducted for the Random Forest to understand how features contributed to HDD failure and not failure classes.

Our suggested machine learning (ML) method, which combines SMOTE, PCA, and LIME to forecast Hard Disk Drive (HDD) failures, has fascinating potential applications in the future. Advanced feature engineering is one such research topic where the incorporation and detection of extra metrics pertaining to environmental conditions, workload patterns, or disk health could improve the predicted accuracy of the model. By integrating knowledge from several models, exploring ensemble approaches and boosting techniques may also improve the HDD failure prediction system's overall robustness.

Acknowledgement. We would like to thank Amrita School of Computing Bengaluru for providing the facilities and resources that allowed this project to be completed. We acknowledge that we used ChatGPT to paraphrase some sentences in this article.

References

1. Cahyadi, Forshaw, M.: Hard disk failure prediction on highly imbalanced data using LSTM network. In: 2021 IEEE International Conference on Big Data (Big Data), Orlando, FL, USA, pp. 3985–3991 (2021). https://doi.org/10.1109/BigData52589.2021.9671555
2. Sobhana, M., Sai Preethi, G.S., Sujitha, K.B., Sri, G.H.: Genetic Algorithm for feature selection in enhancing the hard disk failure prediction using artificial neural network. In: 2022 International Conference on Industry 4.0 Technology (I4Tech), Pune, India, pp. 1–7 (2022). https://doi.org/10.1109/I4Tech55392.2022.9952743
3. Züfle, M., Erhard, F., Kounev, S.: Machine learning model update strategies for hard disk drive failure prediction. In: 2021 20th IEEE International Conference on Machine Learning and Applications (ICMLA), Pasadena, CA, USA, pp. 1379–1386 (2021). https://doi.org/10.1109/ICMLA52953.2021.00223
4. Wang, H., Zhuge, Q., Sha, E.H.M., Xu, R., Song, Y.: Optimizing efficiency of machine learning based hard disk failure prediction by two-layer classification-based feature selection. Appl. Sci. **13**(13), 7544 (2023)
5. Zhang, S., Hai, Q., Wu, W., Han, G.: Hard disk drives failure prediction using the deep learning method based on attention mechanism. In: 2023 5th International Conference on Electronics and Communication, Network and Computer Technology (ECNCT), Guangzhou, China, pp. 133–137 (2023). https://doi.org/10.1109/ECNCT59757.2023.10281160
6. Miller, Z., Medaiyese, O., Ravi, M., Beatty, A., Lin, F.: Hard disk drive failure analysis and prediction: an industry view. In: 2023 53rd Annual IEEE/IFIP International Conference on Dependable Systems and Networks - Supplemental Volume (DSN-S), Porto, Portugal, pp. 21–27 (2023). https://doi.org/10.1109/DSN-S58398.2023.00020
7. Shen, J., Wan, J., Lim, S., J., Yu, L.: Random-forest-based failure prediction for hard disk drives. Int. J. Distrib. Sens. Netw. **14**(11) (2018). https://doi.org/10.1177/1550147718806480
8. Jaswanth, K., Nikhil, M.T., Siddhartha, M.S.S., Jayan, S.: Comparative analysis of COVID detection using chest X-rays by SVM-PCA and deep learning techniques. In: 2023 International Conference on Advances in Electronics, Communication, Computing and Intelligent Information Systems (ICAECIS), Bangalore, India, pp. 188–193 (2023). https://doi.org/10.1109/ICAECIS58353.2023.10170655

9. Kuriakose, S.M., Pati, P.B., Singh, T.: Prediction of diabetes using machine learning: analysis of 70,000 clinical database patient record. In: 2022 13th International Conference on Computing Communication and Networking Technologies (ICCCNT), Kharagpur, India, pp. 1–5 (2022). https://doi.org/10.1109/ICCCNT54827.2022.9984264
10. Yaramalla, D., Singh, T.: A machine learning paradigm for explanatory cases with CKD. In: 2021 12th International Conference on Computing Communication and Networking Technologies (ICCCNT), Kharagpur, India, pp. 1–7 (2021). https://doi.org/10.1109/ICCCNT51525.2021.9580112
11. Ganguly, T., Pati, P.B., Deepa, K., Singh, T., Özer, T.: Machine learning based comparative analysis of cervical cancer risk classifications algorithms. In: 2023 International Conference on Advances in Computing, Communication and Applied Informatics (ACCAI), Chennai, India, pp. 1–7 (2023). https://doi.org/10.1109/ACCAI58221.2023.10200617
12. Varunram, T.N., Shivaprasad, M.B., Aishwarya, K.H., Balraj, A., Savish, S.V., Ullas, S.: Analysis of different dimensionality reduction techniques and machine learning algorithms for an intrusion detection system. In: 2021 IEEE 6th International Conference on Computing, Communication and Automation (ICCCA), Arad, Romania, pp. 237–242 (2021). https://doi.org/10.1109/ICCCA52192.2021.9666265
13. Backblaze. https://www.backblaze.com/cloud-storage/resources/hard-drive-test-data. Accessed 17 Dec 2023
14. Amram, M., Dunn, J., Toledano, J.J., Zhuo, Y.D.: Interpretable predictive maintenance for hard drives. Mach. Learn. Appl. **5**, 100042 (2021). https://doi.org/10.1016/j.mlwa.2021.100042. ISSN 2666-8270

Ethereum Powered Web3 Crowdfunding Platform

S. B. Indra(✉), S. Harshini, and R. Sabitha

Rajalakshmi Engineering College, Chennai, India
{200701087,200701081,sabitha.r}@rajalakshmi.edu.in

Abstract. A project or endeavor can raise money by using a technique called crowdfunding, which involves asking a large number of people to make small donations. Centralized applications, expensive taxes, a lack of transparency, and security vulnerabilities are the platform's current drawbacks. Blockchain is utilized to get around these constraints. This distributed database serves as a public ledger, of all completed transactions and digital events that are shared amongst involved parties. Smart contract technology is another benefit of blockchain. This platform allows users to generate funds for projects or other purposes by providing proper documentation supporting their identity. By confirming that the documents are legitimate for voting and funding, authorized individuals can donate money to the various initiatives they support. Smart contracts will forward monies gathered to the appropriate fundraisers if the majority of donors approve. When their limit is reached, they will be able to access their money using a smart contract. The blockchain keeps track of every transaction. The platform will be safer and more transparent with the use of these smart contracts. Better than the conventional apps, this offers consumers access to a fully functional and safe crowdfunding online application platform.

Keywords: Crowdfunding · Blockchain · Smart Contracts · Decentralized · Ethereum

1 Introduction

One major obstacle for young people who want to start their businesses and want to implement their ideas through a company plan is money. The difficulties associated with traditional fundraising, particularly the absence of a track record of financing coupled with inadequate collateral and stringent bank financial rules, provide a serious obstacle for young entrepreneurs seeking to finance their ventures. Crowdfunding is getting tiny donations from a large number of individuals, usually online, to collect money for a project, business, or idea. Crowdfunding websites are a useful tool for individuals, artists, and entrepreneurs to raise money and publicize their initiatives. Written explanations, images, and videos are frequently included in these presentations. In return for their financial contributions, contributors might get project credits like items, early access to a product, or access to VIP material. Due to its ability to bypass traditional gatekeepers and

Published by Springer Nature Switzerland AG 2025
A. Chandrabose et al. (Eds.): ICCCSP 2024, IFIP AICT 723, pp. 339–353, 2025.
https://doi.org/10.1007/978-3-031-73617-9_27

help people realize their ideas, crowdsourcing has supplanted more traditional forms of money like bank loans or venture capital for many. Blockchain is a distributed transaction record database that is vetted and kept up to date by an international computer network. The records are overseen by a broad community rather than a single central authority like a bank, and no one person has power over them. Additionally, no one can go back and alter or remove a transaction history. The information cannot be changed in a traditional centralized database because of the distributed structure of blockchain and peer-confirmed guarantees. A minimum donation is not required on blockchain-based crowdfunding platforms. Without worrying about hitting any minimum requirements, contributors can give as much money as they like to campaigns. For people who want to invest in a project or support a cause, this kind of system offers more accessibility and flexibility. The potential to contribute in any amount can encourage a more diverse group of people to engage in the crowdsourcing process, thereby expanding its scope and influence. To solve security-related problems and aid in the prevention of fraud, this project intends to employ Ethereum smart contracts on a crowdfunding site. This website aims to boost confidence in the crowdfunding procedure. Blockchain technology offers investors' money a high degree of protection by enabling real-time tracking and monitoring of transactions. Furthermore, it might draw in additional investors to fund a range of projects given its capacity to permit two approved deals while maintaining their integrity.

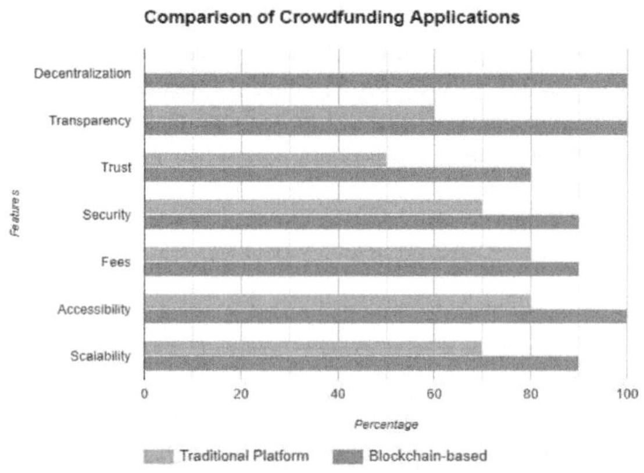

Fig. 1. Comparison bar graph

Figure 1 depicts the comparison of the crowdfunding application with using blockchain and without using blockchain. It compares the features like security, transparency, fees, trust, etc.

Smart Contract

Smart contracts consist of executable code separated by conditions. The conditions are automatically verified, and if they meet particular criteria, the code is performed and posted on the blockchain, which is a distributed, decentralized blockchain network.

Because every smart contract has a unique blockchain address, any user can invoke a function by including the function's hash code in the contract. They eliminate the necessity for an intermediary or central authority to carry out safe transactions involving numerous parties.

Solidity

Solidity is a contract-oriented programming language used to create smart contracts. Solidity is a high-level programming language.It is used for developing Smart Contracts. Smart contracts in the Ethereum state are programs that control account behavior. It was constructed with consideration for the Ethereum Virtual Machine, drawing inspiration from Python, C++, and JavaScript (EVM). Solidity is statically typed, enabling a variety of features including libraries, complex user-defined types, and inheritance.It is possible to design contracts with features like voting, multi-signature wallets, crowdsourcing, and blind auctions thanks to Solidity.

Ethereum

Ethereum is a decentralized blockchain platform that allows anybody to create and manage decentralized applications. A request to have this machine do any computation can also be published by any participant. Other members of the network examine, validate, and perform (or "execute") the computation when a request such as this is broadcast. The execution of this process modifies the EVM's state, which is then committed and spread across the network. Transactions and the current state are recorded on the blockchain, which is subsequently acknowledged and approved by all nodes. Transaction requests are calculation requests. Cryptographic protocols guarantee the integrity of transactions once they are verified as authentic and added to the blockchain.

Ether

The aim of the cryptocurrency Ether is to create a market for computing power. Crypto market participants receive rewards for processing and confirming transaction requests as well as for contributing resources to network computing. The reward will go to the person who finishes the tasks of validating the transaction, executing it, committing it to the blockchain, and disseminating it to the network. The amount of ether paid is correlated with the computation's completion time.

2 Literature Survey

The purpose of the system is to demonstrate a crowdfunding system that aids fundraisers in raising cash and donors in making donations by the deadline. Fundraisers will ultimately pick up the money after all approval requirements have been satisfied, ensuring that all transaction processes are safe and transparent.

[1] This study aims to enhance blockchain payment security by developing a new class of payment assaults known as unfair payment attacks (UP). Three techniques were developed to address this problem: the checkF procedure, the genTX procedure, and the detection of UP. The webpage provides a straightforward, beginner-friendly user interface. A user-interaction/UX website, Smart contract management code written in

Solidity. An ABI (Application Binary Interface) file is produced by the smart contract during compilation. Understanding the smart contract's interface, such as being able to identify a method and its input parameters, is necessary for any external application that wants to interact with a smart contract on the blockchain. All of this information is therefore contained in an ABI file. For the application, the ABI file, which is in JSON format, must be retrieved.

[2] The purpose of the system is to establish a network between investors and investors to make an arrangement that is more resilient to fraud. This network is constructed using Ethereum Contracts. Ethereum contracts are intelligent agreements that take automatic action upon meeting specific criteria. On the blockchain, it is built. This network withholds the investors' donations; the funds are not instantly sent to the investor's bank account. To transfer funds from the contract to a different address, the investor needs to submit a spending request to the smart contract. All of the backers have been informed about this spending request. Spending requests are approved if the majority of backers deem them to be legitimate. If not, the request is denied, the investor is notified to modify it, or else his request will not be approved and no funds will be taken out for the project. Money can be exchanged instantaneously between countries using blockchain. Payment processing times for blockchain-based payment systems can be cut from days to hours due to their exceptional efficiency.

[3] A decentralized platform for fundraising is to be created as part of the proposed effort. Next.js was used for the system's front end, while Tailwind CSS was used to style the entire website. Thanks to the site, people and groups may start crowdfunding campaigns and receive donations in cryptocurrency. By utilizing blockchain technology, all transactions would be guaranteed to be safe, and transparent, and to use the money raised for the intended purpose. The site also has a smart contract capability that, when specific fundraising targets are reached, would transfer money to the campaign creator. The Ethereum development environment was called Hardhat, and Solidity was utilized to build the smart contracts. With each transaction, the blockchain's difficulty increases and records of all transactions are kept, contributing to the creation of a resilient system. The Ethereum development environment controls system security overall. There is also a system in place that restricts the usage of donated funds to requests approved by a predetermined percentage of donors.

[4] A solidity-based Ethereum smart contract is a cryptographic box that stores data, processes inputs, publishes outputs, and is only accessible to the outside world under certain predefined conditions. It is written in a special language. In reality, Ethereum makes it simple to put these smart contracts into action and provides developers with online solidity code generators. The way smart contracts are constructed ensures that the total amount contributed by contributors will be retained securely and that neither tampering nor theft will occur. The money will be stored in the smart contract itself rather than being sent to the campaign creator directly.

[5] Using campaign data from Kickstarter and Indiegogo for three-dimensional printers and smartwatches, the system uses prediction models to show off the methodologies and pinpoint important variables. Each campaign's developers use text, numbers, videos, and tables to describe the project and product on the CFPs. With a long history, researchers have discovered a complete collection of important success variables for

new product development (NPD) projects. For each of the six subcategories, Real, Win, and Worth, the system created a total of 26 comprehensive questions that address 26 potential influencing elements for effective crowdfunding. The campaign descriptions on the CFPs can be read using the 26 guiding questions to determine if there is complete, partial, or no evidence of any of these 26 RWW elements. The rating procedure using the improved 26 questions was successful, as evidenced by the weighted Kappa ratio of 80% that was later obtained.

[6] It is reported that less than 50% of these crowdfunding campaigns are successful, which is defined as successful campaigns that meet their funding targets - GOFUNDME. Several studies indicate that facial expressions, textual and image features, and other factors may influence the success of crowdsourcing by the dataset as of November 19, 2019, totaling 10,974 crowdfunding campaigns worldwide. In addition, dynamic features like the quantity of shares, donors, and followers are included. Demographic, evaluation of image quality, and the count of faces on the cover photo, Age, Ischild, beauty, smile, and gender. The fundraisers with ratios (ratio = money raised/goal amount) higher than 2.5 are eliminated. 0 to 0.5 ratio fundraisers are classified as "highly unsuccessful (−2)"; 0.5 to 1 ratios are classified as "unsuccessful (−1)"; 1 to 1. 25 ratios are classified as "successful (+1)"; 1.25 to 2.5 ratios are classified as "highly successful (+2)".

[7] The aim of the research was to investigate the potential impact of intrinsic versus extrinsic motivational strategies and the timing of rewards on crowdfunding success. The system found that projects with private ownership get funded more highly than those with short-term use. The model has identified when this occurs and what incentive categories work better at drawing contributions. Identifying these trends, the system provides entrepreneurs with advice on how best to arrange their financing requests. Put more simply, they create several situations for campaigns that use crowdsourcing.

[8] The objective is to increase global campaign contributions. By giving donors discretion over how much Ethereum they spend and making it possible for artists to get funding. An Ethereum-based smart contract can be used by users to launch a campaign for tamper-proof tracking. The campaign name, description, target amount, minimum donation, and picture URL are required fields. To launch a campaign, the creator must use MetaMask to connect their Ethereum wallet. The campaign contribution page shows the following important information: fund status, creator wallet address, minimum contribution, campaign details, and contributors. To take part, contributors need to connect MetaMask to their Ethereum wallet. Money is sent to the campaign address for fraud prevention and efficiency. Other users can request withdrawals with their Ethereum wallet addresses and legitimate reasons for needing money for the same purpose. Reviewing requests, approvers determine whether to grant or reject them based on the information supplied. Only with the unanimous approval of approvers can funds be withdrawn, guaranteeing openness and preventing fraud.

[9] This system's recommendation is for a decentralized application that runs on the Ethereum blockchain. All campaign, contribution, withdrawal, and financial data will be kept on a decentralized, public blockchain network. This implies that the data is recorded and visible at each blockchain node rather than being stored in a single, centralized server location. The research reveals that young people who aspire to become entrepreneurs know very little about CF, but they do recognize some of its characteristics, like using

online platforms to fund projects and having a large number of backers who contribute modest amounts of money. It encompasses can be difficult for prospective entrepreneurs, especially when it comes to investment models like equity and loan CF. Although the non-profit sector is more relevant, prospective business owners feel that both types of businesses need to follow the CF philosophy.

3 Proposed Model

The intended system's features include making it easier to create and contribute to campaigns transparently and safely. The Ethereum development environment controls system security, which is dictated by keeping track of all transactions and making the blockchain more complex with each one to build a stronger system. The money contributed by contributors will be carefully stored in smart contracts, where it will remain unaltered and untouchable. This is how smart contracts are written. Instead of being delivered to the campaign creator directly, the money will be stored in the smart contract.

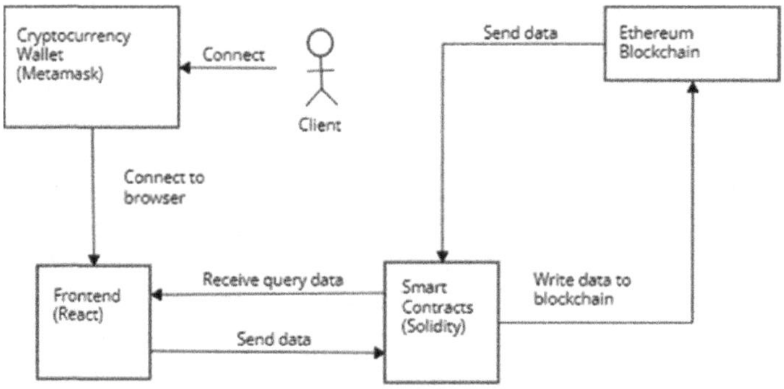

Fig. 2. Data Flow diagram

Figure 2 describes the underlying flow of data starting from wallet registration done with metamask, and how data flows back and forth from the frontend to the Ethereum blockchain.

4 Methodology

The goal of this project is to address security-related problems and aid in fraud prevention by utilizing Ethereum smart contracts on a crowdfunding platform. The other goal of this platform is to raise confidence in the crowdsourcing procedure. Blockchain enables real-time transaction tracking and monitoring, including a high degree of financial security for investors.

User Authentication: All website visitors, regardless of their role as creators or contributors, must go through this process to verify that only reliable people may access the system. MetaMask, a third-party Bitcoin wallet service, assists with the authentication process. MetaMask furnishes users with accounts that enable them to access the system. This account's user-friendly design assists users with all cryptocurrency-related transactions.

Create Campaign: Anyone may launch a campaign in a couple of minutes, much like crowdfunding on other platforms and in the real world. The Ethereum-based smart contract will be in charge of the campaign data, preventing any tampering. For a creator to launch a campaign, he needs to have a clear vision of what he wants to create and how his offering would benefit the platform's investors. The creator of the campaign cannot expect it to be successful if he is not confident in his offering. There's a strong possibility his campaign will be financed if he's completed his proposal, is aware of when his deliverables are due, has the means to construct the product, and has conducted some market research. The goal of any campaign is to provide its creators as much freedom as possible when it comes to the deadline for generating funds. A campaign needs to contain a name, the author's name, a description, a cover image. He also has to give his Ethereum wallet address to get the money, should his campaign be successful.

Campaign Contribution: Campaigns can be shared by users, and contributions can be made to them by anybody with a MetaMask wallet. The money will be paid to the campaign's address, making this strategy more anti-fraudulent and effective.

Withdrawal of Funds: To remove a certain quantity of ether from the fund that has been raised thus far for their campaign, a vendor must first make a withdrawal request. The approval of this proposal needs to come from a minimum of 51% of the campaign's total backers. The vendor must wait for the remaining backers to vote if the 51% voting requirement is not satisfied before they may withdraw the money. Through the campaign creator dashboard, he can acquire a roster of all investors for every campaign, in addition to details regarding their financial and temporal contributions. If the campaign is successful, he can access the funds on the same dashboard.

The novelty of the proposed solution is the reward-based donations for the donors. That is the donors benefited from each donation. Coins can be incremented for each donation for the donors. Also, the donors will get a notification when a new project is added by the fundraisers.

Figure 3 depicts the step-by-step process involved in the overall system like how the fundraiser and donor contribute to the system and how funds get approved and withdrawal happens.

5 Evaluation Techniques

Technical Viability: It will be an application that runs on ReactJS and is compatible with all web browsers. You'll need access to the internet. To sign transactions, users must have the metamask browser extension installed.

Social Feasibility: Over the years, crowdsourcing has benefited many, but it has also been associated with significant fraud. It seeks to increase confidence among contributors to support all causes by bringing openness to the crowdfunding process.

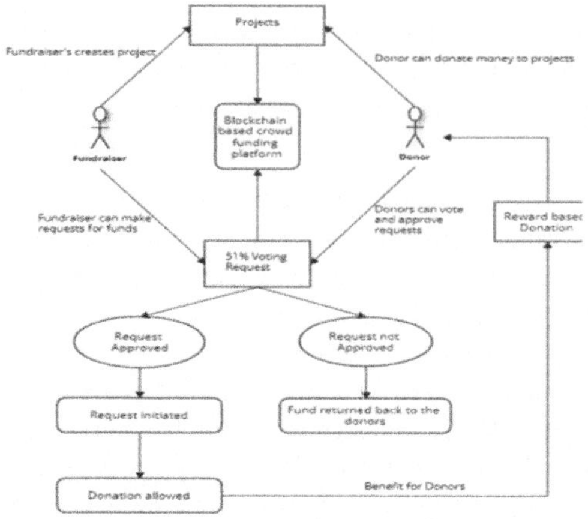

Fig. 3. System Flow Diagram

Economic Feasibility: The majority of the security measures are provided by the Ethereum Blockchain, therefore developing it won't cost much. The cost of the deployed application's server would be the sole expense.

Scope: It is wanted to use crowdfunding to make the process safe, transparent, and devoid of fraud.

6 Results and Discussion

(See Figs. 4, 5, 6, 7, 8, 9, 10, 11, 12, 13 and 14).

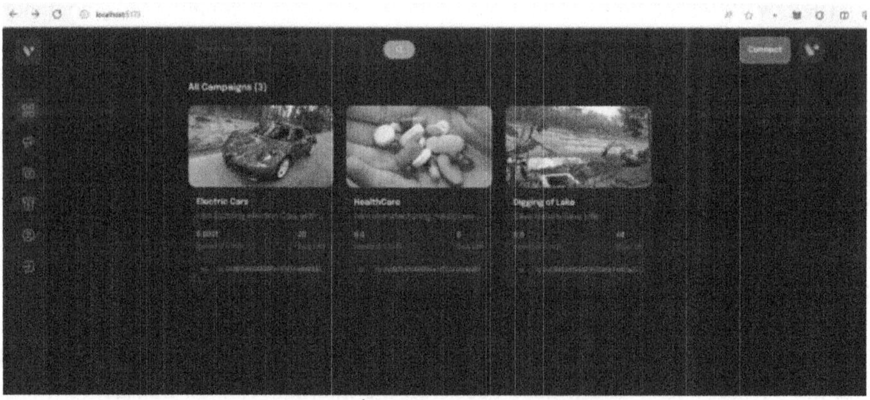

Fig. 4. Dashboard to show all Campaigns.

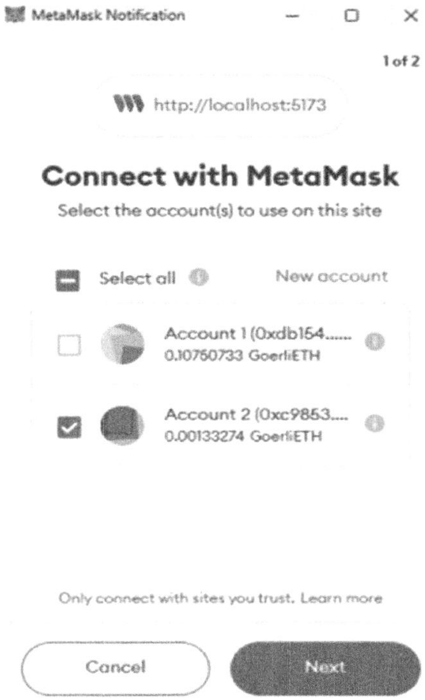

Fig. 5. Connection request with metamask Wallet.

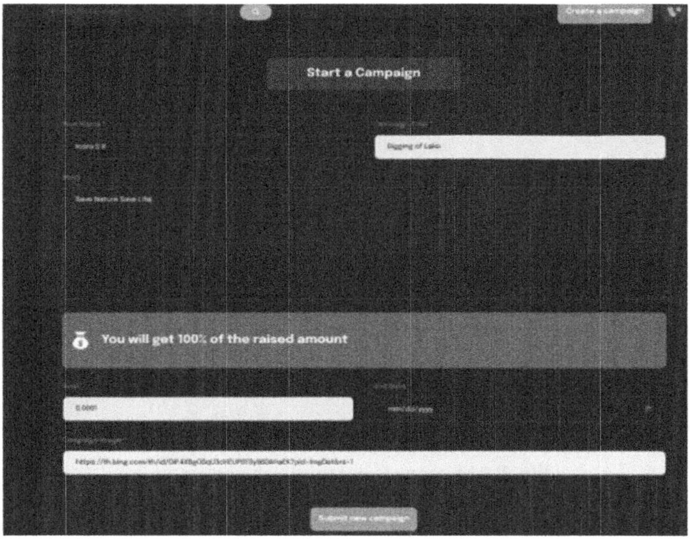

Fig. 6. Create a new Campaign.

Fig. 7. Metamask request for creating Campaign.

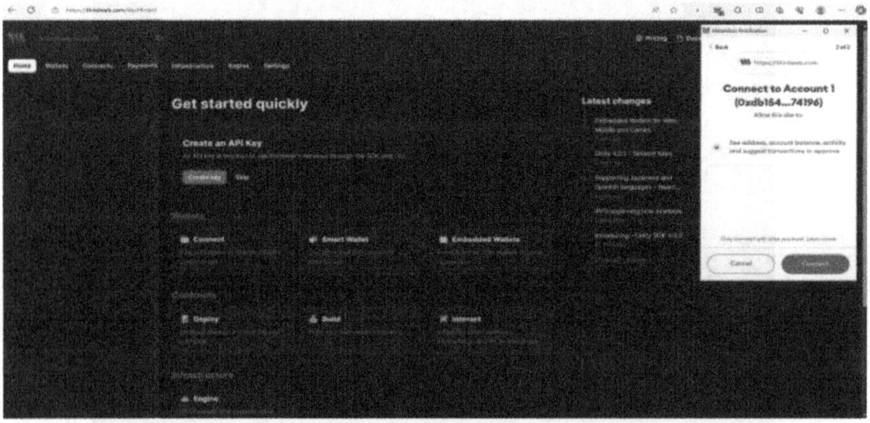

Fig. 8. Metamask and thirdweb connection.

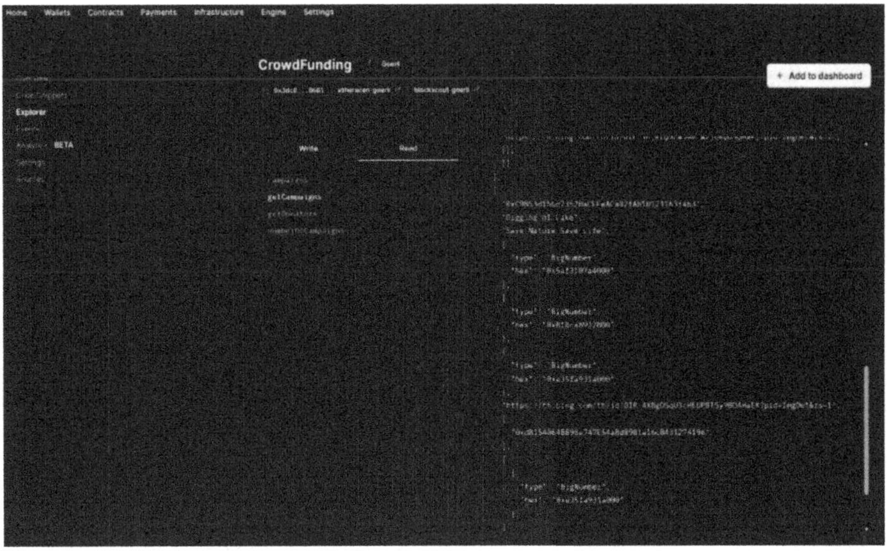

Fig. 9. Campaign Details stored in blockchain.

Fig. 10. Profile Page to show the created Campaigns on that particular account.

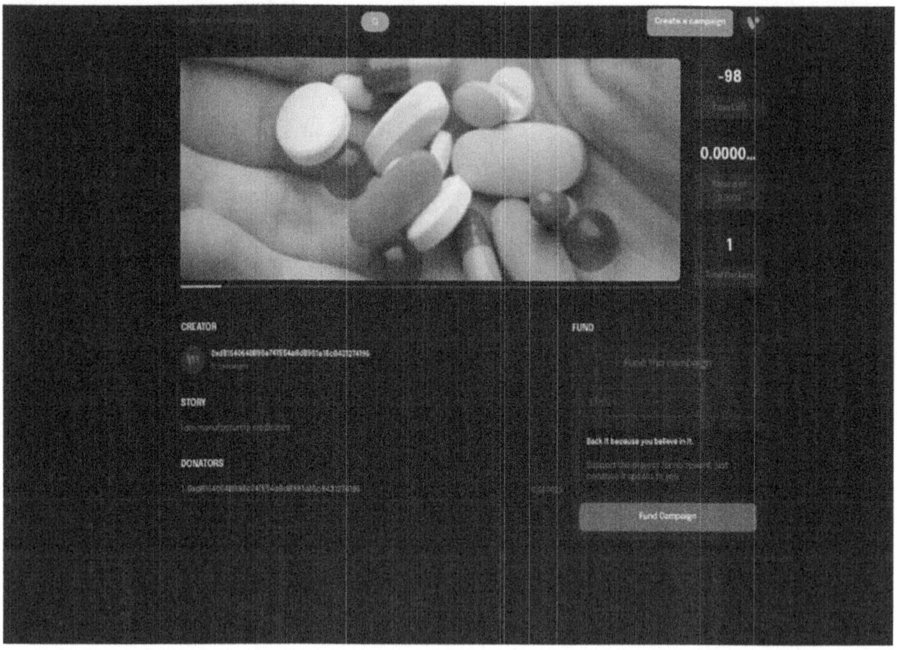

Fig. 11. Campaigns details that can be viewed by the donor.

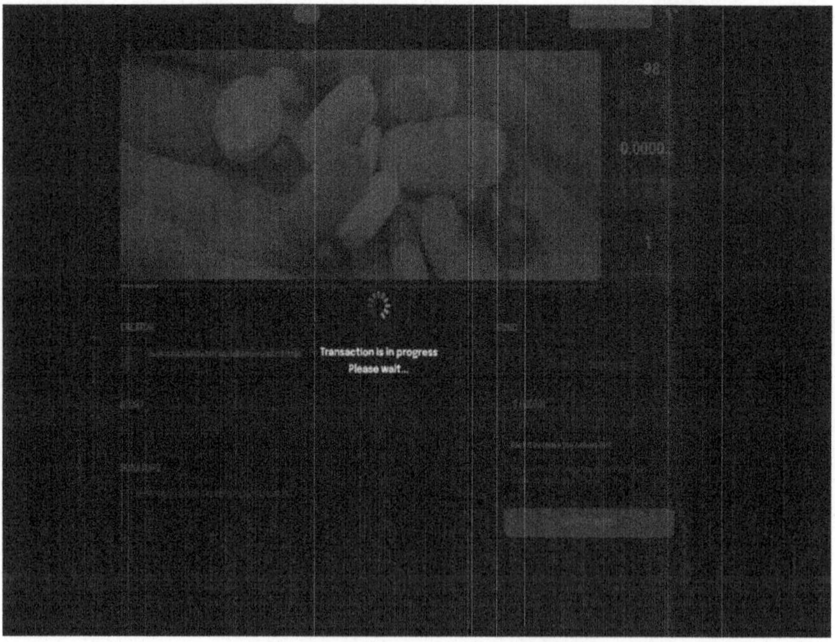

Fig. 12. Donation process- loading page

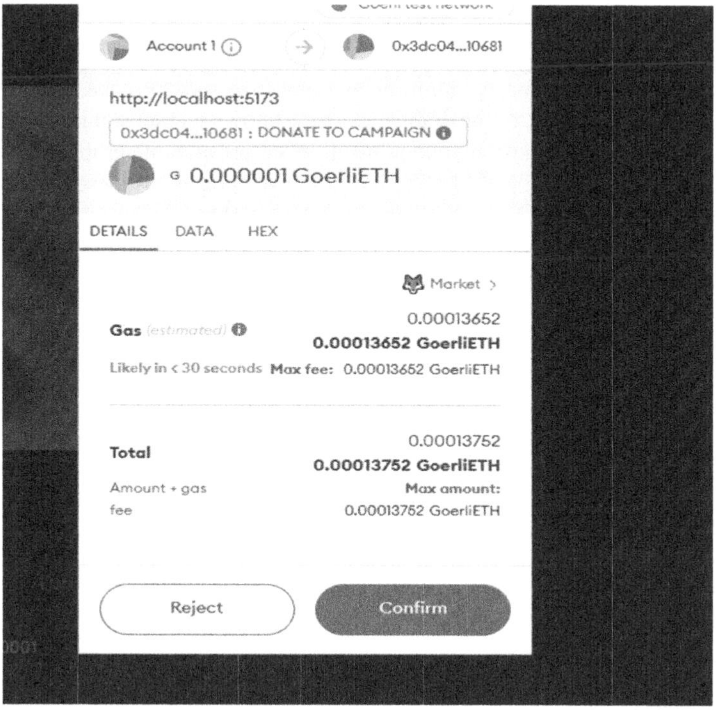

Fig. 13. Metamask confirmation page.

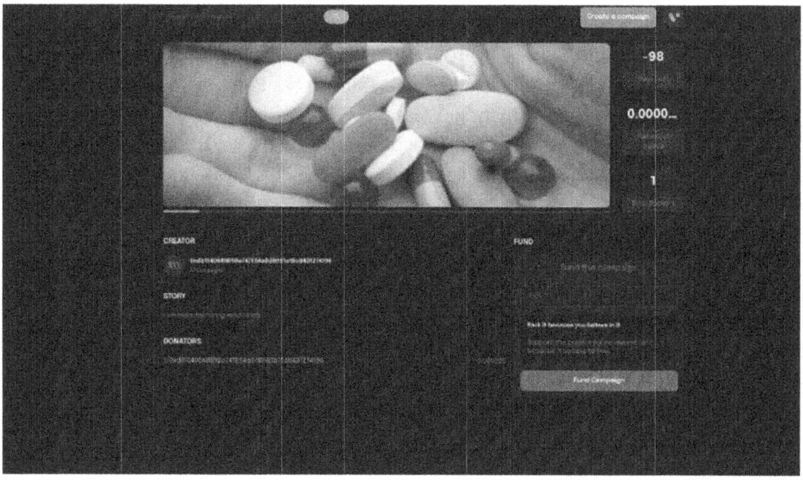

Fig. 14. Made donations will be visible in the page.

7 Conclusion and Future Work

Crowdfunding, which connects entrepreneurs and investors to make tiny investments through an online platform, is one of the most well-known methods of raising money for any project, cause, or to assist anyone in need. It is a preventable problem, and there is a practical remedy in place with this technology that can address these persistent problems. Blockchain provides users with an easy, dependable, and secure way to conduct transactions. A Solidity compiler was used to put together the Solidity code that was written for the campaign contract. Bytecode is generated by the Solidity compiler and is utilized for the deployment of the interface onto the Ethereum network through Metamask. Fundraisers can generate money for projects, and donors can contribute a specified amount to initiatives. These are enabled functionalities. Subsequently, the 51% criteria will be used to determine the approval. If the project is authorized, the fundraisers will withdraw the funds; if not, the funds will be returned to the contributors. It automates the procedure and does away with the need for an intermediary. Future updates for this may include features like an approval rating that offers more details about the campaign raiser after it gains traction.

References

1. Dheeraj, S., Mahesh, B., Rajput, N.K., Joshi, N.S., Vasudevan, V.: A large scale medical crowdfunding platform using smart contracts in blockchain. In: 2022 IEEE North Karnataka Subsection Flagship International Conference (NKCon). https://doi.org/10.1109/NICon56289.2022.10126720
2. Kumar, K., Vashist, R., Vashist, P.C.: A trustful payment system for crowdfunding using blockchain. In: 2023 International Conference on Artificial Intelligence and Smart Communication (AISC). https://doi.org/10.1109/AISC56616.2023.1008564
3. Vhatkar, H.V., Singh, H.G., Sonavane, A.S., Singh, S., Pulgam, N.: Crowdfunding using blockchain. In: 2023 11th International Conference on Emerging Trends in Engineering & Technology - Signal and Information Processing (ICETET - SIP). https://doi.org/10.1109/ICETET-SIP58143.2023.1015161
4. Jhanji, G., Tyagi, V., Gaur, A., Sharma, Y.: Development of a crowdfunding application powered by ethereum blockchain. Iconic Res. Eng. J.|IRE J. **6**(9), 1704204 (2023). ISSN 2456-8880
5. Song, C., Luo, J., Hölttä-Otto, K., Seering, W., Otto, K.: Crowdfunding for design innovation: prediction model with critical factors. IEEE Trans. Eng. Manag. **69**(4) (2022)
6. Zhang, X., Lyu, H., Luo, J.: What contributes to a crowdfunding campaign's success? Evidence and analyses from GoFundMe data. J. Soc. Comput. **2**(2), 183−192 (2021). https://doi.org/10.23919/JSC.2021.0010. ISSN 2688-5255 05/06
7. Maiolini, R., Franco, S., Cappa, F., Hayes, D.: Optimizing reward-based crowdfunding. IEEE Eng. Manag. Rev. **51**(2) (2023). https://doi.org/10.1109/EMR.2023.3243148
8. Senthamil Selvi, R., Surya Prakash, R., Vishnu, C., Priyadarshan, A.S., Prasanna Venkateswara, D.B.: Crowdfunding platform using blockchain technology. Int. J. Innov. Res. Technol. IJIRT **9**(1), 155716 (2022). ISSN 2349-6002
9. Dubey, A.K., Shingte, S.C., Siddiqui, M.S., Patil, S.: Crowdfunding using Blockchain for Startups and Investors. In: 2023 7th International Conference on Intelligent Computing and Control Systems (ICICCS) (2023). https://doi.org/10.1109/ICICCS56967.2023.10142310

10. Baliker, C., Baza, M., Alourani, A., Alshehri, A., Alshahrani, H., Choo, K.-K.R.: On the applications of blockchain in FinTech: advancements and opportunities. IEEE Trans. Eng. Manag. (2022)
11. Bogusz, C.I., Laurell, C., Sandström, C.: Tracking the digital evolution of entrepreneurial finance: the interplay between crowdfunding, blockchain technologies, cryptocurrencies, and initial coin offerings. IEEE trans. Eng. Manag. **67**(4) (2020)
12. Appio, F.P., Leone, D., Platania, F., Schiavone, F.: Evaluating the impact of project and operational complexities on the crowdfunding campaigns of new technologies: an empirical investigation. IEEE Trans. Eng. Manag. (2023)

Enhancing Adaptive Data Management Middleware: Techniques for Federated Cloud Environments

Vikas K. Kolekar[1(✉)] and Sachin R. Sakhare[2]

[1] Department of Computer Engineering, SMT. Kashibai Navale College of Engineering, Pune 411041, India
vikaskolekar2008@gmail.com

[2] Department of Computer Engineering, Vishwakarma Institute of Information Technology, Pune 411048, India
sachin.sakhare@viit.ac.in

Abstract. The adaptive data management middleware is crucial for facilitating efficient and dynamic data management in distributed computing environments. Nevertheless, the widespread adoption of federated cloud environments brings about new complexities and difficulties in data administration, requiring inventive methods to improve the functionalities of current middleware systems. This research paper introduces innovative strategies for enhancing adaptive data management middleware that is especially designed for federated cloud environments. The proposed methodology addresses several fundamental components of adaptive data management middleware. Initially, proposed the methods for dynamically provisioning and allocating resources to enhance the efficiency of data processing and storage across federated cloud environments. In addition, provided the strategies for implementing data governance and enforcing security measures to meet regulatory standards and protect confidential information in federated cloud environments. Furthermore, investigated the techniques for duplicating and synchronization data to improve the accessibility and uniformity of data in federated environments. To evaluate the results of the proposed techniques, we conducted comprehensive experimental evaluations using simulated federated cloud infrastructures. The results demonstrate the substantial enhancements in the performance of data management, utilisation of resources, and capacity to scale when compared to existing methods. Lastly discussed the implications of our findings and emphasised potential areas for further investigation in this rapidly evolving domain.

Keywords: Adaptive data management middleware · Cloud Computing · Federated cloud environments · Data interoperability · Dynamic resource allocation

Published by Springer Nature Switzerland AG 2025
A. Chandrabose et al. (Eds.): ICCCSP 2024, IFIP AICT 723, pp. 354–367, 2025.
https://doi.org/10.1007/978-3-031-73617-9_28

1 Introduction

Adaptive data management middleware is essential in the era of distributed computing as it enables effective processing and storing of data in dynamic contexts. Due to the widespread use of cloud computing, organisations now heavily depend on federated cloud environments. These environments involve numerous separate cloud providers working together to deliver integrated services while yet keeping their autonomy. This collaboration is necessary to satisfy the different computing requirements of organisations. Nevertheless, effectively managing data across such environments presents notable difficulties. The proposed research aims to overcome these difficulties by introducing innovative ways to improve the performance of adaptive data management middleware designed particularly for federated cloud environments. Also, the proposed research aims to enhance the current level of federated cloud computing by providing practical answers to complex data management challenges in remote and diverse contexts. It is achieved by combining theoretical insights with practical experiments. Rest of the paper is organised as follows: Sect. 2 provide reviews about the background and related work to adaptive data management middleware, federated cloud environments and presents the identified research gaps. Section 3 presents the data management challenges in federated cloud environments. Section 4 discusses the context-aware adaptive data management middleware. Section 5 describes the proposed methodology for improving the efficiency of adaptive data management middleware in federated cloud environment. Proposed the principles, implementation consideration and potential benefits. Section 6 discusses the experimental evaluation by providing simulation framework parameters. Results of the proposed system are discussed at the end of section. Section 7 provides the conclusion by highlighting the proposed system and obtained results. At the end provided the potential future scope directions for further investigation.

2 Background and Related Work

In federated cloud environments, addressing data management challenges requires innovative techniques for ensuring interoperability, scalability, and security across heterogeneous cloud platforms. Craig A. Lee et al. [1] outlines a comprehensive framework for federated cloud computing, addressing interoperability, security, and governance challenges. It defines key concepts, components, and interfaces to facilitate seamless integration and collaboration across diverse cloud environments. The architecture emphasizes standardization, modularity, and flexibility, providing guidelines for federated cloud deployment, management, and governance. By having a structured approach to cloud federation, the reference architecture provides organizations to leverage the advantages of distributed computing while ensuring interoperability, security, and compliance with regulatory requirements.

M. R. M. Assis et al. [2] discussed the cloud computing paradigm that has reached a plateau due to limitations such as resource contention, service interruption, and data representation issues. To maintain technology continuity, new approaches had implemented, leading to the formation of inter clouds, which focus on small and medium sized cloud providers. Also mentioned the solutions like hybrid clouds, multi-clouds, and cloud federations are essential in academic, scientific, and industrial environments. Authors presented the desired functional and non-functional properties for cloud federations and evaluates these architectures based on their characteristics.

Yuejin Li et al. [3] presented a novel federated cloud/edge framework for distributed AI tasks, addressing issues like multitasking granularity, privacy constraints, and communication latency. Authors has introduced a new framework called federated cloud/edge (FCE) that is used for distributed medical image processing across various hospital sites. The federated cloud architecture is designed to efficiently train several machine learning models by balancing the workload and minimising communication overhead. The system, tested on a multi-cloud platform at the Chinese University of Hong Kong, reduces total AI processing time by 41.3%, achieves high model accuracy at 87%, and can tolerate multiple cloud failures, making it a viable approach for solving massive AI multitasking problems.

Vingi Patrick Nzanzu et al. [4] presented that the resource management in cloud infrastructure is crucial for service quality and includes discovery, selection, allocation, pricing, disaster management, and monitoring. However, managing resources in a secure and scalable manner is challenging, especially in federated cloud environments. The FEDerated Architecture for Resource Management and Monitoring in cloudS Version 1.0 (FEDARGOS-V1) addresses this by providing a cloud resource monitoring architecture for federated cloud infrastructures. The architecture enables early identification of resource constraints and can be deployed in private or public federated cloud infrastructures for faster and more scalable monitoring.

Faeze Ramezani et al. [5] presented a universal paradigm for managing resources in inter-federated environments, with a specific focus on treating federated clouds as a marketplace for resource exchange. The framework encompasses diverse centralised cloud federation models and categorises the life cycle of the federated cloud into discrete time intervals. Additionally, it presents a resource management approach that is compatible with proposed framework.

Benay Kumar Ray et al. [6] presented a multi-objective optimization problem for cloud federation formation, focusing on profit and quality of service (QoS) trade-off. The authors apply Linear Scalarization and (ε)-constraint method to find a pareto-optimal solution. They proposed integer liner program based heuristic-based algorithm for cloud federation formation, which is tested and found to yield an optimized solution to the general problem of profit/QoS trade-off.

Cloud users need to acquire and analyse data from several Cloud Service Providers (CSPs). In order to ensure that all interconnected cloud computing environments tenants, including both users and CSPs, may take advantage of the top-performing CSPs, it was proposed to implement effective resource management. In addition, it is crucial to periodically check cloud resources. Cloud monitoring is a third-party service that acts as an intermediary between clients and CSPs. Authors presented a comprehensive examination of cloud monitoring in the context of interconnected cloud computing environments, with a specific emphasis on its importance and relevance. Various contemporary open-source monitoring systems are examined. Authors in [7] also presented and examined a taxonomy for the management of cloud resources. This taxonomy encompasses resource pricing, resource allocation, resource exploration, resource gathering, and catastrophe management.

Andriy Luntovskyy et al. [8] focused on Smart Office and Smart Home design, examining protocols, platforms, and best practices. They considered factors like price, easy configuration, data security, privacy, energy efficiency, and compatibility with Internet of Things (IoT) and Industrial Internet of Things (IIoT) components. The authors favour open-source and cloud-free solutions for Smart Home and established commercial platforms for Smart Office with advanced security. Blockchaining contributes to the decentralized world of smart devices, but secured smart devices require a combination of crypto-technologies. The authors proposed an intelligent IoT system that collects data from a specific location and transmits it to an Edge device for on-site processing. This reduces maintenance costs by reducing the volume of messages sent to the cloud platform. An algorithm for predicting temperature values in a smart office server room is proposed and implemented using an Long Short-Term Memory (LSTM) model, increasing server equipment reliability through early prediction, warning, and temperature control measures.

The existing literature provides valuable insights into the challenges and opportunities associated with adaptive data management middleware and federated cloud environments, as well as relevant techniques for addressing associated challenges. By building upon and extending prior research efforts, this paper contributes to the advancement of adaptive middleware solutions tailored by techniques for federated cloud environment, offering practical solutions to the complex data management challenges faced by organizations operating in distributed and heterogeneous environments.

3 Challenges in Federated Cloud Environments

In federated cloud environments, data management faces several challenges due to the distributed nature of the infrastructure and the diverse characteristics of the participating cloud platforms. Here are some of the key challenges:

Data Interoperability: Federated cloud environments often encompass numerous cloud providers that employ distinct data formats, schemas, and storage systems. Overcoming the challenge of compatibility across these diverse data sources requires the use of techniques to transform data, align schemas, and resolve semantic discrepancies.

Data Consistency and Integrity: Ensuring data consistency and integrity in a federated cloud environment poses challenges due to the decentralised nature of data storage and the potential for discrepancies or conflicts among many copies of the same data. In order to ensure the reliability and accuracy of data, it is imperative to employ robust synchronisation techniques and distributed transaction management mechanisms.

Data Security and Privacy: The issue of data security and privacy is heightened in a federated cloud environment, particularly when sensitive data is distributed across multiple cloud platforms. In order to ensure the protection, consistency, and confidentiality of data, it is imperative to incorporate robust encryption, access control, and data anonymization technologies.

Data Governance and Compliance: Data governance and compliance encounter challenges in federated cloud settings since data has the potential to traverse many administrative domains with different policies and laws. In order to assure compliance with data governance standards and regulatory requirements, it is imperative to offer tools that enforce regulations, facilitate auditing, and ensure accountability within federated clouds.

Data Movement and Latency: The process of transferring data between cloud platforms that are located in different geographic locations within a federated cloud system can lead to issues with delays and reduced performance. In a federated setting, it is essential to eliminate delays and efficiently handle data by reducing data flow and improving data transfer protocols.

Resource Constraints and Scalability: Federated cloud infrastructures may have constraints on resources and challenges with scalability, particularly when several users utilise resources across federated clouds. In order to attain scalability and efficiently use resources, it is imperative to adopt adaptive resource allocation methods and scheduling strategies that consider the peculiarities of the workload.

Cross-Domain Collaboration and Trust: Federated cloud environments involve the collaboration of multiple administrative domains that have different levels of trust and conventions for cooperation. To enable safe collaboration across different domains, it is crucial to establish trust connections, handle identity federation, and enforce access control policies in federated clouds.

Addressing these challenges requires a holistic approach to data management in federated cloud environments, encompassing technical, organizational, and regulatory considerations. By developing robust data management strategies and leveraging appropriate technologies and standards, organizations can effectively manage and leverage data across federated cloud environments while addressing security, privacy, and compliance requirements [9–15].

4 Adaptive Data Management Middleware Architecture

The adaptive data management middleware functions as a context-aware and precision-aware mediator between cloud users and federated cloud service providers. The middleware, acting as the core element, integrates policies and algorithms that enhance the adaptability of the overall system. The adaptive middleware serves as a versatile coordinator that facilitates seamless communication and collaboration across different layers of the system.

Figure 1 illustrates the functioning of context-aware middleware, which involves the integration of several crucial components. The figure illustrates the extensive collection of data from many sources such as financial institutions, smart homes, technology-driven businesses, and medical devices. Examples of this data include location, time, device type, network capacity, and other relevant information. The adaptive data management middleware architecture plays a vital role in contemporary distributed computing

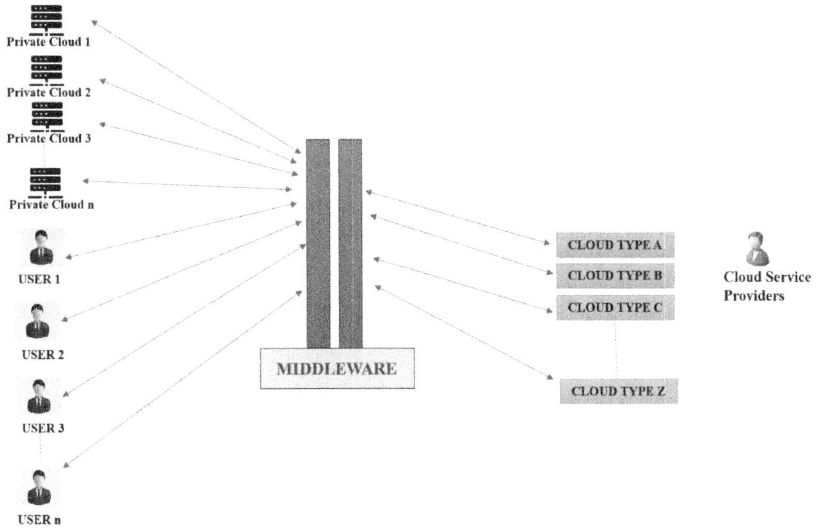

Fig. 1. Proposed overview of cloud users, middleware, and federated cloud service providers [16].

ecosystems by enabling effective and adaptable data management in various and ever-changing situations. This architecture represents a flexible and expandable framework specifically created to efficiently manage data in many scenarios, such as federated cloud environments, edge computing, and IoT ecosystems. The adaptive data management middleware architecture consists of several essential components as data ingestion and integration, data storage and query processing, data governance and security, adaptive resource management, machine learning and analytics, interoperability and integration. The middleware architecture possesses an adaptable character as it can dynamically modify and optimise its components and capabilities in response to changing needs, environmental conditions, and user preferences. The flexibility of the middleware is accomplished by utilising feedback mechanisms, policy-based controls, and autonomic computing concepts. This enables the middleware to constantly monitor, analyse, and adjust its behaviour to meet changing data management requirements.

5 Proposed Techniques for Enhancement

The proposed techniques for enhancing adaptive data management middleware in federated cloud environments are as follows:

5.1 Federated Learning-Based Data Management

Principles: Federated learning is a machine learning approach that allows for training models using data from several sources without the requirement of centralising the data. The fundamental concept is collectively training machine learning models while maintaining the decentralised and confidential nature of the original data. Every node in the cloud platform independently trains the model using its own data and only shares model updates or gradients with a central server. The central server then combines these updates to enhance the global model.

Implementation Considerations: To implement federated learning-based data management, one must integrate federated learning algorithms into the adaptive data management middleware. This involves the creation of communication protocols to exchange model updates across federated nodes, the implementation of federated optimisation algorithms to aggregate model updates, and the guarantee of data privacy and security throughout model training and aggregation.

Potential Benefits

- **Data Privacy:** Federated learning preserves data privacy by keeping sensitive data decentralized and limiting data access to local nodes.
- **Collaborative Learning:** Federated learning enables collaborative model training across distributed data sources, allowing the adaptive middleware to learn from diverse datasets without centralizing data.
- **Scalability:** Federated learning scales well with the number of federated nodes, making it suitable for large-scale federated cloud environments.
- **Adaptability:** By continuously learning from distributed data sources, the adaptive middleware can adapt its data management strategies to changing data distributions and user preferences over time.

5.2 Adaptive Resource Orchestration

Principles: Adaptive resource orchestration refers to the dynamic management and coordination of resources (such as compute, storage, and network) across federated cloud environments to enhance performance, scalability, and resource utilisation. These encompass adaptive allocation of resources, scheduling of workloads, automatic scaling, and strategies for optimising resources.

Implementation Considerations: To implement adaptive resource orchestration, it is necessary to integrate resource management modules into the adaptive data management middleware. This encompasses the creation of algorithms to adaptively allocate resources based on workload characteristics, dynamic workload schedulers to distribute tasks among federated nodes, auto-scaling mechanisms to adjust resource allocations in response to changing demand, and resource optimisation algorithms to enhance resource utilisation and efficiency.

Potential Benefits

- **Performance Optimization:** Adaptive resource orchestration optimizes resource allocation and workload distribution to improve performance and reduce response times in federated cloud environments.

- **Scalability:** By dynamically adjusting resource allocations and scaling policies, adaptive resource orchestration ensures scalability and elasticity, allowing federated clouds to handle varying workloads efficiently.
- **Cost Reduction:** Resource optimization algorithms help minimize resource wastage and reduce infrastructure costs by optimizing resource utilization and efficiency.
- **Fault Tolerance:** Adaptive resource orchestration improves fault tolerance by dynamically shifting workloads and reallocating resources in response to errors or interruptions in federated clouds.

5.3 Secure Data Federation Protocols

Principles: Secure data federation protocols facilitate the secure and efficient exchange and cooperation of data among federated cloud platforms, while guaranteeing the privacy and confidentiality of the data. These protocols employ encryption, access control, and data anonymization processes to protect data during transmission and storage.

Implementation Considerations: Secure data federation protocols involve developing encryption algorithms to safeguard data during transmission and storage, implementing access control systems to enforce specific access policies, and utilising data anonymization techniques to safeguard sensitive information. In addition, by integrating authentication and permission procedures into the adaptive data management middleware, secure access to federated data sources is ensured.

Potential Benefits

- **Data Privacy:** Data federation protocols that are secure preserve data privacy by encrypting data both during transmission and storage, thereby guaranteeing confidentiality and integrity.
- **Compliance:** Secure data federation protocols ensure compliance with regulatory standards by implementing access control policies and data anonymization procedures.
- **Secure Collaboration:** Secure data federation protocols facilitate secure and reliable collaboration between federated cloud platforms, enabling the exchange and sharing of data while reducing the risks of data leakage and unauthorised access.
- **Interoperability:** Secure data federation protocols improve interoperability and compatibility among federated clouds by offering standardised protocols and processes for secure data sharing.

5.4 Dynamic Data Integration and Transformation

Principles: Dynamic data integration and transformation solutions facilitate the seamless retrieval and exchange of data across various cloud platforms in federated contexts. This involves utilising dynamic schema mapping, data transformation, and semantic reconciliation techniques to improve interoperability and facilitate the exchange of data.

Implementation Considerations: The process of establishing dynamic data integration and transformation mechanisms involves developing algorithms for dynamic schema mapping, data transformation, and semantic reconciliation. Subsequently, these mechanisms are incorporated into the adaptive data management middleware. Furthermore, the development of metadata management systems and data catalogues facilitates the identification of data through metadata and the alignment of schemas in interconnected contexts.

Potential Benefits

- **Interoperability:** Dynamic data integration and transformation technologies enhance interoperability and data interchange between diverse cloud platforms, allowing effortless access to federated data sources.
- **Data Consistency:** Dynamic data integration and transformation procedures maintain data consistency and coherence by resolving semantic disparities and resolving data discrepancies across federated clouds.
- **Efficiency:** Dynamic data integration and transformation technologies enhance efficiency and decrease latency in federated data management by minimising data transport and replication overhead.
- **Agility:** Dynamic mechanisms in federated data management promote agility and flexibility by modifying data integration and transformation procedures to accommodate data semantics, schema changes, and system configurations.

5.5 Context-Aware Adaptive Policies

Principles: Context-aware adaptive policies alter data management procedures based on contextual factors such as workload characteristics, user preferences, and system circumstances. The principles enable the adaptive middleware to modify its behaviour and improve performance, scalability, and resource utilisation in federated systems.

Implementation Considerations: The implementation of adaptive policies that are aware of their context requires the development of algorithms that can detect and analyse context, modify policies accordingly, and integrate these operations with the infrastructure responsible for handling adaptive data. Furthermore, the implementation of feedback control circuits and monitoring systems in federated contexts facilitates real-time optimisation and adaptation in response to feedback.

Potential Benefits

- **Performance Optimization:** Context-aware adaptive policies enhance performance and decrease response times in federated environments by optimising data management strategies in accordance with contextual factors.
- **Resource Efficiency:** Context-aware adaptive policies optimise cloud resource utilisation and efficiency through the dynamic adjustment of burden distributions and resource allocations.

- **User Experience:** Federated data management user experience and contentment are enhanced through the implementation of context-aware adaptive policies, which take into account user preferences and application requirements.
- **Adaptability:** Through the continuous monitoring and analysis of contextual information, adaptive policies that are cognizant of context empower the adaptive middleware to modify its behaviour and enhance its performance in accordance with evolving requirements and conditions.

Table 1. Summary of techniques for federated cloud environments

Name of Technique	Description
Federated Learning	Training a collaborative model using data from several sources, while ensuring the privacy and security of the data. Applicable in the fields of healthcare, finance, and IoT
Federated Data Integration	Effortless retrieval and sharing of information across different cloud platforms, enabling data-focused decision-making and analysis
Adaptive Resource Allocation	The resource allocations and scaling rules are adjusted dynamically depending on the workload characteristics and system circumstances, resulting in improved scalability and efficiency
Dynamic Security Protocols	The security measures are modified depending on contextual elements, such as the sensitivity of the data and the degree of danger, in order to improve the capabilities of data protection and threat detection
Federated Resource Orchestration	Efficiently use and optimize resources in dispersed cloud systems via seamless management and coordination
Context-aware adaptive policies	The context-aware policies allows the adaptive middleware to adjust its behavior and enhance performance, scalability, and resource utilization in federated cloud environment

Table 1 presents a brief summary of several methods designed to tackle the difficulties inherent in federated cloud environments, such as data integration, resource management, security, and resource orchestration. These novel approaches collectively enhance the capabilities of adaptive data management middleware in federated cloud systems by addressing the complex challenges of data management while ensuring scalability, security, and performance. Organizations may efficiently manage and use data across distant cloud platforms by using federated learning, adaptive resource orchestration, secure data federation protocols, dynamic data integration, and context-aware adaptive policies. This approach supports a wide range of applications and workloads in federated environment.

6 Experimental Evaluation

Utilized CloudSim, a widely-used cloud computing simulation framework, to construct a virtualized environment that emulates federated cloud environment. CloudSim was configured to simulate the deployment of various cloud nodes across different geographic areas, replicating real-world federated cloud setups. In the configuration, number of cloudlets taken are 20, number of data centers are 5, number of data center broker is 1 and each data center has 2 virtual machines (VM) so in total 10 VMs. This simulation is performed on heterogeneous cloudlets. Where the Cloud service providers are assigned with of the varying length of the cloudlets. Created artificial datasets using CloudSim's data generating features and imported datasets from external sources.

The approach involves generating simulated data and workload patterns to accurately replicate real-world data management scenarios in federated cloud environment. Developed data management middleware that adapts to changing conditions by implementing the suggested strategies using the java programming language. Implemented the integration of the middleware with CloudSim to replicate data management processes and assess performance. Subsequently, the tests were devised using CloudSim to assess both the context-awareness and performance of the suggested strategies. By establishing specific performance indicators and assessment criteria, we can accurately measure the effectiveness and impact of strategies used for data management in federated cloud systems. The experimental findings are also verified by doing analysis inside CloudSim. The results have been generated in terms of response time, cloudlet length, datacenter, and virtual machine id (Fig. 2).

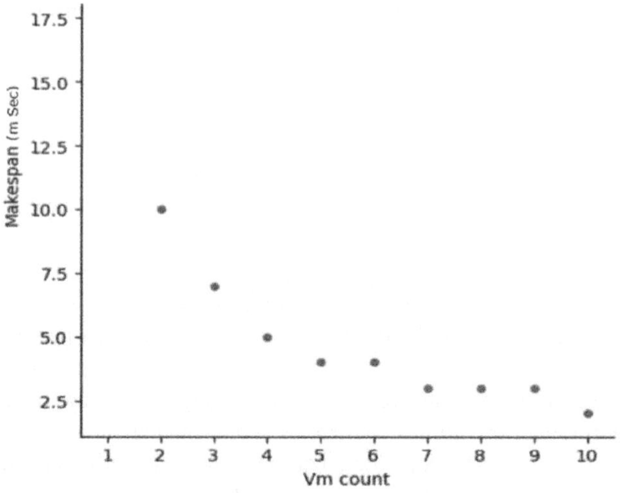

Fig. 2. Relationship between VM count and makespan time (in m sec).

This graph describes the makespan time. It is the total time taken to process a set of jobs for its complete execution. Minimization of makespan can be done by assigning the set of jobs to set of VMs (Fig. 3).

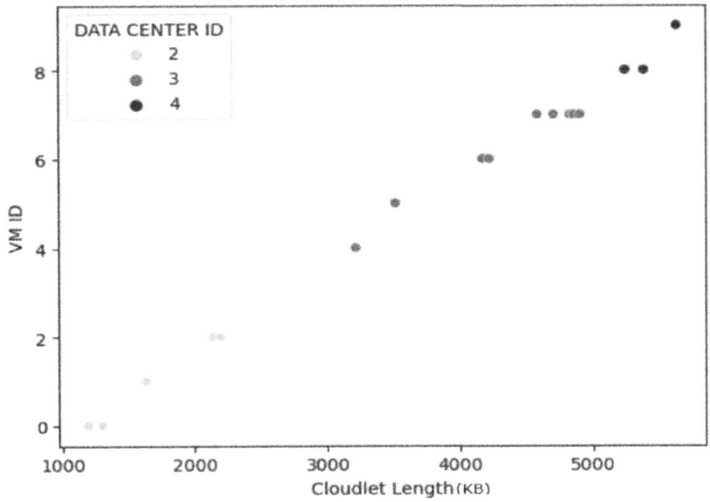

Fig. 3. Relationship between cloudlet length, vm id and data center id.

This graphs shows the linear relationship between the size of the cloudlet and the datacenter. As the aggregation is based on the size. It shows the data of certain size is submitted to the particular data center.

7 Conclusion

The research paper presented a comprehensive evaluation of adaptive data management middleware techniques for federated cloud environments. The proposed system provided a data adaptive middleware that enhances dependability and minimises the need for manual intervention, such as service level agreements, terms, and conditions. The techniques for inclusion of dynamic data placement and the examination of a wide range of characteristics has enhanced the efficiency and modernise the conventional methods of cloud systems. Results demonstrate the effectiveness and potential benefits of the proposed techniques in addressing the challenges of data management, scalability, security, and performance in federated environments. Potential future investigations may explored into refined federated learning methodologies, sophisticated resource orchestration algorithms, and cutting-edge security protocols to boost data administration in federated clouds. In future, it will be fascinating to get the results of federation with realtime and live cloud service providers. Moreover, the integration of current trending technologies like edge computing, blockchain etc. on federated cloud environment will be interesting to investigate.

References

1. Lee, C.A., et al.: The NIST Cloud Federation Reference Architecture. NIST Special Publication 500-32, February 2020. https://doi.org/10.6028/NIST.SP.500-332

2. Assis, M.R.M., Bittencourt, L.F.: A survey on cloud federation architectures: Identifying functional and non-functional properties. J. Netw. Comput. Appl. **72** (2016). https://doi.org/10.1016/j.jnca.2016.06.014
3. Li, Y., Hwang, K., Shuai, K., Li, Z., Zomaya, A.: Federated clouds for efficient multitasking in distributed artificial intelligence applications. IEEE Trans. Cloud Comput. **11**(2), 2084–2095 (2023). https://doi.org/10.1109/TCC.2022.3184157
4. Nzanzu, V.P., et al.: FEDARGOS-V1: a monitoring architecture for federated cloud computing infrastructures. IEEE Access **10**, 133557–133573 (2022). https://doi.org/10.1109/ACCESS.2022.3231622
5. Ramezani, F., Abrishami, S., Feizi, M.: A market-based framework for resource management in cloud federation. J. Grid Comput. **21** (2022). https://doi.org/10.1007/s10723-022-09635-w
6. Ray, B., Saha, A., Khatua, S., Roy, S.: Toward maximization of profit and quality of cloud federation: solution to cloud federation formation problem. J. Supercomput. **75** (2019). https://doi.org/10.1007/s11227-018-2620-2
7. Nzanzu, V.P., et al.: Monitoring and resource management taxonomy in interconnected cloud infrastructures: a survey. TELKOMNIKA (Telecommun. Comput. Electron. Control) **20**, 279 (2022). https://doi.org/10.12928/telkomnika.v20i2.20503
8. Luntovskyy, A., Beshley, M., Guetter, D., Beshley, H.: Technologies and solutions for smart home and smart office. In: van Gulijk, C., Zaitseva, E., Kvassay, M. (eds.) Reliability Engineering and Computational Intelligence for Complex Systems. SSDC, vol. 496, pp. 189–225. Springer, Cham (2023). https://doi.org/10.1007/978-3-031-40997-4_13
9. Shamim, R., Farhaoui, Y.: Enhancing cloud-based machine learning models with federated learning techniques. In: Farhaoui, Y., Hussain, A., Saba, T., Taherdoost, H., Verma, A. (eds.) ICAISE 2023. LNNS, vol. 838, pp. 594–606. Springer, Cham (2024). https://doi.org/10.1007/978-3-031-48573-2_85
10. Somasundaram, P.: Enhancing security in multi-cloud environments through federated access control. Int. J. Comput. Eng. Technol. **14**, 90–96 (2023). https://doi.org/10.17605/OSF.IO/7BMPA
11. AlAnsary, S.A., Latif, R., Saba, T.: Multi factor authentication as a service (MFAaaS) for federated cloud environments. In: Daimi, K., Al Sadoon, A. (eds) ICR 2023. LNNS, vol. 721, pp. 225–236. Springer, Cham (2023). https://doi.org/10.1007/978-3-031-35308-6_19
12. Petrovska, I., Kuchuk, H.: Adaptive resource allocation method for data processing and security in cloud environment. Adv. Inf. Syst. **7**, 67–73 (2023). https://doi.org/10.20998/2522-9052.2023.3.10
13. Saxena, R., Dubey, S., Kumar, U.: A novel approach for service selection and ranking in federated cloud. In: Garg, L., et al. (eds.) ISMS 2022. LNNS, vol. 671, pp. 129–142. Springer, Cham (2023). https://doi.org/10.1007/978-3-031-31153-6_12
14. Souki, O., Djemaa, R., Amous, I., Sedes, F.: A survey of middlewares for self-adaptation and context-aware in Cloud of Things environment. Proc. Comput. Sci. **207**, 2804–2813 (2022). https://doi.org/10.1016/j.procs.2022.09.338
15. Danish, S., Zhang, K., Jacobsen, H.A.: BlockAM: An Adaptive Middleware for Intelligent Data Storage Selection for Internet of Things (2020). https://doi.org/10.1109/DAPPS49028.2020.00007
16. Kolekar, V.K., Sakhare, S.R.: A research perspective on data management techniques for federated cloud environment. IJRITCC **11**(5), 338–346 (2023)
17. Rathi, S.R., Kolekar, V.K.: Trust model for computing security of cloud. In: 2018 Fourth International Conference on Computing Communication Control and Automation (ICCUBEA), Pune, India, pp. 1–5 (2018). https://doi.org/10.1109/ICCUBEA.2018.8697881
18. Kolekar, V.K., Sakhare, S.R.: Scheduling algorithms of cloud computing: state of the art. IJNGC **12**(2), 145–157 (2021)

19. Kolekar, V.K., Vaidya, M.B.: Click and session based—Captcha as graphical password authentication schemes for smart phone and web. In: 2015 International Conference on Information Processing (ICIP), Pune, pp. 669–674 (2015). https://doi.org/10.1109/INFOP.2015.7489467
20. Sakhare, N., Verma, D., Kolekar, V., Shelke, A., Dixit, A., Meshram, N.: E-commerce product price monitoring and comparison using sentiment analysis. IJRITCC **11**(5), 404–411 (2023)
21. Kolekar, V.K., Oswal, M., Wankhade, Y., Shirke, G., Sondur, A., Wable, P.: Smart city IoT data management with proactive middleware. IJRITCC **11**(5s), 319–329 (2023)

SDG 11 Sustainable Cities and Communities

DestiNexus: Probabilistic Framework for Weather- Informed Travel Itinerary Optimization

R. Ranjeeth Kumar(✉), S. S. M. Mahudoom Naina, and V. Muthulakshmi

Department of Information Technology, St. Joseph's College of Engineering, Chennai, TamilNadu, India
ranjeethkumar0909@gmail.com, mahudoomn@gmail.com, computercoordinator@stjosephs.ac.in

Abstract. DestiNexus is revolutionizing travel planning by utilizing a combination of advanced models to provide comprehensive and accurate recommendations. These include the cutting-edge RandomForestRegressor model for precise weather predictions, a RandomForestClassifier for accurate binary rain prediction, and an ARIMA model for effective time-series forecasting. The integration of ReactJS Front End and Backend Server allows for seamless collaboration and personalized suggestions based on factors such as location, date, and time. With a multi-model approach, DestiNexus not only offers specific predictions but also utilizes probabilistic modeling to provide users with valuable prediction intervals. Combining the power of machine learning, probabilistic techniques, and user-friendly design, DestiNexus offers a dynamic and immersive travel planning experience. Rigorous evaluation metrics, including Mean Squared Error and classification accuracy, underscore the reliability of its predictions. In essence, DestiNexus sets a new paradigm in travel planning, catering to a more nuanced and informed exploration of the world.

Keywords: Probabilistic modeling · RandomForestRegressor · RandomForestClassifier · ARIMA model · Multi-model approach · Prediction intervals

1 Introduction

In the ever-changing world of travel technology, where progress is constant, there is an increasing demand for a smooth and individualized travel experience. This has sparked the creation of DestiNexus. This advanced travel planning app goes beyond traditional limits, thanks to its innovative use of machine learning, probabilistic modelling, and client-focused design. With DestiNexus, the definition of intelligent travel planning is being redefined. DestiNexus utilizes not just one, but three cutting-edge models to elevate the accuracy and breadth of its travel suggestions. The dependable and well known RandomForestRegressor model, known for its precise weather forecasts, joins forces

Published by Springer Nature Switzerland AG 2025
A. Chandrabose et al. (Eds.): ICCCSP 2024, IFIP AICT 723, pp. 371–385, 2025.
https://doi.org/10.1007/978-3-031-73617-9_29

with the RandomForestClassifier, introducing a rain pre-diction feature to the platform. Additionally, to capture changes over time and further enhance its forecasting abilities, DestiNexus integrates an ARIMA model, expanding its repertoire to include time-series forecasting. The powerful combination of ReactJS for the Front End and the Backend Server is crucial in creating a seamless connection between user inputs and data processing. Our users enjoy a wide range of customization options, such as being able to specify their location and travel date, as well as taking into consideration the timing of their journeys. This results in a sophisticated and dynamic travel itinerary that effortlessly incorporates weather considerations. What truly distinguishes DestiNexus is its unwavering dedication to providing more than just surface-level fore-casts. Through groundbreaking probabilistic modelling, the application goes beyond simply providing point predictions and instead offers comprehensive insights into potential weather patterns. This inclusion of prediction intervals adds crucial context to weather forecasts, empowering users to make informed decisions about their upcoming travels. With DestiNexus, travellers can feel confident in their journey planning, as they are equipped with a holistic view of weather fluctuations. "Embark on a captivating adventure as we delve into the intricate details of DestiNexus.

This journey not only showcases the impressive technological capabilities of its models but also delves into the practical implications for travellers. With a perfect blend of precision, adaptability, and user-centricity, DestiNexus redefines travel experiences. Through meticulous evaluation metrics such as Mean Squared Error and classification accuracy, DestiNexus proves to be more than just a travel app – it's a trustworthy companion for exploring a world where intelligent planning meets the ever-changing realm of travel. Welcome to the future of travel planning with DestiNexus."

2 Related Works

Numerical Prediction in Weather Forecasting- Recently, there has been a significant rise in the use of machine learning techniques to forecast numerical visibility. Among these methods, regression algorithms like Support Vector Ma-chines and logistic regression have been widely utilized [1]. Moreover, neural network approaches such as Deep Neural Networks and Risk Neural Networks have shown promising results, particularly in forecasting low visibility situations. In addition to these, there have been investigations into utilizing Bayesian-based probabilistic models and Long-Short Term Memory algorithms for this purpose as well. Multimodal Fusion for Improved Predictions - [2]. The concept of multimodal fusion, which involves merging data from various sources, has proven to be advantageous in a wide range of fields [3]. By incorporating a diverse range of data, such as natural elements and human be-haviour, the predictive accuracy has been greatly improved [4]. In particular, satellite imagery has been instrumental in providing crucial multimodal data for tasks such as identifying vegetation and tracking climatic disasters.

Probabilistic Modelling in Weather Prediction - The use of probabilistic modelling has become an essential component in the field of weather forecasting [5]. By introducing prediction intervals and methods for quantifying uncertainty, the decision-making process is greatly im-proved. There is a clear shift towards incorporating Bayesian methods in visibility prediction models, as well as the integration of Risk Neural Network models, further emphasizing the importance of probabilistic elements in numerical weather prediction. Optimization Studies in Weather Prediction Models - Researchers have delved into optimization techniques to enhance the performance of numerical weather prediction models [6]. They have made code modifications and improved I/O libraries to boost the efficiency of high-performance computing applications. In order to optimize I/O performance, genetic algorithms have been utilized [8]. Additionally, automated tuning solutions have been implemented, incorporating machine learning algorithms like random forests. Machine Learning Techniques in Numerical Weather Prediction - [7]. Machine learning techniques, specifically RandomForestRegressor models, have played a crucial role in maximizing the effectiveness of numerical weather prediction models.

Researchers have delved into adapting I/O library codes and fine-tuning various parameters to enhance overall performance [9]. Moreover, the application of black-box optimization methods has yielded promising results in fine-tuning I/O accelerators. DestiNexus: Weather-Informed Travel Itinerary Optimization - [10]. The innovative DestiNexus project presents a cutting-edge probabilistic framework for optimizing travel itineraries with weather information [11]. By incorporating machine learning, specifically the RandomForestRegressor model, it seamlessly integrates with a user-friendly Re-act.js front end and a backend server [12]. What sets DestiNexus apart is its incorporation of probability, which includes prediction intervals, to provide personalized and knowledgeable travel suggestions [Abstract] [13]. This exciting project's incorporation of machine learning, probabilistic modeling, and user-centric design positions it as a notable advancement in intelligent travel planning applications [Introduction]. Evaluation Metrics for DestiNexus - [14]. The effectiveness of DestiNexus is proven through meticulous evaluation using various metrics, such as Mean Squared Error (MSE).

This metric highlights the RandomForestRegres-sor model's ability to accurately capture uncertainties and provide precise predictions [Abstract]. Future Directions and Significance - [15]. DestiNexus paves the way for revolutionary developments in weather-based travel technology. Through its utilization of probabilistic modelling, it not only drives the field forward but also sets a precedent for robust and user-centric applications [16]. The effortless synergy between technology and user agency positions DestiNexus as a game-changing breakthrough in optimizing travel itineraries.

3 Optimization Framework

One of the key elements influenced by a number of factors is travel planning. These factors can include certain events such as festivals, seasonal conditions, etc., as well as uncertainties like local weather and climate factors. Probabilistic models are used to overcome these uncertainties.

3.1 Probabilistic Models

Probabilistic models are versatile mathematical frameworks that incorporate the natural unpredictability and variability of real-world phenomena into their predictions and descriptions. In contrast to deterministic models, which offer precise outcomes, probabilistic models explicitly account for and measure the inherent uncertainty in underlying processes. This makes them especially useful in tackling intricate systems or scenarios where the end result can be affected by a multitude of unanticipated elements. In a probabilistic framework, rather than providing a singular prediction, the model presents a range of possible outcomes through a probability distribution. This distribution conveys the likelihood of different scenarios, empowering decision-makers to not only comprehend the most probable result but also the spectrum of potential outcomes and associated uncertainties. Such models have widespread use in fields such as machine learning, statistics, weather forecasting, finance, and decision analysis, playing a pivotal role in informed decision-making where uncertainty is a critical factor. By offering a more comprehensive and authentic representation of the intricacies of the real world, probabilistic models are essential for navigating complex situations.

3.2 Probabilistic Prediction Intervals

Although point predictions are beneficial, it is essential to comprehend the uncertainty involved with these predictions in order to make well-informed decisions. To tackle this issue, we implemented a bootstrapping approach to incorporate probabilistic prediction intervals. By generating numerous predictions for each data point, we were able to calculate percentiles and assemble intervals. For each prediction yi in the test set, the model generates a set of n bootstrap predictions $\{y_{i1}, y_{i2}, \ldots.., y_{in}\}$. The prediction interval is calculated as follows:

$$\boldsymbol{Predicion\ Interval_i} = [\boldsymbol{Percentile(yi)}, \boldsymbol{Prercentile\{y_{in}\}}]. \quad (1)$$

where:

yi = Individual Predictions
n = Number of Bootstrap Predictions

Percentile function, denoted as $Percentile(x, p)$, returns the p-th percentile of the data x. This approach guarantees that users not only receive a single forecasted value, but also obtain understanding about the potential range of outcomes.

Feature Selection
DestiNexus takes into account some key meteorological factors, including minimum temperature (mintempC), humidity, and wind speed (windspeedKmph). These elements were carefully selected due to their notable impact on weather precipitation patterns and their consistent inclusion in past records.

3.3 Model Selection and Evaluation

RandomForestRegressor
In order to fully comprehend the intricate connections between the selected features and their effect on weather conditions, we made the deliberate choice to utilize the RandomForestRegressor model. This particular model is known for its ability to handle

non-linear relationships and detect subtle patterns within the data. Selecting a regression-based approach was a strategic decision, as it is best suited for the continuous nature of weather parameters and allows for accurate point forecasting. RandomForestRegressor is a dynamic machine learning algorithm expertly crafted for tackling regression tasks. Part of the esteemed ensemble methods family, it harnesses the power of multiple individual models to achieve enhanced overall performance and resilience. Specifically engineered as an extension of the Random Forest algorithm, RandomForestRegressor is tailored to excel in handling regression problems. During the training phase, the algorithm constructs a diverse collection of decision trees. Each decision tree functions independently, generating predictions, and the ultimate output is derived through an averaging or voting process, depending on the specific task at hand. By averaging the predictions from each of its individual decision trees, the RandomForestRegressor arrives at its ultimate prediction. This method guarantees a thorough and precise forecast.

In order to evaluate the effectiveness of the RandomForestRegressor model, we utilized the Mean Squared Error (MSE) as our metric of choice. This powerful tool allows us to gauge the average squared deviation between predicted and observed values, providing us with a quantitative assessment. A lower MSE signifies a more precise model, showcasing the accuracy of our individual predictions. *MSE* measures the average squared difference between predicted and actual values in the test set.

$$\boldsymbol{MSE} = \frac{1}{\boldsymbol{n}} \sum_{i=1}^{n} (y_i - \hat{y}_i)^2 \tag{2}$$

where:

y_i = actual value
$\hat{y}_i$ = predicted value

RandomForestClassifier

The Random Forest Classifier is a powerful ensemble learning approach that goes beyond the capabilities of a single decision tree. During training, it builds multiple decision trees and takes the majority vote of the tree outputs, resulting in accurate classifications. This method not only boosts accuracy, but also ensures the model's adaptability to new data. The algorithm relies on two key principles: individual tree construction and group aggregation. By only using a portion of the data and randomly selecting features, each tree is unique, reducing the risk of overfitting and improving the overall generalization of the model. The decision tree evaluates different features at each node, making splits based on information gain or Gini impurity, and finally assigns a class label to the leaf nodes.

When using DestiNexus, the Random Forest Classifier effectively analyses past weather data such as minimum temperature, precipitation, and wind speed. Its purpose is to categorize days as "rainy" or not based on pre-established benchmarks. This vital classification aids the travel recommendation engine, empowering users to make well-informed choices when planning their trips. At DestiNexus, our Random Forest Classifier has been expertly designed to enhance your travel planning experience. By utilizing a carefully chosen subset of historical data, incorporating key weather variables and precise ARIMA model forecasts, we have trained our classifier to accurately predict the occurrence of rain on a given day. By expertly adjusting its hyperparameters, we have achieved optimal performance, as demonstrated by our assessment measures, which encompass accuracy, precision, recall, and the area under the ROC curve (Fig. 1 and Table 1).

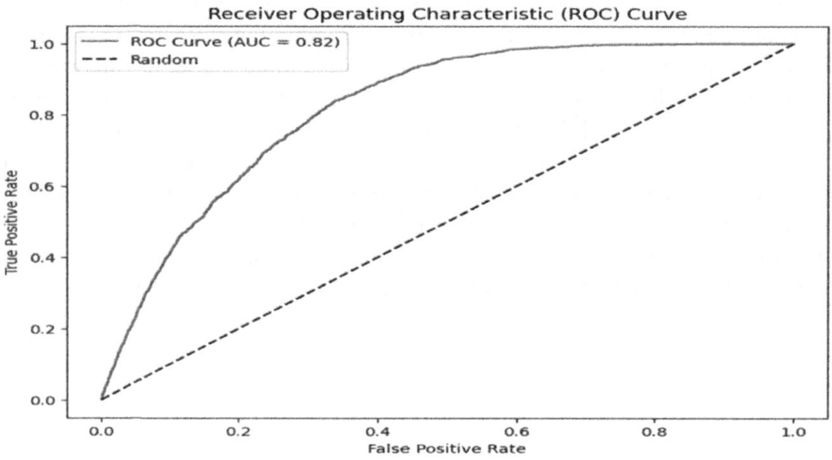

Fig. 1. ROC Curve

Table 1. Classification Report for ROC Curve

	Precision	Recall	F1-Score	Support
0	0.94	1.00	0.97	18042
1	0.00	0.00	0.00	1245
Accuracy			0.94	19287
Macro Avg	0.47	0.50	0.48	19287
Weighted Avg	0.88	0.94	0.90	19287

Accuracy: 94%
ROC AUC: 0.82
Optimal Threshold: 0.051347861712179685

Confusion Matrix:

$$\begin{bmatrix} 18042 & 0 \\ 1245 & 0 \end{bmatrix}$$

Though our classifier provides a binary classification, we have gone the extra mile by also capturing the predicted probability of rain for added transparency. This allows us to convey the level of confidence associated with each prediction, fulfilling our goal of delivering a truly user-centric planning solution.

Entropy is a way to determine how messy or jumbled a set of data is. When it comes to decision trees, it helps gauge how unsure we are about the different categories of data within a specific node. Meanwhile, Information Gain looks at how well a certain attribute can help reduce this uncertainty or chaos. Essentially, it tells us how much insight a feature can provide about the labels of the data. On the other hand, Gini Impurity is another method for measuring data messiness. It calculates the chance of misidentifying an element in the dataset.

1. Entropy (H) and Information Gain (IG)

Entropy:

$$E(S) = -\sum_{i=1}^{c} log_2 p_i \tag{3}$$

Information Gain:

$$IG(S, A) = E(S) - \sum_{v \in A} \frac{|S_v|}{|S|} E(S_v) \tag{4}$$

2. Gini Impurity (G)

Gini Impurity:

$$G(S) = 1 - \sum_{i=1}^{c} p_i^2 \tag{5}$$

3. Random Forest Prediction

Each decision tree in the Random Forest produces a class prediction, and the final prediction in often determined by majority voting.

ARIMA Model

The ARIMA model is a commonly used time series forecasting technique in weather prediction, effectively capturing and predicting temporal patterns and trends in meteorological data. By incorporating autoregression, differencing, and moving averages, ARIMA can accurately model the sequential dependencies and fluctuations inherent in time series data. In order to determine the optimal ARIMA parameters $ARIMA(p, d, q)$, we thoroughly examined the Autocorrelation Function (ACF) and Partial Autocorrelation Function $(PACF)$. The ACF assesses the correlation between a time series and its previous values, while the $PACF$ measures the correlation after removing the influence of intervening values.

An $ARIMA(p, d, q)$ model is represented as:

$$Y_t' = \mu + \phi_1\left(Y_{t-1}^1 - \mu\right) + \ldots + \phi_p\left(Y_{t-p}^1 - \mu\right) + \epsilon_t - \theta_1\epsilon_{t-1} - \ldots - \theta_q\epsilon_{t-q} \tag{6}$$

where:

Y_t' = difference series
μ = mean
ϕ = autoregressive coefficient

θ = moving average coefficient
d = difference order
q = moving average order
ϵ_t = white noise error term

1. Autocorrelation Function (ACF)
   One crucial metric for analyzing time series is ACF, which gauges the relationship between a series and its past observations.
2. Partial Autocorrelation Function (PACF)
   The Partial Autocorrelation Function (PACF) reveals the degree of correlation between a time series and its previous values, without taking into account any intermediate factors (Fig. 2).

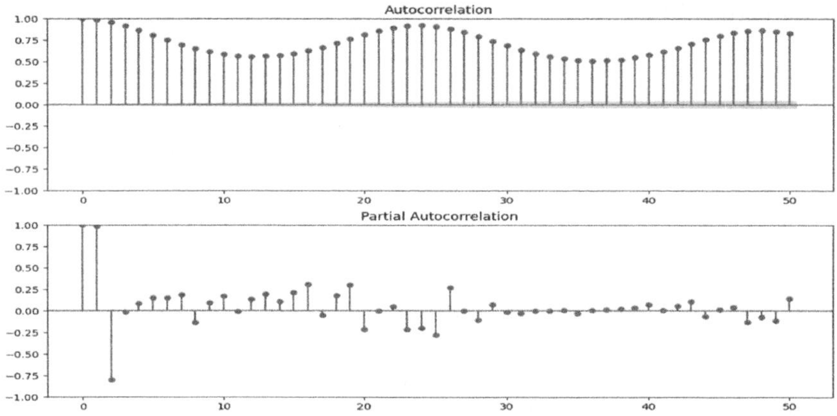

Fig. 2. ACF PACF for Humidity

3. Model Selection Criteria

AIC (Alkaline Information Criterion) and BIC (Bayesian Information Criterion) are often used to compare different ARIMA models. Lower values indicate better-fitting models.

The ARIMA model's performance was assessed through commonly used time series forecasting measurements, such as Mean Squared Error (MSE) and Root Mean Squared Error (RMSE). These metrics allowed for a numerical determination of the ARIMA model's accuracy, particularly in effectively capturing the changing patterns of weather variables.

Best AIC: 274816.45599880896
Best Order (p, d, q): (2, 0, 2)

User Experience Metric
User Experience (UE) metric to evaluate the impact of the system on end-users. The UE metric combines traditional recommendation scoring and application demand attendance, effectively measuring the accuracy of predictions and user engagement at the

same time. A comprehensive User Experience (UE) metric has been devised to gauge the efficacy of the application in providing a holistic and user-centric travel planning experience. The UE metric is strategically designed to encapsulate both traditional recommendation scoring and application demand attendance, ensuring a nuanced evaluation of the system's performance.

Let *UE* represent this metric.

$$\boldsymbol{UE = \alpha\ X\ Recommendation\ Score + (1 - \alpha)X\ Application\ Demand\ Attendance} \tag{7}$$

where:

α = weight parameter.

1. Recommendation Score

At the core of evaluating travel recommendations from DestiNexus is the recommendation score component, which gauges the accuracy and relevance of the system's suggestions in relation to a user's preferences, historical data, and real-time information. This score serves as a measure of how well the application caters to a user's travel expectations.

2. Application Demand Attendance

The application demand attendance component evaluates the system's responsiveness and adaptability towards user engagement. By considering metrics like frequency of usage, duration of interactions, and responsiveness to inputs, this aspect of the metric measures the effectiveness of the application in meeting user demands.

3. **Weighting Parameter** (α).

The weighting parameter α is introduced to allow for a flexible balance between the two components of the UE metric. Users and system administrators can adjust α based on the relative importance assigned to traditional recommendation scoring versus application demand attendance.

4 Architectural Framework

4.1 Dataset Collection

The cornerstone of our DestiNexus undertaking is rooted in the robust and top-notch dataset employed to train and validate our machine learning algorithms. Our dataset encompasses a wealth of historical weather data spanning various locations, gathered from several esteemed providers. By tapping into a vast array of meteorological parameters from these providers, our models are able to effectively capture the distinct intricacies of diverse climates. The dataset consists of precise temporal and spatial data encompassing hourly or daily weather observations. By obtaining data from various locations, including urban, suburban, and rural areas, the dataset offers a comprehensive understanding of weather patterns. This geographic diversity ensures the machine learning models are well-equipped to handle diverse environmental conditions. Furthermore, the inclusion of historical weather data over several years allows for the capture of long-term trends and seasonal patterns, strengthening the models' ability to recognize yearly weather cycles.

4.2 User Interaction

Users interact with the intuitive user interface, inputting their travel details, including location, date, and time. The React.js front end captures the user's input and sends a request to the backend server.

4.3 Backend Processing

Endpoint Handling
The backend server receives the user request through defined endpoints.

Data Processing
The server processes the input data, ensuring it aligns with the requirements of the machine learning models.

Machine Learning Models
The core machine learning models, including the RandomForestRegressor and ARIMA, are invoked to make predictions based on historical weather data.

Probabilistic Framework
The probabilistic framework introduces uncertainty measures into the predictions, calculating prediction intervals that express the range of possible outcomes.

4.4 Recommendation Generation

Travel Recommendations
The backend server combines the predictions from machine learning models with the probabilistic framework results to generate personalized travel recommendations.

Response to Front End
The recommendations, along with associated weather information and prediction intervals, are sent as a response to the React.js front end.

4.5 Continuous Learning and Enhancement

Data Storage and Maintenance
Historical weather data, utilized for model training, is stored and regularly updated to maintain accuracy.

Model Retraining
Periodic model retraining may occur based on newly available data, ensuring the system adapts to changing weather patterns.

Feedback Analysis
User feedback stored in the database is analysed to identify patterns and enhance the recommendation algorithms.

5 Experimental Analysis and Statistics

The temperatures are in a constant state of change, reaching highs and lows between 10.0 °C and 37.5 °C. Predicted for 2025 is a temperature of approximately 24.0 °C, falling in line with previous years' averages. However, the graph fails to display any confidence intervals or error bars, leaving room for uncertainty and variability in the forecast. At the given point of time, the time series graph is found to be in a constant oscillatory motion with no peak readings which indicates that on a given particular datetime constant, the readings implies that there won't be enough temperature of the region to trigger rainfall (Fig. 3).

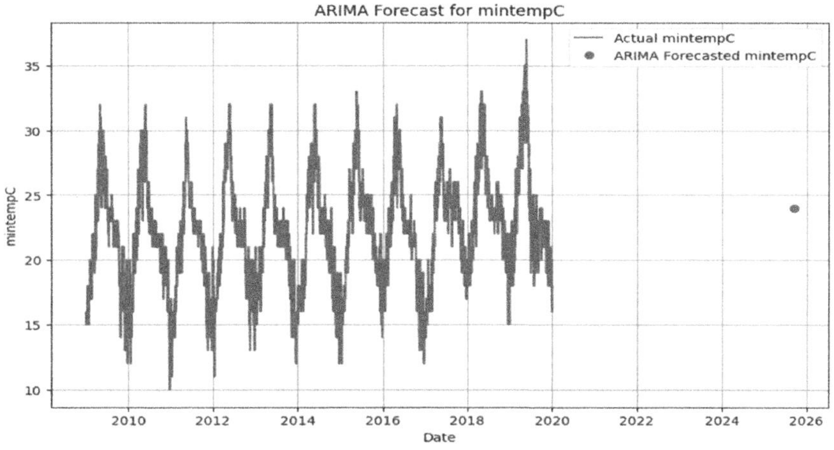

Fig. 3. ARIMA Forecast for mintempC

Over the course of multiple years, there is notable fluctuation in humidity levels between approximately 20 and 100. While some years see higher levels than others, the forecast for 2025 is predicted to have no a certain humidity level. No clear upward or downward trends emerge instead, we observe regular oscillations. At the given point of time in the graph, the predicted humidity level seems to be in between 40 and 50 units, which by the time series correlation is found to an average value with no identifiable peak oscillations, which summarizes that result (Fig. 4).

Over the course of several years, the speed of the wind has been fluctuating, with some years seeing stronger winds than others. Interestingly, the projected wind speed for 2025 is anticipated to be precisely negligible, suggesting minimal wind speed on that particular day. From the Time series graph we can clearly observe that the projected windspeed is not enough to be a catalyst for precipitation for the given datetime constant. No peaks are observed in the projections, instead we can observe an oscillatory value (Figs. 5 and 6).

The model seems to consistently underestimate precipitation values (shown in the blue line) when compared to the actual values (depicted by the green line) throughout the analyzed time period. This points to a general tendency of underestimation by the

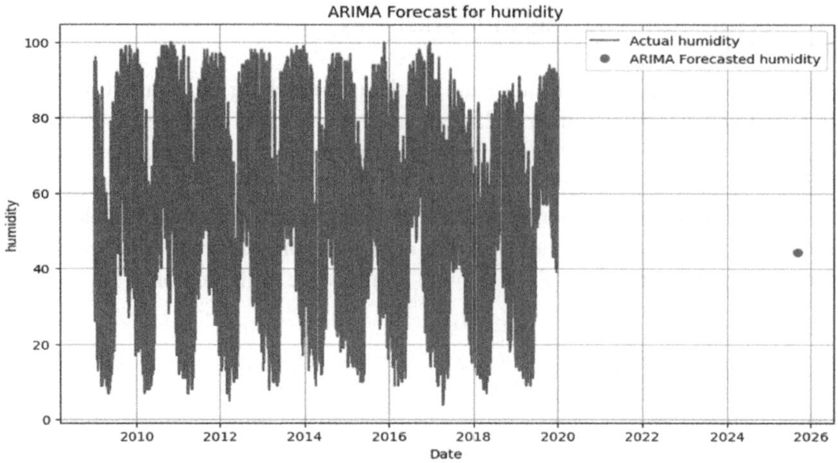

Fig. 4. ARIMA Forecast for humidity

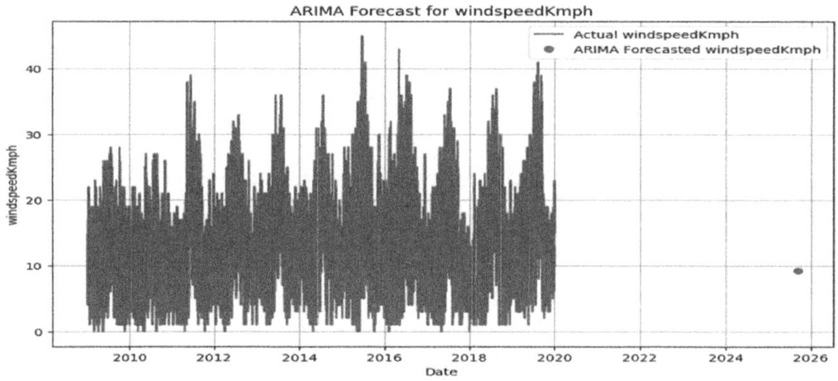

Fig. 5. ARIMA Forecast for windspeedKmph

model. Interestingly, we can observe a clear pattern of seasonality in both the predicted and actual precipitation, with higher values occurring in the latter half of the year, specifically from July to December. However, while the model captures this overall trend, it tends to underestimate the peak levels more than the lower values. Moreover, there is a gradual increase in predicted precipitation over time, whereas the actual values show more variability. This could suggest that the data itself may not be stationary or that the model may have limitations in accurately capturing long-term trends (Table 2).

Confusion Matrix:

$$\begin{bmatrix} 17038 & 478 \\ 1557 & 241 \end{bmatrix}$$

Random Forest Classifier Accuracy: 89%.

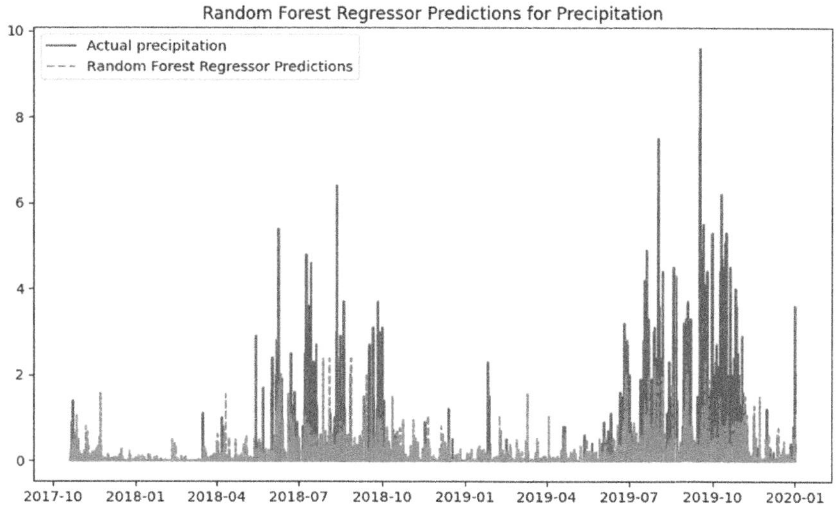

Fig. 6. ARIMA Forecast for windspeedKmph (Color figure online)

Table 2. Classification Report for Random Forest Classifier

	Precision	Recall	F1-Score	Support
0	0.92	0.97	0.94	17516
1	0.31	0.12	0.17	1771
Accuracy			0.89	19287
Macro Avg	0.61	0.55	0.56	19287
Weighted Avg	0.86	0.89	0.87	19287

6 Limitations

The performance of the model appears to be promising for class 0, as demonstrated by its consistently high precision, recall, and F1-score but, the model's handling of class 1 poses a challenge, with noticeably lower values for precision, recall, and F1-score. This suggests that the model has a tendency to incorrectly categorize class 1 points as class 0. While the overall accuracy of 0.89 may seem satisfactory, it should be considered in the context of the significant class imbalance where class 0 has a much larger number of data points. The underestimation of peak precipitation events cannot be solved directly by ARIMA Model, instead we might need to explore feature engineering or hyperparameter tuning in the random forest model itself. The model predicts only for a single data point in the future. It could be extended to provide probabilistic forecasts or predictions for multiple future time steps.

7 Conclusions

To sum up, DestiNexus is breaking new ground in the world of intelligent travel planning apps. By harnessing an advanced probabilistic framework and the impressive capabilities of the RandomForestRegressor model, the system goes beyond traditional methods. Combining cutting-edge technology with a user-focused approach, it not only provides tailored and weather-advised travel plans, but also sets a higher level of transparency through its probabilistic components. DestiNexus empowers users to make well-informed choices by taking into account both accurate forecasts and the inherent unpredictability of weather. By utilizing extensive evaluation metrics, including Mean Squared Error, we have demonstrated the robust performance of the RandomForestRegressor model. Its impressive accuracy and capability to capture uncertainties have solidified its effectiveness. DestiNexus is paving the way for even more advances in resilient and user-friendly travel technologies, ensuring a flawless and well-informed experience when exploring the world.

References

1. Fonseca, F.F., Mamatas, L., Viana, A.C., Correa, S.L., Cardoso, K.V.: Personalized travel itineraries with multi-access edge computing touristic services. In: 2019 IEEE Global Communications Conference (GLOBECOM) Waikoloa, HI, USA, pp. 1–6 (2019). https://doi.org/10.1109/GLOBECOM38437.2019.9013548
2. Nawshin, S., Mukta, M.S.H., Ali, M.E., Islam, A.K.M.N.: Modeling weather-aware prediction of user activities and future visits. IEEE Access **8**, 105127–105138 (2020). https://doi.org/10.1109/ACCESS.2020.3000609
3. Choi, S., Jung, E.-S.: Optimizing numerical weather prediction model performance using machine learning techniques. IEEE Access **11**, 86038–86055 (2023). https://doi.org/10.1109/ACCESS.2023.3297200. (2023)
4. Zhang, C., et al.: Weather visibility prediction based on multimodal fusion. IEEE Access **7**, 74776–74786 (2019). https://doi.org/10.1109/ACCESS.2019.2920865
5. Du, Y., Li, Y., Liu, H.: A new hybrid prediction method of El Niño/La Niña events by combining TimesNet and ARIMA. IEEE Access **11**, 106347–106360 (2023). https://doi.org/10.1109/ACCESS.2023.3319395
6. Dong, L., et al.: Very high resolution remote sensing imagery classification using a fusion of random forest and deep learning technique—subtropical area for example. IEEE J. Sel. Top. Appl. Earth Obs. Remote Sens. **13**, 113–128 (2020). https://doi.org/10.1109/JSTARS.2019.2953234
7. Gupta, V.K., Gupta, A., Kumar, D., Sardana, A.: Prediction of COVID-19 confirmed, death, and cured cases in India using random forest model. Big Data Mining and Analytics **4**(2), 116–123 (2021). https://doi.org/10.26599/BDMA.2020.9020016
8. Jafri, R., Alkhunji, A.S., Alhader, G.K., Alrabeiah, H.R., Alhammad, N.A., Alzahrani, S.K.: Smart travel planner: a mashup of travel-related web services. In: 2013 International Conference on Current Trends in Information Technology (CTIT), Dubai, United Arab Emirates, pp. 181–185 (2013). https://doi.org/10.1109/CTIT.2013.6749499
9. Ambrose, J.K., Bukovsky, D.J., Sedlak, T.J., Goeden, S.J.: Developing a travel route planner accounting for traffic variability. In: 2009 Systems and Information Engineering Design Symposium, Charlottesville, VA, USA, pp. 264–268 (2009). https://doi.org/10.1109/SIEDS.2009.5166192

10. Kaur, R., Sharma, B.: Comparative study for evaluating the usability of web based applications. In: 2018 4th International Conference on Computing Sciences (ICCS), Jalandhar, India, pp. 94–97 (2018). https://doi.org/10.1109/ICCS.2018.00023
11. Javeed, A.: Performance optimization techniques for ReactJS. In: 2019 IEEE International Conference on Electrical, Computer and Communication Technologies (ICECCT), Coimbatore, India, pp. 1–5 (2019). https://doi.org/10.1109/ICECCT.2019.8869134
12. Kiruthika, J., Khaddaj, S., Greenhill, D., Francik, J.: User experience design in web applications. In: 2016 IEEE International Conference on Computational Science and Engineering (CSE) and IEEE International Conference on Embedded and Ubiquitous Computing (EUC) and 15th Intl Symposium on Distributed Computing and Applications for Business Engineering (DCABES), Paris, France, pp. 642–646 (2016). https://doi.org/10.1109/CSE-EUC-DCABES.2016.253
13. Kaur, N., Singh, N.: Comparative analysis of machine learning algorithms for weather prediction using error detection. In: 2023 5th International Conference on Smart Systems and Inventive Technology (ICSSIT), Tirunelveli, India, pp. 1094–1098 (2023). https://doi.org/10.1109/ICSSIT55814.2023.10061132
14. Aravind, M., Thilak, S., Vigneshwaran, B., Jona, J.B.: Weather prediction using random forest method. Int. J. Creat. Res. Thoughts (IJCRT) **10**(2), b542–b545 (2022). ISSN:2320-2882. http://www.ijcrt.org/papers/IJCRT2202187.pdf
15. Aydemir, F., Basciftci, F.: Application of HATEOAS principle in RESTful API design. In: 2022 IEEE 22nd International Symposium on Computational Intelligence and Informatics and 8th IEEE International Conference on Recent Achievements in Mechatronics, Automation, Computer Science and Robotics (CINTI-MACRo), Budapest, Hungary, pp. 000051–000056 (2022). https://doi.org/10.1109/CINTI-MACRo57952.2022.10029427
16. Ahmad, I., Suwarni, E., Borman, R.I., Asmawati, Rossi, F., Jusman, Y.: Implementation of RESTful API web services architecture in takeaway application development. In: 2021 1st International Conference on Electronic and Electrical Engineering and Intelligent System (ICE3IS), Yogyakarta, Indonesia, pp. 132–137 (2021). https://doi.org/10.1109/ICE3IS54102.2021.9649679

Explaining Sentiments in Indian Legal Judgments with LIME and SHAP

T. Hemanth Babu, V. Gopi Kiran, Suhas S. Bhat, Priyanka Prabhakar, and Peeta Basa Pati(✉)

Department of Computer Science and Engineering, Amrita School of Computing, Amrita Vishwa Vidyapeetham, Bengaluru, India
bp_peeta@blr.amrita.edu

Abstract. This paper presents a comparative study on sentiment analysis applied to legal texts, specifically legal opinions, and judgments. This paper uses embeddings such as T5, XLM Roberta and BERT, Roberta, and Legal BERT to convert the textual data into pre-trained language model word representation, to make it easier for ML algorithms to determine the sentiment (positive, negative, or neutral) of legal documents. The dataset was converted into embeddings, and various models, including KNN, ANN, SVM, random forest, XG boost, logistic regression, and decision tree, were employed for sentiment analysis. Each model was subjected to hyperparameter tuning using Grid Search CV, resulting in the highest accuracy of 66.66% with SVM on T5 embeddings. This research provides valuable insights into the emotional degrees within legal texts, demonstrating the effectiveness of our sentiment analysis approach.

Keywords: XLM Roberta · BERT · T5 · LIME · SHAP · Grid Search CV · ANN · Decision Tree · XG boost

1 Introduction

Sentiment analysis in legal texts is a difficult and complex task. Legal documents often contain multiple perspectives, diverse tones, and subtle nuances that require sophisticated techniques to extract sentiment accurately. Additionally, the implications of sentiment in legal contexts can be significant, as it can influence judicial decisions, the interpretation of statutes, and the development of legal precedent.

Sentiment analysis is a subfield of natural language processing, that involves the use of computational methods to determine and understand the sentiments expressed in textual data. In a general context, sentiment analysis is widely applied to social media, customer reviews, and other forms of user-generated content. It involves categorizing the sentiment of a given piece of text into positive, negative, or neutral classes, allowing for a quantitative understanding of public opinion. This technique has proven invaluable in various domains, providing businesses, policymakers, and researchers with insights into public sentiment.

Published by Springer Nature Switzerland AG 2025
A. Chandrabose et al. (Eds.): ICCCSP 2024, IFIP AICT 723, pp. 386–400, 2025.
https://doi.org/10.1007/978-3-031-73617-9_30

In the real-world context, sentiment analysis in legal judgment offers an understanding of the emotional tone embedded in legal texts, helping judges decipher the subjective elements within complex cases. By identifying sentiments, judges can gain insights into the perspectives presented, enabling a more holistic assessment of arguments, and influencing their decision-making process. This approach is anticipated to reduce the challenges associated with manually navigating through extensive legal texts, saving time, and facilitating a more focused consideration of relevant information. The integration of sentiment analysis in legal judgments provides a highlight of the legal ruling so that junior lawyers can get an insight into how higher courts handle faces of different domains. This gives more understanding of the legal argumentation tactics that legal professionals can use. Our analysis indicates (refer Table 1, Sect. 3) that the sentiment polarity present in the judgement document is independent of the judgment outcome for the case.

We address the critical need for specialized sentiment analysis tools in the legal domain by developing a robust model trained on a large corpus of legal documents by utilizing advanced embeddings such as T5, XLM Roberta and BERT, Roberta, and Legal BERT. Trained on these new embedded datasets, machine learning algorithms will accurately determine the sentiment in legal opinions and judgments. The methodology involves employing various machine learning models, including KNN, ANN, SVM, random forest, XG boost, logistic regression, and decision trees, for sentiment analysis. This comprehensive approach provides valuable insights into the most efficient sentiment analysis method for legal judgment texts. Upon completion, the model will be shared with the legal community, offering a powerful tool to enhance their capabilities in navigating and interpreting legal documents.

The key contributions are as follows:

1. A comparative study between T5, Roberta, Bert, XLMRoberta, and LegalBert word embeddings with different classification models, determining the best performance for sentiment analysis of Indian legal judgments.
2. Identification of judgment phrases that influence sentiment polarity detection by utilizing LIME and SHAP.

This research plays a pivotal role in contributing to the United Nations Sustainable Development Goals (SDGs), with a specific emphasis on Goal 16: "Promote peaceful and inclusive societies for sustainable development, provide access to justice for all and build effective, accountable and inclusive institutions at all levels." The insights gained from this research can empower legal practitioners, policymakers, and institutions to make informed decisions, fostering a more just and transparent legal environment in support of the United Nations' vision for sustainable development, as it aligns with the broader SDG 16 objectives.

2 Literature Survey

Rajapaksha et al. [1] explore the application of Aspect-Based Sentiment Analysis (ABSA) in the legal domain, an area less studied. It introduces a rule-based method to assess statement sentiments toward relevant legal parties in a court case. By identifying key elements like involved parties, case facts, and arguments, the method assigns sentiment scores based on predefined rules, with positive scores for commendations and negative scores for criticisms. ABSA has been extensively explored in various fields, yet the legal domain has received limited attention due to the complexity of lengthy and intricate legal opinion writings, making manual sentiment annotation challenging. The unique vocabulary and jargon in the legal field further complicates sentiment identification for ABSA systems. To tackle these issues, Rajapaksha et al. [2] came up with a new text dataset, Sigma Law-ABSA, featuring manually annotated legal opinions that have been proposed. This dataset serves as a valuable resource for ABSA researchers in the legal domain, offering a means to address challenges and enhance the accuracy of sentiment analysis systems. The improved ABSA systems can, in turn, support various legal applications such as document summarization, question answering, and case law analysis.

Yadav et al. [3] offer a comprehensive overview of prominent deep learning models for sentiment analysis, presenting a taxonomy and highlighting the impact of common architectures on sentiment analysis tasks. Focusing on deep learning techniques, the survey summarizes key contributions, addresses sentiment analysis tasks across languages, and provides insights into popular datasets, including the Stanford Sentiment Treebank, IMDB movie review dataset, and Amazon product review dataset. It emphasizes the effectiveness of deep learning models, such as recurrent neural networks (RNNs), convolutional neural networks (CNNs), and long short-term memory (LSTM) networks, comparing their advantages and drawbacks. The conversation emphasizes the importance of deep learning in attaining cutting-edge outcomes in sentiment analysis assignments. This paper serves as a valuable reference for individuals in both research and practical domains who are delving into the realm of deep learning applications for sentiment analysis.

Ratnayaka et al. [4] utilize advanced machine learning and rule-based methods, the paper categorizes sentence pairs based on discernible connections and classifies individual sentences for their contribution to legal arguments. The study introduces inventive techniques, including the application of discourse relationships, to establish meaningful connections within court transcripts. Ratnayaka et al. [5] introduce innovative techniques for creating a sentiment annotator tailored to legal domain-specific sentiment analysis, addressing challenges like limited labeled data and domain expertise. Leveraging the Stanford Sentiment Treebank (SST-5) as a high-resource source domain and legal opinion texts as a low-resource target domain, the authors minimize manual annotation by identifying domain generic, domain-specific, and underrepresented words. They fine-tune the Stanford Sentiment Annotator and adopt a BERT-based approach (BERT) for sentiment classification. To prevent negative transfer, a new training set (L) is generated by removing sentences with deviated sentiments from the original SST training dataset.

Valdez et al. [6] contribute to this evolving discourse by employing sentiment analysis to scrutinize restrictive and protective abortion bills enacted in 2019, aiming to uncover the subtle layers of emotion and framing within the legal language, thus advancing our understanding of how the wording of such legislation may influence interpretations and public discourse. In this study, sentiment analysis (SA) is applied to scrutinize the semantic compositions of both restrictive and protective abortion bills that were passed in the year 2019. Utilizing Natural Language Processing (NLP), SA employs automated methods to extract affective indicators, specifically emotive language, from textual data. Eliot [7] explains Legal Sentiment Analysis and Opinion Mining (LSAOM), at the crossroads of legal theory and practice, and explores nuanced expressions in legal discussions through Sentiment Analysis (SA) and Opinion Mining (OM). Initially reliant on human cognition, recent advancements in AI, particularly in Natural Language Processing and Machine Learning, are automating and transforming LSAOM. This paper traces the evolution, emphasizing the shift to AI-driven automation, and introduces a conceptual framework aligning with Levels of Autonomy in AI Legal Reasoning. The survey offers insights into the potential impact on legal studies and practice.

Pichardo-Lagunas et al. [8] introduce "opposition relations" in Mexican Environmental Laws through sentiment analysis, uncovering entities with opposing sentiments in legal texts. Named Entity Recognition (NER) classifies entities, while Sentiment Analysis (SA) discerns emotional tones, revealing potential conflicts and enhancing coherence in legal documents. This innovative approach addresses a research gap in systematically analyzing relationships between entities in legal texts, particularly in the context of environmental laws and sustainable development. By comprehensively analyzing eight Mexican Environmental Laws, the study highlights complexities in entities with opposing polarities, providing detailed analyses of two cases. Liu et al. [9] propose a methodology for predicting pending judgments using legal documents. Employing text mining techniques like term extraction, stop-word removal, and sentiment term identification, the authors extract features from legal precedents. A multilabel entropy feature selection method is applied, and a Vector Space Representation (VSD) model generates representative vectors. Sentiment analysis, integrating sentiment scores into document vectors, is conducted using a sentiment dictionary. The two-phase testing procedure involves predicting associated articles with a multilabel classifier and forecasting the most suitable judgment category based on sentiment analysis. Sil [10] tackles the challenges arising from India's population surge and its impact on the mounting legal cases, specifically in the context of domestic violence against women, exacerbated by socio-economic imbalances heightened during the COVID-19 pandemic. Focusing on the 'Domestic Violence Against Women Act's sections IPC 498A and IPC 304B, the authors employ aspect-based Sentiment Analysis on argument-based legal documents to predict judgments. Leveraging Machine Learning, Text Classification, and Text Mining, they transform hard-copy legal documents into a PDF format, extracting features to assist legal professionals in predicting judgments.

3 Data Description

The dataset utilized for sentiment analysis consists of 900 legal judgment documents obtained from the Indian Kanoon website [21]. These judgments span a range of legal cases, presenting an array of perspectives, tones, and complexities essential for a robust sentiment analysis. Each document is manually inspected by a legal professional and a sentiment polarity (positive, negative, or neutral) is assigned to the document. The assigned sentiment polarity represents the majority sentiment polarity present in the document across multiple sections and paragraphs. Each document is associated with an outcome (derived based on the judgment given) which is obtained from the data source webpage. These outcomes are "allowed", "dismissed" and "part allowed".

An association analysis is performed to study if the sentiment polarity and the outcome of a case are related. The outcomes of this analysis are presented in Table 1. The data in Table 1 clearly shows that the polarity of the judgment and the final status of the judgment are not highly correlated. For example, all the cases that were allowed need not necessarily have a positive sentiment, and similarly, all the cases with negative sentiment need not be dismissed cases.

Table 1. Matrix displaying the distribution of sentiment polarities across different judgement outcomes.

Sentiment Polarity	Partially Allowed	Allowed	Dismissed
Neutral	51	83	103
Positive	55	112	135
Negative	68	161	132

Figure 1 shows the sample distribution against the 3 sentiment polarity classes, namely, "allowed", "partially allowed" & "dismissed". It may be observed from the bar graphs present in Fig. 1 that the classes are fairly balanced.

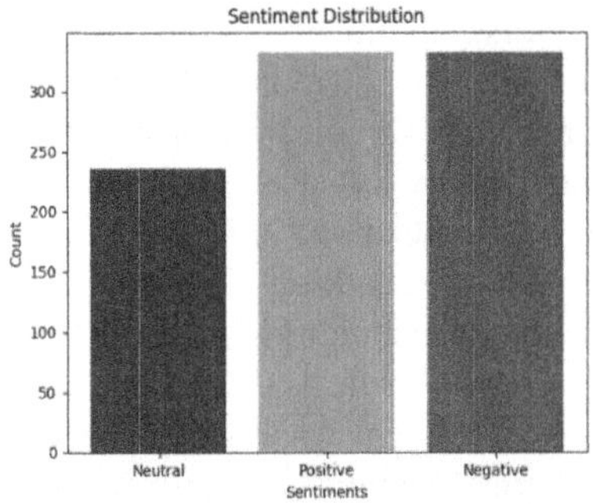

Fig. 1. Sample distribution among the three sentiment polarity classes.

4 Methodology

This section discusses the approach for sentiment analysis on legal judgments. Utilizing transformer models, we apply various machine learning algorithms, including fine-tuning via GridSearch CV. LIME and SHAP text interpretation are used to provide local and global insights into decision-making. Finally, all models were compared based on performance. Figure 2 represents the methodology in the form of a flowchart.

4.1 Word Embedding

In this phase, we utilized three prominent pre-trained transformer models for word embeddings: BERT, T-5, and XLM Roberta, Roberta, and Legal BERT [11]. Applying these transformers to the legal judgments dataset resulted in three distinct datasets, each representing the embeddings from one of the pre-trained models.

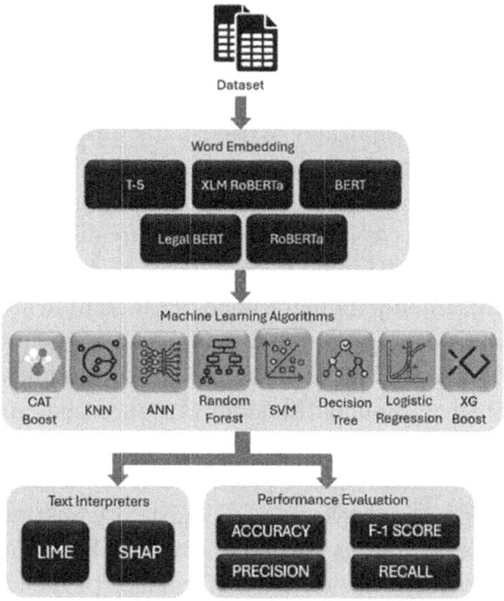

Fig. 2. Architecture diagram

a) T-5 (Text-To-Text Transfer Transformer): T-5 adopts a unified framework for various NLP tasks, treating sentiment analysis as a text-to-text task [12]. This approach allows T-5 to generate informative embeddings by transforming the legal judgments into textual representations, facilitating a holistic understanding of the sentiment conveyed in the legal text.
b) BERT (Bidirectional Encoder Representations from Transformers): BERT, renowned for its bidirectional contextual understanding, captures intricate linguistic relationships within legal judgments [13]. By considering the entire context surrounding each word, BERT embeddings enable the model to grasp nuanced sentiment expressions, enhancing the sentiment analysis capabilities of the classification models.
c) Legal BERT: Legal BERT, fine-tuned specifically for legal domain tasks, incorporates legal vocabulary and context into its embeddings [14]. This specialization aims to capture the unique linguistic intricacies of legal judgments, making Legal BERT a tailored choice for sentiment analysis in the legal domain.
d) RoBERTa (Robustly optimized BERT approach): Roberta, an optimized variant of BERT, further refines the bidirectional training process by removing the next-sentence prediction objective [15]. This modification enhances the model's ability to understand contextual relationships in legal texts, contributing to more accurate sentiment analysis.

e) XLM Roberta (Cross-lingual Language Model - Roberta): XLM Roberta extends the multilingual capabilities of Roberta, making it proficient at handling diverse legal texts. Its cross-lingual pre-training ensures a broader understanding of sentiments expressed in legal judgments across different languages [16].

4.2 Machine Learning Algorithms

For the sentiment analysis classification task, various machine learning algorithms were employed on each of the 5 embedded datasets. These included Artificial Neural Networks (ANN), K-Nearest Neighbors (KNN), Support Vector Machines (SVM), Random Forest, Decision Tree, Logistic Regression, and XGBoost. Each algorithm was fine-tuned using GridSearch CV for hyperparameter optimization, ensuring the best model configuration for classification [17, 18].

Artificial Neural Networks (ANN) were employed for their ability to capture intricate relationships, making them well-suited for sentiment analysis in legal texts. K-Nearest Neighbors (KNN) offered a non-parametric approach to sentiment analysis. Support Vector Machines (SVM) were leveraged for their proficiency in finding optimal hyperplanes for classification. SVM excelled at separating different sentiment classes by identifying the most discriminative features. Random Forest, an ensemble learning method, combined multiple decision trees to enhance the robustness of sentiment analysis. Decision trees, known for their interpretability, provided valuable insights into the decision-making process of sentiment analysis models. Logistic Regression, a widely used linear model, demonstrated its effectiveness in classification tasks. In the context of sentiment analysis, XGBoost effectively boosted the performance of the classification model by iteratively refining weak learners and contributing to robust sentiment predictions in legal judgments. For each of these models, hyperparameter tuning was conducted using GridSearch CV, ensuring the optimal configuration for accurate sentiment classification in legal judgments.

4.3 Text Interpreters

In this phase, two influential text interpretation techniques were employed to shed light on the decision-making processes of the sentiment analysis models: LIME and SHAP [19, 20].

a) LIME (Local Interpretable Model-agnostic Explanations): LIME generates locally faithful explanations for model predictions. In the context of sentiment analysis of legal judgments, LIME perturbs the input data to create instances with subtle variations and observes the corresponding changes in the model's output. This process provides valuable insights into the specific features and their contributions that influenced the sentiment prediction for individual instances. LIME's localized interpretability ensures a nuanced understanding of the model's decision-making, offering transparency in complex sentiment analysis scenarios.
b) SHAP (SHapley Additive exPlanations): SHAP values, based on cooperative game theory, allocate contributions of each feature to the model's output in a global context. Applied to sentiment analysis of legal judgments, SHAP offers a comprehensive

understanding of feature importance across the entire dataset. By quantifying the impact of each feature on the model's predictions, SHAP provides insights into the overall sentiment analysis process, highlighting which legal features play pivotal roles in determining sentiment. The global interpretability of SHAP complements the local insights provided by LIME, offering a well-rounded perspective on the model's decision logic in legal judgments.

4.4 Performance Evaluation

In this final phase, the sentiment analysis models were rigorously evaluated using standard metrics like accuracy, precision, recall, and F1-score providing a comprehensive assessment of their effectiveness. For each combination of ML algorithm and embedded dataset, a classification report and confusion matrix have been plotted to offer a better understanding of the model's performance.

5 Result Analysis

In this section, we take a closer look at the results to better understand their implications. By examining how the optimized machine learning models performed on different datasets, we gain insights into which combinations worked best. Notably, T5 stood out for its strong performance, thanks to its ability to grasp complex patterns in legal text. The analysis also includes LIME and SHAP insights, providing a clearer picture of what influences the sentiment predictions. This deeper examination helps us better grasp sentiment analysis in legal judgments and contributes valuable insights into the field.

5.1 Hyperparameter Tuning with GridSearch CV

Upon Employing GridSearch CV for each machine learning algorithm to systematically explore a range of hyperparameter values, identifying the best configuration for each of the 5 embedding datasets. Table 2 shows the hyperparameter values after hyperparameter tuning obtained for the T5 embedding dataset. With the new hyperparameters, the ML algorithms performed a lot better when compared to their accuracies before tuning, this improvement is depicted in Fig. 3.

5.2 Accuracy Comparison of Different ML Algorithms

Upon performing hyperparameter tuning, the optimized machine learning models were applied to each of the five embedding datasets: T5, RoBERTa, BERT, XLM-RoBERTa, and Legal BERT. The goal was to evaluate the performance of each model across different text representations and identify the combination that yielded the highest accuracy. After thorough experimentation, it was found that the combination of Support Vector Machines (SVM) with the T5 embedding dataset achieved the highest accuracy among all combinations. The SVM model trained on the T5 embeddings demonstrated an accuracy of 66.6%, showcasing the effectiveness of this pairing in capturing sentiments within legal judgments. The results are summarized in Table 3, providing a comprehensive overview of the accuracies obtained by each machine learning model when applied to the different embedding datasets. Figure 3 represents the confusion matrix of the SVM classifier on T5 embeddings.

Table 2. Hyperparameters after tuning using GridSearch CV

Models	After Hyperparameter Tuning
KNN	n_neighbors = 9, p = 2, weights = 'distance'
SVM	kernel = 'linear', C = 10
Random Forest	criterion = 'gini', max_depth = 10, n_estimators = 100
Logistic Regression	C = 10, multi_class = 'ovr', penalty = 'l2', solver = 'lbfgs'
Decision Tree	max_depth = 20, min_samples_leaf = 1, min_samples_split = 2
XG Boost	colsample_bytree = 0.8, learning_rate = 0.1, max_depth = 3, n_estimators = 50, subsample = 1
CAT Boost	depth = 3, learning_rate = 0.1 iterations = 100, subsample = 1 colsample_bylevel = 0.8, bootstrap_type = 'Bernoulli'
ANN	neurons_layer1 = 32, neurons_layer2 = 64 activation = 'relu', optimizer = 'rmsprop'

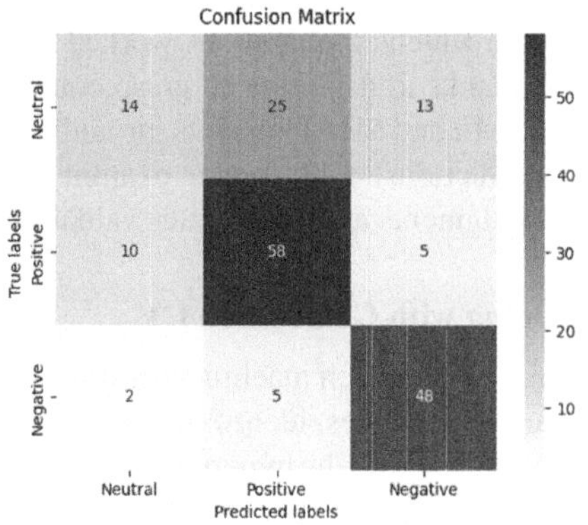

Fig. 3. Confusion matrix of SVM on T5 embeddings.

5.3 Analyzing the Accuracies of Each Embedded Dataset

Table 3 displays the accuracies of each machine learning model across different embedded datasets for both training and testing. Let's delve into the reasons behind the observed accuracies. T5 achieved the highest accuracies across various models during testing. T5's success can be attributed to its transformer architecture's ability to capture intricate patterns and relationships within legal judgments. The contextual understanding provided by T5 embeddings proved effective in discerning sentiment nuances, contributing to superior performance during testing. Despite being extensively trained on legal datasets, Legal BERT exhibited lower accuracies than normal BERT because Legal BERT was not specifically trained on Indian legal datasets. Legal judgments from different regions often exhibit distinct linguistic and contextual nuances, impacting the model's ability to generalize to diverse legal contexts. XLM-RoBERTa, designed as a multilingual model, showed slightly lower accuracy than RoBERTa. The multilingual aspect of XLM-RoBERTa, while advantageous in diverse language tasks, might have led to a slight compromise in performance compared to RoBERTa, which is optimized for English. The dataset's predominantly English content may explain the nuanced difference in accuracies. BERT outperforming RoBERTa contradicts the expectation that RoBERTa, being a derivative of BERT, should exhibit at least similar if not superior performance. This discrepancy can be attributed to the subtle differences in the pre-training objectives. RoBERTa optimizes the mask prediction task, allowing for better representation learning, but the impact on sentiment analysis depends on the specific nuances of the legal text.

Table 3. Comparison of accuracies

Models	Accuracy (%)									
	T5		Bert		XLMRoberta		Roberta		Legal Bert	
	Train	Test	Train	Test	Train	Test	Train	Test	Train	Test
KNN	75.90	65.55	73.60	51.50	67.90	36.36	99.80	61.66	99.86	39.44
SVM	61.66	66.66	99.70	52.22	99.85	43.88	78.05	61.11	93.47	41.11
Random Forest	99.80	65.50	98.10	57.00	99.80	44.88	99.80	60.55	99.86	41.11
Logistic Regression	63.30	65.50	98.19	55.00	99.85	41.66	70.01	58.33	61.52	40.55
Decision Tree	97.50	52.00	93.19	46.11	99.71	37.50	90.13	44.44	91.11	36.66
XG Boost	99.80	65.50	99.86	56.11	99.85	38.63	97.80	55.55	99.86	41.66
Cat Boost	83.61	62.22	84.16	57.22	89.00	38.33	83.00	58.88	87.00	41.11
ANN	79.30	61.66	69.58	52.77	85.00	43.18	90.00	55.55	87.00	38.33

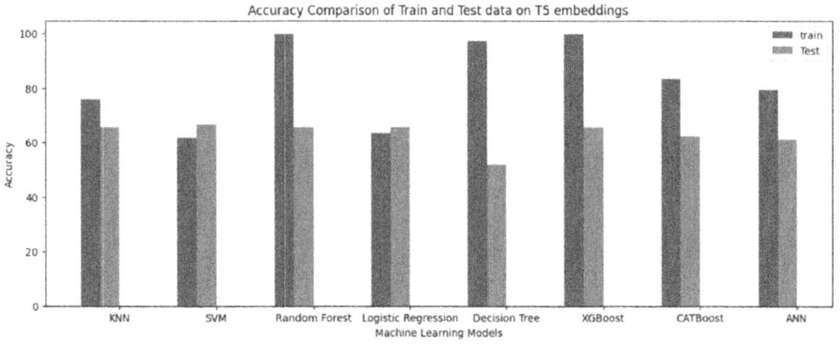

Fig. 4. Train and test accuracy comparison of different classification models with T5 embeddings.

In summary, the choice of embedded dataset plays a crucial role in sentiment analysis accuracy. T5's strong performance highlights its suitability for capturing legal sentiments. Legal BERT's performance underscores the importance of domain-specific training on diverse legal datasets. XLM-RoBERTa's slight dip in accuracy emphasizes the balance between multilingual capabilities and language-specific tasks. The unexpected success of BERT over RoBERTa suggests that the effectiveness of pre-trained models depends on the intricacies of the target task, in this case, sentiment analysis in legal judgments.

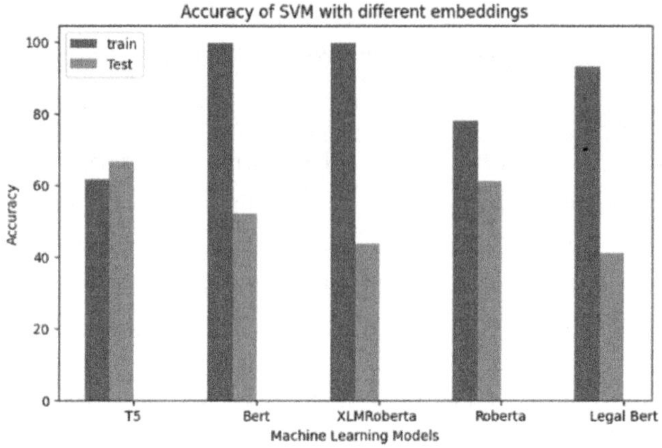

Fig. 5. Train and text accuracy comparison of SVM on different embeddings.

As seen in Fig. 4, the test accuracy of SVM is the highest among T5 embeddings when compared with other ML classifiers. In Fig. 5, T5 performed much better than the remaining transformer models when comparing the accuracies of SVM using different embeddings.

Despite the difference in datasets, upon comparing our accuracy with the recent approaches covered in Sect. 2, ABSA and Sigma Law ABSA implemented in [1] and [2] gave an accuracy of 61.82% and 65.12% respectively. The sentiment analysis in [4] gave an accuracy of 64.93% using the argumentive verb base approach. The methodology specified in [6] gave an accuracy of 56%. The LSAOM approach specified in [7] gave an accuracy of 98.17% while using Naïve Bayes, and 93.54% with SVM classifier.

5.4 Analyzing LIME Text Interpreter

As shown in Fig. 6, the LIME analysis of Instance ID 4, predicted a sentiment score of 1. Feature importance scores revealed that terms associated with family relationships, such as "husband," "dower," and "wife," negatively influenced the sentiment prediction, suggesting a potential negative context. Conversely, positive sentiment was associated with legal terms like "property," "decision," and "entitled." Notably, the model exhibited higher confidence in predicting a more neutral sentiment (0.57) than a positive sentiment (0.35), indicating a level of uncertainty in the classification. In summary, Instance ID 4's sentiment prediction was intricately influenced by a combination of family-related and legal terms, showcasing the model's better understanding of the underlying context. The interplay of negative and positive influences underscored the complexity of sentiment analysis in legal judgments, with the model expressing a certain level of hesitancy in determining the final sentiment score.

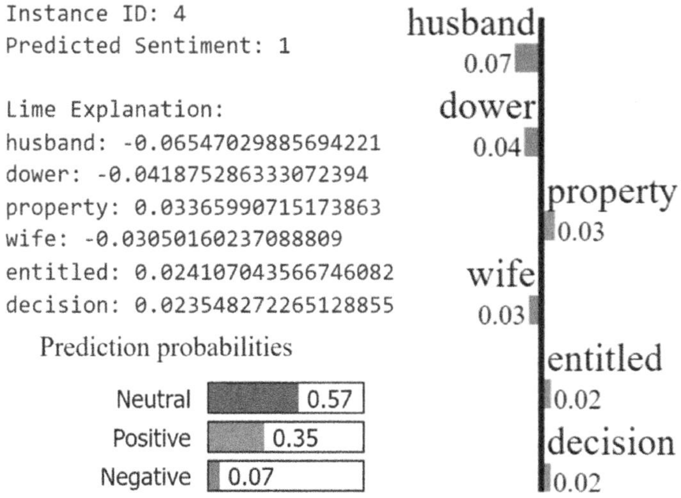

Fig. 6. Output of LIME text Interpreter

5.5 Analyzing SHAP Text Interpreter

In a SHAP analysis output, each feature's contribution to the model's decision is visually represented through colored bars. The colors signify the impact of a specific word on sentiment classification: blue bars indicate influence on the neutral class, red bars indicate influence on positive sentiment, and green bars indicate influence on negative sentiment. This means that if a word has a greater blue bar, it signifies that the presence of that word is more influential in the classification of a neutral sentiment. Conversely, a greater red bar suggests the word's influence in the classification of a positive sentiment, while a greater green bar indicates its influence in the classification of a negative sentiment.

As illustrated in Fig. 7, the word "accused" has a substantial blue bar, thus, it suggests that this word plays a significant role in the classification of neutral sentiment. On the other hand, if like "special" and "observed" have prominent red bars, implying that these words exert more influence on the model's classification of positive sentiment. This visualization provides valuable insights into the specific words driving the sentiment predictions for each class, enhancing the interpretability of the model's decision-making process.

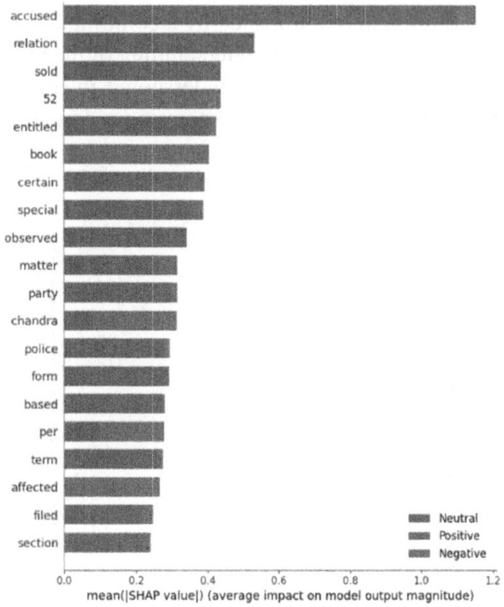

Fig. 7. Output of SHAP text Interpreter (Color figure online)

6 Conclusion and Future Work

A comprehensive study on sentiment analysis applied to legal texts, specifically legal opinions, and judgments. Leveraging advanced word embeddings such as T5, XLM Roberta, BERT, Roberta, and Legal BERT, the study employs a range of machine learning algorithms, including KNN, ANN, SVM, Random Forest, Decision Tree, Logistic Regression, and XGBoost, to accurately determine the sentiment (positive, negative, or neutral) of legal documents. The models underwent hyperparameter tuning using GridSearch CV, enhancing their performance for sentiment analysis. The results reveal that the combination of Support Vector Machines (SVM) with T5 embeddings achieves the highest accuracy of 66.6%, emphasizing the effectiveness of this pairing in capturing sentiments within legal judgments. Additionally, the interpretability of model decisions is enhanced through the incorporation of LIME and SHAP analyses. LIME offered localized insights that revealed specific features' contributions to sentiment predictions, while SHAP provided a global understanding of feature importance across the entire dataset.

Additionally, future endeavors will involve exploring additional pre-trained models like GPT-4 and refining existing algorithms for sentiment analysis in legal texts that can enhance accuracy. Further investigation into domain-specific pre-training on diverse legal datasets may improve global adaptability. We also aim to test the models on diverse legal datasets and extend the analysis to different languages.

Acknowledgment. We would also like to express our sincere gratitude to our university, Amrita Vishwa Vidyapeetham, for providing the opportunity and infrastructure to complete the assignment.

References

1. Rajapaksha, I., Mudalige, C.R., Karunarathna, D., De Silva, N., Rathnayaka, G., Perera, A.S.: Rule-based approach for party-based sentiment analysis in legal opinion texts. In: 20th International Conference on Advances in ICT for Emerging Regions (ICTer), pp. 284–285 (2020)
2. Mudalige, C.R., et al.: SigmaLaw-ABSA: dataset for aspect-based sentiment analysis in legal opinion texts. In: IEEE 15th International Conference on Industrial and Information Systems (ICIIS), pp. 488–493 (2020)
3. Yadav, A., Vishwakarma, D.K.: Sentiment analysis using deep learning architectures: a review. Artif. Intell. Rev. **53**(6), 4335–4385 (2020)
4. Ratnayaka, G., et al.: Classifying sentences in court case transcripts using discourse and argumentative properties. Int. J. Adv. ICT Emerg. Reg. **12**(1), 1–10 (2019)
5. Ratnayaka, G., De Silva, N., Perera, A.S., Pathirana, R.: Effective approach to develop a sentiment annotator for legal domain in a low resource setting. arXiv preprint arXiv:2011.00318 (2020)
6. Valdez, D., Goodson, P.: Neutral or framed? A sentiment analysis of 2019 abortion laws. Sex. Res. Soc. Policy **19**(3), 936–945 (2022)
7. Eliot, L.: Legal Sentiment Analysis and Opinion Mining (LSAOM): Assimilating Advances in Autonomous AI Legal Reasoning. arXiv preprint arXiv:2010.02726 (2020)
8. Pichardo-Lagunas, O., Martinez-Seis, B., Hidalgo-Reyes, M., Miranda, S.: Automatic detection of opposition relations in legal texts using sentiment analysis techniques: a case study. Acta Polytechnica Hungarica **19**(10), 165–184 (2022)
9. Liu, Y.H., Chen, Y.L.: A two-phase sentiment analysis approach for judgement prediction. J. Inf. Sci. **44**(5), 594–607 (2018)
10. Sil, R.: Sentiment analysis-based legal case prediction system. SSRN (2022). https://doi.org/10.2139/ssrn.4145582
11. Prabhakar, P., Gupta, D., Pati, P.B.: Abstractive summarization of Indian legal judgments. In: OITS International Conference on Information Technology (OCIT), Bhubaneswar, India, pp. 256–261 (2022). https://doi.org/10.1109/OCIT56763.2022.00056
12. Ramaneedi, S., Pati, P.B.: Kannada textual error correction using T5 model. In: IEEE 8th International Conference for Convergence in Technology (I2CT), Lonavla, India, pp. 1–5 (2023). https://doi.org/10.1109/I2CT57861.2023.10126228
13. Tanaka, H., Shinnou, H., Cao, R., Bai, J., Ma, W.: Document classification by word embeddings of BERT. In: Nguyen, L.M., Phan, X.H., Hasida, K., Tojo, S. (eds.) Computational Linguistics. PACLING 2019. Communications in Computer and Information Science, vol. 1215, pp. 145–154. Springer, Singapore (2020). https://doi.org/10.1007/978-981-15-6168-9_13
14. Chalkidis, I., Fergadiotis, M., Malakasiotis, P., Aletras, N., Androutsopoulos, I.: LEGAL-BERT: the Muppets straight out of law school. arXiv preprint arXiv:2010.02559 (2020)
15. Bear, D., Cook, P.: Fine-tuning Sentence-RoBERTa to construct word embeddings for low-resource languages from bilingual dictionaries. In Proceedings of the Workshop on Natural Language Processing for Indigenous Languages of the Americas (AmericasNLP), pp. 47–57 (2023)
16. Sai, S., Jacob, A.W., Kalra, S., Sharma, Y.: Stacked embeddings and multiple fine-tuned XLM-RoBERTa models for enhanced hostility identification. In: Chakraborty, T., Shu, K., Bernard, H.R., Liu, H., Akhtar, M.S. (eds.) CONSTRAINT 2021. Communications in Computer and Information Science, vol. 1402, pp. 224–235. Springer, Cham (2021). https://doi.org/10.1007/978-3-030-73696-5_21

17. Priyanka, R., Aravinth, J.: Comparative analysis of different machine learning classifiers for prediction of diabetic retinopathy. In: International Conference on Recent Trends on Electronics, Information, Communication & Technology (RTEICT), Bangalore, India, pp. 233–239 (2021). https://doi.org/10.1109/RTE-ICT52294.2021.9573525
18. Pattanayak, S., Pati, P.B., Singh, T.: Performance analysis of machine learning algorithms on multi-touch attribution model. In: 3rd International Conference for Emerging Technology (INCET), Belgaum, India, pp. 1–7 (2022). https://doi.org/10.1109/INCET54531.2022.9824865
19. Bhattacharya, P., Ghosh, K., Pal, A., Ghosh, S.: Legal case document similarity: you need both network and text. Inf. Process. Manag. **59**(6), 103069 (2022)
20. Krishnan, D., Bharathy, P., Venugopalan, M.: A supervised approach for extractive text summarization using minimal robust features. In: IEEE International Conference on Intelligent Computing and Control Systems (ICCS), pp. 521–527 (2019)
21. Indian Kanoon Webpage. https://indiankanoon.org/. Accessed Oct 2023

An Integrated Framework Utilizing Hybrid LDA and BERT for Enhanced Hotel Recommendation Systems

Neha Bhende(✉), R. Madhumita, R. Ishwarya, and S. Senthamizh Selvi

Sri Venkateswara College of Engineering, Sriperumbudur, Tamil Nadu 602117, India
{2020cs0459,2020cs0539,2020cs0451,senthamizhselvi}@svce.ac.in

Abstract. In the ever-evolving hospitality industry, the need for advanced recommendation systems has become paramount, offering users personalized and dependable hotel suggestions. This paper represents a fusion of Latent Dirichlet Allocation (LDA) for topic modeling and Bidirectional Encoder Representations from Transformers (BERT) for sentiment analysis that enhances the accuracy and relevance of hotel recommendations, addressing the dynamic nature of user preferences. The first core component of our system harnesses the power of LDA topic modeling to unveil latent themes embedded within user-generated content, encompassing diverse sources such as reviews and hotel descriptions. Through this process, topics are categorized, granting the system deeper insights into various facets of hotels that forms the bedrock of more context-aware recommendations, enabling users to receive suggestions that align with their specific preferences and expectations. The second element of the system is the integration of BERT-based sentiment analysis. It undertakes a comprehensive exploration of user-generated content, deciphering the emotional sentiments expressed within the text by analyzing sentiment polarity and intensity. This personalized approach ensures that the system goes beyond the surface-level analysis, delivering a more tailored and satisfying user experience. To assess the efficiency and accuracy of the recommendation system, it is subjected to evaluation by comparing it with three other recommendation systems: LFM (Latent Factor Model), SVD (Singular Value Decomposition)++, and MFFR (Matrix Factorization Fusing Reviews). The benchmarking process employs two robust evaluation metrics, namely Accuracy Score and F-1 Score. Through this comparative analysis, the superior performance and precision achieved through the proposed system has been demonstrated.

Keywords: Latent Dirichlet Allocation · Bidirectional Encoder Representations from Transformers · Context-aware Recommendations · Sentiment Analysis · Hotel Recommendations · Industry · Innovation · and Infrastructure

1 Introduction

In the ever-growing hospitality industry, effective hotel recommendations play a pivotal role in enhancing user experiences. Travelers seek personalized and relevant suggestions to make informed choices. A hybrid recommendation system that combines Latent

Published by Springer Nature Switzerland AG 2025
A. Chandrabose et al. (Eds.): ICCCSP 2024, IFIP AICT 723, pp. 401–412, 2025.
https://doi.org/10.1007/978-3-031-73617-9_31

Dirichlet Allocation (LDA) and Bidirectional Encoder Representations from Transformers (BERT) offers a novel approach to achieving this objective. This system amalgamates the power of topic modelling and contextual understanding, promising an enriched user experience.

The hotel industry is continually evolving, driven by changing TRAVELLER preferences and the surge in online bookings. In this dynamic landscape, the importance of effective hotel recommendations cannot be overstated. Today's TRAVELLERS seek personalized and relevant suggestions to streamline the decision-making process and ensure their travel experiences align with their expectations. To address these needs, we propose the development of a novel hybrid recommendation system that synergizes the strengths of LDA and BERT.

Hotel recommendations are integral to the travel industry, and their impact reaches far beyond mere booking decisions. They influence user satisfaction, brand loyalty, and the overall quality of a travel experience. In a world awash with information, users are overwhelmed with options, and the challenge lies in offering them not just a multitude of choices but recommendations that truly resonate with their preferences.

The hybrid recommendation system proposed here endeavours to bridge the gap between traditional approaches and the evolving landscape of natural language processing and artificial intelligence. By uniting the well-established technique of LDA, a topic modelling algorithm, with the cutting-edge capabilities of BERT, a state-of-the-art language model, this system strives to understand and address the diverse and nuanced needs of travellers.

LDA as discussed in [1] is a probabilistic model designed to uncover hidden topics within a corpus of text. For hotel recommendations, it excels in identifying underlying themes, thereby enhancing our understanding of user queries, hotel descriptions, and reviews. LDA operates by probabilistically assigning words to topics and topics to documents, thus offering a topic distribution for each document. Consequently, it unveils the latent themes embedded within textual data, allowing for categorization based on topics like "Beachfront," "Family-Friendly," or "Luxury." Thus, LDA uncovers the essence of textual information, making it highly applicable in the context of hotel recommendation.

In parallel, as proposed by authors in [2] BERT, signifies a breakthrough in natural language understanding. It revolutionizes the way machines interpret and analyse human language. The essence of BERT lies in its bi-directional and context-aware capabilities. It comprehends not just the words themselves but also the contextual nuances, the interplay of terms, and the subtleties of language. When applied to hotel recommendations [3], BERT excels in understanding user intent, sentiment, and the intricacies of language. It transcends keyword matching and delves deep into the user's intent, allowing it to grasp the essence of queries, even when they are expressed in a conversational or idiomatic manner.. It understands that a user asking for a "budget-friendly hotel with ocean views" is looking for an affordable accommodation option with a scenic waterfront vista. The synthesis of LDA and BERT exponentially improves the performance of recommendation engines. LDA identifies the latent topics, offering a structured view of the corpus, while BERT dives into the rich context of language, understanding the user's intent with precision. This harmony between topics and semantics enables the system to categorize hotels into topics defined by LDA and further refine recommendations based on the contextual and semantic understanding offered by BERT.

2 Literature Review

A methodical approach in the coverage of previous related work in literature from 2015 to 2023 was followed, major online repositories like Google Scholar, ieeexplore and elsevisor were extensively searched. It is important to note that a majority of the previous works in the literature includes various methods and techniques related to the topic.

Authors in [1] proposed a recommendation system, compares the user preferences on a semantic level with the pre-determined attractive features to recommend the tourist destination with the maximum similarity.

Authors in [2] presented a multi-level recommendation engine that can identify the ideal tourist destination that best matches the user preferences and requirements. The recommendation model uses a hybrid filtering methodology, taking into consideration both user preference and destinations liked by similar users.

Authors in [3] proposed a methodology, utilizing topic modelling algorithms such as Latent Dirichlet Allocation and BERT embeddings, and GA based clustering to analyse user-generated content in social media to determine the most significant topics with regards to Moroccan tourist shopping destinations.

Authors in [4] discussed a hybrid recommender system called HybridBERT4Rec, which combines content-based filtering (CBF) and collaborative filtering (CF) techniques based on BERT. The system aims to improve recommendation accuracy by considering both user preferences and item characteristics.

Authors in [5] analysed 242,020 Airbnb reviews associated with a guests' lodging experience in Malaysia to determine the 22 Quality of Service attributes using a structural topic model. It examines the varying preferences of both domestic and international guests and establishes a hierarchy of expectations from the host.

Authors in [6] proposed a model for trend analysis using LDA topic modelling. The model aims to identify latent topics in a document and analyse their trends. The accomplishment of achieving good coherence scores without the complexity of deep learning or graph networks have been highlighted.

Authors in [7] mined implicit information in text reviews to improve the rating matrix and enhance recommendation performance. The algorithm utilizes BERT to quantify sentiment information in reviews and integrate it with the user-item rating matrix. Experimental results demonstrate the effectiveness of the proposed approach.

Authors in [8] proposed a binary classification called Bidirectional Encoder Representations from Transformers (BERT) model to analyse the positive-negative, neutral-negative, neutral-positive sentiments present in online hotel reviews crawled from TripAdvisor. The pre-trained word embedding from the BERT model along with word vectors and TF-IDF of frequent words is given as input to a Random Forest Classifier. Using fuzzy logic, these reviews are grouped and recommended to the user.

Authors in [9] evaluated a system using different performance measures such as Precision@10, Recall@10, F1@10, AUC, and NDCG@10. The system was compared to three state-of-the-art food recommender-systems. The developed system achieved higher Precision, Recall, F1, AUC, and NDCG values compared to the other systems.

Authors in [10] presented a hotel recommendation framework that combines collaborative filtering (CF) with content-based filtering (CBF) to overcome the sparsity issue in hotel rating data. The framework also improves prediction accuracy and uses diversity techniques to optimize the recommendation list. The evaluation metrics used in the system are Mean Absolute Error (MAE), Root of the Mean Square Error (RMSE), and Asymmetric Measures (ASYMM) to help measure the performance of the hotel recommendation framework.

3 Methodology and Approach

The system first identifies the city of preference and performs web scrapping, thus extracting reviews of all the hotels in the city. The reviews stored in a CSV file is pre-processed, following which it is subjected to the LDA processing where stop words are removed and the underlying topics are identified for every hotel. In parallel, BERT generates text embeddings for the reviews and the user query/preference. The recommendation module computes a score for every hotel based on the user preference by comparing the textual similarity between the processed content and the user's processed input. This score will be used to determine which hotel aligns the best with the user's criteria; this is shown in Fig. 1.

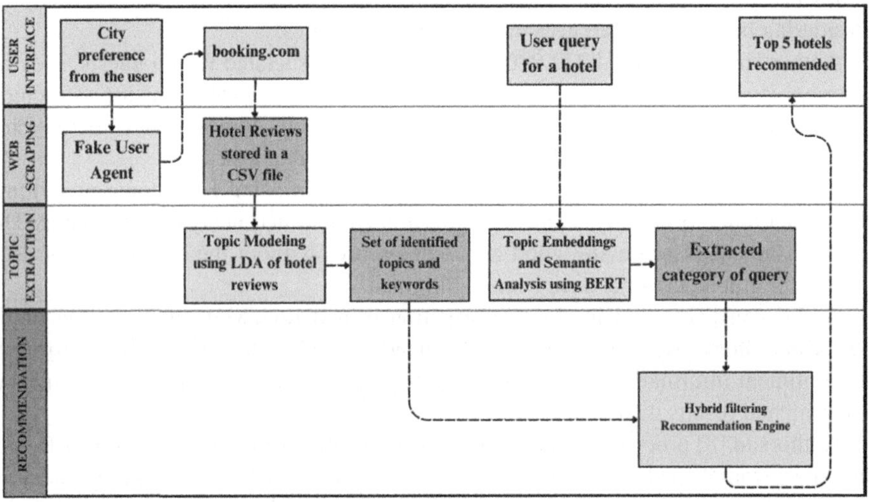

Fig. 1. Proposed System Architecture

3.1 User Preference Processing

The first module is responsible for processing user preferences. When a user inputs their preferences, such as "family-friendly and budget-friendly hotels in Venice," this module parses and extracts the essential keywords, such as "family-friendly" and "budget-friendly." These keywords act as the initial cues for the recommendation process. BERT encoders are used to extract the keywords which will act as the categories.

3.2 Web Scraping and Data Acquisition

The hotel datasets have been created using a Web Scraping process that uses the BeautifulSoup package and a Selenium chrome driver.

This module entails web scraping to obtain valuable data from external sources, specifically hotel reviews from booking.com for the Venice region as shown in Fig. 2. The engine uses web scraping techniques to collect textual data that includes hotel descriptions, reviews, ratings, and other relevant content. This data forms the foundation for generating recommendations. The extracted data contains the name of the hotel, the review title, the review text, score out of 10 and date.

Hotel_Name	review_title	review_text	Reviewer_	date
Antico Panada	Best hotel for first time in venice	If you are going to Venice for the first time this is the perfect hotel. It is central, right by st markâ€	10	Aug-21
Antico Panada	Good	The room was very large and had it's own bathroom attached to it. It was also nicely decorated a	7	Aug-23
Antico Panada	Loved staying here & it was our second time!!	Breakfast was a little bit less than we expected for such a lovely hotel. Need more variety and big	8	Sep-23
Antico Panada	Perfect location, perfect for a solo traveller	I felt very safe in this location, check in really quick, room in a quiet location. Bed and pillows ve	8	Aug-23
Antico Panada	Good stay overall, tiny room but had air conditioning.	Great location	6	Aug-23
Antico Panada	Lovely stay in Venice	Really quirky room beautifully furnished!	8	Aug-23
Antico Panada	Very good	Location if the hotel is great	8	Aug-23
Antico Panada	It worked out perfect for us. Thank goodness they moved us	That location was perfect. They had to put us in a different room because the first room they put	8	Aug-23
Antico Panada	Very good	Nice clean room, well decorated. Excellent location!	8	Aug-23
Antico Panada	Good	Location of property is excellent	7	Jul-23
BW Premier Collection CHC Continental	Good hotel	It has the advantage of being a central location, the hotel is comfortable in general, it was great	10	Jul-22
BW Premier Collection CHC Continental	Great place to stay!	We had a great night in Venice. Our room was upgraded so we were super happy. The room was	9	Aug-23
BW Premier Collection CHC Continental	Very good	Location was great	8	Sep-23
BW Premier Collection CHC Continental	Fantastic location and good value for money	Great location	9	Aug-23
BW Premier Collection CHC Continental	Greta location with comfortable stay but not as luxury as p	Location for ease if only staying a night in Venice, rooms were comfortable with AC and provide	8	Sep-23
BW Premier Collection CHC Continental	I will stay here again	Located perfectly	9	Aug-23
BW Premier Collection CHC Continental	Lovely would stay again.	Very nice room very clean, good coffee	8	Aug-23
BW Premier Collection CHC Continental	Great location, lovely hotel	Great location. Friendly staff. Good breakfast. Lovely views of the canal from our room! It was ve	8	Aug-23
BW Premier Collection CHC Continental	Very good	The hotels location was perfect. The room was nice, clean and big. The staff was polite and kind	8	Jul-23
BW Premier Collection CHC Continental	Loved our experience! Location and restaurant were great.	My experience at this hotel was amazing! I would definitely recommend it. I stayed there with my	9	Aug-23
Hotel Bonvecchiati	excellent on all they do!	the staff exceed my expectations, i forgot some of my Jewerly and they returned to me intact they	10	Jan-23
Hotel Bonvecchiati	Superb	Excellent location in the centre of Venice, nice air-conditioned room, clean bathroom, good bre	9	Aug-23
Hotel Bonvecchiati	Perfect location hotel	The location is perfect, between San Marco Square and Rialto Bridge. Despite being quite small,	8	Sep-23
Hotel Bonvecchiati	Good	Close to everything. Staff helpful, buffet breakfast, view of canal.	7	Sep-23
Hotel Bonvecchiati	Very good	Located in excellent location, near marco square and Rialto Bridge.Wide range of breakfast foo	8	Sep-23
Hotel Bonvecchiati	Good	The location was perfect. The hotel is very pretty from the outside and really enjoyed the restaura	7	Aug-23
Hotel Bonvecchiati	Hotel sa Å¡armom	The hotel is in the center. We asked for a room on a higher floor, to have a view of the roof and a	9	Sep-23
Hotel Bonvecchiati	I would stay here again, itâ€™s a great hotel and good value	It was easy to find and centrally situated with great access to all of the sites.	7	Sep-23
Hotel Bonvecchiati	Very good	Location is excellent, staff are helpful. Classic Venice hotel, feels like you are taking a step back	8	Aug-23
Hotel Bonvecchiati	Had a wonderful stay. Great location and a nice breakfast a	Great location	7	Sep-23
Hotel Carlton On The Grand Canal	Best hotel weâ€™ve ever stayed at in Venice!	Location was so convenient. Staff treated us so warmly when we arrived. Claudia and the guy wi	10	Jul-23
Hotel Carlton On The Grand Canal	Very good	Great location.	8	Sep-23
Hotel Carlton On The Grand Canal	Pleasant stay and hotel sufficient as a base / somewhere to	Staff were extremely helpful , location was perfect . Opposite the train station and only a few mir	7	Aug-23
Hotel Carlton On The Grand Canal	Place to sleep enroute to Ravenna for cruise ship. Nothing i	We stayed at the Carlton twice for 2 nights before and after a Royal Caribbean cruise. The first st	8	Sep-23

Fig. 2. Extracted Hotel Reviews

3.3 Preprocessing and Text Analysis for Keyword Extraction

The preprocessing stage plays a pivotal role in refining textual data for subsequent analysis in the hybrid LDA-BERT recommendation system. It begins with data ingestion, where the CSV file containing the hotel reviews is collected. To ensure consistency and uniformity, the text undergoes a series of steps. Firstly, data cleansing is carried out to remove extraneous characters, punctuation, and non-alphanumeric elements. Following this, the text is tokenized into words or subword tokens, allowing for granular analysis.

The next phase entails stop word removal, where common and less informative words, such as "the," "is," and "and" are filtered out to focus on content-carrying terms. Furthermore, stemming or lemmatization is applied to reduce words to their base or root forms, aiding in uniformity and simplifying the subsequent analysis. This is done using the nltklinary package in python. The result of this is shown in Fig. 3.

```
place clean nice interiors staff extremely cordial
['place', 'clean', 'nice', 'interior', 'cordial']
location room staff
['location', 'room', 'staff']
loved location access canal water comfort room great conditioning
['location', 'access', 'canal', 'water', 'comfort', 'room', 'great', 'c
locationhelpful staff room conditions
['locationhelpful', 'staff', 'room', 'condition']
breakfast great staff exception
['breakfast', 'great', 'staff', 'exception']
central location clean friendly staff ample variety breakfast bonus aft
['central', 'location', 'clean', 'friendly', 'staff', 'ample', 'variety
location fabulous plenty restaurants bars cafes shopping doorstep short
['location', 'fabulous', 'plenty', 'restaurant', 'bar', 'cafe', 'doorst
location perfect minute walking marco square walk square early morning
on't know bookingcom hotel staff responding specific questions promptly
['location', 'perfect', 'minute', 'early', 'morning', 'crowd', 'square'
lovely hotel close everything easy walk around shops restaurants main a
```

Fig. 3. Preprocessed Hotel Reviews

3.4 Topic Distribution Using Latent Dirichlet Allocation

This process begins with an iterative estimation of two key probability distributions: the probability distribution of topics within documents and the distribution of words within topics. These two distributions are interrelated and are at the core of LDA's ability to disentangle the hidden themes within the textual data.

With each iteration, LDA refines these probability distributions to find the optimal combination of topics and their associated words that best explains the observed textual data. This process reveals the hidden themes or topics within the corpus, which are essentially clusters of words that frequently co-occur in the documents. Thus, LDA unveils topics related to various aspects of hotels, such as "service quality," "amenities," "location," or "customer reviews." Each topic comprises a set of characteristic words that capture the essence of that theme.

It uses the cleaned textual data to discover underlying topics that are prevalent in the hotel reviews. Three topics have been identified, Topic 0 shows positive reviews, Topic 1 shows negative reviews and Topic 2 shows reviews for hotels with moderate reviews as shown in Fig. 4. Additionally, the perplexity and coherence score of the model was identified as given in Fig. 5.

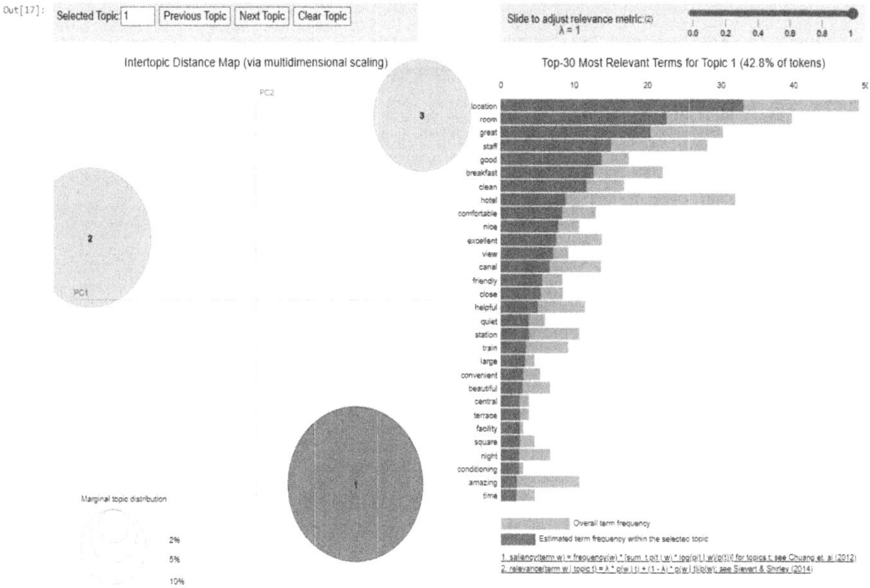

Fig. 4. Topic Distributions of Extracted Keywords

```
Perplexity:  -4.963631661592769

Coherence Score:  0.3649796284766693
```

Fig. 5. Snapshot of Perplexity and Coherence Score

3.5 BERT-Based Text Embeddings

In parallel, the BERT module generates text embeddings for the hotel descriptions, reviews, and user preferences. These embeddings capture the semantic and contextual information in the text, ensuring that the engine comprehends the meaning of words and their relationships within a sentence. This is shown in Figs. 6 and 7.

```
print(num_labels)

{0: 'Gondola Experience', 1: 'Family-friendly', 2: 'Culinary Experiences', 3: 'Opera Per
side', 6: 'Pet-friendly', 7: 'Sunset Views', 8: 'Eco-friendly', 9: 'Tranquil Stay', 10: '
{'Gondola Experience': 0, 'Family-friendly': 1, 'Culinary Experiences': 2, 'Opera Perforr
de': 5, 'Pet-friendly': 6, 'Sunset Views': 7, 'Eco-friendly': 8, 'Tranquil Stay': 9, 'Lu
12

6]: # Load tokenizer
tokenizer = get_tokenizer('basic_english')
```

Fig. 6. Identifying Unique Categories

```
{'pet': 36, 'in': 6, "'": 10, 'ghetto': 201, '<pad>': 0, 'experience': 58, 'canals': 57, 'family': 37, 'water-facing': 484
taway': 346, 'dog': 190, 'with': 5, 'cuisine': 310, 'costs': 305, '.': 2, '<unk>': 1, 'lagoon': 209, 'suggest': 22, 'venet
41, 'venice': 3, 'world-class': 492, 'spots': 125, 'your': 74, 'hotels': 4, 'crowds': 309, 'me': 7, 'sunset': 23, 'talents
0, 'at': 50, 'suitable': 455, 'accommodations': 8, 'that': 32, 'a': 9, 'perfection': 219, 'peaceful': 44, 'for': 11, 'obst
e': 394, 'i': 15, 'ballrooms': 263, 'all': 250, 'to': 12, 'find': 13, 'looking': 55, 'cater': 289, 'visit': 240, 'cats': 1
'show': 16, 'much': 382, 'the': 14, 'canal': 30, 'teatro': 463, 'lodgings': 17, 'both': 276, 'city': 51, 'st': 233, 's': 1
ecommend': 19, 'historical': 352, 'accept': 247, 'attractions': 109, 'gondola': 20, 'stay': 21, 'amenities': 172, 'opera':
'provides': 420, 'near': 25, 'enclosures': 327, 'view': 42, 'm': 40, 'bird-watching': 271, 'activities': 129, 'operatic':
'book': 26, 'pet-friendly': 45, 'help': 27, 'hotel': 28, 'views': 29, 'bike': 269, 'of': 34, 'cheese': 295, 'luxury': 31,
ge': 353, 'romantic': 79, 'and': 33, 'locate': 35, 'best': 38, 'where': 39, 'offering': 43, 'balconies': 174, 'tranquil':
'access': 47, 'prioritize': 417, 'authentic': 132, 'rides': 48, 'shows': 159, 'places': 49, 'canal-side': 66, 'private': 5
rails': 469, 'charm': 113, 'tours': 53, 'on': 59, 'reviews': 432, 'like': 54, 'friend': 342, 'serene': 56, 'calm': 284, 'c
ry': 60, 'travelers': 237, 'd': 61, 'waterborne': 485, 'rooftop': 80, 'experiences': 62, 'my': 90, 'family-friendly': 63,
ries': 259, 'services': 64, 'want': 65, 'setting': 439, 'canalside': 67, 'budget-friendly': 135, 'city-center': 68, 'night
e': 389, 'close': 69, 'care': 183, 'on-site': 152, 'enjoy': 70, 'need': 71, 'over': 216, 'ride': 72, 'immersion': 358, 'tc
06, 'sunsets': 73, 'within': 245, 'along': 130, 'art': 75, 'spending': 448, 'can': 76, 'discover': 77, 'reptiles': 427, 'g
s': 78, 'initiatives': 361, 'wine': 81, '5-star': 82, 'an': 83, 'strollers': 452, 'regular': 423, 'cooking': 84, 'gifts':
'evenings': 85, 'suites': 105, 'events': 86, 'from': 87, 'historic': 88, 'playground': 410, 'savor': 226, 'known': 89, 'cr
e': 308, 'offer': 91, 'kid': 369, 'their': 92, 'beauty': 93, 'center': 94, 'balcony': 175, 'classes': 95, 'away': 260, 'ea
```


Fig. 7. Creating and indexing the BERT Vocabulary

For every category, a positional encoding to order the unsequenced data is assigned. The head is set to 4 and the model size to 300.

The model is put into training mode as shown in Fig. 8, using 80% of the data set to train, 10% to test and the remaining to validate the classification. The epochs is set to 50, learning rate to 1e−4, batch size to 4 and the number of classes to 12. This is performed for the hotel reviews as well.

```
Epochs: 37 | Loss:  0.033 | Accuracy:  0.977
100%|██████████████████████████████████████| 108/108 [00:04<00:00, 23.69it/s]
Epochs: 38 | Loss:  0.034 | Accuracy:  0.972
100%|██████████████████████████████████████| 108/108 [00:04<00:00, 23.55it/s]
Epochs: 39 | Loss:  0.032 | Accuracy:  0.979
100%|██████████████████████████████████████| 108/108 [00:04<00:00, 23.66it/s]
```

Fig. 8. Training the BERT Model with Epochs Set to 50

3.6 Recommendation Generation Using BERT

A classification token is extracted from the search query and is passed through 12 layers of encoding to produce an embedding vector of size 768 which when passed through a multi-class classifier will identify the category the query belongs to. This is compared with the keywords obtained and the corresponding hotel is recommended as shown in Fig. 9.

3.7 Recommendation Scoring

The recommendation scoring module combines the LDA-derived topic understanding and the BERT embeddings. Accuracy and F1-Score is used to test the accuracy of the recommendation engine. These values are compared with LFM (Latent Factor Model), SVD++ (Singular Value Decomposition), MFFR (Matrix Factorization Fusing Reviews) shown in [10]. The same set of reviews and queries have been applied to the above-mentioned recommendation systems and their accuracy has been derived. The precision [11], recall [12], f1-score has been evaluated along with the overall accuracy percentage

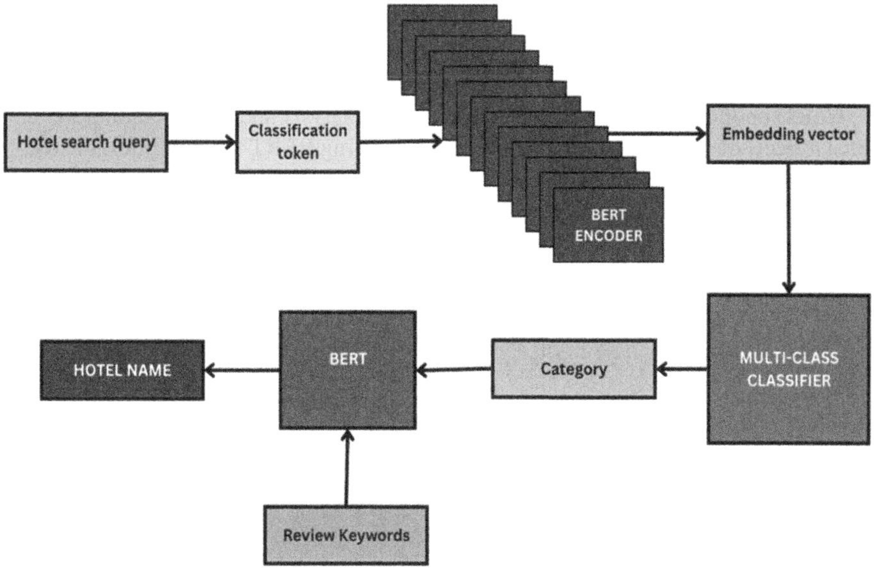

Fig. 9. Text Classification Using BERT

for all. The computation of the relevance scores for each hotel based on the user's preferences, the identified topics, and the textual similarity between the hotel content and the user's input. This scoring mechanism determines how well each hotel aligns with the user's criteria.

4 Results and Findings

The hybrid LDA-BERT hotel recommendation engine has demonstrated remarkable performance, achieving an impressive accuracy score of 82.407%. This outstanding accuracy reflects the system's ability to precisely recommend hotels that align with users' preferences, a significant leap forward compared to traditional recommendation engines.

One of the key highlights of this model is its F1 score, which surpasses that of traditional recommendation systems. The F1 score, a measure that balances precision and recall, is a critical metric in evaluating recommendation systems' performance. In this case, it demonstrates the model's effectiveness in not only providing accurate recommendations but also effectively identifying relevant hotels. The comparison of the hybrid approach with three classical recommendation algorithms, namely Latent Factor Model (LFM), Singular Value Decomposition (SVD)++, and Matrix Factorization Fusing Reviews (MFFR), showing superior performance of the proposed system has been demonstrated. The use of Accuracy Score and F1 Score as evaluation metrics has further confirmed the efficiency and accuracy achieved through the hybrid approach.

The high accuracy can be attributed to the synergistic approach of combining Latent Dirichlet Allocation (LDA) and Bidirectional Encoder Representations from Transformers (BERT). LDA excels at understanding the latent topics in textual data, enabling the system to categorize hotels based on various aspects such as service quality, amenities, and more. These topics provide a contextual foundation for recommendations, ensuring that user preferences are more comprehensively addressed.

BERT, on the other hand, excels in sentiment analysis and understanding the emotional aspects of user-generated content. By harnessing BERT's capabilities, the recommendation engine dives deeper into the user reviews to decipher emotional sentiment, allowing the model to make recommendations that not only match the user's criteria but also align with their emotional preferences. This level of personalization is a significant

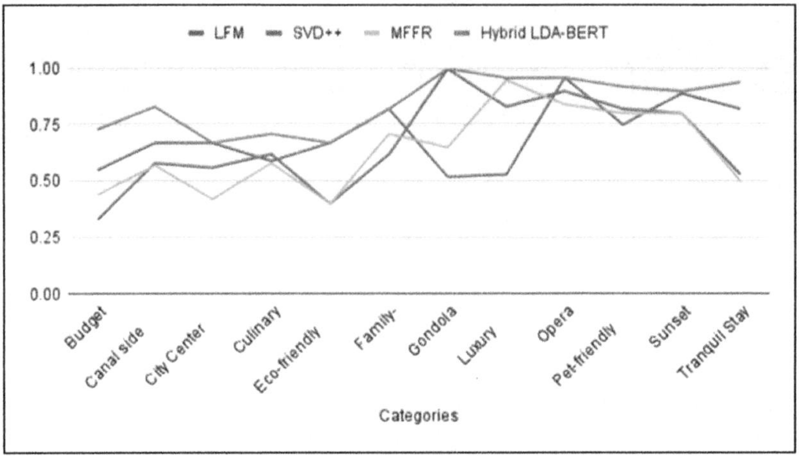

Fig. 10. Comparison of F1 Scores

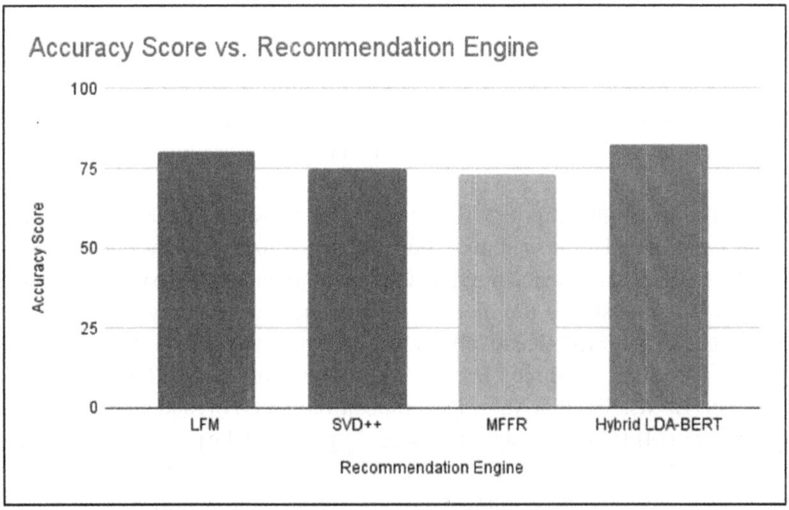

Fig. 11. Comparison of Accuracy Scores

leap forward compared to conventional systems that often focus solely on explicit criteria. Figure 10 and Fig. 11 show the comparison in the form of graphs for accuracy score and F1 score.

5 Conclusion and Future Work

In conclusion, this hybrid LDA-BERT approach has the potential to revolutionize the hospitality industry by providing users with personalized and meaningful hotel recommendations. Through LDA, the latent topics within hotel reviews have been harnessed, uncovering hidden patterns, and extracting valuable insights that go beyond surface-level analysis. This allows it to capture the essence of user preferences and cater to their unique tastes and desires. Furthermore, the integration of BERT, with its advanced natural language processing capabilities, enables a deep understanding of user queries and hotel descriptions. By leveraging the contextual knowledge embedded in BERT, this recommendation system has been empowered to deliver highly relevant and context-aware suggestions, enhancing the overall user experience. The combination of LDA and BERT in a hybrid approach synergistically addresses the limitations of traditional recommendation systems. This led to an improved accuracy, robustness, and adaptability, ensuring that users receive tailored recommendations that align with their preferences, even in complex and dynamic hospitality landscapes. This recommendation engine has shown greater accuracy when compared with three other recommendation engines used as a benchmark in this domain.

Delving into the fine-tuning of BERT for specific domains within the hospitality industry represents an area of exploration. Tailoring the BERT model to cater to distinct sectors like luxury hotels, budget accommodations, or niche travel experiences could significantly boost the engine's capacity to capture domain-specific nuances in user queries and reviews, ultimately leading to more precise and relevant recommendations.

Another promising area involves the integration of user feedback mechanisms. Creating feedback loops that enable users to rate recommended hotels, provide comments, or report issues can facilitate continuous model adaptation and improvement, enhancing user satisfaction over time. The incorporation of multimodal data is a burgeoning frontier. Integrating visual data such as images and user-generated photos of hotels can supplement the recommendation process. However, this endeavor demands the development of advanced techniques for processing and analyzing visual content in tandem with textual information. Further, our recommendation engine works on the assumption that the hotel reviews are authentic, thus allowing room for reviews containing false information to participate in the recommendation. Thus, another area to improve upon would be to validate user reviews.

References

1. Abbasi-Moud, Z., Vahdat-Nejad, H., Sadri, J.: Tourism recommendation system based on semantic clustering and sentiment analysis. Expert Syst. Appl. **167**, 114324 (2021). https://doi.org/10.1016/j.eswa.2020.114324

2. Alrasheed, H., Alzeer, A., Alhowimel, A., shameri, N., Althyabi, A.: A multi-level tourism destination recommender system. Procedia Comput. Sci. **170**, 333–340 (2020). https://doi.org/10.1016/j.procs.2020.03.047
3. Bouabdallaoui, I., Guerouate, F., Sbihi, M.: Combination of genetic algorithms and K-means for a hybrid topic modeling: tourism use case. Evol. Intell. (2023). https://doi.org/10.1007/s12065-023-00863-x
4. Channarong, C., Paosirikul, C., Maneeroj, S., Takasu, A.: HybridBERT4Rec: a hybrid (content-based filtering and collaborative filtering) recommender system based on BERT. IEEE Access (2022). https://doi.org/10.1109/access.2022.3177610
5. Ding, K., Choo, W.C., Ng, K.Y., Ng, S.I.: Employing structural topic modelling to explore perceived service quality attributes in Airbnb accommodation. Int. J. Hosp. Manag. **91**, 102676 (2020). https://doi.org/10.1016/j.ijhm.2020.102676
6. Gupta, R.K., Agarwalla, R., Naik, B.H., Evuri, J.R., Thapa, A., Singh, T.D.: Prediction of research trends using LDA based topic modeling. Glob. Transit. Proc. (2022). https://doi.org/10.1016/j.gltp.2022.03.015
7. Liu, N., Zhao, J.: Recommendation system based on deep sentiment analysis and matrix factorization. IEEE Access (2023). https://doi.org/10.1109/access.2023.3246060
8. Ray, B., Garain, A., Sarkar, R.: An ensemble-based hotel recommender system using sentiment analysis and aspect categorization of hotel reviews. Appl. Soft Comput. **98**, 106935 (2021). https://doi.org/10.1016/j.asoc.2020.106935
9. Rostami, M., Oussalah, M., Farrahi, V.: A novel time-aware food recommender-system based on deep learning and graph clustering. IEEE Access **10**, 52508–52524 (2022). https://doi.org/10.1109/access.2022.3175317
10. Zhang, K., Wang, K., Wang, X., Jin, C., Zhou, A.: Hotel recommendation based on user preference analysis. In: International Conference on Data Engineering (2015). https://doi.org/10.1109/icdew.2015.7129564
11. Precision Score. https://bit.ly/49vKS54
12. Recall. https://bit.ly/3SSJWk9

Road Damage Detection Using Real Time Video

G. Gomathi[1](✉) and G. Niranjana[2]

[1] Department of Computer Science and Engineering, SRM Institute of Science and Technology, Kattankulathur, Tamil Nadu, India
gg2819@srmist.edu.in

[2] Department of Computing Technologies, SRM Institute of Science and Technology, Kattankulathur, Tamil Nadu, India
niranjag@srmist.edu.in

Abstract. This study presents a completely unique deep-learning- powered real-time road damage detection system, paving the way for more secure roads and smarter infrastructure. With the help of convolutional neural networks (CNNs) and an easy to use interface, the system can automatically and clearly identify different types of road damage, such as surface irregularities, detailed fractures, and dangerous potholes. This innovative method surpasses the drawbacks of laborious manual inspections and ushers in a brand new age of advanced road safety and efficient maintenance. A strong CNN model that has been painstakingly trained on an intensive collection of annotated pictures and videos forms the basis of the system. It, as it should be, detects different sorts of damage with an accuracy close to 89%, offering users useful visible information via highlighting particular places on output pictures. However, the creativity doesn't stop there. The system has a clean-to-use Tkinter graphical consumer interface (GUI) that facilitates engagement. It also has real-time alarm triggers that, without delay, inform the appropriate authorities, ensuring timely restoration and decreasing any safety threats. To make the system work better, it is put through a radical testing process using common evaluation standards along with F1-rating, accuracy, precision, and recall. The findings are clear-cut, which is revolutionary pressure in addition to a useful tool for finding road degradation. Beyond the instantaneous safety advantages, it offers better infrastructure management and optimized useful resource allocation, opening the door to a future in which technology protects our lives and creates more secure, more convenient travel.

Keywords: Deep Learning · Real-Time · Road Damage Detection · CNN · Tkinter GUI · AI-Powered Safety

1 Introduction

Road conditions are essential for social and economic growth. In everyday life, potholes, fissures, and other damages may arise from frequent car smashing that damage the road's fundamental layers. Pavement deterioration will negatively impact load-bearing ability

Published by Springer Nature Switzerland AG 2025
A. Chandrabose et al. (Eds.): ICCCSP 2024, IFIP AICT 723, pp. 413–428, 2025.
https://doi.org/10.1007/978-3-031-73617-9_32

and road safety. Rain, snow, and vehicle loads may exacerbate harm to pavement if it is not restored promptly. This is going to have a negative effect on passenger mobility and safety, along with advantages for society. As a result, typical road repair is crucial. Road damage identification that is both reliable and effective is a critical component of road maintenance. In India, degradation of pavement is now mostly detected by physical inspection and assessment, yet manual examination is often time consuming and ineffective. The surface assessment procedure might be negatively impacted by an untrained inspector's erroneous appraisal of the extent of deterioration, even if physical inspection offers clear functional advantages. Due to the limitations of these physical inspections, this approach is no longer able to identify roadway damage in accordance with the rising demands of contemporary society [1]. Techniques for detecting harm to roads encompass the processing of images and videos, automated recognition, and detection by humans. The growing complexity and rising equipment expenses associated with automatic detection technology, including infrared or sensor equipped vehicles [2] are contributing to its expansion. On the other hand, when it comes to identification quickness and precision, it often falls short of the real requirements [3]. By converting a surface into a three-dimensional object in a system of coordinates, laser-measurement-based inspection techniques enable the precise computation of several metrics for pavement condition assessment [4].

When it comes to both expense and efficiency, digital imaging and video technology are much superior to automated recognition. As technologies evolve, identification accuracy also increases, allowing researchers to apply image processing approaches for pavement damage identification. Conventional image processing techniques segment pavement flaws using hand-selected parameters such as colour, appearance, and geometrical characteristics. Machine learning algorithms then categorise and match the segments with the aim of detecting pavement deterioration [5]. In order to identify the main features of fractures in road pictures and videos, Fernaldez et al. preprocessed the images. A decision tree heuristic technique was then used for categorization. Other researchers have used computational image analysis to identify fractures, concentrating on photographs of certain fissures that are noise-free. An automated image processing approach for fast and accurate pavement surface fracture assessment [6] was introduced by Li Q et al. In order to identify pavement cracks on surfaces, Song E. P. et al. presented a novel, optimised two-phase computation approach for primary surface profiles. Nevertheless, because of the intricate nature of road conditions, classical image and video processing methods are unable to match the criteria of robustness and model generalisation capacity in practical engineering applications.

2 Deep Learning Methods

Recent developments in deep learning and artificial intelligence have effectively solved problems with traditional approaches to road deterioration identification. Deep learning is becoming increasingly popular in a variety of domains because of its benefits, which include strong noise resilience and the lack of human extraction of features. Semantic categorization, recognition of objects, and classification of images and videos are prominent applications for convolutional neural networks [7]. Employing masked region convoluted neural networks (RCNN) and optimising the network using a path-enhanced feature pyramid network (PAFPN) and an edge detection branch, numerous scholars have put forward novel techniques for identifying tunnelling faults [8]. In order to fix problems with unstable data in different damage datasets, Wang et al. used data enhancement techniques before training an improved network model based on Faster RCNN to find and classify damaged roads [9]. Kaige Zhang et al. suggested a depth-generating adversarial network (GAN) for finding fractures. It had better training effects and better accuracy in identification [10].

A cross-domain damaged structure recognition technique based on transfer learning was proposed by Yi-zhou Lin et al. and it improved damage recognition performance [11]. Using the DeepLabV3+ model, Wang Zifeng et al. were able to precisely segment building site items and rebuild three-dimensional objects [12]. Although Yang et al. were able to identify fractures at the pixel level in pictures of walls and pavement [13], minor fracture identification remained a problem [14, 15]. A You Only Look Once (YOLO)v5x-based model was enhanced by Jeong et al. using Test-Time Augmentation (TTA), yet the model's detection speed was subpar [16]. Several investigators have tried lightweight models, including the YoLO-MF method by Ma D. et al. the YOLOv5 based model by Guo et al. the semantic segmentation network by Shim et al. and the lightweight CNN model by Sheta et al. These models, however, still have some drawbacks, such as the inability to properly identify fractures in road movies and the ability to only detect fracture damage while optimising identification effectiveness with precision.

The last few years have seen impressive results from deep learning algorithms, especially CNNs, in a number of computer vision applications, such as object identification, semantic segmentation, and picture/video categorization. CNNs are ideal for detecting road fractures because of their capacity to extract intricate structures and features from visual input. In this study, we presented a CNN-based image and video processing model for a road damage detection system. The technique trains CNN to properly identify various forms of road fractures by using a huge collection of annotated road photos and videos. After training, the model is used to examine input photos and video frames and identify regions that could have abnormalities related to roads. We used the Tkinter architecture to create a graphical user interface that would allow for user interaction and real-time tracking. Users can communicate with the system, inspect the identified road damages, and customise alert parameters depending on specified parameters using the GUI, which offers an intuitive platform. It is possible to customise the alarms to sound alerts that inform maintenance personnel or appropriate officials about discovered problems so that servicing and repair may be done on time. This system aims to evaluate several object identification techniques and carry out trials in order to train an exceptionally accurate and broadly applicable framework for road fracture identification. In order to gauge how well road damage detection techniques perform, the study will concentrate on how well the suggested strategy performs in road damage identification and categorization challenges. The method of detecting road damages may be automated to help officials deploy resources more effectively, carry out restorations on time, and reduce the financial losses brought on by unsafe driving circumstances.

3 Literature Review

The researcher emphasises object identification and the utilisation of deep learning and big data in road repairs. The GRDDC requested algorithmic suggestions from those who responded to identify the state of road deterioration autonomously. A picture shot there might show the Czech Republic, Japan, India, or another country. They focus on the detection and categorization of road fractures globally, with particular attention to Japan, the Czech Republic, and India. Potholes, transverse cracks, alligator cracks, and longitudinal gaps are the four main forms of damage that are often seen in it. Considering that data is collected worldwide from nations that are both developed and developing, The significance of road damage identification challenges is emphasised by the fact that they provide a thorough dataset and a uniform assessment system for comparing different strategies. The assignment has seen a sharp increase in involvement since it was first publicised. The same attraction has been shown by the leaderboards and related datasets. When the competition's nominations closed and the rankings were locked, we received numerous inquiries to reactivate them. On the competition's website, new ranking systems have been created to meet these needs and yet keep the task deadline. The Road Damages Identification Initiative aims to classify and identify road fractures worldwide. Summarises the problem and provides useful details for three recipients: scholars fascinated by the latest algorithms for identifying objects; opposition developers intrigued by the detailed planning of the opposition; and transportation professionals fascinated by automated road fracture recognition approaches [17]. The application of deep learning for identifying objects in urban street assessment and the identification and categorization of road fractures are covered in this research. They use CNN regions to concentrate on picture datasets for repositories. They provide object detection (version 3) by enhancing the darknet53 framework. The system is trained using the categories of road degradation. The researchers use one of the most advanced object recognition algorithms (YOLO) to identify the visual characteristics of each sort of road fracture, treating each as a separate object that has to be discovered. After learning that the training visual dataset includes a number of images with overlapping real-world boxes with different categories and multiple overlapping predicted boxes, the researchers raise the parameters of the NMS variable. The researchers concentrate on the dataset's cost, resource, and safety, emphasising cloud computing [18] for the identification, notification, and caution of road fractures. They compile more than seventy-five films, spanning more than forty-nine minutes that depict a wide range of scenarios and lighting conditions. Devices, edges, the cloud, DFRD, HDD, and MDD are examples of structure pieces that make up the elements of architecture. The method of producing pictures and captions is called a "domain mapping problem," where domain is made up of pictures of roads that have been destroyed, and domain Bt is made up of pictures showing roads in the backdrop. The researchers suggest a new EcRD paradigm in order to overcome the drawbacks of the existing techniques. This design makes use of edge computing, particularly when paired with the cloud, to develop programmes for smart road fracture identification and alerting that are speedy, efficient, and reasonably priced [19].

4 Objectives of the Study

1. Create a real-time road fracture detection system that can detect and categorise potholes, cracks, and different commonplace types of street damage with a minimum of 85% accuracy by way of the use of a CNN-based image and video processing model.
2. To show the proposed system's generalizability and efficacy in a range of road settings, evaluate its performance against benchmark datasets consisting of the Road Damage Detection Challenge.
3. Provide a user-friendly Tkinter graphical user interface (GUI) that permits smooth system interactions and allows users to see identified damage regions, regulate alarm parameters, and retrieve pertinent data.
4. Install an actual-time alarm system that, upon detecting road fractures, right away notifies the appropriate officials, enabling faster repairs and reducing viable safety threats.
5. Evaluate the overall performance and cost-benefit of the suggested device in relation to manual inspection strategies, emphasising its potential advantages for reinforcing aid allocation and road maintenance methods.

5 Methodology

The methodology and analysis used in the study include an in-depth explanation of the dataset, a list of all the necessary resources used, and an effective structure combined with the most recent convolutional neural network (CNN) model.

CNNs are used within the technique to become aware of road damage in images and videos. Convolutional layers are used to extract capabilities from input frames, after which pooling is used to decrease dimensionality. These characteristics are incorporated via absolutely related layers, and fracture types are anticipated by way of the output layer. For images, preprocessing techniques consist of binary or grayscale conversion; for videos, they consist of frame extraction or three-dimensional convolutions. Unspecified training parameters include loss characteristic, optimizer, and dataset sizes. Indian road images, Google Images, and Kaggle datasets are used to train the model [20].

6 Dataset Explanation

The pothole dataset was gathered from widely used websites such as Kaggle, along with some photographs and videos from Google and Indian roadways. The dataset utilised in this study is one of the most commonly used and freely accessible datasets for problems involving the categorization and identification of road fractures. There are two test sets (test1 and test2) and one train set (train) in this dataset. Atulya Kumar produced a Kaggle dataset called "Pothole Identification Dataset." It is intended to support the advancement of computer vision-based pothole detection systems. The dataset is made up of a number of photos taken from distinct urban and rural road settings that demonstrate various kinds and dimensions of potholes. To help investigators and programmers train and assess their algorithms, each picture has a tag indicating whether or not there are potholes. Those looking to enhance traffic safety and create computerised pothole detection systems will greatly benefit from this collection [21]. Atikur Rahman Chitholian has compiled a Kaggle dataset called "Annotated Pothole Image Dataset." It is made up of a series of photos that are focused on potholes, which are frequent flaws in roads. Since the dataset is annotated, it contains extra data to help locate and recognise the potholes in the photos, such as bounding boxes or pixel-level comments. Investigators, data scientists, and users of deep learning who are intrigued by creating algorithms or networks that instantly recognise and categorise potholes in photos will find great use in this dataset. A variety of computer vision algorithms for pothole recognition and assessment may be trained and evaluated thanks to the annotations, which offer ground truth data [22].

7 Resources

Employed in order to guarantee the effective deployment of the machine learning (ML) system known as "Smart Road Damage Identification and Warnings," certain resources are necessary. These resources include both technological and human knowledge. Four committed individuals on the task team are essential to the system's development process. There are also external and internal guides that offer direction and assistance. A computer system with an Intel i5 processor, 4 GB of RAM, [23] a 250 GB hard drive, a keyboard, and a mouse are required in regard to infrastructure. The Windows 10 operating system, Python programming language, Spyder IDE, Tkinter GUI, and SQLite database comprise the software stack. The development process is also greatly aided by tools and extra resources, including real-world road fracture video datasets from Kaggle, Jupyter notebooks, access to the internet, and Kaggle datasets. The Smart Road Fracture Identification and Warning System's resilience and efficacy are guaranteed by the incorporation of these resources.

8 The Recommended Methodology's Framework

A number of advantages are provided by the deep learning model-based road fracture detection system. First off, the system is able to precisely recognise and categorise damage to roads in photos or video clips by training the model on annotated datasets and using CNNs for feature extraction. When contrasted with human assessment techniques, this allows the system to deliver accurate and automatic road damage identification, reducing time and effort. Additionally, the system shows the user the outcome, either by giving a binary classification result or by graphically displaying the damaged regions. Road repair work may be planned and prioritised using this data, resulting in prompt repairs and an increase in total road safety. The user may also get messages or warnings from the system, giving them up-to-date information on any identified road fracture. These alerts allow streamlined repair and maintenance and improved transportation networks by facilitating timely response and enabling enhanced oversight of road systems (Fig. 1).

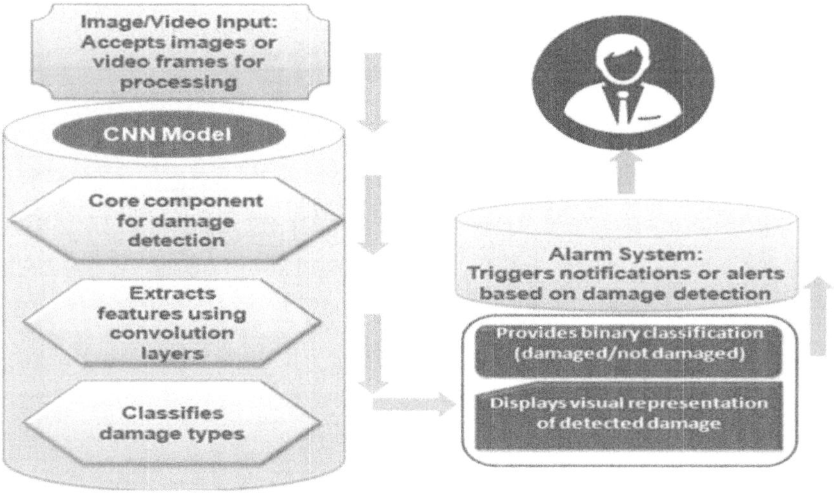

Fig. 1. Smarter Road Fracture/Damage Identification and Warning System Paradigm [26]

9 CNN Categorization

The CNN architecture, which is widely used in image and video processing applications, is used in the CNN framework for road fracture identification. Multiple layers, comprising convolutional, pooling, and totally linked layers, make up the whole framework of the model. Image or video clips are sent to the input layer; for photos, each of the frames is taken into consideration, and for films, a series of frames. By moving filters or kernels over the input and carrying out convolution activities, convolutional layers are in charge of learning and extracting features from the input data. ReLU and other activation features provide network non-linearity. By decreasing computational complexity without sacrificing important characteristics, pooling layers down samples the spatial dimensions of feature maps. The last pooling layer's output is flattened so that fully linked layers may interpret it as a linear representation. Allowing sophisticated feature representations, fully linked layers link neurons across layers and are in charge of the final classification or regression tasks. With many neurons representing various fracture kinds or class labels, the output layer generates the forecasts determined by a particular road damage identification job. Using strategies like reverse propagation and gradient descent, the model minimises the discrepancy among expected output and ground truth labels during training in order to maximise its forecasts [24]. The CNN model may use processes such as 3D convolutions to capture temporal relationships or perform operations on individual frames while interpreting video data. Experiments may be used to fine-tune the unique design decisions of the CNN, such as the number of layers, filters, kernel sizes, and depth, to reach optimal efficiency (Fig. 2).

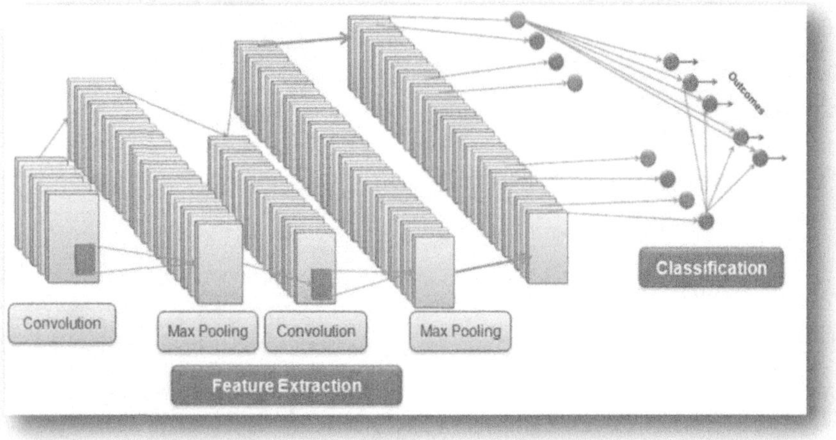

Fig. 2. Classifying Images using CNN [26]

10 Analysis and Results

The "Road Damage Identification System and Warnings" that is being suggested is capable of accurately recognising and categorising a wide range of road fractures, such as cracks, potholes, and uneven surfaces [25]. The system produces output pictures that are accurate and dependable, emphasising the faults that have been discovered. This provides important visual data for additional investigation and service scheduling. Furthermore, a warning system may be included, guaranteeing that the recognised road problems are promptly addressed by informing the appropriate officials or service technicians in real-time (Fig. 7).

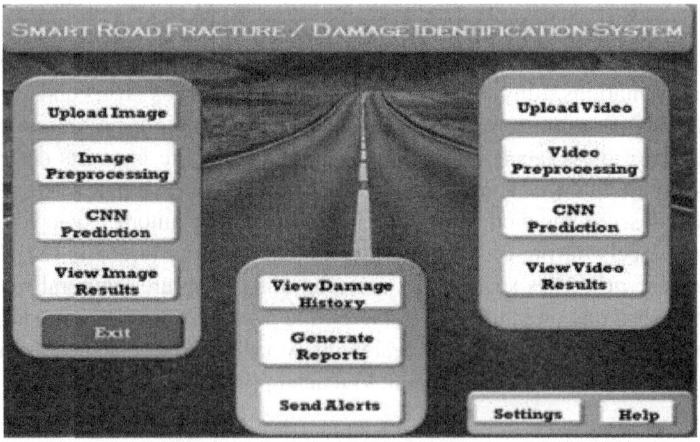

Fig. 3. Uploading a Picture to check if the Road has been cracked

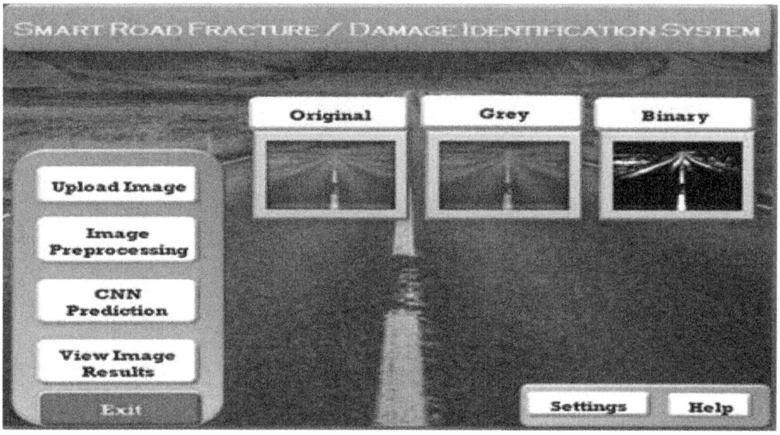

Fig. 4. To Improve Predicting abilities, preparing the CNN Model Using Grey and Binary Image Conversion Approaches

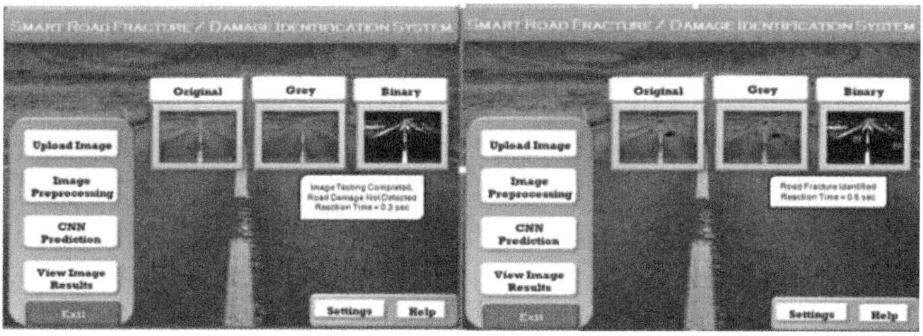

Fig. 5. (a) Road fracture is Not identified by CNN Model: Findings After Image Preprocessing (b) Road Fracture Identified

Fig. 6. Utilize Video Input Data for uploading and Check for fractures to the Road

The Road Damage Identification System's accuracy and effectiveness are proven visually by the figures depicted above. Figure 3 gives a clean visual representation of

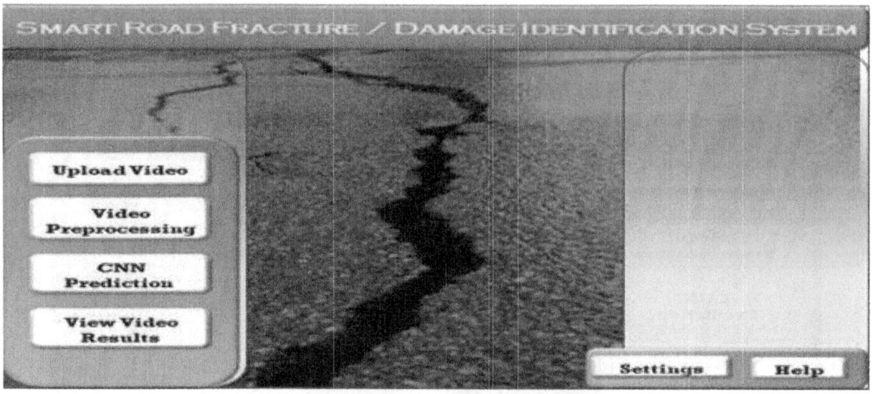

Fig. 7. Road damage is identified by processing video frames based on features and patterns that have been analyzed [26]

the correct road fracture analysis, demonstrating the crack detection abilities of the system. Figures 4 and 5 shed light on the CNN version's instruction procedure by showing how the system's accuracy is better when using binary and grayscale image conversion strategies. The figures show the preprocessing strategies that improve the system's overall performance, in addition to the defects that have been observed. The ability of the system to discover styles of road damage in real time is shown by the effective analysis of video frames in Fig. 6. These numbers, which might be backed by accuracy measures, together provide an intensive and open visual of the system's talent in recognising and classifying road damage, demonstrating its dependability and potential for green infrastructure renovation.

11 Technology and Communication Channels

The Road Damage Identification System makes use of contemporary communication tools to provide well-timed notifications that are powerful.

1. Cloud Computing: The system includes cloud computing to manage and keep records successfully. Rapid evaluation of road damage information is made possible by the speed, performance, and scalability that have been advanced with the aid of cloud technology.
2. Secure Communication Channels: To shield the integrity and security of the information, real-time warnings are dispatched over secure conversation channels. The sent data is blanketed by industry-popular encryption techniques.
3. Central Monitoring Station: A primary tracking station in charge of dealing with road service receives alerts. Instant records of approximately the kind and region of detected road damage are sent to officials on the tracking station.
4. On-Field Technicians: On-subject technicians with the essential tools to quickly manage problems with road maintenance can also get signals. By doing this, road damage can be quickly addressed, maximising useful resource utilisation and reducing downtime. The following are some advantages of generational integration: Efficiency:

Cloud computing speeds up information processing, making it viable to quickly discover and notify people of approximately any damage. Security: The confidentiality and integrity of dispatched warnings are assured through the use of stable communication channels. Real-Time Decision-Making: Rapid indicators and centralised tracking enable the government and technicians to determine road maintenance in a timely manner.

12 Warning System Operation

The warning system of the Road Damage Identification System runs nicely to assure prompt protection and intervention. There are many steps within the procedure, from alarm notification to damage detection:

1. Damage Detection: The device uses pictures and video frames taken by means of cameras to constantly display road surfaces in real-time. Cracks, potholes, and other road abnormalities are most of the several types of road degradation that might be recognised by the CNN-based version through analysis of those pictures.
2. Triggering Criteria: Predefined criteria that keep in mind the type and quantity of the detected road damage are used to prompt warnings. This technology is set up to differentiate between small surface imperfections and more severe issues, like huge cracks or deep craters. Damage severity levels are chosen mainly to make certain that the most prevalent road issues cause notifications right away.
3. Communication Mechanism: The system begins the communication exchange when it detects a road damage zone that satisfies the predetermined criteria. Real-time signals are sent to the appropriate government or a central monitoring station that is in charge of road maintenance. By using stable channels, the communication exchange mechanism ensures the secrecy and integrity of the information that is dispatched. Details like the sort of damage, the area's coordinates, and a severity rating might be covered within the notifications.
4. Recipient Notification: Through the conversation channels, immediate indicators are dispatched to the primary monitoring station. Field technicians who are prepared to respond quickly to road maintenance concerns may get notifications.
5. Reaction and Repair: After receiving notifications, officials or technicians might also determine the urgency of the repairs and set up a concern list. Decisions can be made quickly using real-time facts, which makes it less difficult to provide resources quickly to restore recognised road damage.

13 Areas of Improvement and Limitations

Even though the Road Damage Identification System indicates high-quality accuracy (88%), there's still room for development. Future advances might encompass adding more modern sensor technologies for even more precise identification, exploring new datasets for a number of site visitor conditions, and improving the CNN model structure. Some of the limitations encompass that the video may be suffering from an inclement climate, and the model may also want to be retrained on an everyday basis to modify to converting road conditions.

14 Metrics of Evaluation

Accuracy may be tracked and shown on a graph during the training process to evaluate the strategy's effectiveness. 1. ROC is the statistic used to assess how well an item categorization in the CNN structure is doing. 2. Precision 3. The F1-score 4. Accuracy 5. Recall 6. Loss.

Algorithm: CNN-based Real-Time Road

```
Input:
  - V: Real-time video feed or
static images
  - M: Pre-trained CNN model
  -          GUI:          Tkinter-based
Graphical User Interface
  - A: Real-time alert system
Output:
  - D: Detected road damages
with location and severity
  - T: Real-time triggers to the
alert system
```

```
Procedure:
  Initialize System(M, GUI, A)
  frames ← Preprocess Input(V)
  for frame in frames do
    prediction ← M.Predict
Damage(frame)
    if prediction. Damage Detected
then
      damaged Frame ← Highlight
Damage(frame, prediction)
      GUI. Display Frame(damaged
Frame)
      GUI. Update
Statistics(prediction)
      if A. Is Enabled then
        alert Details ← Compile Alert
Details(frame, prediction)
        A.Trigger Alert(alert Details)
    end if
  end for
```

Damage Detection and Reporting System

```
Performance Metrics ← Evaluate
Performance(M, GUI. Get User
Feedback())
  GUI. Display
Performance(performance Metrics)
  if GUI. UserRequestsRetrain then
    M.Retrain (GUI.GetUser
ProvidedData())
  end if

// Where the sub-procedures are
defined as:
  Preprocess Input(V)
  Highlight Damage(frame,
prediction)
  Compile Alert Details(frame,
prediction)
  Evaluate Performance(M,
feedback)
```

	Predicted Positive	Predicted Negative
Actual Positive	44 (TP)	9 (FN)
Actual Negative	6 (FP)	57 (TN)

Fig. 8. Confusion Matrix

Total Number of Samples: 116
Calculations

Accuracy
The percentage of properly identified samples relative to the overall amount of samples is called accuracy. It is presented as a percentage and shows how effectively the model anticipates the proper class labels. The precision is provided as (Fig. 8)

$$Accuracy = \frac{TP + TN}{Total} = \frac{44 + 57}{116} = \mathbf{0.8894}$$

Precision

The percentage of genuine favourable forecasts among all positive forecasts is measured by precision. It illustrates how well the model can recognise positive samples. One way to write precision is as

$$Precision = \frac{P}{TP + F} = \frac{44}{44 + 6} = \mathbf{0.8800}$$

Recall

The percentage of precise positive forecasts among all real positive samples is determined by recall. It assesses how well the model can accurately identify every positive sample. It is possible to write recall as

$$Recall = \frac{TP}{TP + FN} = \frac{44}{44 + 9} = 0.8302$$

F1-Score

The harmonic mean of recall and accuracy is known as the F1-score. It provides an equitable assessment of the framework's effectiveness by combining the two measures. Whenever there is an unequal distribution of classes in the dataset, the F1-score is helpful.

$$\mathbf{F1 - Score} = \frac{recall^{-1} + precision^{-1}}{2} = \frac{(0.8302)^{-1} + (0.8800)^{-1}}{2} = \mathbf{0.8545}$$

Interpretation

Accuracy: About 89 out of 100 samples are correctly classified with the aid of the framework.

Precision: The system has a high degree of acceptance as true in its forecasts, as it's accurate around 88% of the time because it anticipates a good outcome.

Recall: Approximately 83% of real positive results are as they should be identified by way of the algorithm, indicating that a small number of positive cases may be missed.

F1-Score: 0.8545 is the balanced accuracy and recall rating, indicating typically good but quite uneven achievement (Fig. 9).

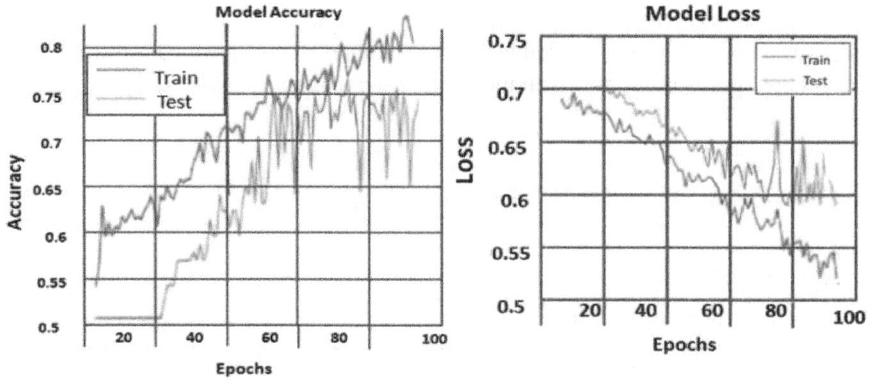

Fig. 9. Comparison between Accuracy vs Epochs & Epochs vs Loss

15 Conclusion

To sum up, the road damage detection system, which uses the CNN framework and the Tkinter GUI, provides a useful way to quickly and precisely detect and categorise fractures on road surfaces. This framework is simple to set up and operate because of its user-friendly interface, which makes use of the power of CNN algorithms. The technology has shown via testing and assessment that it can identify and categorise road damage with an astonishing accuracy of around 88%. This demonstrates how well the system's deep learning classifier algorithm works. The technology improves effectiveness and saves time by automating the process, which decreases the requirement for human involvement in road maintenance tasks. All things considered, this road damage detection system is a useful tool for improving road maintenance procedures.

References

1. Fernald, M., Taylor, D., VanDerslice, J.: Road to ruin: the environmental and social impacts of roads in developing countries. Tufts University (2001)
2. Guan, H., Liu, L., Cao, S., Yu, Y.: Use of unmanned aerial vehicle for quantitative crack detection of concrete structures. Struct. Control. Health Monit. **26**(3), e2308 (2019). https://doi.org/10.1002/stc.2308
3. Li, Q., Liu, X., Zhang, X., Huang, B., Dai, H.: CrackTree: automatic crack detection from pavement images. Pattern Recogn. Lett. **119**, 61–68 (2019)
4. Song, E., Subramanian, V., Choi, Y., Kang, M.B.: Surface profile-based crack detection algorithm for unpaved road surface condition assessments. Transp. Res. Rec. **2636**(1), 75–85 (2017)
5. Mathavan, S., Rahman, M., Stonecliffe-Jones, M., Kamal, K.: Pavement crack detection using OpenCV. Procedia Eng. **114**, 668–675 (2015)
6. Li, Q., Zou, Q., Zhang, D., Mao, Q.: FoSA net: attention-based deep neural network for vibration-based structural damage detection. Struct. Health Monit. **17**(5), 1031–1047 (2018). https://doi.org/10.1177/1475921717747093
7. Tasdizen, O., Akinci, B.: Utilization of Deep Learning Techniques for Automated Detection and Classification of Construction Site Images (2020). arXiv preprint arXiv:2007.03819. https://arxiv.org/abs/2007.03819

8. Gopalakrishnan, K., Khaitan, S.K., Choudhary, A., Agrawal, A.: Deep convolutional neural networks with transfer learning for computer vision-based data-driven pavement distress detection. Constr. Build. Mater. **157**, 322–330 (2018)
9. Wang, Q., Wu, J., Li, M., Wang, Y., Cheng, J.C., Liu, Y.: Deep learning- based automated detection and classification of seismic damage in masonry buildings using drone imagery. Comput.-Aided Civil Infrastruct. Eng. **34**(12), 1117–1132 (2019)
10. Zhang, K., Cheng, H.D., Zhang, B., Huang, F.: Unified convolutional neural network for pavement crack detection and classification. IEEE Trans. Intell. Transp. Syst.ll. Transp. Syst. **22**(10), 6313–6324 (2020)
11. Lin, Y.Z., Nie, Z.H., Ma, H.W.: Cross-domain damage detection based on image translation and transfer learning. Autom. Constr. **122**, 103541 (2021)
12. Wang, Z., Huang, X., Zhao, Z.: Automatic pixel-level crack detection of concrete structure using deep learning technique. Constr. Build. Mater. **314**, 125771 (2022)
13. Gao, F., Li, Y., Han, W.: Pavement crack detection and segmentation based on improved deep convolutional neural network and minimal path selection. IEEE Sens. J. **22**(5), 5125–5136 (2021). https://doi.org/10.1109/JSEN.2021.3121241
14. Yang, F., Zhang, L., Yu, S., Prokhorov, D., Mei, X., Ling, H.: Feature pyramid and hierarchical boosting network for pavement crack detection. IEEE Trans. Intell. Transp. Syst. **23**(4), 4063–4078 (2022)
15. Salman, M., Mathavan, S., Kamal, K., Rahman, M.: Pavement crack detection using the Gabor filter. In: 16th International IEEE Conference on Intelligent Transportation Systems (ITSC 2013), pp. 2039–2044. IEEE (2013). https://doi.org/10.1109/ITSC.2013.6728494
16. Jeong, G.M., Jo, K.H., Park, C.S., Lee, S.W., Park, M.W.: Improved YOLOv5x-based model using test time augmentation for robust detection of cracks on concrete. Autom. Constr. **134**, 104175 (2022)
17. Zohourian, F., Antic, B., Siegemund, J., Meuter, M., Pauli, J.: Superpixel-based road segmentation for realtime systems using CNN. In: VISIGRAPP, vol. 5: VISAPP, pp. 257–265 (2018)
18. Gong, J., et al.: A Pothole detection approach based on 2D surface profile modeling and 3D point cloud processing. IEEE Access **7**, 136819–136831 (2019). https://doi.org/10.1109/ACCESS.2019.2936860
19. Song, W., Jia, G., Zhu, H., Jia, D., Gao, L.: Automated pavement crack damage detection using deep multiscale convolutional features. J. Adv. Transp. **2020** (2020)
20. Gao, Y., Mosalam, K.M., Günay, S.: Deep concrete inspection network (DCIN): automated reinforcement localization and crack detection in concrete using deep fully convolutional networks. Comput.-Aided Civil Infrastruct. Eng. **37**(1), 3–20 (2022)
21. Kumar, A.: Pothole detection dataset. Kaggle (2021). https://www.kaggle.com/atulyakumar98/pothole-detection-dataset
22. Chitholian, A.R.: Annotated potholes image dataset. Kaggle (2023). https://www.kaggle.com/chitholian/annotated-potholes-dataset
23. Maeda, H., Sekimoto, Y., Seto, T., Kashiyama, T., Omata, H.: Road damage detection and classification using deep neural networks with smartphone images. Comput.-Aided Civil Infrastruct. Eng. **33**(12), 1127–1141 (2018)
24. Duarte, F., Nex, F., Kerle, N., Vosselman, G.: Satellite image classification of building damages using airborne and satellite image samples in a deep learning approach. ISPRS Ann. Photogramm. Remote Sens. Spat. Inf. Sci. **4**(2) (2018). https://doi.org/10.5194/isprs-annals-IV-2-25-2018

25. Pauly, L., Hogg, D., Fuentes, M., Ma, X.: Deep learning for surface defect detection. In: 2018 18th IEEE International Conference on Machine Learning and Applications (ICMLA), pp. 827–834. IEEE (2018). https://doi.org/10.1109/ICMLA.2018.00133
26. Mateen, A., et al.: Smart roads for autonomous accident detection and warnings. Sensors **22**(6), 2077 (2022)

Smart Armband with Fall Detection in Elderly

A. R. Fathima Naushin(✉), Nivetha Elango, Jeevesh Krishna Arigala, S. Vikash Anand, and R. Kanchana

Sri Sivasubramaniya Nadar College of Engineering, Rajiv Gandhi Salai (OMR), Kalvakkam 603110, India
{fathima2010192,nivetha2010668,jeeveshkrishna2010708, vikashanand2010015,rkanch}@ssn.edu.in

Abstract. The paper aims to create an affordable wearable fall detection system aimed at accurately identifying falls. The system comprises a smart armband prototype equipped with embedded sensors to capture motion data from elderly individuals during their daily activities. The primary objectives include designing a compact hardware prototype incorporating an accelerometer, and gyroscope, with a microcontroller unity, implementing fall detection algorithms utilizing threshold-based techniques and machine learning models for real-time classification of falls versus other activities, and optimizing the algorithms for on-device execution with limited computing resources. The ultimate goal is to develop a non-invasive, cost-effective solution for elderly fall monitoring that is both accurate and robust. The prototype's development will encompass hardware design and optimization of the fall detection algorithm for on-device inference, with future research potentially integrating this system into assistive technologies to enhance safety for independently living elderly individuals.

Keywords: Internet of Things(IoT) · Wearable Technology · Threshold-Based Detection · Elderly · Good Health & Well Being · Machine Learning(ML)

1 Introduction

The Internet of Things (IoT) refers to a system where numerous devices and sensors are interconnected, enabling them to communicate through computer networks. This network links tangible objects to the internet and offers possibilities for constructing systems utilizing diverse technologies like Near Field Communication (NFC) and Wireless Sensor Networks (WSN).

The healthcare industry has seen the emergence of a range of health monitoring devices enabled by IoT integration. Within IoT healthcare setups, wireless technology aids in gathering crucial data from these devices, which is subsequently shared with medical practitioners and researchers. These medical IoT

Published by Springer Nature Switzerland AG 2025
A. Chandrabose et al. (Eds.): ICCCSP 2024, IFIP AICT 723, pp. 429–438, 2025.
https://doi.org/10.1007/978-3-031-73617-9_33

(MD-IoT) gadgets are crafted for remote accessibility, connecting to various communication tools to consistently monitor patient health. The data collected by these devices is then transmitted to a sophisticated system acting as an interface, before being stored and analyzed securely on a cloud-based platform.

By employing IoT technologies, healthcare professionals can access real-time data, enabling more proactive and personalized care. With applications from this branch of engineering, we hope to improve the healthcare monitoring system for the senior citizens of our society. The remote monitoring capabilities provided by IoT devices offer a means to address healthcare challenges, promoting timely interventions and optimizing the overall healthcare experience for seniors.

In the domain of fall detection systems, camera-based systems were widely known [10]. In this system, a camera is placed in the room or on the person, and a fall is detected based on an algorithm running on the PC. Although it is an effective system, it has limited area coverage, a high cost, and, most importantly, a notable privacy compromise. Following this, some systems incorporate devices employing vibration or a fusion of audio and video data. In the former approach, vibration is detected by sensors (accelerometers) installed within the space [7], and the fall is subsequently computed using a suitable algorithm. On the other hand, the latter strategy, like the former, uses a program that combines aural and visual data to identify the fall. The above-mentioned systems can only detect a fall but fall short of identifying the specific individual who has fallen and transmitting crucial health parameters to doctors. Moreover, these devices are usually placed in the environment; thus, the probability of sending false alerts is high, which causes undue stress to doctors, nurses, and family members.

The focus of this paper lies in wearable systems. These are smart devices which incorporate accelerometers and gyroscopes, and their fall detection capabilities are categorized based on data processing methods and the location of fall detection. Wearables eliminate geographical limitations and streamline communication with relevant parties during falls, offering a promising solution to address the limitations of existing fall detection systems.

Most research, national and international projects, focuses primarily on the collection of data [3] and its analysis [2,3]. Our research, along with more efficient data collection and analysis, would focus on establishing a direct and secure linkage of the patient's health records to the necessary individuals, such as doctors, family members, and caregivers. It also makes it easier for the concerned people to keep track of the progress of the patient and do the needful accordingly. It helps the concerned individuals to act immediately in case of any emergencies or abnormalities in the patient's health condition.

With the increasing elderly population, there has been a surge in fall accidents, leading to numerous strategies proposed for prevention, including technological solutions or tailored fall prevention training programs. However, many of these approaches are costly, complex to implement, or underutilized by the elderly, often failing to produce the desired results. Moreover, the expanding elderly demographic is poised to intensify the workload of medical and nursing personnel [11]. The substantial workload involved in maintaining a patient database and the challenges involved in the senior citizens frequently visiting the hospitals also pose a problem.

This paper aims to gather comprehensive data on vital signs through the utilization of sensors embedded in a smart armband. Subsequently, perform predictive analysis of the collected data and regularly update the health records of the elderly in the application. Through this proactive approach, the system aims to promptly notify healthcare professionals and family members of any deviations or anomalies detected in the data, particularly those indicative of a fall.

This paper focuses on the literature survey, proposed methodology and the results of the ML integration. The organisation of the paper is as follows. Section 2 provides an overview of existing research approaches. Section 3 presents the proposed methodology. Following this, Sect. 4 gives a brief description of the ML integration and its result. Finally, Sect. 5 provides the conclusion of this paper.

2 Literature Review

2.1 Fall Detection Algorithms

In [4], the effectiveness of a fall detection algorithm based on a wearable, wireless sensor system (WSS) with a gyroscope and 3-axis accelerometer is evaluated. To gather real-time motion data from various simulated daily activities, the WSS is positioned near the middle of the chest. 36 human volunteers participated in the tests, and a total of 702 distinct motions were recorded in a lab environment. Half of the dataset was utilised to evaluate the algorithm's sensitivity and specificity, while the remaining 50% was allocated to algorithm development. During a fall, the WSS transmits the accelerometer and gyro data. This paper uses a simple threshold-based algorithm as its method. The gyroscope threshold was established experimentally using preliminary data obtained, and the accelerometer threshold found in the literature was used. A lower fall threshold (LFT) and an upper fall threshold (UFT) are decided for both acceleration and angular velocity. A fall window period is determined from the literature and defined as 0.5 s. When acceleration falls below the LFT (acceleration), data collected during the following fall window, is compared to the UFT for both the acceleration and angular velocity vector. If the acceleration and angular velocity are greater than the UFT of their respective values, then a fall is detected. If only either of them is greater than the UFT, then the fall is not detected. According to the research, the experimental results demonstrate that the algorithm has a sensitivity and specificity of 96.3% and 96.2%, respectively, for detecting falls when compared to other everyday movements.

[1] explores methods for detecting falls using sensors (accelerometer and gyroscope) in smartphones with unconstrained positions. To gather real-time motion data from various simulated daily activities, a smartphone is positioned in six different orientations: face-up, face-down, vertical-bottom, vertical-left, vertical-right, and vertical-top. Multiple human volunteers participated in the experiments, and a total of 84 fall events and 168 non-fall events were captured in an indoor environment. The dataset was divided into training and testing subsets for model development and evaluation. During each activity, the accelerometer and gyroscope data are recorded by the smartphone. This paper proposes a combination of five threshold-based methods: AGVeSR, Alim, $\angle\alpha$, GyroReDi, and AGPeak. The thresholds for each method were established experimentally using preliminary data. According to the results, the accuracy of fall detection using both sensors outperformed using only the accelerometer by over 15%Furthermore, combining the five methods yields a detection accuracy of 95.82% substantially higher than a standard Resultant Acceleration approach. Overall, the multi-modal sensor fusion and ensemble method demonstrates significant improvements in robustness to device positioning compared to existing techniques.

[10] provides a comprehensive overview of elderly fall detection systems using sensor networks and IoT technologies. It discusses the typical system architecture consisting of four main layers. The physiological sensing layer is responsible for data collection. According to the studies surveyed between 2014–2020, accelerometers placed on the body are the most commonly used wearable sensors for fall detection, with a total of 28 studies utilizing them. Depth cameras like the Microsoft Kinect have emerged as the most popular vision sensor compared to RGB cameras alone, with 12 out of the studies reviewed employing Kinect cameras for fall detection in the elderly. The local communication layer deals with transmitting the sensor data to local computing devices or the cloud via protocols like Bluetooth Low Energy to wirelessly transmit accelerometer and gyroscope data from wearable sensor nodes or USB/I2C interfaces to transfer Kinect depth camera data. The information processing layer performs data analysis and classification using machine learning algorithms for individual sensor approaches or feature/data fusion techniques for sensor fusion. The user application layer discusses commercial products and research projects that utilized fall detection systems with sensors and cloud platforms, with tables comparing wearable and vision sensor studies based on aspects like sensors, subjects, datasets, techniques and real-time capabilities. The literature survey highlights the promise of sensor fusion, particularly combining accelerometers and depth cameras, over individual sensors and identifies challenges in realistic evaluation, handling diverse fall types, and ensuring privacy, security and scalability that need further research.

2.2 Health Monitoring Technologies

[6] created a wearable armband device for electrocardiogram (ECG) monitoring during everyday activities. They employed Principal Component Analysis

(PCA) and Normalized Least Mean Squares (NLMS) adaptive filtering to minimize electromyographic (EMG) noise. Additionally, they developed an artifact detector and an optimal channel selector using a Support Vector Machine (SVM) classifier with a Radial Basis Function (RBF) kernel, utilizing features associated with ECG signal quality. Data was collected using wearable armbands, and two ECG channels were synthesized to mitigate noise effects: one utilizing PCA and the other NLMS. Furthermore, they computed four standard heart rate variability (HRV) parameters (SDNN, RMSSD, and powers at low and high-frequency bands) and compared them with data from a commercial Holter monitor. This indicated an error of not more than 1.37%. This armband proved useful for bedtime and non-bedtime monitoring but work has to be carried out to determine its suitability for non-optimal cases such as seizures, arrhythmia etc. The paper gave the team a better understanding of the design of a general armband device prototype.

[8] presents a groundbreaking technique for heart disease detection using the Deep Learning Modified Neural Network (DLMNN) classifier, integrating IoT in healthcare. His approach is divided into two modules: the patient module, which handles patient authentication and data management, and the analysis module, where prediction occurs. Key to this system is a wearable IoT sensor device that securely transmits patient data to the cloud using the PDH-AES technique. This algorithm is notable for its high security (95.87%) and efficient encryption-decryption process. The transmitted data is collected in the cloud, preprocessed and classified into normal or abnormal categories in the cloud. The weights used for classification by the DLMNN classifier are optimized using the Cuttlefish Optimization Algorithm. The classification is made and depending on the output, the heart disease is predicted and alerts are sent out. This classifier notably showcases superior sensitivity, accuracy, and specificity, along with f-measure in disease prediction.

3 Methodology

The proposed system architecture is designed to provide a comprehensive solution for fall detection and activity monitoring. As seen in Fig. 1, the proposed fall detection algorithm is implemented on an Arduino RP2040 Nano Connect Board which establishes a Wi-Fi connection, reads the sensor data as well as communicates the occurrence of a fall, to a remote server using essential libraries. By utilizing the identified thresholds , the system can identify activities such as walking and jogging, contributing to a more comprehensive health monitoring solution. Additionally, from Fig. 2, it can be observed that the design is made to be compact with a simple replaceable battery design that ensures continuous and seamless operation and usage for the elderly.

3.1 Algorithm

The fall detection algorithm focuses on a ten-second average scenario, calculating the rate of change of acceleration and angular velocity between the initial

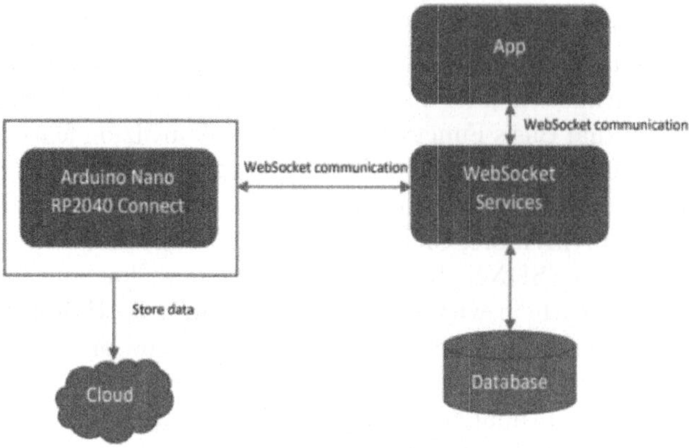

Fig. 1. Proposed System

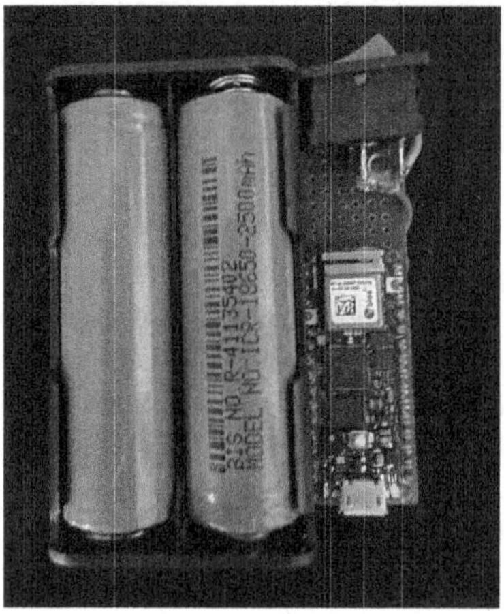

Fig. 2. Hardware Prototype

and final readings. Falls are detected based on predefined thresholds. Notably, a weighted average of acceleration and gyroscope magnitudes ensures a robust approach to movement analysis. Moreover, the system is able to discern various activities like walking and jogging based on the identified thresholds. The thresholds for all these activities are taken from a dataset consisting of all the required values based on which the activity is recognised in comparison with the detected values. The values calculated from the sensors can also be used to detect falls more accurately when integrated with ML Algorithms and the models explored are described in detail below.

4 Results and Discussion

4.1 ML Integration

We explored various machine learning models to improve the accuracy of fall detection compared to just using threshold-based methods. The models were trained and tested on a public dataset containing sensor data for various daily activities and different types of falls.

The models explored include Linear SVC, Logistic Regression, Convolutional Neural Networks (CNN), CNN + LSTM, Two Stream CNN + LSTM, and Bidirectional LSTM [9]. The dataset was pre-processed by normalizing the sensor values, applying signal filtering, and extracting statistical features. Class imbalance in the dataset was handled using weighted loss functions.

Of all the models, Bidirectional LSTM performed the best with an accuracy of 99.5% calculated from Fig. 6. The other top performers were CNN (whose accuracy is calculated from Fig. 3) and Logistic Regression with an accuracy of 98.7% and 98.9% respectively. The deep learning models like CNN, CNN + LSTM and Bidirectional LSTM performed better than linear models like Linear SVC and Logistic Regression as they are able to learn complex non-linear relationships from the time-series sensor data automatically. Specifically, the LSTM and bidirectional LSTM models work very well for sequential data like time series as they can remember long-term context and dependencies through their internal memory cells. This helps in accurately classifying fall events which need contextual information over a time period rather than just instantaneous values. Comparing Figs. 4 and 5, it can be observed that between the LSTM models, the bidirectional LSTM performed better than the unidirectional and CNN+LSTM models as it processes the data in both forward and backward directions, providing additional context for classification. The convolutional layers in CNN and CNN + LSTM models help extract local spatial features from the raw accelerometer and gyroscope signals before the fully connected layers interpret the features. This improves performance compared to feedforward networks. Logistic Regression works reasonably well as the statistical features extracted from the sensor data are linearly separable for the fall and no fall classes. However, it does not learn the temporal relationships that the deep learning models can.

While complex deep learning models like CNN + LSTM performed well during experimentation, we were unable to implement them efficiently on the Arduino board due to limited support for such complex neural network layers and the low memory and processing constraints of the microcontroller board. Therefore, for our final prototype, we implemented a simplified Logistic Regression model that could run effectively on the Arduino with a marginal reduction in accuracy using a platform known as Edge Impulse [5]. The model takes the extracted statistical features from the accelerometer and gyroscope data as input and predicts fall or no fall. This allows us to improve upon just using threshold-based techniques while being feasible to implement on low-power IoT edge devices. The simplified Logistic Regression provided a good tradeoff for on-device execution.

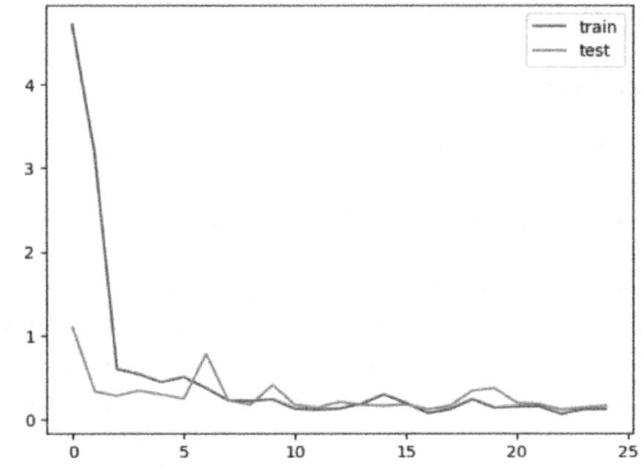

Fig. 3. Graph depicting the accuracy of CNN Model

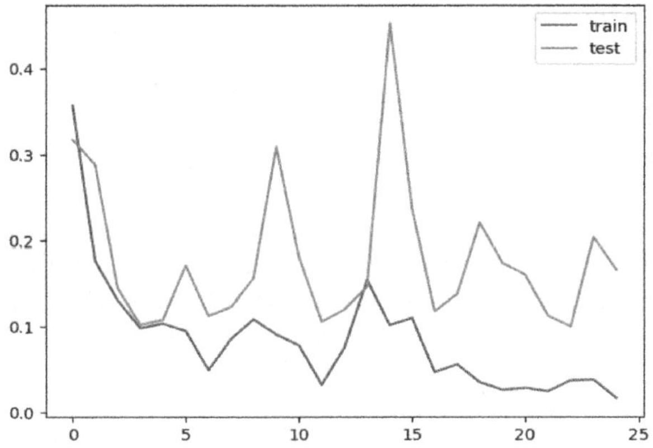

Fig. 4. Graph depicting the accuracy of CNN+LSTM Model

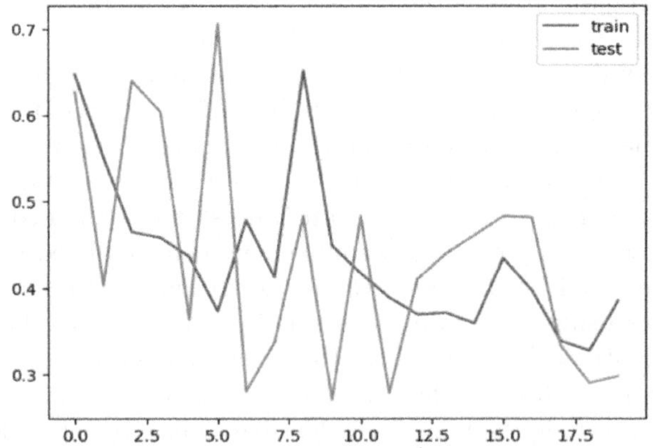

Fig. 5. Graph depicting the accuracy of Two Stream CNN+LSTM Model

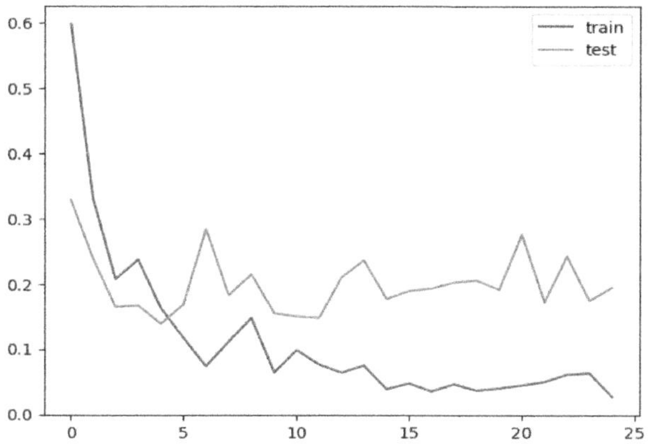

Fig. 6. Graph depicting the accuracy of Bidirectional LSTM Model

Our results demonstrate that the wearable armband sensor paired with a machine-learning model for fall detection provides a significant improvement over just using threshold-based techniques. The on-device ML model allows for low latency predictions while still maintaining high accuracy.

Table 1. Comparative analysis of ML Models

ML Model	Accuracy	Loss
CNN	0.966	0.144
CNN + LSTM	0.987	0.029
Two stream CNN + LSTM	0.884	0.281
BiLSTM	0.995	0.012

5 Conclusion

In this work, the design and implementation of a smart armband prototype for elderly fall detection have been presented. The wearable device incorporates an accelerometer and gyroscope to capture motion data, which is analyzed by an onboard microcontroller running a logistic regression machine learning algorithm to identify falls in real time. While the prototype shows promising capabilities for elderly fall monitoring, further testing is required under diverse real-world conditions. The robustness of the system can be improved by incorporating additional modalities like heart rate monitoring to reduce false alerts. Seamless integration with emergency response systems is also needed to enable timely interventions after dangerous falls.

References

1. Astriani, M.S., Heryadi, Y., Kusuma, G.P., Abdurachman, E.: Human fall detection using accelerometer and gyroscope sensors in unconstrained smartphone positions. Int. J. Recent Technol. Eng. (IJRTE) **8**(3), 69–75 (2019). https://doi.org/10.35940/ijrte.c3877.098319
2. Casilari, E., Santoyo-Ramón, J.-A., Cano-García, J.-M.: Analysis of public datasets for wearable fall detection systems. Sensors **17**(7), 1513 (2017). https://doi.org/10.3390/s17071513
3. Guerrero, J.C.E., et al.: Dataset for human fall recognition in an uncontrolled environment. Data Brief **45**, 108610 (2022). https://doi.org/10.1016/j.dib.2022.108610
4. Huynh, Q.T., Nguyen, U.D., Irazabal, L.B., Ghassemian, N., Tran, B.Q.: Optimization of an accelerometer and gyroscope-based fall detection algorithm. J. Sensors **2015**, 1–8 (2015). https://doi.org/10.1155/2015/452078
5. Reddi, V.J., et al.: Edge impulse: an MLOPS platform for tiny machine learning. In: Proceedings of Machine Learning and Systems, pp. 5 (2023)
6. Lazaro, J., Reljin, N., Hossain, M.-B., Noh, Y., Laguna, P., Chon, K.H.: Wearable armband device for daily life electrocardiogram monitoring. IEEE Trans. Biomed. Eng. **67**(12), 3464–3473 (2020). https://doi.org/10.1109/TBME.2020.2987759
7. Liu, C., Jiang, Z., Su, X., Benzoni, S., Maxwell, A.: Detection of human fall using floor vibration and multi-features semi-supervised SVM. Sensors **19**(17), 3720 (2019). https://doi.org/10.3390/s19173720
8. Sarmah, S.S.: An efficient IoT-based patient monitoring and heart disease prediction system using deep learning modified neural network. IEEE Access **8**, 135784–135797 (2020). https://doi.org/10.1109/access.2020.3007561
9. Seng, K.P., Ang, L.-M., Peter, E., Mmonyi, A.: Machine learning and AI technologies for smart wearables. Electronics **12**(7), (2023). https://doi.org/10.3390/electronics12071509. URL https://www.mdpi.com/2079-9292/12/7/1509
10. Wang, X., Ellul, J., Azzopardi, G.: Elderly fall detection systems: a literature survey. Front. Robot. AI **7**, (2020). https://doi.org/10.3389/frobt.2020.00071
11. Yacchirema, D., et al.: Fall detection system for elderly people using IoT and big data. Procedia Comput. Sci. **130**, 603–610 (2018). https://doi.org/10.1016/j.procs.2018.04.110

Waste Segregation Using Deep Learning Model

K. Jeevitha Bethulakshmi(✉), M. S. Tejasree, S. K. Yasvinippriyaa, and S. Umamaheswari

Department of Information Technology, MIT Campus, Anna University, Chennai, India
jeeviraji2003@gmail.com, uma_sai@mitindia.edu

Abstract. Waste segregation has become one of the crucial tasks which can in turn contribute to efficient recycling of wastes. Manual waste segregation techniques have a lot of issues and also time and efficiency constraints. All these have led to the need for a smart waste segregation system. The main objective is to develop a waste segregation system using a deep learning model built on YOLOv8 architecture, deployed on raspberry pi. The system focuses to classify the wastes to glass, metal, plastic and others by training the model with suitable dataset for each class. The experimental results show that classification model provides high accuracy and fast prediction making it a suitable tool for waste segregation.

Keywords: Waste management · Garbage Classification · Image Classification · Machine Learning · Deep Learning · SDG 11

1 Introduction

Waste management and segregation is one of the major challenges of our time and can pose major threats to resource utilisation and sustainable development, if handled carelessly. Thus, novel yet modern techniques should be incorporated into the process to improve efficiency. If not recycled, those wastes must be eliminated, which is even more tedious compared to the existing volumes of waste that need elimination.

Around 2.01 billion tonnes of waste are generated every year on a global scale, among which only around 19% of what is collected is recycled or used for compost. India generates almost 62 million tonnes of waste every year, of which about 70% is collected. Among the collected waste, only around 28% is treated, while the rest is dumped in landfills. It is estimated that the numbers will shoot up to 165 million tonnes by 2030.

According to the Environment Performance Index ranking for 2022, released by Yale and Columbia Universities on a biennial basis, India is in the bottom position among 180 countries. This is indeed bad news in terms of sustainability, environmental health and the overall development of the country. Thus, there is a need for proper management and recycling of waste to restore environmental health.

Deep learning offers various approaches to use for object detection, among which YOLO is a standard algorithm that has stable and high performance on top of being

Published by Springer Nature Switzerland AG 2025
A. Chandrabose et al. (Eds.): ICCCSP 2024, IFIP AICT 723, pp. 439–449, 2025.
https://doi.org/10.1007/978-3-031-73617-9_34

pre-trained. In comparison with other approaches, YOLO predicts the bounding box of objects and their probabilistic probabilities through CNN, which results in high accuracy. We propose a YOLO-based waste classification methodology that would classify wastes into four categories: glass, plastic, metal and other wastes. Our dataset would focus on three types of recyclable materials (glass, plastic and metal) and others as a separate category. This model would be embedded on a Raspberry Pi board integrated with a camera so as to enable portability. This also enables us to integrate the system into a physical garbage collector setup (a set of 4 bins) for real-time classification, which is explained in the upcoming sections.

2 Literature Review

Over the years, various innovations have been made to improve the segregation of waste and increase the efficiency of recycling. The author in [1] made use of the TensorFlow Object Detection API to train and test the object detection model to classify waste into various categories and utilised OpenCV to test the trained model. They achieved multiple object detections through the use of the faster R-CNN algorithm. The model had an accuracy of about 91% and the time taken for single object detection was nearly 8.05 s, while for multi-object detection, it took 8.09 s. The model had maximum accuracy with respect to white background images.

The approach specified in [2] is classification using SSD and faster R-CNN models. They were trained and tested on images that could classify waste into three categories: aluminium cans, PET bottles and paper cups. The inference was that the faster R-CNN model had more accuracy (97%) than the SSD model (91%), even though SSD had a simpler network architecture than the faster R-CNN model. The approaches discussed to this point were deployed on a local computer system.

The authors in [3] designed a garbage classification model based on YOLOv5 to classify waste into 5 categories: batteries, waste paper, paper cups, bottles and orange peel. This model was deployed on the cloud and had an average accuracy of 99% when trained on a dataset of only 642 pictures. The authors of [4] developed and trained an artificial neural network in Python to classify waste and this was translated to hardware descriptive language (VHDL), which was then embedded on a Raspberry Pi. The model had an accuracy of 80%.

The authors in [5] designed a deep learning-based waste segregation system for six different categories of waste: plastic, metal, glass, organic, medical and e-waste. The model was trained on 2000 images for each class and had the accuracy of 98%. The model was deployed on Raspberry Pi. The authors in [6] used Deep Convolutional Neural Network to segregate waste into four categories: paper, glass, plastic and organic waste. The wastes were classified at 61.67% accuracy in the four-layer DCNN architecture and 70% accuracy in the five-layer DCNN architecture.

3 Methodology

3.1 Proposed System

The intelligent waste segregation system we proposed is shown in Fig. 1. The methodologies to be used in the system include ultrasonic sensing, object classification and the control of servo motors.

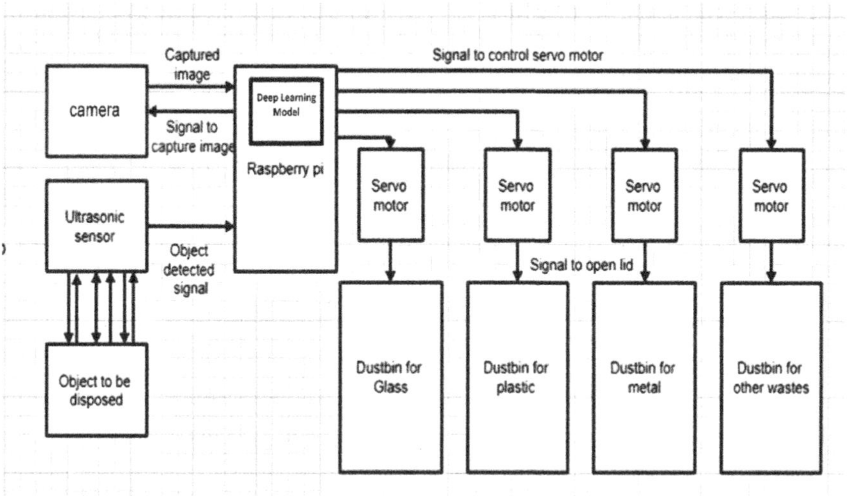

Fig. 1. Architecture Diagram

Ultrasonic Sensing. It is used to send a signal to the camera if an object is detected. This sensor uses ultrasonic waves to find the distance of an object and to detect the presence of an object. It sends high-frequency sound waves, which are reflected by the object. This reflection is detected by the sensor. Based on the time taken, the distance or the presence of the object is detected.

Image Capturing. When the ultrasonic sensor sends the signal, the image of the object is captured by the camera connected to the Raspberry Pi. The image is given as input to the deep learning model.

Image Classification. The image from the camera is classified using the deep learning model. Image classification is the simplest of the three tasks and involves classifying an entire image into one of a set of predefined classes. The output of an image classifier is the class labels and the probability of the prediction. Based on this probability, a threshold is set to 0.75. If the prediction probability is less than the threshold for all three classes, then it is classified as others. If not, the class with the highest probability is the observed class label.

Control of the Servo Motor. The servo motor connected to each dustbin lid is controlled by the Raspberry Pi, depending on the results obtained from the classification model. The servo motor is controlled by sending a pulse width modulation (PWSM) signal.

3.2 Dataset and Data Collection

Dataset. For the classification of waste materials into glass, metal, and plastic categories, we acquired our dataset from two sources: Roboflow and Kaggle. The dataset was customised as per our system needs, including various types of waste items like glass bottles, plastic wraps, plastic cups, metal containers, screws, and various other metallic objects.

Our dataset comprises approximately 3700+ images for training and validation. 80% of the collected dataset is the training set and 20% is the validation set. Table 1 presents the number of images of each class in the train, valid and test datasets.

Table 1. Dataset distribution into training, validation and testing sets.

Class	Train	Valid	Test
Glass	1000	250	20
Plastic	1000	250	20
Metal	1000	250	20

The figures below are some examples of images from each class (Fig. 2):

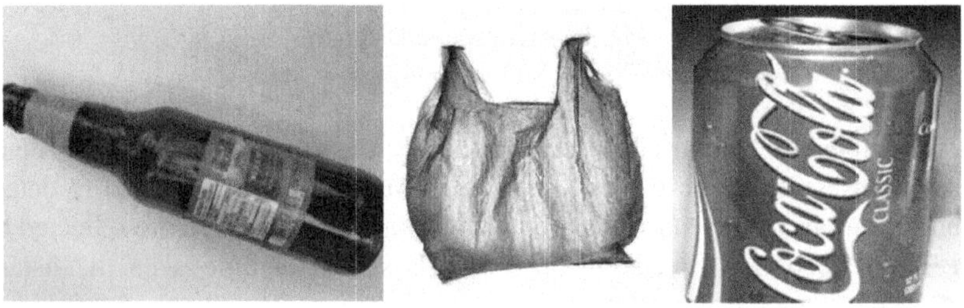

Fig. 2. Sample images from the dataset for glass, plastic, and metal classes

Environment. The images belonging to each class were organised into separate folders named after their respective classes. The training of this dataset was done using Google Colab by uploading the dataset to the cloud (Google Drive) for faster accessibility. We used an NVIDIA Tesla T4 GPU in Colab, 16 GB. The Tesla T4 is a GPU card based on the Turing architecture and targeted at deep learning model inference acceleration.

3.3 Component Specifications

The components utilized in our system are of the following specifications: Raspberry Pi 4 Model B with 4 GB of RAM and 32 GB SD card, a Zebronics Webcam Crystal Pro with a resolution of 640 × 480 and a USB interface for video input, a Robotbanao HC-SR04

Ultrasonic Distance Measuring Sensor, an A.C. 220 V to 6 V Step Down Transformer for voltage regulation, an 8 Pack of LM2596 DC-DC Adjustable Buck Converters capable of converting 3.0–40 V input to 1.5–35 V output for power supply regulation; and a SG90 servo motor for corresponding dustbin lid opening.

The components setup of our system is given below (Fig. 3):

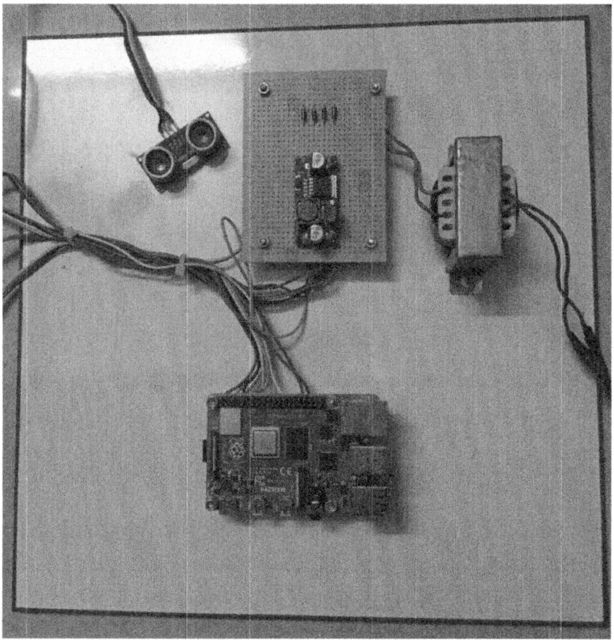

Fig. 3. Component setup

3.4 Deep Learning Model for Waste Segregation

The YOLOv8 classification model was used for training our dataset. The YOLOv8 classification model represents an advancement in object recognition and classification within the YOLO (You Only Look Once) family of models. YOLOv8 has enhanced accuracy and speed compared to the previous versions and it demonstrates significant improvements in detecting small and overlapping objects, making it suitable for diverse real-world applications. Unlike detection models that require annotation files specifying the bounding box of the objects, the classification model operates directly on raw images, simplifying the training pipeline and reducing annotation overhead.

During the training phase, the deep learning model was trained on our dataset, which consists of three classes: glass, plastic, and metal. We trained the dataset for 30 epochs. The final best weight configuration of the model was obtained at the end of the training process and was used for testing on unseen data and use in implementation.

In the classification model, glass is assigned label 0, metal is assigned label 1, and plastic is labelled 2. The train batch images are given below (Fig. 4):

Fig. 4. Train batch images where 0, 1 and 2 represent the class labels for glass, metal and plastic respectively.

Upon completion of training, the model was evaluated on the test dataset to assess its performance. The model classifies input images into one of the predefined categories: glass, plastic, or metal. An image is categorised as a specific class if the confidence score for that class is above 0.75, indicating high certainty in the classification result. Images with confidence scores below this threshold are classified as "others", signifying that the given image does not fall under the predefined 3 classes.

The model's performance was dependable and effective waste sorting was achieved by accurately recognising and categorising waste items using their images, promoting better waste management and environmental preservation.

4 Results

The classification model thus obtained had good accuracy when tested with waste materials like tin cans (metal), glass bottles (glass), reusable cups (plastic), plastic covers, old spoons (metal) and much more. Training loss was 0.65 in the beginning and gradually reduced to 0.018 at the end of 30 epochs. The validation loss gradually decreases from 0.72 at the first epoch to 0.61 at the end of 30 epochs. The validation loss values exhibit consistency in the range of 0.61 to 0.62 after the 19th epoch, with minor fluctuations. The training loss indicates how well the model is fitting the training data, while the validation loss indicates how well the model fits new data. A low value of validation loss indicates that the performance of the model is good with the validation data (Fig. 5).

The model's performance steadily improves throughout the epochs, reaching a maximum top-1 accuracy of 0.947. Top-1 accuracy of 0.94 was reached after 19 epochs itself

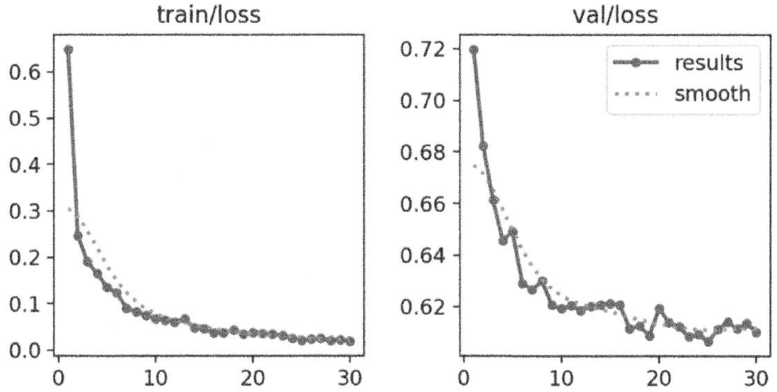

Fig. 5. Training and validation graph

and stayed between 0.94 and 0.93 thereafter. Top-1 accuracy is conventional accuracy; model prediction (the one with the highest probability) must be exactly the expected answer. Top-5 accuracy means any of the model's top 5 highest probability answers match the expected answer. The model consistently achieved a top-5 accuracy score of 1.0, indicating that the model is performing well on the validation data.

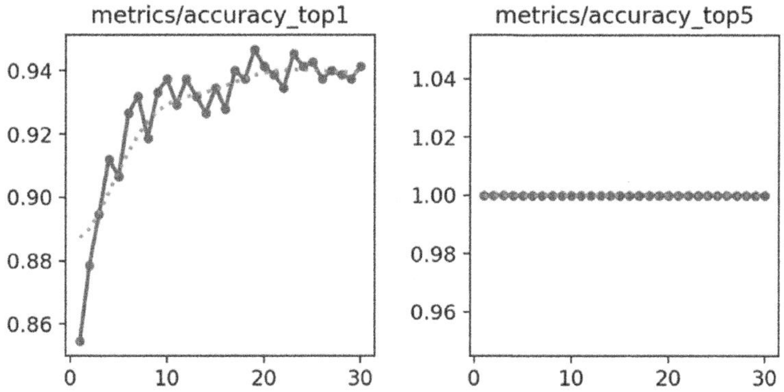

Fig. 6. Top1 and Top5 accuracy scores

The model with an accuracy of 0.947 obtained after 19 epochs was chosen for further testing and implementation. The predictions on validation data are shown in Fig. 6 and the predictions on new test data are shown in Figs. 7 and 8.

With detection models, achieving this level of accuracy is difficult and rare due to the dominance of similar features, but with classification, the process seems seamless. Figures 7 and 8 indicate that the model performs well to new images and classifies them properly. The model also correctly classified images not in any of these classes into the new category "others", when we imparted a probability threshold of 0.75 on it (Fig. 11).

The confusion matrix obtained during validation and testing is provided in Fig. 9 and the corresponding summary is reflected in Table 2.

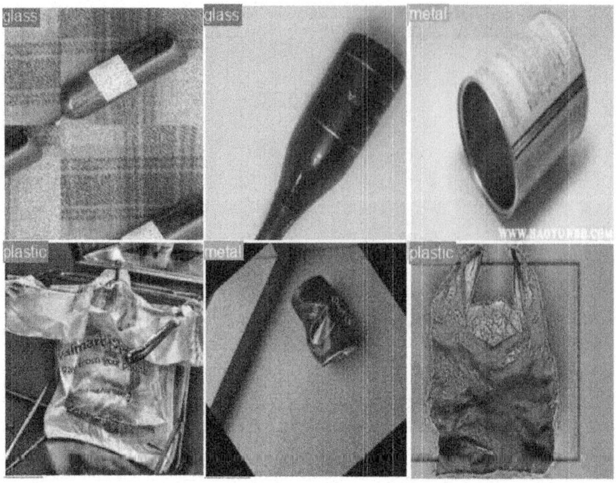

Fig. 7. Prediction results on the validation dataset

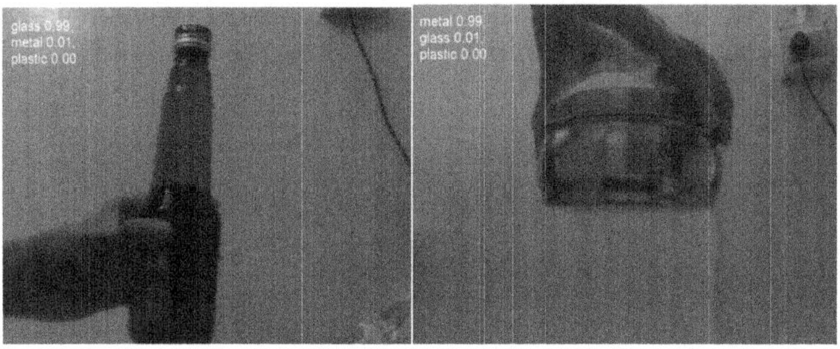

Fig. 8. Prediction results on test data: Glass and Metal

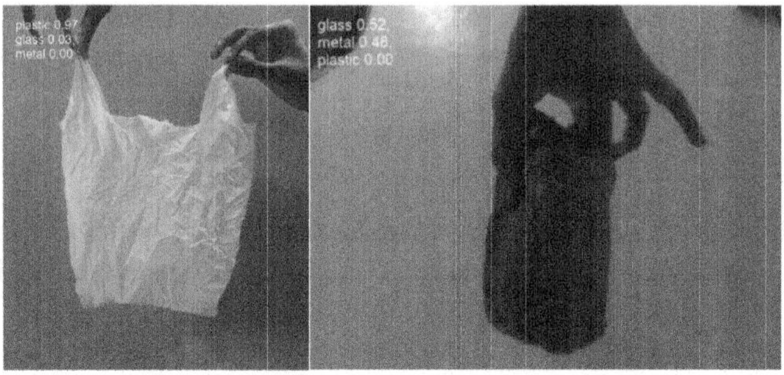

Fig. 9. Prediction results on test data: Plastic and Others

The complete setup of the waste segregation system is shown in Fig. 10. When a waste item is held near the ultrasonic sensor, the image of the waste object is captured

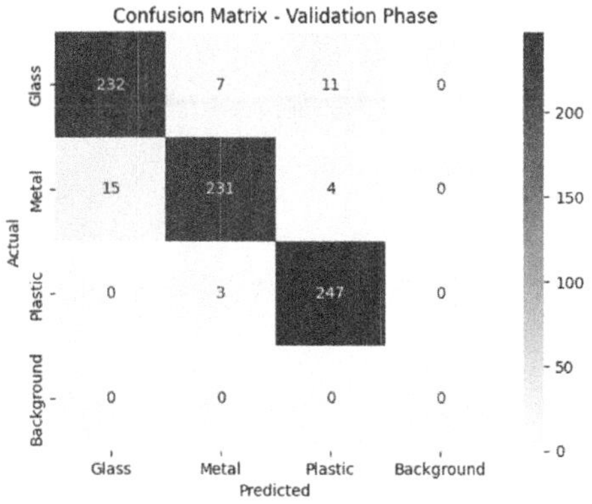

Fig. 10. Confusion matrix for validation phase

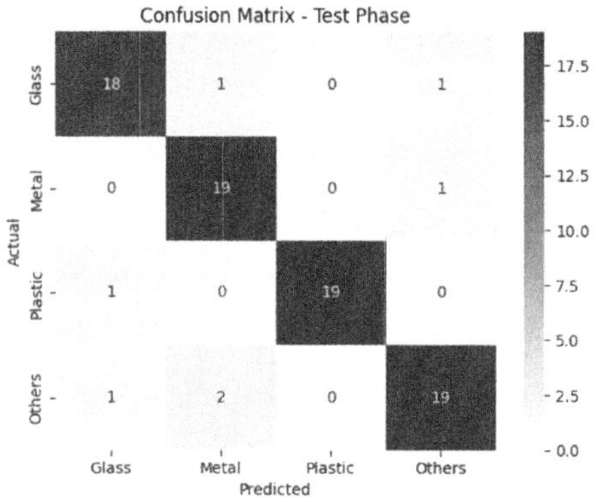

Fig. 11. Confusion matrix for test phase

Table 2. Class-wise accuracies during validation and testing.

Class	Valid	Test
Glass	0.956	0.95
Plastic	0.96	0.95
Metal	0.976	0.9875
Others	-	0.9375

and classified using the classification model. Subsequently, the appropriate dustbin lid is opened with the help of servo motor (Fig. 12).

Fig. 12. Complete setup of the waste segregation system

5 Conclusion

Thus, we have developed a deep learning model that classifies images into four classes: glass, metal, plastic and others. The model, when implemented in the proposed Raspberry Pi setup, performed as expected. The model had an accuracy of 0.99 and was quite fast in terms of computational speed. This classification model has the potential to automate the task of waste segregation on a large scale. Also, since this is a classification model and not an object detection model, it performs well when there is only one object in the image/input. Therefore, this model can be upscaled for use in conveyor belt systems. The model can also be trained to classify more classes. The future scope of this paper can include adding new classes and training the model for the same. In addition to this, the system can also be integrated with IoT techniques there by leading to the remote control of the control system and also monitoring the dustbins capacity and alerting if the dustbin nears full capacity.

Acknowledgement. We would like to thank the Centre for Sponsored Research and Consultancy, Anna University, Chennai, for funding this work. We extend our gratitude to Dr. Umamaheswari S for her valuable guidance throughout the work.

References

1. Mitra, A.: Detection of Waste Materials Using Deep Learning and Image Processing (2020)

2. Lai, Y.-L., Lai, Y.-K., Shih, S.-Y., Zheng, C.-Y., Chuang, T.-H.: Deep-learning object detection for resource recycling. J. Phys.: Conf. Ser. **1583**, 012011 (2020)
3. Wu, Z., et al.: Using YOLOv5 for Garbage Classification (2021)
4. John, N.E., Sreelakshmi, R., Menon, S.R., Santhosh, V.: Artificial neural network based intelligent waste segregator. Int. J. Sci. Eng. Res. **10–10**(4), 367–368 (2019). https://www.ijser.org/researchpaper/Artificial-Neural-Network-based-Intelligent-Waste-Segregator.pdf
5. Nafiz, M.S., Das, S.S., Morol, M.K., Al Juabir, A., Nandi, D.: ConvoWaste: an automatic waste segregation machine using deep learning. In: 2023 3rd International Conference on Robotics, Electrical and Signal Processing Techniques (ICREST), Dhaka, Bangladesh, pp. 181–186 (2023). https://doi.org/10.1109/ICREST57604.2023.10070078
6. Altikat, A., Gulbe, A., Altikat, S.: Intelligent solid waste classification using deep convolutional neural networks. Int. J. Environ. Sci. Technol. **19**, 1285–1292 (2022)

Touchless Doorbell with Face Detection

Rathish Manivannan[1,2](✉), S. Sabesh Raaj[1], S. Vidhusha[1], and P. MadhanKumar[1]

[1] Shiv Nadar University, Kalavakkam, Chennai 603110, India
rathish.manivannan@gmail.com
[2] Indian Institute of Technology Madras, Chennai 600036, India

Abstract. The significance of infrastructure development within households is incomplete without the implementation of an efficient home security solution. Many existing security systems grapple with challenges such as lack of seamless integration, diminished accuracy, and a user-unfriendly experience, often compounded by high costs. Thus, the need for an innovative and effective approach to enhance the safety and security of homes becomes imperative. A groundbreaking solution to address these concerns is the integration of smart IoT-based touchless doorbells with face-detection capabilities. This research endeavors to propose a touchless doorbell system incorporating a face recognition model developed using OpenCV and a Haar cascade classifier. The integration of this system with an Arduino UNO further enhances its functionality. Through this innovative approach, a remarkable improvement in efficiency and accuracy, reaching approximately 93%, has been achieved. This, in turn, contributes to the establishment of a highly reliable and secure home security system. A noteworthy aspect of this research is its positive impact on the safety of visually impaired individuals. The touchless doorbell system has been augmented with features from the Google Text-to-Speech (gTTS) library, providing audio-related functionalities. This not only bolsters the overall accessibility of the security system but also ensures that visually impaired individuals can interact and navigate with the proposed home security system, thereby fostering inclusivity in the realm of home security solutions.

Keywords: Ultrasonic Sensor · Open CV · Arduino UNO · Face Detection · gTTS library · Haar cascade classifier · Industry · Innovation · Infrastructure

1 Introduction

In the contemporary era, ensuring the security of one's home has become a paramount concern for individuals. The prevalence of security challenges necessitates innovative solutions, and among the array of possibilities, smart home security emerges as a formidable deterrent to illegal activities. Researchers have introduced various security systems to fortify and enhance the safety of homes, each contributing unique features to the landscape. Researches were made using Raspberry-Pi, ARMv7 Cortex-A7, and

Published by Springer Nature Switzerland AG 2025
A. Chandrabose et al. (Eds.): ICCCSP 2024, IFIP AICT 723, pp. 450–457, 2025.
https://doi.org/10.1007/978-3-031-73617-9_35

Node MCU to provide home security solutions. However, these approaches had high hardware requirements, cost, and less portability. The proposed solution addresses these needs by introducing a touchless doorbell with integrated face detection capabilities, complemented by advanced audio features with minimal cost and easy portability. This cutting-edge system seamlessly incorporates an Arduino Uno, leveraging the power of machine-learning techniques for face identification and detection. Furthermore, the integration of the gTTS (Google Text-to-Speech) library enhances the system's auditory dimension, contributing to the development of an intelligent and sustainable IoT-based home security system.

This forward-thinking security solution harnesses various machine learning techniques, utilizing datasets that contain images of the household residents. The implementation of such technology enables the system to recognize individuals approaching the doorstep, providing an added layer of security. In essence, the touchless doorbell, with its fusion of facial recognition and audio capabilities, represents a sophisticated and proactive approach to modern home security, underscoring the importance of leveraging technology for the safeguarding of residential spaces. This paper is structured as follows: Sect. 2 covers the literature review; Sect. 3 goes into detail about the proposed system's approach; Sect. 4 explains the results; and Sect. 5 is devoted to the conclusion and future works to improve home safety.

2 Literature Review

This section expounds upon the diverse study endeavors put forward by other researchers concerning face detection and smart home security systems. The Raspberry-Pi, which is powered by an ARMv8 Cortex-A53, was utilized to build the smart doorbell system [1]. Using the recognizer Local Binary Pattern Histogram (LBPH) and Open-Source Computer Vision (OpenCV) library's pre-trained classifier Haar-Cascade, the project attempts to transfer OpenCV to the Raspberry-Pi board for face detection and identification applications. This project uses a real-time Haar-Cascade face detection system [1]. The facial image is captured, extracted, and then converted into an XML or PCD file's fixed-dimension vector with a space vector that contains points and positions.

A study was conducted to investigate the possibility of substituting costly image processing boards with a Raspberry Pi board, which operates the OpenCV library using an ARMv7 Cortex-A7 as its central processor [2]. The primary focus of this project was image processing using the OpenCV library and the Raspberry Pi board. This study introduces facial recognition; Eigen face and Independent Component Analysis (ICA) are two analysis techniques employed by the author to evaluate the suggested system [2]. The system was designed with reduced power consumption, resource efficiency, and faster operation as its foundation. After being extracted, the face picture was reconstructed into a vector with fixed dimensions and an XML file (training file) that had a space vector with points and their respective locations.

A system with artificial intelligence was developed to identify various faces [3]. An app that uses a face recognition algorithm was used to accomplish this recognition. Following this identification, the device using machine learning algorithms determines whether the door's electronic lock has to be opened. If it is new test data, the owner receives a notification so they can take the necessary action. The Arduino UNO was used to control the electronic lock and other parts. The Arduino UNO is linked to a Bluetooth module that the Android phone was connected to. It is evident that the goal was to successfully lock and unlock the door in various scenarios. A particular face could be identified using the principle component analysis (PCA) algorithm by comparing the present face's principal components to those of known people in a facial database that was pre-built [3]. Depending on the given instruction, the lock either unlocks or remains closed. The lock opens if the application recognizes the face. If not, the owner's action activates the lock. Additionally, this action was learned for future use.

The touchless doorbell, a cost-effective device was designed using a circuitry featuring a voltage comparator, potentiometer, and photodiode which ensures touchless operation for enhanced durability and energy efficiency [4]. IoT-based doorbell utilizing NodeMCU and MLX90614 sensor was proposed to alert homeowners about visitors potentially infected with COVID-19, ensuring efficient temperature monitoring with 99% accuracy and data logging via FireBase [5]. A Contactless Doorbell with Arduino, NodeMCU Camera module, and ultrasonic sensor, was proposed to ensure security by autonomously ringing the doorbell, capturing facial images, and sending data to an M-App stored in Firebase, utilizing advanced technologies including AWS cloud services and Computer Vision [6]. IoT-based Contactless COVID-19 doorbell was designed with temperature scanning, app notifications, facial recognition, automatic door control, and a sanitation system for enhanced safety during the global pandemic [7].

The motivation for the proposed system comes from various research works mentioned. The proposed research work is a low-cost and portable system built using Arduino UNO, ultrasonic sensor, OpenCV, and Haar cascade classifier. This system helps in real-time face detection and alerting the household residents. The proposed system leverages the existing approaches by incorporating the Google Text-to-Speech library. Thus, it helps in providing real-time user-friendly interactions and security for visually impaired, and old-aged people.

A study was done to delve into automated image and video analysis through a facial recognition system utilizing deep learning, OpenCV, and Python libraries [8]. Haar Cascade and Local Binary Pattern Histogram proposed advancements in face detection, and employs feature extraction, facilitating human face recognition in live video feeds and images for modern Artificial Intelligence systems [9]. Using the modified AdaBoost algorithm in OpenCV, a real-time face identification method was proposed, showing enhanced simplicity, smoothness, and precision, especially with dual-thread implementation [10].

3 Methodology

3.1 Arduino-Based Touchless Doorbell

One of the most prominent open-source microcontroller boards is the Arduino Uno. The microchip Atmega328p microcontroller serves as the foundation for the Arduino Uno. In the hardware setup of this touchless doorbell system, Arduino Uno is used as a primary device. The Arduino Uno plays a pivotal role by triggering the doorbell if someone is at the entrance, thus it helps in alerting the end-users. Arduino Uno is connected to the ultrasonic sensor in this system. The ultrasonic sensor is set in such a way that it detects and alerts the people at the entrance who are within a distance of 7 cm. Figure 1 shows the circuit connections for the touchless doorbell using Arduino Uno and an Ultrasonic sensor (Fig. 2).

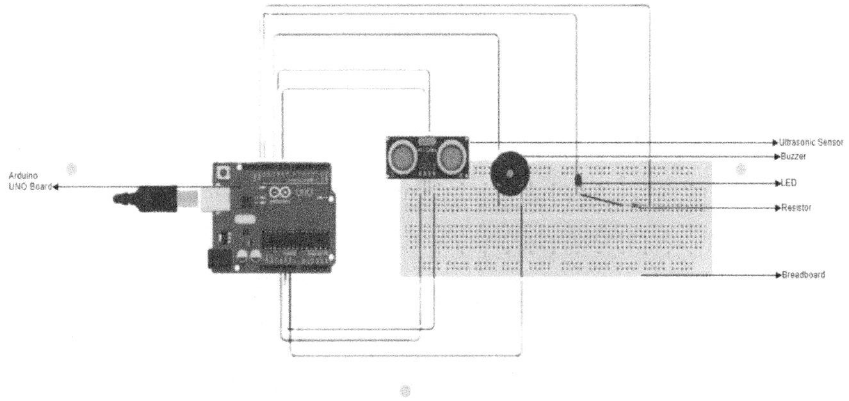

Fig. 1. Touchless doorbell using Arduino Uno.

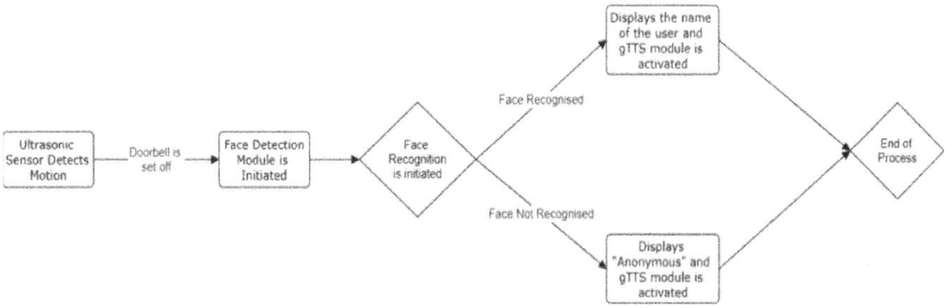

Fig. 2. Methodology of Touchless Doorbell with Face Detection System

3.2 Face Detection

Face Detection is an important phase of this system. The face detection module is initiated after the ultrasonic sensor detects motion. The face detection module is built using the OpenCV module and Haar-cascade classifier. OpenCV module is used to invoke computer vision for face detection. The machine learning-based Haar cascade classifier recognizes faces in a picture by using a cascade of basic features. After the face detection module is initiated, it searches for the face and classifies the face according to the trained dataset.

After the face has been classified, it is displayed on the screen. Figure 3 shows the face detection using the face detection module of the system. If an outsider arrives whose face is not trained in the dataset it displays as anonymous which is shown in Fig. 4. The classified person's name is stored in an mp3 audio file. Further, an additional feature is included using the gTTS (Google Text-To-Speech) library. The Google Text-To-Speech library is used effectively for turning audio files into speech in the language of our choice. Figure 5 shows the label mp3 audio file through which the speech is generated.

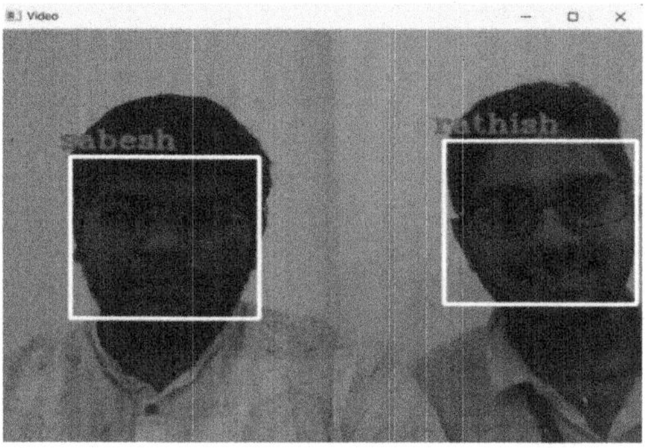

Fig. 3. Face Detection – Displaying the name of trained faces

4 Results and Discussion

The Arduino Uno, ultrasonic sensor, OpenCV, Haar cascade classifier, and Google Text-To-Speech library are used to design a touchless doorbell with face detection. Arduino Uno is highly useful in this system as it is inexpensive and simple, and IDE software operates on any operating system. This system also has a high accuracy for face detection. The accuracy of the system increases with an increase in training epochs. The accuracy graph for the trained dataset is shown in Fig. 6.

Fig. 4. Face Detection – Displaying Anonymous for unknown faces

Fig. 5. Label.mp3 file (gTTS)

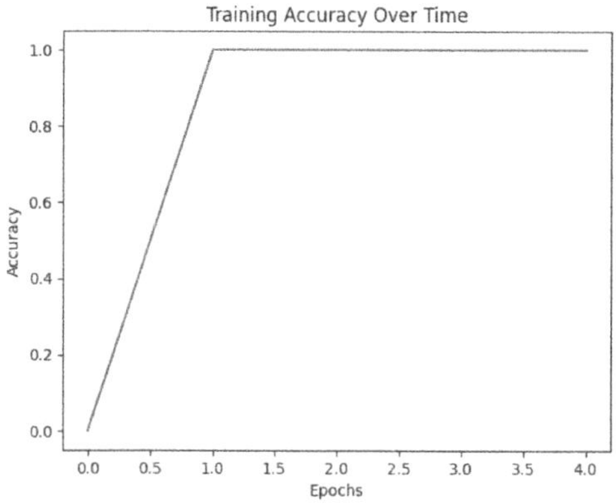

Fig. 6. Accuracy graph

A touchless doorbell has been developed with an ultrasonic sensor and the face of the visitor has been recognized using a face recognition module. The working of a touchless doorbell with the blinking of an LED is shown in Fig. 7. Google Text-to-Speech module has been incorporated for turning audio files into speech and it is very useful for visually challenged people to recognize their visitors.

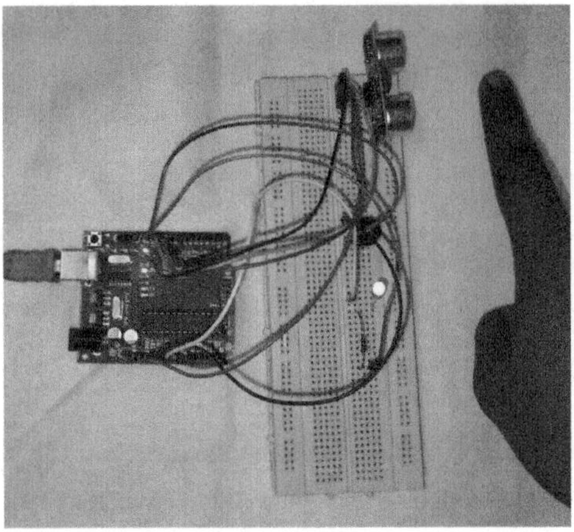

Fig. 7. Working of Touchless Doorbell

5 Conclusions and Future Works

A touchless doorbell with face detection is developed as a modern home security solution that provides homeowners with a secure and convenient way to identify and respond to visitors without physical contact. The existing traditional doorbell systems pose security concerns for the homeowners like sudden trespassing by malicious entrants, burglary, etc., But this system helps in alerting about the person at the doorstep to the house owner. This system is less expensive, portable, and also easy to use as it uses basic components and open-source software, modules, and packages like Arduino Uno, ultrasonic sensor, OpenCV, Haar cascade classifier, and Google Text-To-Speech library.

The proposed touchless doorbell with face detection is also highly useful for visually challenged people as Google Text-To-Speech library gives audio messages of those who are at the doorstep of the house. The practical limitation and constraint lie in the fact that if the total size of the training dataset increases, the total time needed to train the system also increases. There are plans in the future to optimize it as a completely integrated system to enhance its performance. The other future works also include improving battery efficiency, incorporating data privacy, and enhancing facial recognition.

References

1. Malve, S., Morade, S.S.: Face recognition technology based smart doorbell system using Python's OpenCV library. Int. J. Eng. Res. Technol. (IJERT) **10**(06), June 2021. ISSN 2278-0181
2. Upadhyay, J., Rida, P., Gupta, S., Siddique, N.: Smart doorbell system based on face recognition. Int. Res. J. Eng. Technol. (IRJET) **04**(03), March 2017. e-ISSN 2395-0056
3. Jamakhandi, N.M., Harshith, M., Jagriti, P.B.: Smart door lock using face recognition. Int. J. Comput. Sci. Eng. **7**, Special Issue-14, May 2019. E-ISSN 2347-2693
4. Gokul Krishnan, S., Priyadarshi, R., Kumar, A., Tasnin, W.: Cost-effective touch-less doorbell to combat COVID-19. In: 2021 Innovations in Power and Advanced Computing Technologies

(i-PACT), Kuala Lumpur, Malaysia, pp. 1–7 (2021).https://doi.org/10.1109/i-PACT52855.2021.9696966
5. Dadhich, S., Dabre, P., Dabreo, R., Raut, P.: Contactless IoT doorbell for Covid-safe household. In: 2021 IEEE 9th Region 10 Humanitarian Technology Conference (R10-HTC), Bangalore, India, pp. 01–04 (2021).https://doi.org/10.1109/R10-HTC53172.2021.9641565
6. Valarmathi, V., Sathya, T., Nirmala, J., Sivarajeswari, S., Prasanth, R.M., Srihari, V.: Design and implementation of secured contactless doorbell using IOT. In: 2022 International Conference on Computer, Power and Communications (ICCPC), Chennai, India, pp. 187–191 (2022). https://doi.org/10.1109/ICCPC55978.2022.10072073
7. Lokesh, U., Logeshwaran, M., Jeya Sheela, J.J., Shabanabegum, S.K.: Security based contactless Covid-19 doorbell using Internet of Things. In: 2022 6th International Conference on Intelligent Computing and Control Systems (ICICCS), Madurai, India, pp. 885–892 (2022). https://doi.org/10.1109/ICICCS53718.2022.9788357
8. Kumari Sirivarshitha, A., Sravani, K., Priya, K.S., Bhavani, V.: An approach for face detection and face recognition using OpenCV and face recognition libraries in Python. In: 2023 9th International Conference on Advanced Computing and Communication Systems (ICACCS), Coimbatore, India, pp. 1274–1278 (2023). https://doi.org/10.1109/ICACCS57279.2023.10113066
9. Gupta, M., Bisht, K., Sharma, A., Upadhyay, D.: HaarCascade and LBPH algorithms in face recognition analysis. In: 2023 World Conference on Communication and Computing (WCONF), RAIPUR, India, pp. 1–4 (2023). https://doi.org/10.1109/WCONF58270.2023.10235019
10. Fan, X., Zhang, F., Wang, H., Lu, X.: The system of face detection based on OpenCV. In: 2012 24th Chinese Control and Decision Conference (CCDC), Taiyuan, pp. 648–651 (2012).https://doi.org/10.1109/CCDC.2012.6242980

Facial Deblurring and Recognition Using Image Processing and Machine Learning Techniques

B. R. Subrahmanyam(✉), T. S. Janavi, V. Keerthana, Ayesha Jumana Serajudeen, and A. M. Arunnagiri

Department of Electronics and Communication Engineering, College of Engineering Guindy, Anna University, Chennai 600025, India
srisubra0409@gmail.com, janavi.ts06@gmail.com

Abstract. The project addresses the challenge of accurately identifying blurred faces in computer vision and facial recognition. It introduces a novel framework that integrates deblurring techniques, utilizing point spread function deconvolution to enhance facial image quality. Principal Component Analysis (PCA) is employed for feature extraction, and a K-Nearest Neighbors (KNN) classifier is applied for face identification. The combined deblurring and PCA-transformed features improve matching and identification accuracy, particularly in scenarios with initially blurred images. Experimental validation on a real-world dataset demonstrates the efficacy of the proposed methodology. This approach not only enhances facial recognition accuracy but also lays the groundwork for future research in challenging practical applications, such as security and law enforcement.

Keywords: Facial recognition · deblurring · computer vision · image processing · principal component analysis (PCA) · k-nearest neighbors (KNN) · point spread function (PSF) deconvolution · forensic applications · recognition accuracy

1 Introduction

Image deblurring is a pivotal task in image processing that aims to restore sharpness and clarity to blurred images. Blurriness in images can result from various factors, broadly categorized into motion blur and out-of-focus blur. Motion blur occurs when there is either camera or subject movement during the image capture process [15]. This is often observed in low-light conditions or when using slow shutter speeds. Additionally, object movement within the scene can contribute to motion blur, especially in scenarios where fast action is involved. Out-of-focus blur is associated with issues related to focusing. If the camera fails to focus accurately on the intended subject, the resulting image may appear blurry. This can happen due to limitations in autofocus systems or errors in manual focusing. To address the challenges posed by blurred images, there is a need for a robust deblurring technique in addition with a facial recognition system [3].

Published by Springer Nature Switzerland AG 2025
A. Chandrabose et al. (Eds.): ICCCSP 2024, IFIP AICT 723, pp. 458–466, 2025.
https://doi.org/10.1007/978-3-031-73617-9_36

Primarily, the dataset required for this study has been obtained from an open access face database known as CelebFaces Attributes. The dataset addresses real-world challenges, including large pose variations, background clutter, and diverse individuals. The data obtained undergoes pre-processing which includes resizing, augmentation and blurring. Resizing involves changing the dimensions of an image, which is done to ensure that all images in a dataset have a consistent size and augmentation involves applying various transformations to the original images to create new, modified versions which indirectly increases the diversity of the training dataset. Blurring is introduced onto the data which is followed by deblurring by deconvolution methods. The PSF is a mathematical function that defines how light spreads from a point source in the object space to the corresponding image space. Image blurring can often be represented as a convolution operation. The convolution of an image with its PSF describes how each point in the image contributes to the neighboring points in the final blurred image. Deconvolution is the process of reversing the blurring effects applied to an image. By estimating the PSF of an image, it is possible to deconvolution algorithms to recover the original, unblurred image. Feature analysis is performed by K-nearest neighbors (KNN) and Principal component analysis (PCA) techniques. KNN classifies a data point based on the majority class of its k nearest neighbors in the feature space. It indirectly contributes to feature analysis by focusing on the most relevant features for classification. Cosine similarity is applied to assess the similarity between two images represented as vectors. The images are typically transformed into numerical feature vectors, and the cosine similarity is calculated to quantify the similarity between these vectors.

PCA is a technique used for linear dimensionality reduction. It transforms the original features into a new set of uncorrelated features, called principal components, ordered by their variance. PCA allows for the identification of the most important features in a dataset. These features correspond to the principal components with the highest eigenvalues, and they are the ones that contribute to the variance in the data. By combining these techniques, the study benefits from the dimensionality reduction capabilities of PCA while leveraging KNN's ability to classify based on the reduced set of informative features. Finally, the pre-trained weights of the model of a specific dataset are performed along with fine-tuning. Training includes feeding data through the network, optimizing parameters, and updating the model to make accurate predictions [5]. Techniques like grid search or random search help find the best hyperparameter values to improve a model's accuracy and generalization.

2 Methodology

2.1 Data Acquisition

The dataset used for this study has been obtained from an open access face database known as CelebFaces Attributes. The CelebA dataset, comprising 202,599 face images of various celebrities, serves as a crucial resource for the development and evaluation of computer vision and deep learning models, particularly in the context of face detection and attribute recognition. With 10,177 distinct identities and 40 binary attribute annotations per image, the dataset provides a comprehensive and diverse set of facial features for analysis. Notably, the annotations cover attributes such as brown hair, smiles, and glasses, making it a valuable tool for training models to recognize specific facial characteristics. The dataset addresses real-world challenges, including large pose variations, background clutter, and diverse individuals. Additionally, it includes 5 landmark locations for each image, contributing to the dataset's utility in facial analysis applications. Originally curated by researchers at MMLAB, The Chinese University of Hong Kong, this dataset, with its extensive annotations and varied content, significantly contributes to advancements in facial recognition research.

2.2 Pre-processing

With regard to the requirement of identifying blurry faces, this study presents a preprocessing framework for situations where faces are frequently blurry, the preprocessing techniques are intended to improve the facial recognition system's resilience.

Interpolation algorithms are used to scale facial images to a standard dimension, such as 128 × 128 pixels. By guaranteeing consistency in the image dimensions, this phase enables the model to process facial features reliably.

Certain facial photos are purposefully blurred to simulate real-world situations where motion or low quality during image capture could result in facial blurring. The purpose of this stage is to improve the model's capacity to identify faces that are blurry and to mimic difficult situations [12].

2.3 Feature Extraction

Point Spread Function

An imaging system's blurring effects are primarily characterized by the Point Spread Function (PSF). It shows how a point source or object in the scene is transformed, including how that point is blurred or dispersed in the final image. In the paper, the Wiener deconvolution processes a technique used to restore blurred images.The PSF that is used takes on a straightforward form is a matrix of ones split by the size of its square. This decision is in line with a standard procedure in image processing, which models blurring as a result of spatial averaging. In particular, a matrix of ones divided by the square of the blur level is used to form the PSF. This presumption makes things simpler [1] (Fig. 1).

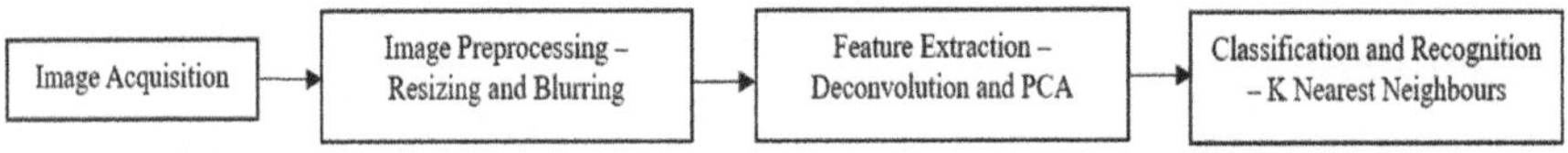

Fig. 1. Block Diagram of the Facial Deblurring and Recognition Process

Deconvolution

The deconvolution technique used in this study is Wiener deconvolution, a method widely used in image processing to restore blurry images [4]. Wiener deconvolution is particularly effective when the blurring process is known and can be modeled, such as in scenarios where a point spread function (PSF) is assumed. In this technique, the blurring effect is essentially reversed by applying a deconvolution filter to the blurred image. The key to Wiener deconvolution is the inclusion of a Wiener filter, which is calculated from the Fourier transforms of the blurred image, the assumed PSF, and the estimated noise variance [13]. The Wiener filter is designed to minimize the effect of noise and improve the signal during the deconvolution process [7]. Using frequency-domain representations, Wiener deconvolution effectively reduces the blur caused by the imaging system, resulting in a restored and clearer representation of the original image. The code implements this technique by applying a Wiener deconvolution process to each color channel of the image separately, helping to improve overall facial features in scenarios where blurring is common.

Principal Component Analysis

For the aim of this paper, Principal Component Analysis (PCA) is the basic dimension reduction technique used to improve the performance of face recognition. PCA is used after the deblurring process to transform the high-dimensional representation of the deblurred face images into a deblurred space while preserving important features. This dimensionality reduction is crucial to optimize the efficiency and effectiveness of subsequent classification tasks. By identifying principal components, which are linear combinations of the original features that account for the most variability in the data, PCA simplifies the representation of facial features [2]. The reduced feature set obtained by PCA not only speeds up computation, but also helps mitigate the curse of dimensionality, which contributes to better generalization of the model. The transformed features are then fed into a K-Nearest Neighbors (KNN) classifier, which improves the accuracy of face recognition. This integration of PCA into the preprocessing pipeline shows its importance in improving the face detection workflow, especially when faced with challenges such as face blurring.

2.4 K-Nearest Neighbours

The K-Nearest Neighbors (KNN) classifier is at the heart of face recognition after deblurring and Principal Component Analysis (PCA) steps. Known for its simplicity and efficiency in classification tasks, this algorithm is used to recognize faces based on modified features obtained by PCA. The training of the KNN classifier involves generating labels for the blurred images that represent each image in the dataset [6]. The dataset is then split into a training and a test set which makes it easy to evaluate the performance of the classifier.

An instance of the KNN classifier is created, which determines the number of neighbors to be considered for classification. The choice of the number of neighbors is key and can be adjusted according to the specific characteristics of the dataset. In this case, the KNN classifier is trained with the PCA-transformed features of the training set using a matching method. A KNN classifier trained in the testing phase can predict the labels from new, unseen data [14]. This careful interplay of PCA, KNN and blurring techniques increases the strength of the face detection system, enabling accurate face detection even in situations where the images were originally blurred.

In this implemented algorithm, a K-Nearest Neighbors (KNN) classifier is employed to predict the label associated with a deblurred input face. This classifier, likely trained using Principal Component Analysis (PCA) features, plays a crucial role in face recognition tasks [9]. The subsequent computation involves measuring the cosine similarity between the PCA features of the input face and those of all faces in the original dataset. This similarity metric aids in identifying the face in the dataset that exhibits the highest resemblance to the input face [8]. This metric provides a measure of angular similarity between vectors, crucial for identifying the most similar face. The Euclidean distance is often employed to measure the straight-line distance between two points in a multi-dimensional space and is commonly used in machine learning scenarios to assess the dissimilarity between vectors [11]. The results, including the predicted label, match status, and paths to identified images, are meticulously organized into a dictionary.

$$CosineSimilarity(A, B) = (A \cdot B)/(\|A\| \cdot \|B\|) \tag{1}$$

where,

A·B is the dot product of vectors A and B.

||A|| and ||B|| are the Euclidean norms of vectors A and B respectively.

The formula for Euclidean distance between two vectors A and B is given by:

$$Euclidean\ Distance(A, B) = \sqrt{\sum_{i=1}^{n} (Ai - Bi)^2} \tag{2}$$

where,

n is the dimensionality of the vectors.

Ai and Bi are the components of vectors A and B respectively.

The visual representation of the identification results is facilitated by creating a figure with four distinct subplots. These subplots showcase the original input face with the predicted label, the blurred input face, the deblurred input face (likely achieved through specific image deblurring techniques), and the identified face or a black image. The decision on displaying the identified face or a black image is contingent on whether the cosine similarity surpasses a predefined threshold. Notably, the implementation incorporates robust error-handling mechanisms, particularly during the loading of the identified image. In case of an error, an appropriate message is printed, ensuring the algorithm's resilience in handling potential issues. Overall, this amalgamation of machine learning [10], image processing, and visualization techniques presents a comprehensive approach to effective face recognition on deblurred images, demonstrating a cohesive and functional implementation.

3 Results and Discussions

The machine learning algorithm operated on a curated subset of 1000 images from the CelebA dataset, a pragmatic choice made to balance computational efficiency and representativeness. Each input image underwent a meticulous process, beginning with blurring and subsequent deconvolution using Wiener filtering. Though the process of deconvolution did not perfectly restore the original image, the output was satisfactory enough to extract features using PCA. The deblurred images served as inputs for Principal Component Analysis (PCA). In this crucial step, 50 principal components were selected as an optimal threshold, ensuring a balance between feature richness and computational efficiency. Beyond this threshold, diminishing returns were observed in the significance of additional principal components for the classification task.

Armed with features extracted from PCA, the K-Nearest Neighbours (KNN) machine learning model undertook the task of classification. The training dataset constituted 80% of the input database, leaving 20% for rigorous testing. The model was trained to recognize matching images with a cosine similarity score of 0.7 – a carefully chosen threshold. Faces falling below this score were deemed non-matching and resulted in the generation of a black image, an unequivocal indicator of a non-match scenario.

Upon achieving model readiness, a comprehensive evaluation was conducted on a diverse set of 150 images. This set deliberately included images both belonging and not belonging to the original database, creating a challenging scenario for facial recognition. The model iterated through each image, providing results that were meticulously analyzed. The results are shown in Fig. 2 and Fig. 3, with the performance metrics being elaborated in Table 1.

Table 1. Performance Metrics of the Prediction Model

Performance Metrics	Score
Accuracy	98.7%
Precision	97.1%
False Acceptance Rate	16.67%
False Rejection Rate	0%
Equal Error Rate	8.34%

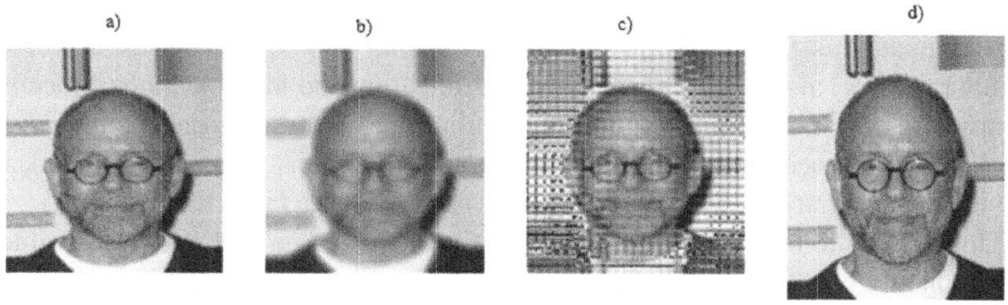

Fig. 2. An output from an image recognized as part of the database: a) Input Image b) Blurred Image c) Deblurred Image d) Recognized Image

As compared to other models, the one developed in this work is significantly optimistic in its results. A brief statistical comparison is as given in Table 2.

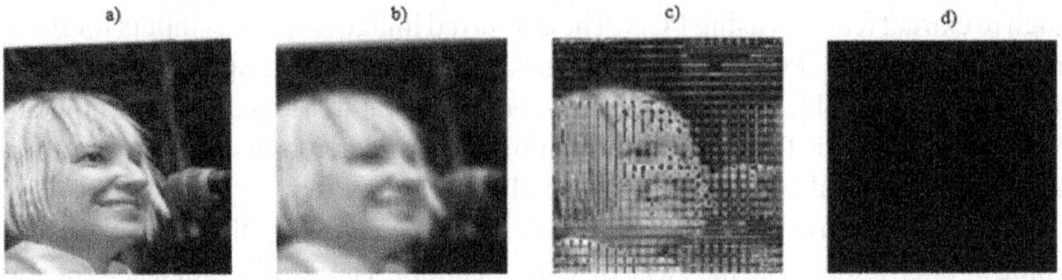

Fig. 3. An output from an image that was not recognized as a part of the database: a) Input Image b) Blurred Image c) Deblurred Image d) Non-matching result in the form of a black image

Table 2. Comparison between different prediction models

Model Name	Accuracy	Precision
Current Model	98.7%	97.1%
FADEIN [16]	96%	-
LPQ [17]	78%	76.4%
UMSN [18]	87.4%	83.2%

4 Conclusion

The integration of facial deblurring and recognition using image processing and machine learning techniques represents a holistic approach to overcoming challenges associated with blurred facial images. The first critical element in this process is the consideration of the Point Spread Function (PSF). By understanding and estimating the PSF specific to facial blurring, it becomes possible to model and address the blurring characteristics effectively. This allows for the development of deblurring algorithms that are tailored to the unique features and nuances of facial images, contributing to the restoration of facial details, and improving overall image quality.

Along with this, the utilization of machine learning techniques, such as the k-nearest neighbors (KNN) algorithm, excels in the classification and identification of facial features by assessing the similarities with neighboring data points while enhancing accuracy, aligning with the need for precise facial recognition systems, especially when dealing with images that may have undergone deblurring to recover facial details.

This extends to techniques like Principal Component Analysis (PCA), valuable for dimensionality reduction and feature extraction, contributing to the efficiency of facial recognition systems. By capturing the essential features of facial images and reducing redundancy, PCA facilitates improved recognition performance and may enhance the overall speed and efficiency of the system.

Ultimately, the combination of facial deblurring and recognition through the application of image processing and machine learning techniques, including the consideration of PSF, the use of KNN for recognition, and the incorporation of PCA for feature extraction, results in a comprehensive approach, addressing challenges in restoring facial details and achieving accurate facial recognition, thereby advancing the capabilities of systems designed for facial image analysis. The synergy of these techniques contributes to more robust and reliable facial recognition systems in various applications, including security, authentication, and human-computer interaction.

References

1. Nishiyama, M., et al.: Facial deblur inference using subspace analysis for recognition of blurred faces. IEEE Trans. Pattern Anal. Mach. Intell. **33**(4), 838–845 (2011)
2. Paul, L.C., Suman, A.: Face recognition using principal component analysis method. Int. J. Adv. Res. Comput. Eng. Technol. (IJARCET) **1**(9), 135–139 (2012)
3. Subban, R., Mankame, D.P.: Human face recognition biometric techniques: analysis and review. In: Thampi, S., Abraham, A., Pal, S., Rodriguez, J. (eds.) Recent Advances in Intelligent Informatics. Advances in Intelligent Systems and Computing, vol. 235, pp. 455–463. Springer, Cham (2014). https://doi.org/10.1007/978-3-319-01778-5_47
4. Menaka, K., Yogameena, B.: Face detection in blurred surveillance videos for crime investigation. J. Phys.: Conf. Ser. **1917**, 012024 (2021). https://doi.org/10.1088/1742-6596/1917/1/012024
5. Song, Z.: Facial expression emotion recognition model integrating philosophy and machine learning theory. Emotion recognition using brain - computer interfaces and advanced artificial intelligence (2021)
6. Wirdiani, A., et al.: Face identification based on k- nearest neighbor. Sci. J. inform. **6**(2), 150–159 (2019)
7. Wang, C., et al.: A new face recognition method for blurred images using a multi-channel wiener filter. In: Conference: Proceedings of the International Multiconference of Engineers and Computer Scientists 2006, IMECS 2006, 20–22 June 2006, Hong Kong, China (2006)
8. Nguyen, H.V., Bai, L.: Cosine similarity metric learning for face verification. In: Kimmel, R., Klette, R., Sugimoto, A. (eds.) ACCV 2010. LNCS, vol. 6493, pp. 709–720. Springer, Heidelberg (2011). https://doi.org/10.1007/978-3-642-19309-5_55
9. Kaur, R., Himanshi, E.: Face recognition using principal component analysis. In: 2015 IEEE International Advance Computing Conference (IACC) (2015). https://doi.org/10.1109/IADCC.2015.7154774
10. Nath, R., et al.: Face detection and recognition using machine learning. UGC Care J. **43**(03(III)) (2020). ISSN:2249-6661
11. Wu, H., Cao, Y., Wei, H., Tian, Z.: Face recognition based on Haar Like and Euclidean Distance. J. Phys.: Conf. Ser. **1813**, 012036 (2021). MBDAS 2020. https://doi.org/10.1088/1742-6596/1813/1/012036
12. Francis, L.M., Sreenath, N.: Pre-processing techniques for detection of blurred images. In: Chaki, N., Devarakonda, N., Sarkar, A., Debnath, N. (eds.) Proceedings of International Conference on Computational Intelligence and Data Engineering. Lecture Notes on Data Engineering and Communications Technologies, vol. 28, pp. 59–66. Springer, Singapore (2019). https://doi.org/10.1007/978-981-13-6459-4_7
13. Biswas, P., Sarkar, A.S., Mynuddin, M.: Deblurring images using a Wiener filter. Int. J. Comput. Appl. **109**(7), 36–38 (2015). https://doi.org/10.5120/19203-0846
14. Guo, X.: A KNN classifier for face recognition. In: 2021 International Conference on Communications, Information System and Computer Engineering (CISCE) (2021). https://doi.org/10.1109/CISCE52179.2021.9445908
15. Flusser, J., et al.: Blur invariants for image recognition. Int. J. Comput. Vis. **131**, 2298–2315 (2023)

16. Shukla, R.K., Das, D., Agarwal, A.: A novel method for identification and performance improvement of blurred and noisy images using modified facial deblur inference (FADEIN) algorithms. In: 2016 IEEE Students' Conference on Electrical, Electronics and Computer Science (SCEECS), Bhopal, India, pp. 1–7 (2016). https://doi.org/10.1109/SCEECS.2016.7509281
17. Nishiyama, M., Hadid, A., Takeshima, H., Shotton, J., Kozakaya, T., Yamaguchi, O.: Facial deblur inference using subspace analysis for recognition of blurred faces. IEEE Trans. Pattern Anal. Mach. Intell. **33**(4), 838–845 (2011). https://doi.org/10.1109/TPAMI.2010.203
18. Kim, Y., Kwon, H., Lee, H., Cho, S., Ko, H.: Deblurring network for accurate facial landmark detection. In: 2022 IEEE International Conference on Consumer Electronics-Asia (ICCE-Asia), Yeosu, Republic of Korea (2022)

Author Index

Published by Springer Nature Switzerland AG 2025
A. Chandrabose et al. (Eds.): ICCCSP 2024, IFIP AICT 723, pp. 467–468, 2025.
https://doi.org/10.1007/978-3-031-73617-9

The manufacturer's authorised representative in the EU is Springer Nature Customer Service Centre GmbH, Europaplatz 3, 69115 Heidelberg, Germany. If you have any concerns regarding our products, please contact ProductSafety@springernature.com

Printed and bound by CPI Group (UK) Ltd, Croydon, CR0 4YY
30/09/2026
02225595-0019